The Cambridge Handbook of Dyslexia and Dyscalculia

In this handbook, the world's leading researchers answer fundamental questions about dyslexia and dyscalculia based on authoritative reviews of the scientific literature. It provides an overview from the basic science foundations to best practice in schooling and educational policy, covering research topics ranging from genes, environments, and cognition to prevention, intervention, and educational practice. With clear explanations of scientific concepts, research methods, statistical models, and technical terms within a cross-cultural perspective, this book will be a go-to reference for researchers, instructors, students, policymakers, educators, teachers, therapists, psychologists, physicians, and those affected by learning difficulties.

MICHAEL A. SKEIDE is a research group leader at the Max Planck Institute for Human Cognitive and Brain Sciences, Leipzig, Germany.

The Cambridge Handbook of Dyslexia and Dyscalculia

Edited by

Michael A. Skeide
Max Planck Institute for Human Cognitive and Brain Sciences

CAMBRIDGE
UNIVERSITY PRESS

University Printing House, Cambridge CB2 8BS, United Kingdom

One Liberty Plaza, 20th Floor, New York, NY 10006, USA

477 Williamstown Road, Port Melbourne, VIC 3207, Australia

314–321, 3rd Floor, Plot 3, Splendor Forum, Jasola District Centre,
New Delhi – 110025, India

103 Penang Road, #05–06/07, Visioncrest Commercial, Singapore 238467

Cambridge University Press is part of the University of Cambridge.

It furthers the University's mission by disseminating knowledge in the pursuit of
education, learning, and research at the highest international levels of excellence.

www.cambridge.org
Information on this title: www.cambridge.org/9781108833196
DOI: 10.1017/9781108973595

© Cambridge University Press 2022

First published 2022

A catalogue record for this publication is available from the British Library.

ISBN 978-1-108-83319-6 Hardback
ISBN 978-1-108-97811-8 Paperback

Contents

Figures and Tables

Contributors

Part III Genetic and Environmental Influences

MARGHERITA MALANCHINI, Assistant Professor of Psychology
Queen Mary University of London, United Kingdom

AGNIESZKA GIDZIELA, PhD student
Queen Mary University of London, United Kingdom

FLORENCE BOUHALI, Postdoctoral Researcher
University of California, San Francisco, USA

FUMIKO HOEFT, Professor of Psychological Sciences, Neuroscience, Mathematics,
Computer Science and Engineering, Psychiatry, Pediatrics and Educational Psychology
University of Connecticut, USA

Part IV Neurodevelopmental Foundations

MICHAEL A. SKEIDE, Research Group Leader
Max Planck Institute for Human Cognitive and Brain Sciences, Leipzig,
Germany

GORKA FRAGA GONZÁLEZ, Postdoctoral Researcher
University of Zurich, Switzerland

KATARZYNA JEDNORÓG, Associate Professor of Language Neurobiology
Nencki Institute of Experimental Biology, Warsaw, Poland

SILVIA BREM, Assistant Professor of Child and Adolescent Psychiatry and
Psychotherapy
University of Zurich, Switzerland

KARIN KUCIAN, Habilitated Scientist of Developmental Pediatrics
University Children's Hospital Zurich, University of Zurich, Switzerland

URSINA MCCASKEY, Postdoctoral Researcher
University Children's Hospital Zurich, University of Zurich, Switzerland

JASON D. YEATMAN, Assistant Professor of Education and Assistant Professor of
Pediatrics
Stanford University, USA

TERESA IUCULANO, Associate Research Professor
Université Paris Cité, La Sorbonne and Centre National de la Recherche
Scientifique, Paris, France

Part V Gender, Ethnicity, and Socioeconomic Background

JESSICA F. CANTLON, Professor of Developmental Neuroscience
Carnegie Mellon University, USA

RACHEL E. FISH, Assistant Professor of Special Education
New York University, USA

Part VI Cultural Unity and Diversity

WAI TING SIOK, Associate Professor of Linguistics
University of Hong Kong

LANG QIN, Postdoctoral Researcher
Peking University, China

BAIHAN LYU, Research Assistant
Beijing Normal University, China

XINLIN ZHOU, Professor of Psychology
Beijing Normal University, China

Part VII Early Prediction

ARNE O. LERVÅG, Professor of Education
University of Oslo, Norway

MONICA MELBY-LERVÅG, Professor of Special Education
University of Oslo, Norway

ELIZABETH A. GUNDERSON, Associate Professor of Psychology
Temple University, USA

Part VIII Intervention and Compensation

KATHARINA GALUSCHKA, Postdoctoral Researcher
German Youth Institute, Munich, Germany

GERD SCHULTE-KÖRNE, Professor of Child and Adolescent Psychiatry and
Psychotherapy
Ludwig-Maximilians University of Munich, Germany

NIENKE E. R. VAN BUEREN, PhD Student
Radboud University, Behavioural Science Institute, Nijmegen, Netherlands

EVELYN H. KROESBERGEN, Professor of Learning and Development
Radboud University, Behavioural Science Institute, Nijmegen, Netherlands

ROI COHEN KADOSH, Professor of Cognitive Neuroscience
University of Oxford, United Kingdom

H. MORIAH SOKOLOWSKI, Postdoctoral Researcher
Rotman Research Institute, Toronto, Canada

LIEN PETERS, Postdoctoral Researcher
University of Western Ontario, London, Canada

Part IX Best Practice: Diagnostics and Prevention

THOMAS LACHMANN, Professor of Cognitive and Developmental Psychology
University of Kaiserslautern, Germany and Universidad Nebrija, Centro de
Investigación Nebrija en *Cognición*, Madrid, Spain

KIRSTIN BERGSTRÖM, Postdoctoral Researcher
University of Kaiserslautern, Germany

JULIA HUBER, Postdoctoral Researcher
University of Tübingen, Germany

HANS-CHRISTOPH NUERK, Professor of Diagnostics and Cognitive Neuropsychology
University of Tübingen, Germany

MARCUS HASSELHORN, Professor of Psychology, Education and Human
Development
DIPF | Leibniz Institute for Research and Information in Education, Frankfurt, Germany

WOLFGANG SCHNEIDER, Emeritus Professor of Educational Psychology
University of Würzburg, Germany

Part X Best Practice: Schooling and Educational Policy

SONALI NAG, Professor of Education and the Developing Child
University of Oxford, United Kingdom

ANTJE EHLERT, Professor of Inclusive Education
University of Potsdam, Germany

LUISA WAGNER, PhD Student
University of Potsdam, Germany

Acknowledgements

The editor would like to thank . . .

. . . all authors for their excellent contributions to this book and their tremendous team effort;

. . . Cambridge University Press editor Stephen Acerra (New York) for triggering the idea for this book project during the 2020 Cognitive Neuroscience Society Annual Meeting;

. . . former Cambridge University Press senior editorial assistant Emily Watton and her administrative assistant Santosh Laxmi Kota for their administrative support; Helen Cooper and Richards Paul at Integra Software Services for copy-editing and typesetting; and Cambridge University Press Senior Content Manager Ruth Boyes for overseeing the publication process.

. . . the SkeideLab members for their help with the thorough scientific evaluation of the submitted contributions; in particular our research assistant Rafael Vinz for his hard work on the bibliography and his creative work on the cover art.

General Introduction

Michael A. Skeide

Almost 150 years after Kussmaul's documentation of 'Wortblindheit' (word blindness) (Kussmaul 1877) the scientific community has generated a number of different theories of dyslexia and dyscalculia. While these theories are still controversially discussed, the converging findings of *longitudinal developmental research* now allow us to draw an increasingly clear picture of the potential origins of these learning difficulties. At the same time, the common understanding of dyslexia and dyscalculia is blurred by persistent myths, such as the notion that dyslexia causes letters to appear out of order or that dyscalculia is a sign of reduced intelligence. Moreover, families, educators, and even specialized practitioners are often not sure how a specific learning disorder is validly diagnosed and which type of support children need to cope with their difficulties. Accordingly, the purpose of this handbook is to provide a *developmentally grounded* perspective on these topics by integrating findings from the life sciences and social sciences.

Starting with the theoretical foundations of dyslexia and dyscalculia (Part I), we move on to key basic scientific questions, including cognitive, behavioural, genetic, environmental, and neural foundations (Parts II–IV). From there, fundamental discussions are centred on culture, gender, ethnicity, and socioeconomic status (Parts V–VI), before addressing applied aspects of prediction, intervention, and compensation (Parts VII–VIII). Finally, we focus on the best practice in diagnostics, prevention, schooling, and educational policymaking concerning dyslexia and dyscalculia (Parts IX–X). Together, the current work represents the field in its full width and across disciplines. Compact summaries at the end of each part will provide the reader with the essential take-home messages regarding what is known about dyslexia and dyscalculia.

The present book is intended to be a one-stop shop for anyone looking for an overview of the state of the art in the field, including researchers, instructors, students, policymakers, educators, teachers, therapists, psychologists, physicians, and, of course, those affected. To keep it accessible to such a broad audience, we took great care to minimize the amount of required prior knowledge of scientific concepts, research methods, statistical models, and technical terms. Furthermore, we tried to maximize its international relevance, wherever possible, by reflecting on the generalizability of the findings to individuals with different national, educational, and cultural backgrounds and by including the currently available literature on non-western-educated-industrialized-rich-democratic (non-WEIRD) populations.

PART I

Theoretical Frameworks and Computational Models

1 Theories of Dyslexia

Usha Goswami

1.1 Introduction

Dyslexia is a disorder of development. Classically, a child has shown apparently typical language acquisition and cognitive development until faced with the task of learning to read. Suddenly the child struggles: 'In spite of laborious and persistent training, he can only with difficulty spell out words of one syllable' (Hinshelwood 1896, p. 1378). Why this apparently specific problem with reading and writing? One hundred years later, a child with dyslexia aged 9 years wrote 'I have blond her, Blue eyes and an infeckshos smill. Pealpie tell mum haw gorgus I am and is ent she looky to have me. But under the surface I live in a tumoyl. Words look like swigles and riting storys is a disaster area because of spellings' (I have blond hair, blue eyes and an infectious smile. People tell Mum how gorgeous I am and isn't she lucky to have me. But under the surface I live in a turmoil. Words look like squiggles and writing stories is a disaster area because of spellings) (author's private notes).

Theories of developmental dyslexia attempt to provide a systematic causal framework for understanding this specific learning difficulty. Most theories aim to identify the critical factor/s or 'core deficits' underlying the child's struggle to learn, in order for remediation to be focused and effective. Yet there are a large number of theories of dyslexia, some mutually exclusive, and there is more heat than light. Many theories are over-reliant on data from a single language or a small set of languages, and no theory is universally accepted by researchers in the field. In this chapter, I focus on some of the most dominant theoretical frameworks, seeking points of unification. Importantly, I will adopt a *developmental* perspective, which means that theories and experiments relying on adult data will not be considered.

A focus on *development* is absolutely critical to identifying core factor/s for effective remediation. Currently, 'multiple deficit' theories of dyslexia are gaining in popularity (Pennington 2006; McGrath et al. 2020). A key developmental question is whether some of the multiple deficits, typically identified in studies of older children with dyslexia, are in fact a downstream developmental consequence of a single atypical factor present from birth that has had multiple systemic effects. Stringent research designs are required to identify such factors, as any deficits found once reading instruction has commenced may be a consequence of the severely reduced reading experience that is inevitable for dyslexic individuals. Both intervention studies and reading-level match studies can help to identify causal factors (Goswami 2015a), as can the study of typical learners.

A focus on development also requires consideration of sensory and neural data regarding how the typically functioning brain creates a speech processing system. Reading is essentially comprehending speech when it is written down. Accordingly, sensory and neural factors that cause individual differences in speech processing may play a role in the emergence of dyslexia. During the acquisition of spoken language, infants and children learn the sounds and combinations of sounds that are permissible in their language/s. Their brains develop *phonological representations* of the sound structures of individual words. As reading is learnt, these phonological structures are linked to visual codes. We know from infant research that phonological representations are developed via auditory, visual, and motor learning: phonological representations prior to reading are already multimodal (Kuhl 2004). Research testing theories of dyslexia must thus begin with infant studies. Taking a snapshot of a single sensory, neural, or cognitive parameter at one age point is insufficient, even with reading-level-match designs. Longitudinal studies beginning in infancy are the key to understanding causation.

To complicate the picture further, studies at multiple levels of developmental description in multiple languages are required. Researchers need to combine the assessment of individual differences in neural learning, sensory processing, cognitive processing, and children's behaviour in the same children, following these children over time using narrow age banding. Studies with pre-readers, including intervention studies, are particularly valuable. Theories that can identify factors for effective intervention prior to learning to read may offer the promise of eliminating dyslexia (Goswami 2020). Unfortunately, few current theories of dyslexia have been tested by studies that include all these important criteria. Nevertheless, these kinds of data will be my focus here.

1.2 Typical Development of Reading

If reading is defined as the cognitive process of understanding a *visual* code for *spoken* language, then, logically, individual differences in acquiring reading could be related developmentally to either spoken language processing or visual code processing, or both. Different cultures have invented a range of visual codes for representing spoken language, and skilled readers appear to access meaning directly from these visual codes. Nevertheless, *phonological activation* (activation of brain areas associated with linguistic sound-structure processing) is mandatory during skilled reading. This suggests that, developmentally, efficiency in learning a visual code cannot be separated from spoken language skills (see Figure 1.1). The visual code is not a neutral visual stimulus. It is a culturally specific code that is taught and learnt using symbol–sound correspondences. This learning typically begins a few years into the development of a spoken language system. The neural spoken language system is then changed forever by this symbol–sound learning. There is developmental *remapping* of phonology with the acquisition of print (Frith 1998).

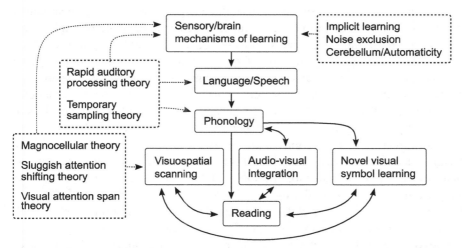

Figure 1.1 *Schematic depiction of key neural, sensory, and cognitive factors in learning to read, highlighting the core factors selected by different theories.*

For example, if young children are asked to choose pictures whose names begin with the same sound as 'truck', child readers will choose items like 'turkey' while preliterate children will choose items like 'chair' (Read 1986). Read argued that this occurs because the 't' sound in 'truck' is affricated and hence is phonologically closer to 'ch', a phonetic distinction still heard by the preliterate brain. Learning via print that the symbol used to represent the 'ch' sound in these words is 't' changes children's phonological judgements. Indeed, the young pre-readers studied by Read would misspell 'truck' as 'chrac' and 'ashtray' as 'aschray', errors that disappear as children learn conventional English spelling patterns.

As might be expected, brain imaging studies across languages show that symbol learning is linked to sound from the very beginning of acquiring reading (Blau et al. 2010; Froyen et al. 2009; Maurer et al. 2005; Maurer et al. 2011; Yang et al. 2020). The brain areas associated with phonological processing also show extensive developmental changes during the first two years of learning to read (Łuniewska et al. 2019). Further, spoken languages differ in the units of sound represented by the chosen visual coding system. For example, Japanese *Kana* represent individual syllables, Chinese *Kanji* represent morphemes, and the alphabet represents phonemes. Further while European languages such as Italian, Greek, and Spanish use alphabetic codes with highly consistent grapheme–phoneme correspondences, languages such as English, Danish, and French use markedly less consistent grapheme–phoneme correspondences (the 'consistency' problem; see Ziegler and Goswami 2005). When one letter can make multiple sounds, this slows learning for *all* children.

The development of 'phonological awareness' (the child's ability to consciously detect and manipulate the component sounds in words) follows a similar developmental sequence across languages. Phonological awareness also predicts reading acquisition in all languages studied to date. Phonological awareness has been called *metalinguistic awareness*, as its measurement depends on the child becoming *consciously aware* of knowledge that is already organized perceptually in her mental lexicon. The perceptual organization of speech information by a child (assigning acoustic, motor, or visual elements to the groupings comprising words in a particular language) contributes to individual differences in phonological representations. Awareness of syllables and onset-rimes (division of any syllable at the vowel, as in H-OP or ST-OP) appears to develop before learning to read across languages, whereas direct tuition is typically required to develop phoneme awareness. A child's access to stressed syllables, syllables, onset-rimes, and phonemes reflects their perceptual organization of the different 'psycholinguistic grain sizes' that comprise words (Ziegler and Goswami 2005). Interestingly, phoneme awareness develops at a faster rate for children who are learning to read orthographies with consistent grapheme–phoneme correspondences (Ziegler and Goswami 2005). This cognitive evidence that development itself changes the mechanisms and operation of the perceptual systems that support reading means that it is imperative to use rigorous longitudinal designs to test theories of dyslexia (see Figure 1.2).

The neural/sensory processes that underpin the development of phonological representations during spoken language acquisition are now better understood. Infants are sensitive to the acoustic boundaries that separate phonetic categories in all human languages, as are other mammals, birds, and insects (Kuhl 2004). This perceptual sensitivity is not equivalent to having conscious access to phonemes. The

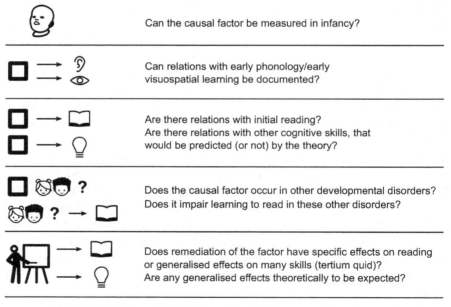

Figure 1.2 *Schematic depiction of key issues to consider when testing the evidence base for different theories of developmental dyslexia.*

infant brain also computes conditional probabilities between phonetic elements, syllables, and other speech sounds, thereby identifying possible 'words' (statistical learning; Saffran 2001). Some recent neurally driven work has revealed another important set of acoustic statistics that relate directly to phonological awareness at different psycholinguistic grain sizes. Statistical learning of interrelated changes in signal intensity (amplitude modulation) at different temporal rates in the speech amplitude envelope provides perceptual information relevant to extracting phonological units such as syllables and stressed syllables (Leong and Goswami 2015). Computational modelling of these amplitude modulation changes reveals that the different rates of amplitude modulation in speech are temporally dependent on each other (*phase dependency*). The amplitude modulations are also arranged in a hierarchy, with the slowest modulations governing the temporal timing of faster modulations. Computational modelling of both infant-directed speech and rhythmic child-directed speech (English nursery rhymes) shows that this amplitude modulation phase hierarchy by itself provides sufficient perceptual information for the brain to extract phonological units of different sizes with more than 90% efficiency (Leong et al. 2014, 2017). Accordingly, the acoustic statistical amplitude modulation structure of both infant-directed speech and rhythmic child-directed speech enables 'acoustic-emergent phonology' (Leong and Goswami 2015).

Neurally, we know that neuroelectric oscillations responsive to speech inputs (rhythmic changes in electrical brain potentials in large cell networks) are also hierarchically organized (Gross et al. 2013), and that the temporal rates of oscillation of these brain rhythms match the amplitude modulation rates in speech (Giraud and Poeppel 2012). 'Rise times' in amplitude (the rates of change between sound onset and sound peak in a given amplitude modulation) provide sensory landmarks that automatically trigger brain rhythms and speech rhythms into temporal alignment, via phase-resetting ongoing neural activity (Doelling et al. 2014). Accordingly, a nascent phonological system can be extracted from the speech signal via the automatic alignment of neuroelectric oscillations to the amplitude modulation information in speech, beginning in infancy (Goswami 2019a, 2019b). This automatic learning can, in principle, enable perceptual organization of the speech stream into syllable stress patterns, syllables, and onset-rime units. Importantly, for languages with consonant–vowel syllable structures, this automatic alignment for onset-rime units also yields information about single phonemes.

This brief survey of typical development suggests that comprehensive theories of dyslexia need to examine putative neural or sensory causes beginning from birth. I first review theories that attempt to explain the origins of the cognitive difficulties with phonology ('phonological deficit') that characterize dyslexia across languages. I then consider theories based on processing visual codes for spoken language, and finally I consider theories that utilize general properties of learning such as statistical learning and neural noise exclusion. In each case, I consider whether the theory is supported by longitudinal data, examine intervention and reading-level-match studies, consider whether the candidate deficit has been tested in other developmental disorders, and consider whether other cognitive difficulties predicted by the candidate deficit are present in children with dyslexia (see Figure 1.2). I also consider whether the available evidence draws on a range of languages.

1.3 Theories Explaining Individual Differences in Phonological Development

Auditory theories of dyslexia propose that sensory processing differences, present from birth, lead affected children to develop atypical phonological representations of spoken language. These impaired phonological representations then affect the efficient learning of a visual code for spoken language. As noted, visual codes for speech are not arbitrary visual stimuli; they are linked to phonology from the onset of learning. Accordingly, if the visual symbols being taught are difficult to match systematically to the perceptual organization of speech-based information in the child's mental lexicon, then learning to read will be slow and inefficient whichever symbol system is being acquired. I review two key theories proposing a sensory basis for the phonological deficit: one based on rapidly arriving pitch cues in speech and one based on slowly varying amplitude modulation-related information (Tallal 1980; Goswami 2011). As auditory learning begins in the womb (the amniotic fluid transmits the low-frequency amplitude modulation information in maternal speech), studies of infants and pre-readers are particularly important tests of causation.

1.3.1 Rapid Auditory Processing Theory

Rapid auditory processing (RAP) theory was first proposed by Tallal and Piercy (1973) to explain developmental language disorder and was later extended to dyslexia. The variations in frequency (pitch) that occur as a speaker moves from producing one phoneme to another are typically rapid (within 40 ms for formant transitions). The core theoretical proposal of RAP was that the ability to process this rapidly arriving and sequential acoustic information was impaired in developmental language disorder. Using tones of different frequencies, Tallal and Piercy showed that twelve children with developmental language disorder (aged 6.5–9 years) had difficulties in processing rapidly arriving information compared to chronological age-matched controls. In a subsequent study with dyslexic children aged 8–12 years, RAP problems were demonstrated in eight of twenty children compared to chronological age-matched controls (Tallal 1980). Accordingly, it was argued that difficulties in processing rapidly changing information in speech (such as the formant transitions that help differentiate phonemes) caused phoneme awareness deficits and thereby developmental dyslexia (Tallal 2004).

Given that conscious awareness of phonemes largely emerges as a consequence of learning to read, these acoustic difficulties should affect phoneme awareness in dyslexia across languages. However, this is not the case. For example, dyslexic 10-year-olds learning consistent alphabetic writing systems such as German become as accurate as chronological age-matched controls in recognizing and manipulating phonemes (Landerl and Wimmer 2000). RAP deficits are also found in a minority of Chinese dyslexic children (e.g., Chung et al. 2008), even though the Chinese writing system is not phoneme based. This may suggest that phonemic awareness is not the causal link between RAP deficits and dyslexia. Recall also that the neural and cognitive representation of phonology changes with reading experience. It is thus logically possible that sensory differences in RAP found with older children are a consequence of poorer reading experience, across languages. Reading-level-match studies are currently not available, but when chronological age-match studies comprise pre-readers or infants who are at family risk for dyslexia, then RAP difficulties are not reported. For example, a longitudinal study of Dutch preschoolers at familial risk for dyslexia failed to show any RAP difficulties, and performance in RAP tasks did not predict later phonological awareness (Boets et al. 2011). Currently missing from the literature are longitudinal studies linking RAP in infancy to phonological measures in different languages and studies of RAP in developmental disorders other than developmental language disorder. Other cognitive impairments that might be predicted on the basis of a RAP deficit, such as perceiving rapid pitch changes in music, have only been studied in dyslexic adults (with null results; see Zuk et al. 2017).

Regarding neural data, US-American pre-readers at family risk for dyslexia showed differences compared to typically developing chronological age-matched controls in brain activity when listening to non-speech stimuli containing either rapid or slow frequency transitions (Raschle et al. 2014). This is potentially important, yet RAP training studies show null results regarding remediation of reading (see Strong et al. 2011 for a meta-analysis). Neural studies measuring the auditory steady-state response in dyslexic children to fast amplitude-modulated noise (rates of 20 Hz+) are also thought relevant to RAP and phoneme awareness (Poelmans et al. 2011; Vanvooren et al. 2014; De Vos et al. 2017, 2020). The auditory steady-state response measures the *amplitude following response* of neural oscillations, and it is claimed that the auditory steady-state response to faster amplitude modulation rates illuminates the integrity of phonemic processing (Vanvooren et al. 2014). The only longitudinal data set (in Dutch) suggests that neural synchronization to 'phoneme rate' (20 Hz) amplitude-modulated noise increases markedly with the onset of learning to read (De Vos et al. 2017). This suggests that differences in older children for rapid rates of amplitude modulation may be driven by reading experience. Differences for dyslexic teenagers and adults regarding 'phoneme rate' auditory steady-state responses are mixed (see Lizarazu et al. 2021 for review). Accordingly, to date, there is no strong evidence that RAP represents a core causal factor in dyslexia.

1.3.2 Temporal Sampling Theory

Temporal sampling theory proposes atypical sensory/neural processing of the *amplitude envelope* of the speech signal by children with dyslexia, particularly at amplitude modulation rates <10 Hz that carry syllabic information (Goswami 2011, 2015, 2018, 2020). The amplitude envelope is the slow-varying energy contour of speech that determines the perception of speech rhythm. The amplitude envelope contains a range of amplitude modulation patterns hierarchically nested at different temporal rates. As noted, the phase relations between these different amplitude modulation rates provide systematic statistical cues to phonological units such as stressed versus unstressed syllables, syllables, and onset-rimes (acoustic-emergent phonology; Leong and Goswami 2015). Notably, these acoustic cues operate at time windows much longer than RAP's 40 ms (50 Hz) window. Yet these slow intensity changes are also relevant to extracting phonemic information. For example, speech-modelling studies show that the critical information in phoneme deletion tasks is related to changes in the phase relations of delta-rate and theta-rate amplitude modulations (Flanagan and Goswami 2018), and brain imaging studies show that these slow amplitude modulations carry phonetic information (Di Liberto et al. 2018). Extracting acoustic-emergent phonology via statistical learning requires successful phase alignment of amplitude modulation information in speech with brain electrical rhythms (oscillations). In turn, this requires efficient discrimination of amplitude rise times. Temporal sampling theory was originally based on studies showing that children with dyslexia in a range of languages were impaired in rise-time discrimination compared to chronological age-matched controls (English, Spanish, French, Finnish, Chinese, Hungarian, and Dutch; Goswami 2015a). Rise-time discrimination was also related to phonological awareness at different grain sizes in these different languages (Goswami et al. 2011).

Longitudinal studies of rise-time discrimination by infants at family risk for dyslexia are now emerging. For example, an Australian study has found impaired rise-time discrimination at 10 months in at-risk infants, who by their second year showed impaired phonological learning in a novel-word-learning task, along with delayed achievement of phonological constancy (Kalashnikova et al. 2018, 2019, 2020). Significant longitudinal associations with language were present: for example, rise-time discrimination in infancy predicted vocabulary size at age 3 years (Kalashnikova et al. 2019). By age 4, non-speech rhythm deficits were present in the at-risk group, but visual–verbal paired-associate learning deficits were not (Kalashnikova et al. 2020). The rhythm deficits were identified using a musical rhythm task that has also been used with Italian dyslexics (Flaugnacco et al. 2015). These infant data are consistent with longitudinal studies of at-risk infants in other languages, which have identified a range of neonate and infant neural auditory weaknesses based on syllabic stimuli that predict later phonological awareness and reading ability (Guttorm et al. 2010; Leppänen et al. 2010; van Zuijen et al. 2013).

Longitudinal studies of preschool children report rise-time deficits in those at family risk for dyslexia (Law et al. 2017). Furthermore, rise time measured in preschoolers aged 3–5 years predicts phonological awareness, letter knowledge, and reading at ages 6 and 7 years (Corriveau et al. 2007; Vanvooren et al. 2014). In these studies, the rise-time measure used accounted for 10–16% of unique variance in later phonological awareness, and up to 10% of the variance in later letter knowledge. Longitudinal studies with school-aged children reveal significant impairments compared to younger reading-level-matched children for rise-time discrimination, musical rhythm perception, and linguistic rhythm perception (Goswami, Huss et al. 2013; Goswami, Mead et al. 2013). The musical rhythm measure can account for up to 42% of unique variance in reading skills (Huss et al.

2011). However, while rise-time discrimination was a significant predictor of phonological development from 8 to 11 years in Goswami et al.'s longitudinal study, phonological development was not a predictor of rise-time development (Goswami et al. 2021), suggesting that the direction of causality is from auditory processing to language skills (Kalashnikova et al. 2019). Rise-time discrimination is also impaired in developmental language disorder, another developmental disorder wherein both speech processing and rhythm perception are affected (Corriveau et al. 2007; Cumming et al. 2015). Comparisons with other developmental disorders where reading is typically unimpaired, such as autism, have yet to be carried out.

Neurally, the accuracy of speech–brain oscillatory alignment in the delta band (~2 Hz, relevant to prosodic organization) is significantly poorer for children with dyslexia compared to both reading-level- and chronological age-matched controls, even when speech recognition accuracy is equated across groups (Power et al. 2016). When rhythmic processing of syllables is equated between dyslexic and chronological age-matched control children (via an acoustic thresholding manipulation), the dyslexic brain shows a phase difference in delta-band speech–brain alignment compared to controls (Power et al. 2013). Accordingly, the brains of children with dyslexia appear to be encoding a significantly less accurate representation of low-frequency envelope information in speech. This finding has been replicated in Spanish (Molinaro et al. 2016). These neural data are important as they provide a direct measure of the quality of children's phonological representations when linguistic behaviour is equated, thereby isolating potential causal loci of impairment.

Intervention studies based on improving rhythmic cognition (typically via music-, motor-, or oral-poetry-based rhythmic tasks) can improve phonological awareness and reading for both typically developing and dyslexic children (e.g., Bhide et al. 2013; Flaugnacco et al. 2015). Furthermore, rhythmic synchronization abilities, such as tapping, clapping, or drumming in time with a beat, predict phonology and reading development in a range of languages (e.g., Ríos-López et al. 2019; Woodruff Carr et al. 2014). These relations for typically developing children would be expected by temporal sampling theory. New insights into the mechanistic role of neuronal oscillations for encoding the speech signal, and of amplitude modulation rise times as automatic triggers for speech–brain oscillatory alignment, thus support a specific developmental pathway from auditory sensory processing to phonology and reading that is impaired in dyslexia (Goswami 2020). Accordingly, temporal sampling theory is supported by longitudinal, neural, infant, and preschool data in many languages (Figure 1.2). The research base suggests that children at risk for dyslexia are encoding poorer-quality representations of the speech signal from birth, in part via impaired automatic (statistical) learning of the amplitude modulation phase hierarchy that facilitates 'acoustic-emergent' phonology (Leong and Goswami 2015). Accordingly, the development of phonological awareness is impaired, which impairs reading acquisition. temporal sampling theory is thus accruing converging developmental data at multiple levels of description (neural, sensory, cognitive, and behavioural). Currently missing from the literature are longitudinal multiple-level data testing temporal sampling theory from infancy in languages other than English, and reading-level-match studies across languages.

1.4 Theories Relating to Atypical Visual Behaviour During Reading

Children with dyslexia do not scan print as efficiently as chronological age-matched controls, showing more fixations and less rhythmic saccades. Sometimes, they complain that print seems to move around on the page. Observations such as these have led to a range of visual theories of dyslexia, of which I consider three prominent examples here.

1.4.1 Impaired Visual Attention Span Theory

During reading, in most languages children are scanning small symbols arranged in rows from left to right. The impaired visual attention span theory proposes that such multi-letter parallel processing is atypical in dyslexia, because the number of individual elements available for simultaneous processing in the 'attentional window' is reduced, limiting reading development (Valdois et al. 2004). A visual attention span deficit has been found to dissociate from a phonological deficit in some French and Portuguese children, which is interpreted to show that impaired visual attention span is an independent cause of dyslexia (Bosse et al. 2007; Germanò et al. 2014). However, the classic visual attention span task used in these studies presents an array of five letters very briefly, and records reaction time for naming either all the letters in the array (full report) or single letters at different cued positions (partial report). The reliance on letters as visual attention span stimuli unfortunately introduces an immediate confound, as letters are a culturally specific code that is taught and learnt using symbol–sound correspondences, and children with dyslexia process letters less efficiently. This may explain why visual attention span tasks account for 24–36% of variance in the reading scores of children with dyslexia (Bosse et al. 2007). Studies using unfamiliar symbols or coloured dots as stimuli do not report visual attention span deficits in dyslexia (Ziegler et al. 2010; Valdois et al. 2012). Nevertheless, visual attention span deficits in dyslexia using the classic task have also been found in Chinese, a non-alphabetic language (Chen et al. 2019). However, Chen et al. used visual attention span tasks based on Chinese characters, Chinese radicals, and digits, and only found a visual attention span deficit on a reading-level match for the Chinese characters, again reminding us that any visual code for representing speech is not a neutral visual stimulus. Zhao et al. (2018) studied Chinese children with dyslexia from grades 2 to 6, using a visual one-back task rather than the classic visual attention span task. Here they only found a visual attention span deficit for older dyslexics (5th and 6th grade). Typically developing Chinese children who were also studied showed no relation between visual attention span and reading development. These effects complicate theoretical interpretation. If visual attention span is a primary causal factor in dyslexia, then it should be present irrespective of reading experience and it should also relate to reading in typically developing children across languages.

Visual attention span has been shown to be related to individual differences in typical reading development in French (Bosse and Valdois 2009). Again, visual attention span contributed significant unique variance to progress in reading, particularly in grade 1 (15%), but again the study relied on letter-based tasks. No studies testing pre-readers are available to determine cause and effect. Further, a reduced attentional window could be expected to cause developmental problems in other areas of cognition that require simultaneous processing of distinct visual elements, for example categorization, but this has not been studied to my knowledge. The sensory and neural factors that may cause impaired visual attention span are unknown, but seem unlikely to be specific to reading. Currently absent from the literature are studies measuring visual attention span in infants or pre-readers that show a reduced span in at-risk children. Ideally, such studies should use non-letter-based visual attention span tasks. Further, visual attention span has not been measured in other developmental disorders to demonstrate specificity to dyslexia.

An interesting visual attention span training study was recently conducted in French (Zoubrinetzky et al. 2019). Children with dyslexia aged 10 years received an adaptive training programme based on visual search, visual discrimination, and visual categorization tasks, developed specifically to train visual attention span (MAEVA: see Valdois et al. 2014, Zoubrinetzky et al. 2019). The children also received a targeted phoneme discrimination training programme (RapDys: see Collet et al. 2012), based on the observation that school-aged children with dyslexia continue to perceive allophones (other possible spoken sounds that could be linked to a letter, but that are typically grouped together as one letter when teaching traditional grapheme–phoneme correspondences: see Serniclaes et al. 2004). The RapDys training was expected to improve phonemic awareness only and MAEVA was expected to improve visual attention span only. A cross-over design was used, in which children first experienced six weeks of training with RapDys or with MAEVA, or vice versa, and then experienced the second intervention (hence acting as their own controls). Unexpectedly, both training regimes improved *both* visual attention span and phonemic awareness, although minor differences could be discerned (e.g., only RapDys improved non-word reading). The finding that training phonemic discrimination improves the visual attention span is difficult to align with the theoretical claim of visual attention span as a causal deficit that is independent of phonological impairments.

A recent visual attention span training study has also been reported for Chinese (Zhao et al. 2019). The study used non-symbolic materials, and compared the effects of visual attention span training for dyslexic children aged 10 years who did show visual attention span deficits in contrast to those who did not. Training improved character reading speed for both groups, and sentence reading speed for both groups when compared to chronological age-matched controls. The lack of specific training effects for the visual attention span deficit group only is suggestive of training affecting a third unknown factor that is causing the changes in reading speed (tertium quid; see Figure 1.2). Accordingly, to date it seems most likely that a reduced visual attention span is a consequence rather than a cause of dyslexia (Goswami 2015b).

1.4.2 Sluggish Attentional Shifting Theory

A second visual attention theory (sluggish attentional shifting theory) argues that the orientation of spatial attention is 'sluggish' in individuals with dyslexia (Facoetti et al. 2010). The dyslexic brain is thought to be unable to move visuospatial attention smoothly from letter to letter when recoding print to sound. This impaired ability to orient spatial attention (while simultaneously suppressing flanking letters) then causes dyslexia. As reading experience itself trains spatial orienting, it is important to establish that reduced reading experience per se is not causing the sluggish attentional shifting deficit. This is particularly important as most sluggish attentional shifting data comes from Italian, a consistent alphabetic orthography where letter-by-letter recoding to sound is the typical reading strategy. Further, only Italian dyslexic children with phonological recoding deficits (poor non-word reading) show a spatial cueing deficit in these studies – a deficit which can account for as much as 32% of unique variance in non-word reading (Facoetti et al. 2010). However, Italian dyslexic children who can read non-words efficiently do not show sluggish attentional shifting. Data such as these suggest that sluggish attentional shifting may arise from reduced practice in recoding print to sound.

Data from pre-reading children and at-risk infants are therefore critical. A longitudinal study of eighty-two Italian pre-readers found that fourteen of the children later classified as poor readers had both reduced pre-reading attentional orienting and poorer pre-reading phonological awareness (Gori et al. 2014). No sluggish attentional shifting studies of infants at family risk for dyslexia are yet available to my knowledge. This is a critical test as impaired attentional shifting should be present from infancy. Sluggish attentional shifting should also affect many other areas of cognition (e.g., visuospatial working memory), though this has yet to be explored. Indeed, studies of children with developmental dyscalculia are converging on visuospatial working memory deficits as a primary impairment (see Chapter 2 Menon and Chang 2022, and Chapter 19, Galuschka and Schulte-Körne 2022), yet a diagnosis of dyscalculia typically depends on reading development being unaffected (Szűcs and Goswami 2013). Utilizing sluggish attentional shifting tasks with children with dyscalculia could thus be important for demonstrating causal specificity.

Regarding intervention data, training visuospatial attention does seem to benefit reading in school-aged children with dyslexia. A series of intervention studies involving action video gaming have documented significant gains in visual–spatial attention, phonological skills, and reading (speed, not accuracy), in both Italian and English dyslexic children, although not in Polish children (Franceschini et al. 2015; Franceschini et al. 2017; Łuniewska et al. 2018). This is interesting and partly supports SAS theory. However, it is intriguing that phonology improves in these studies, despite the lack of any phonological intervention. Reading speed should improve if sluggish attentional shifting is speeded up by action video gaming, but a causal pathway is required to explain why *phonology* improves. For example, a recent action video gaming study showed gains in non-word repetition, a classic phonological task (Franceschini and Bertoni 2019). Such changes again suggest that training is affecting a third, unknown factor that is causing these changes (tertium quid). Phonological interventions do not (to my knowledge) improve visual–spatial attention; they specifically improve phonological skills and phonological decoding. SAS theory does not explain why remediating a primary deficit in shifting spatial attention should affect phonological development.

Mechanistic neural data could possibly help with this conundrum, but such data are still sparse for SAS theory. Functionally, atypical parietal activation is often reported, yet the parietal cortex is also a locus of atypical function in developmental dyscalculia, a disorder diagnosed on the basis of impairments in mathematics accompanied by *intact* reading. A training study in German using pre- and post-intervention brain imaging compared the efficacy of three interventions for 9-year-olds with dyslexia: a phonological intervention, an intervention based on orienting visual attention to word fragments, and an intervention training sight vocabulary (Heim et al. 2015). The children received fMRI scanning during single-word reading before and after the interventions. Differences in post-training neural activation were found for both the phonological and attention groups, who both improved in reading. The attention group showed stronger activation in the left Heschl's gyrus following intervention – a surprising result. SAS theory would not expect visual attention training to affect activation in the primary *auditory* cortex. This neural finding appears consistent with the global improvements in reading and phonology shown in the action video gaming interventions, again suggesting that there may be a yet-to-be identified third factor that is causing the documented changes in spatial attention, reading speed, and phonology. Intervention designs coupled with longitudinal studies beginning in infancy offer one means of improving our understanding of potential causal relationships.

1.4.3 Magnocellular Theory

Dysfunction of the visual magnocellular system has been suggested as a neural cause of dyslexia for decades, and is still a popular theory (Cornelissen et al. 1995; Stein and Walsh 1997; Vidyasagar and Pammer 2010; Stein 2019). The magnocellular visual system plays a key role in eye movements, motion processing, and vergence control (when both eyes converge on the same location). As stable visual fixation is required for processing symbols such as letters, atypical functioning of the magnocellular system could impair reading, for example causing letters to appear to jump around. Numerous studies of visual motion processing find that older children with dyslexia show poorer performance; however, most of these studies rely on chronological age-match designs and so causation is ambiguous (Stein 2019 for recent review). Two reading-level-match studies are available for 11-year-old Italian children with dyslexia: one reporting a deficit in perceiving coherent dot motion (Gori et al. 2015), and one reporting a deficit in the frequency-doubling illusion, a magnocellular-reliant visual illusion based on vertical dark lines (Gori et al. 2014). Gori et al. (2015) also provided longitudinal data, testing seventy-two pre-readers aged 5 years with the same coherent dot motion task. Two years later, the twelve children in the sample who were poor readers were found to have displayed significantly poorer coherent dot motion sensitivity as pre-readers (Gori et al. 2015). Pre-reading coherent dot motion showed a significant predictive relationship with later Italian text reading for all the children, accounting for 10% of unique variance; a similar predictive relationship has been reported in a Dutch study (Boets et al. 2011). Regarding English, a study of pre-readers at family risk for dyslexia used the frequency-doubling illusion as well as coherent dot motion to assess magnocellular function at age 5 years (Kevan and Pammer 2008). The at-risk preschoolers showed poorer performance in both tasks, and preschool thresholds for frequency doubling but not coherent dot motion in the whole sample of fifty-eight children predicted reading accuracy and non-word reading a year later (Kevan and Pammer 2009), accounting for between 5% and 12% of unique variance. These data are supportive of pre-reading differences in magnocellular function, some of which then affect later reading.

Intriguingly, chronological age-matched action video gaming intervention studies with Italian dyslexic children improve coherent dot motion performance (Gori et al. 2015). As found for SAS theory, phonological processing and reading speed also improve in these coherent dot motion/action video gaming studies. A recent study with 7-year-old English dyslexic children trained motion processing directly (using moving stripe patterns), and reported improvements in motion direction detection, reading speed, and phonological awareness, as well as in visual and auditory attention (Lawton 2016). In all these training studies, improved magnocellular function affected phonology, an outcome that cannot be explained by the foundations of magnocellular theory (i.e., by improved vergence control, guidance of saccades, or visual fixation). Again, such data suggest that there may be a yet-to-be-identified third factor that is causing these across-the-board improvements.

To my knowledge, only one training study reporting magnocellular outcomes has included a reading-level match. Olulade et al. (2013) reported significant changes in dyslexic visual motion processing, with the expected enhancement of neural activation in visual cortex (V5), but following a *phonological* intervention. When compared to reading-level controls, the children with dyslexia showed similar levels of V5 activation. These findings suggest that visual motion processing is related to reading, but that the causal relation may be from reading to vision and not vice versa. Atypical visual motion processing in dyslexia in chronological age-match studies may be a consequence of reduced reading experience. A combination of intervention and longitudinal studies, beginning in infancy, are required to clarify the causal connections between phonology, reading, and magnocellular function in children. It is also worth noting that immaturity of the dorsal system (encompassing the subcortical magnocellular system) appears to characterize a number of developmental disorders, including autism, Williams syndrome, and dyscalculia (Atkinson et al. 1997). Children with autism can be hyperlexic, hence much better than expected for their age at recoding print to sound, and children with dyscalculia have intact reading. Accordingly, dorsal-stream deficits are not specific to dyslexia, and children with atypical dorsal-stream function can still develop good reading skills. Clearly, there is a relationship between visual motion processing and reading, but whether it is causal regarding dyslexia remains to be assured.

1.5 Global Theories Based on General Factors

A range of theories based on general neural factors have been proposed to explain developmental dyslexia. The key weakness of all such theories is that they have difficulty in explaining why impairments in the proposed general neural factors only affect children's learning regarding reading, and do not affect learning in other cognitive domains such as categorization, conceptual development, number skills, and long-term memory. For completeness, I briefly consider three such theories. It is notable that none of these theories has yet been tested with infant or longitudinal studies, nor in other developmental disorders, nor via intervention studies.

1.5.1 Cerebellar/Automatization Theory

Atypical activation in the cerebellum is often reported in neuroimaging studies of dyslexia. A general theory based on the idea that deficits in the cerebellar network present prior to learning to read could cause dyslexia was proposed by Nicolson and Fawcett (Nicolson and Fawcett 1990; Nicolson and Fawcett 2018; Fawcett et al. 1996; Nicolson et al. 2001). The theory has undergone a number of updates, but the core idea is that cerebellar deficits cause developmental difficulties in automatizing learnt skills, affecting any form of procedural learning (habit formation), but in particular affecting phonological processing (via articulation) and reading (via automatizing grapheme–phoneme correspondences). Most recently, Nicolson and Fawcett (2018) have linked the cerebellar theory to neural noise theories (reviewed below). Their new cerebellar theory, 'delayed neural commitment', proposes increased noise in the neural circuits associated with hearing, speech, and possibly other processes, and argues that the development of all 'automatic' skills and all forms of implicit learning would be impaired if processing noise were experienced during learning. In particular, it is proposed that this neural noise would impede the development of reading skills via the cerebellum. The neural networks that develop to support articulatory and phonological processes are argued to depend on error-based learning processes that are 'scaffolded *only* by the cerebellum' (p. 112, my italics).

Nicolson and Fawcett (2018) are to be commended for trying to develop a theoretical framework that can encompass a range of both sensory and cognitive theories. However, their reliance on neural noise means that the theory is too general and too under-specified to take the dyslexia field further. Many of the assumptions made in their framework about both cortical neural networks and the operation of noise in cortical networks appear outdated. For example, Nicolson and Fawcett assume that neural commitment is fixed early and cannot be undone by later learning, whereas in vivo animal studies show that even the cerebellar connections underpinning habits are plastic and can be modulated (Vaaga et al. 2020). Indeed, the neural coding of a range of learnt skills appears to 'drift' over time, with no apparent detriment to performance (e.g., for animal navigation; Rule et al. 2020). Similarly, all biological mechanisms are noisy, and in the neural engineering field modelling of noisy synaptic mechanisms suggests that there is an optimal network size for any given task (Raman et al. 2019). For networks below the optimal size, it is actually advantageous for learning to add noise (i.e., to add apparently redundant neurons and connections: 'hyperconnectivity'). Mechanistically, hyperconnectivity reduces the impact of imperfect learning rules. Given the complexity of the brain and of neural learning mechanisms, it is probably too early to propose delayed neural commitment as a theoretical explanation for a *specific* learning difficulty such as developmental dyslexia.

1.5.2 Neural Noise Theory

All sensory systems show impaired functioning in the face of noisy input. For example, trying to understand speech presented in background noise is more difficult than trying to understand speech in a quiet environment. Varieties of noise exclusion deficit theories in dyslexia have been around for more than a decade (Sperling et al. 2005; Hancock et al. 2017). The most recent theoretical instantiation is based on evidence that some genes implicated in dyslexia lead to neural hyper-excitability and increased neural noise in guinea pigs, rats, and other mammals (Hancock et al. 2017). Accordingly, Hancock and colleagues propose that excessive neural noise in cortical areas related to reading may cause dyslexia by disrupting phonological awareness and audiovisual integration. For example, they argue that such hyper-excitability could affect auditory temporal sampling. Although this idea could provide an alternative physiological basis for the temporal sampling (TS) theory, there are currently no data explaining why excessive neural noise should only affect certain areas of the cortex, and indeed the authors acknowledge the substantial evidence gap between animal models and genetic effects in the human brain. Nevertheless, this theoretical effort to unpack neural mechanisms related to impaired temporal sampling, for example via neurochemical messengers such as glutamate and GABA, is highly innovative (Pugh et al. 2014). Hancock et al. (2017) note that their model would be 'directly falsifiable by showing that individuals with dyslexia do not, in general, have noisy, hyper-excitable cortex' (p. 444). The difficulty here is that a generally noisy cortex would also be expected to hamper cognitive processes other than reading. A noisy cortex should affect all areas of cognitive development, yet dyslexia is by definition a specific learning difficulty (although co-occurrence with language and maths difficulties is common; see Chapter 4, Banfi, Landerl, and Moll 2022). On the other hand, as it is already known that the neural system for reading is atypical in dyslexia, the animal work showing that when networks are below the optimal size it is advantageous for learning to add noise could be relevant to neural noise theory (Raman et al. 2019). The difficulty is devising a stringent way to test this idea in humans. Further, it is worth noting that there are neural noise hypotheses regarding a number of other developmental disorders, for example autism and schizophrenia (Rubenstein and Merzenich 2003).

1.5.3 Implicit Learning Theory

A theoretical variant of the procedural learning deficit postulated by the cerebellar theory is that dyslexia is caused by a domain-general deficit in implicit learning. Implicit learning is the ability to automatically extract regularities in environmental input in order to predict future events. The core idea regarding reading is that an impaired ability to learn statistical-sequential patterns would affect learning of grapheme–phoneme correspondences (Arciuli and Simpson 2012). Statistical learning deficits in dyslexia have most typically been explored using either serial reaction time tasks or artificial grammar learning tasks. Serial reaction time tasks are usually motor learning tasks. For example, children may learn to press a button in response to a particular stimulus while experiencing a sequence of stimuli with underlying statistical structure. Children who can learn the implicit sequence get faster at pressing the button. Artificial grammar learning tasks involve strings of letters or other stimuli that reflect statistical regularities, 'rules' that initially are not imparted to the participant. Following a learning phase, new strings are shown, and participants are asked whether they follow the rule. Correct classification shows implicit learning.

The data across languages for both artificial grammar learning tasks and serial reaction time tasks are very mixed, with no clear evidence for a statistical learning deficit in dyslexia (see Schmalz et al. 2017 for review). As with other general factor theories, a key weakness is that the theory fails to explain why domain-general impairments in implicit learning only affect children's reading and do not affect other cognitive domains reliant on implicit learning, such as categorization and conceptual development. Indeed, neuroscience studies make it clear that implicit learning is not a domain-general mechanism. Neural systems do learn the patterns or regularities in environmental input via statistical learning, but the critical statistical patterns in different domains of sensory input are poorly understood and may not be those assumed by theorists (Goswami 2020).

1.6 Towards a Unifying Theory of Dyslexia?

While no single theory reviewed herein is broadly accepted by the field, the current analysis suggests that there are multisensory differences between children with and without dyslexia, across languages, with relatively strong evidence for atypical sensory processing of acoustic aspects of the speech signal and some evidence for atypical processing of visual motion. More of the research strategies shown in Figure 1.2 have been applied to testing acoustic processing theories than visual motion processing theories, however, as the latter theories still lack infant and pre-reader data. Nevertheless, both acoustic differences in rise-time processing and visual differences in peripheral processing are still present in highly remediated adult dyslexics, suggestive of enduring sensory differences (Pasquini et al. 2007; Schneps et al. 2012). These sensory differences are consistent with data from longitudinal neuroimaging studies of children at risk for dyslexia in Norwegian and German. The Norwegian study reported structural brain differences compared to controls in both primary auditory (Heschl's gyrus) and primary visual cortices (V2) prior to the onset of literacy tuition (age 6 years). Structural differences in primary auditory cortex were the only differences found consistently at later measurement points, including after dyslexia had been diagnosed at age 12 (Clark et al. 2014). A German longitudinal neuroimaging study reached similar conclusions (Kuhl et al. 2020). The left primary auditory cortex showed structural differences in at-risk children who later turned out to have dyslexia at all measurement points in the study, including prior to schooling. Functional connectivity between auditory cortex and higher-order speech processing areas also showed differences prior to literacy learning. Combining these structural and connectivity differences predicted later dyslexia with very high accuracy, and more effectively than phonological measures.

Nevertheless, the identification of preliterate differences in primary visual cortex in the Norwegian longitudinal study is thought provoking. In a study exploring the neural circuits underpinning rhythmic pulse pattern recognition in field crickets (insects that rely on transmitting and receiving acoustic rhythmic signals, the signals that are a focus of the temporal sampling theory), the authors noted that the overall network design of the auditory feature detector circuit for pulse patterns was very similar to that of the elementary motion detector circuit found in the visual pathway of these insects (Schöneich et al. 2015). Schoeneich et al. argued that the similarity pointed to a fundamental circuitry layout underlying the temporal processing of sequential events that was shared among different sensory modalities across different nervous systems, also citing studies of flies, crickets, and humans. This cross-species circuitry could suggest that a neural mechanism related to temporal sampling in both auditory and visual domains may be impaired in children with dyslexia.

Recently, a visual analogue to the auditory temporal sampling theory has been proposed by Archer et al. (2020), who suggest that atypical theta sampling in the visual domain could underpin magnocellular differences between individuals with dyslexia and controls, and could also affect oculomotor control. Their proposal encompasses both 'bottom-up' oscillatory mechanisms, which they suggest may exhibit atypical phase-locking to theta frequency fixations during reading (i.e., linked saccades, which typically occur every 300 ms or 3 Hz), and 'top-down' oscillatory control of faster visual signals in order to control oculomotor movements that capture images of alphabetic letters. While currently tied to the act of reading itself, these ideas enable visual temporal sampling mechanisms to be explored in infants. In particular, visual temporal sampling mechanisms related to bottom-up processing should be measurable in infancy.

The account proposed by Archer et al. (2020) is an anatomically and functionally sophisticated version of ideas also proposed by Goswami et al. (2014), who made an early attempt to unify theorizing in developmental dyslexia. Their proposal was based on the function of neuronal oscillations in sensory systems. Goswami et al. suggested that oscillatory temporal sampling mechanisms could have systematic effects in more than one sensory system, which should be detectable from infancy. In principle, deeper understanding of these systematic effects across development could offer explanations for the multiple deficits that are typically seen in older children with dyslexia. Again, the similarity in the fundamental circuitry layout underlying the temporal processing of rhythmic acoustic events and visual motion processing in crickets noted by Schöneich et al. (2015) is thought provoking. In the future, such circuits could potentially offer a neural target for investigation.

However, given the complexity of neural learning, testing a unified multimodal temporal sampling theory of this nature makes it imperative to begin in infancy and to conduct longitudinal studies (see Figure 1.2). Studying developmental trajectories is critical for understanding the complex interplay of auditory and visual sensory/ neural and cognitive processes during the development of reading, particularly as orthographic systems are not neutral visual stimuli. To add to the challenge, studies are required in multiple languages, in order to disentangle core causal features from developmental aspects that arise from the nature of the phonology and/or orthography of a particular language. For example, adult dyslexic readers of Farsi (which is read right to left) show a spatial attention deficit that is a mirror image of Italian dyslexic deficits (Kermani et al. 2018), suggesting that these spatial attention deficits are a consequence of dyslexia rather than a cause. By adulthood, readers in most languages will have read millions of words and practiced reading daily. Those with dyslexia will have read and practiced far less, because of the effort involved in fluent reading. Disentangling the effects of reading experience on the brain across the many different sensory and cognitive components shown in Figure 1.1 is experimentally challenging. Nevertheless, it is mandatory if societies are to devise efficient educational methods for remediating developmental dyslexia.

1.7 Conclusion

I have emphasized repeatedly in this chapter that a focus on *development* is absolutely critical to identifying core factors when testing theories about developmental dyslexia and devising effective remediation. An experimental road map for our field was set out in Figures 1.1 and 1.2, summarizing some of the key developmental issues to consider when testing a unified theory of dyslexia. Computational modelling of different theories is also important (e.g., Ziegler et al. 2020; see also Chapter 6, Malanchini and Gidziela 2022). Nevertheless, remediation methods that work in stringently designed studies should *always* be offered to children with dyslexia, even if there is disagreement over their theoretical basis. For example, using larger print, using shorter sentences in texts, not crowding letters spatially, providing early and explicit instruction in phonological awareness at levels other than grapheme–phoneme correspondences, and using modern multimedia solutions (such as screen reader software for reading aloud words, and speech recognition software for writing and spelling) should all be encouraged (Schneider et al. 2000; Schneps et al. 2013; Zorzi et al. 2012).

An interesting outstanding research question is whether targeted remediation given prior to learning to read could ameliorate dyslexia altogether (Goswami 2020). For example, building on the auditory temporal sampling theory, amplifying the speech signal so that 2 Hz amplitude modulations are exaggerated combined with engineering larger rise-time cues to facilitate sensory triggering of automatic phase entrainment should normalize phonological development across languages. It has already been shown that rise-time enhancement improves the performance of children and adults with dyslexia when listening to speech in noise (Van Hirtum et al. 2019; Van Hirtum et al. 2021). If infants and toddlers always heard speech with such modifications, perhaps through a discrete hearing aid, would a phonological mental lexicon develop that was comparable to not-at-risk children? If so, this would level the sensory playing field before the child entered school and began learning to read. Presenting the deaf brain with a modified speech signal has been very successful in the case of cochlear implants. If used from infancy, these implants support the development of spoken language skills. Which factors to remediate, and how to go about such remediation prior to the onset of learning about print, are critical questions for theories of developmental dyslexia.

Suggestions for Further Reading

Franceschini, S., S. Bertoni, L. Ronconi, et al. 2015. '"Shall We Play a Game?'": Improving Reading Through Action Video Games in Developmental Dyslexia'. *Current Developmental Disorders Reports* 2 (4): 318–29. https://doi.org/10.1007/s40474-015-0064-4.

Goswami, U. 2015. 'Sensory Theories of Developmental Dyslexia: Three Challenges for Research'. *Nature Reviews Neuroscience*, 16, 43–54. http://dx.doi.org/10.1038/nrn3836.

Goswami, U. 2020. *Reading Acquisition and Developmental Dyslexia: Educational Neuroscience and Phonological Skills*. In M. S. C. Thomas, D. Mareschal, and I. Dumontheil (Eds.). pp. 144–68, Educational Neuroscience: Development across the Lifespan. Routledge.

Olulade, O. A., E. M. Napoliello, and G. F. Eden, 2013. 'Abnormal Visual Motion Processing Is Not a Cause of Dyslexia'. *Neuron*, 79(1), 180–90. https://doi.org/10.1016/j.neuron.2013.05.002.

Ziegler, J.C., C. Perry, and M. Zorzi. 2020. 'Learning to Read and Dyslexia: From Theory to Intervention Through Personalised Computational Models'. *Current Directions in Psychological Science*, 29(3), 293–300. https://doi.org/10.1177/0963721420915873.

2 Theories of Dyscalculia

Vinod Menon and Hyesang Chang

2.1 Introduction

Developmental dyscalculia (DD) is a learning disorder characterized by difficulties in reasoning about numbers and performing mathematical calculations (Butterworth et al. 2011; Kaufmann et al. 2013; Kucian et al. 2014). The term DD highlights the specificity of numerical deficits and its developmental origins and is often used synonymously with mathematical disabilities and mathematical learning disabilities (Szűcs and Goswami 2013). Various forms of DD are known to affect up to 14% of school-age children, leading to persistent innumeracy in adolescence and adulthood (Geary et al. 2012). In today's technologically driven world, low numeracy poses a significant barrier to academic and professional success, even more so than low literacy (Butterworth et al. 2011). Gaining a better understanding of this disorder is critical for developing more effective interventions to remediate DD at an early age, with the potential for better long-term professional opportunities individually and increased economic growth collectively (OECD 2016). In this chapter, we take a broad cognitive and systems neuroscience view of DD and describe theories and models that help elucidate cognitive and neurobiological mechanisms underlying poor numerical skills in affected individuals.

Our understanding of the origins of DD is inherently constrained by the criteria used to define the disorder, which tend to vary considerably with respect to diagnostic measures, cut-off scores, stability, persistence of the disorder with development, criteria for co-occurrence, and other exclusion criteria (see Chapter 3, Zorzi and Testolin 2022). We begin this chapter by first summarizing key definitions and measures used to identify DD and address the complexities of the disorder from a theoretical viewpoint that incorporates both dimensional and categorical approaches. We then consider sources of cognitive impairments in DD, including 'domain-specific' processes, such as basic numerical processing, as well as 'domain-general' processes, such as working memory, which impact the ability to perform tasks that involve maintenance and manipulation of numerical information.

Over the past two decades, brain-imaging studies have contributed significantly to our understanding of the neural basis of mathematical difficulties in DD. In particular, neurobiological studies have helped constrain and refine behavioural and cognitive theories of dyscalculia, and have elucidated the mechanisms of poor maths performance and learning in DD. From this vantage point, we provide an overview of the key cognitive and neural theories of dyscalculia. In the following sections, we describe specific domains of numerical cognition that have been extensively investigated in DD and highlight findings in the context of the overarching cognitive and neural theories of dyscalculia. We describe a network of distributed brain regions that show aberrant responses during numerical problem solving in individuals with DD and emphasize that neurocognitive processing deficits in DD are not localized to a single brain region. We present converging evidence from functional and structural brain-imaging studies that demonstrate how distributed brain areas, functional circuits, and white matter pathways are disrupted in DD, leading to the view that DD is characterized by deficits in multiple neurocognitive systems. Finally, we review recent findings on common and distinct neural substrates between individuals with 'pure' DD and those with co-occurring difficulties in maths and reading, which further suggest that domain-general and domain-specific deficits contribute to different aspects of dyscalculia.

The distribution of national backgrounds of samples included in research articles reviewed in this chapter are as follows (number of articles): Austria (2), Belgium (11), Canada (2), China (1), France (2), Germany (3), Israel (4), Italy (2), Netherlands (2), New Zealand (1), Norway (2), Sweden (1), Switzerland (8), Syria/Lebanon (1), United Kingdom (8), and United States (28). Children, adolescents, and adults between 4 and 76 years of age are included (distribution of age groups among the articles with available age information: 4–11 years old: 65%; 12–17 years old: 12%; 18 years old or older: 23%). All articles except for one which included an illiterate sample (Zebian and Ansari 2012) included participants who were receiving/received age-appropriate formal education.

2.2 Definition and Characteristics of Dyscalculia

The revised Diagnostic and Statistical Manual of Mental Disorders (DSM-5) defines DD as a specific learning disorder with persistent difficulties in acquiring academically relevant mathematical skills (American Psychiatric Association 2013). Persistence is defined here as numerical deficits that last six months or more. Children with DD typically perform one to two years below grade level and show difficulties in one or more of the four mathematical domains identified in DSM-5: number sense, arithmetic fact knowledge, accurate and fluent calculation, and mathematical reasoning.

Specific examples of numerical cognition deficits in DD include: (i) weak conceptual knowledge about the principles of cardinality and ordinality of numbers; (ii) poor understanding of numbers, their magnitude, and the relationship between numbers and the quantity they represent; (iii) weak number fact knowledge, often compensated by counting on fingers to add single-digit numbers instead of recalling arithmetic facts from memory as their typically developing (TD) peers do; (iv) switching operations and mixing procedures during arithmetic problem solving; (v) inability to solve verbally presented mathematical problems; and (vi) difficulties with applying mathematical concepts, facts, or procedures to solve quantitative problems (Butterworth et al. 2011; Geary et al. 1992; Geary et al. 2000; Landerl et al. 2004; Mussolin et al. 2010; Piazza et al. 2010; Schleifer and Landerl 2011).

Because of the broad profile of behavioural and cognitive deficits associated with DD, there is considerable variability in criteria used to probe the disorder and its developmental origins. For example, some studies identify the lowest performing individuals (10th percentile or lower on standardized maths achievement tests) as individuals with severe DD and those with persistently low maths performance (25th percentile or lower) as individuals with mild forms of DD (Geary et al. 2007; Mazzocco et al. 2011). Further, some studies use additional criteria to select a sample of individuals who show discrepancy between maths performance and general intelligence to characterize DD as specific deficits in processing numerical information despite normal intelligence (Butterworth et al. 2011; Kaufmann et al. 2013). While strict definitions of DD are critical for identifying and remediating the most severe forms of the disorder, it is also important to recognize that DD, often co-occurring with reading disorders (RD) (Joyner and Wagner 2020; Willcutt et al. 2013), exists in a wider and heterogeneous group of children and adults, and specific exclusion criteria reduce sensitivity to detect all individuals with dyscalculia (Mazzocco and Myers 2003). Given these characteristics, it is important to take a broad view of the disorder that incorporates both dimensional and categorical approaches to consider theoretical viewpoints that incorporate underlying complexities and heterogeneity of the disorder.

2.3 Overview of Cognitive and Neural Theories of Dyscalculia

Behavioural research has shown that, compared to their TD peers, individuals with DD perform poorly on a broad range of numerical tasks, including magnitude comparison, enumeration, and arithmetic (Landerl et al. 2004; Piazza et al. 2010). Individuals with DD also demonstrate weaknesses in higher-level mathematical problem solving that involves working memory or other domain-general cognitive functioning (Geary et al. 2007). Based on behavioural evidence, several theoretical frameworks have been proposed to describe sources of mathematical difficulties in DD from the viewpoints of 'domain-specific' and 'domain-general' cognitive deficits (Ashkenazi et al. 2013).

A notion central to the vast majority of theories is that DD involves core deficits in number sense: the inability to make judgements about quantity (Butterworth et al. 2011; Piazza et al. 2010). A point of departure for various theories is the relative emphasis on 'domain-specific' and 'domain-general' cognitive processes. While some theories emphasize weaknesses in mapping symbolic numbers to their internal magnitude representations (Rousselle and Noël 2007; Rubinsten and Henik 2005), others posit an essential role for deficits in domain-general working memory and attentional processes (Askenazi and Henik 2010; Rotzer et al. 2009; Toll et al. 2011). Thus, for example, children with DD may have weak domain-general spatial skills even in the absence of domain-specific deficits in symbolic or non-symbolic quantity judgement (Peters et al. 2020).

'Hybrid' models seek to reconcile these divergences and explain DD as a heterogeneous disorder with impairments in multiple cognitive domains, including representing numerical magnitude, mapping symbolic numbers to non-symbolic quantity representations, and manipulating numerical information in working memory, as well as cognitive processes not specific to number processing (Fias et al. 2013; Kaufmann et al. 2013; Szűcs et al. 2013). Consistent with this type of model, it has been suggested that different patterns of domain-specific or domain-general impairments may be a prominent feature of heterogeneity in DD (Skagerlund and Träff 2016; Szűcs 2016). This perspective is particularly useful when considering co-occurrence with RD, which represent an important and significant aspect of DD (Wilson et al. 2015), with estimated DD+RD co-occurrence of up to 70% of the DD population (Willcutt et al. 2013).

Neuroimaging studies in children and adults have led to considerable advances in our understanding of the mechanisms of poor numerical abilities and learning in dyscalculia. Early investigations emphasized deficits in the quantity representation system, anchored in the intraparietal sulcus (IPS) of the posterior parietal cortex, which led to the notion of a core neural deficit as a central tenet of DD (Butterworth et al. 2011). With the growing sophistication of research questions and neuroimaging methodologies, multiple lines of evidence point to considerations of DD as a disorder impacting multiple brain regions. Notably, a growing number of studies as well as meta-analyses of fMRI studies indicate that typical development of mathematical skills relies on distinct yet interacting neurocognitive processing systems (Arsalidou et al. 2018; Fias et al. 2013; Menon 2016). Thus, in addition to the quantity representation system, the visual number-form processing system (anchored in the ventral temporal-occipital cortex), the declarative memory system (anchored in the medial temporal lobe), and the cognitive control system (subserved by the prefrontal cortex) have been implicated in mathematical performance and learning (Menon 2016) (Figure 2.1). Importantly, neuroimaging studies of DD have found evidence for atypical patterns of functional activation in each of these areas, consistent with the multicomponent deficit model, which posits that impairments in any of these neurocognitive systems can lead to poor numerical problem solving and to heterogeneous profiles of deficits that are characteristic of DD (Fias et al. 2013).

In the following sections, we focus on specific domains of numerical cognition that have been extensively investigated in DD and highlight findings in the context of the overarching cognitive and neural theories of dyscalculia summarized here.

2.4 Theories and Models of Number Sense Deficits in Dyscalculia

2.4.1 Behavioural Models

Several theoretical models have been proposed to characterize numerical domain-specific deficits in DD. One model describes DD as a core deficit in number sense

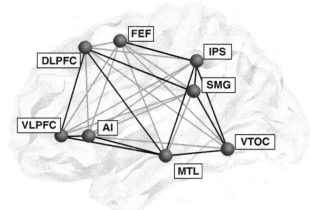

Figure 2.1 *Neurocognitive model of numerical cognition. Schematic diagram of neurocognitive systems involved in numerical problem solving in typical development. The visual number-form processing system, anchored in the ventral temporal-occipital cortex (VTOC), and the quantity representation system, anchored the intraparietal sulcus (IPS), build semantic representations of numerical quantity, which form fundamental building blocks for higher-level mathematical cognition. The declarative memory system, anchored in the medial temporal lobe (MTL), plays an important role in long-term memory formation of number and maths knowledge and binding information together. The fronto-parietal network, including the IPS, supramarginal gyrus (SMG), frontal eye field (FEF), and dorsolateral prefrontal cortex (DLPFC), supports visuospatial attention for objects, short-term representations, and manipulations of quantities, and working memory. Finally, prefrontal control circuits, anchored in the DLPFC, ventrolateral prefrontal cortex (VLPFC), and anterior insula (AI), serve as flexible hubs for integrating information across multiple brain systems, thereby facilitating complex numerical problem solving. Interactions between these functional circuits contribute to both domain-specific and domain-general cognitive processes associated with numerical problem solving. Many of these neurocognitive systems have been shown to be impaired in individuals with dyscalculia. Adapted from Menon (2016).*

(Butterworth et al. 2011; Piazza et al. 2010): the ability to represent or process non-symbolic (e.g., arrays of dots) or symbolic (e.g., Arabic numerals) quantities (Butterworth et al. 2011; Landerl et al. 2004). Consistent with this model, it has been demonstrated that, compared to TD children, children with DD have lower than expected abilities in quantity estimation (Mazzocco et al. 2011; Piazza et al. 2010), abnormal magnitude representations (Ashkenazi et al. 2009), and difficulties processing quantities in both non-symbolic and symbolic formats (Landerl et al. 2009; Mussolin et al. 2010).

An alternative, access-deficit model describes DD as a weakness in mapping symbolic numbers to their internal magnitude representations, which results in specific impairments in symbolic number processing with preserved non-symbolic quantity judgement (De Smedt and Gilmore 2011; Rousselle and Noël 2007). In line with this hypothesis, individuals with DD have difficulties in symbolic but not non-symbolic quantity processing (Holloway and Ansari 2009; Iuculano et al. 2008; Rousselle and Noël 2007), demonstrate weaknesses in automatically accessing internal magnitude representations from symbolic numbers (Rubinsten and Henik 2005), and perform poorly on accessing symbolic quantities but not on accessing non-symbolic quantities (De Smedt and Gilmore 2011).

In this context, there has been considerable debate regarding the relative contributions of symbolic and non-symbolic number sense to overall maths abilities, which may inform our understanding of domain-specific impairments in dyscalculia. Some studies have pointed to the primacy of non-symbolic capacities (Halberda et al. 2008), while others have suggested a stronger relation between symbolic number sense and maths abilities (Holloway and Ansari 2009; Lyons et al. 2014). The emerging consensus based on a meta-analysis of forty-five studies is that symbolic number sense is a more robust predictor of maths skills (Schneider et al. 2017), which coincides with observations of greater impairments in symbolic format in DD (Holloway and Ansari 2009; Iuculano et al. 2008; Rousselle and Noël 2007).

Further studies are needed to clarify how difficulties in symbolic and non-symbolic quantity processing contribute to poor maths abilities in dyscalculia across different developmental stages. One possibility, in line with the access-deficit hypothesis, is that, in earlier stages of development, poor integration between symbolic and non-symbolic quantity representations may contribute to impairments in building semantic associations between mathematical problems and solutions in children with DD. Crucially, the dependence on links between symbolic and non-symbolic quantities in mathematical problem solving may become weaker as individuals acquire proficiency with symbolic numbers over the course of development (Lyons et al. 2012). It remains an open question whether numerical processing deficits in individuals with DD are due to early and persistent difficulties in mapping between symbolic and non-symbolic representation of quantity and how these deficits impact mathematical problem-solving abilities and learning in affected individuals.

2.4.2 Neural Models

The 'domain-specific' core neural deficit model of DD emphasizes impaired representations of numerical quantity in the parietal cortex as the central aspect of the disorder. This framing originated from early lesion studies (Cipolotti et al. 1991; Dehaene and Cohen 1997), and has been supported by functional brain-imaging investigations of numerical magnitude processing, including evidence for impairments in the IPS subdivision of the parietal cortex during numerical processing in DD. To determine representations specific to numerical quantity, while controlling for other perceptual and motor-response factors, neuroimaging studies have manipulated small and large distances between pairs of numbers to investigate these distance effects at the neural level. At the behavioural level, distance effects have been studied in number comparison tasks (Holloway and Ansari 2009; Moyer and Landauer 1967), in which individuals are slower and less accurate when comparing two numbers with a smaller distance (e.g., 1 and 2), compared to two numbers with a larger distance (e.g., 1 and 7). Brain-imaging studies have found that while TD children show greater neural responses in the right IPS for smaller, versus larger, numerical distance, children with DD fail to show such modulation by numerical distance for both non-symbolic (Price et al. 2007) and symbolic (Mussolin et al. 2010) formats. These studies emphasize the crucial format-independent role of the right IPS, which is further supported by a transcranial magnetic stimulation study in adults in which stimulation of the right IPS disrupted magnitude processing (Cohen Kadosh et al. 2007). Structural abnormalities in the left IPS have been also reported in children with DD (Isaacs et al. 2001), consistent with the notion that DD is characterized by neurobiological deficits in the IPS specialized in numerical processing.

The central role of the IPS in DD has also been bolstered by theoretical models emphasizing a crucial role for this region in numerical magnitude processing. For example, the triple code model (TCM) posits an abstract quantity or magnitude processing system supported by the inferior parietal cortex, including the IPS, in contrast to format-dependent representations in the ventral occipito-temporal areas for visual symbols (e.g., the Hindu-Arabic numeral '2') and the perisylvian language network for number words (e.g., the word 'two') (Dehaene and Cohen 1997). A theory of magnitude (ATOM), on the other hand, emphasizes a more general magnitude system in the IPS that represents numbers and other continuous dimensions such as time and space (Walsh 2003), and, furthermore, suggests that neural representations in the IPS are not abstract but format dependent (Butterworth and Walsh 2011; Kadosh and Walsh 2009).

Despite the finding that deficits in the IPS are a prominent neurobiological feature of DD, and despite its central role in theoretical models of numerical representations, it is important to recognize that the IPS and adjoining parietal cortical regions implicated in numerical cognition are also involved in domain-general cognitive processes such as working memory and attention (Szűcs and Goswami 2013). Furthermore, aberrancies in multiple other functional brain systems are also prominent in DD, which calls for a theory that explains a broad profile of deficits from a systems neuroscience perspective. In this vein, Fias et al. (2013) proposed a multicomponent deficit model to overcome the limitations of theories based on a single core deficit in DD. According to this model, impairments in any number of neurocognitive systems typically implicated in maths skill development (Figure 2.1) can lead to poor numerical problem solving (Fias et al. 2013). Moreover, different patterns of neurocognitive impairments may be associated with different subtypes of DD.

Consistent with the view that numerical deficits in DD cannot be localized to one brain region, individuals with DD show atypical functional brain activity not only in the IPS but also in the ventral temporal-occipital and multiple prefrontal cortices during basic number comparison tasks. Decreased activation in relation to the numerical distance has been detected in the prefrontal areas during symbolic (Mussolin, De Volder et al. 2010) and non-symbolic (Price et al. 2007) number comparison tasks, though the specific subdivision and laterality of the prefrontal cortex has not been consistent across these studies. One study which parametrically varied numerical distance during non-symbolic number comparison found evidence for compensatory engagement of the right fusiform gyrus within the ventral temporal-occipital cortex, as well as the bilateral supplementary motor area, but not the posterior parietal cortex, in children with DD (Kucian et al. 2011). Reduced modulation of the left fusiform gyrus by the numerical distance has been also reported in children with DD (Price et al. 2007) during non-symbolic number comparison. Finally, consistent with this model, evidence to date also suggests that maths interventions that target multiple deficits in DD lead to normalization of hyperactivity and hyperconnectivity in distributed brain systems observed in DD, not just in the parietal cortex (Kucian et al. 2011; Iuculano et al. 2015; Michels et al. 2018). Taken together, a wide range of studies made clear that aberrant responses in multiple neurocognitive systems beyond the IPS are prominent in DD, providing support for the multicomponent deficit model.

It should be noted that the direction of these effects has not always been consistent, with evidence for both hyper- and hypoactivation of brain regions typically activated by neurotypical individuals (Kaufmann et al. 2011). The conflicting direction of activation in DD relative to the TD group reported in studies to date may, to some extent, be related to the control task used. While some fMRI studies have assessed neural distance effects as described earlier, others have used low-level non-numerical control tasks. A careful examination of the different types of contrasts reported in studies suggests that children with DD, compared to TD children, often show hyperactivation during magnitude comparison relative to low-level control tasks, whereas hypoactivation (or weak modulation between quantities) has been reported when relatively well-matched conditions are compared, as in the case of numerical distance effects. Thus, for example, despite weak modulation by numerical distance, when activations were compared to passive fixation, children with DD showed greater activation than TD children in several brain regions, including the right supramarginal gyrus and right postcentral gyrus (Mussolin et al. 2010). Similarly, when magnitude comparison was contrasted against judgement of palm rotation, children with DD showed greater activation in the left and right IPS, supramarginal gyrus, paracentral lobule, and right superior frontal gyrus (Kaufmann et al. 2009). These findings suggest that children with DD can engage compensatory mechanisms in task-relevant brain regions. Similar to children, adults with dyscalculia have also been reported to show compensatory hyper-activation in multiple PFC regions, including the right superior frontal and left inferior frontal gyri (Cappelletti and Price 2014).

Recent advances in neuroimaging-analysis techniques have allowed researchers to investigate brain activation patterns on a fine spatial scale, independent of overall differences in signal level (Formisano and Kriegeskorte 2012). This approach has revealed that adults with dyscalculia, compared to healthy controls, show weaker neural discrimination between non-symbolic numbers in multiple parietal, temporal, and frontal regions (Figure 2.2A), suggesting less precise quantity representations in dyscalculia (Bulthé et al. 2019). Importantly, such group differences in activation patterns were not observed in univariate analyses for either non-symbolic or symbolic formats.

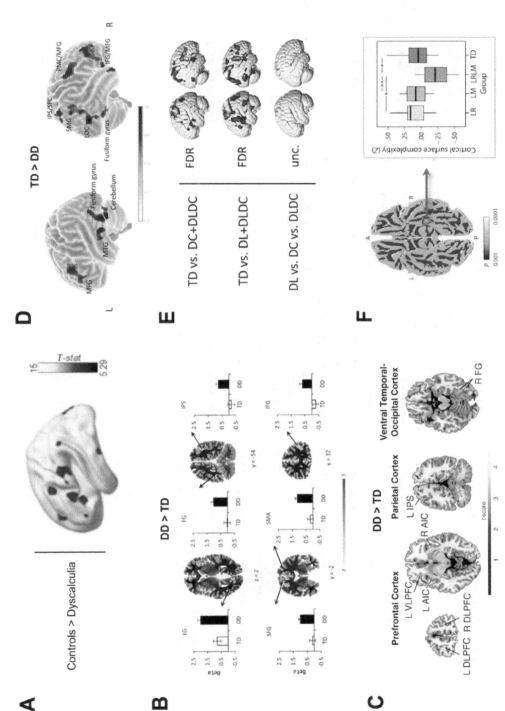

Figure 2.2 *Neurobiological basis of dyscalculia: evidence for a 'hybrid' multicomponent deficit model. Various functional and structural neuroimaging studies suggest 'hybrid' domain-specific and domain-general deficits in multiple neurocognitive systems in dyscalculia. A. Multivoxel pattern searchlight analysis shows less distinguishable neural representations between non-symbolic numbers in adults with*

Caption for Figure 2.2 (cont.)

dyscalculia, compared to controls. Group differences were observed in multiple parietal, temporal, and frontal regions. No significant group difference was observed in the quality of neural representations of symbolic numerical magnitude. Adapted from Bulthé et al. (2018). **B**. Arithmetic problem solving (addition and subtraction), compared to a low-level passive fixation, is associated with hyper-activation in children with developmental dyscalculia (DD), compared to typically developing (TD) children, in multiple brain areas, including the left lingual gyrus (LG), left fusiform gyrus (FG), right intraparietal sulcus (IPS), superior frontal gyrus (SFG) bilaterally, right supplementary motor area (SMA), and right inferior frontal gyrus (IFG). Adapted from Rosenberg-Lee et al. (2014). **C**. Children with DD, relative to TD children, overactivate a distributed set of brain areas in prefrontal, parietal, and ventral temporal-occipital cortices during arithmetic problem solving (addition), compared to low-level control (number identification). AIC: anterior insula cortex; DLPFC: dorsolateral prefrontal cortex; IPS: intraparietal sulcus; VLPFC: ventrolateral prefrontal cortex; L = left, R = right. Adapted from Iuculano et al. (2015). **D**. Modulation of brain responses during 'complex' $(x + y)$ vs. 'simple' $(x + 1)$ arithmetic problem solving is weaker in children with DD compared to TD children. IPS: intraparietal sulcus; LOC: lateral occipital cortex; MFG: middle frontal gyrus; MTG: middle temporal gyrus; PMC: premotor cortex; SMG: supramarginal gyrus; SPL: superior parietal lobule; L = left, R = right. Adapted from Ashkenazi et al. (2012). **E**. Children with dyscalculia (DC), dyslexia (DL), and co-occurring dyslexia and dyscalculia (DLDC) show hypoactivation in frontal and parietal areas, compared to a TD group, during non-symbolic arithmetic problem solving (subtraction). Activation clusters are shown FDR-corrected ($p < 0.05$) or at an uncorrected ($p < 0.001$) statistical threshold for group comparisons between DL vs. DC vs. DLDC. Adapted from Peters et al. (2018). **F**. Cortical surface folding complexity in the right parahippocampal gyrus is reduced in children with co-occurring difficulties in maths and reading (LRLM), compared to children with isolated low reading ability (LR) and low mathematical ability (LM) and TD children. Boxplots show medians (horizontal lines) and standard deviations (vertical lines) of standardized measures of cortical surface complexity in the cluster in each group. *: $p < 0.005$; **: $p < 0.001$. L = left, R = right, A = anterior, P = posterior. Adapted from Skeide et al. (2018).

This study also found greater overall functional connectivity across task conditions between visual regions and ventral temporal-occipital cortex in adults with dyscalculia relative to controls. Although these findings provide important additional insights into impaired numerical processing in dyscalculia, further studies are needed to determine whether similar patterns of altered activation and connectivity profiles exist from early childhood or whether different patterns emerge at different developmental stages.

In summary, the general pattern that is emerging from fMRI studies on basic numerical processing is one of abnormal activity in distributed brain areas that extend beyond the IPS into multiple posterior parietal, prefrontal, and ventral temporal-occipital cortices distributed across both hemispheres. Comparisons with low-level baseline tasks reveal compensatory engagement of these brain areas in ways that may allow individuals with DD to achieve similar levels of performance as their TD peers on basic numerical quantity processing tasks. At the same time, evidence from well-controlled tasks involving numerical distance effects and a refined analysis approach suggests weaker magnitude-related modulation of brain responses in individuals with DD relative to their TD peers. Taken together, these findings reveal converging evidence for the multi-component deficit model of DD and suggest that even for the case of low-level number sense tasks, neurocognitive impairments in DD are more broadly distributed than previously thought.

2.5 Theories and Models of Arithmetic Problem-Solving Deficits in Dyscalculia

2.5.1 Behavioural Models

Arithmetic problem-solving difficulties are one of the most prominent features of DD (Kaufmann et al. 2013). Individuals with DD typically reveal more counting procedure errors, deficits in the use of developmentally appropriate arithmetic problem-solving strategies, and poor fluency in retrieval of arithmetic facts (Geary et al. 2000; Jordan and Montani 1997; Ostad 1997; Ostad 1998). Over the course of arithmetic skill acquisition, children transition from using a mix of procedure-based strategies, such as finger counting, to memory-based strategies, such as direct retrieval from long-term memory (Siegler and Shrager 1984). The speed and accuracy with which individual strategies are executed also improves with development and experience. However, considerable variability in strategy use has been observed across individuals with different levels of maths abilities, and children with DD persist in using less mature strategies (such as finger counting) to solve arithmetic problems for many more years than TD children (Geary et al. 2000; Ostad 1998).

Fluency in arithmetic problem solving may not only require efficient processing of numbers but also more general cognitive abilities to perform calculations or retrieve answers. As such, difficulties in any of these aspects can potentially impact arith-metic problem solving in DD. In this context, behavioural studies have shown that impairments in domain-specific numerical processing (Landerl et al. 2004) as well as weaknesses in domain-general cognitive abilities (Geary et al. 2007) contribute to weak arithmetic problem solving in DD. As reviewed in Section 2.5.2, the evidence from neuroimaging studies is mostly consistent with the view that multiple neuro-cognitive deficits contribute to poor arithmetic problem-solving skills in individuals with DD.

2.5.2 Neural Models

Similar to findings from studies on basic numerical quantity processing, neuroim-aging studies of arithmetic problem solving in DD have also found evidence for atypical functional activation not only in the IPS but also multiple prefrontal regions during mental addition tasks. Crucially, differences in multiple functional systems have been found even when behavioural performance is comparable between groups (Ashkenazi et al. 2012; Kucian et al. 2006). One study of a group of eighteen children with DD in grades 3 to 6 revealed reduced brain activity in the right IPS and the ventrolateral and dorsolateral PFC, but only for addition problems that participants were asked to solve approximately (Kucian et al. 2006). In contrast, Davis and colleagues (Davis et al. 2009) used similar tasks and found hyper-activation of the posterior parietal and prefrontal cortices during both 'exact' and 'approximate' addition tasks in 3rd grade children with DD (Davis et al. 2009). Some of these discrepancies in the direction of brain activation in the DD relative to the TD group might be related to differences between these studies in the criteria used to define DD, the age ranges studied, and developmental changes in arithmetic proficiency that occur during key periods of skill acquisition between grades 3 and 6.

More targeted studies with 7–9 year-old children with DD, carefully matched to their TD peers on intelligence, working memory, and reading, suggest that while atypical responses are common in DD, the precise profile of activation differences depends crucially on the control tasks used (Ashkenazi et al. 2012; Iuculano et al. 2015; Rosenberg-Lee et al. 2014), similar to the case of studies on numerical processing in DD described earlier. When compared to a passive fixation baseline or low-level control, children with DD have been shown to engage multiple parietal, ventral temporal-occipital, and prefrontal cortices at higher levels than their TD peers during arithmetic problem solving (Iuculano et al. 2015; Rosenberg-Lee et al. 2014) (Figures 2.2B–C). However, when 'complex' 'x + y' problems are used relative to a 'simple' 'x + 1' control problem, children with DD fail to show appropriate increases in brain response with increasing arithmetic complexity (Ashkenazi et al. 2012) (Figure 2.2D). Weaker modulatory effects of addition problem complexity (less differentiated neural responses between complex and simple problems) have been detected not only in the IPS but also the adjoining superior parietal lobule in the dorsal posterior parietal cortex, supramarginal gyrus in the ventral posterior parietal cortex, and bilateral dorsolateral prefrontal cortex. These effects suggest that deficits in multiple neurocognitive systems implicated in mathematical cognition contribute to the impairments in numerical problem solving in DD (Fias et al. 2013).

Furthermore, neural representations of arithmetic problems have been shown to be less distinct in children with DD relative to their TD peers (Ashkenazi et al. 2012). Children with DD showed less differentiated activation patterns to 'complex' and 'simple' arithmetic problems in the bilateral IPS, independent of overall differences in signal level. Taken together, these results suggest that children with DD not only have weak modulation of response in key brain regions implicated in numerical cognition, they also fail to generate distinct neural representations for distinct arithmetic problems as seen in TD peers.

Although previous studies of arithmetic problem solving in children with DD have mainly focused on addition problems, there is evidence to suggest that they are especially impaired in their ability to solve subtraction problems (Jordan, Hanich, and Kaplan 2003; Ostad 2000). Despite their surface similarity, subtraction problems rely more on calculation-based procedures and less on memory-retrieval strategies, relative to addition problems (Barrouillet et al. 2008). Contrasting brain responses to these two distinct but related operations has provided further insights into problem-solving deficits arising from weaknesses in executing calculation procedures. Consistent with behavioural findings, relative to TD children, children with DD demonstrated more aberrant brain responses during subtraction than addition problem solving (Rosenberg-Lee et al. 2014). Remarkably, despite poorer performance on subtraction problems, children with DD showed hyper-activation in multiple IPS and superior parietal lobule subdivisions in the dorsal posterior parietal cortex as well as the fusiform gyrus in ventral temporal-occipital cortex.

Together, in line with the multicomponent deficit model of DD, these results suggest that children with DD show extensive dysfunction in multiple posterior parietal, ventral temporal-occipital, and prefrontal cortices during arithmetic problem solving. Critically, hyper-activation observed in multiple brain areas (Iuculano et al. 2015; Rosenberg-Lee et al. 2014) may reflect a need for more processing resources during problem solving, rather than an inability to activate task-relevant brain areas. Furthermore, functional connectivity analyses revealed hyperconnectivity, rather than hypo-connectivity, between the IPS and multiple brain systems including the lateral fronto-parietal and default mode networks in children with DD during both addition and subtraction (Rosenberg-Lee et al. 2014). These findings suggest that the IPS and its distributed functional circuits are a major locus of dysfunction during arithmetic problem solving in DD. Importantly, inappropriate task modulation and hyperconnectivity in critical brain circuits, rather than under-engagement and under-connectivity, are key neural mechanisms underlying arithmetic problem-solving difficulties in children with DD.

2.6 Theories and Models of Domain-General Cognitive Deficits in Dyscalculia

2.6.1 Behavioural Models

Beyond domain-specific numerical impairments, there is growing evidence that deficits in working memory, the ability to maintain and manipulate information in short-term memory (Constantinidis and Klingberg 2016), and other domain-general cognitive abilities, such as attention, executive function, and inhibition, also contribute to weak maths problem-solving skills in individuals with DD (Askenazi and Henik 2010; Bugden and Ansari 2016; Geary et al. 2007; Szűcs et al. 2013; Toll et al. 2011), which has led to the broader framing of a domain-general deficit model in DD.

In line with this model, it has been suggested that poor performance in numerical order judgement in children with DD may arise from verbal working-memory impairments (Attout and Majerus 2015). Similarly, some behavioural evidence suggests that core deficits of DD generalize to difficulties in processing non-numerical magnitudes such as duration (De Visscher et al. 2018) and general deficits in ordering across numerical and non-numerical (e.g., ordering of events) formats (Morsanyi et al. 2018). Furthermore, it has been shown that children with DD have weak domain-general spatial skills even in the absence of domain-specific deficits in symbolic or non-symbolic quantity processing (Peters et al. 2020). Finally, Rotzer and colleagues (2009) found that children with DD have lower visuospatial working memory, measured using a Corsi Block Tapping test, than TD children.

While both verbal and visuospatial working memory deficits have been reported in behavioural studies (Peng and Fuchs 2016; Swanson et al. 2006), neuroimaging studies reviewed herein suggest that visuospatial working memory is a particular source of weak arithmetic problem-solving skills in DD (Ashkenazi et al. 2013; Rotzer et al. 2009).

2.6.2 Neural Models

Consistent with the domain-general deficit model, neuroimaging studies have provided evidence that DD is associated with deficits in multiple frontal and parietal regions implicated in working memory and cognitive control (Davis et al. 2009; Fias et al. 2013). In this context, it should be noted that the IPS – the brain region commonly associated with neurocognitive deficits in DD – is not only important for numerical quantity judgement, but also subserves other domain-general cognitive functions such as visuospatial attention and short-term memory (Hubbard et al. 2005). Such domain-general working memory impairments may occur outside the context of numerical problem solving in DD. For example, Rotzer et al. (2009) found that children with DD have lower activity levels in the right IPS, right inferior frontal gyrus, and right insula during a visuospatial working memory task, and that right IPS activity is positively correlated with visuospatial working memory ability.

Ashkenazi and colleagues (2013) provided further evidence for a neurocognitive link between working memory deficits and arithmetic problem-solving difficulties in

DD (Ashkenazi et al. 2013). Children with DD demonstrated lower visuospatial working memory, despite normal intelligence and preserved abilities on other components of working memory (verbal working memory and central executive). In TD children, responses in the left supramarginal gyrus, bilateral dorsolateral and ventrolateral prefrontal cortex, cingulate gyrus and precuneus, and fusiform gyrus during arithmetic problem solving were positively correlated with visuospatial working memory ability, whereas no such relations were observed in the DD group, which indicates that children with DD do not use visuospatial working memory resources appropriately when solving arithmetic problems. These results suggest that low visuospatial working memory needs to be considered as a specific source of vulnerability in DD and as one of the key components in cognitive, neurobiological, and developmental models of this disorder.

Although evidence is relatively sparse compared to deficits in the fronto-parietal network, some studies have shown that the declarative memory system in the medial temporal lobe, thought to play an important role in long-term memory formation through binding of new and old information (Menon 2016), is impaired in individuals with DD. In neurotypical children and adults, the medial temporal lobe declarative memory system, and particularly the hippocampus subdivision, has been implicated in facilitating the transition of arithmetic problem-solving strategies from more effortful procedural strategies to more efficient memory-retrieval-based strategies in both functional and structural neuroimaging studies (Bloechle et al. 2016; Klein et al. 2019; Qin et al. 2014; Supekar et al. 2013). We propose that difficulties with arithmetic fact retrieval commonly observed in children with DD may be linked to the impairments in the medial temporal lobe system. Consistent with this view, in children with DD, relative to TD children, hyper-activation (Iuculano et al. 2015) and hyperconnectivity (Michels et al. 2018) have been observed in the hippocampus. Converging evidence from structural neuroimaging studies indicate that there are also structural abnormalities in the medial temporal lobe system in DD, as described in the following section. Future studies that employ both domain-specific and domain-general tasks may help determine the sources of deficits in the medial temporal lobe system in DD.

2.7 Neural Circuit and Anatomical Models of Neurocognitive Deficits in Dyscalculia

As reviewed in the previous sections, the profile of aberrant functional activation or connectivity in DD can vary considerably with the level of task difficulty, specific type of task, or control condition used, along with other factors such as age, inclusion criteria for DD, and individual differences in task performance or strategy use. In this context, studies on intrinsic functional connectivity (Greicius et al. 2003) and neuroanatomical investigations of grey and white matter (Johansen-Berg and Behrens 2006; Wilkey et al. 2018) have the potential to provide a general view of neurobiological deficits in DD independent of task engagement. More broadly, systematic identification of alterations in task-free functional network organization and structural integrity can provide convergent evidence for neurobiological deficits in DD and inform the development of brain-based biomarkers.

Using intrinsic functional connectivity analysis, Jolles et al. (2016) observed that children with DD have increased functional connectivity of the IPS with multiple frontal and parietal regions, compared to their TD peers. Further, children with DD, relative to the TD group, showed higher low-frequency fluctuations in the fronto-parietal network, which demonstrates widespread aberrant functional network activity in DD beyond the IPS. These results provide further support for the notion that DD is characterized by deficits in multiple neurocognitive systems.

Structural neuroimaging studies have identified aberrations in multiple distributed posterior brain structures as well as white matter macro- and microstructure in temporo-parietal areas and multiple long-distance pathways as key neuroanatomical correlates of DD. Decreased grey matter volume in multiple parietal, temporal, and occipital areas has been consistently reported in children and adolescents with DD (Ranpura et al. 2013; Rotzer et al. 2008; Rykhlevskaia et al. 2009). Structural abnormalities in DD have been observed in areas that have been implicated in numerical problem solving in typical development, including the IPS and superior parietal lobule in the posterior parietal cortex, fusiform gyrus in the ventral temporal-occipital cortex, and hippocampus and parahippocampal gyrus in the medial temporal lobe. Deficiencies in microstructure and long-range white matter projection fibres linking the right fusiform gyrus with the temporo-parietal cortex have also been reported in children with DD (Rykhlevskaia et al. 2009). Additionally, deficits in the inferior fronto-occipital fasciculus and inferior and superior longitudinal fasciculus, tracts that link parietal, temporal, occipital, and frontal regions, have also been detected. These observations of deficits in multiple white matter pathways linking the posterior parietal cortex with ventral temporal-occipital and prefrontal cortices have raised the possibility that DD may be, at least partly, a disconnection syndrome (Kucian et al. 2014).

Consistent with these observations, a recent longitudinal study showed that children with DD have reduced grey matter volume in multiple parietal, temporal, occipital, and frontal regions across four years of development from 8 to 10 years of age, compared to TD children (McCaskey et al. 2020). Further, reduced white matter volume was observed across this developmental period in multiple tracts, including the inferior fronto-occipital fasciculus and inferior and superior longitudinal fasciculus. These findings suggest that structural abnormalities in grey and white matter are a potential locus of neurocognitive deficits in DD that persist over multiple years of development in school-aged children.

2.8 Models of Reading-related Co-occurrence and Heterogeneity in Dyscalculia

2.8.1 Behavioural Models

While the focus on relatively pure and well-controlled cases of DD is important for characterizing its primary neurofunctional and neuroanatomical correlates, it is important to note that DD, like almost all learning disorders, is highly heterogeneous in its symptom profile. Notably, co-occurrence rates with RD have been estimated to be as high as 70% (Willcutt et al. 2013). A recent meta-analysis indicates that individuals with DD are twice as likely to have RD than those without DD (Joyner and Wagner 2020).

Converging evidence from a number of studies indicates that RD is associated with phonological deficits whereas DD arises from deficits in representation of quantities (Landerl et al. 2009; Rubinsten and Henik 2006). Beyond these 'domain-specific' processes, multiple domain-general cognitive processes are shared between mathematics and reading, including retrieval of abstract symbols, processing speed, attention, working memory, and cognitive control. Impairments in any one of these domain-general skills could conceivably play an important role in both pure and co-occurring conditions (Moll et al. 2016; Willcutt et al. 2013). Notably, in a study of more than 1,000 children, Wilcutt et al. (2013) found that deficits in reading and mathematics are associated with shared weaknesses in working memory, processing speed, and verbal comprehension. In contrast, RD was uniquely associated with weaknesses in phoneme awareness and naming speed, while DD was uniquely associated with weaknesses in set shifting (task switching).

Several lines of behavioural research pinpoint more precisely potential loci of reading-related deficits that can impact DD. First, it has been shown that poor literacy can impair basic symbolic numerical quantity processing (Zebian and Ansari 2012). Second, arithmetic problem solving in a number–word format is found to be a particular source of difficulty for children with co-occurring DD+RD (Jordan et al. 2003; Powell et al. 2009). Third, evidence suggests that deficits in phonological awareness are associated with difficulties in memorizing and retrieving basic arithmetic facts from long-term memory (De Smedt et al. 2010), especially when verbal retrieval is the optimal strategy (Boets and De Smedt 2010).

These findings provide support for multiple neurocognitive deficit models of RD and DD and suggest that RD and DD are distinct but related disorders that co-occur as a result of shared neurocognitive weaknesses in working memory, processing speed, and verbal comprehension.

2.8.2 Neural Models

The neurobiology of 'pure' forms of DD and RD has been generally consistent with the proposal that these disorders are associated with two independent cognitive deficits, namely a core phonological deficit in the case of RD and a deficit in number sense in the case of DD (Landerl et al. 2009). The distinct neurocognitive profiles are reflected in the differential role of the left superior and middle temporal gyri in RD, and the bilateral dorsal IPS and superior parietal lobule in DD. Yet, this pattern of representations may increasingly overlap between these domains as the complexity of numerical processing increases and access to multiple overlapping cognitive resources is needed. This is true even for relatively low-level cognitive processes such as basic quantity processing and verbally mediated fact retrieval. It has been shown that children with DD, RD, or co-occurring DD+RD perform more poorly on both visual perception and non-symbolic number comparison than TD children (Cheng et al. 2018), and adults with RD retrieve fewer arithmetic facts from memory and are less efficient in doing so (De Smedt and Boets 2010). Thus, although domain-specific deficits may exist, co-occurring DD and RD may share multiple overlapping neurocognitive impairments.

The association between phonological awareness and fact retrieval appears to be especially prominent in solving addition problems, as compared to subtraction problem solving, which relies more on calculation-based procedures. For instance, children with RD showed reduced activation in the left supramarginal gyrus and compensatory engagement of the right supramarginal gyrus during addition but not subtraction problem solving (Evans et al. 2014). This finding suggests that children with RD use a suboptimal route for retrieval-based arithmetic operation (addition), engaging the right hemisphere ventral posterior parietal region typically used by TD children for procedure-based arithmetic operation (subtraction). These results suggest a possibility of alternate language pathways for mathematical problem solving in children with co-occurring DD+RD.

For more complex word-based maths problems, which place stronger demands on verbal rehearsal, engagement of the left superior and middle temporal gyri and ventrolateral prefrontal systems involved in phonological and language processing is likely. Consistent with this view, behavioural studies have shown that, when compared with children with DD, children with DD+RD show similar abilities on tasks involving basic numerical processing, but they show profound impairments in word-based maths problem solving (Jordan et al. 2003). Beyond the contributions of verbally mediated mathematical reasoning, deficits in working memory and attentional processes shared between maths and reading (Houdé et al. 2010) may also contribute to co-occurring DD+RD. Such a view is consistent with findings of aberrant engagement of multiple prefrontal regions, including ventrolateral and dorsolateral prefrontal cortices, by children with DD (Rosenberg-Lee et al. 2014).

Comparative neurobiological studies between DD, RD, and co-occurring DD+RD groups can characterize how overlapping and distinct maths- and reading-related deficits contribute to weak numerical problem solving in co-occurring DD+RD. There are several possibilities for neurobiological pathways to co-occurring DD+RD (Ashkenazi et al. 2013): (i) a domain-specific hypothesis that co-occurring DD+RD condition is the 'additive' effect of unique impairments in pure DD and RD; (ii) a domain-general hypothesis that the co-occurrence arises from impairments in domain-general cognitive functions such as working memory and long-term memory formation, mediated by the fronto-parietal network and medial temporal lobe regions; and (iii) a phonological deficit hypothesis that specific impairments in phonological processing systems contribute to difficulties in verbally mediated arithmetic fact retrieval and word-based maths problem solving in co-occurring DD+RD.

Emerging findings on the neural basis of co-occurring DD+RD from comparative neuroimaging studies support the domain-general hypothesis as well as the 'hybrid' of domain-general and domain-specific hypotheses. Peters et al. (2018) observed reduced brain activation patterns in the distributed frontal, parietal, temporal, and occipital regions for children with DD or RD and co-occurring DD+RD relative to TD children during non-symbolic arithmetic problem solving (Peters et al. 2018) (Figure 2.2E). Importantly, no significant differences in brain activation were observed between DD, RD, and DD+RD even at an uncorrected statistical threshold. Additional multivariate classification analysis revealed that the brain activation patterns were distinguishable between TD children and each group of children with learning disorders, but those between DD, RD, and DD+RD were indistinguishable (i.e., generalizable from one disorder to another). Thus, consistent with the domain-general hypothesis, these results suggest that shared neurocognitive deficits across DD and RD may underlie poor numerical problem solving in co-occurring DD+RD.

Skeide et al. (2018) demonstrated reduced cortical surface complexity in the right parahippocampal gyrus in the medial temporal lobe as a distinguishable domain-general neuroanatomical feature in co-occurring DD+RD, as compared to children with isolated DD or RD and TD children (Skeide et al. 2018) (Figure 2.2F). In addition, this study showed that co-occurring DD+RD is characterized by weaker intrinsic functional connectivity of the right parahippocampal gyrus with brain regions specialized for maths(right IPS) and reading (left posterior fusiform gyrus), compared to the DD, RD, and TD groups. These findings provide support for a complex interplay between domain-general and domain-specific cognitive mechanisms that underlie co-occurring learning difficulties, and suggest that multi-dimensional models that incorporate both domain-specific and domain-general hypotheses may be more appropriate for understanding the heterogeneous neurobiological mechanisms that contribute to different types of learning disorders.

2.9 Conclusion

The debate regarding cognitive and neurobiological factors underlying impairments in numerical skills in DD has often been centred around the tendency to focus on a single explanatory cognitive factor or brain region. Cognitive theories of DD as well as neuroimaging evidence reviewed here provide support for a neurocognitive framework involving impairments in multiple functional components and distributed brain circuits that contribute to weak numerical problem solving in DD. Heterogeneity and co-occurrence observed in DD are a natural consequence of deficits in multiple neurocognitive systems (Fias et al. 2013).

By developing neurocognitive models of DD that account for multiple deficits in the disorder, neurobiological studies have significantly contributed to behavioural and cognitive theories of DD, and have advanced our understanding of the neural mechanisms underlying DD. As highlighted in this chapter, it is now increasingly evident that neurocognitive deficits in DD are not localized to a single brain region, and that individuals with DD show deficits in a distributed, interconnected set of brain regions that include multiple parietal, prefrontal, ventral temporal-occipital, and medial temporal lobe regions that integrate key components of numerical information processing. Our chapter has also emphasized the close interplay between deficits in 'domain-specific' and 'domain-general' functional circuitry, highlighting the importance of integrative network models for probing cognitive dysfunction in DD.

Additional studies are needed to further refine theories and models of DD by carefully characterizing different patterns of brain responses, representations, and connectivity in relation to various domains of mathematics and domain-general cognition that contribute to individual differences in mathematical skills. These advances will depend on integrating cognitive and systems neuroscience research with computational modelling. Future studies will also need to investigate processing bottlenecks in DD from the perspective of multidimensional neurocognitive deficits by employing tasks in various cognitive domains, including those that individuals with DD perform relatively well and those that they fail dramatically.

Given the high rates of co-occurrence of DD and RD, cases of co-occurring DD and RD provide a distinct opportunity to clarify the unique and shared brain systems that adversely impact learning and skill acquisition in affected individuals. A more comprehensive understanding of the cognitive and neurobiological factors that contribute to high rates of co-occurrence will inform strategies for remediating deficits in some of the most academically challenged students across various educational systems throughout the world.

Finally, the literatures describing cognitive and neural bases of maths and reading difficulties have evolved largely independently from one another until recently, and further work is needed to extend the models of co-occurrence and heterogeneity to other neurodevelopmental disorders. Across samples included in this review, most of the work has focused on cross-sectional studies in US and European populations. Understanding how different kinds of educational practice in various academic settings across the globe influence numerical skill development and how the proposed neurocognitive systems mature with learning and development will be important avenues for future research.

Suggestions for Further Reading

Fias, W., V. Menon, and D. Szűcs. 2013. 'Multiple Components of Developmental Dyscalculia'. *Trends in Neuroscience and Education* 2 (2): 43–7. https://doi.org/10.1016/j.tine.2013.06.006.

Kaufmann, L., M. M. Mazzocco, A. Dowker, et al. 2013. 'Dyscalculia from a Developmental and Differential Perspective'. *Frontiers in Psychology* 4 (August): 516. https://doi.org/10.3389/fpsyg.2013.00516.

Menon, V., A. Padmanabhan, and F. Schwartz. 2020. 'Cognitive Neuroscience of Dyscalculia and Math Learning Disabilities'. In *The Oxford Handbook of Developmental Cognitive Neuroscience*, edited by K. Cohen Kadosh. Oxford University Press.

3 Computational Models of Reading and Mathematical Difficulties

Marco Zorzi and Alberto Testolin

3.1 Introduction: Computational Modelling for Understanding Typical and Atypical Development

Computational modelling is a powerful tool in cognitive science to evaluate or compare existing theories and to make novel experimental predictions. In contrast to the vague formulation of traditional verbal theories (e.g., box-and-arrow models), computational models need to be formally explicit in any implementational detail and can produce accurate simulations of human performance. Computational modelling has many different flavours that reflect distinct theoretical approaches to understanding human cognition (see McClelland 2009, for a review). When it comes to understanding the acquisition of cognitive skills, as well as how learning might be affected by developmental disorders, we argue that connectionist modelling has proven to be the most suitable and successful approach. Before focusing on reading aloud and numeracy, we briefly review the connectionist approach to cognitive development and highlight recent theoretical and methodological advances that have set the stage for more realistic, large-scale models that can be used to predict individual differences in both typical and atypical development.

3.1.1 Connectionist Models of Learning and Development

The connectionist framework assumes that cognitive processes are implemented in terms of complex, non-linear interactions among a large number of simple, neuron-like processing units that form a neural network (Rumelhart and McClelland 1986). Neurons (units) are usually organized into groups known as layers, typically with at least one layer encoding the networks' input and one layer encoding the networks' output. Any remaining neurons are arranged into one or more intermediate ('hidden') layers that encode the internal representations mediating between input and output. Learning in neural network models is instantiated in terms of changes in the weights of the connections that link any pair of neurons. A variety of learning procedures can be used for training artificial neural networks, but the most widely used in cognitive science has been the error-correction algorithm known as back-propagation (Rumelhart et al. 1986). In this framework, weight changes are computed in a way that reduces the discrepancy between the output generated by the network and the correct (desired) response.

The connectionist framework has been successfully used to explore the emergence of cognitive abilities in a variety of domains. Neural network models are particularly attractive for understanding developmental phenomena (for reviews, see Elman et al. 1996; Mareschal and Thomas 2007) because the trajectories in task performance or in the emergence of internal representations can be examined during learning and serve as a window into human development. It is immediately apparent how this approach can be extended to the study of developmental disorders understood as atypical developmental trajectories that emerge as consequence of alternative starting conditions (e.g., Harm and Seidenberg 1999, for dyslexia; Thomas and Karmiloff-Smith 2003, for language acquisition). These starting conditions can be instantiated using different initial constraints to the network architecture (e.g., different number of hidden neurons or hidden layers) or to the input structure (i.e., how information is encoded across input neurons), noise in the computations, or impoverished environment (i.e., a reduced training set). A key insight offered by the simulation of atypical learning trajectories is that initial differences in a single parameter can lead to very different learning outcomes, as well as that different initial states may produce similar end states (Oliver et al. 2000). More generally, any model component can be 'impaired' to implement a specific hypothesis and its consequences can be analysed through computer simulations (e.g., Harm and Seidenberg 1999; Perry et al. 2019; Ziegler et al. 2008; Ziegler et al. 2014). This allows one to understand the causal relation between deficient model components and behavioural performance.

3.1.2 From 'Toy Models' to Large-scale Models and Deep Learning

A toy model is a deliberately simple model including only the essential details that are required to explain a certain phenomenon of interest. In cognitive science, this notion pertains to how input representations are implemented (e.g., using a small set of hand-coded features as opposed to a full-blown image), to the model architecture (e.g., the number of neurons and layers in a neural network), and to the size of the data set that is used for learning. The use of toy models in cognitive science has been fruitful, and is also justified by the sheer computational burden of simulations carried out on the computer hardware available to cognitive scientists, at least until the last decade. The historical landmarks regarding the computational modelling of reading processes provide a nice illustration of how models have progressively changed in scale. For example, the Interactive Activation Model of letter perception and visual word recognition (McClelland and Rumelhart 1981) had a lexicon that included only 300 four-letter English words, but it offered seminal insights into the role of top-down processing in perception and cognition. The Parallel Distributed Processing (PDP) model of reading aloud (Seidenberg and McClelland 1989) was trained on a set of approximately 3,000 monosyllabic monomorphemic English words; although most words in English have more than one syllable, the model provided a novel (non-conventional) perspective on the functional architecture of reading.

Furthermore, it offered seminal insights into how learning to read is modulated by word frequency and consistency of the spelling–sound mappings. Finally, the Connectionist Dual Process (CDP++) model of reading aloud (Perry et al. 2010) successfully extended a previous model of monosyllabic word reading (CDP+; Perry et al. 2007) to polysyllabic words by incorporating new mechanisms for handling syllabification and stress assignment. With its lexicon of more than 32,000 words, CDP++ is a notable example for successfully scaling up a connectionist model to a size that more realistically approximates the human lexical system. Connectionist models of reading have also been extended to alphabetic languages other than English (e.g., Italian, Perry et al. 2014; French, Perry et al. 2014; also see Paulesu et al. 2021, for a model of bilingual reading) as well as to non-alphabetic writing systems such as Chinese (Yang et al. 2009).

Further improvements in the biological validity of neural network models have been enabled by the advent of *deep learning*, which allows the building of large-scale models composed of many hidden layers (Goodfellow et al. 2016). In analogy with the hierarchical organization of the primate cerebral cortex, these systems exploit multiple levels of representation to encode increasingly more abstract features of the sensory signal (Yamins and DiCarlo 2016). Deep networks achieve impressive performance in a variety of challenging tasks, ranging from image classification (Krizhevsky et al. 2017) to speech recognition (Hinton et al. 2012) and language translation (Sutskever et al. 2014). Notably, the implementation of large-scale simulations has been further boosted by the introduction of efficient parallel computing hardware (Dean et al. 2012; Testolin et al. 2013), which allows creating deep networks that can be trained and tested with the same stimuli used in behavioural experiments (Hannagan et al. 2014; Kubilius et al. 2016), thus allowing for rigorous model validation based on psychophysical measures (Testolin et al. 2020a; Testolin et al. 2017).

3.1.3 From Supervised to Unsupervised Learning

Classical connectionist modelling of cognition has largely used the error back-propagation algorithm for training the model on a given task. Leaving aside the lack of biological plausibility of error back-propagation (O'Reilly 1998; but see Lillicrap et al. 2020 for a recent discussion), its widespread use in psychological modelling implies the assumption that learning is largely discriminative (e.g., classification or function learning) and that an external teaching signal is available at each learning event (i.e., all training data is labelled). One example that is particularly relevant in the present context is the seminal model of reading development of Harm and Seidenberg (1999). The scope of the model and its success in capturing phenomena related to learning to read and dyslexia are discussed in Section 3.2.1. Here we focus on the fact that the model was trained to map the orthography of approximately 3,000 words onto their phonology in a fully supervised way: this implies that the model required an 'external teacher' providing the correct phonology in order to compute error signals for back-propagation learning. The model was able to learn 99% of the training set, but this required 10 million learning trials – a massively supervised learning process that is very different from how children learn to read aloud (Share 1995; Ziegler et al. 2020). In contrast, Ziegler et al. (2014) proposed a radically different learning loop based on the phonological decoding self-teaching hypothesis (discussed in more detail in Section 3.2.2). This loop builds on explicitly teaching a small number of spelling-to-sound mappings at the start of reading development, but most learning is then based on self-teaching. During self-teaching, decoding skills in combination with phonological representations of spoken words provide the system with an internally generated teaching signal, which gradually improves decoding and bootstraps ortho-graphic and lexical development (Perry et al. 2019; Ziegler et al. 2020).

Fully supervised learning is an exceptional scenario in the real world. Reinforcement learning (Sutton and Barto 1998) is a plausible alternative, but there is also a broad range of situations where learning is largely unsupervised and its only objective is that of building rich internal representations of the sensory environment (Fleming and Storrs 2019; Hinton and Sejnowski 1999). In this respect, a particularly interesting class of deep learning architectures is that of *generative models*, such as deep belief networks (Hinton 2007). These models emphasize the role of feedback connections and top-down influences in perception and cognition (Zorzi et al. 2013), at the same time providing a useful bridge to higher-level descriptions in terms of Bayesian computation (Testolin and Zorzi 2016) as well as neuroscientific insights into the functional role of spontaneous brain activity (Pezzulo et al. 2021). In computational investigations of reading, generative neural networks have recently been used to simulate how recycling of natural image statistics could boost letter perception (Testolin et al. 2017), how visual word recognition becomes invariant of spatial location (Di Bono and Zorzi 2013), and how statistical learning mechanisms can support orthographic processing and spon-taneous pseudoword production (Testolin et al. 2016).

3.1.4 From Group Data to Individual Data

The idea of modelling learning difficulties is appealing and somewhat natural within a framework that places emphasis on the emergence of cognitive skills as a result of a learning process. While modelling typical development and skilled performance can be readily carried out with reference to group-averaged human data, one major difficulty with modelling any learning disorder is the heterogeneity of the individual profiles (see Chapter 4, Banfi, Landerl, and Moll 2022). Variability between individ-uals (matched for chronological age) is of course crucial for defining the typical range of performance and the diagnostic criteria for learning disorders (see Chapter 3, Zorzi and Testolin 2022). Nevertheless, the heterogeneity of individual patterns across multiple behavioural scores has led to systematic attempts at categor-izing children into subtypes of deficits (e.g., phonological vs. surface developmental dyslexia) according to their performance in one or multiple outcome measures (e.g., irregular vs. non-word reading; Castles and Coltheart 1993; Manis et al. 1996). Accordingly, connectionist models have been used to simulate group-level perform-ance in the attempt to relate a specific sub-type of a learning disorder to a specific impairment in the model (e.g., Harm and Seidenberg 1999; see Section 3.2.1). However, this approach has been criticized because it does not capture the underlying differences in terms of core deficits (Ziegler et al. 2008). Moreover, as mentioned before, different initial states may produce similar end states. Modelling individuals rather than group averages, thereby producing a personalized model for each individual child (Perry et al. 2019), offers better insights into the underlying (core) deficits and allows prediction of individual outcomes. The use of computational modelling for predicting individual performance (as opposed to just explaining the nature of the deficit) paves the way for assessing the potential benefit of an intervention through simulation (Perry et al. 2019; Thomas et al. 2019).

3.2 Reading Development and Dyslexia

Early attempts to describe the processes underlying skilled reading in a precise and detailed manner were purely verbal and qualitative (box-and-arrow models; e.g., Coltheart 1978). With the emergence of connectionism, verbal theories were successively replaced by computationally explicit models. These models can produce highly detailed simulations of various aspects of the reading process, including word recognition and reading aloud (Coltheart et al. 2001; Harm and Seidenberg 2004; Perry et al. 2010; Perry et al. 2007; Plaut et al. 1996; Zorzi et al. 1998a; Zorzi et al. 1998b). The challenge of capturing the behaviour of brain-damaged patients with various forms of acquired dyslexia (Denes et al. 1999, for a review) by lesioning the models in various ways was also a major driver of theoretical development as well as a benchmark for model comparison. Last but not least, connectionist modelling has been crucial to develop and test specific hypotheses regarding reading acquisition and developmental dyslexia (e.g., Harm and Seidenberg 1999; Perry et al. 2019; Ziegler et al. 2014; Zorzi et al. 1998b). We briefly review the early modelling work and then describe state-of-the-art simulations of developmental dyslexia based on personalized computational models.

3.2.1 Early Computational Models

Starting with the seminal work of Seidenberg and McClelland (1989), connectionist models of reading have explored the role of learning mechanisms for acquiring the mapping between spelling and sound. The initial work (Seidenberg and McClelland 1989; Plaut et al. 1996) aimed at simulating adult skilled performance, as well as some aspects of acquired dyslexia. The model was presented with written words, encoded as distributed patterns of activity over an input layer of grapheme units, and it was trained by error back-propagation to produce the corresponding spoken word, encoded over an output layer of phoneme units. These findings challenged the classic 'Dual-route model' of reading (Coltheart 1978) because a single processing pathway was capable of handling all types of words (including exception words) and able to generalize to novel orthographic stimuli (non-words). The model is known as the 'triangle' model of reading because orthographic and phonological layers are also linked to a semantic layer (Harm and Seidenberg 2004), thereby forming a triangular architecture with the three explicit (i.e., stipulated) levels of representations as vertices. Note that the connectivity between each pair of levels is mediated by a hidden layer, which implies that there are also three levels of learnt internal representations in addition to the explicit representations. Learning in a neural network model, however, does not necessarily imply a plausible simulation of cognitive development.

Modelling reading acquisition and developmental dyslexia within the triangle model was tackled by Harm and Seidenberg (1999). They first trained a recurrent network to learn phonological structure from phonetic input to implement the idea that phonological knowledge is acquired prior to learning to read. Learning to read was then simulated by training the model to map orthography onto the phonological units embedded in the recurrent network. Nevertheless, training was still fully supervised, with the correct (target) phonological representation presented for each of the 3,000 words in the training set and for up to 10 million learning trials. Developmental dyslexia was simulated by impairing the representation of phono-logical information before training the model in the reading aloud task, thereby implementing the mainstream phonological deficit theory of dyslexia (Vellutino et al. 2004). Phonological impairment was imposed on the phonological network in three different ways to hinder learning and simulate increasing severity of the deficit. A mild deficit was implemented using a stronger-than-usual weight decay; a moderate deficit was obtained by removing a set of hidden units as well as lesioning half of the connections between the phonological units; a severe deficit was obtained by adding noise to each connection weight in the phonological network. Importantly, the different types of deficits produced distinct profiles of reading impairment when the model was trained to map orthography onto the impaired phonological network: (1) mild impairment resulted in a non-word reading deficit but typical irregular word reading; (2) moderate impairment produced a mixed pattern, with a severe non-word reading deficit but a weaker irregular word reading deficit; (3) severe impairment produced strong deficits in both non-word and irregular word reading.

3.2.2 Modelling Reading Development Within the Connectionist Dual Process Framework

It is widely accepted that phonological decoding (which is based on learning how letters and groups of letters map onto their corresponding sounds) is the *sine qua non* for reading acquisition (Share 1995; Ziegler and Goswami 2005). Phonological decoding allows children to decode words that they have heard but never seen before, thus giving them access to the thousands of words that are present in their spoken lexicons and the opportunity to set up connections between a given letter string and the spoken word (i.e., developing an orthographic lexicon). This 'self-teaching' mechanism has been successfully implemented in dCDP (Ziegler et al. 2014; Perry et al. 2019), the developmental version of the Connectionist Dual Process (CDP) model of skilled reading aloud (Perry et al. 2007; Perry et al.

2010). The CDP model family maintains a clear distinction between phonological decoding, based on learnt associations between letters and sounds, and lexical processing involving whole-word recognition (see Zorzi 2010, for a review). Specifically, phonological decoding is based on a simple associative neural network (without hidden units) that learns to map graphemes (single letters and letter clusters) onto the most frequently associated phonemes (Zorzi et al. 1998a). In dCDP the decoding network is initially set up by supervised training on a small set of grapheme–phoneme correspondences (without presenting words), similarly to the way children are explicitly taught basic decoding skills during the initial stages of learning to read (i.e., phonics training). From there on, however, learning becomes largely unsupervised. At each learning event, the network is presented with a written word and the decoding network computes its potential (possibly incorrect) pronunciation. This processing step typically results in the activation of one (or multiple) word representations in the phonological lexicon through feedback from the phonemes. If one phonological lexical representation is selected (possibly with the help of contextual or semantic cues; see Ziegler et al. 2020 for a discussion), an orthographic representation is set up and connected to its phonological counterpart. In turn, the activated phonology of the word is used as an internal teaching signal to adjust the connection weights of the decoding network. Note that the self-teaching loop captures both orthographic learning (lexicalization) and consolidation and refinement of the phonological decoding network (see Figure 3.1A).

Ziegler et al. (2014) showed that the dCDP model can learn about 80% of the words in a lexicon of more than 32,000 English words using the self-teaching loop. The remaining 20% of words are those that are too irregular to be learnt through decoding (e.g., aisle, yacht, choir). Indeed, the decoding network progressively learns a richer and more complex set of spelling–sound associations (see Zorzi et al. 1998a, for a developmental analysis), but it cannot learn atypical correspondences (e.g., the pronunciation of 'i' in pint). Learning irregular words requires an additional mechanism: direct instruction (e.g., flashcards), which is the external teaching signal required by supervised learning. Accordingly, dCDP (Perry et al. 2019) assumes that a word can enter the orthographic lexicon through direct instruction when phonological decoding is not successful, with a probability that is a function of word frequency (i.e., a higher probability of learning high-frequency words). Therefore, phonological decoding combined with direct instruction allows the model to learn to read in a developmentally plausible way and with a minimal amount of supervised training.

3.2.3 A Personalized Multi-Deficit Model of Dyslexia

As previously discussed in the context of the Harm and Seidenberg (1999) model, a simulation of developmental dyslexia requires motivated assumptions about the nature of the impairment and the model component that is affected prior to learning to read. Besides the classical phonological processing deficit (e.g., Hulme et al. 2015), children with developmental dyslexia have been shown to present with deficits in visual processing (Stein and Walsh 1997), attention (Vidyasagar and

A   Initial network

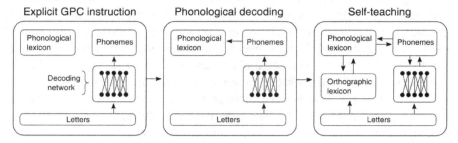

B   Reading performance (proportion correct)

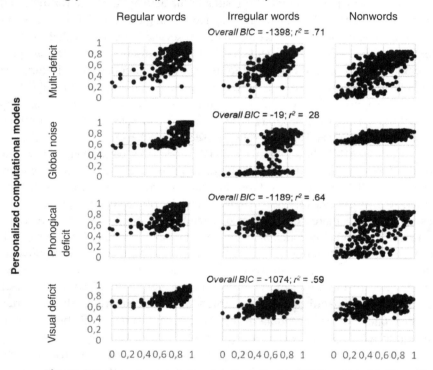

Figure 3.1 *Learning to read and dyslexia in the dCDP model. (A) The self-teaching mechanism in the model. GPC = grapheme–phoneme conversion. (B) Simulations of reading outcomes for 388 personalized models of dyslexic children with different versions of the dCDP model. Each model version differs only in the initial state (before learning to read), which implements a specific deficit hypothesis. For each dyslexic child (represented as a point in the graphs), actual reading performance on regular words, irregular words, and non-words (x-axis) is plotted against the performance predicted by the model at the end of the learning-to-read simulation (y-axis). BIC = Bayesian information criterion.*

Pammer 2010), auditory/temporal processing (Vandermosten et al. 2010), and perceptual noise exclusion (Sperling et al. 2005). Moreover, studies that investigated multiple factors within the same sample revealed that that the presence of a single deficit is more the exception than the rule (e.g., Facoetti et al. 2010; Menghini et al. 2010), thereby emphasizing the multifactorial nature of dyslexia (Pennington 2006; see also Chapter 1, Goswami 2022). Computational modelling is therefore crucial to explore causal links between a given core deficit (or multiple core deficits) and atypical reading development. Importantly, the same model should be used to investigate how different deficits (e.g., phonological vs. visual) impact the developmental trajectory of learning to read (Ziegler et al. 2014).

The dCDP model was used by Perry et al. (2019) to examine the most influential single-deficit models as well as a multi-deficit model. Performance measures of reading aloud (accuracy for regular words, irregular words, and non-words) and of non-reading tasks (e.g., phonological awareness, orthographic choice: e.g., goat vs. gote) were available for a large sample of 622 English-speaking children that included 388 dyslexics (Peterson et al. 2013). The initial state of the model was defined for each child according to their score on one or multiple non-reading tasks that mapped to specific model components. The model was also based on the assumption that the size of the phonological lexicon varied across individuals (weighted towards high-frequency words) as a function of the child's vocabulary score. This procedure yielded a personalized model with an individual learning trajectory, where reading performance was collected as the outcome measure by presenting the same words and non-words used in the empirical study. Importantly, no parameters were manipulated to fit the reading data, so that any discrepancy between predicted (model) and actual (child) reading performance was entirely dependent on the initial state (in interaction with the learning loop). The phonological deficit can be used to illustrate the personalized modelling approach. Performance in a phoneme deletion task taps phonological processing and phoneme awareness, which is a classical predictor of dyslexia (e.g., Landerl et al. 2013; see also Chapter 4, Banfi, Landerl, and Moll 2022, and Chapter 18, Gunderson 2022). Assuming that poor phonological processing leads to phoneme confusions (a common type of error in dyslexia), a phonological deficit can be simulated by switching any phoneme with a phonetically similar one during reading. Accordingly, the child's z-normalized phoneme deletion performance is linearly mapped onto the probability of switching phonemes in the model's phoneme layer. In other words, poorer phoneme deletion performance leads to higher probability of producing incorrect phonemes during decoding in the personalized model.

Figure 3.1B shows that the phonological deficit model provided a better fit to the empirical data than a model instantiating a visual processing deficit (e.g., Stein 2014), where letters were switched with adjacent letters with a probability that was set to be a function of the child's orthographic choice score. In turn, both single-deficit models were largely superior to a model assuming general processing inefficiency due to noisy computations (Hancock et al. 2017), where noise was added to all processing layers in proportion to the child's overall reading performance (see also Chapter 1, Goswami 2022). However, no single-deficit model adequately captured the distribution of reading scores across word types even though the mean results from both phonological and visual deficit models were similar to the human data. This suggests that multiple deficits may combine in different ways for each dyslexic child, thereby leading to heterogeneity of the dyslexic profiles. The latter hypothesis was tested in a multi-deficit model. The multi-deficit model allowed for both a phonological deficit (activation of incorrect phonemes during decoding) and a visual or orthographic deficit (noise in the orthographic lexicon). A simulation was then carried out for each child's personalized model to simulate the learning trajectory and collect the reading outcome measures. The multi-deficit model showed a striking correlation between model predictions and learning outcomes and outperformed all single-deficit models (see Figure 3.1B).

Crucially, a computational model of dyslexia that accurately captures individual performance can be used for predicting the effect of intervention. Each child represents a point in a multidimensional 'deficit space' and the multi-deficit model allows sampling of the entire space by running simulations for any potential combination of deficits (i.e., generating synthetic data). The full deficit space allows one to predict how improving performance in one component task through intervention (e.g., phonological awareness) would change reading performance. Using this approach, Perry et al. (2019) showed that there are important inter-individual differences in the predicted response to intervention and that the optimal intervention depends on the initial conditions. In other words, the effect of an intervention is non-linear, which means that effects cannot be directly predicted without running computer simulations.

3.3 Numerical Development and Dyscalculia

It is widely believed that mathematical learning is rooted in a perceptual 'number sense' that humans share with other animal species (Butterworth et al. 2011; Dehaene 2011) (see Chapter 2, Menon and Chang 2022; Chapter 11, Yeatman 2022; Chapter 15, Siok 2022; Chapter 17, Lervåg and Melby-Lervåg 2022; Chapter 19, Galuschka and Schulte-Körne 2022). Visual numerosity appears to be extracted spontaneously from vision (Burr and Ross 2008; Cicchini et al. 2016) by a specialized mechanism that yields an approximate representation of numerical quantity: the Approximate Number System (ANS; Feigenson et al. 2004). In the primate brain, such approximate numerical processing systematically engages a widespread cortical network, whose key hubs are located in the prefrontal cortex and the intraparietal sulcus of the parietal lobe (Nieder and Dehaene 2009; Piazza et al. 2004).

Notably, the ability to discriminate between numerosities, known as number acuity, improves throughout childhood (Halberda and Feigenson 2008; Piazza et al. 2010). Even newborns seem to be sensitive to numbers, as they can approximately match the numerosity of object sets even when they are presented across different sensory modalities (Izard et al. 2009). Six-month-old infants can discriminate between sets of items with a numerical ratio of 1:2 (Xu and Spelke 2000); at 10 months of age they can successfully discriminate ratios of 2:3; and 2.5-year-old toddlers can master ratios up to 3:4 (Sella et al. 2016). The development of number acuity continues until late childhood, suggesting that learning and sensory experience play an important role in refining numerical representations. Infants are not only sensitive to number, they can also engage in basic operations: for example, 5-month-old infants can carry out simple addition and subtraction operations on small sets of objects (Wynn 1992). It has been argued that such a diverse repertoire of basic numerical abilities provides children with a 'start-up kit' for subsequent learning of more complex mathematical concepts, which in turn implies that a core deficit of these skills might be the primary cause of developmental dyscalculia (Butterworth et al. 2011). Though domain-general deficits can significantly contribute to mathematical learning difficulties (see Chapter 2, Menon and Chang 2022), the modelling studies reviewed in the present chapter offer a domain-specific perspective on numeracy development and dyscalculia. This perspective is supported by the finding that number sense measures correlate with later mathematical achievement (Anobile et al. 2013; Halberda et al. 2008; Libertus et al. 2011; Starr et al. 2013) and are severely impaired in dyscalculia (Mazzocco et al. 2011; Piazza et al. 2010). Nevertheless, we anticipate that computational studies to date have investigated typical development, whereas developmental dyscalculia remains largely unexplored.

3.3.1 Early Computational Models of Numerical Cognition

From a computational perspective, the ANS has been modelled using a variety of approaches. Some authors have proposed that visual numerosity could be approximated by a simple mechanism of density estimation, where an occupancy index is computed by concurrently analysing a circular neighbourhood of all objects in the stimulus (Allik and Tuulmets 1991). A biologically more plausible model based on artificial neural networks was later proposed by Dehaene and Changeux (1993). In their model, numerosity estimation was implemented as a three-stage mechanism: the visual input was first normalized in order to encode the individual items using a size-independent code, and a layer of 'summation clusters' was then used to compute an approximate estimation of numerosity. Specifically, by responding whenever the total activity exceeds a threshold, summation clusters respond whenever the input numerosity exceeds a certain limit. A final layer of 'numerosity clusters' was used to create a more precise number code, with each unit responding only to a selected range of numerosities. However, the numerosity detection system was hardwired, reflecting the assumption that it is present at birth. A successive neural network model revisited this assumption by showing that numerosity detectors can instead be learnt from visual input (Verguts and Fias 2004). Notably, the authors showed that 'number neurons' mimicking the response profiles observed in single-cell recordings (Nieder et al. 2002) could develop through unsupervised learning in response to the activity of a layer of summation nodes, and that their representational efficiency increased when a number encoded in a symbolic format was simultaneously presented at the sensory layer.

A more elaborated connectionist system also incorporated the acquisition of a rudimental counting procedure, using two different mechanisms organized in a modular architecture (Ahmad et al. 2002). A 'subitizing' module was implemented by first applying an object detector system to the visual input, whose goal was to provide a scale-invariant input to a one-dimensional self-organizing map (Kohonen 1990) of ordered numerosity detectors that self-organized into a compressive number line. A separate counting module sequentially scanned each of the visually presented objects by means of two basic networks that run synchronously: a 'pointing next object' feed-forward neural network, and a recurrent neural network that sequentially produced number words. The subitizing and counting modules were combined by means of a gating network that selected the response of either of them. However, the model behaviour was not validated against human performance.

More recently, it has been shown that neural networks can learn to count the number of items in visual displays and that the ability to sequentially point to individual objects helps speed up counting acquisition (Fang et al. 2018). A further step forward has been taken by cognitive developmental robotics, a field that explores the instantiation of these principles in physically embodied agents (Di Nuovo and Jay 2019). Interestingly, pointing gestures significantly improved counting accuracy in a humanoid robot, and learning was more effective when both finger gestures and words were provided as input (De La Cruz et al. 2014; Rucinski et al. 2012).

3.3.2 Deep Learning Models of Numerosity Perception

A step forward in modelling numerosity perception has been made by computational simulations based on deep learning (Figure 3.2A), which showed that approximate representations of numerosity could emerge as a higher-order statistical feature of synthetic images (Stoianov and Zorzi 2012). The key idea was that numerosity is a statistical invariant of highly variable visual input, and for this reason it might be encoded as a higher-order visual feature (summary statistics) in a deep neural network that simply observes images of object sets with variable numerosity. Notably, numerosity-sensitive neurons emerged in the deepest layer of the network (Zorzi and Testolin 2018), supporting numerosity estimation with the same behavioural signature (i.e., Weber's law for numbers; see Chapter 19, Galuschka and Schulte-Körne 2022) and accuracy level (i.e., number acuity) of human adults. Analyses of the emergent computations in the model showed that numerosity was abstracted from lower-level visual primitives through a simple two-level hierarchical process, which exploited the cumulative surface area as a normalization signal (Cappelletti et al. 2014; Stoianov and Zorzi 2017). Deep networks have been successfully tested in subitizing (Wever and Runia 2018) and numerosity estimation tasks (Chen et al. 2018). They also account for congruency effects (e.g., numerosity discrimination is easier when numerical information is aligned with area information; see Zorzi and Testolin 2018) and for the fine-grained contribution of non-numerical magnitudes in biasing behavioural responses (e.g., discrimination choices are modelled better when also considering size and spacing ratios as predictors; see Testolin et al. 2020a).

Deep learning simulations have recently shown that iterative learning can support a gradual improvement of number acuity, in line with developmental studies with human children (Figure 3.2B). The initial numerosity discrimination ability of randomly initialized deep networks was comparable to that of human newborns, and a visual number sense emerged even when deep networks were exposed to a more ecological set of images – that is, when the size and the displacement of the items was obtained by segmenting objects in natural scenes (Testolin et al. 2020b). Interestingly, preliminary work has further shown that the atypical developmental trajectory of number acuity observed in dyscalculic children could be simulated by limiting the computational resources of the deep learning model – that is, by reducing the number of hidden neurons supporting the encoding of numerosity information (Stoianov and Zorzi 2013). Although this result is in line with the finding of reduced grey matter density in the intraparietal sulcus of dyscalculic subjects (Rotzer et al. 2008), it has also been argued that the ANS deficit observed in dyscalculic children could be explained by a difficulty in extracting numerosity information from stimuli in which other visual features (e.g., total area) are incongruent with number (Bugden and Ansari 2016). In this respect, it has been shown that deep networks are more sensitive to non-numerical features early during learning (Testolin et al. 2020a; Zorzi and Testolin 2018), closely mimicking the developmental pattern observed in young children (Starr et al. 2017) and paving the way for a systematic investigation of the role of perceptual cues in atypical number sense development.

3.3.3 Emergence of symbolic numerical abilities and implications for dyscalculia

One of the most pressing questions to be addressed in future research is whether the generic processing and learning constraints incorporated into deep learning models of numerosity perception would suffice for developing more sophisticated types of numerical abilities, such as those underlying symbolic quantification and arithmetic, which likely require enculturation (Núñez 2017) and whose acquisition profoundly reshapes our brain (Kuhl et al. 2020; Ansari 2008).

Indeed, only a few modelling studies so far have investigated how arithmetic could be learnt by artificial neural networks. In early modelling attempts, associative memories have been used to simulate mental calculation as a process of storage and retrieval of arithmetic facts (McCloskey and Lindemann 1992): during the learning phase, the two operands and the result of a simple operation (e.g., single-digit multiplication) are given as input to an associative memory system, whose learning goal is to accurately store them as a global, stable state. During the testing phase only the operands are given, and the network must recover the missing information (i.e., the result) by gradually settling into the correct configuration.

Building on this approach, later modelling work has shown that numerosity-based ('semantic') representations can facilitate learning of addition facts in comparison to symbolic representations that do not convey magnitude information (Zorzi et al., 2005). Incorporating semantic and symbolic representations within the same con-nectionist model rendered it possible to produce simulations of acquired dyscalculia

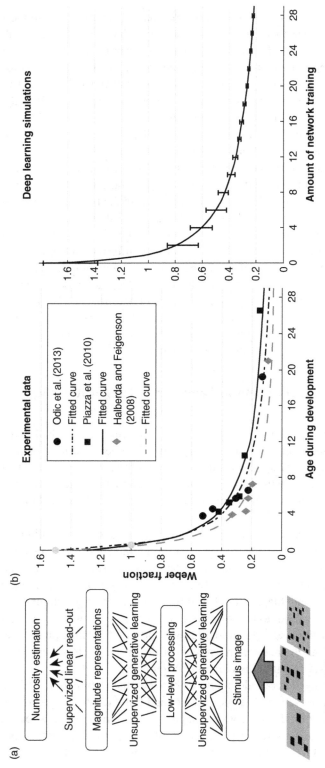

Figure 3.2 (A) Architecture of a deep learning model that simulates numerosity perception. (B) Developmental simulations of number acuity, as measured by the progressive refinement of the Weber fraction (just noticeable difference in numerosity) (adapted from Testolin et al. 2020b). The left panel reports developmental trajectories obtained from three empirical studies. The right panel shows the average developmental trajectory of ten replica (with different random initialization) of the deep learning model represented in panel A, with error bars representing the standard deviation of the mean.

(Stoianov et al. 2004). Interestingly, damage to the semantic component of the network affected addition performance to a greater extent than damage to the symbolic component, supporting the hypothesis that simple mental arithmetic has a semantic basis (see Chapter 2, Menon and Chang 2022, and Chapter 15, Siok 2022).

Despite these initial achievements, symbolic reasoning remains notoriously difficult for connectionist models (Marcus 2003), and deep neural networks still struggle with tasks requiring procedural and compositional knowledge (Garnelo and Shanahan 2019). This constitutes a formidable challenge to the development of neural network models that could simulate high-level mathematical reasoning, and the related deficits caused by learning disabilities (Testolin 2020).

3.4 Conclusion

Reading and mathematical abilities are impressive cultural achievements and hallmarks of human intelligence, as well as a major target of educational efforts: A deeper understanding of their neurocomputational foundations is therefore the key to the possibility of formally assessing the role of different learning strategies for typically developing children and for remediating learning disorders. In this chapter, we have reviewed the most representative computational approaches in the field, with a focus on connectionist models. Despite the seminal insights provided by artificial neural networks and the promise of deep learning to further increase their biological and cognitive validity, several key questions are still open. For example, great advances have been made in modelling reading and dyslexia from a cognitive perspective, but these models have not been systematically linked to neural theories and to neuroimaging findings that relate atypical reading development to specific brain regions and functional circuits. Moreover, the influence of the different writing systems (both alphabetical and non-alphabetical) on atypical learning trajectories still needs to be explored. In contrast, modelling of numeracy development (particularly for the visual number sense) is more closely linked to its brain bases and to single-neuron physiology (see Zorzi and Testolin 2018), but the computational investigation of dyscalculia is still in its infancy. The grand challenge for connectionist models will be to shed light on the mechanisms that allow us to learn and effectively use symbolic numerical knowledge, and how their dysfunctions could lead to mathematical learning deficits. Modelling the acquisition of symbolic numbers would also permit formal assessment of the effect of cross-language differences in the verbal counting system. One additional difficulty is that mathematical learning outcomes are more complex and varied compared to learning to read. In this regard, arithmetic performance might be a viable target for systematic computational investigations of how individual variability in basic numerical abilities shape the developmental trajectory of arithmetic learning. The remarkable success of computational models in simulating individual reading outcomes clearly demonstrates that pushing future research in this direction could be worth the effort.

Funding acknowledgement: This work was supported by the Cariparo Foundation (Excellence Grant 2017 'Numsense' to M. Z.).

Suggestions for Further Reading

Harm, M. W., and M. S. Seidenberg. 1999. 'Phonology, Reading Acquisition, and Dyslexia: Insights from Connectionist Models'. *Psychological Review*, 106 (3): 491–528.

Perry, C., M. Zorzi, and J. C. Ziegler. 2019. 'Understanding Dyslexia Through Personalized Large-Scale Computational Models'. *Psychological Science*, 30: 386–95.

Testolin, A., W. Y. Zou, and J. L. McClelland. 2020. 'Numerosity Discrimination in Deep Neural Networks: Initial Competence, Developmental Refinement and Experience Statistics'. *Developmental Science*, 23 (5): e12940.

Ziegler, J. C., C. Perry, and M. Zorzi. 2020. 'Learning to Read and Dyslexia: From Theory to Intervention Through Personalized Computational Models'. *Current Directions in Psychological Science*, 29 (3): 293–300.

Zorzi, M., and A. Testolin. 2018. 'An Emergentist Perspective on the Origin of Number Sense'. *Philosophical Transactions of the Royal Society B: Biological Sciences*, 373 (1740): 20170043.

Summary: Theoretical Frameworks and Computational Models

1. **Causation vs. correlation**: Longitudinal observation and particularly intervention studies beginning in infancy (which are currently scarce) are the key to understanding the causes of learning disorders.
2. **Multi- vs. monocausality**: The heterogeneous manifestations of dyslexia and dyscalculia (and their co-occurrence) are best explained by multi-causal (vs. mono-causal) theories.
3. **Possible causes of dyslexia**: In alphabetic orthographies, auditory-phonological deficits (at phoneme levels, e.g. auditory temporal sampling, but also at syllable levels) are currently best supported by causal evidence. Audiovisual difficulties in converting print to speech could also be causally related to dyslexia.
4. **Possible causes of dyscalculia**: Difficulties in converting symbolic to non-symbolic quantity representations (and vice versa) likely play a causal role. Deficits in attention, executive functioning, working memory, and long-term memory could also causally contribute to dyscalculia.
5. **Computational evaluation of theories**: Computational models can precisely simulate individual learning trajectories and outcomes and thus are powerful tools for evaluating theories of dyslexia and dyscalculia. They also allow empirical predictions to be made regarding how learning might be affected by developmental disorders (e.g., in terms of difficulty profiles, severity of difficulties, error types) and how individuals respond to intervention.

PART II

Cognitive Profiles and Behavioural Manifestations

4 Cognitive Profiles and Co-occurrence of Dyslexia and Dyscalculia

Chiara Banfi, Karin Landerl, and Kristina Moll

4.1 Introduction

This chapter covers the cognitive underpinnings of dyslexia and dyscalculia and their co-occurrence, from the perspective of the multifactorial deficit model of developmental disorders (Pennington 2006). The two disorders are first defined with respect to their typical behavioural manifestation. Next, prevalence rates of single as well as co-occurring deficits are described and critically discussed in light of methodological challenges. Subsequently, the cognitive bases of each disorder, as well as their comorbidity, are specified in the light of the multifactorial deficit model. Finally, methodological considerations regarding the link between dyslexia, dyscalculia, and other neurodevelopmental disorders are presented. Future avenues of research are also outlined, with a particular emphasis on treating reading and maths performance as a continuous variable, and on longitudinal studies. The studies presented in this chapter are mainly based on children attending primary school (age range approximately 6–12 years old). There are, of course, differences in the organization, duration, and onset of formal instruction across countries. Aside from nation-specific differences, however, this age period is particularly relevant for research on dyslexia and dyscalculia, as this is the typical time window when literacy and arithmetic skills are acquired.

4.2 Behavioural Manifestation

Dyslexia and dyscalculia are neurodevelopmental disorders, characterized by impairments in acquiring specific academic skills (i.e., reading, writing, or mathematical skills). In the ICD-11, International Statistical Classification of Diseases and Related Health Problems (11th ed.; World Health Organization 2020), impairments in reading, writing, and mathematics are classified as three separate diagnostic categories. This classification highlights the fact that problems in the three learning domains can dissociate, such that one learning domain only is affected (e.g., maths problems without reading and spelling problems, and vice versa). This suggests that distinct deficits underlie each learning disorder. In contrast, the DSM-5, Diagnostic and Statistical Manual of Mental Disorders (American Psychiatric Association 2013) summarizes impairments in the three learning domains (reading, written expression, and mathematics) within the same diagnostic category by using the generic term 'Specific Learning Disorder' as an overarching diagnosis. Different manifestations can still be distinguished by means of specifiers that indicate the affected academic domain, but DSM-5 clearly emphasizes the overlap between learning disorders and the common mechanisms underlying impairments in the three learning domains. This difference between the two most important and internationally recognized classification systems of mental disorders is noteworthy, and reflects recent challenges in research on learning disorders (see Chapter 3, Zorzi and Testolin 2022, for a detailed discussion). Any comprehensive developmental model of learning disorders needs to explain both the fact that learning disorders can affect one learning domain only, which suggests that distinct risk factors are associated with each learning disorder, and the fact that deficits in reading, writing, and mathematics frequently co-occur, thus suggesting that shared risk factors affect learning across domains. Against this background, the current section covers the isolated manifestation of dyslexia (Section 4.2.1) and dyscalculia (Section 4.2.2) while Section 4.3 covers their co-occurrence.

4.2.1 Dyslexia

Dyslexia is characterized by significant and persistent difficulties related to reading, such as reduced word reading accuracy, reading fluency, and reading comprehension (American Psychiatric Association 2013; World Health Organization 2019–2021). To receive a diagnosis of dyslexia, children must exhibit problems with basic literacy skills that are unexpected based on their chronological age and general level of intellectual functioning. These basic literacy difficulties are not due to a disorder of intellectual development, sensory impairment (vision or hearing), neurological disorder, lack of availability of education, lack of proficiency in the language of academic instruction, or psychosocial adversity. It is important to note that dyslexia is defined as the lower end of the normal distribution of reading abilities, and therefore the diagnosis follows criteria based on somewhat arbitrary cut-offs.

Reading deficits have varying manifestations within and across orthographies (Verhoeven et al. 2019). Individuals with dyslexia typically encounter problems in mapping written and spoken language units, which in turn affect letter and word recognition. This may be indicated by problems in reading accuracy or in reading fluency. In consistent orthographies, such as Finnish or Italian, reading accuracy can still be very high even among children with reading problems. Accordingly, in consistent orthographies, reading fluency (indicating the number of words or sentences read in a predefined amount of time) is considered a more adequate measure of reading performance (Wimmer 1993). Problems in accurate and/or fluent reading can lead to difficulties in grasping the meaning of what is read. However, reading comprehension difficulties can also occur in the context of intact word recognition skills (Hulme and Snowling 2016). Such deficits in reading comprehension are often the consequence of oral language problems, including problems in vocabulary knowledge and grammar.

Word recognition problems are often accompanied by spelling problems, although this is not necessarily the case. In fact, dissociations between reading fluency and spelling deficits were observed in several orthographies (Hebrew: Bar-Kochva and Amiel 2016; French Fayol et al. 2009; Greek: Manolitsis and Georgiou 2015; German: Moll, Kunze, et al. 2014; Moll and Landerl 2009; Wimmer and Mayringer 2002; Finnish: Torppa et al. 2017), and are as common as combined deficits of reading and spelling, at least in consistent orthographies (Moll, Kunze, et al. 2014).

4.2.2 Dyscalculia

Dyscalculia is characterized by significant and persistent problems in mathematics or arithmetic (American Psychiatric Association 2013; World Health Organization 2020). This includes difficulties in mastering basic number processing, learning arithmetic facts, performing accurate and fluent calculations, and maths reasoning. The exclusion criteria described for dyslexia also apply for dyscalculia (i.e., difficulties with numbers are not due to intellectual disabilities, sensory or neurological disorders, psychosocial adversity, inadequate educational instruction, or lack of language proficiency). Individuals with dyscalculia experience major difficulties in all areas of arithmetic, including basic operations such as learning multiplication tables, complex written calculations, and word problems (Haberstroh and Schulte-Körne 2019).

Similar to dyslexia, dyscalculia has varying manifestations at the behavioural level (Rubinsten and Henik 2009). Children with problems in recalling arithmetic facts, for example, do not necessarily manifest calculation problems (Skagerlund and Träff 2016). Furthermore, symbolic and non-symbolic number processing skills can be differentially affected in the same individual (De Visscher and Noël 2013).

4.3 Prevalence and Co-occurrence

Dyslexia and dyscalculia are among the most frequently diagnosed neurodevelopmental disorders and occur with largely comparable prevalence rates: 4–9% for reading deficits and 3–7% for maths deficits (Moll, Kunze et al. 2014). Although the symptoms of dyslexia clearly differ from those described for dyscalculia, as described earlier, the two learning disorders co-occur more often than would be expected by chance. According to a prevalence study conducted in a German-speaking population-based sample of 2,586 children from grades 2 to 4 (Landerl and Moll 2010), the probability of having a deficit in arithmetic, reading, or spelling is four to five times higher in children who already have problems in one of these scholastic achievement domains. These results have recently been replicated in a representative sample of 1,928 Finnish children (Koponen et al. 2018). Furthermore, a recent meta-analysis (Joyner and Wagner 2020) addressing co-occurrence of dyslexia and dyscalculia based on 33 case-control studies investigated whether the presence of dyscalculia could be considered a risk factor for dyslexia. Results revealed that individuals with dyscalculia were two times more likely to also have dyslexia as compared to individuals who did not have dyscalculia. It should be noted that this meta-analysis included studies with a group comparison design that had (roughly) equal group sizes, which may have induced lower comorbidity rates than in the general population.

While comorbidity rates between learning disorders are consistently reported to be higher than expected by chance, the exact rates vary widely between studies. According to Landerl and Moll (2010), between 17% and 70% of children with dyscalculia also have dyslexia, and between 11% and 56% of children with dyslexia also have dyscalculia. There are several possible explanations for this variability. One possible reason is the arbitrary cut-off that is set to define the disorders. Landerl and Moll (2010) reasoned that finding similar or even higher comorbidity rates with stringent cut-offs implies that the two co-occurring disorders have a strong common neurobiological basis due to genetic pleiotropy (see Chapter 7, Hoeft and Bouhali 2022, and Chapter 12, Iuculano 2022). This hypothesis, however, was only partially supported (Koponen et al. 2018; Landerl and Moll 2010; Moll, Kunze et al. 2014). A further important source of variability for determining comorbidity rates is the task format. For example, Dirks et al. (2008) reported different comorbidity estimates between reading and maths difficulties, depending on whether reading was operationalized as reading fluency or reading comprehension. Furthermore, there is initial evidence showing that arithmetic fluency is more strongly associated with spelling than with reading problems (Dirks et al. 2008; Landerl and Moll 2010; Moll, Kunze et al. 2014), suggesting that arithmetic shares more cognitive resources with spelling than with reading, although the nature of this association is still unclear. In a similar vein, Moll et al. (2019) found that literacy measures (reading and spelling) were more strongly associated with arithmetic fluency than with magnitude processing skills. Accordingly, comorbidity rates were higher between literacy and arithmetic fluency deficits than between literacy and magnitude processing deficits. These findings elucidate potentially shared and non-shared risk factors contributing to the emergence of learning disorders. Specifically, the results reported by Moll and colleagues indicate that language resources are likely a shared risk factor that could explain the overlap between disorders of written language processing and arithmetic fluency, as performance in arithmetic fluency depends at least in part on language skills, while language skills are not involved in magnitude processing tasks (von Aster and Shalev, 2007).

To sum up, studies consistently highlight the contribution of different task-formats to the estimation of comorbidity rates. The underlying source of this variability is due to the fact that different tasks measure different constructs. At the same time, the overlap at the level of the manifested behavioural outcome suggests that there are shared factors at other levels of analysis, such as the cognitive level. To better understand comorbidity as the output of overlapping cognitive mechanisms, Section 4.4 provides a brief overview of the multifactorial deficit framework before describing the distinct and shared cognitive risk factors underlying dyslexia, dyscalculia, and their co-occurrence.

4.4 The Multifactorial Deficit Model

Recent evidence suggests that the high variability in behavioural manifestation of both conditions is associated with heterogeneous cognitive deficit profiles (Kucian and von Aster 2015; Peterson and Pennington 2015). Previous claims that one single 'core' deficit is sufficient and necessary to induce a developmental disorder is untenable, as they do not provide a satisfactory explanation for the interindividual variability in deficit profiles.

According to Pennington (2006), the best model to explain developmental disorders is a probabilistic multifactorial causation model. In this context, 'multifactorial' means that no single risk factor is both sufficient and necessary to explain a learning disorder. Instead, several causal risk factors can induce the behavioural features that characterize the disorder. 'Probabilistic' means that known risk factors are likely to have an impact on the disorder, but are not deterministically related to it. In other words, each disorder has its own continuous distribution of liabilities, rather than one discrete cause. Liabilities can be viewed as risk factors that are placed at different levels within the causal chain that leads to the neurodevelopmental disorder.

The multifactorial framework not only explains the heterogeneity within each learning disorder, but also accounts for the co-occurrence of dyslexia and dyscalculia in terms of partial overlap. Importantly, the concept of partial overlap overcomes the limitations of single deficit models, which proposed a one-to-one mapping between the disorder and its underlying cognitive impairment. While single deficit models could easily account for dissociations between disorders, they did not provide a satisfactory explanation for their co-occurrence, because they assumed divergent and unique underlying causal deficits for each disorder. Within the multifactorial model, co-occurrence can be explained as the outcome of shared probabilistic risk factors at one or more levels of analysis (i.e., genetic, environmental, neural, or cognitive level) (multifactorial causation; Pennington 2006). Risk factors have different weights in different disorders and this may in turn influence their co-occurrence at the level of overt manifestation. This implies that deficits may be 'additive' in two different ways (Cirino et al. 2015): the deficits could result from the association of two groups of risk factors that have a comparable weight on the outcome, or, alternatively, one group of risk factors may be more closely associated with the outcome than the other. For example, phonological processing is required for both reading and maths, but phonological deficits were shown to be more substantial for reading than for maths deficits (Cirino et al. 2015). As a consequence, in a US sample, the group of children with a combined-deficit profile showed a more severe impairment in phonological processing than the group with isolated maths deficits. Phonological deficits thus made an additive, but differential contribution to the disorders.

As a starting point for specifying a multifactorial deficit model of learning disorders, we will first review the comprehensive literature on cognitive underpinnings of each disorder separately, before we discuss cognitive mechanisms that potentially underlie the association of dyslexia and dyscalculia.

4.5 Cognitive Profile of Dyslexia

Reading problems in dyslexia have long been ascribed to a 'core' deficit in phonological processing (Vellutino et al. 2004). A phonological deficit has been proposed to impair the ability to identify and manipulate speech sounds (phoneme awareness) and, in turn, to hinder the mapping of speech sounds to letters (or graphemes) during decoding. As a consequence, word recognition may be slow and inaccurate. In line with this hypothesis, a strong association between phonological deficits and dyslexia has been confirmed for a large number of cases across many different orthographies (Landerl et al. 2013). The assumption that one single phonological impairment is sufficient and necessary to cause dyslexia, however, does not account for the high variability of its manifestation (Peterson and Pennington 2015). Instead, the heterogeneous deficits that manifest in dyslexia can be due to a large variety of co-occurring cognitive impairments that extend well beyond phonological processing skills (Menghini et al. 2010; Italian sample). Importantly, cases of individuals with dyslexia that do not manifest phonological impairments (Bosse et al. 2007; French sample) as well as of typical readers and spellers with weak phonological skills (Saksida et al. 2016; French sample) challenge the idea that phonological impairments are sufficient and necessary to cause dyslexia.

Aside from deficits in phonological processing, several other risk factors are thought to affect the development of literacy skills. For example, there is strong evidence for the role of rapid naming and oral language skills. Other domains with somewhat weaker evidence include verbal working memory, temporal processing, motor skills, and high-level visual processing. In the following passages we describe each of these risk factors and how it might be related to dyslexia.

Rapid naming refers to the ability to sequentially name aloud a series of visual items such as objects, colours, digits, or letters as quickly and accurately as possible. Performance in rapid naming tasks is related to different reading measures, including word, non-word, text reading, and reading comprehension (Araújo et al. 2015). Associations with reading fluency are particularly strong, and deficits in reading fluency related to dyslexia are consistently found to be associated with impaired rapid naming (e.g., Gangl et al. 2018; Moll and Landerl 2009; German-speaking samples). There are several different theoretical accounts that provide an explanation for the association between reading and rapid naming tasks (Moll et al. 2009). Remarkably, all these accounts consistently agree that rapid naming shares a key feature with reading, as both require the timely integration of visual and verbal information to achieve efficient processing of serially presented stimuli (Landerl et al. 2019; Norton and Wolf 2012). Rapid naming deficits in dyslexia hence seem to be related to a problem in efficient visual–verbal processing.

Delayed speech and language development is often observed in children with dyslexia, and is considered a substantial risk factor for the disorder (see also Chapter 18, Gunderson 2022). In a recent meta-analysis, Snowling and Melby-Lervåg (Snowling and Melby-Lervåg 2016) showed that children with a family risk of dyslexia who later develop the disorder have more severe language problems with speech sounds, vocabulary, and grammar at preschool age than children with a family risk of dyslexia who develop typical reading skills. In line with the critical age hypothesis (Bishop and Adams 1990), the risk of developing dyslexia seems especially high when language problems have not resolved at school entry, while language skills earlier in development are less predictive (Thompson et al. 2015).

Verbal working memory was reported to predict literacy skills (Moll, Ramus, et al. 2014) as well as dyslexia (Landerl et al. 2013) across several orthographies (Finnish, Hungarian, German, Dutch, French, English). Compared to phonological awareness and RAN, however, its association with literacy skills is weaker.

Individuals with dyslexia can also have auditory temporal processing problems (Goswami 2011; British sample). Temporal sampling is crucial to differentiate incoming sounds of different frequencies. Deficits in temporal sampling may thus lead to difficulties in differentiating sounds and in turn impair phonological processing. It must be noted, however, that there is large variability in temporal processing skills among individuals with dyslexia (Georgiou et al. 2010; Greek sample), and studies do not always find temporal processing deficits in dyslexia at the group level (Moll et al. 2016; German-speaking sample). Moreover, temporal processing was shown to be strongly related to attention skills and therefore the association between these deficits and dyslexia may be at least partly due to co-occurrent attention problems (Landerl and Willburger 2010).

There is currently little evidence that dyslexia is causally related to low-level visual problems (Handler et al. 2011; Vellutino et al. 2004). A number of studies, however, report associations between reading deficits and higher-level visual processing, specifically problems in visuospatial attention, shifting (Facoetti et al. 2010; Italian sample), and visual search (Sireteanu et al. 2008; German sample). Furthermore, there is evidence that children with dyslexia show stronger effects of visual crowding than typical readers (Zorzi et al. 2012; Italian and French samples). Crowding refers to the negative effect of surrounding elements on target detection (Whitney and Levi 2011), and affects object recognition, visual search, and reading performance. Moreover, dyslexia was related to a reduced visual attention span, which refers to a deficit in the amount of visual information that can be processed in parallel (Bosse et al. 2007). However, not all individuals with dyslexia consistently show visuospatial attention deficits (for a systematic overview, see Banfi et al. 2018). Moreover, it is as yet unclear whether these deficits are causally related to dyslexia (Goswami 2015a).

Finally, motor deficits, including impaired balance function (Rochelle and Talcott 2006) and poor handwriting (Pagliarini et al. 2015), have been found to be related to dyslexia, although studies analysing the association between deficient motor skills and dyslexia are still rare. Deficits in the motor domain may be specifically linked to dyslexia with co-occurring developmental coordination disorders (Downing and Caravolas 2020), and are likely to affect spelling skills more strongly than reading skills (Pritchard et al. 2021). Future studies need to unravel the specific nature of the association between impaired motor and literacy skills.

To sum up, dyslexia is characterized by heterogeneous cognitive profiles, ranging from deficits in phonological and other domains of language processing to deficits in temporal and visuospatial processing. The currently available data indicate that impaired phonological processing and rapid naming have a stronger effect on reading and spelling problems than other deficits that are reported in the literature (Saksida et al. 2016; Wimmer and Schurz 2010).

4.6 Cognitive Profile of Dyscalculia

Dyscalculia has been associated with heterogeneous impairments (Landerl et al. 2021), including number-specific domains such as processing of symbolic and non-symbolic numerosities, number ordering, transcoding (the process that enables conversion of Arabic numbers into number words and vice versa), as well as cognitive skills that do not necessarily require number processing, such as working memory and executive functions.

Dyscalculia has been linked to an impairment in representing non-symbolic numerosities (number sense deficit; Dehaene 2001), which is thought to affect the development of higher-order number processing skills, such as calculation skills. Affected individuals were indeed found to be slower and less accurate than typically developing children when asked to decide which of two sets of dots contains more elements (Landerl and Kölle 2009; Austrian sample; Piazza et al. 2010; Italian sample). However, this deficit was not consistently replicated in other samples with dyscalculia (Rousselle and Noël 2007; Belgian sample), which were shown to have selective weaknesses in symbolic numerosity comparisons of Arabic digits. Rousselle and Noël thus suggested that the main problem associated with dyscalculia is impaired access to numerosities from symbols (access-deficit hypothesis) rather than a deficit in representing non-symbolic numerosities. The association between non-symbolic, symbolic number processing, and mathematical skills is still debated and might at least partly be explained by developmental changes in this three-way association over time.

Order processing refers to the relative position of a number in a given sequence. An increasing number of studies report an association between numerical order processing and mathematical skills (Attout and Majerus 2018; French sample; Goffin and Ansari 2016; English-speaking Canadian sample; Sasanguie and Vos 2018; Belgian sample). Moreover, this relationship seems to increase over the course of development (Lyons et al. 2014). Individuals with dyscalculia were shown to have weaker order processing skills compared to typical maths achievers also in non-numerical domains (Attout and Majerus 2015; Morsanyi et al. 2018). These findings suggest that ordering problems in dyscalculia may not be restricted to numbers, but instead be related to more general weaknesses in manipulating the order of sequences, a construct known as working memory for serial order (Majerus 2019). This evidence, however, is very recent and should be treated with caution until replicated.

Understanding multi-digit Arabic numbers is essential for developing higher-order maths competences. Arabic numbers are arranged according to the place-value system, which is organized as a visuospatial template wherein each position has a specific meaning in the number sequence (e.g. hundreds, tens, and units). Children with low maths achievement were shown to be impaired compared to typically developing children in tasks assessing place-value knowledge (Hanich et al. 2001). Children with dyscalculia are often slower and less accurate in selecting the larger of two multi-digit numbers (Landerl 2013; Landerl and Kölle 2009). They were also found to show a particularly strong compatibility effect, which refers to the finding that comparing two-digit number pairs is generally faster and more accurate when both tens and units are higher in the larger two-digit number (e.g., 82 vs. 61, where 8 is larger than 6 and 2 is larger than 1) than when they are not (e.g., 82 vs. 63, where 8 is larger than 6 but 2 is smaller than 3). These findings indicate that children with dyscalculia experience difficulties in integrating decades and units, thus suggesting impaired understanding of multi-digit numbers.

Transcoding refers to the ability to switch between the structure of numbers in their Arabic form and spoken number words, thus enabling the integration of different representations of numbers. Transcoding is a strong predictor of later arithmetic performance (Göbel et al. 2014; Habermann et al.,2020). Children with low maths achievement were shown to be impaired in transcoding tasks requiring writing and reading multi-digit numbers (Moura et al. 2015; Moura et al. 2013), and problems increased with the number of required transcoding rules (Moura et al. 2015). This indicates that children with dyscalculia lag behind typically developing children in learning transcoding procedures, and this may in turn affect the development of more complex transcoding and number abilities.

Verbal and visuospatial working memory, the ability to temporarily maintain information for further processing, was also found to be affected in dyscalculia. This ability is particularly relevant during mental calculation and maths problem solving, as these tasks require holding a large amount of information online during processing. Recent meta-analyses revealed an association between poor working memory skills and dyscalculia, with a stronger effect size for the visuospatial as compared to the verbal component (Haberstroh and Schulte-Körne 2019; Peng and Fuchs 2016). In line with this picture, Mammarella et al. (2018) found that spatial but not visual components of working memory were impaired in children with low maths achievement. Additional evidence of impaired visuospatial processing in dyscalculia, however, is scarce (Szűcs et al. 2013).

Executive functions is a broad term for cognitive control processes (Miyake et al. 2000), which include updating (monitoring and manipulating of online information), inhibition (the ability to suppress unwanted responses), and switching (the ability to re-allocate attention resources from one task to another). These functions may be relevant for a broad range of mathematical skills (Cragg and Gilmore 2014). For instance, calculations that rely on the sequential implementation of several procedures, for example when multiplying multi-digit numbers ($24 \times 9 = (20 \times 9) + (4 \times 9) = 180 + 36 = 216$), require updating to keep the numerical information online and to manipulate it. Inhibition is necessary to choose the most efficient strategy during maths problem solving, while shifting may be relevant to flexibly change between different strategies. During arithmetic fact retrieval, inhibition may further help to suppress competing but incorrect solutions for the same problem. If the executive functions which are necessary to solve these tasks are impaired, performance in maths tasks will also likely be impaired. Accordingly, deficits in executive functions were repeatedly found in children with dyscalculia (Haberstroh and Schulte-Körne 2019; Szűcs et al. 2013; Wilkey et al. 2020). The evidence, however, is limited, and further replication studies are needed. It is important to note that problems with executive functions are often observed in samples with co-occurring attention deficit hyperactivity disorder (ADHD). Therefore, a major avenue for future research is to investigate whether problems related to updating, inhibition, and shifting are selectively related to dyscalculia or are a result of co-occurring ADHD (see Section 4.8 on methodological considerations for further discussion on this topic).

Taken together, the current literature suggests that dyscalculia is related to a large variety of number-specific as well as more general cognitive deficits that differently affect the way symbolic and non-symbolic number information is processed.

4.7 Cognitive Basis of Comorbidity

As outlined in the previous sections, there is pronounced heterogeneity at the behavioural and cognitive levels for both dyslexia and dyscalculia. This heterogeneity further multiplies when taking the co-occurrence of the two disorders into account. Understanding which cognitive underpinnings are unique and which are shared between dyslexia and dyscalculia is thus a fundamental research question. Studies that addressed this research question mostly relied on the subtyping classification scheme originally devised by Rourke and Finlayson (1978) and Rourke and Strang (1978). This classification scheme comprises four deficit profiles: individuals with selective maths deficits, individuals with selective literacy deficits, individuals with combined maths and literacy deficits, and finally individuals with age-adequate maths and literacy skills (control group). In the following sections, we report results for unique and shared risk factors of dyslexia and dyscalculia. Findings on literacy- and number-specific cognitive dimensions are reported first. Then, we present studies focusing on domain-general risk factors known to contribute to the co-occurrence of learning disorders.

4.7.1 What Is Unique to Dyslexia and What Is Unique to Dyscalculia?

The first research attempts in this direction focused on whether specific cognitive deficits could be selectively related to one but not the other disorder. Shafrir and Siegel (1994), for example, investigated whether English-speaking Canadian adolescents and adults with distinct profiles of isolated or co-occurring reading and arithmetic problems displayed different cognitive profiles. Their results showed that reading deficits with or without co-occurrent arithmetic problems were uniquely related to phonological processing and verbal working memory problems. In contrast, arithmetic problems with or without co-occurrent reading problems were uniquely associated with difficulties in visuospatial processing; the latter findings were particularly evident in a subsample that attained post-secondary education.

Consistent evidence was reported in a younger US sample of first-graders (Geary et al. 1999) that aimed at dissecting the cognitive contributions to low maths achievement as compared to low reading achievement. The findings by Geary et al. revealed that children with low maths achievement (with or without co-occurrent reading deficits) had problems with retrieving arithmetic facts as well as in correctly using finger and verbal counting strategies to solve simple addition problems, such as summing 4 + 5. Children with both reading and maths deficits generally had a more severe deficit profile than the group with isolated maths deficits in tasks related to basic symbolic number knowledge and transcoding. Children in the reading deficit group, however, performed at the same level as the control group on symbolic number tasks. These findings indicate that children with dyslexia have phonological problems that are not shared with dyscalculia, whereas children with dyscalculia have number-specific deficits that are not shared with dyslexia. It should be noted, however, that these initial research findings were not conclusive. The study by Shafrir and Siegel (1994), for example, assessed mostly verbal cognitive skills, whereas number-specific cognitive dimensions were not included. The opposite is true for the study by Geary et al. (1999), which addressed mostly number-related abilities, but not literacy-related skills. Furthermore, these studies selected children with low maths achievement based on different standardized tests. Shafrir and Siegel (1994) used a task which required the participants to perform different written computations in a predefined time window, whereas Geary et al. (1999) used a mathematical reasoning measure, which included a wide range of competences, ranging from basic counting and arithmetic operations to graph interpretation and time information processing. Hence, poor performance in these tasks may have very different sources and thus children with variable maths-related problems may have been included in the groups with low maths achievement.

Other studies applied a more selective strategy by focusing on one specific maths outcome only. For example, Landerl et al. (2004) selected British children with dyscalculia based on their performance on a timed task on arithmetic fact retrieval. The authors tested the hypothesis that an impairment in basic number processing is uniquely related to dyscalculia, with or without co-occurrent dyslexia. As expected, participants in the dyscalculia groups with and without dyslexia revealed a deficit in all tasks tapping into basic number processing, while children with isolated dyslexia showed comparable performance to controls in the vast majority of tasks (with the exception of counting, where they tended to be slower than the control group). Other cross-sectional and longitudinal investigations in school-aged US children largely confirmed these findings, indicating severe and persistent impairments in symbolic number processing, arithmetic fact retrieval, and calculation in children with maths problems with or without co-occurrent dyslexia (Geary et al. 2000; Hanich et al. 2001; Jordan et al. 2003).

4.7.2 Cognitive Profiles of Combined Dyslexia and Dyscalculia: Additive or Interactive Effects?

With respect to combined dyslexia and dyscalculia, an important question is whether the cognitive profile is additive, thus representing the sum of the cognitive deficits observed in the single deficit groups, or if it represents a separate deficit profile. A separate deficit profile in the combined group would suggest that co-occurring dyslexia and dyscalculia should be classified as a separate disorder rather than the combination of dyslexia and dyscalculia. Following this reasoning, a separate diagnostic category was implemented in the ICD-10 (World Health Organization 2015) as 'Mixed disorder of scholastic skills (F81.3)', which is applied when arithmetic as well as reading or spelling skills are impaired (see Chapter 3, Zorzi and Testolin 2022).

To investigate whether the cognitive pattern of combined deficits was additive or interactive, Landerl et al. (2009) assessed phonological processing and a variety of number processing skills in Austrian children with dyslexia, dyscalculia, and co-occurring problems. An additive pattern implies that co-occurrence emerges as the sum of the deficits underlying the two groups with isolated disorders. In contrast, an interactive pattern implies that the combined profile represents a qualitatively distinct disorder compared to both the dyslexia-only and dyscalculia-only profiles. Results revealed that children with dyslexia had deficits in the phonological domain, but not in the number processing domain. In contrast, children with dyscalculia showed problems in basic number processing, but no deficit in phonological skills. In the vast majority of other domains, the combined group displayed an additive profile of co-occurrent deficits that was not qualitatively different from the isolated disorders.

Most studies so far replicated the results reported by Landerl et al. (2009) and provided evidence for an additive deficit in combined profiles in children (Cirino et al. 2015; Downing and Caravolas 2020; Moll et al. 2015; Raddatz et al. 2017; Willburger et al. 2008; Willcutt et al. 2013: US, British, German, and Austrian samples), and adults (Grant et al. 2020; Canadian English-speaking sample; Wilson et al. 2015; New Zealand sample; but see Skeide et al. 2018 for findings of a distinct neural signature in children with co-occurring reading and maths problems). Children, as well as adults, with co-occurring dyslexia and dyscalculia are often reported to have more severe impairments than the isolated groups (Cirino et al. 2015; Grant et al. 2020; Willcutt et al. 2013; Wilson et al. 2015). It is important to point out, however, that their cognitive deficits comprise the same domains as in children with isolated disorders.

4.7.3 Sources of Overlapping Behavioral Manifestations

Another important issue relates to the overlap observed at the level of the manifested behavioral outcome. Children with dyslexia, for example, were reported to have difficulties in counting, transcoding, and retrieving arithmetic facts (e.g., Geary et al. 2000; Simmons and Singleton 2006) even though their ability to process numerosities (e.g. in number comparison tasks) might be unaffected (Gobel and Snowling 2010). How can these manifestations be explained? Should these cases be considered combined deficit profiles? And, crucially, are number problems in children with dyslexia related to the same underlying cognitive risk factors as in children with dyscalculia? Currently available findings indicate that the apparent overlap at the behavioral level likely derives from differential impairments at the cognitive level.

Moll et al. (2015), for example, showed that comparable manifested outcomes such as impaired number reading, number writing, and written arithmetic fact retrieval were associated with distinct underlying cognitive mechanisms in children with dyslexia compared to children with dyscalculia. In fact, impaired number reading, number writing, and fact retrieval skills in children with dyslexia were specifically associated with impaired access to and processing of phonological information, while at the same time the understanding of non-symbolic numerosities (i.e., performance on number line and non-symbolic magnitude comparison tasks) was intact. In contrast, problems with number reading, number writing, and fact retrieval in children with dyscalculia were related to impaired numerosity processing, with no impact of phonological processing and access deficits.

4.7.4 Additional Risk Factors for Co-occurring Deficits: Language, Working Memory, and Processing Speed

So far, we have focused on cognitive deficits that make unique contributions to dyslexia and dyscalculia and produce additive effects in combined deficit profiles. We now focus on risk factors that play a role for both disorders and thus may explain their co-occurrence.

Language abilities, such as verbal comprehension, vocabulary knowledge, and expressive language skills, jointly predict literacy and maths achievement (Peterson et al. 2017; US sample) and are consistently impaired in dyslexia and dyscalculia (Willcutt et al. 2013; US sample). The exact nature of this relation, however, is unclear. While it is obvious that language skills are important to fully grasp and solve oral maths problems (Purpura and Ganley 2014), the association of language with arithmetic calculation procedures is less straightforward. In fact, there is evidence that language predicts performance in maths tasks requiring the manipulation of conceptual meaning, such as data analysis, probability, and geometry, but not arithmetic and algebra, which are based on procedural rules and algorithms (Vukovic and Lesaux 2013). One possible interpretation, introduced by Moll et al. (2015), is that language skills may have an indirect impact on arithmetic: Language skills could explain variance in verbal number knowledge and counting, which, in turn, may predict arithmetic achievement. This hypothesis, however, needs further empirical support.

There is also evidence that phoneme awareness is a shared risk factor for dyslexia and dyscalculia, although this is hotly debated. Indeed, several studies reported that phoneme awareness is a unique risk factor related to dyslexia (Landerl et al. 2009; Moll et al. 2015; Willcutt et al. 2013). In a sample of Dutch school-aged children, however, Slot et al. (2016) found that a model with phoneme awareness as a shared risk factor for both dyslexia and dyscalculia fitted the data best. Moreover, Cirino et al. (2015) reported weaker phoneme awareness in children with dyscalculia as compared to typically developing children, although their deficit was not as severe as in children with dyslexia (with or without concurrent dyscalculia). It should be noted, however, that the groups in the study by Cirino et al. were not perfectly matched on reading and maths achievement: Reading skills were slightly higher in the typical group as compared to the group with dyscalculia. This might, in turn, explain the lower performance in reading-related cognitive skills such as phoneme awareness in the dyscalculia group compared to the typical group. In a sample of US children, Child et al. (2019) found that performance in a phoneme elision task (children were asked to repeat a given word without a specified sound: e.g., say "cat" without the /k/) was associated with both reading and maths, but its contribution to reading was stronger than to maths. It is difficult to reconcile these data with theories of dyslexia and dyscalculia. In fact, phoneme manipulation is an essential prerequisite for decoding, whereas its contribution to arithmetic is less straightforward. One hypothesis (Robinson et al. 2002; Smedt et al. 2010) is that weak phonological skills impair the efficient retrieval of verbal numerical information, including arithmetic facts. This is consistent with recent results in Finnish typically developing children, showing that rapid naming, which is related to retrieval efficiency, predicts shared variance between reading and arithmetic fluency (Koponen et al. 2020). In addition, certain phoneme awareness tasks, such as the spoonerism task used by Slot et al. (2016), impose high verbal working memory demands (Landerl and Wimmer 2000). To specify the unique role of phoneme awareness for arithmetic, future research thus needs to control for verbal working memory capacity as well as oral language skills.

Within the memory domain, verbal working memory was reported as a shared risk factor for dyslexia and dyscalculia (Child et al. 2019; Cirino et al. 2015; Willcutt et al. 2013), whereas visuo-spatial memory seems to be more selectively related to maths deficits (Moll et al. 2016; Dutch sample; Slot et al. 2016; British sample). This is in line with the idea that visuo-spatial processing is specifically related to mathematical skills, whereas the manipulation of verbal codes is a necessary skill for both literacy and maths domains.

Finally, processing speed was repeatedly shown to predict both literacy and arithmetic skills (Child et al. 2019; Peterson et al. 2017; Willcutt et al. 2013; Zoccolotti et al. 2020). However, although discussed as a shared risk factor for dyslexia and dyscalculia, reduced processing speed has not been consistently found in samples with learning disorders (Cirino et al. 2015; Moll et al. 2016). These mixed findings are most likely due to different tasks used to assess processing speed and to the important influence of attentional resources during the execution of processing speed tasks (Moll et al. 2016). Thus, the role of processing speed as a shared risk factor of dyslexia and dyscalculia likely depends on co-occurring attentional difficulties, which are strongly associated with deficits in processing speed. This view is supported by recent findings identifying processing speed as a shared predictor of reading, maths, and attention skills (Child et al. 2019). Additional work is needed to specify how strongly the association between processing speed and the different learning disorders depends on co-occurring attentional deficits and on distinct domains of processing speed (e.g., verbal versus visual processing speed).

Taken together, the reported findings provide evidence in support of the multifactorial deficit view, according to which co-occurrence between dyslexia and dyscalculia is explained by shared risk factors (language, verbal working memory, and processing speed), while at the same time unique predictors (access and processing of phonological information, visuospatial skills, and understanding of numerosity) account for isolated disorders. However, more research is needed to better understand the interaction between shared and unique risk factors and their association with literacy and maths deficits, as well as the impact of different task-formats on this association. In addition, longitudinal studies are needed to assess how the relationship between cognitive risk factors and different literacy and mathematical skills changes over time.

4.8 Methodological Considerations

Based on the multiple deficit framework, this chapter emphasized the importance of studying both isolated and combined learning disorders to better understand each disorder separately as well as the high co-occurrence rates. While we focused on the co-occurrence between dyslexia and dyscalculia, it should not be overlooked that dyslexia and dyscalculia also frequently co-occur with a number of other neurodevelopmental disorders, such as developmental language disorder, developmental coordination disorder, internalizing disorders (depression and anxiety), and externalizing disorders (ADHD and conduct disorder) (American Psychiatric Association 2013). Among those, ADHD represents one of the most intensely studied disorders that co-occur with dyslexia and dyscalculia (Germanò et al. 2010; Haberstroh and Schulte-Körne 2019; Morsanyi et al. 2018). ADHD is frequently related to difficulties in several cognitive domains, including (1) problems in executive functions, such as set shifting, working memory, response inhibition, and planning (Pievsky and McGrath 2018), (2) motivational problems related to delay aversion (Sonuga-Barke et al. 2008), and (3) dysfunctions of cognitive arousal, as reflected in high variability in reaction times (Bellato et al. 2020). These deficits obviously have a negative impact on task performance across multiple learning domains.

The fact that ADHD frequently co-occurs with learning disorders does not necessarily mean that children who also have an ADHD diagnosis should be excluded from studies on the co-occurrence of dyslexia and dyscalculia. Specifically, narrowing down the focus to highly selective samples may have the side effect of introducing a bias towards rare profiles that do not reflect the variability in the general population (Astle and Fletcher-Watson 2020). Moreover, children often display attention problems that are overlooked because they do not reach the threshold for a formal clinical diagnosis, but nevertheless impair everyday functioning and learning. It is thus advisable to statistically take attentional deficits into account in research on co-occurring learning disorders, at least to control for possible attention-related confounding factors (Landerl et al. 2013). This strategy was adopted by Willburger et al. (2008), for example, who assessed attentional skills with a standardized test battery to account for any subclinical attention-related issues that may affect performance in the reading and maths-related tasks of interest.

In the current chapter, we focused on research investigating deficit profiles in groups of children with isolated and co-occurring learning disorders. These findings provide important information on unique and shared risk factors of dyslexia and dyscalculia as well as on additive or interactive profiles in combined disorders. Comparing deficit groups is especially informative for understanding dissociations between learning disorders and the conditions under which these disorders occur in isolation. Group comparisons are also well suited for studying the heterogeneity of each learning disorder across different levels of analysis (e.g., the neurobiological, cognitive, and behavioural levels), as the restricted sample size allows the researchers to assess a large range of risk factors and outcome measures. Given that dyslexia and dyscalculia represent the lower end of the continuum of academic skills, however, the group-comparison approach should be complemented by continuous regression-based approaches (including structural equation modelling) based on large population-based samples which can help with identifying the predictive pattern underlying individual differences in literacy and maths without using arbitrary cut-offs (Peters and Ansari 2019). To identify shared cognitive underpinnings of literacy and mathematical skills, a promising approach is to assess whether a common predictor explains the *covariance* between literacy and mathematical skills, rather than analysing the predictive pattern of literacy and mathematical skills separately (Koponen et al. 2020). This approach is crucial for understanding combined deficits because a certain risk factor might be associated with dyslexia as well as dyscalculia, but for very different reasons, and will therefore not explain their overlap (Pennington et al. 2019).

Another methodological consideration relates to the fact that the majority of studies on co-occurring learning disorders are based on cross-sectional designs. Cross-sectional studies are useful for identifying potential underlying cognitive factors associated with a specific behavioural outcome. Nevertheless, they cannot shed light on developmental trajectories. Therefore, longitudinal studies are needed to assess the stability of isolated and co-occurring deficits and to identify developmental changes in the predictive pattern of risk factors and different literacy and maths outcomes. Longitudinal studies beginning in preschool years, before formal literacy and numeracy instruction starts, will be particularly beneficial for our understanding of early risk factors leading to the emergence of learning disorders. Given that dyslexia and dyscalculia have a genetic basis and share genetic variance (Kovas and Plomin 2006), family risk studies starting before the onset of formal instruction seem particularly promising. These studies render it possible to trace the longitudinal pathways of shared and unique risk factors to a variety of behavioural manifestations associated with isolated and combined learning disorders. While family risk studies have been successfully used in dyslexia research (Snowling and Melby-Lervåg 2016), this approach has not yet been applied to understanding the comorbidity of learning disorders.

4.9 Conclusion

This chapter was centred on the cognitive foundations of dyslexia, dyscalculia, and the co-occurrence of both learning disorders. We emphasized the crucial importance of considering these disorders as the outcome of distinct, probabilistic risk factors in a multifactorial model. A major challenge for the multifactorial deficit model is to fully explain the interactions between risk factors within a level of analysis (e.g., between different cognitive risk factors), and between different levels of analysis (e.g., between a cognitive risk factor and a neural correlate; McGrath et al. 2020). These interactions likely affect the behavioural level in different ways, thus producing distinct manifest outcomes. Furthermore, the causal stream not only travels downwards, but may work in the reverse direction as well: Children's behaviour may influence the environment that they experience, which, in turn, affects neurobiology and cognition.

A key challenge for future studies is to specify the relationship between dyslexia and dyscalculia, for example by differentiating between different outcome measures to account for the heterogeneity of learning disorders, or by identifying the explanatory components of a shared risk factor that elucidate the overlap between learning disorders. In addition, research should be extended to other frequently co-occurring disorders, such as ADHD. It will further be important to specifically target the developmental trajectory of combined deficit profiles based on longitudinal approaches, including family-risk studies (see Chapter 7, Hoeft and Bouhali 2022, and Chapter 12, Iuculano 2022). The longitudinal approach is essential to fully understand the causal pathway that produces co-occurring disorders. An attempt in this direction was made by Koponen et al. (2018), who investigated the longitudinal stability of isolated and co-occurring risk profiles of Finnish children with reading and maths fluency deficits from grade 1 to 4. They found that co-occurring profiles were generally more stable over time than the isolated profiles, with a relatively strong stability from grade 2 onward. We consider it crucial to understand whether the strength of these associations varies as a function of age, and to identify the source of variation. More research is also needed to understand whether difficulties are exacerbated in specific developmental periods due to external environmental factors, such as school demands. Genetically driven neurocognitive processes, for example, sensitive periods during which the effect of learning on brain development is strongest, likely play a role as well. Altogether, the multidimensional interplay between genetic, environmental, and neural risk factors over time should be studied to better understand both the heterogeneity of manifestation as well as the variability in current research results. Moreover, the influence of different national and educational backgrounds on the studied samples is, to date, poorly understood and should be addressed in future studies.

Suggestions for Further Reading

Special Issue: 'Comorbidities between Reading Disorders and other Developmental Disorders', *Scientific Studies of Reading* 24 (1). https://www.tandfonline.com/toc/hssr20/24/1.
Special Issue: 'Interpreting the Comorbidity of Learning Disorders', *Frontiers in Human Neuroscience* 20: www.frontiersin.org/research-topics/12020/interpreting-the-comorbidity-of-learning-disorders.

Pennington, B. F., L. M. McGrath, and R. L. Peterson. 2019. 'Neuropsychological constructs'. In *Diagnosing Learning Disorders: From Science to Practice* (3rd ed., pp. 41–53). New York: Guilford Press.

Willcutt, E. G., L. M. McGrath, B. F. Pennington, et al. 2019. 'Understanding Comorbidity between Specific Learning Disabilities'. *New Directions for Child and Adolescent Development*, 2019(165), 91–109. https://doi.org/10.1002/cad.20291.

5 Reading and Mathematics Anxiety

Dénes Szűcs

[E]very algebra teacher has heard a student say, 'I can do algebra but I can't work stated problems.' … Every time I hear a student of mine give utterance to this expression, I shudder and wonder wherein I have failed, and wherein lies the ability to show these young minds that their failure to grasp reasoning activity comes from their fear and·from the conviction that it is beyond them. (Sister Mary Fides Gough 1954, p. 293)

5.1 Introduction

This chapter primarily considers anxiety associated with mathematics and (to a lesser extent) reading. An overview of relevant research in the field can be found in recent review papers on mathematics anxiety (Barroso et al. 2020; Carey, Hill et al. 2017; Chang and Beilock 2016; Dowker et al. 2016; Mammarella et al. 2019; Namkung et al. 2019; Ramirez et al. 2018; J. Zhang et al. 2019) and reading anxiety (Piccolo et al. 2017). Here the focus is on the latest results in the context of some classical research. Emphasis will be laid on large studies that provide more reliable effect size estimates than small, underpowered studies (see Szűcs and Ioannidis 2017 for a review). Specifically, the current chapter relies on international data gathered in the Program for International Student Assessment (Education at a Glance 2018: OECD Indicators, n.d.; OECD 2013), on meta-analyses collating data worldwide, and on specific data sets collected in Belgium, Colombia, Finland, Germany, Israel, India, Italy, the UK, the USA, Poland, and Switzerland.

5.2 Definition

5.2.1 Anxiety

Broadly speaking, anxiety is a feeling of helplessness focused on future threats or threats to self-esteem (Jalongo and Hirsh 2010). Anxieties can be subdivided into more specific forms of anxiety. General anxiety refers to anxiety felt in everyday situations: 'feelings of nervousness, tenseness, or panic in reaction to diverse situations; frequent worry about the negative effects of past unpleasant experiences and future negative possibilities; feeling fearful and apprehensive about uncertainty; expecting the worst to happen' (Krueger and Markon 2014, p. 481).

5.2.2 Academic Anxiety and Test Anxiety

Academic anxiety is restricted to school or academic settings. Notably, neither the DSM-5 nor the ICD-11 diagnostic manuals recognize academic anxieties, but the psychology and education research literature deals with them extensively (American Psychiatric Association 2013). Test anxiety in turn is a specific form of academic anxiety and can loosely be defined as worry about evaluation (Sarason 1988). Sarason (1984) distinguished between four components of test anxiety: *worry* (cognitive concerns related to anxiety, such as having self-preoccupying thoughts about test situations); *tension* (feelings of unease and anxiety); *awareness of bodily arousal changes* and bodily reactions in response to anxiety; and having *task-irrelevant thoughts* during test situations. In principle, different factors of test anxiety could have different correlations to test performance and to other types of anxieties.

The cognitive interference view of anxiety suggests that anxiety, attention, and cognitive performance interact: 'Anxiety can induce anxious preoccupations, heightened concern over one's inadequacies and shortcomings' (Sarason 1988, p. 4). These preoccupations (task-irrelevant intrusive thoughts) will dominate thought processes during task execution, draining cognitive resources and leaving lesser attentional and working memory resources for task execution. In other words, worrying too much about failure will lead affected individuals to focus on thoughts related to the expected negative evaluation of their work (Sarason 1988). Test anxiety can thus be defined in a more restrictive sense as experiencing 'worrisome, self-preoccupying thoughts that *interfere* with task performance' (Sarason 1984, p. 933). This definition includes a causal mechanism as a defining feature of test anxiety. It also implies that higher levels of test anxiety are associated with worse performance. Accordingly, performance on more difficult tasks may suffer more due to the negative cognitive impact of interfering anxiety (Eysenck et al. 2007; Eysenck and Calvo 1992). Indeed, many studies found that anxiety negatively correlates with academic performance (Hembree 1990). In general, the more cognition-centred and specific the anxiety measures, the stronger the relationship with academic performance (Seipp 1991). Hence, it seems useful to define narrower domains of academic anxieties related to specific aspects of academic performance.

5.2.3 Mathematics Anxiety

Nearly seventy years ago, Sister Mary Fides Gough (1954, p. 291) referred to 'devastating matemaphobia' and Dreger and Aiken (1957, p. 344) reported that many people are 'emotionally disturbed in the presence of mathematics'. They labelled this phenomenon as 'number anxiety' and found a correlation of $r = -0.44$ between 'number anxiety' and maths grades in 704 university students. Subsequently, mathematics anxiety (MA) was defined as 'feelings of tension and anxiety that interfere with the manipulation of numbers and the solving of mathematical problems in a wide variety of ordinary life and academic situations' (Richardson and Suinn 1972, p. 551). MA is now recognized as a major potential stumbling block of maths learning. The manifestation of MA ranges from feelings of dislike, tension, worry, and frustration to fear (Ashcraft and Ridley 2005; Ma and Xu 2004; Wigfield and Meece 1988).

5.3 Measurement

Mathematics anxiety is measured with self-report questionnaires in the overwhelming majority of studies. Richardson and Suinn (1972) and Suinn et al. (1972) developed the Mathematics anxiety Rating Scale (MARS) which first comprised ninety-eight items and was later reduced to thirty items (Suinn and Winston 2003). There is also a very popular nine-item Abbreviated Mathematics anxiety Rating Scale (AMAS) (Hopko et al. 2003) that has been adapted for Italian, Polish, and German (Cipora et al. 2015; Primi et al. 2014; Schillinger et al. 2018).

Some scales were developed specifically for the assessment of children. For example, Carey, Hill, et al. (2017) modified the nine-item AMAS (mAMAS) and validated it in a sample of 1,746 children in the United Kingdom in the age range of 8–13 years. Similar to the original AMAS, the mAMAS captures *learning* and *evaluation* anxiety. Adaptations of the mAMAS have recently become available for Italian (tested on 1,013 children aged 8–11 years) and Spanish (tested on 1,504 children aged 7–19 years) (Caviola et al. 2017; Martín-Puga et al. 2020).

As MA is usually measured by questionnaires, its prevalence depends on exactly how high MA is defined in terms of questionnaire scores. For example, Carey et al. (2017) defined that children have high MA if their score is in the top 10% range. According to other usual definitions (scoring 1 or 2 standard deviations above the mean) about 16% or 2.3% of all children are considered to have high MA.

A notable point is that explicit self-reports have important limitations as they rely on introspection and may be strongly affected by cultural bias (Avancini and Szűcs 2019). Hence, there is a need for developing more reliable measures of MA – for example, based on implicit assessment or psychophysiological measures.

5.4 Specificity of Learning and Test Anxieties

As noted, MA is defined as a specific form of academic anxiety. However, it is correlated with other academic and non-academic anxieties. An important goal for research is thus to assure the construct validity of proposed specific anxiety forms. The meta-analysis of Hembree (1990) reported correlations of 0.33–0.54 between MA and general trait (stable) and state (transient) anxiety. In addition, Hembree's meta-analysis suggests a correlation of 0.29–0.72 between MA and the worry and emotionality components of test anxiety. In general, the relationship of MA and test anxiety is notably stronger than the relationship of MA and general anxiety (Carey, Devine et al. 2017; Carey, Hill et al. 2017; Devine et al. 2012; Devine et al. 2018; Dew and Galassi 1983; Hill et al. 2016).

There is also evidence that MA and reading anxiety can be separated (Punaro and Reeve 2012). For example, in secondary school students, MA was correlated with maths performance when using general anxiety as a covariate. In contrast, MA was not correlated with reading performance in similar analyses (Hill et al. 2016). However, another large study found that children who had high test anxiety and MA scores but comparatively low general anxiety scores performed relatively weakly on both reading and maths tests (Carey, Devine et al. 2017). Hence, further research is necessary to determine how distinct academic, reading, and mathematics anxiety are. In this context, it should not be overlooked that study outcomes can depend on the types of reading and maths achievement tests used as some of these tests are more strongly correlated with each other than alternative tests.

5.5 The Relation between Math Anxiety and Math Performance

Meta-analyses (Barroso et al. 2020; Hembree 1990; Ma 1999; Namkung et al. 2019; J. Zhang et al. 2019) and large primary studies (Devine et al. 2018) (1,757 UK children in grades 8–9 and 12–13) consistently report a correlation of about $r = -0.3$ between MA and maths performance. While this effect is replicable, it is relatively weak: In other words, it is not the case that each child with high MA also shows very poor maths performance. In fact, as much as about 80% of students with high MA have normal to high maths performance (Devine et al. 2018). Hence, this correlation effect size does not allow us to draw conclusions about individuals' maths performance but can only be interpreted at the population level. At the country level, MA is strongly associated with maths performance. Overall, countries with the highest level of MA had a performance lag equivalent to almost one entire school year relative to the countries with the lowest level of MA (OECD 2013; see also Chapter 4, Banfi, Landerl, and Moll 2022).

Importantly, a correlation of $r = 0.3$ is comparable to the correlation between some foundational cognitive skills for maths and maths performance. For example, Pantoja et al. (2020) followed 162 children in grades 1, 2 and 3 longitudinally. Criterion measures were mathematical word problems with increasing difficulty. During the autumn of grade 1, MA was a slightly stronger correlate ($r = -0.355$) of applied maths scores than number line estimation, both on the 0–100 and on the 0–1,000 scales ($r = 0.316$ and $r = 0.327$). Further, in regression models, MA was a significantly stronger predictor of future performance than number line estimation scores. One caveat is that two number line measures were pitted against a single (potentially more reliable) MA measure. Moreover, only number line estimation was used as a potential cognitive predictor of maths learning outcomes. Finally, the correlation reported by Pantoja et al. (2020) is lower than the correlation reported in the meta-analysis of Schneider et al. (2018) ($r = 0.443$ in the same age group of 6–9 years). Meta-analyses, however, typically rely on exaggerated published effect sizes (Szűcs and Ioannidis 2017). A crucial question for similar longitudinal studies concerns the stability of the relationships between maths and mathematics anxiety compared to other factors: While the link between maths and mathematics anxiety is known to be fairly stable (Barroso et al. 2020; Hembree 1990; Ma 1999; Namkung et al. 2019; J. Zhang et al. 2019), the correlations of different cognitive factors and different types of maths performance will probably vary in the course of development (see Chapter 19, Galuschka and Schulte-Körne 2022). Hence, MA might turn out to be one of the most stable correlates of maths performance throughout the school years.

5.6 Is Anxiety a Cause or a Consequence of Math Learning Difficulties?

The correlation of MA and maths performance has been linked to two different causal explanations (see Carey et al. 2015 for a review): The deficit theory suggests that weak maths performance results in MA due to students' justified worries about mathematics (weak maths → MA). In contrast, the debilitating anxiety model suggests that students first experience MA and then this anxiety interferes with their performance, leading to weak maths outcomes (MA → weak math). For example, it has been suggested that MA causes an 'affective drop' in maths performance (Ashcraft and Moore 2009, p. 197.) by interfering with working memory activity (Ashcraft 2002; Ashcraft and Kirk 2021; Hopko et al. 1998; Mammarella et al. 2015).

It is also possible that both views are correct. Specifically, a vicious cycle of experiencing MA and performing poorly may start after experiencing some initial trigger conditions. Specifically, in some cases, anxiety may lead to weak performance, justifying further anxiety that leads to even worse performance, and so on (MA → weak maths → higher MA → weaker maths → . . .). Alternatively, some students may start performing poorly, and hence they experience MA that could further weaken their performance, and so on (weak maths → MA → weaker maths → higher MA → . . .) (Carey et al. 2015). Accordingly, a vicious cycle may be shaped by individually different phenomena, but MA and poor performance would have mutual impact on each other.

5.7 Potential Causes and Triggers of Math Anxiety

Considering only MA and maths performance results in a restricted view of important phenomena that are key aspects of causal explanations of MA. First, as noted earlier, the correlation of MA and maths performance is weak. Hence, MA may have other, equally important or even more important consequences than weak maths performance (e.g., the avoidance of optional maths learning opportunities and career paths; see Section 5.8). Second, there are likely other potential causes or triggers of MA besides low performance (as detailed in Sections 5.7.1–5.7.5). Considering these other factors, causal models can be extended by including various alternative causes and consequences of MA besides weak maths performance.

5.7.1 Cognitive Triggers

A cognitive trigger of MA was suggested by Hopko et al. (1998), who found that adults with high MA were slower to read paragraphs containing distractors than adults with low MA. They concluded that high-MA participants have problems suppressing attention to distractors, similar to high general anxiety being related to low resistance to distractors (Eysenck and Calvo 1992). Hence, in a maths problem solving situation, people with high MA may suffer from failure to inhibit attention to worrisome thoughts. Indeed, higher MA may be associated with lower memory span (Ashcraft and Kirk 2001; Mammarella et al. 2015), potentially impacting performance in tasks requiring higher working memory load (Ashcraft and Krause 2007). The impact of MA on working memory performance can also lead to the seemingly paradox observation that adults (Beilock 2008) and children (Ramirez et al. 2016) (564 1st and 2nd grade children) with high working memory capacity may be more affected by MA than individuals with low working memory capacity because they may fail using advanced problem solving strategies depending on the integrity of their working memory.

Another domain-specific cognitive factor contributing to the high prevalence of MA in students could be that mathematics may in fact be unique in its capability of triggering relatively high anxiety. This could be the case because the solution of many age-appropriate maths exam questions requires mobilizing a large number of cognitive skills under strict time pressure and a single correct outcome must be achieved, leaving no margin of error (Szűcs et al. 2014).

5.7.2 Gender Differences in Math Anxiety

Females often report higher levels of MA than males. PISA surveys, for example, revealed a substantial gender gap (OECD 2013). This gender difference in MA severity seems stable as it has not changed much during the past thirty years (Betz 1978; Hembree 1990). Nevertheless, females' maths performance is typically on par with males at primary and secondary school levels, or even better (Bieg et al. 2014; Devine et al. 2012; Devine et al. 2018; Hill et al. 2016). According to PISA data for 1.5 million 15-year-olds, girls outperform boys in 70% of all countries, including many countries with low gender equality (Stoet and Geary 2015).

MA seems more stable in girls than in boys (Ma and Xu 2004) and many studies also found higher general anxiety, test anxiety, and mathematics anxiety levels in females than in males (Carey, Devine et al. 2017; Hill et al. 2016; Wren and Benson 2004). Hence, women may have a generally more anxious predisposition than men and therefore are more likely to develop higher general anxiety than men. This higher general anxiety could later develop into some form of academic anxiety (Carey, Devine et al. 2017).

MA is most often measured by questionnaires. It is therefore an open question whether higher self-reported anxiety in females reflects biological differences (Malanchini et al. 2020), socially constructed higher levels of anxiety perception in females, or a by-product of self-report measures (e.g., sensitivity to biases). For example, females may be capable of more accurate self-report about their own anxiety, or they may be more willing to admit their anxiety than males (Devine et al. 2018).

Another question concerns the possible separation of trait and state anxiety in females. Goetz et al. (2013) examined about 700 German students in grades 5 to 11. Females and males had similar maths achievement. However, females also had lower perceived maths competence than males. Moreover, females reported higher trait but not state MA (in an actual test situation) than males. That is, females did not experience higher state MA levels than males in an actual test situation.

While gender equality may be increasing worldwide, mathematics is still often considered a male domain, even by many females (Spencer et al. 1999). Accordingly, females may experience stereotype-threat (the perceived threat of fulfilling negative stereotypes about one's group; Maloney et al. 2013; Spencer et al. 1999) due to socially constructed attitudes. Specifically, stereotypes about maths may make them believe that they have lesser aptitude for maths than males (Bander and Betz 1981). Such stereotypical beliefs and worse maths ability perceptions in females than males (Wigfield et al. 1991a) can also contribute to worse maths self-efficacy and self-competence beliefs (see Section 5.7.3) in females. These beliefs, in turn, can also contribute to higher trait MA perceptions in females than in males (Goetz et al. 2013). These results, however, await registered replication (Flore and Wicherts 2015; Stoet and Geary 2015).

Importantly, while it may be that state MA (in actual test situations) does not differ between genders (Bieg et al. 2014; Goetz et al. 2013), gender differences in trait MA can still be highly relevant: negative self-perceptions can substantially bias behavioural choices and, for example, lead to avoiding maths-related careers (see Section 5.8).

5.7.3 Personal Factors

Students' maths self-efficacy (the belief of how successfully one can function in mathematics), self-esteem (positive or negative academic self-evaluation), and confidence in maths are important factors related to MA and maths achievement, even after taking into account gender and socioeconomic status (Giofrè et al. 2017; Pitsia et al. 2017; PISA data and data of 159 Italian children from grade 6 to 8, respectively). Nevertheless, these factors are likely also very important for understanding gender differences in MA. Boys often have higher confidence in maths than girls (Wigfield et al. 1991b). Kyttälä and Björn (2010; 116 students, 13–14 year-olds) found that girls had lower expectations of success in mathematics (lower outcome expectancy) than boys, but attributed similar value (outcome value) to succeeding in mathematics. This combination of attitudes can result in strong perception of uncertainty and uncontrollability (Pekrun et al. 2006; Zirk-Sadowski et al. 2014) with respect to succeeding in a highly valued learning activity. These feelings might result in higher MA and reduced future orientation towards mathematics, which is in stark contrast to the fact that girls perform as well as boys (Kyttälä and Björn 2010). Similar results were also obtained in a larger sample of 805 US children (in grades 3, 4 and 6): Lauermann et al. (2017) found that students who worry about maths and reading typically find maths and reading subjectively valuable. Their subjective self-evaluation of their ability and expected success, however, is relatively negative (low to moderate). In other words, the combination of attributing high value to maths but self-evaluating negatively may be a particular personal risk factor for MA.

Besides questionnaire-based studies, qualitative interviews also proved important for uncovering personal factors contributing to MA. For example, students with MA have similar experiences in school but the interpretation of their experiences is very different. There is evidence for experiences of lack of control as a result of confusing or frequently changing teaching methods used in schools. In line with this, but perhaps surprisingly, MA can be triggered even in high-performing students who are moved into higher achievement groups and suddenly face increased challenges without additional increase in their self-confidence (Carey et al. 2019). These students likely consider maths a valuable subject but their subjective ability and success-expectancy perceptions may be negative when they compare themselves to their high-performing peers (Kyttälä and Björn 2010; Lauermann et al. 2017). Furthermore, personal perseverance and resilience might be protective factors (Donolato et al. 2020; 274 Italian children from grades 5 to 8). As one student put it: 'I felt really frustrated . . . but after two days . . . everything went into my head and I knew everything' (Carey et al. 2019, p. 31; interview excerpt from 9-year-old female student).

5.7.4 Triggers in School

The impact of stereotypes and attitudes towards maths may also be 'passed on' from teachers to pupils. Beilock et al. (2010) studied 17 female maths teachers and their 117 first and second grade pupils. They reported that teachers' MA had a weak relation ($\beta = -0.21$) to female students' maths achievement, presumably because teachers' MA might affect pupils' gender ability beliefs through classroom interaction. Accordingly, female teachers' gender-biased ability beliefs (not measured but indexed by teacher MA) might have been transmitted to their female pupils. In this context, it is notable that in many countries most primary and secondary school teachers are female (*Education at a Glance 2018: OECD Indicators*, n.d.). Hence, female teachers' gender-biased ability beliefs may more readily affect their pupils than male teachers' beliefs. Additionally, girls may more easily identify with their female teachers than boys with the relatively few male teachers. This may then result in higher MA in females than males (as discussed in Section 5.7.2).

Besides passing on gender-biased ability beliefs, teachers can also affect their students' MA in other ways. For example, a study of 181 sixth grade Italian children found that student–teacher relationships (assessed with a questionnaire) were associated with MA, and in turn also with maths achievement ($r = 0.22, - 0.39$) (Semeraro et al. 2020).

5.7.5 Parents

Studies in the USA (Casad et al. 2015; 683 children) and India (Soni and Kumari 2017; 595 children) found that parental MA was a strong correlate of children's MA. This relationship suggests that parents could pass on their attitudes and stereotypes regarding MA to their children. Sister Mary Fides Gough (1954) ironically called this 'hereditary mathemaphobia'.

Maloney et al. (2015) analysed data from 185 first grade and 253 second grade US children. They found that parents' MA correlated with their children's MA and maths achievement – but only if parents often helped with maths homework. Hence, it could be that parent's MA only influenced their children's MA if parents frequently expressed (explicitly or implicitly) their own negative attitudes about maths, paradoxically during activities through which they intended to support their children's learning.

Vanbinst et al. (2020) investigated 172 sixth grade (11-year-old) Belgian children and both of their biological parents. Notably, this study had a relatively high power (0.84) to detect even small effects (r=0.2, one-tailed $\alpha = 0.05$). The authors found a typical correlation between MA and children's maths performance ($r = -0.31$; Bayes Factor [BF] > 100). They also found that girls had higher MA than boys, whereas there was no gender gap in maths performance. Further, mothers had higher MA than fathers. However, very low correlations were found between mothers' and fathers' MA and children's MA ($r = 0.18$; $BF = 1.5$ and $r = 0.13$; $BF = 0.4$). Similarly, weak correlations were found between mothers' and fathers' educational level and children's MA ($r = -0.18$; $BF \approx 1.3$ for both). The MA of the two parents was weakly associated ($r = 0.19$; $BF = 2.3$), while there was a relationship between parents' educational levels ($r = 0.51$; $BF > 100$). Overall, these results did not indicate strong links between parents' MA and their children's MA.

Another recent study of 241 Polish children disentangled potential contributions of fathers' and mothers' MA (Szczygieł 2020). The MA of fathers was associated with the MA of 1st grade children and with the MA of 3rd grade girls. The MA of mothers and teachers was associated with the MA of 3rd grade children. These relationships seem to be variable across grades, and it remains to be seen whether these results reflect stable developmental patterns. It cannot be excluded that low statistical power might cause this variability.

5.8 Short-Term and Long-Term Consequences of Math Anxiety

It has been suggested that students with high MA may avoid maths as much as possible in their daily lives. They may therefore devote less attention to task execution even if they spend more time on a task than low-MA participants (Ashcraft and Faust 1994).

Choe et al. (2019) reported data from two studies including 142 and 332 adults solving maths problems on an online platform. High levels of MA were associated with choosing easier, low-reward maths problems while low levels of MA were associated with choosing harder, high-reward maths problems. This observation may point to the impact of MA on avoiding maths challenges. However, it remains to be seen whether the timed task situation in the online setting is comparable to situations that students encounter in classrooms. It is also unclear whether the adult online sample can be considered representative for student populations.

As noted, MA is negatively correlated with maths performance. However, it is a misconception to assume that all students with high MA are low achievers. Recently, a study of 1,757 English primary and secondary school pupils (8–13 years olds) has shown that 77% of high MA children are typical-to-high maths achievers (Devine et al. 2018). Furthermore, in an actual test situation not all children experience their MA as pronounced as they report on trait MA tests (Bieg et al. 2014; Goetz et al. 2013). For example, while girls report higher trait MA than boys, their overall maths performance is typically not worse. Therefore, it seems that well-performing students often report high MA. Hence, the most important detrimental consequences of MA for maths performance may be medium- and long-term, not short-term consequences (Ashcraft 2002).

People with high MA may avoid further maths learning and practice opportunities, such as taking elective maths classes (Ashcraft and Faust 1994, p. 121). Due to this avoidance, they will thus likely not advance as much in mathematics as students with low MA at the same ability level who do not avoid maths learning opportunities. Another consequence of MA may be to avoid career paths where (intensive) maths learning is required (Ahmed 2018), even if these paths would otherwise be appealing to individuals. This is an especially important factor to consider in light of the finding that 3/4 of children with high MA are normal to high maths achievers (Devine et al. 2018). These otherwise well-performing children may be particularly vulnerable to avoiding maths-related careers. Taking into account the statements made in Section 5.7.2, such long-term avoidance may be a causal factor contributing to the underrepresentation of females in STEM subjects at the university level even though women perform equally well or better in maths in school than males (see Chapter 8, Skeide 2022; see also Stoet and Geary 2015).

5.9 Developmental Pathways

Krinzinger et al. (2009) followed 140 German children from the end of grade 1 until grade 3. They found that MA was increasing during schooling, but they found no relation between MA and later calculation performance. Still, MA and calculation performance were related to children's subjective later evaluation of their maths ability. The atypical lack of a correlation between calculation performance and MA could be explained by the limited construct validity of the rarely used German questionnaire or by lack of statistical power (Krinzinger et al. 2007).

Hill et al. (2016) tested 1,014 Italian children in grades 3–5 and 6–8. MA correlated with general anxiety (about $r = 0.4$), but only weakly with maths performance in primary school (absolute $r < 0.14$). When general anxiety was included in partial correlations, MA correlated with maths performance in secondary school (about $r = -0.25$) but not in primary school. These data suggest that MA becomes a more specific and stronger correlate of maths performance during secondary school compared to primary school. Children's experience in the school system thus may contribute to the emergence of MA.

Carey, Devine et al. (2017; data from 1,720 British children) found that general anxiety, test anxiety, and MA profiles did not differentiate in primary school. That is, children had either consistently low or consistently high anxiety levels, and their anxiety levels correlated with both their maths and their reading performance. In secondary school, however, children already had distinct anxiety profiles: Some had overall low or high anxiety, while others had relatively low general anxiety but high test anxiety and MA, and yet others had relatively low test anxiety and MA but high general anxiety. Maths and reading performance were relatively weak in the high academic anxiety group compared to the other three groups. In line with Hill et al. (2016), these results suggest that academic anxieties become more differentiated and distinct from general anxiety by secondary school. Further research is needed to disentangle subject-specific anxieties as children with high academic anxiety were relatively weak not only in maths but also in reading.

Gender-specific developmental pathways are also possible. For example, Carey, Devine, et al. (2017) found that females were more likely to have higher anxiety than males. However, secondary school boys were more likely to have specific academic anxiety than girls. It is thus possible that girls develop high MA and test anxiety because of their general predisposition to develop higher anxiety levels than boys. Boys seem to develop high academic anxiety even if they do not have a generally anxious predisposition. This discrepancy would suggest that girls and boys may develop academic anxieties through very different developmental pathways and therefore may also have different intervention needs.

5.10 Mathematics anxiety and Dyscalculia

Devine et al. (2018) investigated the co-occurrence of MA and developmental dyscalculia. High MA was defined as a child being in the top 11% of the MA score distribution. Hence, 11% of all children had high MA by definition. Children with poor maths performance but preserved reading performance were labelled with dyscalculia. 22% of all children with dyscalculia had high MA. Accordingly, children suffering from dyscalculia were about twice as likely to have high MA than children in the whole sample. However, this also means that 78% of poorly performing children did not have high MA, falsifying the assumption that maths difficulty is strongly linked to high MA. The results also suggest that emotional and cognitive maths problems strongly dissociate.

Why do most children with low maths performance not have high MA? Perhaps these children do not attribute much value to maths and/or do not have high expectations about their own maths performance and therefore do not develop high MA (Kyttälä and Björn 2010). This may be traced back to parental attitudes towards the subject. For example, parents may not attribute much value to maths learning. It is also possible that some children with dyscalculia do not have the metacognitive awareness needed to self-reflect on their performance and on the impact of their performance on their school progress in general (Devine et al. 2018).

5.11 Intervention

Intervention methods for MA vary in their success rates (Chang and Beilock 2016; Dowker et al. 2016; Hembree 1990). As discussed, MA may have many different triggers, so tailored intervention methods adjusted to specific triggers would most likely yield the best results. A single intervention may not work well for all children with high MA (Juan 2020).

Passolunghi et al. (2020) trained 224 4th grade (10-year-old) Italian children divided into three groups. One training group took part in playful activities designed to alleviate MA, another training group took part in playful maths learning activities, and a control group pursued playful activities related to reading and drawing comics. Activities targeting MA reduced MA (by about 0.4 SD) but did not affect maths achievement. In contrast, activities involving maths learning improved maths achievement (by about 1 SD) and also decreased MA (by about 0.4 SD). It is likely that practice with maths tasks enhanced children's self-confidence and self-efficacy in mathematics and thereby resulted in reduced MA. It remains to be examined how long-lasting these effects are and whether they generalize to other maths tasks.

It is also an interesting question how exactly maths interventions should be structured. For example, low achievers with high MA may benefit the most from basic maths training (Sister Mary Fides Gough 1954) that may help them to avoid entering vicious circles (Carey et al. 2015). In the long run, they may also benefit from training that helps them to increase the perceived value of maths, which in turn may result in more motivation to learn. However, increasing the perceived value of maths may also result in more pronounced MA as students may worry more about a subject that they perceive as important (Kyttälä and Björn 2010). Therefore, care must be taken when implementing such training.

As noted earlier, many high achievers also have high MA (Devine et al. 2018). These students may not benefit much from very basic maths training. Instead, increasing confidence with more demanding tasks may be more useful for them. It has also been suggested that explicitly expressing and discussing worries about mathematics may help students to overcome MA (D. Park et al. 2014; Ramirez and Beilock 2011). This approach may, in fact, work best with higher achievers with high MA who primarily may need to separate their anxious thoughts from their otherwise good maths performance (Juan 2020).

5.12 Reading Anxiety

Similar to mathematics anxiety, the existence of reading anxiety (RA) has been proposed and specific assessment tools have been developed (Zbornik and

Wallbrown 1991). However, most related research concerns learning to read a second language (L2), where students often experience anxiety. There are relatively few studies investigating RA in the first language (L1) (Grills et al. 2014; Horwitz 1986; Horwitz et al. 1986; Piccolo et al. 2017).

Similar to the case of MA, poor readers may experience higher anxiety levels than better readers. In particular, students with dyslexia are often thought to have low self-esteem and higher levels of anxiety than normal readers (Casey et al. 1992). For example, 1st grade US children who were in the top quartile of general anxiety scores at the beginning of the school year were 7.69 times more likely to be in the lowest quartile of reading scores and 2.44 times more likely to be in the lowest quartile of maths scores towards the end of the school year (Ialongo et al. 1994). Arnold et al. (2005) compared data from 94 poorly reading and 94 typically reading US adolescents. Poor readers scored higher on self-reported symptoms of depression, trait anxiety, somatic complaints, and inattention (even when controlling for ADHD status) than control children (Arnold et al. 2005).

A longitudinal study following 153 US children demonstrated that earlier reading performance could predict later RA (standardized beta values about 0.2; Grills-Taquechel et al. 2012). However, different reading scores revealed opposite (positive or negative) relationships with different anxiety scores, which may indicate some inconsistency. Conversely, it was found that earlier anxiety scores did not predict later reading accuracy, but were positively related to later reading fluency. While these results may be explained by referring to the potential performance-increasing effect of anxiety, the variable links between different reading measures may also be a sign of data inconsistency and low power.

A study of 8–11-year-old German schoolchildren compared 60 individuals diagnosed with dyslexia to 64 individuals without dyslexia (Novita 2016). Relative to typically developing individuals, children with dyslexia had significantly lower self-esteem in the school context. Dyslexic children also reported higher generalized anxiety than typically developing children. Effect sizes on other self-esteem scales (self-esteem at home and during free time) and anxiety scales (social phobia, separation anxiety [fear of being away from caregivers]) trended into the same direction but did not reach significance.

Several relevant, non-trivial, and important interactions may exist: For example, more educated parents of (even mildly) reading disabled children may more seriously underrate the scholastic aptitude of their children, thereby inducing more anxiety in them (Casey et al. 1992). Hence, as in the case of mathematics it is likely that the crucial relationship is not simply a direct causal connection between RA and actual test performance. Rather, many subjective, societal, personal, and perhaps genetic factors may contribute to the emergence of RA, and may in fact be more important in generating RA than the measured performance of students. For example, subjectively highly valuing a subject while having low subjective outcome expectations is an important factor for both reading and mathematics anxiety (Lauermann et al. 2017). That being said, studies with large representative samples are needed to confirm that most poor readers really have high RA (Devine et al. 2018).

Similar to MA, females often demonstrate higher RA than males. Females also often have better reading performance than males even if their RA is higher. For example, a study involving 115 Israeli 2nd graders found that girls showed higher RA and a more negative self-concept of their reading ability then boys despite being overall more accurate readers than boys and having the same reading speed as boys (Katzir et al. 2018). Notably, as reading is no longer considered a 'male domain', it seems unlikely that that stereotype-threat could explain the gender difference in RA. Several alternative causes could be considered, as discussed in the case of MA: a generally more anxious predisposition in females or a larger importance attributed to testing on behalf of females.

5.13 Conclusion

This chapter has mainly focused on mathematics anxiety, which has received much more attention in the literature than reading anxiety. However, the major questions emerging from MA research can be generalized to both academic anxiety domains. These questions concern:

(1) the specificity of academic anxiety types,
(2) the directions of causality regarding anxiety vs. performance,
(3) potential triggers, origins, and consequences of anxiety,
(4) the causes and consequences of gender discrepancy,
(5) potential developmental progression and distinct developmental pathways of academic anxieties,
(6) the medium- and long-term impacts of academic anxieties, and
(7) potential interventions for specific anxiety types in specific groups of children and adults.

The responses given in this chapter converge in the observation that MA is influenced by a number of personal factors, including subjective perceptions. Hence, it is likely that the triggers and consequences of MA are under the influence of several culture-specific variables.

To understand the relationships between various possible triggers and consequences of MA and RA, several personal, social, and cultural variables need to be considered in follow-up analyses. Furthermore, future studies should avoid post-hoc groupings of participants and preregister the exact hypotheses and variables that are tested. Future work should also aim for larger sample sizes so that effect sizes can be estimated precisely. In fact, emphasis should be laid on effect size estimation rather than hypothesis testing (Szűcs and Ioannidis 2017).

Suggestions for Further Reading

Devine, A., F. Hill, E. Carey, and D. Szűcs. 2018. 'Cognitive and Emotional Math Problems Largely Dissociate: Prevalence of Developmental Dyscalculia and Mathematics Anxiety'. *Journal of Educational Psychology*, 110(3): 431–444.

Dowker, A., Sarkar, A., and Looi, C. Y. 2016. 'Mathematics Anxiety: What Have we Learnt in 60 Years?' *Frontiers in Psychology*, 7.

Mammarella, I. C., S. Caviola, and A. Dowker (eds.) 2019. *Mathematics Anxiety: What is Known and What is Still to be Understood*. Routledge.

OECD. 2013. *PISA 2012 Results: Ready to Learn: Students' Engagement, Drive and Self-Beliefs (Volume III)*. Chapter 4: Mathematics Anxiety, pp. 98–112. OECD Publishing.

Szűcs, D., and I. C. Mammarella. 2020. 'Math Anxiety. Educational Practices Series 31'. *UNESCO International Bureau of Education*. www.ibe.unesco.org/sites/default/files/resources/31_math_anxiety_web.pdf.

Summary: Cognitive Profiles and Behavioural Manifestations

1. **Behavioural heterogeneity of dyslexia**: Behavioural difficulties of individuals affected by dyslexia are highly heterogeneous: for example, reading accuracy, reading fluency, reading comprehension, spelling, auditory processing, language processing, phonological awareness, visual motion processing, and visual attention.
2. **Behavioural heterogeneity of dyscalculia**: Behavioural difficulties of individuals affected by dyscalculia are highly heterogeneous: for example, understanding (non)symbolic numbers, counting, calculation, number ordering, transcoding, verbal retrieval of number and arithmetic facts, visuospatial attention, working memory, and executive functioning.
3. **Behavioural heterogeneity and causal origins:** While learning disorders manifest themselves heterogeneously and deficits change over time, so far there are few early deficits that have been consistently found to be causally relevant (dyslexia: auditory-phonological deficits, rapid automatized naming deficits; dyscalculia: faulty (non)symbolic quantity representations).
4. **Co-occurrence of learning disorders:** Co-occurrence rates for dyslexia and dyscalculia vary (about 10–70%). Dyslexia and dyscalculia also co-occur with developmental language disorder, developmental coordination disorder, internalizing disorders (depression and anxiety), and externalizing disorders (ADHD and conduct disorder).
5. **Possible causes of co-occurring learning disorders**: Given that early longitudinal data are currently not available, as yet it is unclear whether co-occurring dyslexia and dyscalculia is an independent deficit (e.g., hampered verbal retrieval of number and arithmetic facts, faulty audiovisual long-term memory formation) or 'the sum of its parts'.
6. **Dissociation of cognitive and emotional learning disorders**: Cognitive learning disorders likely have different origins than emotional learning disorders (learning anxiety). Learning anxiety is only weakly related to performance and related to several other social and personal factors (self-efficacy, self-esteem, perseverance, resilience, attitudes, stereotypes, parental influence, school experience).

PART III

Genetic and Environmental Influences

6 Genetic and Environmental Influences on Dyslexia and Dyscalculia

Margherita Malanchini and Agnieszka Gidziela

6.1 Introduction

Dyslexia is one of the most common learning difficulties. Children and adults with dyslexia experience varying degrees of difficulties with reading, writing, and spelling. According to the International Dyslexia Association, key features of dyslexia are impairments in word recognition, spelling, and decoding print – difficulties that are likely to interfere with reading comprehension and vocabulary acquisition. These literacy-related difficulties can be referred to as dyslexia only if accompanied by adequate learning opportunities and intact cognitive, adaptive, and social functioning (Lyon et al. 2003, also see Chapter 3, Zorzi and Testolin 2022). Dyslexia occurs with varying degrees of severity, and it is estimated that one in ten people in the United Kingdom may be affected by some form of dyslexia-related difficulties. These difficulties can range from mild impairments to a diagnosis of Specific Learning Disability (SLD) (Snowling and Hayiou-Thomas 2006). Dyslexia is included in the Neurodevelopmental Disorders category in the Fifth Edition of the Diagnostic and Statistical Manual for Mental Disorders (DSM-V) (American Psychiatric Association 2013).

It has been proposed that clinically diagnosed dyslexia lies at the low extreme of the spectrum of reading ability. As such, studies have suggested that dyslexia is part of a continuum that includes mild reading disability, reading performance in the normal range, and high reading ability (Snowling and Hayiou-Thomas 2006). This in turn suggests that the same factors implicated in dyslexia and milder reading disability are also implicated in reading ability across the entire distribution. But what are these factors? Why do children differ so widely in their ability to read? Behavioural genetic research into individual differences in reading ability has helped us to address these questions and has uncovered the extent to which genetic and environmental factors contribute to variation in reading ability and disability.

6.2 Methodological Approaches

6.2.1 Family Studies

Dyslexia runs in families (Brady et al. 2011). A comprehensive meta-analysis pursued three core questions regarding the familiality of dyslexia (Snowling and Melby-Lervåg 2016).

First, the authors looked at the prevalence of reading difficulties in children with at least one first-degree relative with a diagnosis of dyslexia. After combining evidence across fifteen independent studies, they found that children from high-risk families were four times more likely to develop reading problems than children without a family history of dyslexia (Snowling and Melby-Lervåg 2016).

Second, the authors investigated whether there were significant differences in the home literacy environment between families with vs. without a history of dyslexia. Although few studies had investigated this question, the evidence available suggested that children at family risk read less often than children at low risk and that parents with dyslexia read less frequently and had lower education levels than parents without reading difficulties (Snowling and Melby-Lervåg 2016).

Third, the authors examined what differentiated children from at-risk families who went on to develop dyslexia from those who did not (Snowling and Melby-Lervåg 2016). Overall, the meta-analysis found that all children with familial risk showed delays in speech and language development during the preschool years. However, these difficulties were more prominent in those children who went on to develop dyslexia. The children who did not develop reading problems appeared to overcome delays in the development of vocabulary, grammar, and phonological skills by the time they entered formal schooling.

Findings across the twenty-one independent studies included in this large meta-analysis point to the importance of family risk in the development of dyslexia. However, family studies cannot tease apart the role of genetic and environmental factors, as families share both their genetic make-up and their surrounding environment. Therefore, we need alternative methods that allow us to separate the contribution of genetic and environmental factors to differences in reading ability and disability between children. One way of overcoming this challenge is to investigate reading disability in families with twin siblings.

6.2.2 The Twin Method

The twin design capitalizes on the genetic relatedness between identical and fraternal twin pairs to estimate the extent to which differences between individuals in a given trait are accounted for by genetic and/or environmental factors. The method is grounded in the fact that monozygotic (identical) twins share 100% of their genetic make-up, and dizygotic (fraternal) twins share on average 50% of the genes that differ between individuals, like any other pair of siblings. Furthermore, the twin method is based on the key assumption that both types of twins who are raised in the same family home share their rearing environments to approximately the same extent

(Conley et al. 2013; Kendler et al. 1993). By comparing how similar monozygotic (MZ) and dizygotic (DZ) twins are for a given trait, it is possible, under these assumptions, to calculate the extent to which differences between individuals in that population are due to genetic and environmental influences.

Specifically, the twin method allows the partitioning of variation in a trait into three components: heritability, shared environment, and non-shared environment. Heritability (h^2) describes the amount of variance in a trait that can be attributed to genetic differences in a given population and can be roughly estimated by doubling the difference in the correlation between the MZ and DZ twin pairs (Martin and Eaves 1977). For example, a correlation between MZ twin pairs of 0.50 and one between DZ twin pairs of 0.30 would roughly yield a heritability estimate of 0.40, or 40% (2(0.50−0.30)). Shared environment (c^2) describes the extent to which twins raised in the same family resemble each other beyond their genetic similarity. The proportion of variation due to shared environmental influence can be approximately calculated as the DZ correlation minus half of the heritability. Following the previous example, this would be estimated as 0.10 or 10% (0.30−0.20). Finally, non-shared environment (e^2) describes environmental variance that does not contribute to similarities between twin pairs and can be roughly calculated as the degree to which identical twins raised together are dissimilar – that is, by subtracting the MZ correlation from unity, which, going back to the previous example, results in an e^2 estimate of 0.50, or 50% (1−0.50). Non-shared environmental estimates can also incorporate measurement error (Knopik et al. 2016).

The same three statistics (h^2, c^2, and e^2) can also be calculated for the liability to a given disorder. A method known as the liability-threshold model assumes that disorders would be manifested in all individuals whose liability is above a certain threshold. This cut-off value is usually estimated from the population frequency of the disorder. Following this approach, we can quantify genetic and environmental effects on individual differences in the liability of a population for a given disorder, such as dyslexia or dyscalculia (Knopik et al. 2016).

6.2.3 Disorders Are Quantitative Traits

Looking at families with twin births also contributed to one of the most fundamental discoveries about the genetics of dyslexia and its association with normative variation in reading ability: Dyslexia is the extreme of a continuum of reading ability and disability (Figure 6.1A). That is, the genetic factors that contribute to whether someone is diagnosed with dyslexia or not are also the same genetic factors contributing to reading ability in the normal range. In fact, the same genetic factors contribute to reading ability and disability across the entire spectrum (Kovas et al. 2007).

This can be tested by focusing on the twin siblings of those children scoring above the cut-off for a given disorder (dyslexia, in this case) and comparing their reading scores to the population mean. If the twin siblings of those children meeting the criteria for a dyslexia diagnosis score on average lower than the population mean, this suggests that the same risk factors contribute to clinical diagnoses and reading

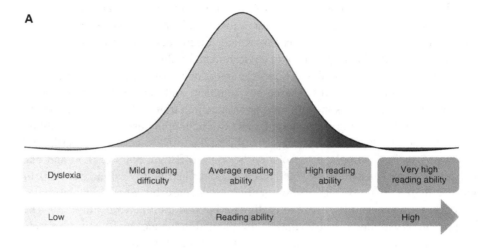

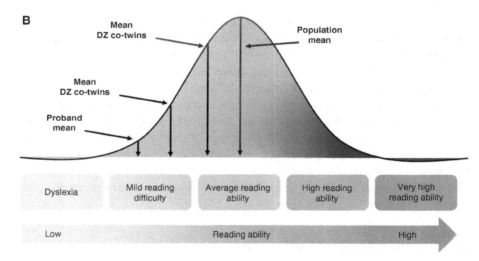

Figure 6.1 *The continuum of reading ability. Panel A shows that dyslexia is the low extreme of a continuum of reading ability. Panel B illustrates the logic behind group heritability. Researchers look at the twin siblings of children meeting the criteria for a dyslexia diagnosis. This way, they can establish that the genetic risk for dyslexia overlaps with the genetics of reading skills across the entire distribution of ability. DZ = dizygotic*

performance above the clinical cut-off for dyslexia. By comparing where unaffected MZ and DZ co-twins fall on average on the distribution of reading ability, it is possible to derive an estimate of heritability, called a group heritability (Figure 6.1B) (Plomin and Kovas 2005).

Importantly, group heritability suggests that genetic influences on disability overlap with genetic influences on ability; and, therefore, that the same genetic effects contributing to neurodevelopmental disorders such as dyslexia are implicated across the entire continuum of reading ability. Put simply, the genes associated with dyslexia are largely the same genes contributing to differences between children in reading ability. Accordingly, research studying the genetic and environmental factors that contribute to individual differences in reading ability is also likely to inform us on the genetic and environmental influences on reading disability.

6.2.4 Limitations of Twin Studies

The knowledge that has emerged from twin studies of reading and mathematics ability should be evaluated considering the limitations that apply to the assumptions the methodology is based on. It is beyond the scope of this chapter to cover all these assumptions and limitations; a detailed account is provided in Knopik et al. (2016). Briefly, one of the main assumptions of the twin method is the idea that environmental similarity is the same for monozygotic and dizygotic twin pairs growing up in the same family: the equal environments assumption. This assumption is often violated, as monozygotic twins are more likely to share similar environmental experiences than dizygotic twins. However, research suggests that this is unlikely to play a major role for the overall similarity of twins for many traits (Conley et al. 2013; Kendler et al. 1993).

A second assumption is random mating: people are assumed to mate at random, and not with other people that resemble them. In reality this assumption is violated as people tend to mate with people who resemble them, a concept known as assortative mating (Ask et al. 2013). Assortative mating can result in a greater genetic similarity between dizygotic twins but cannot increase genetic similarity between monozygotic twins because they are already 100% genetically similar. Accordingly, assortative mating will lead to an underestimation of genetic effects and an overestimation of shared environmental effects (Røysamb and Tambs 2016).

A third limitation of the twin method is its inability to disentangle the interplay between genotype and environment, which happens, as we will discuss later, through the two core processes of gene–environment correlation and gene-by-environment interaction (see Section 6.6; see also Duncan and Keller 2011). These processes are likely to result in increased heritability estimates, which can therefore be thought of as including not only genetic effects but also environmental influences.

A fourth limitation is the possibility that twins may not be representative of the wider population. It is particularly important to consider this limitation when studying early development, as evidence suggests that twins might be at a slight developmental disadvantage during perinatal development if compared to singletons (Martin et al. 1997).

6.3 Twin Research on the Genetic and Environmental Origins of Reading Ability and Disability

Twin studies have helped us establish that genetic factors contribute to explaining why children differ so widely in their reading ability and disability.

Substantial heritability estimates are consistently found for reading ability and disability across samples, countries, and developmental stages. A study investigating genetic and environmental contributions to reading ability in a sample of 6- and 7-year-olds from the United States found that differences in reading ability between children were mostly accounted for by genetic factors, with heritability estimated at 60% (Hohnen and Stevenson 1999). Comparable heritability estimates were obtained by two other studies in cross-sectional samples of 8–20-year-old twins from Colorado (Davis et al. 2001) and 8–16-year-olds participating in the Virginia Twin Study of Adolescent Behavioral Development (Reynolds et al. 1996).

Research conducted in a large sample of twin children from England and Wales examined whether the relative contribution of genetic and environmental factors to reading performance differed when considering different measures of reading. The investigation, conducted as part of the Twins Early Development Study (TEDS) (Rimfeld et al. 2019) sample, revealed that heritability estimates were similar for reading fluency and teacher ratings of reading ability at age 7. Differences between children in reading fluency, measured with the Test of Word Reading Efficiency (TOWRE), were found to be 70% heritable, with the remaining 30% of the variance equally accounted for by shared and non-shared environmental factors. Similarly, teacher evaluations of reading ability based on the UK National Curriculum yielded a heritability estimate of 68%, with shared environmental factors accounting for 7% of the variance and non-shared (child-specific) environmental factors accounting for the remaining 25% of the variance (Kovas et al. 2007).

Heritability estimates were found to be consistent even when considering the low extremes of the distribution of reading ability. At these low extremes, where a large number of children and adolescents met the criteria for a dyslexia diagnosis, heritability was estimated at 65%, in twins aged 8 to 18 (Willcutt et al. 2010). A further study demonstrated consistency in the extent to which genetic and environmental factors contribute to variation in reading ability and disability in a sample of 10-year-old children (Kovas et al. 2007). Heritability, shared, and non-shared environmental influences were estimated to be 60%, 20%, and 20%, respectively when considering both the entire distribution of ability and the bottom 15% of the distribution (Kovas et al. 2007). Similar results were obtained in another sample of 7-year-old children (Hensler et al. 2010).

The degree to which genetic factors influence variability across the distribution of reading ability was found to be comparable for boys and girls. A study conducted in a sample of 7-year-olds from the TEDS found very similar heritability, shared, and non-shared environmental estimates when data for boys and girls were analysed separately. The heritability of a composite measure of reading ability was found to be 65% in boys and 67% in girls. Shared environmental factors were found to account for 19% of the variance in boys and 17% in girls, and non-shared environmental factors accounted for 16% of the variances in boys and girls (Harlaar et al. 2005).

The same study shed light on sex differences in genetic and environmental influences at the extremes of the reading distribution. When the researchers considered the lowest 5% of the distribution of reading ability, differences between boys and girls began to emerge. Very low reading ability in 7-year-old boys was characterized by increased heritability estimates (72%) and a decreased role of the shared environment (16%). In contrast, heritability was significantly lower (37%) for 7-year-old girls scoring in the bottom 5% of the reading ability distribution, while shared environmental influences turned out to be significantly higher (50%). The role of individual-specific, non-shared environmental factors remained comparable for 7-year-old boys and girls (12% and 13%, respectively; Harlaar et al. 2005).

However, not all measures of reading ability show such substantial heritability estimates. Differences in reading comprehension are less heritable, and this was found to be consistent over development. Individual differences in reading comprehension were measured longitudinally in the TEDS sample at ages 7, 10, and 12 with the Peabody Individual Achievement Test (PIAT). At age 7, the heritability of individual differences in reading comprehension was estimated at 39%, with shared environmental factors accounting for 25% of the variance and non-shared environmental factors accounting for the remaining 36% of the variance (Kovas et al. 2007). These results were largely replicated at age 9. Specifically, differences in reading comprehension at age 9 were attributable in similar parts to genetic (39%), shared (28%), and non-shared (33%) environmental influences (Malanchini et al. 2017). This finding suggests that family-wide environmental factors play a more prominent role in the development of reading comprehension compared to reading fluency or teacher-rated performance.

Interestingly, by age 12, the role of family-wide factors was found to be greatly reduced. Differences in reading comprehension were found to be explained moderately by genetic factors (34%), and to a larger degree by non-shared, child-specific, environmental influences (66%) (Malanchini et al. 2017). This is in line with findings of an earlier meta-analysis of five twin studies of reading ability in childhood (5–18 years old) in samples from the United Kingdom and the United States, which obtained a grand estimate of 41% for heritability, 45% for shared environmental factors, and 14% for non-shared environmental factors (Stromswold 2001).

Although heritability estimates are not homogeneous across all aspects of reading ability and disability, twin analyses have also helped us to investigate the extent to which the same or different genetic and environmental factors contribute to performance across different reading measures. This overlap is measured in terms of genetic and environmental correlations. A genetic correlation of 0 implies that the genetic effects on one trait are independent of the other, while a correlation of 1 implies that the genetic influences on the two traits overlap completely. Therefore, the higher the genetic correlation between two traits, the greater their genetic overlap. The same logic can be extended to the interpretation of shared and non-shared environmental correlations.

Strong genetic overlap has been observed for multiple measures of reading ability and disability. For example, a very strong genetic correlation (R = 0.86) was found for two aspects of the TOWRE test which are thought to assess substantially different reading processes: sight-word efficiency, which assesses the ability to read aloud real words; and phonemic decoding efficiency, which assesses the ability to read aloud pronounceable printed non-words (Kovas et al. 2007). A strong genetic correlation of 0.84 was also observed between reading accuracy and year-long teacher assessments of reading based on the UK national curriculum criteria (Harlaar et al. 2007). These findings suggest that genetic influences across multiple aspects of reading performance largely overlap. Therefore, it can be assumed that the genes implicated in variation in reading accuracy are largely the same genes implicated in other aspects of reading ability, such as reading comprehension.

6.4 Finding the Genes Implicated in Dyslexia

While twin studies help us to quantify the extent to which genetic factors contribute to individual differences in reading ability and disability, they do not allow for the investigation of the specific genes and molecular mechanisms underlying reading difficulties (see Chapter 8, Skeide 2022, for neurogenetic studies). Genome-wide association studies (GWAS) on the other hand, are concerned with discovering how genetic variation across many (often hundreds of thousands) of loci in the DNA, called single nucleotide polymorphisms (SNPs), relates to observed individual differences in a given trait. The largest and most recent GWAS that has aimed to identify DNA variants associated with developmental dyslexia is based on a sample of 2,274 dyslexia cases and 6,272 controls of White European ancestry (Gialluisi et al. 2020).

After accounting for multiple testing, the study failed to identify SNPs that were significantly associated with developmental dyslexia, likely due to the lack of statistical power provided by the relatively small sample (Gialluisi et al. 2020). Although a sample of more than 2,000 cases and 6,000 controls might seem large for psychological investigations, genome-wide significance is only obtained after accounting for hundreds of thousands of tests. Therefore, GWAS require incredibly large samples to meaningfully separate signals from noise across the entire genome.

While this recent genome-wide association study did not identify specific DNA variants that were significantly linked to developmental dyslexia, it allowed researchers to calculate heritability estimates from SNP data using a method called Linkage Disequilibrium (LD) Score Regression (Bulik-Sullivan et al. 2015). SNP heritability provides an estimate of the proportion of variance in a trait (developmental dyslexia, in this case) that is additively explained by all DNA variants, not only those SNPs reaching genome-wide significance. SNP heritability estimates ranged between 20% and 25% depending on the threshold set for the prevalence of developmental dyslexia in the population (5% and 10%, respectively; Gialluisi et al. 2020). Few other studies have investigated the heritability of reading ability and disability using DNA-based methods. However, results are consistent across studies and developmental time courses. For example, the heritability of reading ability was estimated to be 21% in a sample of 7-year-olds and 27%–29% in the same sample at age 12 (Davis et al. 2014; Harlaar et al. 2014).

However, these heritability estimates are substantially smaller than the estimates obtained from the twin studies previously discussed. This gap in the heritability estimated from classical twin design and DNA-based methods is called *missing heritability* (Maher 2008). Several processes have been proposed to account for this missing heritability, including the possibility that the stringent cut-off that is applied to each SNP in GWA analyses may conceal the significant contribution of SNPs of modest effects (Manolio et al. 2009). A second proposition is that missing heritability can be explained by the current inability of GWAS to test for interactive effects between genes (epistatic effect), and between genes and environments (Aschard et al. 2012).

6.5 Non-Cognitive Processes That Contribute to Reading Development: A Genetically Informative Perspective

There is a consistent association between reading achievement, measured as reading comprehension, and aspects of reading motivation, such as enjoyment and self-perceived ability, indicating that more motivated readers are generally more skilled readers. Although several studies report modest to moderate correlations between reading achievement and several aspects of reading motivation, the findings are mixed with respect to the developmental nature of this association (Baker and Wigfield 1999). One unresolved issue is how the motivation–achievement association develops and to what extent genetic and environmental factors contribute to this association.

Our research group applied a twin design to investigate the development of the association between reading comprehension and reading motivation from age 9 to age 12 in the UK-based TEDS (Rimfeld et al. 2019). We were particularly interested in the developmental period from 9 to 12 years because it is assumed that during this period children make the transition from 'learning to read' to 'reading to learn' (Harlaar et al. 2007). Our results revealed a reciprocal relation between reading motivation and achievement: early reading achievement predicted subsequent reading motivation over and above the effects of early reading motivation; conversely, early reading motivation also predicted subsequent reading achievement controlling for the effects of early reading achievement. Compared to their peers, children with more confidence and a stronger interest in reading were more likely to become more competent readers over time, and more skilled readers were also more likely to become more confident in their ability to read and more interested in reading (Malanchini et al. 2017).

As part of the study, we also examined the extent to which genetic and environmental factors contributed to variation in reading comprehension and reading motivation and to their reciprocal developmental links. Individual differences in reading achievement at age 9 were attributable in similar parts to genetic (39%), shared (28%), and non-shared (33%) environmental influences. Variation in reading achievement at age 12 was explained moderately by genetic (34%) and mostly by non-shared environmental influences (66%). Individual differences in reading motivation at both ages were largely accounted for by non-shared environmental factors (~65%). Although non-shared environmental factors explained a substantial portion of variance in reading motivation and reading achievement at both ages, the developmental links between motivation and achievement were largely genetic in origin (Malanchini et al. 2017).

It is possible that children at genetic risk of poorer reading abilities experience more obstacles in learning to read and subsequently become more avoidant of reading activities (Harlaar et al. 2011). As a result, the less they read, the less pleasure and confidence they gain from reading. Similarly, reading achievement was not only traceable to genetic and environmental influences specific to reading performance, but was partially attributable to motivational processes by means of genetic influences (Malanchini et al. 2017).

6.6 Gene–Environment Interplay

It is important to consider that genes and environments do not operate independently. Therefore, the research discussed so far needs to be interpreted in light of the dynamic interplay between genes and environments. Two basic types of gene–environment interplay may be at work: gene–environment correlation and gene-by-environment interaction.

Gene–environment correlation describes the processes through which individuals experience environments that correlate with their genotype, rather than being exposed to random environmental experiences. This can happen through three processes: (1) *Passive* processes: children and adolescents tend to grow up with their parents who shape the rearing environment on the basis of their own genotype, which they share with their offspring; (2) *Evocative* processes: individuals may elicit their experiences on the basis of their partly genetically influenced traits, such as dispositions and characteristics; (3) *Active* processes: individuals actively select and modify their experiences based on their genetic propensities, dispositions, and appetites (Plomin et al. 1977; Plomin 2014).

For example, children who have a genetic predisposition for high reading motivation may actively seek out reading activities, which in turn provide them with opportunities to practice and improve their reading skills (active gene–environment correlation). Children with a genetic predisposition for good reading skills may also elicit more praise and recognition from their parents and teachers, which further fosters their interests and confidence in reading activities (evocative gene–environment correlation; Tucker-Drob and Harden 2012). Twin analyses do not allow us to disentangle these dynamic processes. To investigate gene–environment correlation processes, future studies should focus on examining whether relevant environmental experiences *mediate* the longitudinal relations between motivation and achievement through genetic pathways (Malanchini et al. 2020).

Genetically influenced individual differences drive dynamic gene–environment correlation processes, but the existence of adequate opportunities in the environment is a necessary condition for such processes (Tucker-Drob 2017). Children who are genetically disposed to high reading motivation can only practice their reading skills when reading materials and opportunities are available to them; genetically influenced better reading skills may not result in more motivation to read or better reading skills without feedback and help from parents and teachers. Limitations in the environment may constrain the expression of genetic disposition, whereas optimal environmental exposure may facilitate the translation from genetic propensity to outcomes (Taylor et al. 2010). This process through which the environment *moderates* genetic effects on outcomes is known as gene-by-environment interaction.

6.7 Genetic and Environmental Origins of Mathematics Ability and Disability

Dyscalculia is another common neurodevelopmental learning disorder, affecting between 3% and 6% of the population (Butterworth 2011). This disorder is characterized by difficulties in understanding arithmetic, number reasoning, manipulating numbers, and performing calculations (Shalev et al. 2001). As with dyslexia, the deficits associated with dyscalculia are observed in the absence of broader deficits in general cognitive ability (American Psychiatric Association 2013). In addition, similar to dyslexia, dyscalculia is best conceptualized on a spectrum of mathematical ability and disability, with dyscalculia reflecting the lower extreme of the distribution.

Investigations into the genetic and environmental origins of dyscalculia and low mathematics ability have furthered our understanding of how dyscalculia represents the low end of the continuum of mathematics ability (Kovas et al. 2007). Consequently, investigating the whole range of mathematics ability informs us on the genetics of dyscalculia.

Compared to the large body of work that has investigated the origins of variation in reading ability and dyslexia, there is a paucity of genetically informative research into variation in mathematics ability. One of the earliest studies on the genetics of dyscalculia included a small sample of 40 MZ and 23 DZ twin pairs, which were selected based on at least one co-twin showing deficits in mathematics. The study found that 58% of MZ co-twins and 39% of DZ co-twins of the probands showing maths deficits also met the criteria for dyscalculia. This resulted in a proband-wise concordance rate (the degree to which, on average, twin pairs were phenotypically similar) of 0.73 for MZ and 0.56 for DZ twins, respectively, and a heritability estimate of 38% (Alarcón et al. 1997).

A large body of research on the genetic and environmental origins of mathematical ability and disability is based on the TEDS sample comprising rich data on mathematics ability and achievement from early childhood through to the end of compulsory education. At age 7, the heritability of maths abilities, measured as teacher ratings of three core aspects of the UK National Curriculum (using and applying mathematics; numbers and algebra; and shapes, space, and measures), was found to be substantial: 65% on average (Oliver et al. 2004). The magnitude of genetic effects was found to be similar when considering both the entire distribution of maths ability and the lowest 15% of the distribution. Moreover, not only did the magnitude of genetic and environmental influences turn out to be similar, but the same genetic and environmental factors were also found to be involved in variation at the low end as well as the rest of the distribution (Oliver et al. 2004).

The same study also found that for both mathematics ability and disability, shared environmental factors only played a small role, which indicated that family-wide environmental factors did not contribute to similarities between siblings beyond their genetic similarity. On the other hand, non-shared, child-specific environmental factors were found to account for between 17% and 43% of the variation in mathematics ability and disability across the three teacher-rated measures (Oliver et al. 2004).

Another study examined the genetic and environmental contribution to mathematics ability when the TEDS twins were 10 years old (Kovas et al. 2007). Web-based testing was used to assess three core aspects of mathematics: numerical and algebraic problem solving; understanding of non-numerical mathematical concepts; and fact retrieval and computation. Consistent with what was observed for the teacher ratings at age 7, the study found moderate genetic influence (ranging between 32% and 45%) and environmental influence mainly due to non-shared environmental factors (ranging between 42% and 48%; Kovas et al. 2007). Results were consistent across the entire distribution of ability, even when considering mathematics disabilities by selecting the lower end of the spectrum. In addition, the genetic and environmental origins of mathematics ability and disability were not found to differ between males and females (Kovas et al. 2007). Findings were also consistent at later developmental stages, when the twins were 12 years old: more than half of the variance (56%) in mathematics disabilities could be attributed to genetic factors (Haworth et al. 2009).

Genetic research into mathematics ability and disability has contributed to a fundamental shift in the conceptualization of dyscalculia as the extreme of a continuum of ability, rather than a neurodevelopmental disorder characterized by a qualitatively different ability profile. This implies that research on mathematics performance and its correlates, causes, and consequences across the entire range of abilities can inform us about the factors that contribute to dyscalculia. Research has shown that several factors beyond cognitive skills play a role in explaining variation in mathematics performance (Krapohl et al. 2014; Malanchini et al. 2019). For example, mathematics anxiety has been identified as one of these factors contributing to low mathematics performance, independently of general cognitive ability (Ashcraft and Moore 2009; see also Chapter 5, Szűcs 2022). Students struggling with mathematics anxiety also tend to show lower levels of mathematics motivation. In a recent study, we explored how mathematics anxiety was related to different aspects of mathematics motivation and ability, and to what extent these relations were explained by overlapping genetic and environmental factors. We investigated these questions in a sample of more than 5,000 TEDS twins aged 16 to 21 (Malanchini et al. 2020).

We found that estimates of heritability ranged from 36% to 63% and that the remaining variance was mostly accounted for by child-specific environmental experiences. Although genetic factors contributed differently to different aspects of mathematics performance, the majority of genetic effects overlapped across almost all aspects of mathematics performance (understanding numbers, problem solving ability, and exam scores), mathematics motivation (interest and self-perceived ability), and mathematics anxiety, as indexed by strong genetic correlations. The only exception was approximate number sense. This points to the existence of a common genetic network that underlies performance, attitudes, and emotions related to mathematics, although this network seems to be either specific to symbolic number representation, or to relate to the learnt mathematical content, as opposed to the innate ability to discriminate between approximate quantities (i.e., approximate number sense; Malanchini et al. 2020).

These findings provide a starting point for delving deeper into the observed common genetic links between attitudes and performance in mathematics. Specifically, this work paves the way for examining how the experiential processes through which children select, shape, and modify their mathematical experiences interact with genetic predispositions to produce variation in mathematics anxiety, attitudes, and performance. The findings also lay the foundation for future genetic research aimed at identifying the specific genes implicated in variation in the cognitive and non-cognitive factors of mathematics across the entire distribution. No genome-wide association studies to date have investigated the specific DNA variants associated with mathematics ability and disability.

6.8 Conclusion

Genetic research into reading and mathematics ability and disability has provided crucial insights into why children differ so widely in these fundamental academic skills. Twin studies point to the importance of genetic variation for the emergence of dyslexia and dyscalculia. Fundamentally, these studies have shown that these two neurodevelopmental disorders are at the low end of a continuum of reading and mathematics abilities. Rather than being influenced by different genetic risk factors, genetic influences on dyslexia overlap with the genetic factors contributing to normative variation in reading ability, and the same has been observed for dyscalculia and normative variation in mathematics. These genetic influences, however, do not operate in isolation, but rather are shaped by their interplay with the environment.

It must be noted that virtually all currently existing studies are confined to White European and US-American samples. Accordingly, substantial additional work is needed to determine to which degree the currently available findings generalize to samples that are not WEIRD (western-educated-industrialized-rich-democratic).

Suggestions for Further Reading

Snowling, M. J., and M. Melby-Lervåg. 2016. 'Oral Language Deficits in Familial Dyslexia: A Meta-Analysis and Review'. *Psychological Bulletin* 142 (5): 498–545.

Kovas, Y., C. M. Haworth, P. S. Dale, and R. Plomin. 2007. 'The Genetic and Environmental Origins of Learning Abilities and Disabilities in the Early School Years'. *Monographs of the Society for Research in Child Development*, 72: 1–156.

Malanchini, M., K. Rimfeld, Z. Wang, et al. (2020). 'Genetic Factors Underlie the Association between Anxiety, Attitudes and Performance in Mathematics'. *Translational Psychiatry*, 10 (1): 12.

7 Pre- and Postnatal Environmental Effects on Learning to Read and Mathematical Learning

Fumiko Hoeft* and Florence Bouhali*

7.1 Introduction

The foundations of academic abilities in reading and mathematics are established early in life, long before formal schooling begins. One major source that impacts the outcome of academic abilities is the prenatal (or antenatal) and postnatal environment. Exposures during prenatal or postnatal development that cause permanent changes to the biology and outcome of an individual are known as 'developmental programming' (Sutton et al. 2016). These exposures include but are not limited to drugs, alcohol, maternal psychosocial stress, and teratogens such as pollutants. Earlier studies of pre- and postnatal environmental impact on the brain and behaviour have primarily focused on outcome measures such as mortality, physical growth, and internalizing and externalizing neurodevelopmental disorders. Later studies have, however, begun to focus on more fine-grained cognitive as well as academic outcomes, and their neural correlates, notably as cognitive and academic performance provide important measures of life outcome, including future well-being, health, and employment (Shuey and Kankaraš 2018). Thus far, links have been identified through animal models and epidemiological, prospective, and intervention studies in humans to identify the causal relationships and underlying mechanisms.

The prenatal period is defined as the developmental period between conception and birth, typically divided into the germinal (approximately the first 2 weeks), embryonic (the following 6 weeks), and fetal stages (from 2 months to birth). The postnatal period begins immediately after the birth of the baby, and extends up to 6 weeks (42 days) after birth. It is typically divided into the immediate (the first 24 hours from birth), early (from Days 2 through 7), and late postnatal stages (from Days 8 through 42). The perinatal period is not simply a combination of pre- and postnatal periods but begins at 22 completed weeks (154 days) of gestation, and ends 7 completed days after birth. For the purpose of this chapter, however, in order to provide a better overview of the relevant literature, we adopt a looser definition of pre- and postnatal impact, and include roughly the prenatal, labour, and postnatal periods.

There are several other caveats to this chapter. First, while genetic and environmental impact have often been dichotomized in the past ('nature vs. nurture'), we now understand that genes and the environment are largely intertwined, as reflected in large and pervasive gene–environment correlations (Hart et al. 2021; Krapohl et al. 2017; see also Chapter 6, Malanchini and Gidziela 2022). Thus, many factors that we believe are environmentally mediated also have a substantial genetic origin. For example, breastfeeding has been linked to positive effects on general intellectual ability and academic achievement in the offspring. While these associations seem at least partly mediated by breast milk's high content in fatty acids important for brain development (see Section 7.3.3), they may also be explained by genetic factors shared between mothers and their offspring. Indeed, mothers who breastfeed have overall higher intelligence quotients (IQs) themselves (Walfisch et al. 2013; Der et al. 2006), thus also transmitting to their offspring a genetic predisposition for higher IQ and better academic achievement. Consistently, it was found that when controlling for maternal IQ, the association between breastfeeding and children's general cognitive abilities is largely reduced (Horta et al. 2015). As most studies do not control for genetic confounding and as environmental effects generally survive the genetic control, we nonetheless treat these variables as environmental in this chapter. Still, we mention, where possible, whether a given environmental factor has been reported to have an effect over and above genetic confounds. Genetic factors may, in addition, modulate the effect of given environmental exposures on a child's development (gene–environment interactions; see Chapter 6, Malanchini and Gidziela 2022). For instance, breastfeeding tends to increase children's IQ to a different extent depending on their variant in the gene *FADS2*, involved in the control of fatty acid pathways (Caspi et al. 2007). In this chapter, we focus on the average effect of environmental factors on children's cognitive and academic development, but do not delve into subtleties of gene–environment interactions.

Second, some factors may be questionable to be categorized as environmental in origin. For example, medical conditions such as bronchopulmonary dysplasia (see Section 7.2.1) in a child may lead to perinatal asphyxia (causing hypoxic-ischaemic brain injury), a complication in turn associated with later learning disability. As the cause is not 'endogenous' (e.g., stemming from genetic risks for a learning disability), we consider such factors that are 'exogenous' to the immediate and direct cause of reading and mathematics impairment as environmental for the purpose of this chapter. Note, in addition, that the boundary between 'endogenous' and 'exogenous' factors is inherently blurry and/or hard to draw. For example, according to the three-hit model (Daskalakis et al. 2013), stressful experiences including exposure to substances during early life can modulate the genetic programming of specific brain circuits that make one vulnerable to dyslexia, which may be further exacerbated by later life experiences such as poor home environment or schooling.

Third, we differentiate the various environmental factors into three broad categories: child-centric, maternal, and exogenous. Some of these boundaries, however, are ambiguous. For example, we categorize prematurity as a child-centric factor. However, the cause of prematurity could be preterm birth, which may have been induced by maternal use of a substance. Prematurity is an umbrella term, including many causes and risk factors, many of which are indeed due to the environment (see Section 7.2.1). Hence, when studies examine prematurity without differentiating the maternal or other causes leading to prematurity, we include them in child-centric factors. On the other hand, when the study focuses on particular causes such as the maternal use of cocaine, even though it is a risk factor of prematurity, we include those studies as maternal factors. Therefore, there is significant overlap in what is reported in these three categories. In addition, many of these factors are highly correlated (confounded). For instance, maternal tobacco and alcohol use, malnutrition, cannabis consumption, pollutant exposure, and socioeconomic status (SES) all differentially, as well as interactively, have an impact on an offspring's academic abilities. Whether an influence was primarily prenatal or both pre- and postnatal is also difficult to disentangle in human research. With future research when causal pathways become better known, these boundaries should become clearer.

Finally, because the focus of this chapter is on reading and mathematical learning, we do not focus on all dimensions of neurocognitive behaviour. We focus instead on reading and mathematics abilities (and disabilities) as well as some critical cognitive processes (such as IQ and memory) known to significantly impact academic skills, and neurodevelopmental disorders such as attention deficit hyperactivity disorder (ADHD) that frequently co-occur with reading and mathematics disabilities.

Consequently, and despite these challenges, in this chapter we describe key perinatal factors that have been shown to impact reading and mathematics outcomes. We categorize them into the following (Figure 7.1):

(1) *child-centric* factors such as prematurity, perinatal asphyxia, and hyperbilirubinemia;
(2) *maternal* factors such as substance use – nicotine, alcohol, cannabis (marijuana), cocaine, psychostimulants, opioids, and caffeine; psychosocial stress, including mental health issues such as anxiety and depression; breastfeeding;

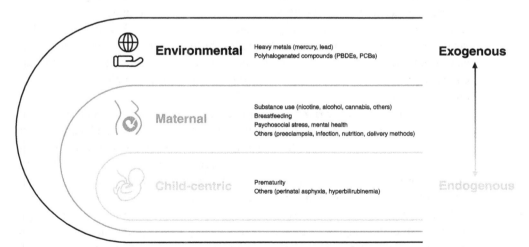

Figure 7.1 *Key perinatal factors that have been shown to impact reading and mathematics outcomes described in this chapter.*

and other maternal factors – hypertension diseases including (pre-)eclampsia, nutrition, infection, and delivery method; and

(3) *exogenous* factors such as heavy metals, in particular lead and mercury; and polyhalogenated aromatic hydrocarbon compounds, including polybrominated/ polychlorinated biphenyls (PCBs) and related chemicals, given their prevalence and the body of evidence.

For the core factors listed, we describe global prevalence rate, risk factors, biological mechanisms, key neuroimaging findings, details of research that examined academic impairment, and possible mediators. Whenever possible, we include the country and cultural population examined in the specific study. We conclude with a summary, and future directions.

7.2 Child-centric Factors

7.2.1 Prematurity

The preterm birth rate has been increasing, and was estimated to be approximately 11% in 2010 worldwide (Blencowe et al. 2012). Preterm birth can be categorized as spontaneous onset of labour, pre-labour rupture of membranes, and medically indicated labour onset. A myriad of different pathways can lead to any of these preterm births. These include distal factors such as sociodemographic factors, genetic traits, reproductive history, and maternal medical conditions; and factors that are more proximal to the birth, such as complications of pregnancy and delivery (Goldenberg et al. 2008). More specifically, causes for spontaneous preterm births include maternal infection or inflammation, vascular disease, and uterine overdistension; and for indicated preterm births, pre-eclampsia (maternal high blood pressure during pregnancy causing fetal organ damage), and intrauterine growth restriction. While genetic risks contribute to prematurity and low birth weight, the different underlying causes of preterm birth are rarely dissociated. Since many causes and risk factors are environmental (see Section 7.1), we include preterm birth as a child-centric environmental factor.

Preterm birth is a major risk factor for neurodevelopmental disorders (Saigal and Doyle 2008) as well as poor academic outcomes, including reading and mathematics. Studies have repeatedly shown that preterm birth is associated with low intelligence and learning difficulties (Jaekel et al. 2013; Kerr-Wilson et al. 2012). In a meta-analysis on reading abilities in school-age children born preterm, worse decoding (d=−0.42) and reading comprehension abilities (d=−0.57) were found in preterm children compared to controls (Kovachy et al. 2015). Another meta-analysis found that preterm children showed broader neurodevelopmental problems. They notably scored 0.7 standard deviations (SD) below full-term peers on arithmetic, 0.4 SD lower on reading, and 0.5 SD lower on spelling. They were also almost three times more likely to receive special educational assistance (Twilhaar et al. 2018). Similar estimates were obtained in an older meta-analysis in very preterm and/or very low birth weight children (<32 weeks of gestation): mathematics, 0.6 SD; reading, 0.5 SD; spelling, 0.8 SD; attention, 0.4–0.6 SD; and executive function, 0.3 to 0.6 SD (Aarnoudse-Moens et al. 2009). These studies generally show that gestational age, birth weight, and postnatal complications of the neonate (e.g., ventilation or intubation, severe anaemia, and cerebral haemorrhage) predict outcome. The relationship is either a linear dose–response relationship (Kerr-Wilson et al. 2012), and/or a curvilinear relationship that is detected only with increased cognitive load (Jaekel et al. 2013).

Interestingly, some have argued that the nature of academic difficulty in children born preterm is different from typical developmental learning disorders (Simms et al. 2015). For example, one study found that the mathematics difficulties in very preterm children are associated with deficits in working memory and visuospatial processing, and not numerical representations (Simms et al. 2015). Based on these findings, the authors concluded that very preterm children's mathematics difficulties are different in nature from those of children with developmental dyscalculia. These academic challenges are generally not accounted for by low intelligence (Simms et al. 2013). While a recent large-scale study in China (n = 34,748) found a significant association between the risk of dyslexia and preterm birth (odds ratio [OR] = 1.30) even after adjustment of possible confounding variables (Liu et al. 2016), there is currently no evidence that reading difficulties of children born preterm are different in nature from those of children with dyslexia, unlike for mathematics difficulties. Other risk factors for dyslexia in that study included maternal infectious diseases (dyslexic 9.17% vs. non-dyslexic 5.83%; OR = 1.59), difficult vaginal delivery (dyslexic 3.12% vs. non-dyslexic 1.75%; OR = 1.58), and neonatal asphyxia (dyslexic 3.76% vs. non-dyslexic 1.42%; OR = 2.38), all factors that have been associated with preterm birth (see Section 7.3.4).

There is a wealth of neuroimaging research in preterm birth. Brains of neonates born prematurely are highly prone to injury from hypoxia, ischaemia, and inflammation (Bruckert et al. 2019; Back et al. 2007; Khwaja and Volpe 2008; Volpe 2009). These early insults primarily affect the myelin-producing cells, or oligodendrocyte precursors, and result in cell maturation arrest, cell death, and myelination failure (Bruckert et al. 2019; Back et al. 2007; Khwaja and Volpe 2008). Abnormal white matter microstructural properties, notably in terms of fractional anisotropy (FA) or apparent diffusion coefficient (ADC), have been found in preterm children using diffusion MRI (dMRI) at near-term equivalent age, and up to adolescence (Nagy et al. 2003; Groeschel et al. 2014; Travis et al. 2015), although inconsistently across studies (Bruckert et al. 2019; Anjari et al. 2007; Knight et al. 2018; Giménez et al. 2008). These studies often find that moderate and late preterm children (infants) show widespread brain white matter abnormalities when compared to full-term controls (Kelly et al. 2016; Liu et al. 2016). In particular, poor reading skills may result from structural abnormalities in several tracts of the dorsal and ventral reading pathways. These include dorsally, the left superior longitudinal fasciculus (SLF), connecting in part ventral premotor articulation regions with inferior parietal language regions (Frye et al. 2010), and the left arcuate fasciculus (AF), which connects the inferior frontal and superior temporal regions, important for sensory-to-motor mapping and complex syntax (Dodson et al. 2018; Skeide and Friederici 2016). Additionally, they also include a ventral tract (Travis et al. 2016), the uncinate fasciculus (UF) that connects the inferior frontal cortex and the temporal pole implicated in language (Dodson et al. 2018; Skeide and Friederici 2016). The association between the microstructure of these tracts and reading skills is often altered in individuals born preterm (Frye et al. 2010), with typically more bilateral involvement (Mullen et al. 2011). These subtle but significant white matter abnormalities, as well as more prominent and visible abnormalities such as cerebellar injury, are likely to have implications for cognitive skills and learning (Brossard-Racine et al. 2015). The findings support the view that plasticity and reorganization following early white matter injury result in atypical neural processing during reading in individuals born preterm.

Within the realm of factors leading to preterm birth, some risk factors specific to academic challenges in preterm birth have been identified, although these risk factors may be interrelated. For example, preterm children suffering from bronchopulmonary dysplasia (a breathing disorder of premature babies where an infant's lungs become irritated and do not develop normally, resulting in chronic lung disease) have increased risks for academic difficulties (Hughes et al. 1999). Other factors predictive of adverse neurodevelopmental outcomes are cerebellar injury, which has been linked to poor expressive/receptive language and cognitive deficits; periventricular leukomalacia and intraventricular haemorrhage, linked to general sensory, cognitive, and language deficits; and neonatal infectious diseases, linked to poor head growth, especially in low birth-weight and very preterm birth (Limperopoulos et al. 2007; Stoll et al. 2004; Patra et al. 2006). A recent meta-analysis showed that bronchopulmonary dysplasia explained as much as 44% of the variance in academic performance (78% when only examining very preterm birth), revealing a major impact of such perinatal factors (Kovachy et al. 2015). While the exact mechanisms underlying the detrimental effects of bronchopulmonary dysplasia on brain development are unknown, it is hypothesized that it may be related to infection and inflammation affecting lung maturation and interfering with cerebral development, which is in turn related to episodic and chronic hypoxia impacting neurocognitive outcomes. It might also be an epiphenomenon and a marker of adverse outcome without a causal relation.

In summary, mathematics and reading abilities of preterm children are impacted, with mathematics difficulties (but not reading difficulties) which may differ in nature from those of children with dyscalculia (or dyslexia, respectively). Regardless of the exact mechanisms, poor reading and mathematics abilities stemming from preterm birth have significant consequences. For example, in two large British population-based birth cohorts born in 1958 and 1970, the relationship between preterm birth and decreased wealth in adulthood was mediated by decreased intelligence, reading, and, in particular, mathematics attainment in middle childhood (Basten et al. 2015). Long-term disadvantages in SES were found even in late preterm birth (34 to 36 weeks of gestation; Heinonen et al. 2013).

7.2.2 Other Child-centric Factors

Neonatal encephalopathy following perinatal asphyxia is a main cause of long-term disabilities such as intellectual disability, cerebral palsy, and other neurodevelopmental disorders with impaired language skills, learning, executive functions, or social ability (van Handel et al. 2007). *Perinatal asphyxia* can occur during the antepartum (predelivery), intrapartum (during delivery), or postpartum (postdelivery) periods, and is estimated to occur in 0.1 to 0.8% of live births (American College of Obstetricians and Gynecologists 2004). While perinatal asphyxia may occur from factors that are typically not considered as environmental factors (e.g., bronchopulmonary dysplasia, described in Section 7.2.1), there are many environmental risk factors, such as maternal hypothyroidism, pre-eclampsia, premature rupture of the membranes, and bacterial infection before or during labour (i.e., chorioamnionitis), many of which are maternal factors and described in Section 7.3 (Badawi et al. 1998). Most studies about the long-term outcomes of infants with perinatal asphyxia are focused on the first two years of life. These studies have shown that mild encephalopathy typically has positive outcomes, moderate encephalopathy is most variable, and severe encephalopathy is associated with increased risk for intellectual disabilities (and cerebral palsy) (van Handel et al. 2007; Gonzalez and Miller 2006). Some studies that examined longer-term outcomes, especially in moderate encephalopathy, have found difficulties in the domains of reading, spelling, and arithmetic/ mathematics of about 1 SD below the norm (OR = 2.38), in the absence of intellectual disability (van Handel et al. 2007; Liu et al. 2016). Deficits have also been found in receptive vocabulary, visual-motor integration, phonological memory, auditory verbal learning and delayed recall, auditory binaural integration, and auditory sequencing and labelling (Robertson 2003; van Handel et al. 2007), despite attention, executive functions, and visuospatial abilities being within normal range (Low et al. 1988; Mañeru et al. 2003). Some studies have also shown elevated rates of hyperactivity in children with moderate neonatal encephalopathy (van Handel et al. 2007).

A rodent model suggests that moderate hypoxia-ischaemia reduces cortical activity (measured using electroencephalography [EEG]), hampers dendrite development, and impairs cortical plasticity, similar to what is observed in humans (Ranasinghe et al. 2015). In a primate model of term neonatal brain injury, the authors also found different durations and severities of ischaemia to be associated with regional vulnerability to injury. Partial asphyxia, on the one hand, causes injury to the cerebral white matter in primates (Myers 1975; Myers 1972). In human term newborns, watershed cerebral infarctions (observed by MRI) occur in cerebral regions at the border between cerebral vascular territories, furthest from arterial supply, and thereby most vulnerable to hypoxia. Subsequent abnormalities are predominantly observed in the white matter, and, when severe, in the cortical grey matter (Miller et al. 2005; Sie et al. 2000). On the other hand, acute and profound asphyxia in primates causes injury to deep grey nuclei (basal ganglia and thalamus; Myers 1975; Myers 1972). Human MRI also predominantly found basal ganglia–thalamus patterns involving deep grey nuclei and perirolandic cortex, and, when severe, extending to the entire cortex (Miller et al. 2005; Sie et al. 2000). In summary, these studies show selective vulnerability of the developing brain to hypoxia-ischaemia, with injury often reported in the hippocampus, striatum, and parasagittal cortex (Gonzalez and Miller 2006). These injuries often cause impairment in memory, learning, and spatial orientation requiring cognitive interventions, often in the absence of clear MRI abnormalities and gross motor deficits (Gonzalez and Miller 2006).

Neonatal *hyperbilirubinemia* (or jaundice) – the building up of bilirubin in the blood resulting in yellow discoloration of the skin and eyes – is another child-centric risk factor that can lead to impairments in reading, writing, and mathematics persisting even in adulthood, over and above prematurity and other confounding factors (Hokkanen et al. 2014). The overall risk for these neurodevelopmental disorders is five-fold in infants presenting with vs. without neonatal hyperbilirubinemia (Hokkanen et al. 2014). While jaundice often naturally occurs postnatally (also termed *physiological jaundice* when within normal limits), pathological jaundice is problematic and is often caused by a medical condition in the child (e.g., poor liver function, blood disease such as Rh disease, and/or inherited or acquired risk). Some maternal environmental factors can lead to hyperbilirubinemia, including breastfeeding failure in the first week of life, or feeding on breast milk in the second or later weeks of life (former due to increased reabsorption of bilirubin in the intestines, and the latter likely due to the mother's milk inhibiting the ability of the infant's liver to process bilirubin).

7.3 Maternal Factors

7.3.1 Substance Use

7.3.1.1 Nicotine

Cigarettes (where nicotine is the principal active ingredient) are among the most commonly used and abused legal drugs. The global prevalence of smoking during pregnancy between 1985 and 2016 is estimated to be 1.7%, although there are large regional differences, with Europe being the highest at 8.1% (Lange et al. 2018). In the United States about 1 in 14 women (7.1%) who gave birth in 2016 smoked cigarettes during pregnancy (Kondracki 2019). Nicotine exposure is thought to be a major risk factor for fetal neurotoxicity that stems from hypoxia of the foetus and toxic increase in carbon monoxide, as well as structural and functional defects (teratologic effects) on the developing central nervous system (Wakschlag et al. 2002). Nicotine crosses the placental barrier (with fetal concentrations typically being 15% higher than maternal levels; Walker et al. 1999), acts as a neurotransmitter on nicotinic acetylcholine receptors (nAChRs) (Kovachy et al. 2015; Koren 1995), and can reduce noradrenaline and dopamine levels (Sharma and Brody 2009; Brennan and Arnsten 2008). Prenatal nicotine exposure produces persistent cholinergic hypoactivity throughout life (Abreu-Villaça et al. 2004). Hypoxia, alterations at the neurotransmitter level, and oxidative stress-induced cell damage may account for deficits in learning, memory, and behaviour described in Section 7.3.4 (Steckler and Sahgal 1995; Huizink and Mulder 2006). Further, a recent and small-scale review on the effect of maternal smoking during pregnancy (MSDP) on fetal structural and functional brain development showed decreased volume/thickness of the cerebellum and corpus callosum, increased auditory brain-stem responses, and lack of coordination across brain regions during information and auditory processing (Bublitz and Stroud 2012).

Paralleling these neurobiological findings, studies show that MSDP increases the risk of abnormal outcomes such as preterm birth and low birth weight (Kazemi et al. 2020), and causes a myriad of health problems in their children, including developmental, cognitive, and behavioural deficits such as learning disabilities, and ADHD (Hill et al. 2000). When children are exposed to nicotine both pre- and postnatally, they are twice as likely to be classified as abnormal according to the total Strengths and Difficulties Questionnaire at 10 years of age (Rückinger et al. 2010). Prenatal exposure resulted in a 90% higher risk, whereas postnatal exposure resulted in a 30% higher risk, which was not explained by confounding factors such as parental education, father's employment, child's time spent in front of a computer or television screen, being a single father or mother, or mother's age. Such impact was largest for ADHD symptoms (Braun et al. 2006).

A study on school-aged children, the Avon Longitudinal Study of Parents and Children (ALSPAC), found that prenatal nicotine exposure was associated with poor performance in specific reading skill outcomes, especially in single word decoding (Cho et al. 2013). The effect on academic achievement, measured by mathematics and language abilities, appears to persist throughout schooling in a population-based longitudinal study following children from 4th to 10th grade (Kristjansson et al. 2018). Furthermore, a review supported the impact of fetal nicotine exposure (Huizink and Mulder 2006), and confirmed a cumulative adverse effect on academic achievement in interaction with other risk factors. Such risk factors include: MSDP, parents' disability status, being born to a young mother, number of children in the household, family income, number of visits to school nurses, and reports of maltreatment (Ragnarsdottir et al. 2017). Further, in another study on the Avon sample that demonstrated a relationship between nicotine exposure and language (oral comprehension and phonological memory), an association was found between a known nicotine dependence gene *ANKK1/DRD2* and language impairment (Eicher et al. 2013). Interestingly, it has been shown that MSDP interacts with the dyslexia candidate gene *DYX1C1* but not with *DCDC2*, *KIAA0319*, and *ROBO1*, and impacts reading and memory (Liu et al. 2016; also see Chapter 8, Skeide 2022).

The causality and the degree of how strongly MSDP impacts academic scores, however, remain contentious. For example, in a large-scale study of 654,747 Swedish children, the authors showed that the effect disappears when compared to their control siblings (D'Onofrio et al. 2010), in line with their later report that genetic factors explain 74% of the association between MSDP and low academic achievement (Kuja-Halkola et al. 2014). Yet, a tightly controlled study recently showed that MDSP is significantly associated with reading and language skills within siblings discordant for exposure to MSDP, above several environmental factors and genetic confounds (e.g., corresponding maternal skills; Micalizzi et al. 2021), in support of a direct causal effect of MSDP on later reading development.

7.3.1.2   Alcohol

Alcohol is a teratogenic agent that can cause fetal alcohol spectrum disorder (FASD), which includes brain dysfunction and impaired later academic skills, amongst other effects. The most severe end of the FASD is known as fetal alcohol syndrome (FAS). In 2019, about one in nine pregnant women in the United States reported drinking alcohol, and about one-third engaged in binge drinking (Denny et al. 2019). Alcohol can cross the placenta and has been linked to several mechanisms that impact the developing fetal brain, and likely lead to the cognitive and behavioural impairments observed in FASD. These include (but are not limited to): cell death through necrosis and apoptosis; oxidative stress and mitochondrial dysfunction; dysfunctional regulation of neurotransmitters such as the glutamatergic and serotonergic systems; and excitotoxicity from excess in glutamate, especially when mothers binge-drink (Goodlett and Horn 2001; Ehrhart et al. 2019).

Neuroimaging studies have shown widespread abnormalities in children who were prenatally exposed to alcohol, affecting many areas and metrics of the brain (for recent reviews, see Mattson et al. 2019; Donald et al. 2015; Moore et al. 2014). Correlations have also been found between volumes of brain structures such as the diencephalon, including the thalamus, basal ganglia, and facial dysmorphology in FASD, which suggests anatomical correlates of the severity of FASD (Mattson et al. 2019; Roussotte et al. 2012; Suttie et al. 2017). The neuroanatomical structures that are most consistently negatively impacted in this population are the parietal and frontal lobes, corpus callosum, basal ganglia (especially the caudate nucleus), hippocampus, and cerebellum. Importantly, more recent brain imaging studies have taken an individual difference approach to examining processes related to reading and mathematics. For example, neuroanatomically, several surface area clusters have been identified as being differentially related to mathematics (left superior parietal and right lateral/middle occipital regions) and spelling performance (bilateral inferior and medial temporal regions) in control and FASD groups (Glass et al. 2017). Specifically, the larger the surfaces, the worse the mathematics and spelling scores in controls, whereas no association was observed in the FASD group. Another study of cognitive processes linked to reading and mathematics showed that a smaller left hippocampus is associated with decreased verbal learning skills and spatial memory performance in youth with FASD compared to controls (Mattson et al. 2019; Willoughby et al. 2008). Smaller caudate volume was associated with poorer verbal learning and recall skills and cognitive control (Mattson et al. 2019; Fryer et al. 2012). Functional neuroimaging studies have also shown abnormalities in individuals with FASD. They demonstrate altered brain activation patterns during functional MRI (fMRI) tasks, electroencephalography (EEG), magnetoencephalography (MEG), and other approaches (Moore et al. 2014). These notably concern: medial temporal regions during a verbal learning task (Sowell et al. 2007), the prefrontal-striatal (caudate) circuit during a response inhibition task (Fryer et al.

2007), an occipital region during a visual attention task (Li et al. 2008), and frontal regions during verbal and spatial working memory tasks (Malisza et al. 2005; Astley et al. 2009; Spadoni et al. 2009; O'Hare et al. 2005). Studies that looked at academic skills more directly showed prenatal alcohol exposure to be associated with decreased arithmetic performance and fMRI activation in the intraparietal sulcus and medial frontal regions in a dose-dependent fashion (Santhanam et al. 2009). At the same time, activation of a broader and more diffuse network of brain regions has been observed in this population, suggesting verbal and other processes being recruited to overcome their deficits (Meintjes et al. 2010). Taken together, these studies demonstrate the impact that prenatal alcohol exposure can have on the development of the offspring's brain and the subsequent effects on cognitive abilities.

Prenatal alcohol exposure has also been linked to birth complications, including preterm births, and developmental disabilities, including FASDs, and cognitive, academic, and behavioural problems (Flak et al. 2014; Kazemi et al. 2020). Studies suggest that levels of exposure and cognitive/behavioural outcome show dose–response effects (Sood et al. 2001), and the amount of variance uniquely explained by prenatal alcohol exposure ranges between 0.6% and 2% (Huizink and Mulder 2006; Sood et al. 2001; Jacobson and Jacobson 2002). While reading and mathematics are both impacted, some studies have reported that challenges in mathematics are greater and more common than difficulties in reading in children exposed to alcohol. For example, a study in 8–16-year-old children with heavy prenatal alcohol exposure found that mathematics reasoning was significantly lower than numerical operations, which in turn was significantly lower than spelling and word reading (Glass et al. 2017). In this study, 58.2% of the alcohol-exposed group demonstrated low achievement in one or more academic domains. In another study, alcohol-exposed children demonstrated a unique pattern of spelling deficits compared to reading deficits (Glass et al. 2015). The association between working memory and reading, as well as spelling, was specific to the alcohol-exposed group. A recent paper reviewed domains that are specifically impaired and are characteristic of FASD compared to ADHD controls. They found that general intelligence, cognitive set-shifting, shifting and encoding attention, visuospatial ability, verbal encoding, arithmetic, fluency, problem solving, and planning were specifically impaired in FASD (Mattson et al. 2019). Further, deficits in mathematics were found in FASD compared not only to typically developing controls (Howell et al. 2006; Jirikowic et al. 2008; Jacobson et al. 2011; Rasmussen and Bisanz 2011; Crocker et al. 2015), but also to ADHD controls (Coles et al. 1997), and IQ-matched controls (Jirikowic et al. 2008; Crocker et al. 2015). The impairment in mathematics in FASD has been linked to spatial processing (Crocker et al. 2015), working memory (Rasmussen and Bisanz 2011), and numerosity (Mattson et al. 2019; Jacobson et al. 2011). Reading impairment, on the other hand, is typically similar between FASD and ADHD (Coles et al. 1997), and IQ-matched controls (Jacobson and Jacobson 2002; Olson et al. 1998); or maybe even lower in FASD than in ADHD (Mattson et al. 2019; Coles et al. 1997).

In summary, there are many mechanisms that lead to FASD and impact reading and mathematics. The most prominently impacted neurocognitive domains appear to be visuospatial processing, working memory, and mathematics abilities.

7.3.1.3   Cannabis (Marijuana)

Cannabis is the most widely consumed illicit drug, even among adolescents and pregnant women (Higuera-Matas et al. 2015), with a prevalence rate of 3.9% worldwide (United Nations Office on Drugs and Crime 2013). While many surveyed countries have a prevalence rate of about 4–5%, there are regional differences. For example, Ibiza (a Spanish island) reported a Δ^9-tetrahydrocannabinol (THC; an active psychoactive [mind-altering] component of cannabis) positivity of 10.3%, compared to 5.3% when THC positivity was examined across the country (Spain) overall (Lozano et al. 2007; Friguls et al. 2012). Some view cannabis use as harmless in pregnancy (Jaques et al. 2014; Forray 2016), but it can lead to preterm labour, low birth weight, and admission to the neonatal intensive care unit (Hayatbakhsh et al. 2012). Prenatal cannabis use has also been linked to subtle but negative impact on the fetal and adolescent brains (Jaques et al. 2014; Forray 2016), attention (and ADHD), academic achievement, and behaviour, with a particular effect on executive functions (Warner et al. 2014; Roncero et al. 2020).

Some of the original research that led to the discovery of the mechanism of the impact of prenatal cannabis use was on endocannabinoids (eCBs), which are endogenous neurotransmitters that bind to cannabinoid receptors. eCBs are known to affect the development of the central nervous system (CNS) by regulating early neural stem cell survival and proliferation (Lubman et al. 2015), interneuron migration and morphogenesis (Berghuis et al. 2005), synaptogenesis (Kim and Thayer 2001), and by modulating synaptic transmission in the developing hippocampus (Higuera-Matas et al. 2015). Rats treated with a cannabinoid(-like) substance show alterations in dopaminergic activity of the dorsal and ventral striatum/nucleus accumbens (Bortolato et al. 2014). Cannabis readily crosses the placenta, although fetal exposures appear lower than maternal exposures (Grant et al. 2018; Zhu and Lovinger 2010). THC is also secreted in breast milk and can accumulate to high concentrations (Garry et al. 2009). In preclinical studies, the prenatal cannabinoid-like substance WIN 55,212–2 (WIN) has been shown to alter the migration of early-born glutamatergic neurons and GABAergic interneurons in the rat cerebral cortex (Saez et al. 2014). Repeated THC exposure disrupts eCB signalling, but the consequences of in-utero THC exposure for the development of the CNS in humans are still largely unknown.

A large-scale study targeting low-income families (the Maternal Health Practices and Child Development Project [MHPCD]) found a significant relation between heavy prenatal marijuana exposure (PME) and impairment in academic achievements such as reading, reading comprehension, and spelling at age 10 (Goldschmidt et al. 2004). These children's poor academic achievement was in contrast to their relatively intact intellectual ability, and remained significant after controlling for their home environment and sociodemographic status (Goldschmidt et al. 2004). At age 14, a significant negative correlation was found between PME and reading, mathematics, and composite scores of academic achievement. This impairment in school achievement was mediated by the effects of PME on IQ at age 6, as well as attention problems and depression symptoms at age 10 (Goldschmidt et al. 2012).

Additional findings were that PME predicted poor short-term memory and verbal reasoning at ages 3 to 6 (Day et al. 1994; Goldschmidt et al. 2008; Fried and Smith 2001). In another large-scale longitudinal study of PME in middle- rather than low-income families (the Ottawa Prenatal Prospective Study [OPPS]), the effect was observed in spelling only, and only in older ages (13 to 16) (Fried and Smith 2001; Fried et al. 1997; Fried et al. 2003). The different findings between the MHPCD and OPPS may be due to differences in SES between the cohorts.

In summary, prenatal cannabis exposure impacts spelling in offspring across SES. In low-SES families, there is broader impact on academic achievement beyond spelling that includes reading and mathematics. While IQ is relatively spared, the impact on academics appear non-specific and mediated by general cognitive and socio-emotional factors.

7.3.1.4   Other Substances

The most frequently used substances in pregnancy internationally are the aforementioned tobacco, alcohol, and cannabis (Forray 2016). In 2015, the estimated prevalence among all adults was 15.2%, 18.4%, and 3.8%, respectively (Peacock et al. 2018). There are, however, other illicit substances such as cocaine (0.35%), stimulants (0.37%), and opioids (0.77%) that are widely used, and that impact the offspring when used during pregnancy. Further, polysubstance use is a major issue; for example the majority of opioid use in reproductive-aged women co-occurs with the use of at least one non-opioid drug (90%), with higher prevalence in those with low educational attainment (Cicero et al. 2020; Jarlenski et al. 2017). The impact of these substances on the fetal and neonatal brains, and subsequently on cognition and academic performance, has been investigated to varying degrees (for a recent review in neuroimaging, see Morie et al. 2019).

Prenatal cocaine exposure (PCE) has been shown to impact brain development and cognitive outcome of children through several mechanisms. For example, PCE blocks the presynaptic reuptake of monoaminergic neurotransmitters such as dopamine predominantly, but also serotonin and norepinephrine (Martin et al. 2016). PCE also causes vasoconstriction, resulting in elevated plasma catecholamine levels, and damages the fetal-placental neuroendocrine environment (Landi et al. 2017).

Cocaine use during pregnancy is associated with premature rupture of membranes, placental abruption, preterm birth, low birth weight, and small infants for their gestational age (Forray 2016). The negative impact of PCE on cognition, affect, and behaviour has also been shown repeatedly. Systematic reviews, however, show that the overall negative impact of PCE on cognitive and language functions, as well as academic achievement, is generally small (Ackerman et al. 2010). Environmental variables play a key moderating role, in particular the caregiving environment and violence exposure. Yet, when these are controlled, PCE still has significant and reliable long-term negative associations with sustained attention and behavioural self-regulation (Ackerman et al. 2010). Despite the overall small effects on cognition, one of the only studies that examined detailed effects of PCE on reading and their neural correlates, and the longest prospective study, found PCE-associated deficits across a number of reading and language assessments such as single word reading, reading comprehension, and verbal short-term memory, after controlling for SES and exposure to other substances (Landi et al. 2017). The analysis of these children's neural event-related potentials (ERPs) revealed atypical orthography-to-phonology mapping (reduced N1/P2 response), and atypical rhyme and semantic processing (N400 response). Observationally, the behavioural deficits associated with PCE appear to get stronger over development, as they were more pronounced in late teenage years than at a younger age in the same cohort.

Amphetamines, often used for the treatment of ADHD, and the more potent methamphetamine, often used illegally, are synthetic psychostimulants that are increasingly being misused in pregnancy (Terplan et al. 2009; Pong et al. 2010). Psychostimulant use during pregnancy has been linked to preterm birth, low birth weight, and small size for gestational age (Ross et al. 2015). The effects of these psychostimulants are mediated through the modulation of dopamine, serotonin, and norepinephrine. The impact on the developing brain and its clinical relevance are uncertain, but prenatal exposure to psychostimulants may result in decreased recruitment of the fronto-striatal circuit during visuospatial processing and working memory; smaller striatal structures; and abnormal frontal, parietal, and fronto-striatal white matter, with elevated total creatine (Morie et al. 2019). The reported effects on cognition and behaviour are very small. In the most extensive large-scale longitudinal study, however, a variety of adverse physical, cognitive, emotional, and social effects, including increased prevalence of ADHD, aggression, and learning difficulties attributed to deficits in attention, memory, and motivation, were found. Specifically as it relates to academics, a Swedish study found that 15% of the 14-year-old children who were exposed to amphetamine prenatally were one grade lower than indicated by their biological age (vs. less than 5% in the general population in Sweden; Cernerud et al. 1996). Academic grades in mathematics and Swedish language were also below those of their classmates.

Opioids are a class of drugs that include the illegal drug heroin, synthetic opioids such as fentanyl, and pain relievers available legally by prescription, such as oxycodone, and morphine. Between 1999 and 2014, the United States saw a three-fold increase in prenatal exposure to opioids, coincident with an 'epidemic' of opiate prescription misuse (Conradt et al. 2019). Opioid use during pregnancy is higher among lower SES groups and has been associated with a 60% increase in risk of preterm birth as well as low birth weight (Corsi et al. 2020). A majority (50% to 80%) of newborns exposed to opioids develop neonatal opioid withdrawal syndrome (NOWS), also known as neonatal abstinence syndrome (NAS), which includes symptoms such as inconsolability and high-pitched cry, tremors, feeding difficulty, hypertonia, watery stools, and respiratory problems (Conradt et al. 2019).

It has been suggested that prenatal exposure to opioids may have adverse effects on the developing brain, such as neuronal migration, cell survival, modification of synaptic plasticity, decrease of dendrite length and branch number, and long-lasting neurochemical changes (Bajic et al. 2013; Beltrán-Campos et al. 2015; Miller et al. 2012; Rozisky et al. 2013). Further, in human neuroimaging, reduced whole-brain and basal ganglia volumes (Yuan et al. 2014) and microstructural white matter alterations have been reported (Monnelly et al. 2018; Walhovd et al. 2012). These alterations seem to persist into school age (Walhovd et al. 2007; Sirnes et al. 2017; Walhovd et al. 2010). A recent review of the literature shows that the long-term negative neurodevelopmental outcome is equivocal, with 8 of 27 studies showing no impairment in cognitive outcome (Conradt et al. 2019). While some have reported impaired IQ, language, and executive functions, for example, the results have not held when controlling for confounds, and the studies have most often been retrospective chart reviews. What appears most consistent is that boys are more impaired than girls, and the manifestation of behavioural issues such as aggression, anxiety, and attention difficulties more than other neurodevelopmental consequences. Further, children who faced NOWS at birth are more impaired in these areas as well as in educational test scores than children without NOWS (Oei et al. 2017). For example, one large-scale study showed that literacy and mathematics scores were significantly lower in children with NAS compared to controls (adjusted odds ratio of not meeting minimum requirements: OR = 2.5), a gap that widened with advancing grades (Oei et al. 2017). This effect was larger, in comparison, than that of male gender on meeting minimum requirements in literacy and maths (OR = 1.3), or that of low parental education (OR = 1.5; Oei et al. 2017).

Methadone maintenance treatment (MMT) is the most common treatment approach for opioid-dependent women, and a recent prospective study showed that when children are exposed to methadone prenatally, they performed worse than non-exposed children in many areas of reading and mathematics (decoding, reading fluency/comprehension, calculation, maths fluency, and maths problem solving), and showed four-fold educational delay (57% vs. 15%; OR = 7.5; when adjusted for confounds, OR = 3.6) at age 9.5 years, regardless of severe intellectual impairment (Lee et al. 2019).

While caffeine is not of major concern as a substance use disorder, it is the most widely consumed psychoactive drug in the world. Caffeine is metabolized by the cytochrome P450 oxidase enzyme system. Because this system also metabolizes steroid hormones (Chang et al. 2009), caffeine is metabolized up to 4 times more slowly during pregnancy (20 h) (Zaigler et al. 2000). Regardless, low to moderate caffeine consumption during pregnancy is generally not associated with any adverse effects on cognition and neurodevelopment in the offspring according to recent large-scale studies (up to 8 years of age) in 2,197 and 64,189 mother-child dyads (Klebanoff and Keim 2015; Berglundh et al. 2021). There are, however, a few human and animal studies that have shown an association between high caffeine consumption and negative neurodevelopmental outcomes (Temple et al. 2017). For example, in animals, caffeine slowed the migration of neurons by 50%, which had negative consequences such as mild cognitive deficits in adult mice (Silva et al. 2013). In addition, concurrent use of caffeine and morphine are often medically indicated for apnoea treatment of prematurity and pain control in neonatal intensive care unit (NICU) neonates, respectively. Their combined use increases apoptosis (cell death) in the developing brain compared to individual use of caffeine and morphine (Kasala et al. 2020). Therapeutic doses of caffeine may hence significantly augment the neurotoxicity of sedative/anaesthetic drugs such as morphine (Cabrera et al. 2017).

The preclinical findings challenge the clinical assumption that caffeine is safe for premature infants when used in combination with sedative drugs, and suggest needs for future research.

In summary, evidence of a negative impact of prenatal substance exposure on academic outcome is stronger for some substances (e.g., nicotine, alcohol, and cannabis) compared to others (e.g., caffeine), while more evidence is needed for other substances (e.g., cocaine, opioids). Across various types of drug abuse, preclinical and human neuroimaging studies suggest a negative impact of prenatal substance exposure, especially in the area of cognitive control (Morie et al. 2019). Some of these studies have reported increased neural activation in exposed children, often interpreted as compensatory neural 'effort'. There are currently very few neuroimaging studies pointing directly to the neural correlates of academic abilities in these children (except for cocaine). Overall, research to date also indicates that boys are more susceptible than girls to dysfunctions in cognitive processing related to prenatal substance exposure (Traccis et al. 2020).

7.3.2 Psychosocial Stress and Mental Health

Depression and *anxiety* are highly prevalent in mothers during the perinatal period, with an estimated prevalence of 11.9% for depression, that is higher in low- to middle- than in high-income countries (OR = 1.8) (Woody et al. 2017) and a prevalence of 15.2% and 9.9% for anxiety disorders during the prenatal and postnatal periods, respectively (Dennis et al. 2017; Bleker et al. 2019). In this chapter, we operationally include psychopathology such as depression and anxiety symptoms and disorders within the broad spectrum of *psychological stress*. Mild to moderate stress is reported by 30–50% of generally healthy pregnant women across the globe (Bleker et al. 2019). Maternal psychological stress during pregnancy is a risk factor for preterm birth and low birth weight (Dunkel Schetter 2011). Fetal or neonatal exposure to maternal psychosocial stress has long-lasting consequences on the offspring's neural and cognitive development, including negative affect, difficult temperament, and psychiatric disorders, as shown in numerous epidemiological and case-control studies (Bleker et al. 2019; Matas-Blanco and Caparros-Gonzalez 2020; Graham et al. 2021; Rogers et al. 2020; Van den Bergh et al. 2020). Stressors that have shown strong negative associations with the child's outcome include major life events such as the death of a family member, and catastrophic community-wide disasters such as earthquakes or terrorist attacks; chronic stress such as general strain, household strain, and length and severity of homelessness; and neighbourhood stressors such as poverty and crime (Dunkel Schetter 2011). Pregnancy anxiety (compared to state anxiety and perceived stress) is another strong predictor of a child's outcome such as preterm birth; other stressors, such as depression, chronic strain, and racism, seem to predict outcomes such as low birth weight. While paternal stress also likely contributes to the offspring's outcome, research in this area is only beginning (Rafferty et al. 2019).

The mechanisms explaining how maternal stress might act on a child's outcome are increasingly being understood. Key mediating processes to which these effects are attributed are neuroendocrine, inflammatory, and behavioural mechanisms (Graham et al. 2021; see also Dunkel Schetter 2011; Van den Bergh et al. 2020; Franke et al. 2020; Glover 2015; Scheinost et al. 2017 for reviews on biological mechanisms). For example, maternal stressors have been associated with atypical activation of the hypothalamic-pituitary-adrenal (HPA) axis, and increased release of corticotropin-releasing hormone (CRH), which controls the production of cortisol – known as the 'stress hormone' – from the placenta. While there is only a weak association between maternal prenatal stress and cortisol level, especially in later stages of pregnancy as the maternal HPA axis becomes gradually less responsive to stress, there may be increased transfer of maternal cortisol across the placenta to the foetus, and/or reduced placental enzyme metabolizing cortisol to inactive cortisone. Cortisol levels in the amniotic fluid are in turn negatively correlated with infant cognitive development (Glover 2015). Maternal stress also influences immune pathways, notably inducing atypical upregulation of cytokines, and likely acts through several alternative mediators such as serotonin, the autonomic nervous system, the gut microbiome, as well as epigenetic mechanisms (i.e., molecular modifications which modulate gene expression without altering the DNA sequence, e.g., DNA methylation) and telomeric mechanisms (e.g., alterations or programming of a structure at the end of a chromosome in a manner that accelerates cellular dysfunction, ageing, and disease susceptibility over the lifespan; Glover 2015; Van den Bergh et al. 2020). Finally, maternal stress may also pose risk to their offspring through their health behaviour such as smoking, alcohol, and other substance use, as well as through poor nutrition. Specifically for postpartum mechanisms including postpartum depression, impoverished parent–child interaction and enrichment activities such as reading, reduced breastfeeding, and gene–environment correlation likely play a role (Hay et al. 2008; Rafferty et al. 2019). Higher maternal education likely buffers the impact of perinatal stress (Kotimäki et al. 2020).

An increasing number of studies have examined offspring's anatomical, functional, and chemical neural correlates of exposure to maternal psychosocial stress. For instance, with regard to brain development, animal studies convincingly demonstrated that prenatal stress (or early postnatal stress in rodents, a time-period which parallels the prenatal period in humans) affects neuronal and synaptic development – changes most often studied in the limbic system such as the hippocampus and amygdala, prefrontal cortex, and cortico-limbic circuitry – and alters the excitatory-inhibitory balance of cortical neurons (Van den Bergh et al. 2020; Scheinost et al. 2017). In humans, several behavioural and neuroimaging studies using techniques such as EEG, ERP, fMRI, structural MRI, and diffusion-weighted imaging (DWI) have shown that prenatal exposure to maternal psychosocial stress leads to neurodevelopmental abnormalities in the offspring that encompass changes in the amygdala and hippocampus, their connectivity to other subcortical and cortical regions, cerebellar development, cortical thinning, cortical gyrification in frontal and temporal lobes, and neurochemical choline and creatine levels (Van den Bergh et al. 2020; Scheinost et al. 2017; Wu et al. 2020). Many of the findings are consistent with the behavioural profiles of impaired affective processes and stress circuitry, with sex differences being equivocal (Scheinost et al. 2017).

Few studies have examined the influence of perinatal psychosocial stress on academic outcome. One study found associations between self-reported maternal prenatal stress events related to socioeconomic issues (e.g., financial problems) and psychological factors (e.g., isolation), and their child's poor literacy and numeracy reported by their teacher at 6 years of age (Niederhofer and Reiter 2004). Another study using data from the Western Australian Pregnancy Cohort (Raine) Study examined the relationship between maternal exposure to common life stress events in pregnancy (a more objective measure than subjective experiences of emotions and tensions) and achievement in numeracy, reading, spelling, and writing using a standard state-wide test among children at age 10 (Li et al. 2013). Maternal exposure to four or more stressful life events during pregnancy, such as the death of a relative and/or the death of a friend, was associated with lower reading scores in girls. The findings were independent of maternal sociodemographic characteristics, family income, maternal smoking in pregnancy and common life stress events in infancy and middle childhood. They also found, counterintuitively, that boys demonstrated higher reading and writing scores with moderate maternal stressful events during pregnancy. The findings were interpreted as a process similar to the 'feminization' of neurobiological structures, hormones, and neurotransmitters found in male animals. Indeed, male animals during maternal psychological stress in pregnancy show a decrease in fetal testosterone and brain aromatase activity, and alteration of brain catecholamine activity, approaching female activity levels, with corresponding effects on anxiogenic (anxiety-causing) behaviour (Zagron and Weinstock 2006; Weinstock 2005). Interestingly, some studies have shown associations between mild stress during pregnancy and improved learning in male rats (Cannizzaro et al. 2006; Fujioka et al. 2001; Li et al. 2013). Fetal testosterone concentration in utero has also been shown to inversely correlate with emerging language skills in humans (Lutchmaya et al. 2001).

A more recent study based on the large UK population cohort (ALSPAC) showed that prenatal anxiety and maternal postpartum depression were independent predictors of poor mathematics abilities. For example, adolescents with postnatally depressed mothers were 1.5 times as likely as those without depressed mothers to fail to achieve a 'pass' grade in mathematics (Pearson et al. 2016). Further, working memory explained 17% of the association with prenatal anxiety, and attentional control explained 16% of the association with postnatal depression. A similar pattern was seen for language grades, but associations were confounded by maternal education. Paternal factors were not predictive of academic outcome (nor of executive functions). Other studies on postpartum depression found similar effects in children of postpartum-depressed mothers compared to controls, especially in boys. In one study, 11-year-old children had lower IQs, more attentional problems, and greater difficulty with mathematical reasoning after controlling for possible confounds such as parental IQ, later depression in the mothers, and sociodemographic variables, and the effect was more pronounced in boys than girls (Hay et al. 2001; Bernard-Bonin 2004). In another study, 16-year-old boys of postpartum-depressed mothers, but not girls, showed poorer General Certificate of Secondary Education (GCSE) exam performance than control children. This effect was accounted for by the children's early cognitive functioning and their maternal interactions through childhood (Murray et al. 2010).

In summary, maternal psychosocial stress has a negative impact on academic performance, which is possibly most severe in the context of mathematics. The effect seems to be generally more pronounced in boys. Whether boys have improved learning when exposed to milder stress warrants replication.

7.3.3 Breastfeeding

Breastfeeding, as opposed to *formula feeding*, is known to be associated with a number of positive short- and long-term outcomes, ranging from physical health (decreased child infection, blood pressure, serum cholesterol, lower prevalence of obesity and type-2 diabetes) to cognition, including decreased risk for ADHD and ASD, and higher intelligence and academic achievement (Victora et al. 2016; Horta et al. 2007; Bar et al. 2016; Westmark 2013; Petryk et al. 2007). The World Health Organization (WHO) recommends exclusive breastfeeding until 6 months of age (see Infant and young child feeding 2018), a recommendation met only by 40% of 0–6-month-old infants worldwide (WHO: Breastfeeding) and 37% of infants in low- to middle-income countries (Victora et al. 2016). Adequate complementary food is recommended after 6 months in addition to breastfeeding up to 2 years and beyond (WHO: Breastfeeding; see Infant and young child feeding 2018; OECD and The World Bank 2020; 71st world health assembly 2018). Low-birth-weight or preterm infants seem to especially benefit from breastfeeding in terms of general cognitive development (Anderson et al. 1999), in line with higher protein and fat concentrations in preterm milk vs. term milk, thought to better support their brain development (Ballard and Morrow 2013).

Breastfeeding has consistently been associated with better scores in reading and mathematics across ages and into adulthood. In the UK Millennium Cohort Study, children who had been breastfed for more than 4 months were more likely at age 5 to have reached a good level in tests of communication, language, and literacy (adjusted OR = 1.13), and of problem solving, reasoning, and numeracy (adjusted OR = 1.08) (Heikkilä et al. 2014). Similarly, a study in Ireland of 8,226 children showed that breastfed children continued to have a significant test score advantage of 3.24% and 2.23% in reading and mathematics, respectively, compared to those who were never breastfed (McCrory and Layte 2011; Richards et al. 2002; Victora et al. 2005). At age 10, Australian children who were predominantly breastfed for 6 months or longer in infancy had higher scores in mathematics, reading, and spelling than children who were breastfed for less than 6 months (Oddy et al. 2011). Interestingly, benefits were only evident for boys (see also Nyaradi et al. 2015 for similar results). Several studies in Brazil, Great Britain, and New Zealand have further related breastfeeding or breastfeeding duration to educational attainment (Horwood and Fergusson 1998), demonstrating significant positive effects into adolescence and adulthood. Of note, an advantage of breastfeeding on reading and verbal memory scores was observed at age 53, partially explained by cognitive ability at age 15 (Richards et al. 2002). Finally, the Helsinki Birth Cohort Study showed a cognitive advantage of breastfeeding in Finnish men persisting at age 68, notably with higher verbal ability and arithmetic scores (Rantalainen et al. 2018). Importantly, while verbal scores decreased between 20 and 68 years of age in men breastfed for 3 months or less, they increased in men breastfed for more than 3 months, suggesting that longer duration of breastfeeding may benefit ageing-related changes. These studies generally controlled for many variables related to the environment, including demographics and socioeconomic and socio-environmental characteristics, and some studies controlled for substance exposure and home cognitive stimulation.

The mechanisms underlying the positive impact of breastfeeding on cognition include biochemical substances in breast milk, better mother–child bonding while breastfeeding, and the child's genetic predisposition, which can influence breastfeeding success (see Petryk et al. 2007 for a review). An important factor may also be the change in composition of human milk across time from colostrum to mature milk, both in terms of nutritional substances and non-nutritive bioactive factors (Ballard and Morrow 2013). Among many important substances found in breast milk that can influence neural development (including growth factors, trophic factors, and other hormones), long-chain polyunsaturated fatty acids (LCPUFAs) have received particular interest. These fatty acids are preferentially incorporated into neural cell membranes during the last trimester of pregnancy and first months of life, and are thought to be essential in cellular differentiation and synaptogenesis of the maturing brain and retina. LCPUFAs are present in breast milk, but not in most brands of formula (Koletzko et al. 2007), and are found in higher concentrations in the phospholipids of the cerebral cortex of breastfed compared to bottle-fed infants (Makrides et al. 1994). Interestingly, the benefits of breastfeeding on child IQ have been found to be moderated by a genetic variant of FADS2, a gene involved in the genetic control of fatty acid pathways (Caspi et al. 2007). This gene–environment interaction supports the potentially causal involvement of fatty acids found in breast milk on children's cognitive development.

At the neural level, breastfeeding, compared to formula feeding, has been associated with larger white and grey matter volumes (Isaacs et al. 2010; Ou et al. 2016), in particular in boys. Increased brain volumes were also associated with higher IQ in boys (Isaacs et al. 2010). A recent longitudinal neuroimaging study further demonstrated that children exclusively breastfed for at least 3 months had higher myelin content in their cerebral and cerebellar white matter than formula-fed children, a difference detectable by 18 months of age and persisting at least until 5.5 years of age (Deoni et al. 2018). Additional differences in myelin content were observed between different brands and compositions of formula, with a significant impact notably of LCPUFAs and sphingolipids. Cognitive ability and rates of cognitive development, including verbal and non-verbal functioning, were also higher in breastfed than formula-fed children, with the best performances observed for formulas rich in LCPUFAs and sphingolipids, paralleling findings in myelin content.

The effects of formula feeding vs. breastfeeding on cognition and academic skills are vastly confounded by other factors, such as maternal intelligence, cognitive stimulation, SES, or MSDP (Scott et al. 2006; Walfisch et al. 2013; Fergusson et al. 1982). Thus, some studies concluded that there is no significant effect of breastfeeding on cognition when controlling for environmental and genetic confounds such as maternal IQ (Walfisch et al. 2013; Der et al. 2006). Yet, many studies of high quality have reported significant effects of breastfeeding on cognition over and above these confounds (Horta et al. 2015; Evenhouse and Reilly 2005; Caspi et al. 2007). For example, according to a meta-analysis, breastfeeding has an average impact on IQ of 2.62 points when controlling for maternal IQ (Horta et al. 2015). A randomized study of breastfeeding promotion in Belarus also found a significant difference in IQ of 7.5 points on average in 6.5-year-old children. This effect was in favour of the group whose mothers received a breastfeeding promotion intervention compared to a control group (Kramer et al. 2008). The causal role of breastfeeding on IQ is also supported by the observation that genetic variation in fatty acid metabolism moderates this link (Caspi et al. 2007). Although no study supporting the role of breastfeeding on academic performance used strict study designs and genetic controls, breastfeeding most likely also has a causal role on academic performance, especially as intelligence and academic abilities (such as reading) have bidirectional causal relationships (Ferrer et al. 2007).

In short, breastfeeding seems to have a beneficial effect on intelligence and academic performance persisting throughout the lifespan. This association is most likely partly mediated by the high content of fatty acids crucial for neural development in breast milk. Boys and preterm babies benefit from breastfeeding to a larger extent.

7.3.4 Other Maternal Factors

There are many other maternal factors during and shortly after pregnancy that impact offspring's neurodevelopmental outcome. For example, prenatal exposure to maternal *hypertension diseases including (pre-)eclampsia* in utero has been shown to result in mild cognitive impairment affecting working memory, executive control, and verbal reasoning (including vocabulary) in the absence of non-verbal reasoning impairment. These exposures were also found to be related to poorer performance on mathematics (but not language) exams after controlling for confounds such as gestational age and small for gestational age status in a national Icelandic cohort of 68,580 children between 4th and 10th grades (see Sverrisson et al. 2018 and Gumusoglu et al. 2020 for a review). Maternal hypertension is also associated with brain morphological, white matter, and vascular abnormalities in small-scale human neuroimaging studies, with such effects likely mediated by hypoxia, and dysregulation of immune responses, oxidative stress, growth factor, and angiogenic processes. In addition to the literature on decreased volume and reduced connectivity, few studies suggest overgrowth of grey and white matter volumes as well as increased functional connectivity of brain regions important for social processing, threat detection and appraisal, and goal-oriented behaviour (Rätsep et al. 2016; Figueiró-Filho et al. 2017; Mak et al. 2018). Consistent with these findings, serum taken from women with pre-eclampsia increases neuronal growth and branching in rat fetal cortical neurons, suggesting that maternal serum-secreted factors may play a role in enlargement of some brain regions (Curran et al. 2018).

Prenatal exposure to *maternal infection* is another risk factor for a myriad of neurodevelopmental disorders such as autism spectrum disorders, schizophrenia, and intellectual disability (for a review, see Labouesse et al. 2015). Possible mechanisms mediating the influence of maternal infection on offspring include: transplacental transfer of maternally produced inflammatory cytokines, placental production of cytokines, or increased fetal cytokine synthesis (known as maternal immune activation [MIA]); oxidative stress that may cause cytotoxic effects and tissue injury; cytokine-associated inflammatory reactions leading to activation of the HPA axis by stimulating the release of CRF, eventually increasing glucocorticoid levels; reduced maternal and fetal availability of several micronutrients, including iron and zinc, and macronutrients; and alteration of the placental microbiome (Labouesse et al. 2015). The impact of prenatal infection on academic outcome, however, is limited and equivocal. One study examined a large Chinese sample of 45,850 children in grades 3 to 6 using retrospective questionnaires of pregnancy, checklists for dyslexia and learning disabilities completed by parents and teachers, and a Chinese language exam done at their schools. After adjustment for possible confounding variables, the risk of dyslexia (poor reading) remained significantly associated with maternal infectious diseases (OR = 1.59), which was higher than the association with preterm birth (OR = 1.30) (Liu et al. 2016). Data from the Danish National Birth Cohort collected during 1996–2002 in 71,850 children in grades 2 to 8, however, showed no difference in academic performance measured using the Danish National Test Program, a mandatory computerized test in Denmark (Dreier et al. 2017). Estimates of academic performance were based on measures of language comprehension, decoding, and reading comprehension for language; numbers and algebra, geometry, and applied mathematics for mathematics; and an overall score. Specifically, there was no significant effect of prenatal exposure to fever (OR = 1.01), any infection (OR = 1.00), genitourinary infection (OR = 1.01), prolonged cough (OR = 1.00), or diarrhoea (OR = 0.99). The findings were supported by the use of different types of academic assessments (overall, language, and mathematics), with different timings of exposure, and in sibling comparisons.

Further, *maternal nutritional status* (anthropometry, macro- and micronutrients) before and/or during pregnancy is a potential predictor of offspring cognitive function. Prenatal exposure to severe malnutrition has been shown to be negatively associated with visuo-motor skills, mental flexibility, and selective attention in adulthood (Li et al. 2015). Regardless, maternal nutrient restriction and folate deficiency during early pregnancy seem to have a global effect on neurodevelopment, reflected in decreased overall brain volume and disturbances in white matter organization (see Franke et al. 2020 for a review). These effects occur even in the absence of low birth weight. However, a review of maternal nutrition impact on cognitive functions and academic abilities shows that the influences of maternal nutritional status during pregnancy as defined by body mass index (BMI), single micronutrient studies, or macronutrient intakes on offspring cognitive function is inconclusive (see Veena et al. 2016 for a review). Further, those studies that examined reading and mathematics abilities show generally small effect sizes. Children of *obese* compared to normal-weight mothers scored ~0.3 SD lower in general cognitive and non-verbal abilities but not in verbal or motor abilities at age 5 years; and ~0.1–0.2 SD lower in reading and mathematics scores at age 5–7 years (Tanda et al. 2013). Children of *underweight* compared to normal-weight mothers showed very small non-significant differences in general cognitive, verbal, and non-verbal abilities (0.06-0.1 SD) at age 5, and reading and mathematics scores (0.02–0.05 SD) at age 5–7 years (Tanda et al. 2013).

The final maternal risk factor we consider relates to *delivery methods*. A recent large-scale study showed that even after adjusting for neonatal asphyxia and other factors, *difficult vaginal delivery* was an independent risk factor for dyslexia (poor reading) (OR = 1.58) (Liu et al. 2016), even though an older study found no elevated risk for cognitive abnormalities such as speech delay and learning disabilities (Rosen et al. 1992). Since it is hard to disentangle the causes and manifestations of difficult vaginal delivery, more research in this area is needed, and the neurodevelopmental outcome should be interpreted with caution. *Caesarean section* has also been associated with adverse outcomes in terms of health (Stinson et al. 2018; Peters et al. 2018) and psychiatric disorders (notably autism spectrum disorders [ASD] and ADHD; Zhang et al. 2019), as well as in cognitive and academic domains. Despite these negative associations, rates of caesarean sections are well above the WHO's recommended 15% ceiling in most developed countries (Gibbons et al. 2010), suggesting a large portion of medically unnecessary but potentially harmful procedures. In the Longitudinal Study of Australian Children (based on 3,666 children), caesarean-born children were found at age 8–9 to perform significantly below vaginally born children on national standardized tests in reading, writing, and particularly in numeracy, by up to 0.1SD (Polidano et al. 2017). While approximately 30% of these effects were mediated by lower rates of breastfeeding (see Section 7.3.3) and adverse child and maternal health outcomes in caesarean-born children, strict controls and sensitivity analyses point to the importance of other mechanisms, such as disturbed gut microbiota (but see Stinson et al. 2018 for a critical review), in explaining the relationship between caesarean section and academic outcome. A previous study found that children's risk of falling within the lowest 10% in Australian national academic assessments during their first year of school was increased by factors of caesarean vs. vaginal delivery and induced vs. spontaneous labour (Bentley et al. 2016). The risks were highest in caesarean deliveries with induced labours, with adjusted risk rates compared to spontaneous vaginal deliveries of 1.18 for language and cognitive skills, 1.12 for basic literacy, and 1.14 for basic numeracy. Pre-labour caesarean deliveries were also associated with increased risks for poor academic outcomes compared to spontaneous vaginal birth, but to a smaller extent. The association between labour induction and academic achievement, however, seems to be the result of other genetic or environmental familial confounders, as it is fully attenuated when investigating the effects of labour induction within families (Wiggs et al. 2017).

7.4 Exogenous Factors

7.4.1 Heavy Metals

7.4.1.1   Methyl Mercury

Methylmercury (MeHg) is characterized by the WHO as an environmental pollutant of major public health concern (Sheehan et al. 2014). MeHg contamination occurs particularly in aquatic environments, risking human populations primarily on islands and in coastal regions, where fish consumption tends to be high (Sheehan et al. 2014). The neurotoxic effects of MeHg have been documented in both animal (Burbacher et al. 1990) and human research (Castoldi et al. 2003). Among humans, perinatal exposure to MeHg, often through maternal consumption of fish and seafood (Sheehan et al. 2014), is associated with impairment in cognition and academic performance in children (Crump et al. 1998; Grandjean et al. 1997; Sheehan et al. 2014). A large-scale report shows that the incidence of mild intellectual disability (IQ scores 50–70) associated with prenatal exposure to MeHg varied nearly forty-fold across countries, with the greatest incidence rates generally in coastal countries or islands (Bellinger et al. 2016). Countries with high birth rates and greater consumption of seafood and rice made the largest contributions. Because the risk of harm to the developing nervous system from perinatal exposure of MeHg is well established, major public health organizations such as the United States Food and Drug Administration (FDA), the Canadian Minister of Health, the European Food Safety Authority, and WHO encourage minimized consumption of aquatic apex predators (Sheehan et al. 2014) and certain fatty fish (Center for Food Safety and Applied Nutrition 2020; Health Canada 2009; EFSA n.d.). These predators and fish have been shown to carry disproportionately high levels of organic mercury in their tissues.

Anthropogenic processes (i.e., pollution caused by humans through mining operations, combustion of fossil fuels, waste incineration or such) and natural processes (e.g., volcanoes, forest fires, weathering of rock) induce wide dispersion of inorganic mercury in the atmosphere, which is later methylated by microorganisms. These microbial emissions of mercury compounds lead to MeHg contamination. MeHg has been associated with neurotoxicity, cytotoxicity, and genotoxicity in in-vitro research involving human tissues (Pieper et al. 2014). Inorganic mercury has also been associated with serious adverse effects, but it is far less readily absorbed in the gastrointestinal tract and far less likely to cross the placental and blood–brain barriers (Biomonitoring Summary 2019). Evidence from animal model research indicates that ingested MeHG readily bonds with free L-cysteine and with proteins and peptides containing L-cysteine (Kerper et al. 1992). The resulting methylmercury-L-cysteine complex resembles methionine, an essential amino acid, and is freely transported throughout the body, and across the placental and blood–brain barriers (Roos et al. 2010), thus inhibiting methionine transport and accumulating in body tissues, in particular the brain and liver (Roos et al. 2010). In primate model neural tissue, organomercury has been found to accumulate preferentially in astrocytes, though it has also been detected in neurons (Charleston et al. 1996). Following exposure, MeHg has been shown in animal models to directly impair monoamine neurotransmission, interfering with both the serotonin (Tsai et al. 1995) and dopamine (Eddins et al. 2008) systems. Organomercury complexes also appear to promote calcium and glutamate dyshomeostasis and provoke the production of reactive oxygen species (highly reactive molecules), resulting in oxidative stress and the consequent death of neurons and glial cells (Farina et al. 2011; Ni et al. 2012). Compounding these adverse effects, MeHg and its metabolites are not readily eliminated from the body.

Acute perinatal exposure to MeHg is clearly associated with a host of adverse neurobiological and neurodevelopmental outcomes. In the mid-twentieth century, two major incidents of aquatic MeHg contamination led to widespread organic mercury poisoning among inhabitants of Niigata (Myers et al. 2020) and Minamata (Harada 1995), Japan, who largely depended on local fish catches for their protein intake. The effects of acute exposure included sensory disturbances, dysarthria, and tremor. Individuals heavily exposed in utero showed generally more severe symptoms, including extensive lesions of the brain, intellectual disability, seizure disorders, cerebellar ataxia, visual and auditory impairments, and other significant neurological abnormalities (Myers et al. 2020; Harada 1995; Rice et al. 2003). In the decade following the contamination of Niigata's waterways, Iraqi residents were exposed to high levels of MeHg by way of organomercury-treated grain. Similar to the children of Niigata and Minamata, Iraqi children exposed perinatally to MeHg showed symptoms such as paralysis, cerebral palsy, intellectual disability, motor disorders, sensory disturbances, blindness, deafness, and various other neurodevelopmental impairments (Amin-Zaki et al. 1981; Amin-Zaki et al. 1976; Rice et al. 2003).

In regions of the world with particularly high levels of fish consumption or routine marine mammal consumption by the indigenous population, perinatal exposure to MeHg has been associated with decreased intellect and increased prevalence of attentional difficulties. For example, a Faroese cohort study examining the cognitive abilities of approximately 7-year-old children who had been perinatally exposed to MeHg through maternal pilot whale consumption showed a clear pattern of neuro-psychological dysfunction among children with higher levels of exposure (n = 917; Grandjean et al. 1997). Regression analyses indicated an inverse relationship between MeHg exposure and cognitive abilities across numerous standardized measures. Greater deficits were found in the areas of language, attention, and memory; however, visuospatial and motor functions were also found to be affected. The effects remained significant, even after controlling for a number of covariates and the exclusion of children who were outliers in terms of levels of MeHg exposure. Similarly, a New Zealand cohort study (n = 237) found a significant negative association between perinatal MeHg exposure and children's overall cognitive, perceptual reasoning, reading, and grammatical skills, as measured by standardized tests ($\beta = -0.50$ to -0.60; Grump et al. 1998).

While the results of the Faroe Island and New Zealand studies tend to support the hypothesis that perinatal MeHg is associated with cognitive and scholastic deficits among perinatally exposed children, other researchers have failed to report similar results, even when evaluating comparably exposed populations. For example, in the Seychelles Child Development Study a cohort of 779 mother–child pairs was followed to investigate the relationship between maternal fish consumption, perinatal MeHg exposure, and cognitive abilities, as well as academic achievement, among exposed children. For most academic and standardized cognitive and behavioural measures, no significant association was detected at either 9 (van Wijngaarden et al. 2009) or 17 years of age. The only exceptions to this pattern were a significant but small performance decrease in fine motor skill tasks (using the non-dominant hand) in boys at age 9, a significant improvement in hyperactivity index scores on the Connor's teacher-rating scale among children of both sexes at age 9 (Myers et al. 2003), and a significant negative association between MeHg exposure and performance on a standardized test of mathematics and reading comprehension among male children from a subset (n = 215) of children in grade 6 (Davidson et al. 2010).

A combined analysis of these three data sets (i.e., the Faroe Islands, New Zealand, and the Seychelles Islands studies) revealed a dose–response relationship between prenatal MeHg exposure and deficits in cognitive abilities (as measured by Wechsler Intelligence Scales for Children [WISC]; Axelrad et al. 2007). Following preparation and scaling of data derived from the aforementioned studies, these analyses indicated a decrease in childhood intelligence of −0.18 points for every part per million of methylmercury in maternal hair samples. Moreover, they reported a linear inverse relationship between MeHg exposure and cognitive abilities, which was consistent with the findings of the United States Environmental Protection Agency obtained in their analyses used to derive a reference dose for MeHg exposure (Rice et al. 2003).

A detrimental effect of MeHg on cognitive abilities and academic achievement, especially in individuals with high levels of prenatal exposure, and a dose–response relationship is relatively well established. Further studies are needed, however, to examine the relative contributions of the various factors affecting cognitive abilities and academic achievement among children exposed to MeHg. A large part of the controversy may be related to the timing of exposure; for example, it is difficult to dissociate prenatal exposure from postnatal exposure during breastfeeding. The critical exposure indicator is also not well established (White et al. 2011). Further, MeHg exposure often goes together with exposure to other substances, such as PCBs. Finally, it is hypothesized that there are also protective effects of fish consumption, which is often the source of maternal MeHg contamination. Fish contains minerals (e.g., iron, selenium, and iodine), vitamins (e.g., D and E), and long-chain fatty acids (e.g., n-3 polyunsaturated fatty acids [PUFAs]) that are critical for fetal brain development (Lauritzen et al. 2001; Cohen et al. 2005). For example, a US-American cohort study of mother–child pairs (n = 135) examined the association between maternal fish consumption, MeHg exposure, and infant cognition. An increase of one-part-per-million in maternal hair-sample MeHg levels was associated with a 7.5-point decrease in visual recognition memory among participating infants (Oken et al. 2005). In contrast, each additional weekly serving of fish was in turn associated with a 4-point increase in visual recognition memory. While the sample size did not allow full exploration of the interaction between rates of fish consumption and levels of mercury exposure, the authors concluded that visual recognition memory scores appeared to be highest among infants of mothers with high fish intake and low mercury levels, whereas scores appeared lowest in infants of mothers with low fish intake and high mercury levels.

7.4.1.2   Lead

Like mercury, lead is a potent environmental pollutant and neurotoxicant (Nava-Ruiz et al. 2012). Unlike mercury, however, human exposure to lead is almost entirely attributable to anthropogenic activity. Since the eighteenth century, environmental lead contamination has increased by approximately three orders of magnitude, mostly in the twentieth century, following the introduction of automobile fuels enriched with organolead anti-knock compounds (Nava-Ruiz et al. 2012). Other prominent sources of lead exposure include mining, industry, plumbing, drinking water, soil, and contaminated consumer products such as ceramics, food storage containers, cosmetics, jewellery, paint, hardware, and toys (Cleveland et al. 2008). While the efforts of national and international regulatory bodies have resulted in steep declines in blood-lead levels in recent decades (Cleveland et al. 2008; Naranjo et al. 2020), lead exposure remains an important cause of morbidity and mortality, particularly in low- and middle-income countries. The United Nations Children's Fund (UNICEF) reports that 1 in 3 children worldwide (about 800 million children) has blood-lead levels in excess of the US Centers for Disease Control and Prevention (CDC) reference value of 5 µg/dL (Paulson and Brown 2019). Lead exposure is estimated to be responsible for more than 1,000,000 deaths and nearly 600,000 cases of intellectual and developmental disability annually, which is equal to approximately two-thirds of the cases of idiopathic intellectual and developmental disability globally (Naranjo et al. 2020). In particular, perinatal exposure to lead is associated with intellectual disability, hyperactivity, and impaired academic achievement, among other adverse outcomes (Papanikolaou et al. 2005).

Foetuses, infants, and young children have been shown to be particularly vulnerable to the harmful effects of lead exposure. Between 40% and 50% of lead ingested by children is absorbed by the immature gastrointestinal system (Mushak 1991), while adults only absorb approximately 20–30% of that amount. Likewise, the half-life of lead in the adult human body is approximately 35–40 days, whereas the half-life of lead following perinatal, infant, and childhood exposure can span years or even decades (Biomonitoring Summary 2019). Compounding these vulnerabilities, lead absorbed by adult bodies is largely fixed in hard tissue ($\approx$ 90%), such as bones and teeth; however, lead absorbed by developing bodies more readily accumulates in soft tissue (Barbosa et al. 2005). Moreover, the proportion of lead that does become bound to immature bones and teeth ($\approx$ 70%) is continuously released into the bloodstream as the skeleton grows, creating a persistent, internal source of contamination (Gulson et al. 1996). Pregnant and lactating women also experience rapid bone-tissue turnover, rendering them vulnerable (Mason et al. 2014). Once lead enters the bloodstream, whether via inhalation, gastrointestinal absorption, or bone-tissue turnover, it is carried throughout the body by erythrocytes and is readily transported across the placental and blood–brain barriers (Biomonitoring Summary 2019).

Myelinating cells and neurons are particularly vulnerable to the cytotoxic effects of lead, although astroglia have also shown to be vulnerable (Tiffany-Castiglioni 1993). Lead exposure is associated with direct alterations to the normal development of the central nervous system during the perinatal period and in childhood (Mason et al. 2014), as well as indirect effects resulting from damage to other body systems (Mason et al. 2014). Adverse effects of lead exposure to the developing brain include impairment of synapse formation and neuronal migration, as well as neuronal and glial differentiation (Bressler and Goldstein 1991; Mason et al. 2014). Lead exposure has also been associated with alterations to physical development during the perinatal period. As an example, researchers have detected a significant negative association between newborn head circumference, a measure that correlates with intelligence and academic achievement, and umbilical cord-blood lead levels, even after controlling for potential confounds (Al-Saleh et al. 2008). MRI studies in humans corroborate the effects on these biological pathways, reporting altered myelin microstructure (Brubaker et al. 2009; Sahu et al. 2010), reduced structural brain volume (Brubaker et al. 2010; Cecil et al. 2008), altered brain metabolite levels (Cecil et al. 2011; Trope et al. 1998), and reduced activity in task-relevant brain circuitry (Yuan et al. 2006) in individuals exposed to lead.

With respect to sub-acute exposure to lead, epidemiological meta-analytical studies performed in wealthy countries (all from high-income Western countries except Shanghai) have reported significant but subtle adverse effects. A 1994 systematic review and meta-analysis of research on the relationship between environmental lead exposure and children's intelligence revealed a significant negative association between lead exposure and childhood IQ (mostly between the ages of 5 and 9 years) (Pocock et al. 1994). This association was, however, not present across all samples. In studies in which blood was collected at birth (from the umbilical cord) or within weeks of birth, no consistent relationship was found between lead levels and childhood IQ (Pocock et al. 1994). By contrast, in studies in which blood samples were collected at age 2 or in which deciduous teeth were collected for evaluation, significant negative associations were consistently reported after adjusting for potential confounds such as maternal IQ and demographics (Pocock et al. 1994). The results of a meta-analysis (n = 4,594) showed that a doubling of body-lead burden (from 10 to 20 µg/dL in blood lead or from 5 to 10 µg/g in tooth lead) was associated with a decrement in full-scale IQ of 1–2 points (Pocock et al. 1994).

A UK-based study also found a significant but less pronounced negative association between early childhood lead exposure and academic achievement (using the UK national Standard Assessment Tests [SATs] for Key Stage One), as well as behavioural difficulties (using the Strengths and Difficulties Questionnaire [SDQ] and the Development and Well-being Assessment [DAWBA]; attention was measured using the Test of Everyday Attention for Children [TEACh]). Blood-lead levels at age 30 months negatively predicted academic achievement at age 7–8 years (n = 488) (Chandramouli et al. 2009). After controlling for potential confounds, researchers observed that a doubling of lead levels from 5 to 10 µg/dL was associated with a reduction in scores for reading (OR = 0.51) and writing (OR = 0.49) of approximately 0.3 point. A significant positive association between blood-lead levels and hyperactive and antisocial behaviour was also detected. Similarly, researchers examining the association between low-level lead toxicity and academic performance amongst children across the Chicago Public School system (n = 58,650) reported that when blood-lead levels were less than 10 µg/dL at a mean age of about 45 months, lead level was negatively associated with reading (β = −0.60) and mathematics achievement (β = −0.50; Illinois Standard Achievement Tests [ISAT]) in children in grade 3 (Evens et al. 2015). A 5 µg/dL increase in blood-lead levels (from 0-4 µg/dL to 5-9 µg/dL) was associated with a 32% increase in the risk of failure in reading and mathematics after controlling for the effects of potential confounds including demographic factors, prematurity/low birth weight, and maternal education. Approximately 13% of reading failure and 15% of mathematics failure amongst Chicago public school children in grade 3 was explained by low-level lead exposure (<10 µg/dL).

In research involving participants in middle-income countries, the impact of sub-acute levels of lead exposure is generally larger. For example, authors of a large-scale study of Filipino children (n = 877; mean blood-lead level of 7.1 µg/dL) reported that among sample participants, each 1 µg/dL increase in blood-lead level was associated with a 3.3-point decrease in cognitive abilities (using Wechsler-based measures and the Bayley Scales of Infant Development) in children aged 6 months to 3 years, and a 2.47-point decrease in children of 3 to 5 years of age – even after controlling for numerous factors, including maternal education and/or IQ (Solon et al. 2008). The large deficits found in this Filipino study may be partially attributable to the overall nutritional status of the participants, many of whom were chronically malnourished and deficient in essential nutrients. Children who were deficient in folate were particularly vulnerable to the negative effects of lead on cognitive abilities. In a study in which wealthy and middle-income countries were pooled, there was also a significant negative relationship between environmental lead exposure and children's intelligence, but the overall effect was smaller (Lanphear et al. 2005). These children showed a decrease of 3.9 points in cognitive abilities with an increase in blood-lead levels from 2.4 to 10 µg/dL; a decrease of 1.9 points with an increase from 10 to 20 µg/dL; and a decrease of 1.1 points with an increase from 20 to 30 µg/dL (n = 1,333, mean blood-lead level of 12.7 µg/dL in early childhood). Taken together, the adverse effects of environmental lead exposure on cognitive abilities and academic achievement show a dose-dependent response, with steeper effects amongst children with blood-lead levels inferior to 10 µg/dL. This relationship may depend in part on the socioeconomic level of the country/region and factors such as nutritional status.

7.4.2 Polyhalogenated Aromatic Hydrocarbons

7.4.2.1 Polybrominated Diphenyl Ethers

The production and use of polybrominated diphenyl ethers (PBDEs) grew rapidly in the 1970s, as an alternative to polybrominated/polychlorinated biphenyls (PCBs), a closely related class of organohalogens that was linked to serious adverse environmental and health effects (Dingemans et al. 2011; Costa and Giordano 2014; Epa and OP 2016). Exposure to PBDEs arises from many sources including contaminated air, water, soil, and sediment, as well as consumer products (Siddiqi et al. 2003), even though the production and use of most PBDEs has been banned in the European Union (Brominated flame retardants [EFSA]) and phased out in the United States (Epa and OCSPP 2015) in recent years. Individuals in low- and middle-income countries, especially those involved in the processing and disposal of electronic and consumer waste, are at elevated risk of exposure (Cai et al. 2020), despite an international treaty designed to protect human health and the environment from the harmful effects of persistent organic pollutants, including PBDEs (Convention).

PBDEs are commonly found in the environment and in the human body. They persist in the human body as they are lipophilic and tend to accumulate in adipose tissue (Frederiksen et al. 2009). Human exposure to environmental sources of PBDEs, such as dust from furniture containing PBDE-treated foam, is compounded by the consumption of lipid-rich oils (Frederiksen et al. 2009) and meat from exposed farm animals (Pietron et al. 2019) and aquatic predators, the latter of which been shown to accumulate particularly high levels of PBDEs in body tissues (Frederiksen et al. 2009). PBDEs are known to cross the blood–brain barrier and have been detected in human blood, cord blood, and breastmilk, as well as placental, fatty, and brain tissues (Siddiqi et al. 2003). US-Americans in particular tend to have elevated levels of PBDE congeners in their blood. Specifically, there is evidence that mean US-American blood-PBDE levels exceed those of populations in Asia and Europe by approximately ten-fold (Frederiksen et al. 2009). Moreover, blood-PBDE levels in infants and toddlers have been shown to be 3–9 times higher compared to those of adults (Costa et al. 2014), and evidence from animal models suggests that infants may be less able to excrete PBDE congeners than adults (Staskal et al. 2006).

PBDEs have been associated with a host of adverse effects, including developmental neurotoxicity, endocrine disruption, thyroid toxicity, and immunotoxicity (Epa and OLEM 2013). While the consequences of PBDEs' neurodevelopmental toxicity are not fully understood, there is evidence for calcium dyshomeostasis (Kim et al. 2011) and altered prenatal thyroid levels. Calcium dyshomeostasis may partly explain the association between prenatal exposure to PBDEs and cognitive, attentional, and behavioural decrements deficits later in life (Dingemans et al. 2016). Calcium signals regulate various processes within the developing nervous system, including modulating the length of axons and dendrites, sculpting dendritic arborization, and influencing growth-cone motility (Kamijo et al. 2018). Thyroid hormones are implicated in basic neurodevelopmental processes, including neurogenesis, myelination, dendrite proliferation, and synapse formation (Williams 2008).

MRI studies investigating the impact of perinatal PBDE exposure on the brain are rare. One preliminary study, however, used resting state fMRI to examine associations between prenatal PBDE concentrations measured in maternal serum and intrinsic functional network organization in 5-year-old children (n = 34) (de Water et al. 2019). The authors examined whether PBDE serum concentrations were associated with executive functioning (EF) assessed using a parent-report questionnaire known as

Behavior Rating Inventory of Executive Function (BRIEF-P) (n = 106), and whether changes in intrinsic functional network organization linked the association between prenatal PBDE serum concentrations and EF problems. Children with higher prenatal PBDE showed increased global efficiency, estimated using a graph-theoretical approach, in brain areas involved in visual attention (e.g., inferior occipital gyrus) (β = 0.01), and more reported EF problems (β = 0.001). Further, higher global efficiency in these brain areas was associated with more EF problems (β = 0.01). This preliminary study suggested that intrinsic functional network organization of visual-attention-related brain areas may link prenatal PBDE concentrations to EF problems in childhood.

In addition, there is growing evidence that PBDEs cause neurodevelopmental delays, particularly when exposure occurs during the perinatal period. For example, an Ohio-based US-American study of 309 mother–infant pairs reported that an increase of one order of magnitude in serum PBDE congener concentrations during early pregnancy was associated with a 4.5-point decrement in FSIQ (measured using the Wechsler Preschool and Primary Scale of Intelligence-III [WPPSI-III]), and a 3.3-point increase in hyperactivity scores (measured using the Behavioral Assessment System for Children-2 [BASC-2]) at age 5 after controlling for demographic covariates and maternal IQ (Chen et al. 2014). Similarly, in a California study involving more than 300 mother–child pairs, prenatal PBDE serum concentrations were significantly associated with impaired attention at age 5, decreased fine motor coordination at ages 5 and 7, and decreased full-scale IQ at age 7 (Eskenazi et al. 2015). Decreased full-scale IQ at age 7 was attributable primarily to impairment in verbal comprehension, particularly amongst participants in the top quartile of serum concentration. These associations remained even after adjusting for demographic factors and maternal education. In a study following 329 mother–child pairs in New York City, cord-blood concentration of PBDEs was negatively associated with outcomes on tests of cognitive and physical development, even after adjustment for demographic factors and maternal IQ. Significant negative associations were detected for psychomotor development at 12 months (using the Psychomotor Development Index of the Bayley Scales of Infant Development, Second Edition [BSID-II]); mental development at 12 and 36 months (using the Mental Development Index of the BSID-II); full-scale, verbal, and performance IQ at 48 months, and performance IQ at 72 months (using the revised Wechsler Preschool and Primary Scale of Intelligence).

There is scarce literature regarding the impact of PBDE on academic achievement. A study involving participants from the aforementioned Ohio-based US cohort reported that an increase in maternal PBDE congeners by 10 times was not significantly associated with reading scores at age 5 years (measured using Woodcock-Johnson Tests of Achievement-III [WJ-III]) but was inversely associated with reading at age 8 (β = –6.2; Wide Range Achievement Test – 4 [WRAT-4]; n = 239 mother–child pairs; Zhang et al. 2017). However, when childhood PBDE congener serum concentration (measured between the ages of 1 and 8) was examined, researchers reported negative associations between PBDE levels and reading achievement at 5 and 8 years, although the associations were no longer significant after controlling for covariates (n = 230 mother–child pairs; Liang et al. 2019). In the same study, a ten-fold increase in PBDE congener concentrations at ages 3 and 5 years was associated with a −4.5 to −5.5-point change in reading ability at ages 5 and 8. The data thus far support the link between perinatal PBDE exposure and reasoning (IQ), executive functioning, language, and reading abilities. Nevertheless, additional research is needed to uncover the biological pathways that mediate these effects.

7.4.2.2   Polychlorinated Biphenyls

As described earlier, PCBs are a class of organohalogens with a high degree of structural similarity to PBDEs. PCBs have been associated with cancer and adverse effects on the nervous, endocrine, immune, and reproductive systems in animal models, similar to PBDEs (Epa and OLEM 2015). Between the 1930s (when commercial production began) and the 1970s there was increasing research documenting PCBs' harmful effects (Kodavanti 2017; Markowitz 2018) and environmental accumulation (Kodavanti 2017). Global PCB contamination peaked in the 1970s, along with public attention to its adverse effects (Markowitz 2018). The production and use of PCBs was banned in the United States in 1979 (Epa and OLEM 2015) and globally in 1986 (Weiner 2008); by this time, however, PCBs had already become a long-term threat to human health and the environment as a persistent organic pollutant (Convention). Some regions of the world remain heavily contaminated even thirty-five years after the implementation of a global moratorium on production. Northeastern Europe, in particular, carries a high relative burden of environmental PCBs, with PCB concentrations up to two orders of magnitude greater than in other regions of the world (Undeman et al. 2018).

While not fully understood, the mechanisms underlying the neurodevelopmental toxicity of PCBs appear to be similar to those proposed for PBDEs. As with PBDEs, exposure to PCBs has been linked to thyroid hormone dyshomeostasis (Zoeller 2005) and calcium dyshomeostasis (Holland et al. 2017; Wong et al. 1997). Like for other exogenous factors described here, there are not many human neuroimaging studies investigating the effects of PCB poisoning. One noteworthy study found associations between prenatal exposure to PCBs, the surface area of the splenium of the corpus callosum, and response inhibition using the continuous performance test in 4.5-year-old children (n = 189) (Stewart et al. 2003). Results revealed a dose-dependent association between cord blood PCBs and errors of commission. Splenium size but not other brain areas negatively predicted errors of commission ($R^2 = 0.20$). There was also an interaction between splenium size and PCB exposure indicating that the smaller the splenium, the larger the association between PCBs and errors of commission. This study and other preliminary studies may represent both causal deficits as well as compensatory mechanisms.

Perhaps reflecting these neural differences, prenatal PCBs exposure is associated with alterations in cognitive abilities, IQ, attention, motor abilities, and behaviour. For example, researchers following a cohort of 156 9-year-old participants in the New York region detected a 3-point-decrease in full-scale IQ and a 4-point-decrease in verbal IQ for every 1 ng/g increase in PCB in placental tissue. This association remained significant after controlling for maternal IQ, numerous demographic factors, and burden of other toxicants in placental tissue (Stewart et al. 2008). Similar results were reported in a Dutch cohort study following 395 mother–child dyads (Patandin et al. 1999). After controlling for covariates, including maternal education and demographic factors, a negative association was observed between maternal blood-plasma PCB levels and children's scores on the overall cognitive as well as sequential and simultaneous processing scales of the Kaufman Assessment Battery for Children (K-ABC). Children whose mothers had the highest levels of exposure scored on average four points lower on the K-ABC when compared to children in the group with the lowest level of maternal exposure. Authors of another study involving 94 First Nations mother–infant pairs in Canada reported a negative association between cord-blood PCB levels and visual recognition memory in infants, assessed with the Fagan Test of Infant Intelligence (Boucher et al. 2014). Researchers in Japan have reported a negative association between cord-blood PCB concentrations and social behaviour using a biological motion paradigm, and expressive language development using the KIDS questionnaire. By contrast, a study performed in the Netherlands (n = 90) produced mixed results. After controlling for potential confounds, cord-blood concentrations of PCBs were correlated to poorer fine motor abilities, better attention, and better visual perception abilities on standardized measures (Roze et al. 2009).

With regard to academic achievement, the aforementioned Ohio study showed a significant negative association between (maternal) prenatal PBDE congener and reading ability (β = 7.0; n = 239 mother–child pairs; Liang et al. 2019). The sum of prenatal PCBs congeners was, in contrast, not significantly associated with children's reading skills (Liang et al. 2019). In a US-based multi-site study (n = 883), the Collaborative Perinatal Project, 3rd trimester PCB serum and reading (adjusted effect size estimate = 0.68) as well as arithmetic abilities measures (adjusted effect size estimate = 0.45) obtained using the Wide Range Achievement Test were nominally significant, including covariates such as study centre and gender of the child (Gray et al. 2005). The effect was no longer significant, however, when including other covariates such as race, SES, smoking status, number of days breastfed, educational level of mother/caregiver, emotional environment, age of child, and pesticide level (n = 890). Accordingly, more research is needed to determine the impact of perinatal PCB on academic achievement.

7.5 Conclusion

In this chapter, we have reviewed pre- and postnatal environmental factors that impact neurocognitive function and academic performance, in particular in reading and in mathematics. In addition to the research focusing on pre- and postnatal influences on academic performance, we covered the available literature on prevalence, neurobiological foundations, and cognitive mechanisms. Despite varying quality and quantity of the currently available work, we provided unequivocal evidence that many of the risk factors reviewed here have a negative impact on children's neurocognitive and academic outcomes (except for breast-feeding, which appears to have positive impact on cognitive outcomes). Evidence for an influence on academic outcome was strongest in the context of prematurity and neonatal asphyxia for child-centric factors; nicotine, alcohol, cannabis, psychosocial stress, and breastfeeding for maternal factors; and mercury, lead, and PBDEs for exogenous factors. Systematic reviews, however, also show other developmental toxicants not elaborated in the current chapter. These include, for example, arsenic, toluene, manganese, fluoride, chlorpyrifos, dichlorodiphenyltrichloroethane, and tetrachloroethylene (Grandjean and Landrigan 2014). However, this literature generally lacks concrete evidence of their impact on academic achievement, and hence these toxicants were not included in the current chapter. Most of the negative environmental exposures reported here were also associated with increased rates of neurodevelopmental disorders and lower general cognitive abilities.

Many of the environmental factors described here likely share common biological pathways, such as dysregulation of the HPA axis, immune responses, oxidative stress, neurochemistry, the microbiome, and epigenetics. However, none of these mechanisms, in particular epigenetic and gene–gene interaction, gene–environment correlation, and sexual dimorphism, were described in detail in this chapter, as their complex nature would require an independent chapter focused on biological pathways. Turning to cognitive mechanisms that mediate the effects of adverse early environmental exposures on reading, mathematics, domain-general executive, attentional, and cognitive functions seem to mediate these effects. Interestingly, a few of these perinatal environmental factors showed some unique characteristics (although false-negative findings cannot be ruled out at present). For example, prenatal alcohol exposure and pre-eclampsia seem to impact mathematics more than reading, while neonatal encephalopathy seems to impact reading more than mathematics. In addition, premature birth appears to impair children's mathematics skills via different mechanisms than the mechanisms thought to underlie developmental dyscalculia. Further, maternal hypertension during pregnancy showed regional neural overgrowth, which in turn was associated with impaired neurodevelopment, rather than the typical undergrowth observed in other risk factors. The effect of prenatal exposure to psychostimulants, opioid, caffeine, infection, nutrition, and several of the exogenous factors on academic outcome were negligible and/or controversial. These observations could be due to reporting biases inherent to the small (but growing) literature. A further bias might be introduced by the degree to which reading and math researchers are actively conducting research on a particular risk factor.

It must be noted that the field also faces a number of challenges. For example, a common research design in this area is retrospective chart review, which is far from ideal as important (control) measures may be missing, and/or not systematically and objectively quantified. Multiple risk factors also frequently co-occur within the same individuals, such as stress, substance use, and low SES.

Considering the likely contribution of genetic risk, and the frequent continuation of adverse prenatal exposures during the postnatal period, it is exceptionally difficult to dissociate true causal mechanisms of academic failure from correlated factors. It is noteworthy that the effect sizes of these environmental factors are generally small, and likely additive, akin to the contributions of individual genetic contributions to academic achievement. We provided effect sizes adjusted for other confounds whenever the literature allowed. Finally, even in cases where the negative impact of perinatal exposure to environmental contaminants is well established, it is likely that child-centric, maternal, and other environmental factors in addition to genetic factors interact and influence an individual's vulnerability to neurodevelopmental disorders and learning difficulties. While these effects deserve detailed discussion, they were not described here due to limited space.

We did not provide independent sections for paternal risk factors because of the small number of currently available studies. Nevertheless, we acknowledge that fathers do have an impact on children's developmental cognitive outcome (see, for example, Section 7.3.2). We also did not include SES as an independent category, even though many studies have examined the impact of SES on academic outcome (see Chapter 14, Fish 2022), and this too is likely due to both environmental and genetic contributions. The rationale for excluding SES as an independent factor is that SES is often treated as a confounding factor to the more specific perinatal factors highlighted in this chapter (e.g., substance use, nutrition), and continues to impact child development well beyond the perinatal period considered here through several other mechanisms.

Looking into the future, comprehensive studies of these perinatal factors that include prospective, longitudinal, and/or genetically sensitive designs combined with sophisticated statistical analysis frameworks, such as path analyses, will be helpful for moving the field forward. Specifically, studying sibling pairs discordant for exposure to a specific risk factor and/or controlling for corresponding parental academic skills may help mitigate some of the effects of genetic confounds, and can hence lend support for causal relationships between a given risk factor and children's outcomes. Future studies should also specifically focus on buffering effects introduced by factors such as maternal education (Kotimäki et al. 2020) and other socioeconomic metrics, as well as sex (particularly, being female). Finally, it should not be overlooked that there are medical interventions for some of the factors described here. For example, caffeine, which we described here as only having a minor impact on offspring's cognitive outcome, has been used for over a decade to treat prematurity, hypoxemia, and bronchopulmonary dysplasia. Treating such perinatal factors may help mitigate the negative neurodevelopmental outcomes associated with these risk factors, although it must be noted that the results to date are mixed (including many null findings; Gentle et al. 2018). Knowing the positive and negative mediators and mechanisms of these perinatal factors related to cognitive and academic outcomes can have a large impact on intervention options, not just in the early medical context, but also on reading and maths interventions later in life.

Suggestions for Further Reading

Pulli, E. P., V. Kumpulainen, J. H. Kasurinen, et al. 2019. 'Prenatal Exposures and Infant Brain: Review of Magnetic Resonance Imaging Studies and a Population Description Analysis'. *Hum Brain Mapping* 40: 1987–2000.

Morie, K. P., M. J. Crowley, L. C. Mayes, and M. N. Potenza. 2019. 'Prenatal Drug Exposure from Infancy through Emerging Adulthood: Results from Neuroimaging'. *Drug and Alcohol Dependence* May 1, 198: 39–53.

McBryde, M, G. C. Fitzallen, H. G. Liley, H. G. Taylor, and S. Bora. 2020. 'Academic Outcomes of School-Aged Children Born Preterm: A Systematic Review and Meta-analysis'. *JAMA Network Open* 3 (4): e202027.

D'Onofrio, B. M., Q. A. Class, M. E. Rickert, et al. 2016. 'Translational Epidemiologic Approaches to Understanding the Consequences of Early-Life Exposures'. *Behavior Genetics* 46, 315–28.

Van den Bergh, B. R. H., M. I. van den Heuvel, M. Lahti, et al. 2020. 'Prenatal Developmental Origins of Behavior and Mental Health: The Influence of Maternal Stress in Pregnancy'. *Neuroscience and Biobehavioral Reviews* Oct, 117: 26–64.

Summary: Genetic and Environmental Influences

1. **Familial clustering of learning disorders:** Dyslexia and dyscalculia run in families – that is, in individuals who share both their genetic make-up and their surrounding environment. Children with at least one diagnosed first-degree relative are up to approximately four times more likely to develop learning difficulties themselves.

2. **Interplay of genetic and environmental factors:** Learning difficulties are caused by genetic *and* environmental influences (e.g., via gene–environment correlation and interaction).

3. **Genetic and environmental contributions:** Depending on several factors (e.g., age, domain tested), genetic variance explains about 30–70% of the variance in reading and maths ability while the remaining variance is explained by (shared and non-shared) environmental factors. Genes and environments have small effect sizes, usually explaining only up to 2% of the variance.

4. **Continuity of behavioural genetic effects:** Genes related to typical performance likely overlap with genes related to dyslexia and dyscalculia.

5. **Homogeneity of behavioral genetic effects:** Genetic associations with behavioural performance often generalize to several domains of reading (e.g., reading accuracy and comprehension) and maths (e.g., number understanding and maths problem solving).

6. **Molecular genetic null findings:** So far, no DNA variants have been found to be reliably associated with dyslexia and dyscalculia at the whole-genome level.

7. **Early environmental influences:** Early environmental factors (that in fact also have a genetic basis) such as preterm birth, prenatal substance exposure (e.g., alcohol, nicotine, and cannabis), maternal psychosocial stress, and developmental toxicants (e.g., mercury, lead, and polybrominated diphenyl ethers) are negatively related to reading and maths ability (e.g., via general deficits in working memory, cognitive control, and visuospatial processing). Breastfeeding is positively related to reading and maths learning outcomes.

PART IV

Neurodevelopmental Foundations

8 Neurogenetic Insights into the Origins of Dyslexia and Dyscalculia

Michael A. Skeide

8.1 Introduction

Reading and maths ability are shaped by an interaction of genetic and environmental factors. Roughly half of the behavioural variance that is measured when assessing reading and maths performance is explained by genetic variance, while the other half is explained by environmental variance (see Chapter 6, Malanchini and Gidziela 2022, and Chapter 7, Hoeft and Bouhali 2022). In this context, it is often overlooked that there is a large explanatory gap between what genes do and how behavioural performance is regulated. Genes do not act directly but *indirectly* on reading and maths ability, most notably by playing a role in the development of the brain, the biological information processing system that makes learning to read and do maths possible. More specifically, many candidate genes for dyslexia and dyscalculia encode protein structures in developing neural circuits that ultimately form the brain systems underlying reading and maths. This explanatory pathway involving genetic variation, brain systems for reading and maths, and learning difficulties in these two domains is the key topic of the present chapter. Particular emphasis will be given to neurogenetic association studies in which naturally occurring DNA variants (single nucleotide polymorphisms [SNPs]) or copy number variants (in particular deletions) were related to magnetic resonance imaging (MRI) or electroencephalography (EEG) measures that were in turn used to differentiate between children with dyslexia or dyscalculia and typically developing control groups.

8.2 Neurogenetic Association Studies of Dyslexia

Neurogenetic association studies are effortful and expensive since they require resource-intensive techniques, in-person assessment of participants, and large samples to produce reliable results. These challenges multiply in developmental samples in which high-quality data are harder to get than in adults (e.g., due to head motion or face muscle artefacts during brain recordings). Accordingly, neurogenetic association studies of dyslexia are scarce.

8.2.1 Neuronal Migration Genes and the Inferior Parietal Cortex

The first study in the field was based on a small US-American sample of 56 typical adults without dyslexia (Meda et al. 2008). Here, the authors compared the whole-brain grey matter volume of 13 individuals with an intron-2-deletion on the gene *DCDC2* vs. 43 individuals without this mutation. In carriers of the deletion, grey matter volume was larger, particularly in right middle fusiform, right middle temporal, right superior parietal, right inferior frontal, and left anterior temporal cortices (at a threshold of $P < 0.01$ uncorrected). These uncorrected results, however, would not meet current standards for statistical reliability and therefore should not be interpreted.

Another line of research focused on the genes *DCDC2*, *DYX1C1*, and *KIAA0319*, which have been most consistently found to be associated with reading ability at the behavioural level, although none of the associations reported so far have reached genome-wide significance ($P < 5$ x 10^{-8}; Mascheretti et al. 2017). In a sample of 76 Swedish participants aged 6–25 years, Darki and colleagues investigated whether candidate SNPs on these genes are related to a white matter volume index calculated from structural MRI data (Darki et al. 2012). The SNPs rs793842 on *DCDC2*, rs3743204 on *DYX1C1*, and rs6935076 on *KIAA0319* revealed overlapping associations with the volume of two clusters encompassing the left inferior parietal white matter. Specifically, the white matter volume of this area was significantly reduced in individuals carrying the T allele of these SNPs. In follow-up structural MRI work on the identical sample, rs793842 was also found to be related to the thickness of the left inferior parietal cortex, with T-allele carriers showing significantly increased cortical thickness (Darki et al. 2014). Brain-structural measures were significantly correlated with reading ability in both studies. While the authors did not provide an explanation for the opposite genetic effects on white and grey matter, they highlighted the role of these genes for neuronal migration. Neuronal migration occurs in the first years of life when young nerve cells move to a final target position in the cortex (Nguyen 2019). The cortical thickness results reported by Darki et al. 2014 could thus indicate that certain variants of *DCDC2* may promote excessive radial migration from medial to lateral target layers of the inferior parietal cortex. The biological validity of this finding, however, is limited by the observation that *DCDC2* downregulation effects in rodent models are bidirectional, leading to both increased and reduced migration of nerve cells (Gabel et al. 2010). Furthermore, the link between increased neuronal migration in cortical grey matter and reduced white matter volume remains unclear. An alternative explanation offered by the authors is that *DCDC2*, *DYX1C1*, and *KIAA0319* might indirectly influence neuronal migration and axonal growth by regulating primary neuronal cilia functioning. Cilia are sensors signalling migrating nerve cells at which position these cells are in the extracellular space. A closer look at the available literature, however, indicates that this particular role is only documented for a different gene, not for *DCDC2*, *DYX1C1*, or *KIAA0319* (Higginbotham et al. 2012).

An intron-2-deletion on *DCDC2* was also found to be most strongly associated with functional MRI data in an independent US-American sample of 82 children aged 7–12 years (Cope et al. 2012). Specifically, compared to non-carriers, carriers of the deletion demonstrated significantly increased activation in the left inferior parietal cortex when performing high-level phonological tasks. There are many possible explanations why this increase in activation might co-occur with the increase in cortical thickness reported by Darki et al. 2014. It is conceivable, for example, that an accumulation of nerve cells at the white matter and cerebrospinal fluid boundary leads to a stronger hemodynamic response in these zones. The link between the increase in activation and reduction in white matter volume, however, is not straightforward.

In a related study including an Italian adult sample, Marino et al. compared the white matter fractional anisotropy of twenty-one carriers and twenty-six non-carriers of the *DCDC2* deletion (Marino et al. 2014). The authors reported that individuals with the deletion had a significantly lower fractional anisotropy in the left middle temporal white matter. The specific relevance of this effect for dyslexia, however, is unclear as it was found regardless of whether individuals actually had dyslexia or not.

8.2.2 A Glucose Transporter Gene and the Fronto-Temporal Phonological Processing System

In their seminal work with children, Roeske and colleagues conducted a genome-wide association study (GWAS) combined with EEG. They examined an exploration sample (n = 200) and a replication sample (n = 186) of 8–19-year-old German individuals with dyslexia (Roeske et al. 2011). The authors found a significant association between the SNP rs4234898 on chromosome 4 and a mismatch negativity (MMN) EEG component in the exploration sample (P < 1 x 10^{-5}, exact P not reported) and the replication sample (P = 1.46 x 10^{-3}). In the combined sample (n = 386), this association trended towards genome-wide significance (P = 5.14 x 10^{-8}). The interpretation of the role of rs4234898 for brain development is complicated by the fact that this SNP is located in a gene desert – that is, beyond any protein-coding genes. Nevertheless, rs4234898 may have a trans-regulation effect on *SLC2A3*, a gene on chromosome 12 that is involved in controlling the energy supply (glucose transport) in nerve cells. Accordingly, the observation that carriers of the T allele of rs4234898 showed a significantly reduced MMN compared to carriers of the C allele could be explained by a reduced glucose supply in inferior frontal sources (Tsolaki et al. 2015). The late time window of the MMN (peak at 300 to 710ms) induced during the basic syllable oddball task (standard: /da/, deviant: /ba/) suggests a link to high-level phonological processing that remains to be determined (e.g., working memory, attention, prediction).

In a follow-up study, Skeide et al. explored associations of rs4234898 and its neighbouring SNP rs11100040 with resting-state functional MRI in a small sample of 34 typically developing German children aged 9–12 years (Skeide et al. 2015). This work was guided by the hypothesis that if these SNPs indeed contribute to glucose transport in the left inferior frontal cortex, this region could also reveal different hemodynamic time courses as a function of carrying either the C or T allele.

In line with this hypothesis, it turned out that the inferior frontal time course of C-allele carriers vs. T-allele carriers of rs11100040 was significantly more strongly correlated with the time course of the left superior temporal gyrus. The superior temporal cortex is thought to mainly contribute to low-level phonological processing, like phoneme detection, and has also been identified as a source of the late MMN (Boets et al. 2013; Maurer et al. 2009). In this context, it is important to point out that the direction of the influence of these two regions on one another was not determined in the study of Skeide and colleagues (2015). Accordingly, it remains an open question whether the potential link between *SLC2A3* and the inferior frontal and superior temporal cortices relates to high-level or low-level phonological processing (or both).

8.2.3 A Neurite Extension Gene and the Posterior Fusiform Cortex

Skeide et al. examined gene–brain associations in a German sample of 3–6-year-old children without formal literacy instruction (n = 101) and followed them longitudinally until school, when they were 7–8 years old and underwent literacy assessment (Skeide et al. 2016). This focus on an unschooled sample made it possible to disentangle the neurogenetic predisposition for developing dyslexia from the consequences of having developed dyslexia (i.e., different learning quality and quantity). The authors related grey and white matter volume to 69 SNPs on 19 candidate genes with a documented link to literacy skills and found multivariate associations for five genes. Only one grey matter volume cluster associated with *NRSN1* and located in the left posterior fusiform cortex performed significantly above chance in classifying the participants into future dyslexic and control individuals (yielding an accuracy of 75%). Neurensin-1, the protein encoded by *NRSN1*, is involved in the extension of neurites by transporting vesicles to the growing ends of dendrites and axons (Araki et al. 2002). The left posterior fusiform cortex develops a selective response to letter strings in the course of literacy learning (Saygin et al. 2016). It can be concluded that the link between genetic variants of *NRSN1*, individual differences in the formation of fusiform cortex neurites, and developmental dyslexia is biologically plausible. Still, it has not been replicated yet in an independent sample. Furthermore, the functional consequences of this structural effect remain to be specified.

8.2.4 Associations with Genes of Unknown Function

Wilcke and colleagues reported an association between rs12533005 on *FOXP2* and hemodynamic activation during a high-level phonological rhyming task in a German sample (Wilcke et al. 2012). Specifically, carriers of the G allele of this SNP (n = 25) showed a significantly stronger response than carriers of the C allele (n = 8) in left inferior frontal and inferior parietal cortices. The interpretation of this finding is complicated by the fact that the functional role of rs12533005 is currently unknown, especially since this SNP has no influence on the protein sequence of *FOXP2*.

In an Icelandic sample of 18–65-year-old adults, Ulfarsson and colleagues examined the whole-brain grey and white matter volume of 51 individuals with a rare deletion occurring in less than 0.2% of the population (Ulfarsson et al. 2017). This deletion is located on chromosome 15 between breakpoints 1 and 2 (15q11.2(BP1-BP2)) and spans the genes *TUBGCP5, CYFIP1, NIPA1*, and *NIPA2*. They compared the structural images of the 51 individuals with the deletion against those of 104 individuals with a reciprocal duplication at that location and against those of 552 controls without the relevant copy number variants. The authors discovered that carriers of the deletion had significantly reduced grey matter volume in the left middle fusiform cortex compared to controls and an even more pronounced differ-ence compared to carriers of the duplication. The volumetric indices were not significantly related to reading test scores, but carriers reported a history of develop-mental dyslexia. In line with this structural finding, a subsample of 29 carriers of the deletion also showed a significantly reduced left middle fusiform cortex response to unfamiliar words in a visual lexical decision task. While this line of research seems promising, the functional role of the genes affected by the deletion is currently unclear. Moreover, individuals carrying the deletion not only had a specific history of dyslexia, but also a history of dyscalculia.

8.3 Neurogenetic Association Studies of Dyscalculia

Despite comparable prevalence and educational relevance, developmental dyscalculia is understudied compared to developmental dyslexia (Butterworth et al. 2011). To the best of my knowledge, the currently available literature comprises only three neurogenetic association studies.

8.3.1 Associations With Genes of Unknown Function

The pioneering work in the field was published in 2013 by Ludwig et al. who explored associations between the SNP rs133885 on the gene *MYO18B* and sulcus depth in a sample of 79 typical German adults with a mean age of 42 years (Ludwig et al. 2013). The starting point of this study was a GWAS of a sample of 699 children with dyslexia in which the authors detected a significant association between rs133885 and mathematical ability ($P = 7.71 \times 10^{-10}$). In the next step, they compared sulcus depths in relation to different genotypes of this SNP using the right intraparietal sulcus as a region of interest. In this analysis, which was run on an independent sample of adults, the authors found that GG-carriers had a significantly lower average intraparietal sulcus depth than AA/AG-carriers. Although the intra-parietal sulcus is known to underlie mathematical information processing (Nieder 2016), the lack of a brain–behaviour association limits the implications of this study for dyscalculia. In a similar vein, the SNP was not specifically related to dyscalculia but identified in a sample with dyslexia. Lastly, and most importantly, it is not clear via which intermediate phenotype *MYO18B* might be linked to dyscalculia since this gene does not express proteins in brain tissue.

The study by Ulfarsson et al. on carriers of the 15q11.2(BP1-BP2)-deletion (see Section 8.2.4) also informed our understanding of the neurogenetic foundations of dyscalculia (Ulfarsson et al. 2017). Carriers reported a history of developmental dyscalculia and showed significantly reduced grey matter volume in the left middle fusiform cortex compared to controls and carriers of a duplication. This result is potentially relevant for dyscalculia since the fusiform cortex plays a role in recognizing number symbols (Price et al. 2007). More direct evidence for an intermediate neural phenotype comes from the additional observation that 18 deletion carriers significantly underactivated the left inferior parietal cortex compared to 40 controls and 52 duplication carriers during a functional MRI task in which they had to determine whether a visually presented multiplication equation was correct or not. As pointed out earlier, these findings are limited by the lack of specificity with respect to the behavioural profile (co-occurrence of dyscalculia and dyslexia) and the unknown functions of the relevant genes.

8.3.2 A Neuronal Migration Gene and the Parietal Cortex

Most recently, Skeide and colleagues explored associations between known candidate genes for mathematical ability and grey matter volume (Skeide et al. 2020). To this end, they followed 3–6-year-old children that had not yet received mathematical instruction to examine longitudinally whether gene–brain associations would predict test scores in school at 7–9 years of age. The rationale behind focusing on a young unschooled sample was to capture potential neurogenetic predispositions of individual mathematical learning outcomes by controlling for the different learning experiences of children with dyscalculia. Associations between 18 SNPs on 10 genes and whole-brain grey matter volume were calculated in an exploration sample (n = 101) and, guided by power analyses, in an independent replication sample (n = 77) of 3–6-year-old children. A significant replicated association was only detected for the gene *ROBO1* and localized in the right parietal cortex, a key region for mathematical processing (Arsalidou et al. 2018). Individual grey matter volume in this cluster was in turn significantly related to individual mathematical test scores at 7–9 years of age in school. The biological plausibility of the link between *ROBO1* and grey matter volume is supported by molecular evidence from rodent models suggesting that this gene regulates prenatal neuronal migration during intrauterine brain maturation (Gonda et al. 2013; Hernandez-Miranda et al. 2011). The effects of *ROBO1*-related differences in parietal cortex development on specific functional processes (in particular, numerosity detection and mathematical problem solving) require further investigation.

8.4 Conclusion

Currently, the best-supported neurogenetic pathways for both dyslexia and dyscalculia include multiple genes (*DCDC2*, *DYX1C1*, *KIAA0319*, and *ROBO1*) that encode proteins guiding young nerve cells to a final target position in the developing parietal cortex (*neuronal migration*). Certain variants of these genes are related to differences in parietal cortical volume that in turn might hamper brain responses underlying processes relevant for reading (e.g., phonological storage) and mathematics (e.g., numerosity detection, mathematical problem solving). These hypothesized structure-to-function links, however, remain to be established and further specified empirically.

The present literature raises a number of open questions. Many other genes (e.g., *SLC2A3*, *NRSN1*) may be involved in the emergence of learning disorders (*polygenetic inheritance*). Given the small sample sizes of the currently available studies, it is likely that only a fraction of the relevant candidates has been discovered so far. Additionally, some genetic hits might even turn out to be non-replicable false positives, especially since most of the SNPs have never yielded genome-wide significant associations. It should also not be overlooked that the reported genes may play multiple independent roles for the development of reading-related brain systems (*pleiotropy*). *ROBO1*, for example, may be involved not only in neuronal migration, but also in the proliferation of parietal cortex neurons (Yeh et al. 2014). Another unsolved puzzle is the discrepancy between the very general functions of the known genes and the confined brain regions and specific cognitive domains they are associated with (*specificity*). Gene–environment interactions might be a key to answer this question, but how, for example, *ROBO1* interacts with home learning environments during certain developmental time windows is currently not known. Finally, it remains to be seen whether the present findings in US, Swedish, German, and Icelandic samples generalize to individuals with different national and educational backgrounds.

Suggestions for Further Reading

Darki, F., M. Peyrard-Janvid, H. Matsson, J. Kere, and T. Klingberg. 2014. 'DCDC2 Polymorphism is Associated with Left Temporoparietal Gray and White Matter Structures During Development'. *The Journal of Neuroscience* 34(43): 14455–62.

Mascheretti, S., A. De Luca, V. Trezzi, et al. 2017. 'Neurogenetics of Developmental Dyslexia: From Genes to Behavior through Brain Neuroimaging and Cognitive and Sensorial Mechanisms'. *Translational Psychiatry* 7 (1): e987–e987.

Skeide, M. A., K. Wehrmann, Z. Emami, et al. 2020. 'Neurobiological Origins of Individual Differences in Mathematical Ability'. *PLOS Biology* 18 (10): E300087.

9 Longitudinal Neural Observation Studies of Dyslexia

Gorka Fraga González, Katarzyna Jednoróg,
and Silvia Brem

9.1 Introduction

Learning to read is a remarkable feat with extraordinary consequences for cognitive and personal development. This learning process involves substantial changes in the function and structure of underlying brain networks. In most western industrialized societies, these changes take place across several years in early and middle childhood, from the onset of formal schooling at around 5 to 7 years of age to 3rd grade of primary school at around 7 to 9 years. Over this period, brain maturation processes co-occur with cognitive development shaped by learning and literacy experience (Dehaene et al. 2015). Longitudinal designs are useful for disambiguating the contribution of maturational changes from those associated with cognitive development and the individual trajectories of reading skills. This knowledge is important for advancing our understanding of the specific neurodevelopmental basis of both typical reading and dyslexia.

This chapter focuses on two types of longitudinal studies of reading and dyslexia. The first type includes multiple measurements of brain structure or function. Results of these studies reveal whether children with dyslexia, relative to typical readers, show delayed but otherwise comparable development of the brain network for reading or whether their trajectories of brain changes differ. The second set of studies consists of single neuroimaging measurements that are used to predict later reading skills or learning rates. These studies often combine neural and behavioural variables to anticipate future reading difficulties. Intervention studies examining the effects of training on the brains of individuals with dyslexia are not within the scope of this chapter but are reviewed in Chapter 11 (Yeatman 2022).

Most of the studies reviewed here deal with alphabetic languages and with samples from western-educated-industrialized-rich-democratic (WEIRD) countries. National backgrounds are identified for the samples of those studies that are most relevant to the central topics of this chapter. To facilitate clear navigation through the literature, the first part of this chapter provides an overview of the main neural systems implicated in reading and its development as delineated by decades of neuroimaging research.

9.2 The Developing Brain Network for Reading

The process of learning to read leads to changes in the sensitivity to print, which is commonly described as the 'tuning' or 'specialization' of particular brain regions. This is not limited to regional activations and involves detectable changes in the patterns of functional coupling or synchronization between regions. Moreover, these regions and their connections also undergo changes in the course of learning to read, mainly in their grey matter properties, mostly relating to nerve cell bodies, and white matter properties, mostly relating to nerve fibres. These distributed reorganization processes are in line with the notion that reading relies on coordinated activity of multiple sensory and associative neural systems. Consequently, the neural development of reading can be better understood by envisaging a network. The canonical 'reading network' comprises a set of posterior brain regions involved in auditory processing and multisensory integration (temporal and temporo-parietal cortices, including superior temporal, supramarginal, and angular gyri) and visual processing (ventral occipito-temporal cortices). In addition, anterior regions (including inferior frontal cortices) are considered as part of this network, but their functional interpretation is less well defined. Among the functions attributed to this circuitry are phonological processing, speech planning, comprehension, and other general attentional and inhibition processes (see review in Ozernov-Palchik and Gaab 2016). The term 'language network' is sometimes used to indicate a broader context not limited to written language.

The vast majority of the neuroimaging evidence available comes from studies on alphabetic orthographies. This evidence implies that the association between speech sounds and letters plays an important role in the formation of the reading network, and this will be used as a conceptual framework in this chapter. An established view of reading development in alphabetic languages (Ehri 2008) suggests four major milestones in learning to read (Figure 9.1). First, in the pre-reading stage, auditory processing areas become tuned to speech and subsequently to smaller units such as syllables and speech sounds, called phonemes, while logographic icons gain familiarity in visual areas. Next, audiovisual integration areas start specializing when learning the alphabetic code, so that associations between visual letters and speech sounds are established in the first months of schooling. These associations allow slow reading through letter-by-letter word decoding. In parallel, increasing interaction with visual areas facilitates specialization in processing letters and eventually words, enabling sight word reading. Here, an occipito-temporal region, the widely reported visual word form area (VWFA) in the left fusiform gyrus, consistently shows sensitivity to words and allows whole-word recognition (Glezer et al. 2009; US sample). The functional connections in the developmental framework can be divided into a dorsal (superior) phonological route employed by beginning readers using the grapheme–phoneme decoding strategy, as opposed to a ventral (inferior) orthographic route used by expert readers relying on fast visual word recognition and direct access to meaning. The structural foundations of these functional routes are white matter fibre tracts connecting these regions (see Figure 9.1, bottom panel).

Maturational and experience-dependent changes in these connections include myelination and axonal pruning, as we elaborate in Section 9.3.

Longitudinal and cross-sectional evidence suggests that specialization in the posterior regions of the reading network does not entail a linear increase of responsiveness to orthographic or phonological stimuli (see review in Chyl et al. 2021). Instead, the pattern emerging from the literature is that audiovisual integration areas and visual areas undergo an inverted U-curve trajectory of responses to print (see Figure 9.1, top panel).

A Functional network development

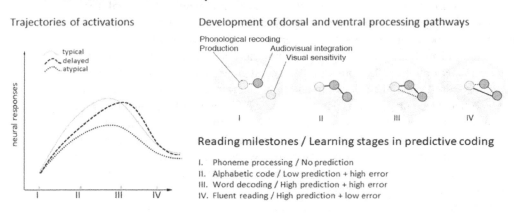

B White matter pathways

Figure 9.1 *(A) Development of the main functional brain systems for audiovisual letter–sound integration and visual sensitivity to orthography. Multisensory integration areas facilitate specialization of visual areas that enable a transition from a slower, indirect dorsal route to a direct ventral route that is dominant in advanced readers. Longitudinal data suggest an inverted U-curve of neural activations with growing expertise. An interactive perspective explains this curve in terms of predictions from other areas and the errors between predicted and sensory information (Price and Devlin 2011). From this perspective, processing in those areas is optimized with further learning and practice by updating these predictions. There is mixed evidence for both delayed and atypical trajectories in dyslexic readers. (B) Illustration of the main white matter tracts forming the dorsal and ventral routes for reading. The schematic shows a model of white matter development as reflected by a connectivity measure, fractional anisotropy (FA). Learning is proposed to interact with connectivity development through the processes of myelination and axonal pruning.*

This trajectory shows a peak of response amplitudes at the initial stages of learning followed by a decrease with increasing expertise. A broader conceptual framework describing this pattern proposes different stages of learning characterized by top-down predictions and prediction errors that gradually adjust processing sensitivity (Price and Devlin 2011). In this account, efficient processing, for instance of visual words, is facilitated by top-down predictions, which emerge in early learning stages. This emergence is followed by high prediction error signals indicating the mismatch between predicted and sensory inputs, which is used to optimize predictions. The combination between high prediction and prediction error signals at this stage explains the peak in neural responses. As learning progresses, predictions become better and error signals decline, resulting in reduced activation. We can draw a parallel between these general learning stages and the milestones in learning how to read in alphabetic languages shown in Figure 9.1. Alternatively, research on general skill learning suggests an 'expansion-selection-renormalization' pattern for plastic brain changes to explain inverted U trajectories (Wenger et al. 2017). This model predicts that the brain areas involved in a specific task would show an initial 'expansion', as shown by an increase of activation, volume, and/or connectivity, which may reflect a growth in neural resources such as, for example, in the number of neurons or connections (synapses). As learning progresses, the most efficient circuits are 'selected' while those that are not required are pruned away, leading to a 'renormalization'. The results reviewed in Section 9.4.4 reveal mixed findings that could reflect either delayed or altered trajectories in readers with dyslexia. Accordingly, further longitudinal studies are needed to shed light on these theoretical accounts.

The framework introduced here characterizes the developmental trajectories that may be associated with typical reading skills. Top-down predictions and interactions between various brain areas seem to be important in explaining some of the findings. The following sections summarize neuroanatomical and functional aspects of this reading network and evidence for altered development in dyslexia.

9.3 Neuroanatomical Changes Emerging When Learning to Read

Learning to read in childhood and adolescence coincides with a developmental period in which the brain structure and function undergoes major maturational changes with regional variations in the trajectories of grey and white matter development. These changes have a critical impact on the emergence, formation, and maturation of specialized brain circuits including the reading circuit, as discussed in Sections 9.3.1 and 9.3.2.

9.3.1 Morphological Alterations in Cortical and Subcortical Regions

The main metrics for quantifying brain morphology include grey or white matter volume, cortical thickness, surface area, and gyrification. In early child development (birth to 6 years of age), various patterns of changes, from linear to logarithmic and quadratic, were observed depending on the brain region (Remer et al. 2017; US sample). Although cortical thinning and surface expansion dominated most brain regions, some posterior brain structures showed initial thinning that was followed by thickening of the cortex. After the age of 5 years, grey matter volume development can be described as a predominantly linear decline (Norwegian, Dutch and US samples: Mills et al. 2016); US sample: Brain Development Cooperative Group 2012) but again with some regional variations. Prefrontal and temporo-parietal cortical thickness, for example, shows a somewhat later peak in growth at around the age of 8 years (Ducharme et al. 2016). Further, minor sex differences pointed to more inverted U-curve developmental trajectories of grey matter volume in girls compared to linear declines in boys (Brain Development Cooperative Group 2012) and a faster cortical thinning in occipital areas in boys (Ducharme et al. 2016). Such declines in grey matter volume have been related to neuronal pruning processes and the concurrent increase in intracortical myelination (Paus 2005).

To obtain a better understanding of the trajectories of brain morphology development in children and adolescents with dyslexia, it is important to characterize changes related to typical reading acquisition. Two studies examined the development of grey matter volume in typically reading children at school age and alterations associated with gains in reading (German sample: Linkersdörfer et al. 2015; US sample: Houston et al. 2014). These studies related reading skills to grey matter changes in mainly, although not exclusively, the regions of the classic language network, including parietal, temporal, and frontal regions. In the study by Linkersdörfer et al. (2015), the grey matter volume in the left superior temporal gyrus (STG), including parts of the planum temporale, was positively correlated in children in the first grade of elementary school (aged 7.5 years) with their gains in reading skills one year later. This finding suggests that early structural differences in areas for multisensory integration may be important in explaining individual variability in the acquisition of written language (Linkersdörfer et al. 2015). In contrast, three clusters in the left inferior parietal lobe, including angular and supramarginal gyri, and the left precentral and postcentral gyri showed a negative association between grey matter volume changes from grade 1 to 2 and reading proficiency in 2nd grade (Linkersdörfer et al. 2015). Similar decreases in grey matter volume of parietal and frontal cortical regions over time were associated with better baseline performance on rapid naming, word reading, and fluency in a sample of children and adolescents (5–15 years) in which participants were scanned twice over two years (Houston et al. 2014). Such findings indicate that maturational trajectories of brain regions critical for reading are associated with reading proficiency and may already differ in poor readers at an early stage (Linkersdörfer et al. 2015; Houston et al. 2014).

The most consistent differences in cortical morphology associated with dyslexia are mainly derived from case-control studies, which have been summarized in several meta-analyses. These differences include a reduced grey matter volume in bilateral superior temporal areas (English, German, Italian and French samples: Richlan et al. 2013; Linkersdörfer et al. 2012; Eckert et al. 2016); in temporo-parietal, cerebellar, and left occipito-temporal areas (Richlan et al. 2013); and in inferior frontal and orbito-frontal areas (Eckert et al. 2016). Longitudinal observation studies on brain morphology in dyslexia that include more than one MRI session are rather scarce. Two studies focused on the initial phase of reading acquisition from preschool or kindergarten age to school age in children with and without dyslexia (Kuhl et al. 2020), (Clark et al. 2014). The study by Kuhl and colleagues (2020) in a German sample found consistently higher gyrification of the left primary auditory cortex in children with dyslexia than in typical readers. This group difference was detected at age 5 years and persisted until age 8 years (Kuhl et al. 2020). Gyrification refers to the surface folding patterns of the brain (White et al. 2010). These morphological alterations accompanied alterations in the structural connectivity of the arcuate fasciculus and reduced functional connectivity of the primary auditory cortex to the planum temporale in pre-reading children (Kuhl et al. 2020). These results are partly in line with the findings of a study in a Norwegian sample by Clark et al. (2014) which used structural MRI data at a pre-reading age (6–7 years), beginning reading age (8–9 years), and a more advanced reading age (11–12 years) that were collected from two longitudinal samples of seven dyslexic and ten typically reading children. Reduced cortical thickness was found in auditory areas in pre-reading children with dyslexia, as were additional reductions in the lingual gyrus and medial, cingulate, and orbitofrontal gyri. Group differences at the last test time point at age 11.8 years remained only for the auditory cortex. The study by Clark et al. (2014) is so far also the only longitudinal study that specifically examined and reported sex differences. However, the group sizes in these comparisons, limited to five and six subjects, prevent further discussion and interpretation of their results. The two studies thus converge in showing alterations in the thickness and folding of the cortical structure of auditory processing areas in pre-reading children and suggest an atypical maturation of the speech processing network that precedes reading acquisition.

To summarize, brain development is characterized by increasing grey matter volume at the beginning of reading acquisition in regions related to auditory and speech processing and decreasing grey matter volume in regions associated with phonological processing and covert articulation. Children at the lower end of the reading continuum, including individuals diagnosed with dyslexia, show atypical maturational patterns in speech-related brain structures, especially in the auditory cortex.

9.3.2 Development of White Matter Tracts

Efficient communication between brain systems is necessary to combine orthographic, phonological, and semantic information when reading. The large-scale white matter tracts, which are bundles of axons, constitute the neuroanatomical basis of the neural reading networks. Diffusion tensor imaging (DTI) can be used on diffusion-weighted MR images to examine these tracts non-invasively and to quantify white matter properties. A popular measure is fractional anisotropy (FA). FA values are influenced by a combination of macroscopic factors, such as axonal orientation and the tissue-to-water ratio, and microscopic factors, such as myelination, number of axons, and axonal density and calibre. Therefore, FA measurement can be confounded, yielding lower values, especially in brain regions with a large proportion of crossing fibres. The macroscopic and microscopic factors in FA cannot be directly disentangled, although other DTI-derived measures, such as radial and axial diffusivity, may more specifically reflect myelination and axonal properties, such as coherence of orientation and calibre, respectively (Weiskopf et al. 2015). Another popular measure is mean diffusivity (MD), which quantifies the magnitude of water diffusion within the brain, with lower values reflecting tissue boundaries, including myelin. Studies often explore several of these measures, although most of the results reviewed here are based on FA data. In addition, studies vary in how many tracts of interest they focus on, with some also allowing quantification of segments within each tract. Nevertheless, a consistent pattern across clinical and developmental studies is a decrease in FA associated with pathological processes (Assaf and Pasternak 2008; Horsfield and Jones 2002) and an increase in FA with maturation (Cascio et al. 2007; Lebel et al. 2008).

The development of white matter can be described as resulting mainly from an interaction between two factors: growing myelination, which facilitates faster transmission of information, and pruning or elimination of some axonal connections (Yeatman et al. 2012). Importantly, because both of these processes are known to be influenced by learning and experience, individual variability in their timing and rate is an important contributor to cognitive development. Longitudinal studies that examine typical and dyslexic readers have provided valuable insights into the relation between white matter maturation and reading acquisition.

The major tracts connecting the main regions of the reading network can be grouped into two main sets of pathways. The dorsal pathways involve connections between temporo-parietal regions and frontal regions via the arcuate fasciculus and the superior longitudinal fasciculus. The ventral pathways connect temporal, occipital, and frontal regions via the inferior fronto-occipital fasciculus, inferior longitudinal fasciculus, and uncinate fasciculus. In typical readers, studies have found an association between white matter connectivity increase in several tracts of these two pathways and emerging reading skills (e.g., Moulton et al. 2019; French sample; Reynolds et al. 2019; Canadian English-speaking sample).

Two longitudinal studies examined white matter development from pre-reading stages onwards in typical and poor readers. Vanderauwera et al. (2017; Belgian, Dutch-speaking sample) tested children with and without familial risk for dyslexia in kindergarten and 3rd grade. The results showed the expected increase in FA values over time. However, the group of children that went on to develop dyslexia initially showed lower FA in the long segment of the arcuate fasciculus compared to typical readers. In the right hemisphere, this group difference persisted in 3rd grade, but in the left arcuate fasciculus the difference was no longer detected in 3rd grade. Interestingly, FA in the left arcuate fasciculus was the only significant predictor of reading skills in a regression model combining FA values from ventral and dorsal tracts, cognitive tests, and familial risk: 45% of dyslexic readers were correctly classified. Regarding familial risk, the right arcuate fasciculus across both measurements and the left inferior fronto-occipital fasciculus in kindergarten revealed a reduced FA in children with vs. without risk for dyslexia. In another study, Wang and colleagues examined English-speaking US children at three stages of reading: pre-reading, beginning reading, and fluent reading. They focused on left dorsal tracts: arcuate fasciculus, superior longitudinal fasciculus, and ventral inferior longitudinal fasciculus (Wang et al. 2017). The authors found that white matter development, reflected in FA increase over time, was slower in poor readers than in typical readers in a segment within the left arcuate fasciculus. This segment was selected because it showed lower FA in children at risk than in children without risk for dyslexia. In addition, the rate of WM development was positively associated with reading development across groups. Moreover, within the risk group, right superior longitudinal fasciculus development was slower in those children that would become poor readers than in those that would be classified as good readers. Backwards step-wise regression analyses were used to find the optimal set of variables for predicting later reading abilities. The regression models that combined familial risk, white matter changes, and cognitive tests performed best at predicting later reading comprehension and fluency.

Another study examined children at the age of 9.5 years and approximately 1.5 years later (Lebel et al. 2019; US sample). Focusing on temporo-parietal tracts, the authors reported an increase in FA in the right superior longitudinal fasciculus and bilateral corona radiata in typical readers but not in poor readers. The corona radiata contains fibres from precentral, frontal, and parietal lobes and converges towards the internal capsule. Interestingly, the MD measure in this study was sensitive to differences within poor readers. Specifically, dys-fluent and inaccurate readers showed a steeper decrease in diffusivity in the right corona radiata and the left uncinate fasciculus than did dysfluent but accurate readers. This study also found a significant correlation between changes in diffusion parameters and development of reading skills. A broader time window of three years was used in a study by Yeatman et al. (2012). They followed a group of 7–12-year-old children over four time-points (Yeatman et al. 2012; US sample) and focused on the arcuate fasciculus and inferior longitudinal fasciculus. In the left arcuate fasciculus and inferior longitudinal fasciculus, above-average readers showed initially low FA values that increased over time, whereas the reverse pattern was found in children with below-average reading skills. The rate of change in white matter connectivity in these tracts covaried with the children's reading skills.

The longitudinal DTI studies reviewed here examined somewhat different age ranges, yet they all detected an increase in connectivity of white matter fibre tracts in typically developing readers. Importantly, they all also found atypical development of dorsal and ventral tracts in poor readers. FA seems more sensitive to these effects than other diffusion measures. However, differences in diagnostic criteria, such as cut-off values, and analytic approaches, such as reconstructing the whole tract, mean tract, or a region of interest within a tract, complicate direct comparisons across studies and the derivation of diagnostically valid diffusion-based MRI markers. Despite these caveats, the studies discussed here demonstrate that measures of white matter change are relevant when searching for combined neural and behavioural predictors of reading problems.

9.4 Development of Functional Networks in Dyslexia

9.4.1 Insights from Electro- and Magnetoencephalography

The time-resolved electroencephalography (EEG) and magnetoencephalography (MEG) techniques provide information about how brain responses change with reading expertise. Most longitudinal studies available used event-related potential (ERP) designs to examine neural responses to orthographic, phonological, or semantic stimuli. These responses are often found to be attenuated in poor or dyslexic readers. Here, we should briefly discuss two considerations for interpretation. First, stronger ERP amplitudes are typically interpreted as reflecting facilitated processing, which is less demanding of attentional or cognitive resources, or advanced 'sensitivity' or 'specialization' (e.g., Swiss-German-speaking samples: Maurer et al. 2011; Pleisch et al. 2019). However, some results have also been explained with the opposite interpretation: larger amplitudes could indicate higher recruitment of attentional or cognitive resources (e.g., Dutch sample: Fraga González et al. 2014; US samples: Vogel and Luck 2000; Yoncheva et al. 2010). Thus, depending on the experimental context, differences between groups and/or conditions may be explained by somewhat divergent functional interpretations. A second important consideration is changes in EEG responses across the lifespan. Some ERP amplitudes become smaller, and their latencies become shorter, in adults as compared to children (e.g., Swiss-German-speaking samples: Maurer et al. 2006; Brem et al. 2009). A few longitudinal developmental EEG studies have also focused on frequency analysis of oscillatory activity: the rhythmic patterns of neural activity at different frequency ranges. One of the key findings of this line of work is that the individual alpha peak (i.e., a peak in the EEG power spectra typically within the alpha band, 8–12 Hz) seems to shift towards higher frequencies with increasing maturation (see, e.g., Smit et al. 2012; Rodríguez-Martínez et al. 2017).

9.4.2 Insights from Functional Magnetic Resonance Neuroimaging

Functional magnetic resonance imaging (fMRI) measures the change in the blood-oxygenation-dependent (BOLD) signal during rest or tasks. The BOLD signal is a relative, slow, and indirect measure of neural activity in the brain. In contrast to the high time-resolution of EEG and MEG, it provides insights into neural function of cortical and subcortical structures at high spatial resolution. Higher BOLD signals are usually interpreted as a net increase in neural activity. However, many factors modulate the BOLD signal, and its interpretation remains a challenge, especially in a developmental framework. Signal changes with age may often not reflect altered information processing in the brain (Harris et al. 2011) but could be due to concomitant task-independent changes. Such task-independent factors include changes in the consumption of oxygen, often referred to as 'neural energy use', and changes in the neurovascular coupling, the mechanism that links the increase in neural activity with an increase in cerebral blood flow (Harris et al. 2011). Despite these factors, the BOLD signal can provide insights into important aspects of network development, such as changes in the activation of specific regions and systems, and the connectivity and functional interaction of regions in the brain. Functional connectivity measures are based on the interregional temporal correlations of the BOLD signal time series and provide information about the coupling of spatially distinct regions during rest and experimental tasks. However, these measures do not allow conclusions to be drawn about how the regions influence each other. In contrast, effective connectivity can explain the direction of interaction and the influence of experimental manipulations on the network. A large number of fMRI studies have investigated reading and reading-related skills in dyslexia. The most consistent findings in fMRI studies on reading are shown in meta-analyses (Richlan et al. 2009; Maisog et al. 2008; Martin et al. 2016) and multicentre studies (Dutch and German-speaking samples: Brem et al. 2020). These suggest that reduced BOLD signal amplitudes in key regions of the reading network such as the left ventral occipito-temporal cortex and temporo-parietal regions and increased amplitudes in bilateral precentral gyri and anterior insula relate to overt or covert articulation processes (Brem et al. 2020). Underactivation of the left occipito-temporal cortex seems universal to the reading process in dyslexia, as shown in a meta-analysis that compared shallow and deep orthographies (Martin et al. 2016) and in comparisons of widely differing writing systems, such as English, French, and Chinese (Siok et al. 2004; Feng et al. 2020). However, compensatory mechanisms such as whole-word guessing and covert articulation may diverge depending on orthographic depth and writing system (Martin et al. 2016).

9.4.3 Phonological and Auditory Language Processing

A phonological processing deficit is reported across numerous behavioural studies as one of the core factors underlying impaired reading acquisition in dyslexia (see meta-analytic review in Melby-Lervåg et al. 2012). However, it is still unclear whether this deficit occurs primarily at the level of representations, storage and/or access, and/or manipulation of speech sounds. Longitudinal studies can help to clarify whether such impairments are transient states and characterize specific stages of learning to read, or may reflect a stable trait and are persistently associated with reading difficulties.

One example of an ERP thought to reflect several aspects of phonological representations is the late positivity component (LPC), an ERP component with positive polarity detected in temporo-parietal regions at around 500–900 ms after stimulation. It is slower than more basic auditory and visual responses, and it has been suggested to reflect access to and recognition of phonological representations in memory. Differences in the LPC have been previously reported between dyslexic and typical German readers in childhood (Hasko et al. 2013), adolescence

(Schulte-Körne et al. 2004), and adulthood (Rüsseler et al. 2003). A recent study examined the development of the LPC across five time-points in kindergarten and primary and secondary school using a phonological decision task involving words or pictures (German sample: Wachinger et al. 2018). In typical readers, LPC amplitudes elicited by words increased from kindergarten to 1st grade and then gradually decreased over time. In dyslexic readers, LPC amplitudes in left temporo-parietal channels were attenuated compared to typical readers in kindergarten and 1st grade. The findings of the study were limited to words that require grapheme-to-phoneme conversion to access phonological information, which unlike pictures allow access to phonology via semantic information. This finding suggests an atypical developmental curve in dyslexic readers related to this specific form of phonological access.

The development of phonological processing was also extensively studied using fMRI to provide insights into the activation and connectivity of the underlying brain networks. Changes in the phonological network from pre-readers to beginning readers (age 5–7 years) was reflected in decreased activation in the left temporo-parietal cortex (Polish sample: Łuniewska et al. 2019; US sample: Yu et al. 2018) and inferior frontal regions (Łuniewska et al. 2019). These changes, observed during an auditory rhyme or initial sound matching task, were interpreted as reflecting growing automatization of phonological processing. This maturation of functional activation was accompanied by parallel changes in functional connectivity from the left inferior parietal cortex to the left inferior frontal, left posterior occipito-temporal, and right angular gyri (Yu et al. 2018). Importantly, a developmental increase in functional connectivity was detected in children showing above-average gains in phonological skills, whereas a reduction was found for children with low gains in phonological skills (Yu et al. 2018). In addition, children with developmental dyslexia and children with familial risk for dyslexia showed altered developmental patterns of the phonological processing network during an auditory rhyme judgement task. Children with impaired reading presented delayed development of phonological network activation, including the middle and superior temporal gyri, insula, and right frontal sites. In contrast, children with familial risk showed atypical development by increasingly activating pre- and postcentral gyri, which may reflect enhanced silent articulation as a potential compensatory mechanism (Łuniewska et al. 2019). More insights on putative protective and compensatory neural activations were provided by a retrospective longitudinal study in a US sample (Yu et al. 2020). This study examined preschool children with familial risk that showed either typical or poor reading outcomes at school age, and these risk groups were also compared to typically reading children without risk. Underactivation of the left temporo-parietal cortex at a preschool age was suggested as a potential neural marker of familial risk for dyslexia. Moreover, typically reading children with familial risk showed hyper-activation of the right inferior frontal cortex during phonological processing at the pre-reading stage and more interhemispheric connectivity than children without risk. Because the activation of the right frontal region also correlated with later reading outcomes in all children with familial risk, this activation difference may reflect a putative protective mechanism supporting reading development in children at familial risk (Yu et al. 2020).

In emergent typical readers, the dominant reading strategy shifts from a phonological decoding strategy implemented in a dorsal stream involving the superior longitudinal and arcuate fasciculi to orthographic recognition implemented into a ventral stream involving the inferior fronto-occipital, uncinate, and inferior longitudinal fasciculi. This is supported by a longitudinal study in a US sample which found that reading practice can lead to reduced dorsal connectivity between the temporo-occipital and inferior parietal cortex and maintained ventral occipital-fusiform cortex connectivity (Wise Younger et al. 2017). Importantly, children with low gains in reading over time showed weaker connectivity in the dorsal stream and a decrease in ventral connectivity, indicating deviant reliance on ventral and dorsal stream resources for reading (Wise Younger et al. 2017). The transition from dorsal to ventral streams has received additional support from another longitudinal report of increased activation in superior temporal and inferior frontal gyri together with stronger occipital activations with reading practice (US sample: Smith et al. 2018).

The establishment of stable and accurate phonological representations depends upon other basic auditory mechanisms, such as processing of temporal information in speech. According to some sensory deficit theories, these may underlie phonological and reading impairments in dyslexia (Goswami 2011). Sensitivity to modulations in speech at different rates has been associated with synchronization of oscillatory activity of the auditory cortex across different frequency bands (Giraud and Poeppel 2012). This sensitivity was tested in a group of Dutch-speaking children with and without risk of dyslexia in kindergarten and 1st and 3rd grade (De Vos et al. 2017). EEG responses to auditory stimulation with 20 and 4 Hz speech modulations were recorded to trace the development of processing stimuli at phoneme and syllable rates. The authors found that phoneme-rate sensitivity increased with reading onset in 1st grade. Somewhat counterintuitively, this change was negatively correlated with reading and phonological skills. Moreover, the auditory evoked responses were stronger in children that would develop dyslexia after reading onset than in typical readers. This is consistent with similar group differences reported in adolescents and adults (Dutch-speaking: De Vos et al. 2017; Spanish-speaking: Lizarazu et al. 2015). Since these results emerged after reading onset, it is possible that they reflect the consequences rather than causes of poor reading. Importantly, these results suggest that dyslexic readers may present differences in the general auditory domain related to information-sampling processes (Giraud and Ramus 2013).

In sum, the first years in elementary school reflect a period when the phonological system's contribution to reading changes, along with a transition from a more indirect to a more direct reading strategy with increasing practice. There are signs of both protracted development of involved brain networks and altered processing in children with dyslexia and children with familial risk for dyslexia. Such alterations include additional activations of areas that support covert articulation, which are usually interpreted as compensatory mechanisms and might be pronounced in tasks challenging phonological processing.

9.4.4 Visual and Audiovisual Processing

A fundamental feature of writing systems is the link between phonological and visual information. Thus, several studies have focused on early responses to print in the ventral occipito-temporal cortex. A widely investigated ERP component in the visual domain is the N1, a response with negative polarity detected in occipito-temporal scalp electrodes and peaking around 150–220 ms after stimulus. N1 amplitudes have been linked to visual expertise, and familiar stimuli typically elicit larger amplitudes than unfamiliar stimuli (e.g., Tanaka and Curran 2001; Maurer et al. 2010), although they can be modulated by such factors as task demands and focus of attention (Yoncheva et al. 2015; Vogel and Luck 2000). In reading research, studies have frequently compared N1 responses to words with those to strings of false fonts, which are similar in their basic visual features. Most studies do not require explicit reading and use a paradigm that ensures visual attention with a simple target detection task that can be performed by young children. Maurer and colleagues used this approach and reported a non-linear trajectory of N1 sensitivity to words vs. symbols, emerging from kindergarten to 1st grade and levelling off with more extended practice from 2nd to 5th grade in German-speaking children (Maurer et al. 2006, Maurer et al. 2011). The stronger responses to words than to symbols were considered to indicate growing sensitivity to words that, in addition to mere visual familiarity, is driven by phonological and semantic associations after learning to read. Importantly, in dyslexic readers, the trajectory of this coarse N1 word-vs.-symbol sensitivity differed from that of typically reading children. The increase of the N1 amplitude observed in typical readers from kindergarten to 2nd grade was not detected in children with dyslexia, who also developed less sensitivity to words than did typical readers (Maurer et al. 2007). The group difference, however, levelled off in 5th grade (Maurer et al. 2011). This effect was taken as an indicator that dyslexic readers may be delayed in reaching the peak of the ventral occipito-temporal cortex word sensitivity curve.

Longitudinal fMRI studies on the typical development of print-sensitive processing provide convergent evidence for tuning of the ventral occipito-temporal cortex to print. One aspect of this tuning process is an increasing sensitivity to the visibility of words presented in noise (English-speaking sample: Ben-Shachar et al. 2011). The conjoint increase in sight word reading efficiency and the sensitivity to word visibility in the left ventral occipito-temporal cortex underline the importance of this region in extracting visual word forms for quick and efficient further processing. Another aspect of tuning to print is related to training studies in preliterate children and studies covering the first months and years of reading acquisition in children. This work shows a rapid emergence of print-sensitive processing of letters and words in the ventral occipito-temporal cortex after only a few weeks of grapheme–phoneme association training (Swiss-German-speaking sample: Brem et al. 2010) or after sensory-motor training in which participants copied letters and words on paper

(English-speaking sample: James 2010). These findings were also supported by studies that involved repeated measurements during the initial phase of formal reading acquisition. The children in these fMRI studies were assessed from preschool to the end of the first year at school at two-month intervals (French-speaking sample: Dehaene-Lambertz et al. 2018) or twice as 5-year-old pre-readers and 3 years later as emergent readers (English-speaking sample: Saygin et al. 2016). Both fMRI studies presented print as well as stimuli of other visual categories, such as faces, objects, and false-font strings, and provided important additional insights into the location and time-course of ventral occipito-temporal cortex specialization. Accordingly, specialization for novel, culturally defined categories (words and numbers) emerges in ventral occipito-temporal cortex areas that are not dedicated to processing specific visual categories such as faces (Dehaene-Lambertz et al. 2018), and the exact location is predetermined by early-developing extrinsic connections to other brain regions in the language network in pre-readers (Saygin et al. 2016).

A couple of longitudinal fMRI studies on adults from India with varying degrees of literacy have provided an interesting contribution to our understanding of visual specialization for reading in non-WEIRD populations (Skeide et al. 2017, Hervais-Adelman et al. 2019). The first study examined brain changes in illiterate adults associated with learning to read for 6 months (Skeide et al. 2017). The study found changes in functional connectivity between occipital cortex and subcortical regions in the midbrain and thalamus. In addition, these subcortical regions showed increased functional coupling with V1 and V4 right occipital areas. Although the symbols in the learnt script, Devanagari, represent pronunciation as in other alphabetic scripts, it is possible that their visual complexity elicited stronger recruitment of low-level visual areas. The second study focused on the same script and examined adults that varied in their literacy levels to characterize changes in the visual cortex after reading training (Hervais-Adelman et al. 2019). The longitudinal analysis showed that training induced additional responsivity to sentence reading in proximity to the VWFA. Interestingly, there were no differences after training in neighbouring visual areas sensitive to non-orthographic categories such as faces and houses. This result was interpreted as suggesting that literacy learning in adults enhanced the responses of a specific region rather than extending this sensitivity to a broader area in the occipito-temporal cortex.

Only a few studies have collected longitudinal fMRI data on the development of orthographic processing networks in children at risk for dyslexia or with poor reading skills. A small-scale longitudinal (3 months) training study focused on kindergarten English-speaking children with and without dyslexia risk that received supplemental teaching on phonological and alphabetic skills (Yamada et al. 2011). Seven no-risk children showed a shift from a bilateral to an increasingly left-hemispheric engagement of temporo-parietal regions in a letter vs. false-font visual task. In contrast, seven at-risk children showed delayed emergence of bilateral temporo-parietal print-sensitive responses. The children at risk recruited frontal regions, which was interpreted as reflecting articulatory and attentional compensatory strategies, and anterior cingulate regions, which may reflect motivational compensatory strategies (Yamada et al. 2011). A larger sample of 25 children with typical reading outcomes and 25 with poor outcomes was examined from the beginning of schooling at age 6–7 years to the age of 8–9 years (Polish sample: Chyl et al. 2019). Print processing was examined with fMRI at the first and the last (third) test time, and the results of the group of 8–9-year-old poor readers were also compared with those of younger children matched for reading level. Words and symbol strings were presented to the children, but no explicit decision was necessary to complete the task. Although no differences in print and print-sensitive processing emerged between the children with dyslexia and typically reading children at the first test time, differences were detected in the course of development: Typical readers showed developmental increases in activation to print in bilateral inferior frontal, precentral, bilateral parietal, and fusiform cortex regions, indicating the emergence of a canonical neural circuit for reading. However, children with dyslexia showed only increases of activation in the right occipital and left precentral areas. Similarly, print-sensitive processing yielded a stronger activation for print in left inferior frontal areas in typical readers but not in children with dyslexia, who showed increased activation for print in pre- and postcentral and occipital areas. The comparison with age-matched and reading-level-matched control groups indicates that the hypoactivation of the left fusiform and inferior frontal gyri in children with dyslexia can be explained as a dyslexia-specific atypical developmental trajectory rather than a consequence of lower expertise with reading (Chyl et al. 2019).

Changes in fMRI effective connectivity were observed during a reading task across development in a Norwegian sample (Morken et al. 2017). The study examined children from preliterate stages of reading (6 years) through the emergent (8 years) to the fully literate (12 years) stages. The network connectivity model included the inferior frontal gyrus, precentral and superior temporal gyri, and the occipito-temporal and inferior parietal cortex of the left hemisphere. Typical readers showed stable connectivity or a decrease over time in all five connections. However, children with dyslexia showed a different developmental course of connectivity: Connections from occipito-temporal to inferior frontal and precentral areas increased with emergent reading skills from 6 to 8 years and decreased afterwards from 8 to 12 years. Interestingly, no group differences were detected in connectivity at the fully literate stage even though the reading skills of the children with dyslexia were still significantly lower than those of typically reading peers. These first insights into effective connectivity suggest that the delayed development of functional interaction in children with dyslexia may critically affect early literacy development (Morken et al. 2017).

Different developmental trajectories from beginning to emergent readers in processing audiovisual information were also shown in a study presenting non-words together with matching and non-matching sounds (Wang et al. 2020). Gains in pseudoword reading performance were positively associated with emerging sensitivity to audiovisual matching of the stimuli in the left STG. Furthermore, functional connectivity analyses emerging from the left ventral occipito-temporal cortex showed different patterns of changes in connectivity over time between typical and poor readers. Typical readers exhibited increased coupling from the ventral occipito-temporal cortex to the right superior parietal lobe when processing matching stimuli. In poor readers, coupling from the ventral occipito-temporal cortex to inferior frontal and superior temporal gyri increased over time for processing of non-matching pairs. These results indicate that different processing strategies develop in typically and poorly reading children. For instance, the groups may differ in how they allocate attention to matching audiovisual information to support the decoding of non-words (Wang et al. 2020).

To summarize, the findings on visual and audiovisual processing suggest a delayed and altered trajectory of print-sensitive processing in the reading network of children with dyslexia. The studies currently available converge in showing a later and weaker sensitivity of the left ventral occipito-temporal cortex in affected children, which is possibly compensated by articulatory or attentional strategies. We assume that these effects indicate persistent rather than transient differences, but further longitudinal studies tracking development into adolescence or even adulthood are needed to confirm this hypothesis.

9.5 Early Markers of Future Reading Skills

So far, we have reviewed how various aspects of phonological and visual information processing in the brain may contribute to the development of dyslexia. But to what extent can neuroimaging data inform us about the development of future reading skills? A number of studies have linked various brain-functional, brain-structural, and behavioural measures at baseline to additional behavioural assessments several months or years later. The baseline measurements in these studies are often taken in kindergarten or at the very beginning of schooling. The studies examine the predictive value of cognitive and neuroimaging measures for literacy learning trajectories or outcomes. EEG is cost-effective and easy to apply in young children. Accordingly, this technique is often used to detect early biomarkers. Similar studies have also been conducted with various MRI metrics. The application of MRI is significantly more expensive than EEG measures. Moreover, the motion sensitivity of this technique poses a further challenge when examining young children. This caveat might, at least partly, explain the often rather small group sizes of MRI-based prediction studies. That said, MRI provides a range of metrics, such as functional activation, connectivity, and morphometric measures, that may explain important aspects of variation in children's reading skills. Therefore, MRI has the potential to complement prediction with behavioural and/or EEG measures and thus maximize accuracy.

Most prediction studies with EEG have focused primarily on variations of auditory oddball paradigms that elicit the automatic detection of deviances in tones and/ or phonemes. In one study, ERPs recorded as early as a few days after birth in a Finnish sample correlated with phonological skills, naming, and letter knowledge at 6.5 years (Guttorm et al. 2010). This study also found evidence for atypical right-hemisphere processing of speech in children at familial risk for dyslexia compared to children without risk. A Dutch study using similar auditory ERPs at 2 months of age found group differences between poor and fluent readers, but no significant correlations between the ERPs and reading in 2nd grade (van Zuijen et al. 2013). However, another study with a focus on reading abilities used EPRs in newborns to classify children as typical, poor, or dyslexic readers, as they were labelled eight years later (US sample: Molfese 2000). Correct classification rates of up to 81.25 % were achieved using the ERP measures. In another study in a Finnish sample, ERPs recorded in 6-month-old infants predicted 44% of variability in reading speed at the age of 14, and the prediction was mediated by letter naming at an intermediate age (Lohvansuu et al. 2018). Similarly, another study using EEG recordings in kindergartners showed that ERPs mismatch responses of automatic phoneme and tone deviances (e.g., /ba/ vs. /ta/, 1,000 Hz vs. 1,060 Hz tones) could improve prediction of future reading skills in 2nd and 3rd grade by 16% to 36% over using only behavioural measures (German-speaking sample: Maurer et al. 2009). Interestingly, in this study the mismatch response to a deviant phoneme was found to be particularly relevant for the long-term prediction of reading outcome in 5th grade, when behavioural predictors were no longer significant (Maurer et al. 2009). Altogether, these studies indicate that very early deficits in the developing auditory system may play an important role in the emergence of dyslexia, at least in some individuals.

Besides ERPs, less specific and task-independent measures derived from EEG have been explored as potential predictors of dyslexia. Since neuronal oscillations may be relevant to several aspects of language and cognition through development (e.g., multisensory integration: Bauer et al. 2020; working memory: Roux and Uhlhaas 2014; phonemic processing: Lehongre et al. 2011), Schiavone et al. (2014) explored markers derived from EEG frequency power during rest in a group of 3-year-old Dutch children. The study found differences in spectral amplitudes of lower delta and alpha bands between fluent and dysfluent readers, and correlations between these EEG measures and reading and phonological processing in 3rd grade. The results suggest that general aspects of brain maturation and oscillatory activity may be involved in dyslexia, but the functional significance of these brain measures remains to be clarified.

One of the first prospective longitudinal MRI studies examined the reading skills of typically and poorly reading children and adolescents 2.5 years after they underwent MRI scanning and baseline behavioural assessment (US sample: Hoeft et al. 2011). Interestingly, although behavioural measures could not reliably predict reading gains in subjects with dyslexia, a combination of functional activation in the right prefrontal cortex during a reading task and right superior longitudinal fasciculus white matter organization (measured by FA) predicted future reading gains in dyslexic readers with 72% accuracy (Hoeft et al. 2011). This seminal MRI study thus confirmed earlier EEG findings and obtained superior prediction accuracy when applying a combination of behavioural and neural measures. A series of other studies subsequently confirmed the potential of MRI to contribute to or even outperform behavioural prediction of reading gains or reading outcomes. They used a variety of measures ranging from brain structure (grey and white matter) through functional activation (auditory, phonological, and visual language processing) to connectivity between regions and measured these at preschool or school age (Kraft et al. 2016; Kuhl et al. 2020; Yu et al. 2018; Marks et al. 2019; Preston et al. 2016; Smith et al.

2018; Bach et al. 2013; Karipidis et al. 2018; Liebig et al. 2020; Borchers et al. 2019; Zuk et al. 2021). One study applied a logistic regression model and demonstrated a higher prediction success (80%) for distinguishing children at a pre-reading age who went on to develop dyslexia and typically reading children in the first two school years. This study compared measures of myelin concentration (T1) in the left anterior arcuate fasciculus to a purely behavioural model (German-speaking sample: Kraft et al. 2016). In another structural MRI study, children underwent DTI when starting to read at 6 years of age and were followed longitudinally to predict reading outcome at 8 years (US sample: Borchers et al. 2019). Mean FA of the left and right superior longitudinal fasciculus and left inferior cerebral peduncle significantly contributed to the prediction of later reading outcomes even when preliterate language skills and demographic covariates such as sex and family history of reading problems were controlled for. Another DTI study focused on kindergartners at risk for dyslexia that did not go on to develop poor reading at the end of 2nd grade (US sample: Zuk et al. 2021). These authors reported a significant prediction of reading skills with a combination of cognitive, demographic, and neural factors; a positive association with better word decoding was found for FA in the right superior longitudinal fasciculus in conjunction with socioeconomic background, age, sex, and phonological awareness (Zuk et al. 2021). In contrast to these findings, FA outperformed cognitive measures in a study examining an age range of 8–14 years with a gap of 2–4 years between behavioural tests (US sample: Gullick and Booth 2015). This study found that initial FA along the long segment of the arcuate fasciculus contributed uniquely to prediction of reading gains between baseline and follow-up assessments.

Similar contributions to early prediction have been made by functional MRI studies. In a phonological task on first sound matching of object words, the connection strength of the left inferior parietal cortex and the left posterior occipito-temporal cortex in pre-reading children predicted reading performance in 2nd and later school grades (Yu et al. 2018). Furthermore, the convergence of brain responses to speech and print in the superior and middle temporal gyri of kindergartners was shown to be a valuable measure for predicting reading outcome one year later (US sample: Marks et al. 2019). Print–speech convergence in the bilateral inferior frontal gyrus, left inferior parietal cortex, and fusiform gyrus in a group of beginning readers at around 8.5 years of age also predicted reading ability two years later (mean age 10.5 years). Interestingly, convergence in the left inferior frontal gyrus was associated with better reading skills later on, but convergence in the right inferior frontal gyrus predicted poor reading outcome (US sample: Preston et al. 2016). Another study focused on changes in the organization of functional connectivity within the reading network and reading skills in young readers (8–14 years). BOLD activations during a phonological rhyme judgement task and reading skills were measured longitudinally with ~2.5 years between baseline and follow-up. The results revealed a decrease in functional segregation in a network of auditory and visual regions that is important for reading and was associated with pseudoword reading at the second time point. Better pseudoword reading was thus related to a stronger interdependence between auditory and visual processing regions (US sample: Smith et al. 2018).

In a recent study, functional and structural data were combined in a prospective classification model that included brain measures of auditory cortex gyrification, its functional connectivity to the planum temporale, and the streamline density of the arcuate fasciculus at a preliterate age of 5–6 years (Kuhl et al. 2020). This model achieved considerable power to distinguish children with dyslexia from typical readers at age 8 years (area under the receiver operating characteristic curve = 0.86; a value of 1 indicates perfect prediction). Interestingly, a combined model including the same brain data and established gold-standard behavioural predictors only slightly outperformed the brain-based model (area under the receiver operating characteristic curve = 0.91).

Finally, a combination of EEG and fMRI measures has also been used to achieve better accuracy compared to purely behavioural prediction. The study by Bach and colleagues focusing on Swiss German-speaking children (Bach et al. 2013) showed that the combination of behavioural literacy precursors and sensitivity to print in the left ventral occipito-temporal cortex (indexed EEG and fMRI) in preschool could explain 84% of the variance in reading skills two years later and differentiate between typical and poorly reading children. A somewhat lower prognostic accuracy for reading outcomes in 2nd grade was achieved in another study with a Swiss German speaking sample (Karipidis et al. 2018). A recent prediction study in a larger sample combined demographic, genotypic, and behavioural measures with EEG auditory brainstem response to predict reading and spelling in 1st–3rd graders. Apart from standard behavioural measures, demographic, neural, and genotypic information added significantly to the detection of a risk for dyslexia in preschool children and to the prediction of reading and spelling outcomes (German-speaking sample: Liebig et al. 2020).

Most prediction studies are limited by small sample sizes, which may induce biased, unstable, and overfitting prediction models that perform poorly on new data (Ogundimu et al. 2016). Replication and comparison of the particular neural measures in independent studies are thus urgently needed to verify and confirm the predictive value reported in previous studies. Despite this limitation, the studies currently available converge in showing the potential of complementing the behavioural prediction of reading gains and reading outcomes with neural measures. Currently, the most promising neural predictors are EEG and MRI measures related to phonological and auditory information processing at a preliterate age. It remains to be seen whether other modalities, such as the visual processing of word forms, may also add value to early prediction models.

In sum, early auditory brain responses have shown considerable potential to inform researchers about future reading skills. Several studies also highlight the benefit of combining cognitive and brain data for predicting reading outcomes.

9.6 Current Limitations of Longitudinal Neural Studies of Dyslexia

Currently available studies vary widely in their methodological approaches, specific research questions, and observational time scales. Therefore, aggregating these findings into a coherent framework of the developmental trajectories in dyslexia requires additional empirical evidence. Moreover, virtually all dyslexia studies reviewed here are based on samples of children learning alphabetic orthographies in WEIRD countries. Therefore, any neurodevelopmental model of dyslexia that can currently be developed is restricted to such specific study populations and writing systems. Moreover, factors such as socioeconomic status and educational background are often homogenized in the study recruitment process. This can blur important information on potential differences in brain structure and function (Noble et al. 2005, Monzalvo et al. 2012) that may contribute to reading difficulties and explain divergent responses to supportive interventions. For example, SES was reported to affect both gains in reading performance and corresponding changes in neuroanatomy during intervention (Romeo et al. 2017). Similarly, exposure to reading material, additional training, and home literacy environment are often not taken into account despite increasing evidence of their influence on the development of the brain networks underlying language and literacy (Hutton et al. 2020, Hutton et al. 2017, Hutton et al. 2015). These environmental factors might have a particularly strong influence on brain development and the formation of functional networks in the early preliteracy stages, when the basis for later reading acquisition is laid. In addition, despite moderate sex differences in prevalence rates of dyslexia (Peterson and Pennington 2012), this factor is rarely considered in longitudinal studies. This is likely due to the very limited group sizes in longitudinal studies, which make further subgrouping difficult. Thus, the developmental pathways that may lead to the potential sex differences reported in the literature, including cortical thickness, grey and white matter volume, asymmetry of surface area, and white matter architecture, need to be studied in more detail in longitudinal studies to derive a better understanding of the underlying factors (Krafnick and Evans 2018). In future work, it would be important to consider more complex samples as well as environmental and genetic factors that could mediate between brain development and cognitive performance (see Chapter 6, Malanchini and Gidziela 2022; Chapter 7, Hoeft and Bouhali 2022; Chapter 8, Skeide 2022). This would improve current classification and prediction models and advance our biological understanding of dyslexia.

9.7 Conclusion

In this chapter, we reviewed the longitudinal neuroscientific literature on reading and dyslexia. Although it is difficult to draw a clear picture from this large body of heterogeneous results, the evidence consistently indicates that an atypical development of auditory, phonological, and audiovisual processing systems plays a key role in atypical learning in the domain of reading. In line with these functional findings, the emergence of dyslexia is related to the atypical development of grey matter in speech and phonological areas and a range of white matter tracts connecting the main regions of the language network. Studies that focus on the prediction of reading outcomes demonstrate that the detection of atypical neural responses in these systems improves the accuracy of early detection of future reading difficulties.

However, the data that are currently available are strongly biased towards children in WEIRD countries learning alphabetic writing systems; hardly anything is known about atypical learning trajectories in other cultural and educational environments. Furthermore, little is known about how sex differences and environmental, educational, or socioeconomic factors may interact with reading development. Collaborative multicentre studies that include larger samples of individuals with diverse social and cultural backgrounds are needed to examine the specific roles of these factors.

Suggestions for Further Reading

Chyl, K., G. Fraga González, S. Brem, and K. Jednoróg. 2021. 'Brain Dynamics of (a)typical Reading development: A Review of Longitudinal Studies'. *NPJ Science of Learning* 6 (1): 1–9.

Dehaene, S., L. Cohen, J. Morais, and R. Kolinsky. 2015. 'Illiterate to Literate: Behavioural and Cerebral Changes Induced by Reading Acquisition'. *Nature Reviews Neuroscience* 16 (4): 234–44.

Hannagan, T., A. Amedi, L. Cohen, G. Dehaene-Lambertz, and S. Dehaene. 2015. 'Origins of the Specialization for Letters and Numbers in Ventral Occipitotemporal Cortex'. *Trends in Cognitive Sciences* 19 (7): 374–82.

Price, C. J., and J. T. Devlin. 2011. 'The Interactive Account of Ventral Occipitotemporal Contributions to Reading'. *Trends in Cognitive Sciences* 15 (6): 246–253.

Skeide, M. A., U. Kumar, R. K. Mishra, et al. (2017). 'Learning to Read Alters Cortico-subcortical Cross-talk in the Visual System of Illiterates'. *Science Advances* 3 (5): e1602612.

10 Longitudinal Neural Observation Studies of Dyscalculia

Karin Kucian and Ursina McCaskey

10.1 Introduction

In this chapter, we summarize the current state of research that relates the inability to mentally operate with numbers to the development of brain mechanisms. Before looking at the details about longitudinal development of the neurocognitive underpinnings in numerical disorders we would like to briefly address the neural bases of typical numerical cognition and developmental dyscalculia. Here, we refer to the clinical classification of developmental dyscalculia, which defines it as a specific learning impairment affecting numerical cognition that emerges at a very early stage of development and cannot be explained by inappropriate schooling or lack of learning opportunities. Therefore, when we talk about developmental dyscalculia, we do not include acquired numerical disorders due to loss of an established ability (e.g., after brain damage). Rather, we focus on the inability to acquire numerical concepts or procedures due to developmental issues. Based on the knowledge generated in cross-sectional studies investigating numerical cognition, we elaborate on developmental changes in brain function and structure during typical development and in developmental dyscalculia. Finally, we discuss the predictive relation between brain characteristics and numerical skills.

10.2 The Brain Basis of Numerical Cognition

10.2.1 Brain Correlates of Typical Numerical Cognition

In recent years, we have gained a clearer image of neurocognitive processes during number processing and calculation. Specifically, brain imaging revealed the neural networks needed to carry out numerical operations (for reviews, see Arsalidou and Taylor 2011, Kucian et al. 2018, Menon 2015, Peters and De Smedt 2018). The intraparietal sulcus (IPS) has been confirmed as the core area of numerical processing within this distributed network. The IPS is activated whenever numbers or magnitudes are involved in a cognitive process. This key region processes numerosities even in the absence of numerical task demands. For instance, subjects may only have to look at changing amounts of dots (Notebaert et al. 2011). However, recent findings highlight that areas adjacent to the IPS in the parietal lobe, as well as frontal areas, are also crucial for number processing and calculation (Sokolowski et al. 2017). The neurocognitive network for numerical cognition includes brain areas for sensory processes such as visual or auditory identification of numbers or magnitudes, but also brain areas serving higher cognitive functions, which are mandatory cognitive skills for processing numbers and calculations. We will now introduce some of the major brain areas involved in number processing (see also Kucian 2016; and Chapter 2, Menon and Chang 2022). These areas are also illustrated in Figure 10.1.

10.2.1.1 Number Sense

The intraparietal sulcus (IPS) and superior parietal lobe (SPL) form a visuospatial representation of quantity. The right parietal lobe is more strongly involved in basic

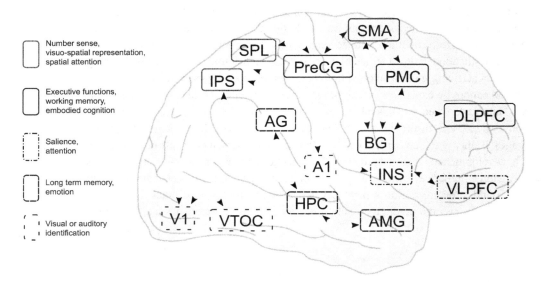

Figure 10.1 *Neural network of numerical cognition. Depicted are brain areas supporting numerical cognition including regions related to the number sense, visuospatial representation of quantities, or visuospatial attention; areas for decoding visual or auditory input; areas for storing numerical facts in long-term memory and emotional processes. Various brain regions in the frontal lobe involved in executive functions, short-term retention of numerical information, and embodied numerical cognition, and areas related to saliency and attentional processes are also depicted. Abbreviations are (in alphabetical order): A1: primary auditory cortex, AG: angular gyrus, AMG: amygdala, BG: basal ganglia, DLPFC: dorsolateral prefrontal cortex, HPC: hippocampus, INS: insula, IPS: intraparietal sulcus, PMC: premotor cortex, PreCG: precentral gyrus, SMA: supplementary motor area, SPL: superior parietal lobe, V1: primary visual cortex, VLPFC: ventrolateral prefrontal cortex, VTOC: ventral temporal-occipital cortex. Taken together, numerical cognition is implemented in the parietal lobes, the prefrontal cortices, and the dorsal and ventral visual pathways, as well as subcortical areas and the cerebellum. Within this network, a brain region is not devoted to one specific task, but its role depends on the cognitive demands placed by a certain numerical task.*

non-symbolic magnitude processing and the left parietal lobe contributes more strongly to the processing of symbolically presented numbers (Arabic digits) (Ansari 2007).

The SPL plays an important role for counting larger sets. SPL activation has been associated with spatial attention shifting (Piazza et al. 2003; Sathian et al. 1999; Zago et al. 2010).

10.2.1.2 Embodied Numerical Cognition

Counting has been related to finger representation involving a somatosensory integration located in the cortical motor system (precentral gyrus [PreCG]) and therefore represents an important example of embodied cognition in number processing (Krinzinger et al. 2011; Tschentscher et al. 2012).

10.2.1.3 Primary Identification

The primary visual cortex (V1) and ventral temporal-occipital cortex (VTOC) decode the visual input (Arabic digits, magnitudes, etc.). Specifically, parts of the right inferior temporal gyrus have been claimed to host the number form area (Yeo et al. 2017). Furthermore, the posterior occipital cortex has been reported to support subitizing, which is the enumeration of small quantities without counting (Demeyere et al. 2012). However, another study implicated bilateral posterior temporo-parietal areas in subitizing, which presumably relates to the function of the ventral visual stream (Vuokko et al. 2013).

The primary auditory cortex (A1) decodes auditory input. For the decoding of number words, primary auditory stimuli are further processed by the ventral auditory pathway, which is responsible for sound recognition, and is accordingly known as the auditory 'what' pathway.

10.2.1.4 Executive Functions and Short-term Memory

The frontal lobe is responsible for executive functioning, which plays a role in numerical problem solving. These functions include attention, working memory, planning and organizing, forethought, reasoning, problem solving, and impulse control.

The prefrontal cortex (dorsolateral prefrontal cortex [DLPFC]), premotor cortex (PMC), supplementary motor area (SMA), and parietal areas (IPS, supramarginal gyrus), together with subcortical areas (basal ganglia [BG]), create a hierarchy of short-term representations that allow manipulation of numerical input over several seconds.

The PMC has also been implicated in ordinality processing and counting, or the integration of quantity and ordinal processing (for a review, see Lyons et al. 2016).

Left-lateralized activation in premotor and temporal areas has been reported, which most likely reflects the verbal component of counting (subvocal articulation, verbal working memory) (Piazza et al. 2003; Zago et al. 2010). The activation of frontal areas during counting indicates the involvement of task guidance and attention (Vuokko et al. 2013).

10.2.1.5 Salience and Attention

Prefrontal processes related to saliency and attentional functions include the anterior insula (INS) and ventrolateral prefrontal cortex (VLPFC) and support the guidance and maintenance of behaviour in goal-directed mathematical problem solving.

10.2.1.6 Long-term Memory Formation

Long-term memory formation of numerical facts is anchored in the left angular gyrus (AG) in the parietal cortex as well as important subcortical areas such as the hippocampus (HPC) and the amygdala (AMG) (Menon 2015, McGaugh et al. 1996).

Finally, the AMG has been related to emotional responses in numerical cognition, such as maths anxiety (Kucian et al. 2018, Supekar et al. 2015, Young et al. 2012).

10.2.2 Brain Correlates of Developmental Dyscalculia

There is growing evidence that developmental dyscalculia is associated with alterations in brain function and brain structure. However, we are far from being able to draw a clear picture capturing the neural correlates of developmental dyscalculia. Differences in brain function, brain structure, functional and structural connectivity between different brain areas, or brain metabolism have been reported across almost the entire numerical brain network.

This wide range of differences in neural networks for numerical cognition might be explained by the heterogeneity of maths learning difficulties, but also by the differences between numerical tasks that have been used. At the behavioural level, we know that developmental dyscalculia is associated with a wide range of possible difficulties in numerical cognition, affecting non-symbolic magnitude processing, subitizing, counting, transcoding between number words, digits and quantities, spatial number representation, calculation procedures, the establishment and retrieval of numerical facts, written calculations, and the use of mathematical symbols (for further information on symptoms of developmental dyscalculia please, see, e.g., Castaldi et al. 2020; von Aster et al. 2005; von Aster, Kaufman, McCaskey, and Kucian, 2021). As outlined in the previous section, these numerical functions do not map onto the same parts of the number network in the brain. Also, considering the fact that each child with developmental dyscalculia reveals an individual behavioural pattern of problems, it is clear that the neural underpinnings of dyscalculia cannot be expected to be uniform. Furthermore, dyscalculia is often associated with domain-general cognitive problems, such as deficits in working memory, attention, or executive functions (planning, control, inhibition, monitoring, shifting). Here, the picture is again rather diverse. For example, impairments in visuospatial working memory have repeatedly been reported in some, but not all children with dyscalculia (Ashkenazi et al. 2013b; Rotzer et al. 2009; Szűcs et al. 2013; Geary et al. 2012; Geary et al. 2007). Consequently, not all affected children will show alterations in brain areas responsible for visuospatial working memory. Numerical cognition thus comprises a multitude of different numerical and non-numerical competencies, and children with dyscalculia differ in their individual profiles of strength and weaknesses. To make the story even more complex, co-occurring difficulties, such as attention deficits or dyslexia, are very common and have differential effects on the neural emergence of developmental dyscalculia.

So far, only a few studies have faced the challenge of examining the neural correlates of dyscalculia by means of electrophysiology and magnetic resonance imaging (MRI). The following sections will provide a short overview of neural alterations in dyscalculia focusing on brain structure, connectivity, metabolites, and function.

Brain structure: The acquisition of high-resolution anatomical brain scans by means of MRI allows the examination of structural brain differences between subjects with and without dyscalculia. Specifically, these images offer the opportunity to differentiate between grey and white brain matter, and to compare structural differences in these tissues. Numerous studies have shown that children with developmental dyscalculia show peculiarities in brain structure (Rotzer et al. 2009; Rykhlevskaia et al. 2009). Reduced grey matter volume has been reported in and adjacent to the IPS and in frontal and subcortical areas, which are important for the development of numerical as well as general cognitive abilities (working memory, attention, logical reasoning). A more recent approach is to investigate the folding complexity of the brain surface. Moreau et al. (2019) reported no differences in surface folding complexity between adults with dyscalculia or dyslexia or combined dyslexia/dyscalculia. Similarly, Skeide et al. (2018) reported reduced surface folding associated with reading and mathematical difficulties – but not with isolated difficulties. This effect was found in the right parahippocampal gyrus, a region implicated in visual associative learning. Ranpura et al. (2013) reported a reduction in cortical thickness in children with dyscalculia, most prominently in the left temporal and right inferior frontal lobes – areas associated with setting up and monitoring ongoing tasks. They argue that cortical thickness is reflective of genetic and environmental factors affecting brain development in dyscalculia.

Brain connectivity: Since an entire network is involved in number processing and calculation, it is relevant to examine white matter tracts that allow communication between distant areas. Successful numerical cognition depends on the development and organization of these networks in the brain. So far, only a few studies have looked at structural connectivity in developmental dyscalculia (Kucian et al. 2014; Rykhlevskaia et al. 2009). Results indicate altered fibre connections between parietal, temporal, and frontal areas of the numerical network. In particular, the superior longitudinal fasciculus seems to be affected, especially in parts that are adjacent to key areas for number processing, namely the intraparietal sulcus (Kucian et al. 2014; for reviews of typical development of numeracy, please see Matejko and Ansari 2015; Peters and De Smedt 2018).

Most functional connectivity studies in children with dyscalculia revealed increased functional coupling between parietal, occipital, temporal, and frontal areas (Jolles et al. 2016; Michels et al. 2018; Rosenberg-Lee et al. 2011). We assume that the enhanced synchronization of activation between these areas is a consequence of the impaired structural connectivity. It could mean that poorly connected brain areas increase their coupling to compensate and execute numerical tasks. A recent study also showed that the hyperconnectivity in children with dyscalculia disappeared after numerical intervention, while their maths abilities improved (Michels et al. 2018).

Brain metabolites: Magnetic resonance spectroscopy provides a measure of brain metabolite concentration. To our knowledge, only one case study of an 18-year-old man with dyscalculia employed this method to investigate changes in brain metabolites related to dyscalculia (Levy et al. 1999). Findings revealed decreased choline and creatine levels, as well as a mild focal decrease in N-acetyl-aspartate. The authors concluded that changes in these brain metabolites are due to an alteration in cell density, impaired cellular energy metabolism in neurons, and mild general neural loss. The maturation of brain metabolites is clearly a field that has been neglected in dyscalculia research so far. However, recent findings suggest that neurotransmitter concentrations in the adolescent brain are associated with the individual mathematical education level (Zacharopoulos et al. 2021).

Brain activation: Several studies have investigated brain activation in children, adolescents, or adults with dyscalculia using different types of numerical tasks. The reported findings are mixed, indicating both decreased and increased activation in affected individuals (for reviews, see Kaufmann et al. 2011; Kucian 2016). One likely explanation is the variety of numerical tasks chosen, which may have a great influence on brain activation. Reduced activation in the parietal lobules has been detected using different numerical tasks ranging from basic number sense (Price et al. 2007) to the understanding of ordinality (Kucian et al. 2011), from symbolic number comparison (Mussolin et al. 2010) to arithmetic (multiplication: Berteletti et al. 2014), approximate addition (Kucian et al. 2006), and even for non-numerical tasks that are processed by overlapping networks (spatial working memory: Rotzer et al. 2009). In addition to decreased activation in key areas for numerical cognition, brains of people with dyscalculia do not seem to be modulated like brains of typically developing people. Specifically, typically developing people show greater activation the more complex and demanding the numerical tasks become, whereas people with developmental dyscalculia do not show such a modulation (Ashkenazi et al. 2013a; Ashkenazi et al. 2012; De Smedt et al. 2011; Mussolin et al. 2010; Price et al. 2007; Soltész et al. 2007).

In contrast to reported reduction of brain activation in the parietal lobe, two studies have reported enhanced activity in parietal regions (Kaufmann et al. 2009; Rosenberg-Lee et al. 2015). The authors argue that the increased parietal activation might be driven by compensatory mechanisms (Kaufmann et al. 2009), or may be a result of inappropriate connectivity, rather than substantial underactivation (Rosenberg-Lee et al. 2015).

Non-symbolic number comparison has not revealed activation differences between children with and without dyscalculia (Kovas et al. 2009; Kucian et al. 2006). This fits the observation that non-symbolic number processing deficits are less consistently found in dyscalculia than symbolic number processing deficits (Smedt et al. 2013).

Increased activation of the postcentral gyrus in dyscalculic children has been argued to result from the dependence on finger-based strategies (using finger counting) when solving arithmetical tasks (for review, see Kaufmann et al. 2011; Kaufmann et al. 2008).

As highlighted in the previous section, frontal areas have been claimed to be equally important for number processing and calculation (Sokolowski et al. 2017). In particular, several imaging studies have reported altered brain activation in distributed frontal areas, including the superior, middle, and inferior frontal gyrus, the medial prefrontal cortex, paracentral gyrus, cingulate gyrus, and the insula (Kaufmann et al. 2011; Kucian et al. 2011; Kucian et al. 2006; Kucian et al. 2011; Mussolin et al. 2010; Price et al. 2007; Rosenberg-Lee et al. 2011; Rotzer et al. 2009). These frontal areas host executive functions, which are crucial for number processing and calculation. These findings are in line with behavioural deficits in executive functioning found in children with dyscalculia (attention, e.g. Askenazi and Henik 2010; working memory, e.g. Geary et al. 2012; problem solving, e.g. Osmon et al. 2006). Similar to the lack of brain modulation in parietal areas, no modulation in frontal areas was found for individuals with dyscalculia while performing easier versus more complex arithmetic tasks (Ashkenazi et al. 2013a; Berteletti et al. 2014).

Occipito-temporal areas and subcortical structures such as the thalamus, basal ganglia, and hippocampus also seem to be affected in children with dyscalculia (Ashkenazi et al. 2013a; Delazer et al. 2004; Kaufmann et al. 2011; Kucian et al. 2006; Kucian et al. 2011; Price et al. 2018; Rosenberg-Lee et al. 2011). Altered brain activation in these areas is thought to be related to deficits in Arabic digit processing as well as the memorization of numerical facts.

The stronger recruitment of areas associated with executive functions, memory formation, or finger representation in children with dyscalculia may relate to compensatory mechanisms, or may be a consequence of deficient automatized access to number representations.

10.3 Development of Neural Functions in Numerical Cognition

In this section, we provide an overview of the neural development underlying the emergence and refinement of numerical cognition. The focus of the first part is on functional brain development, while the focus of the second part is on structural brain development. In both sections, we will first present results for typical development, before elaborating on the few studies focusing on dyscalculia.

10.3.1 Changes in Brain Function During Numerical and Arithmetical Development

10.3.1.1   Neural Development of Non-symbolic Numerical Processing

The IPS is known as one of the core regions of numerical processing (see Section 10.2.1). As mentioned earlier, the right IPS seems to be more strongly involved in non-symbolic magnitude processing (e.g., comparison of dot arrays), while the left IPS is more strongly activated when processing numerical symbols (e.g., Arabic digits) (Ansari et al. 2005).

Infants are already able to discriminate between numerosities (Xu and Spelke 2000) and this ability refines gradually (e.g., 2:3 ratios are mastered earlier than 7:8 ratios), peaking rather late in development at the age of about 30 years (Halberda and Feigenson 2008; Halberda et al. 2012). During this kind of non-symbolic numerical processing activation in the IPS is already found in 4-year-old children. Adults solving the same task showed robust bilateral activation of the IPS, while children's activation was predominantly in the right IPS (Cantlon et al. 2006). In a further study targeting non-symbolic magnitude comparison, adults showed greater modulation by numerical distance specifically in the left IPS, as compared to school children (Ansari and Dhital 2006). The authors of a recent study used steady-state visual evoked potentials (SSVEP) to measure the neural sensitivity for numerosity and non-numerical properties (e.g., total area, size) of dot arrays in children between 3 and 10 years of age as well as adults (Park 2018). Similar to adults, children exhibited strong SSVEP sensitivity to numerosity in the right occipital cortex. However, the data further revealed that this neural sensitivity to numerosity was almost non-existent in 3-year-olds and then gradually emerged as a function of age. Together, the existing studies show that non-symbolic numerical processing elicits neural activation in right parieto-occipital regions in early childhood. In the course of development, this predominantly right-lateralized neural activation eventually shifts to a bilateral activation and shows a greater sensitivity with increasing age.

10.3.1.2   Neural Development of Symbolic Numerical Processing

At the age of 2 or 3 years, children learn number words and acquire basic counting skills. Furthermore, they successively connect these verbal concepts to Arabic digits. Results of imaging studies indicate that the left IPS plays an important role in the processing of numerical symbols (Ansari 2007; see Piazza et al. 2007 for Arabic digits and Cohen Kadosh et al. 2007 for number words). How the contribution of the left IPS to symbolic processing changes in the course of development has been examined in several studies (Emerson and Cantlon 2015; Vogel et al. 2015; Matejko and Ansari 2019). Emerson and Cantlon (2015) investigated the number-related neural response in children aged 4 to 9 years by means of longitudinal fMRI. They found that the neural response amplitude in the right IPS correlated significantly between the first and the second measurement 2 to 3 years later, indicating a stable response to numbers. In contrast, the left IPS showed a correlation between the change of neural activation and number acuity, suggesting that the neural response develops along with the refinement of numerical skills (see also Kaufmann et al. 2011). Similarly, Vogel et al. (2015) observed stable activation of the right IPS and age-related changes in the left IPS in children between 9 and 14 years, and Matejko et al. (2019) found the same effect for symbolic ordinal processing.

Although the parietal lobe and specifically the IPS play a key role in numerical cognition, several studies reported developmental changes in the entire brain. For example, choosing the larger of two Arabic numerals revealed greater activation in parietal regions of adult participants, while children engaged frontal brain areas to a larger extent. The authors relate the observed differences to an increased automaticity in mapping numerical symbols and their magnitudes, which in turn requires less engagement of frontal areas (Ansari et al. 2005). However, some studies investigating non-symbolic as well as symbolic number processing did not find this fronto-parietal shift over the developmental course. Comparisons between adults and school-aged children showed greater activation in parietal (e.g., SPL) and frontal regions (e.g., insula) and in the number form area for adults (Holloway and Ansari 2010; Vatansever et al. 2020).

As the mapping between symbols and underlying magnitudes emerges, changes also occur with respect to the communication of the right parietal cortex and other brain regions involved in numerical symbol processing. Park et al. (2014) scanned children aged between 4 and 6 years while they performed non-symbolic (dot arrays) and symbolic (Arabic numerals) magnitude comparisons. Using psychophysiological interaction (PPI) analyses, they found that two brain regions show increased effective connectivity with the right SPL specific to symbol number processing, namely the supramarginal gyrus and the superior precentral gyrus. The strength of connectivity was further shown to be correlated with age and mathematical performance, indicating that these connectivity patterns may be crucial for mastering symbol-to-number mapping.

A recent study investigated children's brain activity during naturalistic viewing of educational movie clips (with contents related to counting, word reading, and phonetics). Developing regions related to numbers were mainly found in the parietal and occipital cortex, indicating a gradual strengthening of the emerging network. In contrast, child-specific activity was observed in the anterior temporal lobe and inferior frontal gyri located within the reading and numerical network. The authors also reported, amongst others, child-specific patterns of functional connectivity between the bilateral inferior frontal gyrus with regions of the prefrontal cortex. This pattern likely vanishes across development, possibly reflecting the acquisition of new skills and the abandonment of child-unique strategies (e.g., counting from one instead of from the larger addend) (Kersey et al. 2019). We think that this work could serve as a role model for developmental science, as the authors take into account that children not only show a gradual acquisition of adult-like behaviour, but also may take neurocognitive 'detours' to acquire a certain skill.

In summary, the literature reveals that the acquisition of Arabic symbols and their mapping to the underlying magnitudes mainly leads to a developmental increase in activation in the left IPS, while the right IPS shows stable activation across development. Furthermore, children show increased activation in frontal regions while neural activity in adults is more confined to parietal regions. However, establishing symbol-to-number mapping not only alters brain activation but also leads to developmental changes in connectivity between the right SPL, left parietal and right frontal areas. It is important to bear in mind that some of the observed developmental changes might reflect the successive refinement towards an adult-like network, while others might be related to transient stages of numerical development. However, one study found that children and adults recruit the left IPS to a similar extent when the cognitive demands of the arithmetic task are comparable (Matejko and Ansari 2019).

10.3.1.3   Neural Development of Arithmetical Processing

Soon after children have learnt to count, which happens before formal schooling, they start to solve simple arithmetic problems. They use finger counting to solve addition problems (such as 2+2), eventually leading to the memorization of arithmetic facts (through repetition). The acquisition of fact knowledge is a crucial step in mathematical learning that enables children to solve arithmetic problems efficiently and subsequently progress to more difficult mathematical operations. There has been considerable research investigating the neural changes underlying arithmetical processing over the course of typical development. Despite a substantial overlap between children and adults, children show greater activation in the prefrontal and anterior cingulate cortex, as well as in the hippocampus and basal ganglia. This observation could point to the fact that children need more working memory, attentional, and memory resources to perform mental arithmetic. Young adults, however, show increased activation in left parietal regions, such as the IPS, the supramarginal gyrus, and the occipito-temporal cortex, suggesting a functional specialization of the left parietal cortex for arithmetic (Rivera et al. 2005; Kucian et al. 2008).

Rosenberg-Lee and co-authors explored arithmetic problem solving over a shorter period of development (Rosenberg-Lee et al. 2011). After one year of schooling, they found that, compared to 2nd graders, 3rd graders showed increased activation in the bilateral IPS, the right AG, and the bilateral SPL. In addition, occipital regions, the parahippocampal gyrus, and the left DLPFC revealed greater neural response. Parallel to the increases in activation, 3rd graders also showed significantly higher functional connectivity between the left DLPFC and posterior brain regions. Qin et al. (2014) focused on the transition from finger counting to fact retrieval in 7–9-year-old children and reported a longitudinal activation increase in the bilateral hippocampi during addition problem solving. They also demonstrated that children's retrieval-strategy use was positively correlated with the strength of hippocampal connectivity with prefrontal and parietal areas. Comparing the results of the children with adolescent and adult data sets further revealed that the initial increase in hippocampal engagement during middle childhood decreases thereafter, reaching adult-like levels by adolescence. These results suggest a non-linear development of arithmetic processing in the hippocampus, raising the question of whether this is also the case for parietal brain regions. Chang et al. (2016) demonstrated that the activation in subsections of the parietal lobules (namely the bilateral ventral IPS, the anterior AG, and the posterior SMG) increases steadily from childhood to adulthood. In contrast, they observed an inverted u-shaped growth in the left anterior SMG across age, with a peak in activation during adolescence. Moreover, the same region exhibited greater functional connectivity with temporal and prefrontal areas. As adolescents performed equivalent to adults, these results suggest that during adolescence SMG activation might be upregulated to reach the proficiency level of adults.

One study did not investigate age-related effects but focused on children's retrieval fluency to examine changes in brain activity and connectivity. Children with higher retrieval fluency showed greater activation in hippocampal and prefrontal regions and the AG. Moreover, effective connectivity analyses identified strong interactions of the hippocampus with the DLPFC and VLPFC, regions known to be involved in memory retrieval (Cho et al. 2012).

Most of the studies on arithmetic processing were conducted with paradigms measuring addition. Not all arithmetic operations rely on the same strategy, however, and therefore also differ with respect to their underlying neural response. An age-related activation increase in the hippocampus and the left MFG was only found for addition, while subtraction was related to the opposite effect in the same regions (Evans et al. 2016). In line with this, a developmental decrease of activation was found in the MFG and IFG during subtraction in adolescents (Artemenko et al. 2018), while addition and multiplication lead to an increase in AG and middle temporal gyrus activity in childhood and adolescence (Prado et al. 2014; Artemenko et al. 2018). Furthermore, subtraction is related to an increase across school grades in the right posterior SPL (Prado et al. 2014). In general, these results suggest that a developmental shift from effortful counting strategies to memory-based verbal strategies (e.g., addition and multiplication) is related to an increase in activity of the hippocampus, AG, and MTG. In contrast, operations that rely to a greater extent on calculation (e.g., subtraction) result in developmental changes in number-related areas, such as the IPS and SPL.

To summarize, during the acquisition of arithmetic fact knowledge, a fronto-parietal activation shift can be observed from childhood to adulthood. While activation in some of the parietal regions follows a linear increase during development, the anterior SMG and the hippocampi show an inverted u-shaped development, peaking during adolescence. Connectivity between the hippocampus and frontal and parietal areas increases, emphasizing the importance of these memory-related circuits for the transition from counting to arithmetic fact retrieval. Finally, arithmetic operations that are calculation-intensive are related to developmental activation increases in number-related areas, while operations that depend on the transition to fact retrieval show developmental increases in memory-related areas.

10.3.1.4 Functional Changes in Children with Developmental Dyscalculia

The picture of the development of numerical abilities in children with dyscalculia is far from complete. Behavioural longitudinal studies show that although children with mathematical difficulties show growth in mathematical abilities, they do not catch up to their peers, suggesting that the deficits in numerical abilities are stable over time (Nelson and Powell 2018). Findings from neuroimaging studies are mixed – that is, both increased and decreased activation has been reported in the numerical processing network of children with dyscalculia (see Section 10.2.2). To date, only one study has examined the longitudinal brain-functional development of children with dyscalculia (McCaskey et al. 2017). At baseline, children with dyscalculia aged between 8 and 11 years mainly recruited a right-lateralized network when performing symbolic ordinal judgements, while typically developing peers showed a bilateral activation of the IPS. At follow-up four years later, dyscalculic adolescents showed age-related activation increases in parietal (e.g., bilateral IPS) as well as frontal (e.g., IFG, insula) regions compared to typically developing adolescents. These results point to delayed maturation of parietal regions in children with dyscalculia. At the same time, the data also indicate that affected children might rely on compensatory mechanisms or different but less effective task solving strategies. Interestingly, an intervention study found an increase of activation in parietal areas in children with dyscalculia after the completion of a 5-week number line training (Kucian et al. 2011; see also Chapter 12, Iuculano 2022). A recent study investigated children's brain activity before the start of formal mathematical education (at 3 to 6 years of age) and related this data to mathematical abilities measured four years later. Children who later developed dyscalculia could be distinguished from control children by the regional functional activity of the right posterior parietal cortex, the network-level functional activity of the right DLPFC, and the effective connectivity of these regions measured in early childhood (Kuhl et al. 2021). It is important to note that there is an urgent need for additional studies confirming these first results and further investigating developmental aspects of the numerical network in dyscalculia.

10.3.2 Changes in Brain Structure Related to Numerical and Arithmetical Development

10.3.2.1 Structural Changes in Typical Development

To date, there are only a few studies investigating the anatomical changes in relation to numerical and arithmetical abilities (Rivera et al. 2005; Schel and Klingberg 2017; Torre et al. 2020). Moreover, several different anatomical measures are examined in these studies. The results are somewhat mixed, giving an incomplete and patchy picture. Rivera et al. (2005) investigated if the observed functional fronto-parietal shift (see Section 10.3.1) was accompanied by changes in brain anatomy in these regions. They found no age-related changes in grey matter volume in any of the parietal and frontal regions between 8 and 19-year-old participants. Another study looked at the relationship between individual differences in reading and mathematical abilities with cortical thickness and surface area in 6 to 22-year-olds. The results revealed a positive correlation between cortical thickness and reading ability in the left SMG and the fusiform gyrus in adolescents and young adults only (15–22 years). However, no such relationship was found for mathematical abilities (Torre et al.

2020). In contrast, Schel and Klingberg (2017) demonstrated that the cortical thickness of the right IPS is related to mathematical abilities over development. Interestingly, they found that thinner cortex is associated with better mathematical and working memory performance in children below 12 years. In participants aged 14 years and older, this association was only found for mathematical performance. The authors concluded that this sub-region of the right IPS (connected to the frontal cortex) possibly transforms into a maths-specific region during development.

In general, the literature on anatomical changes in relation to numerical abilities is scarce. Up to now, we can conclude that anatomical changes seem to be less prominent compared to the functional changes reported here.

10.3.2.2 Structural Changes in Children with Developmental Dyscalculia

To date, only two studies looked at developmental anatomical changes in children with dyscalculia (Ranpura et al. 2013; McCaskey et al. 2020). The first study investigated the correlation of grey and white matter volume, cortical thickness, and surface area between 8 and 14 years. Age-related changes were found for the cingulate cortex, revealing a decrease of cortical thickness over time for typically developing children and an increase in dyscalculic children. Cortical surface area increased in frontal and left supramarginal areas, but only in typically developing individuals. In children with dyscalculia, but not in typical controls, grey matter volume decreased in the primary motor cortex and increased in the superior occipital gyrus and the DLPFC. Moreover, dyscalculics showed delays in white matter volume development. While age-related increases were found in parietal and frontal areas of typically developing children, the dyscalculic participants showed stable or decreased white matter volume over time in these areas (Ranpura et al. 2013). The authors concluded that their results provide evidence for disrupted cortical maturation of the neural basis for number processing, which may result from learning and experience, but also point to genetically shaped individual differences (Ranpura et al. 2013). The second study investigated grey and white matter volumes by means of longitudinal data of typically developing and dyscalculic children. In children affected by dyscalculia, persistently reduced grey matter volume was found in bilateral parietal areas (inferior parietal lobule, IPS, SMG, precuneus), right superior occipital gyrus (SOG), and bilateral frontal regions including the insula. In line with that, white matter volumes were mainly reduced in the bilateral inferior and superior longitudinal fasciculi. These results indicate that, in dyscalculia, the known structural differences in the fronto-parietal numerical network and the long association fibres persist from childhood into adolescence (McCaskey et al. 2020).

In general, the literature to date suggests that children with developmental dyscalculia exhibit a different developmental trajectory of the cortical surface area and persistently have lower grey and white matter volumes over time. More studies in typically as well as atypically developing children are needed, however, to draw conclusions about the structural development of brain networks related to numerical and arithmetic abilities. For instance, to our knowledge, there is currently no study investigating the development of structural connectivity and its association with mathematical skills (but see Kuhl et al. 2021). Of particular interest would be research investigating the trajectory of fibre tracts during the acquisition of symbol-magnitude associations or the transition from counting to fact retrieval. Finally, it is important to mention that, to date, the relationship between function and structure and its changes is not fully understood (Zatorre et al. 2012), meaning that better performance can, for example, be associated with functional and structural increase, but also with functional and structural decrease depending on the brain region or cognitive task demands. Filling this gap is essential to detect developmental deviations at an early stage.

10.4 Prediction of Brain Development and Numerical Abilities

Dyscalculia-specific severe numerical learning problems are very common in our society and create significant obstacles in daily lives, school settings, and professional careers. Therefore, a major societal goal should be to identify affected children as early and reliably as possible and offer them adequate support (see Parts VIII to X).

At the behavioural level, there is growing longitudinal evidence that early numerical competencies are good predictors for later development of calculation skills. Early basic numerical skills include number knowledge, verbal counting, object counting, non-symbolic magnitude comparison, number comparison, rapid enumeration of small quantities without counting (subitizing), and simple calculations, which have all been identified as strong predictors for later mathematical achievement in primary school (e.g., Gallit et al. 2018; Jordan et al. 2009; Krajewski and Schneider 2009; Toll et al. 2016). In general, one can differentiate between symbolic numerical abilities, including the comparison of two sets of objects, and symbolic skills, including actively handling Arabic digits (e.g., number comparison, linking numbers and magnitudes, reading numbers). Particularly these symbolic skills are the most powerful predictors of later mathematical skills (Caviola et al. 2020; Göbel et al. 2014; Kolkman et al. 2013; Krajewski and Schneider 2009; Missall et al. 2012; Szkudlarek and Brannon 2017; Toll et al. 2016). Accordingly, one can conclude that numerical difficulties manifest as early symbolic processing deficits, eventually leading to dyscalculia.

As outlined in the previous section, longitudinal studies are scarce, especially in children and in combination with brain imaging. So far, there have been only a few attempts to combine brain-imaging with behavioural data to predict numerical abilities. One study investigated whether the behavioural numerical skill level predicts the corresponding brain activation (Grabner et al. 2007). It turned out that adults with higher mathematical competencies displayed stronger activation of the left AG, indicating a stronger reliance on automatic, language-mediated numerical fact retrieval (Grabner et al. 2007). Another line of research explored whether a neural biomarker predicts numerical abilities (Boulet-Craig et al. 2017; Cantlon and Li 2013; Emerson and Cantlon 2012; Matejko et al. 2013; Skagerlund et al. 2019). Matejko et al. (2013) used diffusion tensor imaging to investigate whether differences in white matter fibre tracts predicted performance on a maths test in young adults. Their findings suggest that the white matter connectivity of the left parietal lobe (including the left superior longitudinal fasciculus, left superior corona radiata, and the left corticospinal tract) is critical for complex mathematical processing (Preliminary Scholastic Aptitude Test [PSAT] including word problems, geometry, algebraic equations, and complex arithmetic). Similarly, functional connectivity between the right IPS and the left supramarginal gyrus and premotor cortex bilaterally has been demonstrated to be a unique predictor of mathematical ability in adulthood (Skagerlund et al. 2019) – unique in terms of excluding confounding effects of different executive functions that are known to be processed as well by the parietal cortices. This identified network comprising the IPS, premotor cortex, and the supramarginal gyrus may support the ability to integrate symbolic and non-symbolic magnitudes in ordered sequences, which subsequently facilitates arithmetic calculation procedures (Skagerlund et al. 2019). In addition, the amplitude of parieto-occipital activity during a visual short-term memory task has been found to be associated with mathematical reasoning and calculation fluency in adults (Boulet-Craig et al. 2017).

In children, two studies examined brain activation while watching educational videos focusing on mathematical abilities (Cantlon and Li 2013; Emerson and Cantlon 2012). It turned out that the functional connectivity between frontal and parietal regions predicted children's basic numerical matching skills as well as their scores on a standardized maths test (Emerson and Cantlon 2012). The link between this fronto-parietal connectivity and mathematical skills was domain-specific in the sense that it was independent of individual verbal intelligence, age, or other functionally connected networks, such as the face processing network. fMRI also demonstrated that the degree to which children showed adult-like brain activation of the IPS was correlated with their performance on a maths test (Cantlon and Li 2013). In addition, the IPS activation was selectively driven by numerical content both when watching videos with numerical content and when the children were engaged in a number matching task. Furthermore, activation induced by watching videos with numerical content was more closely related to children's maths performance than the activation induced by solving the numerical task. Accordingly, the authors concluded that the natural viewing paradigm was better suited for predicting children's mathematical development than the traditional experimental paradigm (Cantlon and Li 2013).

All these studies provide important insights into the relation of neural characteristics and numerical skills by identifying neural network components which are linked to better numerical abilities or to impaired numerical cognition. However, it is important to note that these studies are based on a correlational approach, which cannot reveal causation. Furthermore, all studies described herein investigated the association between neural measures and numerical abilities at the same time. Longitudinal studies testing whether a certain neural biomarker has the potential for forecasting future mathematical development are of higher causal relevance.

A handful of studies tested the predictive value of neurobiological measures on mathematical development in children (Dumontheil and Klingberg 2012; Evans et al. 2015; Price et al. 2018; Schwartz et al. 2020; Supekar et al. 2013). Supekar et al. (2013) investigated the neural predictors of individual responses to an 8-week maths intervention in 3rd grade children. After maths tutoring, a significant improvement in arithmetic problem solving strategies from counting to fact retrieval was observed. Interestingly, the volume of the hippocampus (r = 0.55) and its functional connectivity with dorsolateral prefrontal cortices and the basal ganglia before the intervention (mean r = 0.62) predicted individual performance improvements after tutoring. In contrast, no initial behavioural measure, such as intelligence, working memory, or mathematical abilities, predicted performance improvements.

Evans et al. (2015) provided important insights into brain structure and connectivity relating to the longitudinal growth of children's mathematical skills over a 6-year period. Specifically, grey matter volume in the ventral temporo-occipital cortex, the posterior parietal cortex, and the prefrontal cortex predicted the development of numerical skills from age 8 into adolescence. In addition, the strength of functional connectivity among these regions also predicted individual gains in numerical abilities. In contrast, behavioural measures, such as mathematical or reading skills, intelligence, and working memory, did not predict learning trajectories, demonstrating the unique value of neurobiological approaches for forecasting future numerical skills.

In line with this work, resting-state connectivity of the right IPS and the contralateral IPS at the end of 1st grade has been shown to be a strong predictor (mean r = 0.63) of arithmetic performance at the end of 2nd grade (Price et al. 2018). These findings implicate that a well-established interhemispheric IPS connection is important for arithmetical development in children. In contrast, stronger connectivity between the left IPS and the left AG with mainly ipsilateral areas of the frontal and temporal cortices were negatively correlated (mean r = −0.59) with arithmetic competences one year later. These different findings suggest that parietal sub-regions are functionally and structurally heterogeneous subdivisions of the neural network underlying numerical development.

Recent work conducted functional and structural MRI in 3–6-year-old children without formal mathematical learning experience and identified those children at the age of 7–9 years who developed dyscalculia (Kuhl et al. 2021). Future development of dyscalculia could be predicted with up to 87% accuracy based on the functional activity of the right posterior parietal cortex, the network-level functional activity of the right dorsolateral prefrontal cortex, and the effective functional and structural connectivity of these regions. Accordingly, Kuhl et al. (2021) were able to identify a neurobiological early-childhood predisposition for dyscalculia characterized by altered spontaneous activity, functional interaction, and structural connectivity of a fronto-parietal network in the developing brain.

Brain responses to non-numerical cognitive processes have also been shown to predict calculation skills in children. Recent work by Schwartz et al. (2020) provided evidence that neural processing of transitive relations (such as A > B, B > C, therefore A > C) in the IPS predicted mathematical skills at both the first measurement time point (r = 0.60) and 1.5 years later (r = 0.39). In their preceding study, the authors showed that a transitive reasoning task activated the IPS in typically achieving children, but not in children with maths learning difficulties (Schwartz et al. 2018). Therefore, these findings support the notion that maths learning does not only rely on numerical understanding, but also critically involves the ability to infer logical relations (Schwartz et al. 2020). In line with other reports (Dumontheil and Klingberg 2012; Evans et al. 2015; Supekar et al. 2013), their findings also suggest that neural measurements may be more sensitive than behavioural assessments, because calculation skills were not related to transitive reasoning performance.

Finally, left (but not right) IPS activation during a visuospatial working memory task predicted arithmetical performance two years later in children, independently of behavioural measures ($r^2 = 0.69$) (Dumontheil and Klingberg 2012). Behavioural measures alone, including non-verbal reasoning and verbal and visuospatial working memory, were also independent predictors of arithmetical skills. However, the combination of brain and behavioural data improved (more than twice) the classification of children as typical vs. poor arithmetic performers two years later.

Taken together, there is growing evidence that neurobiological markers are able to provide additional value to predicting the development of numerical abilities from childhood into adolescence. Activation of the IPS during numerical tasks, but also during domain-general processing like visuospatial working memory or logical reasoning of relations, turned out to be a particularly powerful predictor. Predictive markers can also be derived from the grey matter volume of diverse brain regions of the numerical network that are either associated with numerical understanding (e.g., the IPS) or support memory formation (hippocampus). Furthermore, the functional connectivity of these areas has been repeatedly identified as a predictor of numerical learning gains. Accordingly, distributed nodes of the numerical network provide a structural scaffold that supports the typical or atypical development of numerical skills in children (Evans et al. 2015). Remarkably, a number of studies highlighted the potential of neural measures to predict future mathematical competencies beyond behavioural data. However, a combination of brain function, structure, and connectivity data with behavioural performance measures taken outside the scanner may have the best predictive power (Dumontheil and Klingberg 2012). That being said, the authors of a very recent study demonstrated that it could be possible to identify children at an early age who will most probably develop severe difficulties in numeracy by the help of neural biomarkers (Kuhl et al. 2021).

10.5 Theoretical and Methodological Challenges for the Developmental Cognitive Neuroscience of Dyscalculia

Longitudinal designs are the optimal way to study development as they allow us to avoid the pitfalls of generalizing from observational snapshots (Paterson et al. 2016). However, longitudinal studies are practically challenging, as they are resource-intensive and often have high drop-out rates, to name only a few issues. Several publications provide an overview of important points that should be considered when measuring and modelling longitudinal neural data (e.g., Paterson et al.

2016; Ansari 2010; King et al. 2018). We will now take up some of these aspects in detail.

Theoretical explicitness. Firstly, a theoretical model of development should be specified that explains what change over time means, when change is expected to occur, and how developmental processes influence change (King et al. 2018). Moreover, it is crucial to focus on the process of change itself, not just on outcome measures (Paterson et al. 2016). Following work in adults, it is often assumed that development occurs linearly (Ansari 2010; Paterson et al. 2016). Numerous studies demonstrate, however, that this is not always the case, corroborating the view that developmental models should account for different linear and non-linear neurodevelopmental trajectories.

Measurement issues. Secondly, a design that enables the observation of change is needed. This includes careful consideration of the timing, frequency, and spacing of observations (Paterson et al. 2016; King et al. 2018). Furthermore, the availability of consistent MRI equipment and software, and measures suitable for a broad age range, should be ensured (King et al. 2018). It is also noteworthy that investigating individual trajectories of change is particularly important when studying developmental disorders (Paterson et al. 2016). Additionally, the observed variability in longitudinal fMRI signals and the test–retest reliability of fMRI is another point that should be considered in the field of developmental studies. Variability can, for instance, be reduced by standardizing data acquisition and performing quality measurements of the scanner before data collection. Reliability of fMRI measures can be validated by using sub-samples to correct for reliability error bias for a given task and brain region (for an overview, see Herting et al. 2018).

Statistical modelling. Finally, appropriate statistical models are necessary to test theoretical models of change (King et al. 2018). General linear models can be used to answer basic questions regarding change for data sets comprising two measurement time-points. For data with more than two measurement time-points, growth curve models can be used to model within-individual change, while auto-regressive panel models or latent change score models can quantify between-person differences (for detailed information and additional methods, see King et al. 2018).

To conclude, the measurement of neural trajectories imposes several practical and theoretical challenges that researchers have to overcome. Nevertheless, this work is crucial for understanding development.

10.6 Conclusion

In this chapter, we have summarized the current state of longitudinal neuroscientific research on typically developing children and children with dyscalculia. Research on typically developing samples reveals that with increasing acuity of non-symbolic and symbolic number processing, bilateral activation emerges in the parietal lobe and in particular in the IPS. The acquisition of arithmetic fact knowledge leads to a decreasing involvement of executive frontal regions, and an increasing recruitment of memory-related hippocampal and temporal areas. Moreover, the functional connectivity of these areas increases when reaching certain maths competence levels. Remarkably, neural measures have been shown to predict future mathematical skills beyond behavioural measures, although a combination of behavioural and brain-imaging data would probably show the best performance in predicting the development of mathematical learning disorders.

Despite substantial efforts, the understanding of how the numerical network develops from childhood to adulthood is still far from complete. First studies show that developmental trajectories do not always follow a linear pattern and that children sometimes show unique activation patterns that vanish with the acquisition of more efficient strategies for number processing. This clearly shows that findings from adult studies cannot be directly applied to developmental processes. There is preliminary evidence that the neurodevelopmental trajectory of children with dyscalculia differs substantially from the trajectory of typically developing peers. Further research is needed to better understand when numerical ability and its neural correlates start to deviate in the course of development. This would render it possible to pinpoint when targeted interventions are necessary and enable us to better understand the effects of intervention.

Suggestions for Further Reading

Arsalidou, M., Pawliw-Levac, M., Sadeghi, M., and Pascual-Leone, J. (2018). 'Brain Areas Associated with Numbers and Calculations in Children: Meta-analyses of fMRI Studies'. *Developmental Cognitive Neuroscience* 30, 239–50.

Kucian, K. (2016) 'Developmental Dyscalculia and the Brain'. In Berch, D. B. , Geary, D. C. , Mann Koepke, K. (Eds.), *Development of Mathematical Cognition: Neural Substrates and Genetic Influences* (Vol. 2, pp. 165–93). Amsterdam: Elsevier Inc.

McCaskey, U., M. von Aster, U. Maurer, et al. (2018). 'Longitudinal Brain Development of Numerical Skills in Typically Developing Children and Children with Developmental Dyscalculia'. *Frontiers in Human Neuroscience* 11, 629.

McCaskey, U., von Aster, M., O'Gorman, R., and Kucian, K. (2020). 'Persistent Differences in Brain Structure in Developmental Dyscalculia: A Longitudinal Morphometry Study'. *Frontiers in Human Neuroscience* 14. https://doi.org/10.3389/fnhum .2020.00272.

Peters, L., and De Smedt, B. (2018). 'Arithmetic in the Developing Brain: A Review of Brain Imaging Studies'. *Developmental Cognitive Neuroscience* 30, 265–79.

11 Neuroplasticity in Response to Reading Intervention

Jason D. Yeatman

11.1 Introduction

Understanding the neurobiological underpinnings of learning difficulties, particularly developmental dyslexia, has received substantial attention since functional MRI and diffusion MRI first became widely available in the 1990s. Now, a couple decades later, there are hundreds of studies documenting differences in brain structure and function in people with dyslexia. Despite vast differences in educational systems, writing systems, and languages around the world, and differences in methodologies and samples across labs, there are at least three points that are broadly accepted. First, differences in neural activity in ventral occipito-temporal cortex (VOTC), in the broad vicinity of the visual word form area (VWFA), are among the most consistently reported differences in children with dyslexia (Wandell et al. 2012; Richlan et al. 2011; Kubota et al. 2019; Shaywitz et al. 2002; Olulade et al. 2015). Differences in neural responses within this region of high-level visual cortex are likely related to the difficulties that people with dyslexia have with automating word recognition. Moreover, they are a characteristic of the dyslexic brain across many different languages (Paulesu 2001; Richlan 2020). Second, lower or absent activation in phonological processing regions in superior temporal cortex is also likely to be a core deficit of dyslexia, at least for those learning to read in English (Xia et al. 2017; Black et al. 2017; Pugh et al. 2012; Maisog et al. 2008; Wandell et al. 2012; Kovelman et al. 2012; Joo et al. 2019; Hoeft et al. 2007; Kuhl et al. 2020b). Third, differences in white matter connectivity are apparent in children and adults with dyslexia (Yeatman et al. 2012; Wandell and Yeatman 2013; Vandermosten et al. 2012; Ben-Shachar et al. 2007; Kuhl et al. 2020b). Two left-hemisphere white matter pathways have been consistently implicated in reading development: the arcuate fasciculus and the inferior longitudinal fasciculus (Wandell and Yeatman 2013; Yeatman et al. 2012).

The fact that reproducible patterns of differences in brain structure and function have been replicated across labs operating on nearly every continent should be seen as a major success for the field. However, distinguishing aspects of neurobiology that cause reading difficulties from the neurobiological consequences of differences in educational experience for those with dyslexia has been a major challenge (Goswami 2015a; Huber et al. 2018; Huettig, Kolinsky, et al. 2018; Huettig, Lachmann, et al.

2018). More broadly, we might ask whether the relationship between brain imaging measures and behavioural measures: (1) reflects a static property of the brain that constrains cognitive abilities, or (2) emerges as the result of environmental influences on brain development (i.e., plasticity). The question of stability versus plasticity need not be an 'either/or' question. Many brain circuits are highly plastic, but only under certain circumstances (e.g., critical periods: Wandell and Smirnakis 2009; Werker and Hensch 2014). It is also possible that certain brain circuits are less malleable to experience in people with learning difficulties. Thus, intervention studies where children are assigned to specific, controlled learning environments are critical for understanding the balance between stability and plasticity in the dyslexic brain.

An emerging body of work has highlighted the dynamic interplay between brain development and learning, revealing that many neurobiological differences change and evolve in relation to children's learning environments (Black et al. 2017; Huber et al. 2018; Wandell and Yeatman 2013; Wang et al. 2016; Yeatman et al. 2012). Thus, even though there are a variety of differences in the structure and function of the dyslexic brain, these differences should not necessarily be interpreted as static traits that will forever impede progress in reading. There is a wealth of evidence demonstrating the brain's impressive capacity for plasticity when children are provided with high-quality, evidence-based intervention programmes (Huber et al. 2018; Barquero et al. 2014; Keller and Just 2009). The following sections highlight exciting findings from longitudinal and intervention studies exemplifying the dynamic interplay between education, brain development, and learning to read. Most of the longitudinal developmental data discussed in this chapter are based on samples from the United States (18), followed by Germany (3) and then England, France, Switzerland, and Austria (1 sample each).

11.2 Neural Plasticity in Ventral Occipito-Temporal Cortex

VOTC contains a mosaic of regions that are specialized for processing different categories of visual stimuli, such as faces, bodies, objects, scenes, and words. Situated at a high level in the hierarchy of visual processing regions, category-selective regions of VOTC are critical for rapid and automatic visual recognition (DiCarlo et al. 2012; Felleman and Van Essen 1991; Grill-Spector and Weiner 2014; Riesenhuber and Poggio 1999). Moreover, VOTC is highly plastic throughout childhood and adulthood. The tuning properties of VOTC regions are known to reflect visual expertise – be it expertise with cars and birds (Gauthier et al. 2000), cartoon characters (Gomez et al. 2019), or reading (Dehaene and Cohen 2011; McCandliss et al. 2003). Indeed, the capacity for experience-dependent plasticity within VOTC is at the foundation of reading development. As children learn to read, a particular location within VOTC develops a specialization for processing words. This 'visual word form area' plays a fundamental role in reading, serving as the intermediary between vision and language.

A collection of longitudinal studies have emphasized the link between plasticity in VOTC and learning to read. For example, Brem and colleagues randomly assigned non-reading, preschool children to one of two intervention programmes focusing on either (1) letter–sound knowledge or (2) number knowledge. By comparing the electrophysiological response to text (measured with EEG) before and after the intervention, they found that learning letter–sound correspondences led to text-selective responses in the VOTC (Brem et al. 2010). Thus, reading instruction quickly establishes the foundations of the reading circuitry. Even the simple act of learning to associate letters with their corresponding phonemes induces the development of visual circuits that selectively respond to text above other visual stimuli.

Two longitudinal studies following pre-readers through the first year of elementary school have confirmed similar findings. Saygin and colleagues collected fMRI data in a group of pre-readers (5 year olds) while they viewed images of text, faces, and objects. Prior to formal reading instruction, they could localize visual regions that selectively respond to faces but they could not detect regions that preferentially respond to text. They collected follow-up data three years later, after all the children had learnt to read, and localized the VWFA in each child. Retrospectively analysing the response properties of the patch of cortex that was destined to become the VWFA in the pre-readers, they found that it did not preferentially respond to any specific image category. Prior to reading instruction, this same patch of cortex responds to a variety of visual stimuli with no selectivity for text (Saygin et al. 2016). Dehaene-Lambertz and colleagues ran a longitudinal study in which a small group (n=10) of pre-readers were scanned seven times over the first year of reading instruction and found that, as children learnt to read, the VWFA emerged from a particular patch of VOTC that responded broadly to many types of visual stimuli (Dehaene-Lambertz et al. 2018). Thus, within the first year of reading instruction a region is established in VOTC that is specialized for processing text.

Longitudinal studies of elementary school children have revealed the link between changes in the VWFA and improvements in reading skills: as children gain expertise in reading, the VWFA is increasingly tuned for words (Ben-Shachar et al. 2011). For example, Ben-Shachar and colleagues conducted a four-year longitudinal study in which they measured the sensitivity of the VWFA to words embedded in noise (Ben-Shachar et al. 2011). Each child's yearly growth in reading skill was coupled to a proportional increase in their VWFA's sensitivity to visual word forms (R~0.5). Moreover, training studies in adults have confirmed that VOTC even remains highly plastic in adulthood. For example, Glezer and colleagues demonstrated rapid changes in VWFA tuning properties as adults learnt to recognize new words (Glezer et al. 2015; Riesenhuber and Glezer 2017). Taylor and colleagues trained adults to read a new made-up alphabet and demonstrated changes in the representation of this alphabet within VOTC over the course of two weeks (Taylor et al. 2019). Hervais-Adelman and colleagues trained illiterate adults to read and observed the emergence of the VWFA in a patch of high-level visual cortex that was not previously tuned for any specific stimulus category (Hervais-Adelman et al. 2019). Thus, even after the foundations of the reading circuitry have been established, VOTC broadly, and the VWFA specifically, show changes in neural tuning properties that are linked to changes in reading skills (Taylor et al. 2019; Hervais-Adelman et al. 2019).

Since the development of the VWFA is tightly linked to reading development from preschool through adulthood, it might come as no surprise that children with dyslexia show dramatic differences in VWFA response properties. For example, Kubota and colleagues recruited a sample of elementary school children of varying reading levels, performed an fMRI experiment to localize the VWFA in each participant, and then quantified the VWFA response to images of text, faces, and objects (Kubota et al. 2019). They found that, for highly skilled readers, VWFA activation to words was much higher than activation to faces and objects. For struggling readers (and those with dyslexia) activation to words and objects was equivalent. In many of the struggling readers no region could be identified that preferentially responded to words compared to objects. Olulade and colleagues reported similar findings by comparing the fMRI response to words versus symbol strings (false fonts) in children with dyslexia and typical readers (Olulade et al. 2015). They found that, on average, there was not the characteristic text-selective response in the VOTC for the children with dyslexia.

The findings from Kubota et al. (2019) and Olulade et al. (2015) provide an intriguing explanation for those children's difficulties with automatizing word recognition, but also exemplify the difficulty with resolving causality in the neurobiology of dyslexia. Kubota et al. (2019) reported that only strong readers had a VWFA that was selective for words compared to objects, while those with dyslexia did not. This finding might either reflect the fact that: (1) deficits in this region of cortex cause children to struggle with automatizing word recognition, or (2) the VWFA develops with reading expertise and the struggling readers had not yet achieved a sufficient level of expertise. Only intervention studies can resolve this question and, currently, there is clear evidence of intervention-driven plasticity in VOTC broadly. However, intervention studies have yet to target the computations of the VWFA specifically.

11.3 Intervention Studies Revealing Plasticity in the Reading Circuitry

Shaywitz and colleagues conducted one of the earliest studies on neural plasticity in response to intervention in children with dyslexia (Shaywitz et al. 2004). Thirty-seven children with dyslexia (6–9 years old) were enrolled in a phonological intervention programme that was delivered for 50 minutes a day for 8 months through their schools. The intervention systematically trained components of reading, including phonological awareness, letter–sound correspondences, oral reading, and other phonics-based activities that are widely known to improve reading skills in children with dyslexia. The intervention improved reading fluency scores in the intervention group, and a letter identification fMRI experiment revealed increased activation in inferior frontal cortex and posterior temporal cortex in the left hemisphere immediately after the intervention. Interestingly, there was no change in the

VOTC response to text immediately after the intervention. However, at one year follow-up, the authors did observe a significant increase in VOTC activation. Thus, they concluded that the intervention induced a sequence of changes that culminated in increased VOTC response levels for words.

Subsequent intervention studies have also reported changes in the VOTC (Gebauer et al. 2012; Simos et al. 2007). It appears that, under certain circumstances, the VOTC can change as children with dyslexia improve their reading skills. However, as revealed by a recent meta-analysis of intervention studies, results are variable across studies and it is difficult to clearly summarize mechanisms of plasticity that are common across interventions (Barquero et al. 2014). There are three reasons for this. First, due to variability in intervention approaches and fMRI paradigms, we shouldn't expect to see the same results across studies. For example, most intervention studies employ phonological processing tasks with auditory stimuli and we would not expect these tasks to tap VOTC (Barquero et al. 2014). Indeed, the meta-analysis by Barquero and colleagues found that the lateral temporal cortex is the most common location to observe intervention-driven changes in brain activity and this most likely reflects that most studies have employed tasks designed to tap phonological processing circuits in the lateral temporal cortex (Barquero et al. 2014). For example, another early dyslexia intervention study used a training programme that focused on auditory and language processing skills and employed a rhyming task to assess changes in phonological processing circuits (Temple et al. 2003). They found that, after the intervention, activation in the temporal-parietal cortex was more similar between dyslexic and control subjects than before the intervention. Second, most intervention studies have very small samples: only 4 out of the 22 studies summarized by Barquero et al. 2014 (table 1) included more than 20 participants. Thus, based on those small samples, we should expect to find variable and inconsistent effects. Finally, most intervention studies employ fMRI tasks that tap general reading-related processes (e.g., phonological processing) as opposed to testing hypotheses about specific computations performed by specific components of the reading circuitry. For example, no intervention studies have specifically focused on the VWFA, and therefore data is lacking as to how this critical component of the reading circuitry develops and changes during targeted intervention in children with dyslexia.

11.4 White Matter Plasticity and Learning

Traditionally, white matter was viewed as static infrastructure of the brain; research on plasticity and learning generally focused on the synapse (Bullock et al. 2005). However, a series of observations about white matter plasticity have spurred a sea change in how neuroscientists view the white matter. First, oligodendrocytes, the glial cells that are responsible for myelination in the white matter, actively monitor neural activity, allowing them to adjust white matter properties in response to neural activity (Barres and Raff 1993; Fields 2015; Ishibashi et al. 2006). Second, diffusion-weighted magnetic resonance imaging (dMRI) measurements of white matter tissue properties are correlated with most, if not all, aspects of cognitive function, differ in children with learning deficits such as dyslexia, and differ as a function of lifetime experiences (e.g., socioeconomic status, adverse childhood events, expert musicians) (Wandell and Yeatman 2013; Zatorre et al. 2012). Third, experimental studies in humans and animal models have revealed a surprising capacity for experience-dependent white matter plasticity throughout the lifespan (Gibson et al. 2014; Huber et al. 2018; Matuszewski et al. 2020; McKenzie et al. 2014; Mount and Monje 2017; Sampaio-Baptista and Johansen-Berg 2017). Pharmacological interventions blocking white matter plasticity have further demonstrated that this previously ignored form of plasticity is critical for learning (Gibson et al. 2014; McKenzie et al. 2014). Indeed, it is now largely appreciated that white matter not only plays an essential role in complex behaviours such as reading, but also that white matter plasticity is essential for learning. The goal of this section is to provide an overview of what has been learnt about human white matter plasticity from intervention studies targeting reading skills. We highlight two areas of the literature that have revealed insights into white matter plasticity and reading development: (1) correlational studies relating reading development to individual differences in white matter development; (2) intervention studies that have systematically manipulated environmental factors (e.g., reading instruction) and studied the impacts on white matter development.

11.4.1 Reading Development Is Correlated with White Matter Properties

Seminal work by Klingberg and colleagues demonstrated that diffusion MRI measures of temporal-parietal white matter are correlated with reading skills and differ in people with dyslexia (Klingberg et al. 2000). This observation – that individual differences in white matter properties are related to individual differences in performance on standardized reading tests – opened the floodgates to a flurry of papers investigating the relationships between specific aspects of reading, structural properties of different white matter tracts, and the developmental time-course of these effects. For example, three different labs quickly published papers extending Klingberg's observation to children with dyslexia (Beaulieu et al. 2005; Deutsch et al. 2005; Niogi and McCandliss 2006). These studies established the relationship between structural properties of temporo-parietal white matter and reading skills in children and adults. This work further inspired two important questions:

(1) Are different white matter tracts specifically related to different cognitive functions and different components of skilled reading? Early work by Klingberg and others employed voxel-based approaches wherein values are analysed on a grid in the three-dimensional brain volume. The effect they discovered was in a cluster of voxels around the vicinity of the temporal-parietal junction. Moreover, these voxels were at the intersection of three different tracts: the arcuate fasciculus, the superior longitudinal fasciculus, and the corticospinal tract (Ben-Shachar et al. 2007). Subsequent meta-analyses (Vandermosten, Boets, Wouters, et al. 2012), reviews (Wandell and Yeatman 2013), and empirical studies (Vandermosten, Boets, Poelmans, et al. 2012; Yeatman et al. 2011, 2012) capitalized on

evolving tractography approaches to better localize the microstructural difference to specific anatomical connections. These studies revealed effects localized to the arcuate fasciculus (Yeatman et al. 2011; Yeatman et al. 2012; Vandermosten et al. 2012; Kraft et al. 2016) but also suggested that, additionally, there are differences in the macro-anatomical configuration of these major fascicles in people with dyslexia (Ben-Shachar et al. 2007; Schwartzman et al. 2005).

(2) Do correlations between white matter structure and reading ability reflect a static property of the brain that constrains learning, or do correlations emerge as a result of environmental and educational influences on brain development? Most studies relating white matter to reading skills have interpreted group differences in dyslexia (and correlations with reading skills) as reflecting static deficits. The predominant assumption has been that white matter is not sufficiently plastic over short timescales to explain effects that are present in early childhood. However, longitudinal investigations have revealed a dynamic interplay between an individual's white matter development and their learning trajectory (Wang et al. 2016; Yeatman et al. 2012). Moreover, recent experiments in model organisms and human subjects have called this assumption into question (Fields 2015). It is now widely accepted that the white matter is a dynamic system. White matter tissue properties change over rapid timescales and adapt to environmental demands (Huber et al. 2018; Sampaio-Baptista and Johansen-Berg 2017). For example, myelination and axon calibre can change over the course of days and weeks, and new glial cells can proliferate in response to new experiences (McKenzie et al. 2014; Mensch et al. 2015; Gibson et al. 2014).

Two longitudinal studies capitalized on the evolving knowledge of the neuroanatomical correlates of reading ability to investigate the relationship between individual differences in white matter development and reading ability (Wang et al. 2016; Yeatman et al. 2012). The first important finding from Yeatman and colleagues was that correlations between white matter diffusion properties and reading skill changed over time (Yeatman et al. 2012). Children with better reading abilities displayed more rapid rates of development for both the left hemisphere arcuate fasciculus and the inferior longitudinal fasciculus compared to children with lower reading abilities. Thus, due to individual differences in growth rates of these two key reading pathways, the cross-sectional correlations between diffusion and behaviour computed at any particular time-point changed year to year. Wang and colleagues confirmed similar findings showing more rapid rates of development in better readers compared to children at risk for dyslexia (Wang et al. 2016). Thus, longitudinal studies have revealed a dynamic interplay between white matter development and reading skills and lent support to the notion that the experiences associated with being a strong reader might influence the developmental trajectory of white matter connections that support reading.

11.4.2 The Causal Influence of Reading Intervention on White Matter Development

Educational interventions have redefined our understanding of white matter plasticity. These interventions offer a particularly compelling tool to support causal inferences as researchers can manipulate specific aspects of a child's learning environment and measure the impact of that environmental factor on white matter structure. For example, Keller and Just were the first to use diffusion MRI to measure intervention-driven changes in the white matter in children with dyslexia (Keller and Just 2009). They enrolled 35 struggling readers in a supplemental reading instruction programme that involved 100 hours of training in word-level decoding skills delivered over six months of the school year. After the six-month training period, they found changes in diffusion measures localized to voxels in the centrum semi-ovale. Interestingly, the region showing changes after the intervention co-localized with a region that showed differences between the dyslexic and control groups prior to intervention (but anterior to the original temporal-parietal white matter region reported by Klingberg and colleagues; Klingberg et al. 2000). This study provided compelling evidence of white matter plasticity following an intervention for dyslexia. However, the improvements in reading skill were small and only reached significance for a measure of pseudoword reading. Thus, the fact that the intervention-driven changes in the white matter were localized to a small region of the centrum semiovale, and not elsewhere in the reading circuitry, might reflect the limited behavioural effects or the fact that the intervention was spread out over a long period of time.

To better understand the link between white matter plasticity and learning in children with dyslexia, Huber and colleagues enrolled a group of struggling readers in an eight-week, intensive (four hours a day, five days a week), one-on-one reading intervention programme conducted over summer vacation (Huber et al. 2018). Conducting the intervention over summer vacation, while children were not attending their typical schools, allowed the researchers to isolate the impacts of a high-intensity, evidence-based intervention programme without the variability introduced in a typical school setting. They collected diffusion MRI data and measures of reading ability at 2.5 week intervals and used tractography to identify the white matter tracts that are conventionally associated with reading (left arcuate fasciculus and left inferior longitudinal fasciculus) and charted the time-course of plasticity in each individual's brain. They found that white matter plasticity occurred over a more rapid timescale, and across a broader network of white matter tracts, than conventionally assumed. Within the first couple of weeks of instruction the left hemisphere arcuate fasciculus and inferior longitudinal fasciculus already showed significant changes in diffusion properties. This growth persisted over the course of the eight-week intervention as reading skills improved. Individual time-courses of white matter plasticity tracked reading improvements, revealing a coupling between plasticity and learning over the eight-week intervention period. Surprisingly, beyond the plasticity observed within the core reading circuitry, they observed large-scale changes (effect sizes ranging from $d = 0.5-1.0$) throughout an extensive network of tracts in the left and right hemisphere. These data highlight the surprising capacity for rapid, extensive, and experience-dependent remodelling of the white matter. Notably, the intervention produced large improvements in decoding accuracy, reading rate, and reading fluency (effect sizes ranging from $d = 0.5-1.1$ across different reading measures) that were associated with similarly large changes in white matter structure. More broadly, intervention studies reveal the powerful impact of high-quality reading instruction on white matter development, emphasizing how a child's environment sculpts white matter architecture over timescales ranging from weeks to months to years.

11.5 Looking Forward: What Does Research into Plasticity Reveal About Learning Disorders?

We have focused on plasticity of a couple of key components of the reading circuitry. First, we reviewed studies on plasticity in high-level visual cortex, namely the VWFA, which develops as children gain reading expertise. It is clear that this region is sculpted by education and remains plastic throughout the lifespan, and there is evidence that it is amenable to intervention. Second, we reviewed studies that have linked individual differences in white matter connectivity to individual differences in reading development. Longitudinal studies have made it clear that there is a dynamic interplay between white matter development, reading education, and learning, and that a child's educational environment has a profound impact on the physical structure of the reading circuitry. Despite our focus on these two systems, it should not be inferred that they are unique examples of intervention-driven plasticity. In fact, most aspects of brain structure and function that have been linked to reading have also been shown to be amenable to change, at least under certain circumstances. For example, phonological processing regions in the posterior temporal lobe are linked to dyslexia (Hoeft et al. 2007; Joo et al. 2019; Xia et al. 2017), and neural response properties of these regions change when children (Barquero et al. 2014; Temple et al. 2003) or adults (Eden et al. 2004) receive high-quality interventions. Moreover, differences in grey matter volume have been linked to dyslexia (Krafnick et al. 2014; Skeide et al. 2016) and dyslexia candidate genes (Skeide et al. 2016; see also Chapter 8, Skeide 2022), but are also known to change rapidly with intervention (Krafnick et al. 2011; Romeo et al. 2017).

Reconsidering the question of causality in light of data from longitudinal and intervention studies suggests that causality is more likely to be reciprocal than unidirectional. When children have access to high-quality, evidence-based intervention programmes, many aspects of brain structure and function that are associated with dyslexia are remarkably plastic. However, many of the major differences in the dyslexic brain reviewed here have also been reported in preschool children, prior to formal reading instruction. For example, neural response properties of the VOTC and temporal-parietal cortex are different in preschool children who are at risk for dyslexia (Centanni et al. 2019; Vandermosten et al. 2019) or go on to develop dyslexia (Kuhl et al. 2020; see also Chapter 14, Fish 2022). Moreover, diffusion properties of the arcuate fasciculus differ in preschool children who are at risk for dyslexia, and this difference can even be detected in infancy (Langer et al. 2015; Vandermosten et al. 2015). Thus, we might infer that differences emerge early in development and that these differences are likely to remain stable if dyslexic children do not receive an appropriate intervention. Hopefully data revealing the profound impact that high-quality education has on the developing brain will inspire policies ensuring that every child has access to the educational resources they need to reach their full potential.

Suggestions for Further Reading

Barquero, L. A., N. Davis, and L. E. Cutting. 2014. 'Neuroimaging of Reading Intervention: A Systematic Review and Activation Likelihood Estimate Meta-Analysis'. *PloS One* 9 (1): e83668.

Huber, E., P. M. Donnelly, A. Rokem, and J. D. Yeatman. 2018. 'Rapid and Widespread White Matter Plasticity during an Intensive Reading Intervention'. *Nature Communications* 9 (1): 2260.

O'Brien, G., and J, D. Yeatman. 2021. 'Bridging Sensory and Language Theories of Dyslexia: Toward a Multifactorial Model'. *Developmental Science* 24 (3): e13039. https://doi.org/10.1111/desc.13039.

Ozernov-Palchik, O., and N. Gaab. 2016. 'Tackling the "Dyslexia Paradox": Reading Brain and Behavior for Early Markers of Developmental Dyslexia'. *Wiley Interdisciplinary Reviews. Cognitive Science* 7 (2): 156–76.

Yeatman, J. D., and A. L. White. 2021. 'Reading: The Confluence of Vision and Language'. *Annual Review of Vision Science* 7 (June): 487–517. https://doi.org/10.1146/annurev-vision-093019-113509.

12 Neuroplasticity in Response to Mathematical Intervention

Teresa Iuculano

12.1 Introduction

Neuroplasticity refers to the ability of the brain to reorganize itself following experience and, as such, it represents a foundational milestone to any type of learning. At the microscopic level, neuroplasticity can be described via modifications of neuronal morphology or changes in neurobiochemical balance (Fuchs and Flügge 2014). These microscopic changes, in turn, can lead to macroscopic alterations in the morphology or functionality of certain brain regions (i.e., structural and functional changes, respectively), and to circuit reorganization, at the regional or network levels (i.e., connectivity changes), as a function of learning.

By its very nature, the learning of formal mathematics – including the ability to acquire new cultural symbols (i.e., Arabic numerals) and being able to reason on them via the systematic application of defined algorithms – entails (and gives rise to) long-lasting mechanisms of neuroplasticity as the brain starts to repurpose some of its domain-general cognitive resources (e.g., visual recognition, memory processes) for tasks that are domain-specific and evolutionarily recent (e.g., decoding number symbols, remembering rules and procedures, consolidating arithmetical facts in long-term memory).

This chapter presents existing evidence describing macroscopic neuroplasticity changes in response to mathematical learning, both in childhood and adulthood, and in typical and atypical cohorts. I will outline studies which have adopted a training/intervention paradigm to unveil structural, functional, as well as connectivity changes across brain regions (and systems) considered to be important for (1) processing numerical stimuli (i.e., domain-specific), as well as those that subserve (2) domain-general cognitive skills, such as working memory, executive functions, and knowledge-consolidation in long-term memory. Notably, all these functions serve as the neurocognitive scaffolds of mathematical knowledge acquisition. Initial evidence for this view comes from *one time-point neuroimaging studies* which, over the last twenty-plus years, have contributed to identifying the neural substrates of these functions during numerical tasks (see Iuculano et al. 2018 for a review; see also Chapter 2, Menon and Chang 2022, and Chapter 10, Kucian and McCaskey 2022). Altogether, such evidence supports the notion that multiple brain regions and systems encompassing the fusiform gyrus, the intraparietal sulcus, the superior temporal gyrus/sulcus, the supramarginal gyrus, the parieto-frontal system, the medial temporal lobe, and the ventral prefrontal system aid the hierarchical cascade of processes that ultimately lead to successful arithmetical learning. Yet, when and how these systems get recruited across development and as a function of skill acquisition remains an open question. More specifically, is there a fixed developmental period when a certain brain region/system plays its (time-limited) role in mathematical skill acquisition? Or does its recruitment rather depend on the novelty of the material to be learnt? Moreover, at the network level, how are these systems remodelled to cohesively contribute to the successful development of arithmetical competences, and in different populations? What are the neurocognitive processes that fail to adequately develop in children and adults with mathematical learning difficulties, such as developmental dyscalculia? Could brain aberrancies in these cohorts be remediated through intervention? Finally, and more generally, what is the neural profile that supports the most efficient 'sedimentation' of arithmetical problems at the brain level, and how is it 'mechanistically' achieved?

In this chapter, I outline evidence from the emerging literature of *neuroimaging training studies*, in different age and ability cohorts, which – I argue – represent a powerful methodological approach to shed light on these questions and, ultimately, refine neurocognitive models of mathematical skill development and learning. Note that, given the comprehensive nature of this review – encompassing experimental evaluations on both typical and atypical populations – the term 'training', rather than 'intervention', is used, to better reflect the broad range of evidence covered.

The distribution of national backgrounds of samples (by number of studies) presented in this chapter is: Austria (N = 4), China (N = 5), Germany (N = 5), Japan (N = 1), Switzerland (N = 2), USA (N = 7). The samples include children and adults (age-range: 6–49 years; distribution of age groups: 6–12 years old = 54.2% of studies, 18–49 years old = 45.8% of studies). All reported research articles include participants with age-appropriate formal education.

12.2 Training Studies Targeting the Neural Correlates of Math Learning

As a general rule, *neuroimaging training studies* are defined here as studies comprising brain-related data within the context of a training/intervention paradigm while behavioural measures are also collected on, at least, two time-points (i.e., before and after the given intervention). However, the format of these types of studies may differ on various parameters.

A first distinction relates to the fact that certain studies collect brain data at both time-points (i.e., before and after the given intervention), while others limit brain data collection to one time-point, either before (see for example Supekar et al. 2013) or after (see for example Chang et al. 2019) the intervention.

Another aspect is the presence or absence of a control group alongside the experimental training group. The control group could be either a no-contact control group (i.e., receiving no training) (see for example Rosenberg-Lee et al. 2018) or an active control group (i.e., receiving a different training than the experimental group) (see for example Takeuchi et al. 2011). Control-group designs are highly preferable as they allow analyses within and between subjects (Rosenberg-Lee et al. 2018). Yet, it is worth noting that studies which only test one experimental training group can also be very informative with respect to brain plasticity mechanisms underlying maths learning (Chang et al. 2019).

A distinction should also be made between studies on neurotypical populations and those focusing on cohorts with a significant performance-deficit. In the case of maths learning, these are individuals with a form of mathematical learning difficulty, including developmental dyscalculia (Iuculano 2016). The aim of the latter studies often includes assessing the potential benefits of a given intervention, both at the behavioural as well as at the brain levels (see for example Iuculano et al. 2015). In these studies, the control group often consists of a neurotypical cohort, well matched to the experimental group on parameters such as age, education, sex, and IQ, but without the given difficulty or disability.

The type of training and its administration, as well as its duration, may also differ across studies.

For the specific case of mathematical problem solving, interventions could be focused on training a particular skill (e.g., numerosity representation; see Kucian et al. 2011; Michels et al. 2018), or they could be designed to tap onto various processes simultaneously (e.g., number knowledge, counting principles, calculation strategies, etc.; see Iuculano et al. 2015; Jolles et al. 2016; Supekar et al. 2013).

Other training approaches have also been exploited and tested. For instance, a recent series of studies assessed the benefits of an abacus-based mental calculation training in relation to various features of brain plasticity (Li et al. 2016; Xie et al. 2018).

Regardless of the type of training, most studies within this domain assess the behavioural outcome of a given intervention as a function of performance gains on tests of maths fluency that are either standardized (e.g., the Wechsler Individual Achievement Test, the Woodcock-Johnson, etc.) or custom-made (e.g., a predefined set of trained and untrained arithmetic problems) – with moderate to large effect sizes, when reported (Supekar et al. 2013; Rosenberg-Lee et al. 2018; Iuculano et al. 2015; Michels et al. 2018; Jolles et al. 2016; Zamarian et al. 2018; Jolles et al. 2016; Soltanlou et al. 2018). In terms of performance outcomes, studies have also directly assessed behavioural transfer effects to untrained material (e.g., untrained problems/ stimuli, or untrained operations) (Chang et al. 2019; Ischebeck et al. 2009) – also with moderate to large effect sizes, when reported (Zamarian et al. 2018; Soltanlou et al. 2018).

The pedagogical approach adopted in the training may also differ between studies: some use more conceptual or procedural trainings (Kucian et al. 2011; Tenison et al. 2014), others more drill-based ones (Chang et al. 2019; Klein et al. 2019), or a mix between the two (Iuculano et al. 2015; Jolles et al. 2016; Supekar et al. 2013). Moreover, the training could be delivered either in person (i.e., 1:1 training/tutoring) (Iuculano et al. 2015; Jolles et al. 2016; Supekar et al. 2013) or via digital platforms, which are often created ad-hoc (see, e.g., Kucian et al. 2011; Michels et al. 2018).

In terms of neuroimaging variables, two-time-points designs are centred on structural, functional, or connectivity changes across sessions (i.e., before versus after a given intervention/training), and their link to behavioural performance (see for example Iuculano et al. 2015). Studies featuring only one neuroimaging time-point assess forward (see for example Supekar et al. 2013) or backward (see for example Chang et al. 2019) correlates of structural, functional, or connectivity brain measures as a function of behavioural gains. Both of these approaches have revealed moderate to large effect sizes, when reported (Rosenberg-Lee et al. 2018; Iuculano et al. 2015; Jolles et al. 2016; Klein et al. 2019; Jolles et al. 2016; Soltanlou et al. 2018; Supekar et al. 2013).

Notably, within the aforementioned frameworks, both children and adult cohorts have been assessed. In studies with children, the material taught usually follows the maths curriculum and is based on educational and developmental milestones that are set according to it. For instance, when testing primary school children in their early grades (i.e., 2nd or 3rd graders), single-digit arithmetical problems are often used, with (e.g., '3 + 8 = 11'; '11 − 8 = 3') and without (e.g., '3 + 5 = 8'; '8 − 3 = 5') carrying or borrowing aspects (Iuculano et al. 2015). Sometimes, double-digit operands are presented together with a single-digit operand (e.g., '6 + 72 = 78'), also with carrying or borrowing variants (e.g., '75 + 8 = 83') (Chang et al. 2019).

With adult cohorts, more complex, multi-digit arithmetic problems – often featuring multiplications – are usually employed (e.g., '28 x 3 = 84') (Bloechle et al. 2016; Delazer et al. 2003; Grabner et al. 2009; Ischebeck et al. 2009; Klein et al. 2019). In this case, all problems require a carrying/or borrowing approach. In other studies, adult participants are taught the application of new, artificially created procedural algorithms: for example, '11$4'. In this example, the starting number '11' represents the 'base', and '4' is the 'height'. The 'height' indicates the total number of terms to add together, where each item is one less than the previous. So, in this example: '11 + 10 + 9 + 8 = 38' (Tenison et al. 2014; see also Delazer et al. 2005 for another example of a study using a procedural training paradigm in adults).

Stimuli used for abacus mental calculation trainings are often adaptive, and operate along a continuum that can reach very complex calculation problems featuring very large numbers (i.e., with more than ten digits) (Li et al. 2016; Xie et al. 2018). During this training, participants are initially provided with a device (i.e., the abacus) which can be used to represent the arithmetical problem (i.e., via the abacus beads). As participants get more and more proficient, they move away from the abacus and start to solve problems solely via visual mental imagery.

It is important to note that this particular training – contrary to other types of trainings whose duration spans from 5 days to 8 weeks – often lasts a very long time (i.e., at least 1 year, and for at least 2 hours a week), and groups of trained experts and non-experts are compared. Given its long-lasting nature, and the fact that it capitalizes heavily on visuospatial processes for arithmetic problem solving, this type of training can reveal brain plasticity correlates related to strategy use that differ between experts and non-experts.

The level of adaptivity of the training may also vary across studies. Some experimental evaluations have opted for more adaptive approaches, wherein the material to be learnt changes as a function of participant's responses to it (Kucian et al. 2011; Michels et al. 2018; Takeuchi et al. 2011; Xie et al. 2018), while others settled on administering exactly the same material across subjects (Bloechle et al. 2016; Chang et al. 2019; Delazer et al. 2003; Delazer et al. 2005; Grabner et al. 2009; Ischebeck et al. 2009; Ischebeck et al. 2006; Iuculano et al. 2015; Jolles et al. 2016; Jolles et al. 2016; Klein et al. 2019; Rosenberg-Lee et al. 2018; Supekar et al. 2013). Both approaches have their merits: the 'adaptive approach' ensures a better, more equal distribution of time-on-training, while the 'fixed approach' allows for a more controlled comparison between trained and untrained stimuli (or groups), both at the behavioural and at the brain levels.

Finally, aspects of persistence should also be assessed within the context of *neuroimaging training studies* of arithmetical learning (see Chapter 21, Sokolowski and Peters 2022). Yet, thus far only one study has assessed the long-term brain effects of intervention, albeit on a rather small (sub)sample of participants (N = 5) (Kucian et al. 2011).

In the next section, I will review the contribution of these studies and approaches to our understanding of neuroplasticity effects following maths training/intervention. Notably, the global picture that emerges is that maths skill acquisition is gradually refined through the dynamic engagement and disengagement of multiple cortical and subcortical brain systems alongside their on-and-off interactions and concurrent specialization.

12.3 The Brain Bases of Learning to Master Arithmetic Problems

Neuroimaging training studies have the potential to unveil how the human brain starts (and finishes) learning to master arithmetic problems, from simple (e.g., '3 + 8') to more complex ones (e.g., '28 × 3 = 84'). Notably, when a child approaches the problem '3 + 8', but also when an adult is presented with the problem '28 × 3', the whole brain is 'at work', and in a similar way. Regions of the prefrontal cortex involved in planning and working memory get recruited to tackle the problem, and to store and manipulate intermediate rules and results 'online'. Regions of the posterior parietal cortex are also engaged at this time, as these are the areas of the brain that underlie our 'sense' for numbers. More specifically, these regions provide resources to perform simple numerosity judgements and to understand what numbers mean. Other cortical regions are also involved during initial arithmetic learning, including high-level visual cortices and lateral temporal phonological processing regions for the decoding of visual number symbols ('3') and auditory number words ('three'), respectively. Over time, the hippocampus in the medial temporal lobe (MTL) starts to establish associations between '3 + 8' and '11' (or '28 × 3' and '84'), and to bind operands and solutions together. The bound-information is then sent to cortical systems for long-term memory storage, and cortico-cortical connections are gradually strengthened to become less and less dependent on the hippocampus. This is the stage at which the arithmetical problem is finally mastered, rather than effortfully computed, so that an over-recruitment of multiple brain regions engaging numerous mental functions is no longer required. Brain activation for learnt problems is therefore more fine-tuned and efficient, ultimately leading to segregated neural modules within large-scale brain networks, reflecting arithmetical expertise.

In Sections 12.3.1 and 12.3.3, I will present evidence in support of these trajectories provided by *neuroimaging training studies* of arithmetical learning across different developmental stages and ability levels.

12.3.1 Brain Reorganization During Arithmetic Learning

In a series of seminal studies, Delazer and colleagues trained neurotypical adult participants – for 5 days, for about 25 min a day – on a list of multiplication problems that are not normally memorized in school (e.g., '28 x 3 = 85'?) (Delazer et al. 2003). After their five-day training, participants underwent a functional magnetic resonance imaging (fMRI) session (i.e., one time-point fMRI design). During the fMRI session, the same list of trained problems (along with a list of untrained ones, matched for difficulty and format) was presented. Notably, after the training, participants were significantly faster and more accurate on trained compared to untrained problems. Furthermore, the authors showed that untrained problems (compared to trained problems) activated a distributed network of brain regions that included the bilateral intraparietal sulcus (IPS) and the bilateral frontal cortex, as well as regions of the occipito-temporal cortices. This result suggests a decrease in activation for trained versus untrained problems, compatible with the idea that untrained problems require greater neural resources than well-practiced ones. In contrast, trained problems elicited greater and highly focal activation within the angular gyrus (AG), in the inferior aspect of the parietal cortex, near the superior edge of the temporal lobe (for similar results, see also Grabner et al. 2009; Ischebeck et al. 2009; Ischebeck et al. 2006). The AG is known to be implicated in language processing (Price 2000), and thus, within the context of maths problem solving, its engagement has been proposed to be related to the verbal retrieval of learnt arithmetic facts (Dehaene et al. 2003; Grabner et al. 2009). Yet, more recently, competing hypotheses have been put forward in relation to the specific role of the AG during arithmetic fact retrieval. Some authors have claimed that activation's increases within this brain region actually reflect decreases in deactivation (relative to baseline) as problems become more and more automatized (Wu et al. 2009). Another view is that AG activation corresponds to bottom-up attentional processes (Bloechle et al. 2016). Despite these different interpretations, all theoretical accounts acknowledge the role of this region for the processing of well-mastered arithmetical problems.

Reduction of activation in fronto-parietal regions as a function of learnt material has also been shown in primary school children with a neurotypical profile (Rosenberg-Lee et al. 2018). These children were trained by a tutor in a 1:1 set-up for a total of 8 weeks, 3 times a week, with sessions lasting about 45–50 min each. During these sessions, children learnt and practiced efficient strategies to solve simple arithmetic problems such as '3 + 8 = 11'. Before and after training, all children also took part in fMRI sessions where they were asked to solve arithmetic problems inside the scanner (i.e., two-time-points fMRI design). Critically, this study also collected data on strategy use (Wu et al. 2008): children were asked to self-report whether they were solving the problem by counting (i.e., 'I counted on to the final result' or 'I counted on my fingers'), by decomposing it (i.e., 'I went to 10, and then I just added 1'), or by retrieving the answer from memory (i.e., 'I just knew the answer by heart'). The authors found that children who underwent training showed a significant relationship between higher rates of retrieval for arithmetical problems and decreases in activation in fronto-parietal regions. Notably, this effect was not evident in a no-contact control group who did not take part in the training. (For similar results indicating functional activation decreases after arithmetic trainings of ≥1 week, see also Chang et al. 2019; Soltanlou et al. 2018).

Using the same paradigm and stimuli, Iuculano and colleagues reported training-contingent decreases in activation across multiple brain regions in a group of 7–9-year-old children with developmental dyscalculia. More specifically, the authors showed that in this cohort of children, widespread over-activation during arithmetic problem solving that was evident in prefrontal, parietal, temporal, and ventral temporo-occipital cortices prior to training, was significantly reduced after 8 weeks of training, and no longer differed from a neurotypical group. Critically, neuroplasticity effects in these children were significantly correlated with improvements in maths performance following training (Iuculano et al. 2015).

A similar pattern of activation's decreases was also reported by Kucian and colleagues in a cohort of 8–10-year-old children, following a number line training aimed at improving spatial number representations (Kucian et al. 2011). In this study, training took place for 5 weeks, 15 min a day, 5 days a week, via a computer software ('Rescue Calcularis') at home. Task-based fMRI data during an ordinality judgement task (i.e., 'Indicate whether this list of numbers is in ascending, descending, or not in order: "3 5 8"') were collected both before and after the training. After training, performance-improvements were reported on the number line task, and minimal gains were also seen on an arithmetic problem-solving task. At the brain level, training led to significant decreases in task-related functional activation across distributed parietal and prefrontal regions, including the posterior parietal and insular cortices. Interestingly, exploratory analyses conducted on a subgroup of children at the lower end of the distribution of abilities (N = 5) revealed focal increases in parietal activation at a follow-up scanning session 5 weeks after the end of the training (Kucian et al. 2011), suggesting reconfiguration of activation similar to that seen in adults (Delazer et al. 2003).

Another interesting finding in line with these results comes from studies of procedural training in adults. In these types of protocols, subjects learn and practice, over a short period of time, a given algorithm such as: {[(2nd op. − 1st op.) + 1] + 2nd op.} using natural numbers (Rickard 1997). An example of a problem is: {[(11 − 3) + 1] + 11}. After 5 consecutive days of training, participants showed greater activity for new compared to practiced problems in regions of the prefrontal and parietal cortices (Delazer et al. 2005). Similar results were obtained with a single training session lasting ~35–45 minutes. In this case, neurotypical adults were trained on so-called 'pyramidal problems' (Anderson et al. 2011), wherein an artificial algorithm such as '11$4' is taught and practiced prior to a scanning session. As mentioned in the previous section, the solution to this problem is: '11 + 10 + 9 + 8 = 38'. Notably, after training, subjects displayed reduced activation for practiced compared to novel problems in multiple cortical regions, with the largest effects in the IPS (Tenison et al. 2014).

At the structural level, cortical thinning of frontal and parietal as well as superior temporal regions has also been reported following a short-term working-memory-based mental calculation training (Takeuchi et al. 2011). In this training, neurotypical adults were encouraged to implement step-wise checks during their mental computations. For instance, while solving the problem '37 x 45', participants were asked to focus on the intermediate result of the first column ('37 x 5 = 185'), and that of the second 'column' ('37 x 4 = 148'), before proceeding to solving the problem. Structural neuroimaging data were collected before and after the training, which lasted for a total of 5 days, 4 hours a day. After training, participants in the experimental group showed larger arithmetical performance gains and reduced grey matter volume in the dorsolateral prefrontal cortex, in the inferior parietal cortex, and in the superior temporal gyrus compared to a no-contact and an active control group. In this case, reduced grey matter volume may be related to a morphological brain feature of increased 'neural efficiency' (Durston and Casey 2006) as a function of gained expertise.

Together, the results of these studies suggest that when approaching a novel arithmetic problem, the brain of both adults and children – and even more so that of children with maths learning difficulties – places high demands on various neurocognitive processes, including those responsible for quantity manipulation, symbol recognition and decoding, counting strategies, working memory, cognitive control, and other types of executive functions anchored in parietal, occipital, temporal and prefrontal regions of the cortex. With training, and as arithmetical problems become more and more automatized, a decrease in activation in these brain regions is observed, indicating a lower use of neural resources while solving the task. Moreover, the studies presented in this section suggest that neural decreases may precede more focal engagement of other brain regions as a function of trained, well-practiced problems (Delazer et al. 2003). What does this functional brain reorganization reflect? And how is it achieved? Sections 12.3.2 and 12.3.3 describe a series of *neuroimaging training studies* suggesting that such functional reorganization may be the end-product of a dynamic neural process that is initially orchestrated by the MTL and its connections with cortical systems. A progressive strengthening of cortico-cortical connections and a gradual disengagement from the hippocampus may ultimately lead to the emergence of highly segregated neural modules within large-scale brain networks, reflecting high automatization of the learnt mathematical material.

12.3.2 The Interim Role of Hippocampal Structures for Integrating Arithmetic Problems and their solutions

Neuroimaging training studies have been pivotal in uncovering the time-limited role of the MTL, and particularly of the hippocampus, during arithmetic learning.

In the first study of its kind on mathematical learning, Supekar et al. (2013) trained 2nd and 3rd graders on efficient counting and retrieval strategies to solve addition and subtraction problems (the conceptual part of the training). Children then substantially practiced all these problems – which were of increasing difficulty – on a weekly basis (the drill part of the training), for a period of eight weeks. Structural brain data (MRI) and task-free resting-state fMRI data were collected for all children prior to the training, and both brain measures highlighted the key role played by the hippocampus in arithmetic learning. More specifically, values of hippocampal volume prior to training were a strong predictor of individual differences in performance gains: the greater the volume of the hippocampus, the higher the gains contingent to the training. Critically, this relationship was not evident in a no-contact control group who underwent no training for those two months.

Moreover, in the trained group, intrinsic functional connectivity between the hippocampus and regions of the prefrontal and temporal cortices before training was the strongest predictor of performance gains in arithmetic problem solving. Together, these results corroborate the hypothesis of an instrumental role of hippocampus morphology and task-free connectivity to individual differences in response to mathematical training.

Functional activity and task-based functional connectivity of the hippocampus have also been proven to be critical for the successful consolidation of arithmetical facts. Using the same training protocol as Supekar et al. – yet with two neuroimaging acquisition time-points (i.e., pre- and post-training) – Rosenberg-Lee and colleagues found that 2nd and 3rd graders who were part of the training group showed greater post-training engagement of the hippocampus as a function of higher rates in retrieval-use, during an arithmetic problem-solving task (Rosenberg-Lee et al. 2018). Critically, and also in this case, this effect was not observed in a no-contact control group who underwent no training. Furthermore, hippocampal-parietal functional connectivity during task increased with training and was positively correlated with changes in retrieval rates. Again, the no-contact control group did not show such relation.

These results are in line with longitudinal findings demonstrating the transient engagement of the hippocampus in a sample of slightly older children showing increases in retrieval rates during arithmetic problem solving (Qin et al. 2014). More specifically, hippocampal engagement during a simple arithmetic problem-solving task (e.g., '3 + 5 = 8') was not observed in younger (7–8-year-old) learners who were mostly solving the arithmetical problems via counting strategies, nor in adolescents or adults who were solving the problems via highly efficient retrieval strategies. Hippocampal engagement, and greater hippocampal–cortical connectivity as a function of fact retrieval, was only seen in children aged 10–11 years. This suggests that, in line with prominent theories of memory and learning (Frankland and Bontempi 2005; Smith and Squire 2009; Takashima et al. 2009), the hippocampus plays a pivotal, yet time-limited, role in the integration and initial consolidation of arithmetic facts.

Another series of studies on neurotypical adults further support this theory and hint at the idea that the number of times an arithmetic problem is repeated could be critical in determining the transient role of the hippocampus in arithmetic fact acquisition. For instance, Bloechle and colleagues (2016) – using a similar training paradigm as Delazer et al. (2003), but with fewer repetitions (i.e., thirty instead of ninety) and a larger set of multiplication problems – showed hippocampal activation (which was never reported by Delazer et al., 2003) for trained versus untrained problems after training. Furthermore, using exactly the same training paradigm, Klein and colleagues demonstrated that structural connectivity — defined as the number of white matter fibers — passing through the left hippocampus was higher after training, in a population of neurotypical adults (Klein et al. 2019). Together, these studies suggest that the frequency of item repetition may be a crucial factor in determining which brain structures are involved, at any given time-point, during arithmetic learning.

Additional hippocampal neural features have recently been associated with individual differences in maths learning profiles following training. In a recent study, Chang et al. (2019) trained 8–10-year-old neurotypical children on a set of double-digit plus single-digit addition problems (e.g., '75 + 8') across 5 sessions, over a 1-week period. After training, fMRI data was collected, together with behavioural data. During these sessions, children were tested on the problems they had learnt as well as on novel problems that were matched for difficulty and format to the trained ones. Unlike in other studies, behavioural performance was assessed not only at pre- and post-training sessions, but also at each day of the training. Hence, individual learning profiles could be determined for each child, allowing identification of specific neural features associated with faster and slower learners. While all children showed improved performance on trained problems, children who were identified as faster learners also showed better transfer effects to untrained problems. Notably, these children displayed higher degrees of overlap in the spatial patterns of hippo-campal activity between trained and untrained problems, hinting at mechanisms of near transfer. More specifically, in line with classical memory models (Collin et al. 2015; Bowman and Zeithamova 2018; Schlichting et al. 2015; Shohamy and Wagner 2008; Tompary and Davachi 2017), the hippocampus may be crucial for integrating local neural representations across structurally similar problems (i.e., trained and untrained), thereby generalizing representations of recently learnt items. More generally, these findings support the theory that the hippocampus plays a pivotal role in integrating information during maths learning, eventually leading to neocor-tical consolidation of arithmetic facts (Frankland and Bontempi 2005; Qin et al. 2014).

How are these arithmetic memory traces further strengthened at the neocortical level? One hypothesis is that as memory traces mature, connections between different cortical modules are enhanced, allowing newly formed memories for arithmetical facts to gradually function independently from the hippocampus (Frankland and Bontempi 2005). Accordingly, as the 'learning brain' acquires mathematical expertise, specific functional pathways would be preferentially strengthened (over others) to support such knowledge-consolidation (Jolles et al. 2016). A series of recent *neuroimaging training studies* of arithmetic learning and neural connectivity support this hypothesis.

12.3.3 Emergence of Specific Functional Brain Pathways and Systems for Mathematical Cognition

Along with brain changes indicative of (1) less neural demand for domain-general and domain-specific cognitive resources, and (2) memory consolidation processes orchestrated by the hippocampus, other neuroplasticity effects may underlie the emergence of efficient arithmetic problem-solving skills. More specifically, at the connectivity level — similarly to what we have seen for the remodulation and reconfiguration of brain activity (see section 12.3.1)— a general pattern seems to emerge, supporting the idea of an initially noisy system that gets progressively fine-tuned to ultimately strengthen the most efficient neural pathways and favour the development of segregated functional systems that can best aid mathematical cognition.

Neuroimaging training studies in children with developmental dyscalculia have been pivotal in assessing this hypothesis. Using the same training paradigm and design proposed by Kucian et al. (2011), Michels and colleagues demonstrated heightened levels of functional connectivity during a numerical ordering task between the IPS and regions of the prefrontal, parietal, occipital, and temporal cortices, in a group of 8–10-year-old children with developmental dyscalculia (Michels et al. 2018). Similar results were obtained with task-free connectivity data (Jolles et al. 2016). Critically, Michels et al. went on to show that such hyperconnectivity normalizes with numerical training: in the post-training neuroimaging session, the functional connectivity profile of children with developmental dyscalculia no longer differed from the profile of a neurotypical group. These results echo the notion that atypical mathematical processing may be characterized by widespread activity (Iuculano et al. 2015) and connectivity (Jolles et al. 2016) aberrancies. Moreover, these findings support the hypothesis of an initially noisier – yet highly plastic – system for problem solving underlying inefficient performance. After the system has normalized (Michels et al. 2018), more efficient, refined connections can start to develop as a function of successful arithmetic skill-acquisition. Indeed, using the same eight-week training program and design as other studies (Iuculano et al. 2015; Rosenberg-Lee et al. 2018 – featuring two neuroimaging acquisition time-points), Jolles and colleagues showed that white matter tracts innervating the prefrontal and temporal cortices were strengthened with maths training, and as a function of behavioural gains. More specifically, changes in performance efficiency during an arithmetic problem-solving task were correlated with changes in fractional anisotropy (an index of fibers' density and orientation, axonal diameter, and myelination of the white matter). This effect was found in the fronto-temporal part of the left superior longitudinal fasciculus, in a sample of 7–9-year-old children (Jolles et al. 2016). In a follow-up study, the same authors also reported functional reconfiguration of parietal circuits anchored in the IPS as a function of maths training and individual differences in performance (Jolles et al. 2016). More specifically, greater intrinsic functional connectivity following training was detected between the IPS and regions of the medial inferior and ventral temporo-occipital cortex, as well as the prefrontal and superior temporal cortices, as a function of behavioural gains. Critically, no effects were evident in a no-contact control group. Together, the results of these studies highlight the behavioural significance of neuroplasticity changes within cortical circuits, and further support the hypothesis of the emergence of efficient cortical systems underlying successful arithmetic learning.

Fine-tuned connectivity could eventually give rise to more segregated large-scale brain circuits for mathematical knowledge. Interestingly, functional segregation of cortical circuits (from the hippocampus) was recently demonstrated for faster arithmetic learners in a group of neurotypical primary school children, following a five-day arithmetic training (Chang et al. 2019). Specifically, the authors showed that better learning-rates were associated with greater differentiation of connectivity patterns between trained and untrained problems at the large-scale network level. Additional analyses revealed lower hippocampal–cortical connectivity for trained compared to novel problems (Chang et al. 2019). These results suggest that during successful arithmetic learning, large-scale network segregation may first occur across functional systems anchored in the hippocampus.

By contrast, *neuroimaging studies* of long-term arithmetic *training* can provide evidence for large-scale network reconfiguration at the cortical level, likely reflecting long-lasting strategy-dependent mechanisms for arithmetic problem solving. For instance, a recent study based on an abacus mental calculation training reports greater local efficiency and greater intra-module connections within the visual network in a population of children following training over more than a year (Xie et al. 2018). The abacus is a traditional visual calculator that has been used in China, Korea, Japan, and India since 1200 AD. It represents numbers via a special arrangement of beads in columns, where each column codes for a place value that increases from right to left. When trained on this device, expert subjects have the ability to mentally calculate numbers with up to ten digits at an incredible speed and a high level of precision (Stigler 1984). This remarkable performance is achieved gradually: first, subjects learn to operate the abacus beads with both hands; then, they learn to imagine and operate the beads in their mind with the help of finger movements; finally, as their calculation skills improve, they can manipulate numbers via an imagined mental abacus without actual finger movements (see also Chapter 11, Yeatman 2022). Thus far, a series of neuroimaging studies have demonstrated that this type of training can elicit high degrees of neuroplasticity in terms of structural and functional features, both in adults and children (see Li et al. 2016 for a review). Across the board, abacus experts tend to show greater reliance on brain regions important for visuospatial manipulations and motor control, compared to groups of non-experts (Chen et al. 2006; Li et al. 2013). In line with this, connectivity across visual and motor brain structures has also been found to be altered by this type of training (Hu et al. 2011). More specifically, after undergoing an abacus mental calculation training for 3 years (3–4 hours per week), a group of ~10-year-old children showed increased fractional anisotropy values across tracts of the occipito-temporal conjunction area, the corpus callosum, and the premotor projection (see also Li et al. 2013 for a similar result).

Critical to our argument here, abacus mental calculation training also seems to elicit neuroplasticity changes of large-scale network properties (Xie et al. 2018). As outlined earlier, Xie and colleagues reported greater local efficiency and intra-module connections within the visual network (Xie et al. 2018) in a group of children who underwent more than a year of abacus training. These findings indicate that abacus experts may indeed be using unique visuospatial strategies when solving arithmetic problems, suggesting that reconfiguration of large-scale functional brain systems following training could be strategy-dependent. More generally, these results support the idea that arithmetical expertise may be ultimately achieved via mechanisms of functional segregation at the large-scale network level.

Given the findings outlined here, a testable model may predict that initial (temporary) increases in connectivity across relevant brain regions (Jolles et al. 2016) can eventually support the emergence of segregated large-scale functional brain systems to successfully master arithmetical problems. Data from short-term maths training studies suggest that an initial functional segregation, supporting faster arithmetic learning, may occur across large-scale brain systems anchored in the hippocampus (Chang et al. 2019), while a longer training may induce functional segregation of large-scale cortical systems (Power et al. 2011), which may underlie differential strategies for expert trainees compared to novices. This is in line with recent findings from graph-theory studies showing that neurocognitive normative development may be characterized by a gradual, increased segregation of large-scale functional networks (Grayson and Fair 2017; Gu et al. 2015). More generally, this theoretical prediction resonates well with data from animal studies suggesting that functional segregation is related to enhanced clustering of cortical ensembles (Fang and Yuste 2017), indicating imprinted representations implemented into neighbouring groups of neurons with strong synaptic connectivity (i.e., intra-module connections) (Carrillo-Reid et al. 2016). Following this notion, well-mastered arithmetic problems could be stored as cortical ensembles that are easy to retrieve (Delazer et al. 2003; Kucian et al. 2011).

12.4 Brain-Level Effects of Remediating Math Learning Difficulties

Compared to the literature on developmental dyslexia, studies on neuroplasticity following maths training in individuals with developmental dyscalculia are rather scarce. To date, a total of three investigations – two of them using the same training paradigm – have been conducted (Iuculano et al. 2015; Kucian et al. 2011; Michels et al. 2018). These studies are described in Section 12.3, as they have also significantly contributed to the advancement of our knowledge on neuroplasticity as a function of maths learning. Yet, an additional value of imaging clinical cohorts in the context of a maths training paradigm is the possibility to evaluate the neural consequences of a given behavioural intervention. Notably, even when an intervention improves performance, the question that remains is whether the neurocognitive profile has become more typical or whether compensatory mechanisms have emerged (Butterworth et al. 2011).

The first study aimed at investigating the effects of a behavioural intervention at the brain level assessed a group of 8–10-year-olds with and without developmental dyscalculia, before and after a mental number line training (Kucian et al. 2011). This training, focused on strengthening the link between numbers and space, did improve performance in the clinical group, yet not to the level of neurotypical peers. Nevertheless, even if children with developmental dyscalculia did not fully catch up to their peers, significant decreases in brain activation across multiple parietal and prefrontal regions were observed in this group. Together, this study was the first (1) to provide evidence that a numerical training could trigger brain-related changes in a clinical cohort; and, most importantly, (2) to show that neuroplasticity may follow a similar trajectory as that seen in neurotypical individuals (e.g,. Delazer et al. 2003; Grabner et al. 2009; Ischebeck et al. 2009; Ischebeck et al. 2006), characterized by an (initial) disengagement of multiple cortical regions, reflecting lower neural demands for cognitive resources. Yet, this study did not formally assess neuroplasticity models of normalization and compensation. This was tested by another study which systematically evaluated the effects of a behaviourally-validated maths intervention (Fuchs et al., 2009; Fuchs et al., 2008; Fuchs et al., 2010; Fuchs et al., 2013; Powell et al., 2009; see also: Rosenberg-Lee et al., 2018) on brain function, in a group of 7-9-year-olds with developmental dyscalculia and a group of age-, IQ- and gender-matched neurotypical individuals (Iuculano et al. 2015). The authors showed that, in parallel with performance normalization on an arithmetic task, this training elicited extensive functional brain changes in the clinical cohort, normalizing their aberrant hyperactivation to the level of neurotypical peers (i.e., normalization model). More specifically, machine learning algorithms revealed that brain activity patterns in children with developmental dyscalculia were significantly discriminable from the patterns of neurotypical peers before training, but indistinguishable after training. This is in stark contrast with a compensatory model of neuroplasticity, which would have posited that after training, children with developmental dyscalculia would recruit additional and distinct (compensatory) brain systems, compared to neurotypical peers, still resulting in distinguishable (quantitative or qualitative) brain differences across groups. Moreover, these results do not support a persistent neural aberrancy model, which would have predicted that children with developmental dyscalculia would have continued to show atypical functional responses in the same brain areas as they did before training. In the interventional context, these findings suggest that a comprehensive training, designed to tap onto various cognitive competences simultaneously (e.g., number knowledge, counting principles, calculation strategies, etc.), and integrating conceptual- and drill-type approaches may effectively remediate deficits in this clinical group. Last but not least, the degree of brain normalization was significantly correlated with individual gains in maths performance, highlighting the neurocognitive significance of the findings. This datum is particularly informative on a translational level as it underlines the vast heterogeneity of learning outcomes, pushing for the development of other types of training approaches for non-responders. Michels and colleagues also demonstrated normalization of hyperactivity and functional connectivity in a group of 8–10-year-old children with developmental dyscalculia following a mental number line training (Michels et al. 2018). Effects were found in multiple brain circuits connected with the

IPS, and were accompanied by performance normalization on the number line task these children were trained on. Notably, the co-occurrence of multiple neuroplasticity effects (i.e., activity and connectivity features) is in line with the hypothesis that network-level aberrancies in developmental dyscalculia may hamper the ability of affected children to properly allocate neural resources for maths problem solving (Jolles et al. 2016), thereby contributing to their over-activation profile (Iuculano et al. 2015). Normalization of hyperconnectivity may, eventually, contribute to restoring neural activity-levels in this group (Michels et al. 2018). However, this hypothesis remains to be tested empirically.

In sum, the available literature suggests that behavioural maths interventions can elicit significant neuroplasticity effects in clinical developmental cohorts. Effects are evident across multiple brain systems in frontal, parietal, temporal, and occipital lateral regions known to support planning and working memory functions, numerosity judgements, counting procedures, and high-level decoding of visual and auditory number-stimuli (see Section 12.3 and Iuculano and Menon 2018 for a review). Critically, the (few) studies conducted so far indicate that neuroplasticity effects in children with developmental dyscalculia are characterized by marked functional activation and connectivity decreases during task performance. As we have seen, an initial disengagement of these cortical systems represents the first of a series of neuroplasticity processes ultimately leading to successful maths knowledge acquisition. Follow-up studies are needed to test whether neuroplasticity effects in clinical cohorts may follow the same hierarchical cascade of neural processes as in typical development.

Intervention studies aimed at remediating maths performance following a brain incident are even more scarce. Thus far, only one study has tracked the neural effects of a behavioural intervention – focused on rehabilitating simple arithmetical skills – in a patient who had suffered damage to the left-side posterior parietal cortex (Zaunmüller et al. 2009). Notably, after an intensive training spanning four weeks, the patient showed an increase in retrieval-based strategies for trained problems. At the brain level, activation increases in the right posterior parietal cortex for trained compared to untrained problems were reported. Interestingly, the effects were observed in the contralateral lesion area. These findings suggest that neuroplasticity can be successfully triggered by maths training even following brain insults. Moreover, it can be speculated that these compensatory mechanisms seem to anchor – wherever possible – on homologue systems that may have been in charge prior to the incident, and which correspond to those displaying learning effects in neurotypical adults (Delazer et al. 2003).

Overall, the studies outlined in this part of the chapter suggest that tracing the time course of learning-related brain modifications – first in typical, and then in atypical cohorts – can ultimately provide insights into the benefits and limitations of intervention approaches aimed at restoring maths performance in vulnerable learners.

12.5 Conclusion

In this chapter, I have reviewed the nascent literature on *neuroimaging training studies* of arithmetical learning and illustrated how this work has enhanced our understanding of the neural bases of mathematical cognition.

These types of studies render it possible to assess learning-contingent neuroplasticity in a dynamic yet controlled way. They can uncover, for example, the time-limited role of brain systems for the successful acquisition of maths problem solving skills, and in response to training. They can also demonstrate which neurocognitive systems may show aberrancies in populations with mathematical difficulties, and ultimately reveal the benefits of an intervention. Critically, by characterizing the hierarchical cascade of neurocognitive steps leading to successful (or unsuccessful) maths learning, these studies can ultimately inform remediation and educational strategies. More specifically, delineating the neural profile corresponding to a certain developmental stage or ability-level could provide guidance on the (best) type of intervention – or pedagogical strategy – to implement.

Thus far, the available literature suggests that mathematical proficiency is engendered via a series of progressive neurocognitive steps: (1) an initial over-engagement of multiple brain systems encompassing parietal, ventral temporo-occipital, temporal, and frontal cortices that support basic quantity manipulations, symbol recognition and decoding, counting strategies, working memory and other types of executive functions. This is followed by (2) a gradual disengagement of all these brain regions, reflecting lower demand for neurocognitive resources. Successively, (3) a (transient) recruitment of hippocampal systems aids the integration and consolidation of arithmetical facts in memory. Finally, (4) increases in selective connectivity across relevant cortical systems accompanied by (5) a gradual disengagement of the hippocampus ultimately leads to (6) the full specialization for maths problem solving at a more segregated large-scale systems' level, within stable functional constructs (i.e., cortical ensembles) that allow for flexible access to stored knowledge.

At the educational level, this information could be particularly useful to identify teaching and intervention programs that are targeted to the neurocognitive profile of the learner. For instance, a child or individual showing heightened activity levels across multiple cortical brain regions may benefit more from a comprehensive intervention tapping onto the fundamentals of arithmetical knowledge (e.g., number concepts, number words/symbols' recognition, efficient counting strategies, etc.) than from an associative training that 'stimulates' hippocampal consolidation mechanisms when this system is not yet ready to be targeted/engaged. Such an approach could instead be well suited for a child or individual whose brain systems are not at a stage of 'overload'. Climbing up the hierarchy, targeted practice to aid the sedimentation of successfully acquired arithmetical associations can support the emergence of segregated cortical neural networks for efficient maths problem solving. Yet, this type of approach may only be beneficial at a slightly later phase/stage, when hippocampal–cortical connections are established, and prior to the system becoming hippocampal-independent.

As mentioned earlier, *neuroimaging training studies* of arithmetic learning could differ on many parameters: length of the training, population studied (i.e., clinical versus neurotypical; children versus adults), type of training (i.e., conceptual/procedural versus drill-based), material (i.e., type of operation trained; curriculum-based versus custom-stimuli), and number of neuroimaging data acquisitions. The systematic manipulation of these parameters will provide the data-basis for refining models of mathematical cognitive development that can ultimately inform educational and clinical practices that are targeted to individual needs and neural profiles. As such, *neuroimaging training studies* represent one of the most promising means of investigation within the flourishing discipline of educational neuroscience.

Finally, it should be noted that the findings presented in this chapter are limited to North America, Asia, and Europe. Accordingly, it remains to be examined whether the reported results systematically generalize cross-culturally to individuals with different national and educational backgrounds.

Suggestions for Further Reading

Iuculano, T., A. Padmanabhan, and V. Menon. 2018. 'Systems Neuroscience of Mathematical Cognition and Learning: Basic Organization and Neural Sources of Heterogeneity in Typical and Atypical Development'. In *Heterogeneity of Function in Numerical Cognition*, edited by A. Henik and W. Fias, 287–336. Cambridge, MA: Academic Press.

Iuculano, T., and V. Menon. 2018. Development of Mathematical Reasoning. In: *Steven's Handbook of Experimental Psychology and Cognitive Neuroscience, Developmental and Social Psychology.* 4th ed., vol. 4: Developmental and Social Psychology. J. T. Wixted and S. Ghetti (Eds.). John Wiley and Sons Inc. pp. 183–223.

Zamarian, L., A. Ischebeck, and M. Delazer. 2009. 'Neuroscience of Learning Arithmetic: Evidence from Brain Imaging Studies'. *Neuroscience and Biobehavioral Reviews* 33 (6): 909–25.

Summary: Neurodevelopmental Foundations

(1) **Neuronal migration genes:** Dyslexia- and dyscalculia-related variants of the genes *DCDC2*, *DYX1C1*, *KIAA0319*, and *ROBO1* might not properly guide young nerve cells to their target position in the cortex (neuronal migration). These associations have been most consistently found for the parietal cortex, which is related to reading (e.g., phonological short-term memory) and maths (e.g., numerosity detection).

(2) **Dyslexia – auditory-phonological system:** The development of the auditory cortex and downstream phonological processing regions (superior temporal, inferior parietal, and inferior frontal cortices connected via the arcuate fasciculus) plays a causal role for the emergence of dyslexia in alphabetic learners. Auditory-phonological processing deficits occur already at the level of representations in the first two months of life. Imprecise phonological representations then in turn seem to affect the storage, access, and manipulation of speech information.

(3) **Dyslexia – print-to-speech conversion system:** The developing brains of children with dyslexia persistently reveal different activation (typically under-activation) of the left ventral occipito-temporal cortex and the superior temporal sulcus, which may hamper converting print to speech.

(4) **Dyslexia – articulation system:** The developing brains of children with dyslexia differently activate (typically overactivate) inferior frontal and premotor cortices which may support silent articulation as a potential compensatory mechanism for imprecise phonological representations.

(5) **Dyscalculia – (non-)symbolic number (manipulation) system:** Within the first years of life, children who develop dyscalculia reveal distinct parietal cortex activation and distinct functional and structural connectivity with the prefrontal cortex, which is possibly related to their difficulties in understanding and manipulating (non-)symbolic number information. These differences disappear after intervention, but the persistence of these effects is currently unknown.

PART V

Gender, Ethnicity, and Socioeconomic Background

13 Gender and Sex Differences in Dyslexia and Dyscalculia

Jessica F. Cantlon

13.1 Introduction

There are intrinsic similarities between boys and girls in the cognitive and neural mechanisms characterizing typical reading and mathematics development, with few and small behavioural differences emerging between genders in older age groups. The similarities between the cognitive and neural processes of boys and girls in these domains are sometimes surprising because folk beliefs about differences between males and females pervade scientific discourse in psychology and even impact empirical research (Hyde and Linn 1988) and clinical practices (Shaywitz et al. 1990). The universal patterns of cognitive and neural development across gender groups are important to appreciate, not only because they are potentially surprising empirical facts, but also because they expose candidate sources of disorder in reading and mathematics. Research on typically developing children can reveal the specialized cognitive and neural mechanisms at the core of reading-specific and mathematics-specific deficits in boys and girls.

Gender differences in cognition largely range from small to zero, and the small effect sizes of gender differences in cognition are important to consider when hypothesizing about the impact of gender on learning (Figure 13.1). Hyde (2005) showed that although a very large sample size might yield statistically significant gender differences in test scores, the actual sizes of the effects are often trivial – that is, effects so small that they are irrelevant in practice (i.e., effect sizes < 0.10). Zell and colleagues (2015) used a metasynthesis to test this claim and found that indeed most effect sizes on gender differences in cognition fell into this category.

Similarly, although biological sex differences manifest in aspects of the body and brain function, particularly those bound to sexually dimorphic neuroendocrinology, many measures indicate that neural variability is a continuum wherein the brains of males and females reflect one heterogeneous population rather than two distinct groups, much like other internal organs (Joel and Fausto-Sterling 2016). When gender differences do exist in reading and mathematics, there is significant evidence for environmental causes and little evidence of any biological or genetic causes that could be teased apart from social and

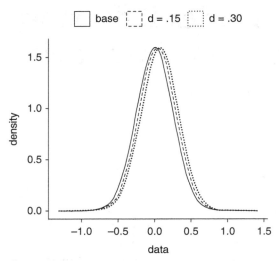

Figure 13.1 *Typical effect sizes of gender differences in reading and mathematics. The base distribution is shown in a solid black line and the other two distributions show how far the distributions would diverge at effect sizes of* d *= 0.15 (dashes) and* d *= 0.30 (dots). This is the typical range of effect sizes for gender differences in cognition, including mathematics and reading.*

environmental ones. A wide array of social factors generate different educational experiences for boys and girls.

Disordered reading and mathematics can take many forms. The terms 'dyslexia' and 'dyscalculia' are clinical categories used to describe a range of performance deficits, rather than designations of specifically impaired cognitive or neural mechanisms (see also Chapter 22, Lachmann, Bergström, Huber, and Nürk 2022). Evidence of the impact of gender on dyslexia and dyscalculia disorders is variable, with some studies showing differences and others showing similarities between gender groups. In the following sections, I show that this variability depends partly on the criteria used to diagnose impairment. Moreover, there are at least three possible non-exclusive explanations for equivocal findings of gender differences across studies: 1) dyslexia and dyscalculia diagnoses are not solely based on specific mechanisms for reading and mathematics; 2) dyslexia and dyscalculia impairments and/or diagnoses are yoked to social differences between boys and girls; and 3) dyslexia and dyscalculia disorders are linked to cascading psychological impairments with distinct risks in boys and girls. Here we discuss these potential causes of gender differences in reading and mathematics diagnoses, and argue that the existing evidence casts doubt on the cognitive and physiological specificity of gender differences in dyslexia and dyscalculia. We use the term 'gender' rather than 'sex' because most studies group children based on verbal reports of their gender and not on their chromosomes or other biological markers of sex.

13.2 Intrinsic Similarities between Boys and Girls in Development

13.2.1 Mathematics

Boys performed higher than girls on formal mathematics tests through the 1980s, but now both gender groups perform equally. Gender differences in mathematics performance are declining, or even non-existent, in countries with more gender-equal cultures (Else-Quest et al. 2010; Guiso et al. 2008). In an analysis of 2003 TIMSS (Trends in International Mathematics and Science Study) scores from nearly half a million students in 69 countries, the mean effect size of gender difference in maths performance was small, $d < 0.15$, with a range across countries centred over zero (d's = -0.42 to 0.40). In the United States, the male advantage in mathematics has been eliminated: state mathematics tests between 2005 and 2007 for grades 2–11 found equal mathematics performance for boys and girls, even in adolescence ($d = 0.0065$) (Hyde et al. 2008). The 2011 TIMSS showed no global gender differences in mathematics ability (Reilly et al. 2019). Furthermore, recent cognitive studies find no gender differences in the core components of mathematical cognition during childhood (Hutchison et al. 2019; Kersey et al. 2018; Lindberg et al. 2010).

Some older behavioural studies claimed that gender differences in performance *variance* could drive gender differences in mathematics outcomes, even in the absence of mean differences in performance (Hedges and Nowell 1995). This idea began in the 1800s and proposed that males, as a group, are more cognitively variable than females because they are the heterogametic sex. There is no good evidence, however, that this hypothesis applies to human cognition. Most claims about unique male variance in mathematics are based on older US data, and recent studies do not support those hypotheses (Lindberg et al. 2010). In recent data, boys and girls show no reliable gender difference in mean mathematics performance or in their variance ratio (Lindberg et al. 2010). Moreover, the magnitudes of variance ratios between genders vary considerably between countries (Reilly et al. 2019). Cultural variability in the gender variance ratio implicates a role for cultural and educational environment in causing the variability ratios, such as the range of available intellectual opportunities for males compared to females.

Spatial cognition is often claimed to engage distinct faculties in males and females. However, boys and girls typically do not perform differently on the Block Design task, the main spatial subtest of general IQ in childhood (Jirout and Newcombe 2015). This suggests that young children do not exhibit gender differences in overall spatial ability. A study of 4–7-year-olds (N = 847) found no gender differences in spatial performance, despite the fact that parents engaged in more spatial and maths play (i.e., board games, puzzles, blocks) with boys than with girls (Jirout and Newcombe 2015). Early environmental differences between boys and girls could thus lead to differences in mathematical or spatial cognition later in development.

In adults, males tend to perform higher than females on some dynamic spatial tasks, whereas females outperform males on some static object location tasks (Uttal et al. 2013). Training studies have shown that performance on these tasks is malleable, even with short-term interventions, and some studies have found that spatial training can even eliminate adult gender differences in spatial tasks (Feng et al. 2007). Adults perform equally on Raven's Progressive Matrices, independently of gender (see Halpern et al. 2007 for review). Thus, adults might show gender differences in performance on some specialized maths-related tasks. Nevertheless, in those studies it is impossible to disentangle intrinsic cognitive differences from sociocultural effects because there are known environmental differences between boys and girls and performance is highly malleable.

Children's brains function similarly during mathematics tasks in early childhood, independently of gender. These findings are based on functional neuroimaging data from typically developing children, using methods such as functional magnetic resonance imaging (fMRI). First, it is important to point out that the neural networks we consider mathematics-related are established by random effects analyses of neural activation (relative to either a baseline or control condition) across mixed gender groups, usually half male and half female. Observations of large-scale similarities across people in these analyses indicate that human brains process mathematical content similarly across gender groups.

The specific impact of gender on mathematical processing in the brain has been tested in a few studies. In a recent study of 3–10-year-old children (N = 104), girls' and boys' brains exhibited common functions during mathematical processing across analyses (Kersey et al. 2018; Kersey et al. 2019). Children watched educational lessons about counting and arithmetic during fMRI scanning. The network of brain regions systematically engaged by mathematical content included the intraparietal sulcus (IPS), anterior cingulate (ACC), and inferior frontal gyrus (IFG) – regions commonly engaged during mathematics processing in adults (see Chapter 10, Kucian and McCaskey 2022). There were no gender differences in children's neural responses to mathematics content, neither in their neural responses during educational video viewing, nor in their rates of neural development for mathematical processing. In fact, statistical equivalence emerged between boys and girls throughout the brain. Tests of statistical equivalence were based on positive evidence of distribution similarities between genders using Bayes Factor analysis, rather than from simple failures to reject the null hypothesis. Furthermore, boys' and girls' maths abilities related to their rates of neural development within the same brain regions. Specifically, amplitude patterns in neural time courses were equally correlated across children of the same and of different genders.

The network of brain regions that adults engage during mathematical processing is consistent across adults, and, like in children, includes activation in the IPS, IFG, and ACC, among other regions (e.g., Amalric and Dehaene 2017; Cantlon 2012). Studies reporting maths-related gender differences in the brains of adults are rare. Moreover, any observed gender differences are subtle and difficult to interpret in terms of their functional significance. One fMRI study compared twenty-four men and twenty-five women and found that both groups engage the same network of brain regions during three-digit identification and calculation; however, men showed greater differences in activation between identification and calculation, whereas women showed more similar activation on both tasks (Keller and Menon 2009). There were no significant behavioural differences between gender groups. It is difficult to interpret the meaning of subtle group differences in task activation, especially when the neural network and behaviours are equivalent between gender groups.

Interestingly, gender differences in *attitudes* about mathematics are larger than any gender difference in mathematics ability. Meta-analytic studies show consistent gender differences in attitudes and affect towards mathematics, with boys holding more positive attitudes about maths, particularly in high school where the effect size of the gender difference in self-confidence in mathematics is $d = 0.25$ (Hyde et al. 1990). In the 2003 TIMSS data, boys reported more positive maths attitudes and affect (d's $= 0.10$ to 0.33); cross-national effect sizes ranged from $d = -0.61$ to 0.89. Similarly, results from the 2011 and 2015 TIMSS data indicate that gender differences in students' self-concepts are significant in most countries, favouring boys (Mejía-Rodríguez et al. 2020; Reilly et al. 2019). Girls also tend to report lower confidence and higher anxiety about their mathematics abilities compared to boys (Hyde et al. 1990; Beilock et al. 2010; Casey et al. 1997; Fredricks and Eccles 2002: Australian, US, and German samples). Effects of gender differences in attitudes tend to be small, but those effect sizes often are larger than gender differences in mathematics abilities (Else-Quest et al. 2010). Moreover, gender differences in attitudes remain even after effects of student achievement and parental involvement are controlled (Mejía-Rodríguez et al. 2020). This suggests that students' attitudes are not solely caused by ability – though a direct causal test is needed.

For decades, the default position was that gender differences in cognition are biological and fixed (e.g., Jensen 1998) but this view is changing as new data emerge (Ceci et al. 2014). Any test of cognitive ability that shows evidence of gender differences, however, faces the difficulty of disentangling biological from social factors. As described earlier, some narrow tests of spatial skills show gender differences in childhood and adulthood (Halpern et al. 2007). For example, one study showed that boys outperform girls on the Mazes subtest of the Wechsler Preschool and Primary Scale of Intelligence, with a small effect size of $d = 0.30$ (Levine et al. 1999). Additionally, adults show gender differences on mental rotation tasks (e.g., Miller and Halpern 2014), but the causes of those differences are likely environmental (Ceci et al. 2014). One example of evidence for such environmental influence is that gender differences in cognition are decreasing over time due to changes in their sociocultural causes (Miller and Halpern 2014).

Social differences between boys and girls in early environments and social attitudes are a likely source of behavioural differences. For instance, although 4–7-year-old boys might show advantages over girls in tests of spatial skills, their parents also report more spatial play with boys compared to girls, suggesting a likely sociocultural influence on gender differences in spatial cognition (Jirout and Newcombe 2015; US sample). Similarly, in maths and science, teachers tend to show gender-based allocations of time spent encouraging students, praising students, and explaining concepts to students, with boys receiving more time than girls (Wellesley College: Center for Research on Women 1992; Jones and Wheatley 1990; Kelly 1998; Becker 1981). This is important because adults' perceptions of a child's ability predict that child's later maths achieve-ment scores (Bleeker and Jacobs 2004).

Parents' expectations about their children's success also correlate with children's own self-concepts of their abilities and their performance on maths tasks (Jussim and Eccles 1992; Bleeker and Jacobs 2004). In this context, it has to be taken into account that male self-concept in mathematics tends to be higher than females' (Hyde et al. 2008; Mejía-Rodríguez et al. 2020). A central concern in maths education is that gender differences in mathematics self-concept may be caused by gender stereotypes that characterize mathematics as a male domain (Cvencek et al. 2011; Master et al. 2017), and that those stereotypes are conveyed to children by significant adults, such as parents or teachers (Gunderson et al. 2012). A recent study provided causal evidence of gendered socialization in mathematics (Bian et al. 2017). Specifically, Bian and colleagues showed that by the age of 6 years girls are sensitive to the stereotype that boys are smarter than girls, and they believe that this difference makes boys more likely than girls to excel in mathematics – which in turn caused girls to shy away from novel mathematical activities that were said to be for 'really smart' people. A sociocultural influence on mathematical development is demon-strably strong. Thus, although there is speculation that gender differences in a subset of maths abilities might emerge from interactions between maths training and sexually dimorphic qualities (i.e., behaviour resulting from differences in hormone levels; Geary 1989; Arnold et al. 2004), there simply is no firm evidence for the existence of any innate, mechanistic, and immutable gender differences in mathem-atics ability. Instead, there is evidence for early cognitive and neural similarities between gender groups in core mathematics abilities, and for gender differences in auxiliary social factors such as attitudes and inclusion.

13.2.2 Reading

Gender differences in reading skill typically are not observed in children younger than 10 years, but they are robust and reliable in older children. In a recent study of 1,075 2nd- and 3rd grade children (8–9 years old), boys and girls performed equally on reading comprehension at all levels: the word, sentence, and text levels (all d's < 0.1; Stutz et al. 2016, German sample). However, girls at this age reported slightly greater involvement in reading compared to boys ($d = 0.14$). Specifically, girls reported marginally higher values than boys on a four-point scale to questions such as 'Do you read because books and stories are often fascinating?' Boys, on the other hand, reported slightly higher values than girls on questions such as 'Do you read because you want to outperform others in your class?' ($d = 0.24$). Thus, in early childhood there are no gender differences in core reading comprehension, but there are slight differ-ences in reading interest and motivation.

Empirical evidence shows that reading motivation is related to reading amount, and that reading amount in turn contributes to reading skill (McElvany et al. 2008; Schiefele et al. 2012; Stutz et al. 2016). By 4th grade, girls read more frequently than boys and have more positive attitudes than boys towards reading and schoolwork (Logan and Johnston 2009; PIRLS 2006). Thus, it is no surprise that slight gender differences favouring girls are observed in reading comprehension scores in 4th grade and higher. International studies examining reading comprehension in 10-year -old children have observed a gender difference favouring girls in most countries (PIRLS 2001; PIRLS 2006; PIRLS 2016). However, the effect sizes of these gender differences are small. In 2016, they ranged from d = 0.05 (Austria) to d = 0.2 (Saudi Arabia). In the United States, the effect size of the gender difference in reading achievement favouring girls is small: d = 0.05 (Mullis et al. 2017; PIRLS 2016). In some countries, such as Portugal and Macao, boys and girls perform equally on reading tests. This suggests that gender differences in reading comprehension are environmental.

Older adolescents show larger gender differences in reading, spelling, and writing scores because gender differences in reading emerge gradually with age (Reilly et al. 2019). Hedges and Nowell (1995) examined public databases of test scores from US 15–22-year-olds and found both mean gender differences in reading ability favouring girls and an overrepresentation of boys who are poor readers compared to girls – but these effects were small and variable. In one data set based on the National Assessment of Educational Progress (US) they found that girls showed significantly higher reading scores in each of seven years of assessment between 1971 and 1992, with effect sizes ranging from $d = 0.18$ to 0.30. The ratio of boys to girls in the bottom 10% of the distribution ranged from 1.07 to 1.20. In the other five large data sets, gender effects were smaller: boys and girls scored similarly on reading comprehension in three data sets (ds −0.002 to +0.09), and the other two data sets showed a small advantage for girls (ds <0.18). Variance ratios across these data sets were nearly equal (VRs = 1.03 to 1.16), and the gender distribution was asymmetrical, with more boys in the bottom tail and generally more girls in the upper tail. Hedges and Nowell argued that there are gender differences in average reading skill and also that males are more variable than females in performance – a finding that contributed to an overarching hypothesis of greater male cognitive variability.

It must be noted that the evidence for the male variability hypothesis in the original Hedges and Nowell study is questionable because it did not neatly describe boys' reading performance and, though it was initially met with enthusiasm and claims of genetic origins (Jensen 1998), support for it has since waned. For example, Reilly et al. (2019) found that boys were not overrepresented in both tails of the reading distribution of recent NAEP assessments. More boys than girls were poor readers in grade 12, but the effect was reversed at the upper tail of the reading distribution: more girls than boys achieved advanced literacy. This performance asymmetry, which is also evident in the original Hedges and Nowell analysis, is inconsistent with a genetic male variability hypothesis. Instead, social differences are considered a likely source of the patchy gender differences observed in variance between boys and girls (Deary 2003; Feingold 1994).

Gender differences in reading scores are often small, vary across tests and cohorts, are culturally variable, and increase gradually from 10 to 18 years of age. In a recent study of reading comprehension in 113,000 Canadian adolescents, the effect size of the female reading advantage was trivially small (White 2007). Gender differences in reading favouring girls accounted for less than 1% of variance in reading achievement. For contrast, group differences in 'topic of study', whether academic or applied, accounted for 22.8% of the variance in reading. 'Topic of study' is a curriculum, not a supposed 'trait' like gender, yet it accounts for more variance in students' reading comprehension than gender. 'Topic of study' is also influenced by social factors such as family income and parental education level. Irregularities in the effects of gender on reading have led some to conclude that gender differences in reading ability have been overstated. Gender differences are small, slow-developing, and inconsistent perhaps because they are a product of society.

Just as for mathematics development, reading ability differences between boys and girls are smaller than their differences in *attitudes*, and those differences relate to reading frequency (UK sample: Logan and Johnston 2009). In fact, gender differences in reading comprehension are known to disappear when motivation and reading strategies are controlled (German sample: Artelt et al. 2010). The already small gender gaps in reading further approach zero when informational reading is tested compared to literary reading, which also may reflect differing attitudes towards content types between boys and girls (Mullis et al. 2017; White 2007; international sample; PIRLS 2016; White 2007). Reading is socially regarded as feminine in nature, and gender stereotypes about language are held by both males and females (Halpern et al. 2011; Canadian sample: Plante et al. 2013). Logan and Johnston (2010) argue that girls are generally socialized to read more and better than boys. Differing social pressures between gender groups can have cascading effects on cognitive development. Attitudes and motivation for reading and schoolwork are strongly associated with reading skill, especially in boys but also in girls (Baker and Wigfield 1999; Logan and Medford 2011; Stutz et al. 2016). Together, this research suggests that social experience, and consequently interest and motivation for reading, distinguishes the reading development of boys from that of girls.

If boys and girls show different motivations to read, and different attitudes towards reading, then their reading outcomes could be different, including their behaviour and brains. A general confound in behavioural and neural studies of complex cognition is that a wide range of thoughts, motivations, and emotions can modulate behavioural and neural output. For example, behavioural and neural output during cognitive tests can be modulated by anxiety (US samples: Ashcraft and Krause 2007; Young et al. 2012) and motivation or engagement (US samples: Berch and Mazzocco 2007). Moreover, structural and functional neural signatures of reading are not exempt from short- and long-term social influences, and they are not fixed properties of the body, but rather can change even with short-term training (e.g., US sample: Poldrack et al. 1998). Yet, even considering the vast potential influences on reading development and notable social and environmental differences between boys and girls, males and females show remarkably similar reading development.

Studies of gender differences in reading are mostly based on global assessments of reading comprehension. These reading comprehension scores cannot tease apart component processes, and thus are not a good measure of the mechanisms underlying reading. Reading is composed of word decoding and recognition, lexical and semantic identification, grammatical rules, semantic connections within and between sentences, background knowledge and inference, working memory, and executive function (Castles et al. 2018). Any one component, or a combination of these components, could be a source of gender differences in reading comprehension (not to mention sources such as attention, attitudes, and motivation). In order to claim that males and females differ in reading, as opposed to some other aspect of cognition, it is important to measure the specific cognitive components of reading.

When narrower tests of reading skill are assessed, there are no major gender differences. For example, word decoding is a well-defined and precise measure of reading cognition, and is a primary component underlying early reading acquisition. Seymour et al. (2003) measured 1st grade word and non-word decoding in a large sample of 684 children across multiple countries. Boys and girls performed equally in reading accuracy and speed across conditions. This is evidence that orthographic decoding, perhaps the most significant reading-specific cognitive component in early childhood, functions similarly in boys and girls. Similarly, a study of 140 19-year-olds that were tested on Bell and Perfetti's (1994) word decoding task found no statistically reliable differences in decoding ability between males and females ($d = 0.17$; US sample: Hannon 2014). Word decoding ability was highly and equally predictive of reading comprehension in both gender groups (R = 0.48 females, R = 0.61 males). Thus, whether measuring 6-year-olds or 19-year-olds, word decoding functions similarly between gender groups. When reading ability is precisely defined as 'speed and accuracy of word and non-word reading', there are no gender differences. Gender differences only sometimes emerge when the diagnostic criteria shift to more complex skills in older children, such as reading comprehension or writing, which are aggregates of multiple underlying mechanisms with multiple causal influences.

The neural bases of reading also show large-scale similarities across gender groups, both in children and in adults. As for mathematics, it is important to point out that what we know about the neural basis of reading is determined by random effects analyses of neural activation across mixed gender groups, typically half male and half female. This means that the networks we consider reading-related are by definition engaged by boys and girls, men and women. The neural regions engaged across male and female subjects during reading tasks include the left occipito-temporal cortex and the left perisylvian language cortex, including the superior temporal sulcus and the planum temporale (see Chapter 9, Fraga González, Jednoróg, and Brem 2022). There is large-scale similarity in how human brains process words, phrases, and sentences independently of gender, and, thus far, there are no robust and reliable language-specific gender differences.

One often-cited study that is interpreted as evidence of gender differences in the neural basis of reading is a study by Clements and colleagues (US sample: Clements et al. 2006). In that study, fifteen men and fifteen women aged 19–35 years completed a phonological task in which they read two four-letter nonsense words and pushed a button if they rhymed. There were no gender differences in task performance. fMRI analyses of subjects' neural activation showed that both groups engaged the left IFG during the task, and between-group whole-brain statistics showed no group differences between males and females. All participants, regardless of gender, showed left-hemisphere dominance. Region-of-interest (ROI) analyses of the number of suprathreshold voxels in atlas-defined IFG (BA 44/45) and inferior parietal lobe (IPL) revealed a greater number of suprathreshold voxels in the left hemisphere IFG for men (89% of suprathreshold voxels across the right + left IFG) compared to women (66%). Thus, whole-brain patterns of activation during this task were similar between males and females, and subtle differences were observed in a narrower atlas-based ROI analysis. Because the samples are so small, a number of factors could distinguish the subjects in the male and female groups, including age and life history, meaning that the subtle activation differences between groups could have explanations other than gender. Importantly, the overall results support large-scale gender similarities in the functional network underlying word processing. Moreover, since the subtle gender differences in lateralization are unrelated to any performance differences, it is unclear how this phonological task and its neural correlates might relate to individual reading development or ability.

Many studies have investigated gender differences in language lateralization using neuroimaging techniques (see, e.g., Eliot 2011; Wallentin 2009). Importantly, however, neuroimaging studies of language processing with small samples are more likely to report gender differences than studies with larger samples, and studies with large samples do not find reliable gender differences in brain structure or function (Wallentin 2009; Bishop and Wahlsten 1997; Sommer 2004; Sommer et al. 2008). Although the hypothesis that females show more bilateral language-related activity than males might seem well-established, its basis in empirical data is weak (Wallentin 2009). Recently, Sommer and colleagues (Sommer 2004; Sommer et al. 2008) conducted a meta-analysis on 26 neuroimaging studies, with more than 2,100 subjects, and found no effect of gender on language lateralization, neither in children nor in adults. Instead, large-scale gender similarities in structure and function were observed throughout the human brain, despite documented social, environmental, and attitude differences towards reading in boys and girls.

Finally, there are no major gender differences in reading comprehension and vocabulary in adults. Composite reading comprehension scores and vocabulary scores are equivalent for adult males and females, and there is no difference in the number of males and females in each tail of the distribution ($d = -0.02$; Hannon 2014; Hyde and McKinley 1997). Any gender differences that might appear in childhood appear to have little impact on adult vocabulary and reading comprehension. This suggests that any gender differences observed during early childhood are superficial: they are rare, erratic, small, mutable, or temporary.

13.3 Gender-Specific Prevalence Ratios Depend on Diagnostic Criteria

Gender ratios reported for dyscalculia are inconsistent. Some studies report prevalence higher in boys (Barbaresi et al. 2005), some note prevalence as higher in girls (Dirks et al. 2008), while other studies report equal prevalence between genders (e.g., Badian 1986; Badian 1999; Gross-Tsur et al. 1996; Koumoula et al. 2004; Lewis et al. 1994; Mazzocco and Myers 2003). Ramaa and Gowramma (2002) found that gender ratios varied depending on whether dyscalculia was diagnosed using a maths test only (prevalence higher in boys), teacher referral (prevalence higher in girls), or maths test impairment excluding reading and writing test impairments (equal prevalence).

A more recent study examined gender differences against multiple diagnostic criteria in 1,004 children aged 7–10 years (Devine et al. 2013). The gender ratio in dyscalculia was equivalent when the diagnostic threshold was defined in absolute terms, meaning that boys and girls were equally likely to show learning impairments. Using relative thresholds like IQ-discrepancy, there also were no gender differences in dyscalculia diagnoses. When using relative thresholds defined with a mathematics-reading discrepancy, a gender difference emerged wherein girls were more likely to be diagnosed with dyscalculia than boys. However, those gender differences were driven by high reading performance in girls, not poor mathematics performance. Children who had 1–1.5 SD difference between mathematics and reading performance often had average mathematics performance and high reading performance – a profile that does not reflect mathematics impairment but instead reflects gifted reading perform-ance. When gifted readers were excluded, the same number of boys and girls had average or above-average reading performance and mathematics performance below 1 SD of the mean. Thus, diagnostic cut-offs greatly affect the prevalence of dyscalculia and the emergence of gender differences, which suggests that gender differences in dyscalculia are unreliable and may have superficial causes.

Gender comparisons in dyslexia are similarly fraught with complications. Peterson and Pennington set the prevalence rate of dyslexia at 7%, defined as reading achievement scores 1.5 standard deviations below the mean (Peterson and Pennington 2012). Dyslexia is diagnosed at a rate of 1.8:1 to 2:1 in boys compared to girls (Flannery et al. 2000; Wheldall and Limbrick 2010), though some report higher ratios. The reliability and causes of this gender difference are debated. Shaywitz et al. (1990) noted that more boys than girls are identified as poor readers by educational institutions, but in epidemiological studies, girls and boys approach equal representation (Hawke et al. 2009; Jiménez et al. 2011; Rutter et al. 2004). Similarly, Siegel and Smythe (2005) reported no gender differences in reading disorder prevalence in a large-scale longitudinal study. That study used cut-off criteria of 1 and 2 standard deviations below the mean on standardized reading tests. The prevalence of boys in referred samples for dyslexia screening is higher than in population samples, which is known to reflect social biases (Hawke et al. 2009). The implication is that the prevalence of reading impairment in girls may be under-reported, and that there is an elevated referral bias for boys. Just as for dyscalculia, the diagnostic cut-offs and control tests make a big difference in how many and which children are considered reading impaired and dyslexic.

Absolute cut-offs on the reading test distribution, which are often used to diagnose dyslexia, do not discriminate among the underlying mechanisms or causes of dyslexia. Claims about high rates of dyslexia in boys are sometimes based (circu-larly) on evidence that there are more boys than girls who are 'poor readers'.

Children subsumed in the category 'poor reader', however, could be impaired in a range of mental operations, ranging from word recognition and working memory to semantic memory, executive function and theory of mind – all of these components are necessary in skilled reading, and one or many of these components could be impaired in poor readers.

Gender differences in the neural bases of dyslexia and dyscalculia have not been observed. Yet even if such differences were confirmed, it would be difficult to determine whether those differences were causes or consequences of different reading and mathematics behaviours. A wide array of factors can land a student in the bottom 10–20% of the distribution on a maths or reading test. The causes and profiles of those performance levels are likely not uniform across students. Wide variability in cause is possibly the reason that gender differences in dyscalculia and dyslexia are so unreliable and fluctuate under different diagnostic criteria and assays.

13.4 Dyslexia and Dyscalculia Diagnoses Are Sensitive to Social Differences between Boys and Girls

As reviewed earlier, mathematics and reading development in typically developing children are impacted by social factors. The social impact on gender differences in mathematics and reading is evident in a global decline in gender gaps on school tests over time. Gender differences in mathematics performance are declining, or even non-existent in countries with more gender-equal cultures (Else-Quest et al. 2010; Guiso et al. 2008). Gender differences in reading, favouring girls, have also declined from the 1970s to the present, in national and international data sets (e.g., Loveless 2015), especially in elementary school children. Nevertheless, the magnitude of these differences in reading remain larger than those in mathematics (Reilly et al. 2019).

In young children, there are environmental differences between boys and girls in their social engagement with reading and mathematics. Parents engage in more spatial and physical play with boys compared to girls, whereas girls are socialized to read more than boys by parents and teachers (Jirout and Newcombe 2015; Jirout and Newcombe 2015). Attitudes and motivation distinguish older boys and girls in reading and mathematics and yield effect sizes more than double the typically small performance differences in these domains (Else-Quest et al. 2010; Logan and Johnston 2009). In mathematics, boys report higher confidence than girls beginning around 8th grade, whereas in reading girls report more positive attitudes than boys and higher motivation beginning around 4th grade. In high school, there are comparable gender differences in attitudes and motivations, with slightly larger performance differences between boys and girls, albeit still small effects (Else-Quest et al. 2010; Reilly et al. 2019). The path from social gender differences in early childhood, to attitude and motivation differences in mid-childhood, to performance differences in late childhood suggests a major social influence on reading and mathematics development. Social factors affect the amount of practice that children get with reading and mathematics. In extreme or even in moderate forms, the social influences which push boys towards mathematics and girls towards reading could, probabilistically, yield more boys in the bottom of the reading distribution, versus more girls in the bottom of the mathematics distribution, and result in gender differences in diagnoses of dyslexia and dyscalculia from distributional scores (i.e., 1 SD below mean).

Social influences can also impact children's performance directly. Negative emotional reactions to reading and mathematics, such as maths anxiety, can develop during the early school years (Newstead 1998), and are associated with learning disorders (Rubinsten and Tannock 2010; Devine et al. 2012). Parents and teachers have certain beliefs and emotions regarding mathematics that can influence the performance of girls and boys differently (Beilock et al. 2010). The behaviour of significant adults in the social environment can impact children's performance. Although it is unclear whether maths or reading anxiety is a cause or a consequence of learning disorders, the association of learning-related anxiety with maths and reading disorders suggests that some cases of impairment could have social origins. Social influences on learning-related anxiety are observed more commonly in girls than boys (Maloney et al. 2013), though it is unclear why (see Chapter 5, Szűcs 2022, for a discussion of this issue).

Finally, dyscalculia and dyslexia referrals by significant adults, such as parents and teachers, are also permeable to social influences. For example, teacher- and parent-referrals for childhood dyslexia are higher for boys than for girls, but epidemiological studies of dyscalculia do not show nearly the same gender asymmetry as the referrals (US sample: Shaywitz et al. 1990). The discrepancy between the gender ratio in the referrals versus the population suggests that teachers and parents are more likely to think that boys are poor readers compared to girls. This social difference could be related to stereotypes about boys and reading, or it could be a social judgement based on maturational differences in boys versus girls, including higher rates of social misconduct in boys compared to girls (Berkout et al. 2011; Chaplin and Aldao 2013; Costenbader and Markson 1998; Veenstra et al. 2010).

13.5 Dyslexia and Dyscalculia Are Linked to Gender Differences in Antecedent Impairments

Researchers sometimes intuit that if boys and girls show differences in rates of dyslexia and dyscalculia then those differences must be genetic. Currently there is no known direct genetic cause of these disorders, let alone one that distinguishes boys from girls (Meaburn et al. 2008; Ludwig et al. 2008; see also Chapter 6, Malanchini and Gidziela 2022, and Chapter 8, Skeide 2022). Instead, a wide range of biopsychological factors influence reading and mathematics impairments (Massand and Karmiloff-Smith 2015). Basic-level deficits early in development cascade over developmental time and impact children's phenotypic outcomes variably across domains. Children may show gender differences in their frequencies of dyslexia and dyscalculia due to the cascading effects of psychosocial disorders which show early gender differences but are not specifically related to mathematics or reading. For example, if a child has an extreme temperament or developmental delay early in development, that child may be more likely to struggle generally with formal education. It may initially appear that the child has a reading-related deficit, since reading is the first intensive, formal learning in which children engage. However, the reading deficit is not caused by reading-specific mechanisms, it is caused by an antecedent disorder that exercises its influence first and most noticeably in reading. Gender differences in children's susceptibility to early mental health adversity could cascade into gender differences in early learning that impact some domains worse than others.

Boys are more prone to early mental health adversity than girls. For example, males may be more vulnerable than females to neurological impairments during fetal and infant development (see Chapter 7, Hoeft and Bouhali 2022). The rate of premature birth is approximately 1% to 5% higher for males versus females (e.g., Cooperstock and Campbell 1996; Zeitlin et al. 2002). Males also have higher rates than females of fetal and neonatal mortality and are more vulnerable to long-term neurological impairments after preterm birth (Peacock et al. 2012). In one study of infants born prematurely (23–28 week gestational age), male sex was associated with higher incidents of cranial ultrasound abnormality than female sex (20% vs. 12%), and males were more likely than females to experience cognitive delay, measured by a Bayley Mental Development Index (≤ 70 at 24 months; Peacock et al. 2012). There are multiple hypotheses for why this sex difference emerges, including simple mechanisms such as earlier conceptions for boys, relative to the reproductive cycle, yielding earlier births for boys (James 2000). Regardless of the underlying mechanisms, boys appear to begin development with greater vulnerability to neurocognitive impairments than females, and this early difference in vulnerability could have cascading effects on their academic development.

Later in development, there are several cognitive disorders that are more common in boys compared to girls (Halpern et al. 2011). Neurodevelopmental disorders including speech, language, and learning disorders, attention deficit hyperactivity disorder (ADHD), cerebral palsy, Tourette's syndrome, and autism are all diagnosed more often in boys than in girls (e.g., Abramowicz and Richardson 1975; Bauermeister et al. 2007; Gualtieri and Hicks 1991). Developmental Language Disorder (DLD) is a condition in which a child has a persistent deficiency in language acquisition including phonology, vocabulary, sentence structure, and discourse (American Psychiatric Association 2013). DLD affects 7–8% of children (Norbury et al. 2016). In children who were referred for speech and language testing and considered at risk for DLD, boys outnumbered girls 2:1. Relatedly, Specific Learning Disorder (SLD) is defined by persistent difficulties with learning and academic skills (American Psychiatric Association 2013). It may be more or less selective for skills related to reading, writing, or maths. As indicated earlier, boys outnumber girls in the lower end of the distribution of reading competences, and the lowest percentiles are likely to be diagnosed with SLD or dyslexia (by definition). The gender ratio of SLD is around 2:1 for males versus females (Miles et al. 1998), which accords with gender ratios found in reading impairments. A recent meta-analysis estimated that males are 1.83 times more likely than females to have reading difficulties between ages 6 and 14 years (Quinn 2018). Thus, multiple disorders show similar gender disparities and may be interdependent. In particular, a dyslexia diagnosis with a co-occurring deficit is much more common than a dyslexia diagnosis without a co-occurring deficit.

The causes of these gender differences in childhood neurodevelopmental disorders are unclear, and many researchers argue that they have simply been over-diagnosed in boys. Accumulating evidence suggests that girls have been under-referred for special education services, and boys have been over-referred (Anderson 1997; Vogel 1990; Shaywitz et al. 1990; Liederman et al. 2005). One likely reason why boys are over-diagnosed with learning disorders by clinicians and educators is that they display behavioural or attentional difficulties more frequently than girls (McGee et al. 2002). Conduct disorder, for example, is associated with poor impulse control and ADHD in both boys and girls, but it is significantly more common in boys (Berkout et al. 2011; Veenstra et al. 2010). Longitudinal research with 5th to 8th grade children shows that poor effortful control predisposes children to school behavioural problems and that boys show lower effortful control and higher school behavioural problems than girls (US sample: Atherton et al. 2019). Gender differences in children's behavioural dispositions in school could lead to differences in referrals and diagnoses for learning disorders, as well as to differences in academic achievement.

Externalizing and inattention disorders are more commonly reported in boys than girls, and can interfere with educational outcomes, particularly reading in boys. Externalizing behaviour in kindergarten is known to predict reading impairment at older ages (Rabiner and Coie 2000; Prior et al. 2001). The causes and specificity of the relation between early inattention, externalizing, gender, and reading development are currently unknown. However, the relation between psychopathological factors, gender, and mathematics development seems to show a different pattern than reading development (Wu et al. 2014). This could mean that the developmental pathway for how early effortful control and school behavioural problems impact reading is different from how they impact mathematics, and that these early pathways also interact with children's gender.

Antisocial behaviour and misconduct are not only more common in boys but also are more tightly correlated with genetic factors in boys than in girls (Meier et al. 2011). Genetic correlations are difficult to interpret because the correlations could be driven by indirect biological factors (those not directly linked to conduct disorder – e.g., retaliating after experiencing bullying over a physical characteristic) or result from environmental modulators. But the gender difference in correlation strength suggests at least a different set of influences on boys versus girls, which could result in different behavioural outcomes. These observations raise questions about whether the higher prevalence of reading disorders in boys arises indirectly from other gender-specific problems.

Reading shows a different pattern of gender differences than mathematics, and this may be related to differences in how these skills are acquired. Reading is acquired hierarchically, meaning that learning to read requires acquiring and embedding knowledge sequentially across different levels of granularity from phonology to word morphology to syntax and semantics. Children master these different knowledge levels incrementally, and their learning progress depends on integrating their prior knowledge both cumulatively and hierarchically (e.g., Frith 2017).

Although mathematics is also hierarchical to some extent, many mathematical skills can be learnt independently and are more mutualistic than hierarchical. For example, children can make progress on single-digit addition and subtraction before they master the decades sequence in verbal counting, or vice versa. In contrast, for reading, the phonology and morphology of a word must be mastered before its syntax and semantics can be understood. There is considerably more variability in the strategies that children use to acquire mathematics compared to reading (Farrington-Flint et al. 2009), which reflects the less rigid acquisition process in mathematics. Thus, disorders that impair early reading are more likely to impair subsequent reading, whereas the trajectory of mathematics learning is more flexible. The rigid hierarchical learning during reading development lends itself to cascading effects of early psychosocial problems on reading acquisition.

Differences in the developmental demands for acquiring reading and maths skills could interact with children's vulnerabilities in early childhood. As described earlier, boys show greater vulnerability than girls to early neurodevelopmental impairments affecting or delaying their attention, language, learning, and social behaviour. Additionally, as described in Section 13.5, reading development might be more vulnerable to cascading effects during acquisition due to its rigid acquisition structure. These developmental constraints could yield the greater prevalence of boys developing disordered reading than disordered mathematics, and higher rates of reading impairment in boys than girls. As noted earlier, children aged 10 years and older show gender differences on reading comprehension assessments disfavouring boys, whereas boys and girls perform equally in mathematics assessments during childhood and adolescence. One possibility is that gender differences disfavouring boys in reading emerge because of boys' unique vulnerability to cascading impairments during early childhood, combined with the strict structure of reading acquisition.

13.6 Conclusion

Gender differences in the diagnosis of dyslexia and dyscalculia are sometimes thought to be explained by differences in the specific mechanisms underlying reading and mathematics. There are a number of reasons why this logic does not hold. In typically developing children, there are no gender differences in reading and mathematics attributable to any gender-specific cognitive or biological mechanisms. Instead, the types of tests that suggest gender differences are often broad skills tests administered to children 10 years of age and older. Performance on these broad tests invokes mechanisms that cross-cut many cognitive domains and are correlated with many other measures, such as language ability and domain-general skills like working memory and attention. Moreover, the effect sizes of gender differences on these broad skills tests tend to be insignificant, and many are changing over time cross-nationally.

In mathematics, gender differences are unreliable across tests, variable across cultures, and effect sizes hover around zero. Attitudes towards mathematics, such as confidence and anxiety, show more reliable gender differences than ability. Numerous factors indicate a role for social and cultural influences in gender differences in mathematics favouring boys; these include gender differences in social play, social stereotypes, the physical environment (e.g., masculinized spatial toys and games), and feedback from parents and teachers.

Gender differences in reading ability emerge in children ages 10 years and older, with small effect sizes. Interestingly, some evidence suggests a possible role for social influences. Reading and language are associated with feminine stereotypes, and gender differences favouring girls emerge in children's attitudes, reading interest, and in the content types that children find engaging.

In the past, when researchers' understandings of mechanisms involved were more limited, gender differences were speculatively attributed to simple direct causes. Specifically, gender differences in reading and mathematics were attributed to genetic factors (Jensen 1998). However, there is no known direct genetic causal mechanism for reading and mathematics, and no known genetic cause for mathematics or reading that distinguishes boys from girls. Genetic correlations are variable in these domains (Peterson and Pennington 2012) and gene correlations cannot be interpreted as direct causation of genes on cognition because indirect genetic effects are likely. Moreover, a narrow genetic cause of any gender differences in higher-order cognition is unlikely, given our current understandings of the role of social and cultural factors, significant plasticity in children's learning, and the major role of practice and experience in reading and mathematics development.

Gender differences in the diagnosis of dyscalculia appear to be largely a consequence of diagnostic criterion selection. Girls and boys show equal rates of dyscalculia when absolute cut-offs are used on the normal distribution of performance. Girls show higher prevalence than boys when their (higher) scores on reading tests are weighed in the baseline. The role of the baseline test in determining whether or not gender differences in dyscalculia are observed indicate that observed gender differences are not maths-specific. Moreover, boys and girls who exhibit the most severe deficits in mathematics might have working memory deficits, suggesting that mathematics impairments could be linked to broader learning impairments (Geary 2010), and that similar factors influence mathematics disorder across gender groups.

Gender differences in dyslexia are more complex. A subset of researchers believe that gender differences in dyslexia are reading-specific. Others argue that boys show higher rates of dyslexia because of referral bias, and yet others argue that gender differences in dyscalculia are a consequence of co-occurring impairments with greater frequencies in boys than girls. Observed gender differences in dyslexia could arise from gender differences in early childhood vulnerability to neurodevelopmental impairment in attention, language, learning, and social behaviour, regardless of whether these observations are biased or measuring reading-specific effects. Such impairments are more common in boys and could uniquely affect reading acquisition because learning to read is both hierarchical in nature and the first rigorous exercise in formal learning during development. Yet another potential source of gender differences in dyslexia is socialization. Boys and girls experience different frequencies of reading, different reading attitudes, different reading content, and different stereotypes about learning. These factors influence reading development in typically developing boys and girls, and could also influence the probability of developing dyslexia.

Suggestions for Further Reading

Devine, A., F. Soltész, A. Nobes, U. Goswami, and D. Szűcs. 2013. 'Gender Differences in Developmental Dyscalculia Depend on Diagnostic Criteria'. *Learning and Instruction* 27 (October): 31–9.

Kersey, A. J., K. D. Csumitta, and J. F. Cantlon. 2019. 'Gender Similarities in the Brain during Mathematics Development'. *NPJ Science of Learning* 4 (November), 19: 1–7.

Massand, E. and A. Karmiloff-Smith. 2015. 'Cascading Genetic and Environmental Effects on Development: Implications for Intervention'. In K. J. Mitchell (ed.), *The Genetics of Neurodevelopmental Disorders*, 275–88. Hoboken: John Wiley and Sons, Inc.

Reilly, D., D. L. Neumann, and G. Andrews. 2019. 'Gender Differences in Reading and Writing Achievement: Evidence from the National Assessment of Educational Progress (NAEP)'. *The American Psychologist* 74 (4): 445–58.

Zell, Ethan, Zlatan Krizan, and Sabrina R. Teeter. 2015. 'Evaluating Gender Similarities and Differences Using Metasynthesis'. *The American Psychologist* 70 (1): 10–20.

14 The Role of Socioeconomic and Ethnic Disparities for Dyslexia and Dyscalculia

Rachel Elizabeth Fish

14.1 Introduction

The 'overrepresentation' of racially/ethnically marginalized and socioeconomically disadvantaged children in special education has been of concern to researchers, policymakers, and practitioners since at least the late 1960s (Dunn 1968; Mercer 1973; Coard 1971). The prevailing wisdom has long been that racially/ethnically and socioeconomically marginalized children are both at higher risk of disability due to cognitive and social–emotional–behavioural effects of structural inequalities, and that schools make racially/ethnically and socioeconomically biased decisions to qualify students for special education services (e.g., National Research Council 2002). Newer research has identified more nuanced and complex mechanisms in racial/ethnic inequalities in particular, in which racially/ethnically marginalized students are more likely to need services due to structural inequality, but are largely less likely to gain access to those services when they need them than their White peers (Shifrer and Fish 2020).

In this chapter, I first describe the current knowledge on the nature of these disparities, and then discuss research that aims to disentangle the complex origins of these inequalities. Unlike the majority of the chapters in this handbook, this discussion relies on understanding disability as, in part, a socially constructed category. My focus in this chapter is on the ways that the social environment shapes disparities in disability by race, ethnicity, and socioeconomic status (SES). Moreover, disability intersects with race, ethnicity, and SES. Race and ethnicity are socially constructed categories, and have real social meaning because of racism, marginalization, and structural inequalities in our society. Thus, the discussion here focuses on the social and environmental processes that lead to these disparities.

It is important to note that here I attempt to provide an overview of racial/ethnic and SES disparities in dyslexia and dysgraphia that is inclusive of international patterns. However, most research on these disparities has occurred in the United States and the United Kingdom (Strand and Lindsay 2009). Synthesizing research on patterns of inequality, as well as research revealing the mechanisms of these inequalities, is difficult due to limitations in data collection, as well as variations in the measurement of disability. Extant research on international patterns has focused on a limited set of countries with available quantitative data on race, ethnicity, SES, and disability. For example, citizens in Finland are not registered according to their ethnic origin, and their special education supports are so flexible that they can be provided without officially classifying students as disabled (Anastasiou et al. 2011), rendering analyses of racial/ethnic disparities in disability impossible in that context. Relatedly, countries have different classifications that may or may not include dyslexia and dysgraphia. To include the greatest proportion of relevant research, I will discuss research that focuses on *specific learning disability* or *learning disability* (SLD or LD), which typically includes dyslexia and dysgraphia in administrative datasets. However, it should be noted this definition is imperfect: for example, in Germany, the term for LD includes both learning disabilities *and* mild intellectual disability (Pfahl and Powell 2011). Additionally, due to limitations in data collected and extant research, I will, at times, discuss research that includes students with any disabilities that have not been disaggregated by category.

14.2 Descriptive Patterns of Socioeconomic and Ethnic Disparities

Research and reports documenting disparities in receipt of special education in the raw data (i.e., without statistically adjusting for correlates) largely suggest overrepresentation – but also some underrepresentation – of racially/ethnically marginalized and low-SES students relative to their more advantaged peers. In the United States and United Kingdom, where available data includes both disability category and race/ethnicity, and also where the greatest research and policy focus has been directed, racially/ethnically marginalized and low-SES students are generally overrepresented in SLD relative to their more advantaged peers (IDEA 2019; Strand and Lindsay 2009). In the United States, this includes Native American, Black, Latinx, and Pacific Islander students, as well as low-income students, while Asian students are underrepresented relative to White students (IDEA 2019). Evidence is more mixed in the UK, where Afro-Caribbean and Roma students are overrepresented in SLD relative to their White British peers, while Black African students are not (Anastasiou et al. 2011).

Similar patterns are evident in countries that do not document or define learning disabilities as in the USA and the UK. In Germany, where the category of learning disability also includes students with mild intellectual disability, research has documented overrepresentation of students from immigrant backgrounds and low-income students (Werning et al. 2008; Bruce and Venkatesh 2014). Across multiple European countries, Roma children are overrepresented in special education relative to their peers (Gabel et al. 2009). In New Zealand, Maori and low-income students are overrepresented relative to White and higher-income students (Wynd 2015). While most research and reports suggest that in the raw data, identification of SLD and other disabilities is associated with socioeconomic disadvantage, Bruce and Venkatesh (2014) note that in Kenya and India, where poor children have limited access to education, socioeconomically disadvantaged children are underrepresented in special education.

14.3 The Contested Roots of Disparities in Special Education

Given the patterns in the raw data, racial/ethnic disparities in special education (at least in the US context) have long been treated by policymakers and researchers as likely evidence of bias and inappropriate identification of students of colour as disabled (National Research Council 2002; Losen and Welner 2001; Oswald et al. 2001; Skiba et al. 2005), with less attention or problematizing of socioeconomic disparities. However, new research challenges these previous conclusions, examining racial/ethnic disparities in special education while also accounting for confounders of race/ethnicity (e.g., SES, which is associated with race and also with risk of special education receipt) and by analytically accounting for the nesting of students within school contexts (Hibel et al. 2010; Shifrer 2018; Shifrer and Fish 2020; Fish 2019). This research suggests that once factors associated with race are accounted for, students of colour are not overrepresented – and may actually be *underrepresented* in special education (Hibel et al. 2010; Morgan et al. 2015; Morgan et al. 2015). While the vast majority of this research has used US data, similarly robust analyses of UK data suggest that, among comparable students, there is no increased risk of learning disabilities for Black students relative to White peers in that context either (Strand and Lindsay 2009). Examining international evidence, Gabel et al. (2009) suggest that racial/ethnic variation in special education is attributable to socioeconomic inequality, age shifts in populations, and immigration policies, as well as linguistic backgrounds, cultural expectations, and life experiences.

The newer findings and subsequent interpretations have instigated a heated debate over the nature of racial disparities in special education (as discussed by Artiles 2019): Are racially/ethnically marginalized students actually overrepresented in special education? Do their higher rates reflect higher need for services, or are these students being inappropriately placed in special education? Research suggests that racially/ethnically marginalized students and, likely, lower-SES students are simultaneously overrepresented and underserved (Shifrer and Fish 2020). This seemingly paradoxical inequality arises from the role of racism and other structural inequalities in predisposing racially/ethnically marginalized and socioeconomically disadvantaged children to have difficulties in school, yet also making them less likely to be identified than similarly performing peers from more advantaged backgrounds (Shifrer and Fish 2020). Yet the relations between SES, race/ethnicity, and disabilities such as SLD are complex, dependent on context, and vary both across and within disability categories (Artiles 2019, Fish 2019).

14.4 The Social Construction of Specific Learning Disability

To work towards a better understanding of the complex inequality in diagnosis and access to services for SLD and other disabilities, it is necessary to critically examine what we mean by disability, and how this social category intersects with race and class.

14.4.1 Disability As Social Construction

Education researcher and practitioner frameworks of disability are generally rooted in the medical model, treating disability as objective, natural categories of human pathology. Yet disability is also constructed through social practices (Shakespeare 2013), with boundaries defined by 'cultural values of normalcy' (Frederick and Shifrer 2019) in the 'ability/disability system' (Garland-Thomson 2020). Like gender, race, and class, disability is a key axis of stratification (Frederick and Shifrer 2019). The boundaries between disabled and non-disabled are fluid, ambiguous, and often invisible (Maroto et al. 2019), and disability is a contested category, seen by some as pathology, by others as a source of pride and identity (Frederick and Shifrer 2019).

Disabilities in schools, and SLD in particular, not only reflect impairments in cognitive processing, memory, and other neurological processes, but are also created by the context and structure of schooling (Blanchett 2010; Dudley-Marling 2004), by the medicalization of underperformance (Leonard and Conrad 1978), and by socio-political processes that define disability categories in schools (Blanchett 2010; Connor and Ferri 2010; Ong-Dean 2009; Sleeter 2010). For example, schools define the skills and behaviour that are salient (e.g., pre-reading skills), and treat the failure to learn those skills as a deficit that resides in the individual student, rather than as the result of social interactions with particular teachers in a particular social context (Dudley-Marling 2004; Gerber 2005).

14.4.2 Subjectivity in Diagnosis

This social construction is, in part, made visible through subjectivity in diagnostic processes (Shifrer and Fish 2020; see also Chapter 22, Lachmann, Bergström, Huber, and Nürk 2022). In the United States, for instance, teacher suspicions of disability largely drive the diagnosis of the more subjective categories, as they make the vast majority of referrals to testing (Klingner 2006; Lloyd et al. 1991), and their suspicions are largely confirmed by the diagnostic process (Klingner 2006). Additionally, many of the referrals that are officially made by parents and doctors appear to be driven by teacher pressure for diagnoses (Brinkman et al. 2009; Cormier 2012; Sax and Kautz 2003). The pre-referral interventions and processes rarely prevent special education placement as intended (Balu et al. 2015; Klingner 2006). Psychoeducational testing procedures may involve test after test to find a 'hidden disability' (Mehan et al. 1986), and team decisions of disability qualification are shaped by teachers' informal diagnoses of students (Klingner 2006). Additionally, racial bias, social status, parental social networks, and parental advocacy have been shown to affect various stages of the diagnostic process: both *whether* a student is diagnosed with a disability and also *which* disability category is diagnosed (Eyal 2013; Fish 2017; Liu et al. 2010; Ong-Dean 2009).

14.4.3 The Construction of Specific Learning Disability as a Stratified-status Category

Additionally, disabilities in schools are constructed very differently by category, with some categories (e.g., speech/language impairment, autism) having higher social status, lower stigma, and more inclusive services than others (e.g., intellectual disability, emotional disturbance; Saatcioglu and Skrtic 2019; Fish 2019). SLD stands out among disabilities for its differentiated meaning and implications for students – within a single category (Fish 2019; Ong-Dean 2006; Blanchett 2010). Scholars examining this category in the US context have noted that SLD rose in incidence as academic achievement expectations increased, as one response to low achievement among more advantaged children (Blanchett 2010; Ong-Dean 2006; Sleeter 2010). Yet the disability category shifted over time such that more racially/ ethnically marginalized students were identified with SLD (Ong-Dean 2006). Now, it appears that SLD is a 'stratified status' disability category (Fish 2019), providing extra resources, accommodations, a destigmatizing label, the presumption of normal or superior intelligence, and inclusive service provision for racially/ethnically and socioeconomically advantaged students, while also, in part, serving as a 'dumping ground for children of colour' (Blanchett 2010) that excludes these children from the general education classroom (Saatcioglu and Skrtic 2019; Blanchett 2010; Ong-Dean 2006; Fish 2019). Moreover, while services for SLD appear to be beneficial for most students (Hurwitz et al. 2020; Schwartz et al. 2021), they do not appear to support academic achievement for Black children (Schwartz et al. 2021). Understanding the stratified status and implications for students identified with SLD is key to the examination of the complex patterns of inequality by race/ethnicity and SES, particularly as we consider how advantaged families may seek to deploy the label and associated services (see Section 14.5).

14.5 Disentangling the Roots of Racial/Ethnic and Socioeconomic Disparities in Specific Learning Disabilities: Multilevel, Multi-directional Processes

A multitude of factors work together, often in contradictory directions, to create racial/ethnic and socioeconomic overrepresentation in special education while simultaneously underserving marginalized students. It is important to consider multiple, complex, and sometimes contradictory effects of racism and economic inequality at macro-, meso-, and micro-levels, and how these shape the risk of students exhibiting the kinds of difficulties that may be identified as disabilities (Fish 2019).

To understand how both overrepresentation and reduced access to diagnosis and services are possible for racially/ethnically marginalized and low-SES children, we must consider that identification with disabilities generally depends on three distinct processes. First, variation across children's academic and social–emotional skills occurs through the combination of biological, home, environmental, and community factors, presenting for some as difficulties that may or may not eventually be diagnosed as disabilities. Second, adults in the child's life recognize the difficulties and interpret them as potential disability, shaped by the social construction of disability, perceptions of the child, and the availability of institutional resources of disability knowledge and testing. Third, adults in the child's life mobilize resources to test for and diagnose a disability, and acquire services. Note that while the first of these stages presents fairly objective (though socially and context-dependent) differences in student difficulties for different populations, the latter two are social processes that depend on constructions of disability, and on variation in access to resources.

14.5.1 Socioeconomic Status and Racial/Ethnic Disparities in Children's Presentation of Difficulties

First, let us consider how a child's SES shapes the first of these three processes: the difficulties experienced by the child. Research suggests that socioeconomic disadvantage increases children's risk of learning difficulties that may be diagnosed as SLD or other disabilities, through effects on cognitive development and exposure to learning experiences. Specifically, family income and wealth are strongly associated with cognitive development (Paxson and Schady 2007), operating through a variety of factors. One mechanism appears to be health care access and health outcomes associated with SES and with risk of disability, such as the child's birth weight (Morgan et al. 2015). Children in low-SES households are also more likely to be exposed to environmental toxins, such as lead, that affect cognitive development and risk of SLD (Marshall et al. 2020; see also Chapter 7, Hoeft and Bouhali 2022). Growing up in a low-SES family is also associated with higher levels of family stress and lower access to home literacy resources, which have been shown to increase risk of dyslexia – with stronger associations than familial genetic risk factors for SLD (Dilnot et al. 2017; see also Chapter 7, Hoeft and Bouhali 2022). Additionally, low-SES children also experience effects on cognitive development and risk of SLD via neighbourhood disadvantage, via stressors and access to community resources, with effects on children's cognitive ability that even extend across generations (Sharkey and Elwert 2011). This discussion is not meant to be exhaustive, but rather to demonstrate that SES disadvantage early in life shapes children's cognitive development and predisposes poorer children to have the kinds of difficulties that might be identified as SLD and other disabilities that impact their educational trajectories.

Racial/ethnic marginalization is also associated with children's academic and socio-emotional difficulties that might be diagnosed as SLD and other disabilities. As discussed, racial/ethnic minorities are generally overrepresented in the raw data. Research using analytic models with robust sets of student-level predictors of special education receipt generally finds that this overrepresentation is fully 'explained' by factors such as the child's SES, measures of academic and socio-emotional readiness for school, and low birth weight (e.g., Strand and Lindsay 2009; Shifrer and Fish 2020; Hibel et al. 2010; Morgan et al. 2015). This suggests that racially/ethnically marginalized students have a greater need for special education services, due to structural, racial/ethnic inequalities external to the diagnostic process.

It is difficult to disentangle the effects of racism and ethnic marginalization from those of socioeconomic inequality because of the vast racial/ethnic inequalities in income and wealth (e.g., Oliver et al. 2006). Thus, a great deal of the relationship between race/ethnicity and children's academic and socio-emotional difficulties operates through the pathway of structural racism and ethnic marginalization's effects on socioeconomic inequality; however, this does not explain the entire relationship. For example, particularly in the US context, high levels of racial segregation mean that racially/ethnically marginalized children are isolated in neighbourhoods with disadvantages for cognitive development, such as higher levels of environmental toxins like lead, lower levels of social trust and institutional resources, and other neighbourhood effects (e.g., Moody et al. 2016; Sampson et al. 2002). Research also shows that racial segregation is associated with preterm birth (Anthopolos et al. 2014), a risk factor for special education receipt (Morgan et al. 2015). Moreover, the many mechanisms through which racial/ethnic marginalization creates stress for families, such as discrimination, are associated with lower health and well-being for children (Priest et al. 2013), likely shaping the risk of SLD and other disabilities. It is key to understand the roles of racism and ethnic marginalization, and to understand how these structural features shape children's academic, cognitive, and socio-emotional skills and difficulties, without treating racial/ethnic minority status as a deficit that resides in individuals, families, or communities (Artiles 1998).

14.5.2 Beyond Risk of Difficulties: Socioeconomic Status and Racial/Ethnic Disparities in Recognition and Diagnosis

As outlined earlier, in the first process leading to diagnosis of SLD and other disabilities, the pathway between racial/ethnic and socioeconomic disadvantage and children's enhanced risk of academic or socio-emotional difficulties is rather clear. In the next stages, in which those difficulties are recognized, assessed, diagnosed, and lead to the provision of services, the relationship between race/ethnicity, SES, and SLD is more complex. In general, while disadvantages due to SES and marginalization by race/ethnicity are associated with a greater risk of displaying the kinds of difficulties that might be identified as disabilities such as SLD, racially/ethnically and socioeconomically advantaged students with those same difficulties are more likely to access diagnosis and services. Yet the relationship is complicated by the nuances of school context, the kinds of needs that the child has, whether linguistic dominance might be playing a role in the child's needs, and other factors, discussed in Sections 15.5.3–15.5.6.

14.5.3 Disparities in Access

One mechanism through which racial/ethnic and socioeconomic advantage drive higher levels of diagnosis and service provision is access to diagnosis and services. Susan Bruce and Kavita Venkatesh (2014) illustrate this clearly in their discussion of the underrepresentation of disabilities among impoverished children in Kenya and India, where poor children are often excluded from schooling entirely, and also lack access to assessment centres. They note that this is particularly true for disabilities such as SLD in India, where disabilities with more significant effects on day-to-day life, such as blindness and physical disabilities, are more likely to be identified

(Bruce and Venkatesh 2014). Similarly, Hibel et al. (2010) find that students attending schools with more White students are more likely to be identified with disabilities, potentially because these schools have greater resources available to diagnose students' difficulties.

14.5.4 Bias in Testing and Diagnosis

In addition to access to testing, the testing process itself also appears to shape socioeconomic and racial/ethnic disparities in SLD and other disabilities. For schools and assessment centres using the 'discrepancy model' of diagnosis, in which a significant discrepancy between IQ and achievement is considered an indicator of SLD, the diagnostic process favours identifying SLD among higher-SES students (Siegel and Himel 1998; see also Chapter 22, Lachmann, Bergström, Huber, and Nürk 2022). Specifically, IQ tests measure, to some extent, the environmental experiences a child has, leading higher-SES children to have higher IQ scores. Siegel and Himel (1998) found that while SES was not correlated with reading performance, it was correlated with IQ, meaning that lower-SES children are less likely to qualify as having a significant discrepancy as similarly performing higher-SES children, and therefore less likely to be diagnosed with dyslexia than their peers. McLeskey et al. (1990) found a similar pattern in racial disparities in the discrepancy model. Specifically, Black students were less likely to be identified as having SLD than White students when the discrepancy model was used with the standard score method of determining a discrepancy and an IQ cut-off. Regardless of the model of diagnosis, research also suggests that racialized discourses shape qualification decisions by psychologists and other gate-keepers of diagnosis or access to special education services (e.g., Fish 2022; Harry and Klingner 2014).

14.5.5 Disparities in Recognition of Difficulties As Potential Disability

In addition to the relatively straightforward processes outlined here, of access to assessment, and of racial/ethnic and SES bias in testing and qualification procedures, the processes leading to the *recognition* or suspicion of a potential disability are more complex. As I argue earlier, SLD and other disabilities are in part socially constructed, and are rooted in social context. This is particularly evident in the subjective and context-dependent process in which an adult recognizes a child's difficulty as potential disability and refers them to testing procedures.

Teacher decisions to refer children to special education testing or pre-referral processes are of particular importance in this process. While teachers do not make the decision to diagnose a student with a disability, they make the vast majority of referrals to special education testing (Harry and Klingner 2014) and pressure parents to pursue diagnoses (Cormier 2012). Additionally, teacher referrals are largely confirmed by the diagnostic process (Balu et al. 2015; Mehan et al. 1986; Harry and Klingner 2007). Moreover, their decisions to refer children to testing and pre-referral processes are shaped by their perceptions of students' abilities, performance, and behaviours, which are affected by social biases. In my own research, teachers were asked to read case studies of fictional boys experiencing academic and behavioural difficulties in the classroom, in which only the race of the fictional student varied across otherwise identical narratives (Fish 2017). I then asked teachers whether they would refer the child for special education testing/pre-referral. My findings demonstrated that while teachers were more likely to refer Black and Latino boys with behavioural difficulties (e.g., oppositional behaviour) than identical White boys, they were less likely to refer Black and Latino boys with academic difficulties (e.g., reading level below their peers) than their White counterparts (Fish 2017). The latter finding, relevant to referrals for SLD, likely reflects teachers' perceptions of greater academic competence in White students than their Black and Latinx peers (e.g., Tenenbaum and Ruck 2007). Thus, when a White child struggles academically, the teacher is likely more alarmed, and mobilizes potential supports through diagnosis, allowing SLD to serve as a beneficial resource for that student. In contrast, when a Black or Latinx child experiences similar academic difficulties, the teacher likely interprets their performance as meeting the lower expectations they have for those students, and are less likely to refer them for disability testing.

In addition to teacher interpretations of White students' struggles as disability, parent conceptualizations of disability, and differential resources for advocacy by race and SES, likely shape disparities in SLD. Particularly for more advantaged families that expect their children to perform above the average, a disability label – and the associated services and accommodations – is preferable to 'mere underperformance' (Leonard and Conrad 1978). A disability label can relieve the child, family, and school of the burden of perceiving low performance as a failure, and instead attribute it to a neurobiological difference. This is particularly true for disability categories that have higher social status, like SLD does, particularly for the more advantaged students that receive this label (Fish 2019). Indeed, more privileged families advocate for SLD, preferring it to intellectual disability (Gottlieb et al. 1994; Ong-Dean 2006). Thus, both parent and teacher conceptualizations of disability, and how these intersect with race and class, appear to increase the likelihood that racially/ethnically socioeconomically advantaged students will be diagnosed with SLD, as compared to similarly performing marginalized peers.

In addition to biased expectations, research also suggests that for racially/ethnically marginalized, low-SES, and, in particular, language minorities, it is difficult to isolate potential disability from other needs, such as language proficiency (see Chapter 22, Lachmann, Bergström, Huber, and Nürk 2022). For example, children from immigrant families are overrepresented in special schools in Germany and in special education in Finland, likely due to linguistic background (Anastasiou et al. 2011). In New Zealand, schools do not even apply for special education funding or services for children that speak Maori because of a lack of special education professionals proficient in the language (Chapman et al. 2003). In the United States, research suggests that children of immigrants are less likely than their non-immigrant peers to receive special education services when they are younger, and then more likely when they are older, likely because educators prioritize English instruction over special education (Hibel and Jasper 2012), or because discerning between language-dominance and disability is difficult for educators. Similarly, for children that are racially/ethnically marginalized and low-SES, educators likely struggle to distinguish indicators of disadvantage from those of disability (Harry and Klingner 2014). For instance, if a child is highly transient due to poverty, and is also struggling to learn to read, educators will struggle to distinguish effects of the lack of consistent reading instruction from those of potential dyslexia.

14.5.6 The Role of School Context

Finally, the schools that students attend appear to play an important role in whether a child is diagnosed and receives services for SLD, particularly in regard to disparities by SES and race/ethnicity. Lower-SES and racial/ethnic minority students are more likely than their peers to attend schools with lower levels of resources, with teachers that are less prepared to meet their needs. Conceivably, this could increase students' likelihood of SLD diagnosis, as students may be more likely to experience difficulty in reading, writing, and other academic skills. Yet it is also possible that attending a school with more racial/ethnic minorities and/or a lower-SES population might have the opposite effect, as these schools may be less equipped to identify and diagnose struggling students, or struggling students may simply blend in with their lower-achieving peers more in these schools (Hibel et al. 2010). When researchers have examined the role of school context in students' risk of special education receipt, their findings have varied greatly, perhaps due to these multi-directional mechanisms (Hibel et al. 2010; Bal et al. 2019).

It is more likely, however, that the variation in findings of the role of school context is explained by variation in school-level effects on students of different racial/ethnic backgrounds. Recent studies, using a variety of datasets and methods, have found that standing out racially/ethnically or linguistically, or 'distinctiveness,' shapes a student's risk of receiving special education (Fish 2019; Shifrer and Fish 2020; Elder et al. 2019). In my own work, for example (Fish 2019), I found that as the proportion of White students increases, the risk of lower-status disabilities, such as intellectual disability, increases for Black, Latinx, and Native American students. As the proportion of White students decreases, White students' risk of higher-status disabilities, such as speech/language impairment, increases relative to students of colour. For SLD – described here as a stratified-status category – the moderation by school racial composition mirrors the higher-status categories for White students and the lower-status categories for students of colour. In addition to providing compelling evidence of how school racial/ethnic composition matters for the association between student race/ethnicity and disability, these findings also suggest empirically that SLD is, indeed, a stratified-status category, with different implications depending on the racial/ethnic background of the child.

While this new body of literature has not yet been able to identify contributory mechanisms, theory and related research suggest a few potential explanations for these findings (Fish 2019). It is possible that racial/ethnic distinctiveness among students triggers teachers' reliance on racial/ethnic stereotypes (Fish 2019). It is also possible that when racially/ethnically marginalized children attend school with more

White children, political pressures from White families encourage educators to sort the marginalized children into special education, in part to remove them from the classroom (Fish 2019). Conversely, in predominantly non-White schools, White parents may advocate for diagnosis and special education services for their own children, in part, to allocate additional resources (Fish 2019). In sum, it appears that school racial/ethnic composition is a crucial organizational feature of a school, shaping the nature of racial/ethnic disparities in diagnosis of and services for SLD. Moreover, this research shows empirically that SLD has different meanings and implications for students depending on their own racial/ethnic (and likely, socioeconomic) background, as a coveted resource for more advantaged families to acquire, but also, in part, as a category and placement for marginalized children that does not benefit them.

14.6 Conclusion

The processes leading to the overrepresentation and underserving of racially/ethnically marginalized and socioeconomically disadvantaged children with SLD is complex, and continued research is necessary to understand the socio-historical and contextual factors that produce and maintain inequality at the intersection of disability, race/ethnicity, and SES (Artiles 2019). As part of a qualitative study I am working on at the time of writing this chapter, I recently interviewed a 3rd grade teacher in rural Wisconsin, Ms. Johnson, about a Black, lower-income girl in her class, Vanessa (both names are pseudonyms). While Vanessa's peers, who were almost all White, were reading on grade level, Vanessa struggled to decode words at a Kindergarten level. Ms. Johnson explained to me that when she asked Vanessa's previous teachers about her academic difficulties, the common response was 'Oh Vanessa is just so sweet'. Her academic skills and difficulties were simply not noticed by her teachers, who focused on her good behaviour. Vanessa's mother had advocated for her with school staff, but the school had not responded with testing or services. How had Vanessa reached 3rd grade with no one noticing that she might have dyslexia, or, at the very least, require additional supports?

The synthesis of the research presented here suggests that Vanessa is unlikely to be alone in her experience, but does not fully explain the case. Her position as a lower-income Black girl has exposed her to the effects of structural inequality by race/ethnicity and SES, increasing her risk of having academic difficulties. Yet she attended a predominantly White school where, because her behaviour was not seen as a problem, she completely slipped through the cracks and her reading difficulties went unnoticed. Vanessa, and other students, do not fully fit the patterns suggested by research on school context. This case suggests that while research has revealed some pathways through which racial/ethnic marginalization and SES might matter for diagnosis with SLD and other disabilities, there is still a great deal of research that needs to be done to understand the roots of these disparities.

It is important to note that the vast majority of the research presented in this chapter, particularly the research on the causes of racial/ethnic inequality in SLD, are based on the extant literature, which, to the best of my knowledge, is largely from the US context. It does appear that across contexts, racial/ethnic marginalization and socioeconomic disadvantage are associated with higher risk of exhibiting the kinds of difficulties that might be diagnosed as dyslexia, dysgraphia, and other disabilities. It also appears to be the case that, across contexts, racial/ethnic and socioeconomic advantage allows greater access to diagnosis and services. It is unclear if the more nuanced patterns of racialized perceptions of students and the role of school context extend beyond the US context. Attempts to generalize the discussion of mechanisms, here rooted in the US context, should proceed cautiously, and the need for further research is clear.

Suggestions for Further Reading

Fish, R. E. 2019. 'Standing Out and Sorting In: Exploring the Role of Racial Composition in Racial Disparities in Special Education'. *American Educational Research Journal* 56 (6): 2573–2608.

Artiles, A. J. 2019. 'Fourteenth Annual Brown Lecture in Education Research: Reenvisioning Equity Research: Disability Identification Disparities as a Case in Point'. *Educational Researcher* 48 (6): 325–35.

Gabel, S. L. , S. Curcic, J. J. W. Powell, K. Khader, and L. Albee. 2009. 'Migration and Ethnic Group Disproportionality in Special Education: An Exploratory Study'. *Disability and Society* 24 (5): 625–39.

Shifrer, D., and R. Fish. 2020. 'A Multilevel Investigation into Contextual Reliability in the Designation of Cognitive Health Conditions among US Children'. *Society and Mental Health* 10 (2): 180–97.

Summary: Gender, Ethnicity, and Socioeconomic Background

(1) **Effect size of gender differences:** Effect sizes of gender differences in reading and maths ability are small. A moderate effect size is currently only reported for a related domain (male advantage in visuospatial mental modelling tasks).

(2) **Origins of gender differences:** Gender differences in reading and maths ability are related to social-environmental factors (e.g., educational experiences, inclusion in learning-related activities, attitudes towards competition, self-concepts of performance, gender equality culture) whose interplay with other biological factors is currently not understood.

(3) **Gender and prevalence:** Boys are diagnosed with dyslexia about twice as often as girls, for currently unknown reasons (e.g., performance stereotypes, referral bias, higher male susceptibility to early psychosocial adversity, rigid hierarchical nature of learning to read). Gender ratios in the absolute prevalence of dyscalculia diagnoses are comparable.

(4) **Ethnic marginalization and socioeconomic disadvantage:** Racially/ethnically marginalized students (e.g., Native American, Black, Latinx, and Pacific Islander students in the USA; Roma students in Europe; Maori students in New Zealand) and socioeconomically disadvantaged students are *overrepresented* in special education and more likely to need special education services, *but underserved* – that is, less likely to gain access to those services when they need them than their White (or Asian) peers. This discrepancy can be explained by the partial subjectivity of the diagnosis, which is prone to social biases and stereotypes (e.g., related to racialized performance constructs and social status), but also by a number of other factors (e.g., preterm birth, low birth weight, early stress, exposure to environmental toxins, limited access to health care and learning resources).

PART VI

Cultural Unity and Diversity

15 Cross-Cultural Unity and Diversity of Dyslexia

Wai Ting Siok and Lang Qin

15.1 Introduction

In the simplest sense, reading acquisition is a process of learning how a writing system represents a spoken language. It requires conscious awareness of how the basic graphic symbol, the *grapheme*, represents a spoken unit. However, unlike language acquisition, which occurs naturally, rapidly, and automatically in most children, learning to read is a lifetime developmental process that requires effort, explicit instruction, and conscious awareness of the language structure (known as *metalinguistic awareness*). Many children fail to achieve full proficiency in reading, and some exhibit specific problems with reading, writing, and spelling despite adequate intelligence, motivation, and educational opportunity. This specific learning difficulty, known as *developmental dyslexia*, has varying incidence rates depending on the diagnostic criteria and the language examined. The divergent incidence rates, together with some findings suggesting that dyslexia has different behavioural and neural manifestations within and across cultures, has led to the question of whether the underlying causes of dyslexia differ across writing systems and whether it is possible to be dyslexic in one language and not dyslexic in another. The aim of this chapter is to review the cross-cultural behavioural and neuroimaging findings on dyslexia and discuss how the common and unique characteristics of different writing systems may affect the underlying cognitive and neural mechanisms of dyslexia.

15.2 The Universality vs. Specificity Debate

In contrast to spoken languages, which emerged more than 100,000 years ago, written languages are relatively recent in human evolution, with a history of approximately 6,000 years. Thus, reading acquisition is unlikely to be supported by a dedicated, genetically evolved neurobiological architecture that enables rapid, automatic acquisition. To accommodate the new skills, the brain has to make use of the already existing neural system to process this new cultural invention. A prominent debate among reading researchers is whether writing systems worldwide share common features, and whether a universal neural network is used by all writing systems. Universal reading theories assume that since all writing systems encode spoken language, reading skills should be universally constrained by language skills (Ziegler and Goswami 2005). As spoken languages worldwide are commonly processed in the perisylvian language network comprising Broca's and Wernicke's areas, reading of any orthography should recruit the same spoken language network and rewire it with the visual cortices that are tuned to process the salient novel visual features of print (e.g., Dehaene and Cohen 2007; Skeide et al. 2017). The neuronal recycling hypothesis (Dehaene and Cohen 2007) argues further that because the graphic symbols of all writing systems share similar features (e.g., lines, curves, angles, vertices, and junctions) with objects in the everyday context (Changizi et al. 2006), the visual cortices that evolved to process these features should be adopted, or recycled, to process new graphic symbols.

These universal reading accounts have gained support from studies showing that typologically different writing systems activate a coarsely similar neural network; the visual word form area (VWFA) is commonly and invariably recruited to process visual-orthographic information (Bolger et al. 2005; Dehaene and Cohen 2011; Nakamura et al. 2012). Moreover, dyslexics show phonological processing deficits in different languages, including English (Gabrieli 2009; Cao et al. 2017; Siok et al. 2004; Siok et al. 2008), French (Mahé et al. 2018; Maïonchi-Pino et al. 2010), German (Landerl et al. 1997), Japanese (Kita et al. 2013), Italian (Paulesu et al. 2001; Tobia and Marzocchi 2014), and many other languages.

However, universal reading theories may overemphasize macroscopic similarities and underrate the featural, configural, and mapping differences among writing systems (Coltheart 2014; Tan et al. 2005). While it is true that graphemes represent speech sounds in all writing systems and that phonological skills universally correlate with early reading development, the visual configuration of graphemes and the speech units they represent, as well as the nature and consistency of print-to-sound mappings, differ substantially across languages in various aspects and may elicit different cognitive, metacognitive, and neural processes. Notably, the prevalence of dyslexia varies across cultures: 5–17% for English (Shaywitz 1998), 3.5% for Italian (Barbiero et al. 2019), 0.2–2.5% for Japan Kana (Koeda et al. 2011; Makita 1968), 1–7% for Japanese Kanji (Makita 1968; Uno et al. 2009), 4–5% for simplified Chinese (Lin et al. 2020; Sun et al. 2013), and 10% for traditional Chinese (Chan et al. 2007). The behavioural manifestations of dyslexia also differ across languages. For example, German people with dyslexia often achieve higher reading accuracy than their English counterparts, although both show equivalent impairments in phonemic awareness (Landerl et al. 1997) and decoding speed (Ziegler et al. 2003). Furthermore, there are more Japanese people with difficulties in Kanji (logographic script) than in Kana (syllabic script) (Makita 1968), and Kana reading is predicted by phonological skills, whereas Kanji reading is predicted by visual memory capacity (Koyama et al. 2008). Chinese people with dyslexia exhibit multiple types of deficits, including rapid automatized naming (Tan et al. 2005), visual processing (Siok et al. 2009), orthographic processing (Ho et al. 2004), phonological processing (Siok et al. 2004; Siok et al. 2008), morphological awareness (Peng et al. 2017), and handwriting skills (McBride-Chang et al. 2011), but none of these is a core cause of dyslexia.

These findings may suggest, on the one hand, that the underlying causes of dyslexia are the same cross-culturally, with the core deficit lying in the phonological domain while the severity and behavioural manifestations of the disorder vary across languages. On the other hand, there is also evidence that the underlying causes of dyslexia vary across cultures and are affected by linguistic, psychological, and educational factors. This controversy will be further explored in the following sections.

15.3 Cross-cultural Differences in Learning to Read Alphabetic Scripts

At the end of the nineteenth century, the French neurologist Jules Déjerine argued that the left angular gyrus, a parietal brain region located at the junction of the occipital cortex and Wernicke's area, played an important role in the visual memory of words and letters (Déjerine 1891). However, Déjerine's view that there was specific storage for holistic visual word images did not go unchallenged. Wernicke (1874) posited that concept or semantic information did not have localized representations but was distributed over the whole brain, and the meaning of either spoken or written words must be derived through sound memory of words that are stored in the superior temporal gyrus (or Wernicke's area). Since the pronunciation of visual words could be derived through letter-by-letter decoding, Wernicke doubted the necessity of storing visual images of entire words and argued that storing letter images would suffice for visual word processing (Wernicke 1906, cited in Bub et al. 1993). Interestingly, as noted by Bub et al. (1993), the contrasting views of Wernicke and Déjerine could be due to linguistic differences between their native languages. German, the native language of Wernicke, has a *shallow* orthography that has an approximate one-to-one mapping between phonemes (the smallest contrastive speech unit) and graphemes. French, Déjerine's native language, has a *deep* orthography, such that one phoneme is represented by many graphemes and one grapheme maps to many phonemes. It is thus difficult to derive word pronunciation reliably based on letter-by-letter decoding in French. This remark on the effects of culture on reading highlights the possible influence of linguistic differences on learning to read and the conceptualization of the nature of dyslexia.

15.3.1 The Alphabetic Principle and Its Effect on Learning to Read

The brain findings reviewed herein are based on alphabetic languages, including German and French. An alphabetic orthography uses graphemes (letters or letter clusters: e.g., *l* or *th*) to systematically represent all the phonemes of the spoken language (e.g., /l/ or /θ/). It allows a learner to derive the pronunciation and meaning of written words by applying grapheme–phoneme conversion rules. A grapheme (or a phoneme) does not carry meaning on its own; meaning is derived in the process of phonological computation. As most languages use approximately 30–60 phonemes, this mapping principle is economical in the sense that it significantly reduces the number of graphemes (e.g., 26 letters in English) needed to represent all spoken words, which could be as many as hundreds of thousands. This feature of an alphabetic system may have provided the rationale for Wernicke to reject the necessity and feasibility of visual storage of whole words.

Since changing the phoneme sequence changes a word's meaning, such that *blog* becomes *glob* and *tab* becomes *bat*, temporal processing skills may also underlie alphabetic reading development (Tallal 1980). Moreover, this linear, piecemeal representation of words may elicit analytic rather than holistic processing (Ben-Yehudah et al. 2019). At the neural level, the left inferior frontal region (LIFG) has been shown to play a more general function in temporal, analytic processing, whereas the left supramarginal gyrus is more specifically involved in phoneme sequencing (Gelfand and Bookheimer 2003). These two regions have been found to be strongly activated during alphabetic word processing (see Maisog et al. 2008; Martin et al. 2016; Richlan et al. 2011 for meta-analyses).

These features of alphabetic systems corroborate the central importance of phoneme identification and grapheme–phoneme conversion in reading (Ziegler and Goswami 2005). Indeed, cognitive research in the past several decades has established that the ability to detect, extract, and manipulate smaller sound units, or *phonological awareness*, plays a central role in alphabetic reading and spelling acquisition. In support of this view, the phonological deficit hypothesis holds that developmental dyslexia arises from impairments in phonological processing and representation (Ramus 2003). Moreover, effective remediation programmes emphasizing phonological training can yield substantial improvements in reading (Bradley and Bryant 1983).

Neuroimaging findings have consistently revealed that the left-lateralized perisylvian language network comprising the IFG (or Broca's area) and temporo-parietal (TP) regions (coinciding with Wernicke's area) and visual cortices comprising the ventral occipito-temporal cortex (vOT) including the VWFA are recruited during silent or overt reading (Fiez et al. 1999; Horwitz et al. 1998; Hoeft et al. 2007). These findings show that the neural network for reading overlaps with the oral language network, supporting universalist theories of reading. Functional activation reduction in the left posterior mid-superior temporal gyrus, the angular gyrus, and the supramarginal gyrus is associated with poor reading ability (Martin et al. 2016; Shaywitz et al. 2003; Temple et al. 2001), which might be related to a decrease in grey matter volume in the same brain regions (Hoeft et al. 2007). This abnormal brain development may arise well before children start to read (Kuhl et al. 2020; see also see Chapter 9, Fraga González, Jednoróg, and Brem 2022), and may have a genetic basis (Müller et al. 2017; Skeide et al. 2016; see also Chapter 8, Skeide 2022).

In general, these findings support Déjerine's proposal of the importance of the left angular gyrus (AG) and the left vOT in reading. However, contrary to Déjerine's belief that the left AG is a storage for visual word images, research has now shown that this brain region subserves the phonetic analysis of spoken words (DeWitt and Rauschecker 2012) and audiovisual integration (Booth et al. 2002). In line with this view, Pugh et al. observed that a disruption in functional connectivity between the left AG, posterior superior temporal gyrus (pSTG), and vOT is confined to tasks that make explicit demands on grapheme–phoneme mapping (Pugh et al. 2000). Accordingly, they proposed that the dorsal circuit including the left AG and pSTG is responsible for rule-based analytic phonological processing, whereas the ventral circuit including the left vOT is responsible for memory-based word recognition (Pugh et al. 2000; but see Richlan 2014 for a different proposal). Meta-analyses confirm that these dorsal and ventral regions are the brain regions that show the most robust hypoactivity in readers with dyslexia relative to non-impaired readers (Maisog et al. 2008; Martin et al. 2016; Richlan et al. 2011). These findings together support that alphabetic readers with developmental dyslexia have a central deficit in the phonological domain.

15.3.2 The Effects of Orthographic Depth and Syllable Structure Complexity on Learning to Read

As mentioned, German has a shallow orthography and French has a deep orthography. This linguistic feature, known as *orthographic depth*, refers to the degree of consistency of grapheme–phoneme correspondence. Alphabets vary markedly in orthographic depth due to different historical factors, such as cultural mixing and hybridization, historical sound changes, language contacts, and the adoption of loan words. Grapheme–phoneme correspondence rules are easy to detect and use in shallow (or transparent) orthographies, but are more difficult to learn in deep (or opaque) orthographies. Note that orthographic depth has two sides: one refers to the consistency of the mapping from print to sound, as in word decoding (*graphematic transparency*), and the other is the consistency of the reverse mapping from sound to print, as in word spelling (*orthographic transparency*) (Joyce and Borgwaldt 2013). The two sides can be asymmetric in some orthographies. According to Marjou (2019) who estimated the transparency scores of fifteen alphabetic scripts, Arabic, Finnish, Korean, and Turkish have the highest transparency in both directions (with scores above 80%). French has the lowest orthographic transparency (28%) but high graphematic transparency (78%), meaning that it is easy to read but difficult to spell. English has low transparency in both directions (approximately 30% in both directions).

Paulesu et al. (2000) compared the brain activation patterns of English and Italian during word and pseudoword reading. They observed that readers of the deep and shallow orthographies recruited a common left-lateralized network including the left middle temporal gyrus (MTG), inferior temporal gyrus (ITG), precentral gyrus, ventral occipito-temporal cortex (vOT), and bilateral superior temporal gyrus (STG). Within this network, Italian readers had stronger activity in the left pSTG, while English readers had stronger activity in the left vOT and anterior IFG. These findings suggest that orthographic depth is evident quantitatively but not qualitatively, with more transparent orthography activating the brain region responsible for rule-based phonological processing (left pSTG) more strongly and more opaque orthography activating the memory-based brain region (left vOT) more strongly. Paulesu et al. (2001) further showed that dyslexia in deep (English and French) vs. shallow orthographies (Italian) had the same biological origin characterized by a reduced activation of left mid-inferior occipito-temporal regions during word and pseudoword reading. They concluded that phonological processing deficits are a universal problem in dyslexia in both shallow and deep orthographies. It must be noted, however, that their claim might not be directly applicable to non-alphabetic systems.

The complexity of syllable structures may also affect the ease of phoneme detection (Seymour et al. 2003). Some languages, such as Italian and French, have simple syllable structures, with CV (consonant + vowel) and CVC being the dominant syllable patterns and no or a limited set of consonant clusters (a cluster of two or more consonants). Other languages, such as English and Danish, have complex syllable structures that allow a large set of consonant clusters to appear at both ends, such as CCV (e.g., *blue*), VCC (e.g., *old*), CCVC (e.g., *blur*), CVCC (e.g., *boost*), CCVCC (e.g., *drums*), and CCCVCC (e.g., *streets*). Thus, languages around the world vary significantly in syllable structure as well as the number of distinct syllables in use, ranging from a few hundred in Japanese to several thousand in English (Coupé et al. 2019). Detecting phonemes in a language with many complex syllables is more challenging than in a language with fewer and simpler syllables (Seymour et al. 2003).

Taken together, alphabetic languages differ in their orthographic depth and complexity of syllable structure, which affect the effort of learning to read and shape the brain reorganization for reading (see Richlan 2014 for a review). The combination of a deep orthography and a complex syllable structure makes English probably the most difficult writing system within the alphabetic family (Seymour et al. 2003), which may also explain the high prevalence of dyslexia in English-speaking countries. Orthographic depth also modulates the predictive power of phonological awareness as it plays a more important role in deep than shallow orthographies (Ziegler et al. 2010). Finally, people with developmental dyslexia in transparent orthographies show more difficulties in reading fluency than accuracy, and their reading impairment is less severe than in opaque orthographies (Ziegler et al. 2003). These findings suggest that developmental dyslexia has the same core deficit in the phonological domain but different behavioural manifestations in different cultures.

15.4 The Chinese Writing System and Its Underlying Cognitive and Neural Mechanisms

As one of the world's oldest writing systems that has been in continuous use for more than 3,000 years, Chinese orthography retains a logographic form. Written Chinese uses characters as the basic written symbols, which consist of unpronounceable strokes determined by stroke order rules and are confined to the same size square space irrespective of the number of strokes they contain. This two-dimensional visual configuration of a Chinese character may enhance holistic orthographic processing similar to facial processing (Mo et al. 2015; Wong et al. 2012), in contrast to the linear, letter-by-letter array of an alphabetic word, which may involve analytic orthographic coding (Ben-Yehudah et al. 2019). Indeed, neuroimaging studies have found that Chinese reading elicits activation in bilateral vOT cortices, in contrast to alphabetic reading where activation is mostly left-lateralized (Tan et al. 2005; Wu et al. 2012). Thus, even though Chinese characters share basic visual features such as lines, vertices, and junctions with alphabetic words, their face- or picture-like square configuration may activate additional brain regions for holistic visual–spatial processing.

A Chinese character typically represents a syllable and a morpheme or a word, but it does not transcribe phonemes. Hence, written Chinese is also known as morpho-syllabic (DeFrancis 1989), although the mapping between characters and syllables is not systematic and grapheme–phoneme-conversion rules are not available in Chinese. The pronunciation of a character cannot be computed from its strokes or components and must be retrieved from stored memory (addressed phonology). Thus, prelexical, rule-based assembled phonology is not viable in Chinese, making the nature of phonological mapping very different from that of an alphabetic orthography. Accordingly, the neural circuitry for assembled phonology, supposedly the dorsal circuit including the left TP regions, is unlikely to be involved in reading Chinese. This view has gained support from brain imaging studies that have consist-ently shown that reading-related phonological processing in Chinese is subserved by a neural network that does not commonly involve the left TP regions (particularly the pSTG), but the left middle frontal gyrus (LMFG) and other visual or memory regions, such as the bilateral fusiform gyrus, superior parietal lobule, lingual gyrus, and cuneus. Indeed, a range of experimental paradigms involving phono-logical tasks (e.g., Kim et al. 2016; Siok et al. 2003; Siok et al. 2004; Siok et al. 2008; Tan et al. 2003), orthographic tasks (Cao et al. 2013), semantic tasks (Booth et al. 2006; Siok et al. 2004;Wu et al. 2012), morphological tasks (Liu et al. 2013), syntactic processing (Luke et al. 2002), and writing (Cao et al. 2013) unanimously corroborated the central role of the LMFG in reading Chinese.

In Chinese samples, dyslexia is characterized by weak activation of the LMFG, LIFG, left VWFA, and left precentral gyrus compared to typical readers (see Xu et al. 2019 for a meta-analysis). Hypoactivity of the LMFG is related to the dysfunction of neural circuits responsible for morphosemantic processing (morphological processes combined with the interpretation of meaning) (Liu et al. 2013), phonological work-ing memory (Xu et al. 2015) and the mapping of orthography to phonology (Siok et al. 2004; Siok et al. 2008; Yang et al. 2020) and orthography to semantics (Hu et al. 2010; Siok et al. 2004). The reading-related functional disruption in the LMFG of dyslexia in Chinese may be a consequence of reduced grey matter volume in that region (Siok et al. 2008). Specifically, when compared with typically reading controls, Chinese children with dyslexia exhibited reduced grey matter volume in the left middle frontal region and reduced activation in this same brain region during a reading task, and there was a significant correlation between grey matter volume and reading-related brain activation in this area. By contrast, Chinese readers with dyslexia did not show functional or structural differences in the more posterior brain systems identified in children with difficulties in learning alphabetic scripts. Siok et al. (2009) further discovered that Chinese poor readers performed worse than their normal-reading counterparts not only in a phonological processing task but also in a visual–spatial task, the font-size judgement task, in which they were instructed to judge whether two characters presented simultaneously had the same font size. It turned out that the impaired readers who performed slower and less accurately than normal readers had weaker activity in the left anterior intraparietal sulcus and the lingual gyrus. This finding suggests that developmental dyslexia in Chinese individuals is associated with a visuospatial deficit and a phonological disorder. Overall, these results suggest that the structural and functional basis for dyslexia varies between alphabetic and non-alphabetic languages. Specifically, the activation differences in the LMFG are hypothesized to be responsible for difficulties with integrating morpho-semantic and phonological information and orthographic information (Liu et al. 2013; Siok et al. 2004; Tan et al. 2005).

Since a Chinese character represents a syllable that is considered a salient perceptual unit, in contrast to a phoneme that is transient, abstract, and difficult to perceive, some linguists believe that this mapping principle makes learning to read Chinese easier than alphabetic languages because a syllable is more readily 'available' than a phoneme (Wydell and Butterworth 1999; Ziegler and Goswami 2005). On the other hand, the logographic nature of written Chinese has resulted in the formation of a huge number of distinct written symbols to represent spoken words. Specifically, there are more than 85,000 distinct Chinese characters listed in the Zhonghua Zihai dictionary (Leng and Wei 1994). Although only approximately 4,000 characters are required to understand ordinary written texts and not more than 6,500 characters cover 99.99% of all occurrences in formal modern Chinese texts (Da 2004), children still need 6 years to acquire 2,500–3,000 characters during primary schooling. This large number of graphic symbols needed for rote memorization has created a different type of learning problem, termed the 'granularity problem' by (Ziegler and Goswami 2005). As Chinese has a simple syllable structure with mostly CV and CVC syllables and uses only approximately 1,200 distinct syllables (when tones are considered), many characters share one syllable, resulting in a high incidence of homophones that could be visually similar or dissimilar. For example, the characters 饭, 贩, 畈, 范, 笵, 犯, 泛, 梵, 飰 are all pronounced as /fan4/. This suggests that print-to-sound mappings in Chinese are not one-to-one but indeed many-to-one, meaning that a syllable maps onto many characters and represents many different meanings (Perfetti et al. 2005). Assessing the meaning of a character thus cannot rely solely on its pronunciation but also requires subtle visual discrimination and rote memorization of visual forms. One common strategy to help children memorize and distinguish character forms is letting them hand-copy new characters repeatedly and sound them out simultaneously (Tan et al. 2005).

Thus, compared to alphabetic reading, reading in Chinese requires more advanced visual analytic and memory skills, and reading difficulty may evolve not only from a low-quality mapping of orthography to phonology but also from low-quality orthographic representation of characters. Indeed, in the memory literature, the LMFG is known to play important roles in working memory (WM) functions (for review, see D'Esposito and Postle 2015). Various tasks tapping verbal WM, visual WM and executive control processes such as selection, monitoring and manipulation, and resource allocation and coordination have been found to involve LMFG activations. Thus, the LMFG may be recruited to serve these functions during reading Chinese.

Studies using Hangul characters (Korean symbols) have shown that silent reading (Yoon et al. 2005), meaning judgement (Lee 2004), and rhyme judgement (Kim et al. 2016) of characters elicit LMFG activations. Korean Hangul is an alphabetic (or phonemic) writing system in which letters map onto phonemes rather consistently. Unlike other alphabetic scripts that are written linearly, Hangul letters are grouped into square blocks. Each Hangul block maps onto a syllable and contains two to six phonemes. In this sense, a Korean Hangul character bears some resemblance to a Chinese character. The LMFG may thus play a role in visuospatial analysis or print–sound mapping at the syllable level. Indeed, recent fMRI studies have shown that activations in the posterior LMFG are involved in visual imagery (Hayashi et al. 2014) and are parametrically modulated by the stroke number of Chinese characters (Chen et al. 2016). It also plays a role in syllable processing (in contrast to phonemic processing) and syllable–character integration in Chinese (Yang et al. 2020), and is involved in reading Japanese Kana, which is a highly transparent syllabary script (Kita et al. 2013). The recruitment of the LMFG in these writing systems may thus be related to the square-shaped visual array, visual complexity, and/or character-to-syllable mapping.

Behavioural findings from the past two decades have shown that phonological skills, including phonological awareness and phonological memory, correlate with typical and atypical reading in Chinese. This relationship, however, involves larger sound units such as rhymes, syllables, and tones, but not phonemes (Siok and Fletcher 2001). These findings align well with the linguistic features of the Chinese orthography in which phonemes are not encoded. Besides phonological awareness, various other factors have been reported to be correlated with reading performance in Chinese, including rapid automatized naming (RAN) (Tan et al. 2005), visual processing skills (form constancy and sequential memory) (Siok and Fletcher 2001), visual-motor integration or hand-copying skills (Meng et al. 2019; Tan et al. 2005), orthographic awareness (Siok and Fletcher 2001), morphological awareness (Ruan et al. 2018), and working memory (Peng et al. 2018), but none of these correlations differ significantly from each other. People with developmental dyslexia in Chinese have shown multiple deficits in phonological, visuo-ortho-graphic, and morphological processing (Ho et al. 2004;Ho et al. 2007; Siok et al. 2009; see Peng et al. 2017 for a meta-analysis and review). Interestingly, some studies suggest that phonological awareness does not play a significant role in Chinese reading (Liu et al. 2013), challenging the view that phonological deficits are a universal cause of dyslexia.

In sum, both behavioural and neuroimaging studies have shown that dyslexia could have different behavioural and biological underpinnings in Chinese compared to alphabetic scripts. Chinese people with dyslexia typically may have multiple deficits and there may not be a universal cause of dyslexia across cultures. Nevertheless, this cultural difference hypothesis awaits support by longitudinal studies beginning before literacy instruction begins, ideally in infancy (see Chapter 1, Goswami 2022).

15.5 Direct Comparison of Neural Networks for Reading between Writing Systems

The neural and cognitive networks for reading may reveal universal and idiosyncratic features across writing systems, with the fundamental difference lying in visual configurations and print–sound mapping principles. In a meta-analysis comparing the neural correlates of phonological processing while reading Chinese characters (sound-like judgement, homophone judgement) and alphabetic words (rhyme judgement, letter transformation, phonological decision, letter–sound matching), Tan et al. (2005) reported that the two writing systems showed convergent and divergent brain activation patterns. Both systems commonly activated the left dorsal inferior frontal region and the left ventral occipito-temporal region. The alphabetic system, however, also elicited activation in the left posterior TP regions covering the mid-superior temporal gyri and the ventral inferior parietal cortex (supramarginal region), while the Chinese system also includes the LMFG, the left dorsal inferior parietal lobule (IPL), and the right vOT. Tan et al. (2005) argue that the LMFG is responsible for visuospatial analysis and syllable processing, and the left dorsal IPL serves as short-term phonological storage. The left dorsal IFG, together with the supplementary motor cortex, is thought to be relevant for grapheme–phoneme conversion and subvocal rehearsal functions. Since Chinese does not require grapheme–phoneme conversion, this region might play a more important role in alphabetic languages. Tan et al.'s (2005) findings demonstrate that the neural circuit for reading is shaped by the linguistic demands of a writing system. It is important to note that some studies have found the LMFG to be involved in alphabetic reading (e.g., Feng et al. 2020; Hu et al. 2010). Additionally, extended lesions covering the middle frontal gyrus in addition to Broca's area have been found in Broca's aphasics (Mohr 2006). Other studies, however, including Kim et al. (2017), did not find LMFG activation during reading processing in alphabetic readers, which suggests that the LMFG is not as robustly recruited in alphabetic reading as it is in Chinese reading (but see Murphy et al. 2019).

A few neuroimaging studies have attempted to directly compare brain activation between alphabetic and non-alphabetic learners with dyslexia. Using a semantic word matching task, Hu et al. (2010) found that typical Chinese and English readers showed brain activation differences in the left mid-inferior frontal region (Chinese > English) and the left posterior superior temporal sulcus (pSTS) (English > Chinese). Chinese individuals with dyslexia had weaker brain activation than the Chinese controls in the LMFG, whereas English individuals with dyslexia had weaker activation than the English controls in the left pSTS, but the two dyslexic groups did not differ in these two brain regions. Hu et al. (2010) argued that the two dyslexic groups used a similar neural mechanism during semantic word processing, implying a universal neural substrate of developmental dyslexia in two contrastive writing systems. In a more recent study comparing brain activation during a passive reading task in Chinese and French children with and without dyslexia, Feng et al. (2020) identified a common functional network, including the bilateral fusiform gyri, bilateral precentral gyri, bilateral MFG, left STS, and right middle occipital gyrus, that was found to correlate significantly with the reading scores of both Chinese and French readers. Feng et al. (2020) argued that since both Chinese and French children showed an effect of reading ability in the LMFG, this region was not specific to Chinese reading. They concluded that the reading network was largely universal, even though Chinese children (both typical and atypical readers) showed significantly stronger activity than their French counterparts in the LMFG, the left STG, and the left parietal region and had more bilateral activation in the occipital regions. Similar universal reading proposals were made by Nakamura et al. (2012), who compared the neural networks for orthographic and handwriting processes between Chinese and French normal-reading adults, and Rueckl et al. (2015), who examined semantic processing among Spanish, English, Hebrew, and Chinese speakers.

15.6 Dyslexia in Bilingual Readers

Research on bilingual individuals provides another perspective on the impact of language structure on reading acquisition. Since metacognitive awareness (such as phonological awareness) can be transferred from the native language (L1) to the second language (L2) and vice versa (e.g., Holm and Dodd 1996), it is not surprising that the cognitive and neural processes in the two languages are similar and interactive in bilinguals. Indeed, many English-as-second-language (ESL) learners in Hong Kong and China learn English words as holistic units without dividing the whole words into letters and mapping the letters onto phonemes. Moreover, they typically have poor phonemic awareness even if they have learnt an alphabetic script as their L2 (e.g., Cheung et al. 2001). An fMRI study showed that Chinese ESL adults recruit the canonical brain network for reading Chinese to read English. Specifically, the left TP region turned out to be inactive during Chinese and English visual-phonological processing (visual word rhyme judgement), suggesting that they did not activate the regions for rule-based phonological processing in both language conditions (Tan et al. 2003). A similar lack of a language transfer effect was observed in a group of Hong Kong Chinese–English bilingual children. Ho and Fong (2005) reported that the concomitance rate of dyslexia in Chinese and English was high in Hong Kong, with twenty-four out of twenty-five of their Chinese participants with dyslexia having concurrent difficulties reading English. Interestingly, one boy with dyslexia in reading Chinese had above-average English reading performance. The boy had good phonemic awareness in English but poor rhyme awareness in Chinese. Ho and Fong (2005) suspected that the boy might have learnt English using phonics, but the phonological knowledge did not transfer between the two languages. Therefore, the high co-occurrence rate of dyslexia in these bilinguals is likely due to the fact that they adopted the same strategies when learning to read these two contrastive orthographies.

Wydell and Butterworth (1999) reported a different form of dissociation in a case study. A 16-year-old English–Japanese bilingual boy, AS, had reading difficulties in English only. AS was born in Japan to highly literate Austrian parents. His proficiency in Japanese reading of both logographic Kanji and syllabic Kana was equivalent to that of Japanese undergraduates or graduates, but his performance in reading and phonological processing in English was poorer compared to his Japanese peers. AS's phonological deficit and reading difficulties in English persisted into adulthood (Wydell and Kondo 2003). In general, these findings suggest that the underlying cognitive and neural network of two structurally different writing systems may be functionally dissociated and that readers may have deficits in only one but not both languages.

The notion that learning strategy may shape the neural network of reading is corroborated by an fMRI study comparing US-American Chinese-as-foreign-language learners (CFL) with Chinese English-as-second-language (ESL) learners (Nelson et al. 2009). Nelson and colleagues replicated Tan et al.'s (2003) finding that Chinese ESL learners used the network typically seen in Chinese to read words in their first language (L1) and second language (L2) (*assimilation pattern*). In addition, they found that US-American CFL learners used the typical English reading network to process English words but implemented the new Chinese writing system by adding new neural resources (the LMFG and bilateral occipital cortices) to meet the specific visual processing demands of Chinese (*accommodation pattern*). In other words, using the same cognitive strategy for both writing systems might lead to an assimilation pattern, while using different strategies (phonics for English and whole word recognition for Chinese) might result in an accommodation pattern.

It could also be that the functional dissociation of the two writing systems may be traceable to overlapping networks with different functional connections between regions. This speculation has received support from recent studies indicating that distinct neural patterns can be observed in two structurally different orthographies such as Chinese and English (Xu et al. 2017) but not in two structurally similar orthographies such as Spanish and English (Willms et al. 2011). In fact, seemingly overlapping neural networks for L1 and L2 reported in most bilingual neuroimaging studies might turn out to blur different language-specific association patterns.

15.7 Limitations of Current Research on Universal vs. Specific Features of Dyslexia

Although studies reporting common brain networks for typologically different writing systems may suggest that the neural correlates of reading and dyslexia are largely universal across cultures, multiple issues must be considered when interpreting these findings. First, most of these studies focused on a deep alphabetic orthography such as French or English (e.g., Feng et al. 2020; Hu et al. 2010). Compared to more transparent orthographies, these deep orthographies elicit more lexical-level but less sublexical phonological processing during reading (Coltheart 2014), implying that their underlying cognitive mechanism may be more similar to reading Chinese. Indeed, studies have shown that French reading involves more visual memory skills than transparent orthographies such as Spanish (Valdois et al. 2014), and both French and Chinese have higher graphematic transparency but lower orthographic transparency than Spanish. It then makes sense that dyslexia in these cultures shares similar attributes.

Second, these studies often used simple semantic categorization tasks such as animate/inanimate judgement (Dehaene and Cohen 2011; Hu et al. 2010; Nakamura et al. 2012; Rueckl et al. 2015) or a passive viewing task (Feng et al. 2020) with high-frequency words (e.g., *train*, *window*). These tasks may elicit mostly conceptual processing that is likely universal across writing systems (Buchweitz et al. 2012). As emphasized, writing systems differ fundamentally in their visual configurations and print–sound mapping principles but not in their conceptual semantic representations. Reading ability is contingent on the construction of an orthographic constituent that links to the already existing phonological and semantic constituents, with the strength and nature of connections between the three constituents shaped by reading experience (Perfetti et al. 2005). To better examine the universal reading hypothesis, tasks tapping into orthographic and phonological processing should be included in future studies.

Third, the design and statistical analysis used in many studies may not be optimal for detecting differences between writing systems. Most studies use statistical thresholding to identify the functional localization of activated regions in typical and atypical readers of different orthographies. Conjunction analysis is then performed to identify the shared neural network across orthographies, followed by a quantitative analysis of neural activity in each activated region. As impaired readers cannot recruit the typical neural system for reading, they may adopt different compensatory mechanisms, potentially resulting in heterogeneous patterns of neural activity within the group. Not surprisingly, group analysis of their activation patterns typically reveals overall weak neural signals in almost all brain regions, leading to a null difference between impaired readers in different orthographies. Even for typical readers, it would be unrealistic to expect two distinct networks for two contrastive writing systems, or that the neural correlates of two writing systems differ in one or more localized brain regions. Instead, cross-linguistic differences could be quantitative rather than qualitative in nature (Paulesu et al. 2000), or could be system-level rather than region-level differences. More sensitive statistical analysis techniques, such as multivariate pattern analysis (Xu et al. 2017), and more system- or network-based analysis, such as functional connectivity analysis, are needed to capture these subtle differences within culture-specific networks for reading.

Fourth, the neural circuit for reading reveals different patterns of development in different orthographies. Using a task that isolates reading-related brain activity and minimizes confounding performance effects, Turkeltaub et al. (2003) conducted a cross-sectional fMRI study with participants aged 6 to 22 years. They found that learning to read is associated with two patterns of change in brain activity: increased activity in the left-hemisphere middle temporal and inferior frontal gyri, and decreased activity in the right inferotemporal cortical areas. In a series of fMRI studies, Booth and colleagues found that cortical regions associated with children's reading performance largely overlap with those associated with adults' reading performance (Booth et al. 2002; Booth et al. 2004). Increasing age is correlated with greater activation in the left MTG and IPL, suggesting that older children have more elaborate semantic representations and more complete semantic integration processes, respectively. Decreasing age, in contrast, is correlated with activation in the right STG, and decreasing accuracy is correlated with activation in the right MTG, suggesting the engagement of ancillary systems in the right hemisphere for younger and lower-skilled children (Chou et al. 2006). This pattern of findings coincides with that of Turkeltaub et al. (2003) in that reading development is associated with the development of an increasing left-lateralized neural network. However, the neural development of Chinese reading reveals a different pattern. In a lifespan study with 125 participants aged 6–74 years, Siok et al. (2020) found that beginning and fluent readers recruit an overlapping neural network for reading that is typically involved in reading Chinese. Reading development is evident in more focused brain activation of the same brain network, and brain regions show either the same or reduced activation intensity with increasing reading experience. Although children and adults use the same neural circuitry to process the logographic orthography, they show different connectivity patterns between the cortical areas associated with reading, suggesting that the associations among specialized brain regions are modulated by learning experience. Thus, longitudinal data should be used to capture developmental changes of the reading networks and examine cross-cultural differences.

15.8 Conclusion

While writing systems worldwide share common features, they also differ in (1) the visual configuration of letters, (2) the speech units they represent, and (3) the nature and consistency of print-to-sound mappings. Each of these dimensions shapes the cognitive and neural underpinnings of reading and dyslexia to different extents in different cultures. Cross-cultural research has widened our understanding of the nature of dyslexia by revealing its common and idiosyncratic features. On the one hand, the VWFA is commonly and invariably recruited to process visual-orthographic information of any writing system, and dyslexic readers of different orthographies have phonological processing deficits. On the other hand, the nature of phonological skills important for reading differs across cultures and shapes the brain in distinctive ways, with sublexical, rule-based phonological processing recruiting the left TP regions and lexical, memory-based phonological processing recruiting the left middle frontal region. In addition, graphic symbols with complex stroke configurations may induce more activity in the left middle frontal region and the bilateral visual cortices, and dyslexic children reading a logographic script have more difficulties in the visual-orthographic domain. However, current research using simple localizations cannot reveal the fundamental mechanism underpinning normal or dyslexic reading. Accordingly, the debate regarding universality and specificity continues. Future studies should be guided by a focus on (1) more diverse languages, (2) statistical techniques that uncover differences in overlapping brain activation clusters and capture the connections between different brain areas, (3) imaging techniques with better temporal and spatial resolution, and (4) readers at different developmental stages, in particular the first years of life.

Suggestions for Further Reading

Gabrieli, J. D. E. 2009. 'Dyslexia: A New Synergy between Education and Cognitive Neuroscience'. *Science* 325 (5938): 280–3.

Kuhl, U., N. E. Neef, I. Kraft, et al. 2020. 'The Emergence of Dyslexia in the Developing Brain'. *NeuroImage* 211 (May): 116633.

Maisog, J. M., E. R. Einbinder, D. L. Flowers, P. E, Turkeltaub, and G. F. Eden. 2008. 'A Meta-Analysis of Functional Neuroimaging Studies of Dyslexia'. *Annals of the New York Academy of Sciences* 1145 (December): 237–59.

Paulesu, E., Danelli, L., and Berlingeri, M. 2014. 'Reading the Dyslexic Brain: Multiple Dysfunctional Routes Revealed by a New Meta-Analysis of PET and fMRI Activation Studies'. *Frontiers in Human Neuroscience* 8 (November): 830.

Richlan, F. 2014. 'Functional Neuroanatomy of Developmental Dyslexia: The Role of Orthographic Depth'. *Frontiers in Human Neuroscience* 8, 347. https://doi.org/10.3389/fnhum.2014.00347.

16 Cross-Cultural Unity and Diversity of Dyscalculia

Baihan Lyu and Xinlin Zhou

16.1 Introduction

At an international conference in China, we were asked by a non-Chinese colleague: 'Since Chinese students are already so good at mathematics, why are you studying dyscalculia?' Advantages in the development of early mathematics ability have been generally documented in favour of Asian Pacific countries/regions including China, Japan, Korea, and Singapore (e.g., Miller et al. 2005; Leung 2014). However, this advantage does not translate to an 'immunity' from problems related to maths learning in children. Problems in arithmetic (termed dyscalculia) that are encountered in most western countries are found with equal prevalences in Asian Pacific countries/regions. Thus, the work we do in China along with other research is still important for understanding dyscalculia in a universal context.

We wish to emphasize that the type of dyscalculia discussed in this chapter is primarily of developmental origin, as opposed to acquired dyscalculia, which is often caused by brain damage. In the Diagnostic and Statistical Manual 5th Edition (DSM-5), developmental dyscalculia is defined as a specific learning disorder characterized as an impediment in mathematics, evidenced by problems with number sense, memorization of arithmetic facts, accurate and fluent calculation, and accurate mathematical reasoning (American Psychiatric Association 2013). Many studies have determined cases of dyscalculia automatically using the lower tail of a standardized mathematical test rather than using a specialized dyscalculia screener. The test content, target population, language, and relevant factors can vary considerably across studies, and thus large inconsistencies exist in how dyscalculia is detected (Moeller et al. 2012; see also Chapter 22, Lachmann, Bergström, Huber, and Nürk 2022). In this chapter, we consider dyscalculia to be present when performance in number and arithmetic tasks is persistently low when measured in experimental, educational, and clinical settings.

Most dyscalculia research comes from North America and Europe. While populations in other regions have been studied less, this trend has been changing in recent years. However, very little cross-cultural comparison has been conducted in order to understand dyscalculia in an international context. There are several reasons for this. First, an international consensus for the maths content relating to dyscalculia has not yet been achieved. In the DSM-5 (American Psychiatric Association 2013), dyscalculia covers a range of mathematical difficulties, whereas the World Health Organization (WHO) has specified a different set of deficits in arithmetic skills (World Health Organization 2015). Second, because the cut-off points range widely across studies (i.e., 1–2 standard deviations (SDs) below the average maths performance), the reported prevalences vary (Devine et al. 2013). This could also mean that these difficulties in mathematics might have different origins, but this remains to be examined. Very few studies so far have adapted a cross-cultural cohort design that carefully controls demographics, diagnostics, and educational contexts (see Rodic et al. 2015). In the following section, we will discuss findings from individual studies conducted in different countries to present an overall picture of the common and culture-specific features of dyscalculia.

16.2 Prevalence

The first recorded dyscalculia study in Slovakia revealed that 6.4% of all school children suffered from difficulties with number processing or maths problem solving (Kosc 1974). Studies since then have generally found prevalences between 5% and 7%. However, a closer look at individual studies reveals a large variation. One reason for this is the broad range of cut-off points used to define the deficit (from 3% to 25% of the lower tail of mathematical performance). Devine et al. (2013) reviewed 17 studies with varying cut-off points below the average maths performance (2 SD to 0.68 SD, or 1.3% to 10.3% in percentiles). According to the review, the average prevalence was approximately 5.3%.

In Table 16.1, we summarize prevalence-related information for dyscalculia from 22 studies across 14 countries. We believe that the diverse findings result from three potential sources of variation. First, the main source of variation across studies was the cut-off points. A study conducted in Iran (Barahmand 2008) used a cut-off of 2 SD below the mean and reported a prevalence of 3.8%. In contrast, studies that used a 1.5 SD cut-off and controlled for at least average intelligence mostly reported prevalences around 5%–7%, including work in Greece (6.3%: Koumoula et al. 2004), Germany (6%: von Aster and Shalev 2007; 5.4%: Moll et al. 2019), and the United Kingdom (6%: Devine et al. 2013; 5.7%: Morsanyi et al. 2018). However, exceptions existed in Serbia (9.9%: Jovanović et al. 2013) and China (4.2%: Cheng et al. 2018). The high prevalence in Jovanović et al. (2013) might be due to the lack of control for general cognitive ability (including intelligence).

Second, according to the DSM-5, *persistent* difficulties in arithmetic should be considered since studies that adopted a one-time test were more likely to lead to false-positive diagnoses of dyscalculia. This was true for studies in Brazil (7.8%: Bastos

Table 16.1 *Summary of prevalences of dyscalculia across different cultures*

Study	Country	Sample	Grade	Prevalence	Comorbidity with dyslexia	Cut-off criterion
Lewis et al. (1994)	UK	1.056	5	3.6%	64%	< 16%
Gross-Tsur et al. (1996)	Israel	3.029	4	6.5%	17%	< 20%
Badian (1999)	USA	1.075	K–8	3.9%	–	< 25%
Hein et al. (2000)	Germany	181	3	6.6%	–	< 17%
Ramaa and Gowramma (2002)	India	1.408	1–4	5.5%	51%	grade level[2]
Mazzocco and Myers (2003)	USA	209	K–3	9.6%	–	< −1SD
Desoete et al. (2004)	Belgium	3.978	2–4	5.5%	51%	< −2SD
Koumoula et al. (2004)	Greece	240	2–5	6.3%	25%	< −1.5SD
Barbaresi et al. (2005)	USA	5.718	1–9	5.2%	–	regression[3]
von Aster and Shalev (2007)	Germany	378	K–2	6.0%	70%	< −1.5SD
Barahmand (2008)	Iran	1.171	2-5	3.8%	–	< −2SD
Dirks et al. (2008)	Netherlands	799	4–5	6.6%	43%	< 10%
Geary (2010)	USA	238	K–9	5.4%	–	< 15%
Reigosa-Crespo et al. (2012)	Cuba	11.652	2–9	3.4%	–	< 15%
Devine et al. (2013)	UK	1.004	2–4	6.0%	–	< −1.5SD
Jovanović et al. (2013)	Serbia	1.078	3	9.9%	–	< −1.5SD
Bastos et al. (2016)	Brazil	2.893	3–5	7.8%	–	regression[4]
Keong et al. (2016)	Malaysia	448	7–9y[1]	3.8%	–	low score[5]
Wong et al. (2017)	China	211	K–1	9.2%	–	< 10%
Morsanyi et al. (2018)	UK	2.421	4–7	5.7%	–	< −1.5SD
Cheng et al. (2018)	China	1.142	3–5	4.2%	38%	< −1.5SD
Moll et al. (2019)	Germany	1.454	3	5.4%	22%	< −1.5SD

[1] years of age [2] arithmetic performance at least 2 years below grade level [3] Minnesota Regression Table [4] logistic regression formula [5] qualitatively determined poor performance

et al. 2016) and a first-stage screening conducted in Cuba (12.4%: Reigosa-Crespo et al. 2012). On the other hand, when using multiple screening procedures or persistent monitoring, the reported prevalence was relatively low. Reigosa-Crespo et al. (2012), for example, reported a prevalence rate of 3.4% in a sample of 1,966 individuals. Other studies focusing on persistent difficulties also reported relatively low prevalences (5.7%, UK: Morsanyi et al. 2018; 5.5%, Belgium: Desoete et al. 2004), even when using a lenient cut-off point of < 25% (3.9%, US: Badian 1999).

Third, small sample sizes and uncontrolled random sampling may not generate representative data and thus may lead to a substantial deviation of prevalence rates. Interestingly, the prevalence of dyscalculia is typically larger than 5% in studies with sample sizes smaller than 1,000 (Table 16.1).

In summary, based on the 22 studies from 14 countries reviewed here, we conclude that the prevalence of dyscalculia is consistently around 5–7%. Based on Table 16.1, we obtained an average prevalence across studies (weighted by sample sizes) of approximately 5.6%. The average prevalence for three samples from Asian Pacific countries was about 4.7%. Therefore, although East Asian students typically have higher average mathematical achievement (e.g., Miller et al. 2005), the need to study and treat dyscalculia is equally urgent across cultures.

16.3 Cognitive Profiles

The main underlying causes of dyscalculia could be domain-specific or domain-general deficits. The domain-specificity hypothesis proposes that the core deficits of dyscalculia are the ability to understand and manipulate numerical magnitudes (e.g., Piazza et al. 2010). In contrast, the domain-generality hypothesis (Fias et al. 2013) proposes that dyscalculia originates from several domains, such as working memory (e.g., Bull and Scerif 2001; Szűcs et al. 2013), attention (e.g., Hannula et al. 2010), executive control (e.g., Blair and Razza 2007; Gilmore et al. 2013), and visual perception (Cheng et al. 2018).

Is there a culture-specific difference in cognitive profiles of dyscalculia? Chia et al. (2014) compared dyscalculia in Singaporean and US-American students based on their performance on the *Test of Mathematical Abilities-2nd Edition* (TEMA-2), which measures calculation, mathematical vocabulary, mathematical concepts, word problems, and attitudes towards mathematics. The results suggested a consistent relationship between calculation and total maths performance in both countries. However, although vocabulary was not a significant predictor for calculation in Singapore ($r = 0.19$), the correlation was high in the US-American sample ($r = 0.62$). According to the authors, this discrepancy could be due to different sample selection procedures or due to different curricula given that the 40 US-American students with dyscalculia were tested during 1990–2 (age 8–18 years) whereas the 40 Singaporean students (age 9–11 years) were tested in 2011 (Chia). To elaborate on the shared and unique cognitive profiles of dyscalculia, we compare and discuss findings from studies of populations in different regions and countries across the world.

16.3.1 Domain-Specific Ability

Number skill is an innate ability to represent non-symbolic or analogue quantity that relies on the approximate number system (ANS). The domain-specificity hypothesis proposes that the core deficit of dyscalculia is an impaired ANS (Butterworth et al. 2011). Among a broad range of task paradigms, the most popular way to assess the ANS is through non-symbolic dot comparison tasks. In its typical form, the task requires participants to compare the quantities of two dot arrays while ignoring the dot size (Zhou et al. 2015). The difficulty increases as the ratio of dots between the arrays approaches 1.

Numerous studies have shown that children with dyscalculia have impairments in the ANS (e.g., Italy, the United Kingdom, USA, Belgium, Sweden, China; Piazza et al. 2010; Iuculano et al. 2008; Mazzocco et al. 2011; Cheng et al. 2018; Olsson et al. 2016; Mejias et al. 2012). Piazza et al. (2010) tested school-aged children in Italy and found that their performance in non-symbolic numerosity discrimination was much lower than that of their peers. In the USA, Mazzocco et al. (2011) showed that ANS impairment was observed in severe cases of dyscalculia in which scores were below the 10th percentile, but not in poorly performing children whose scores were in the 10th to 25th percentile range. Similar findings have been obtained in other countries (e.g., Israel, China; Furman and Rubinsten 2012; Chan et al. 2013; Wong et al. 2017). For instance, Chan et al. (2013) investigated first-grade Chinese children and found two distinct types of mathematical learning difficulties. One type was a specific deficit in non-symbolic processing in which symbolic number processing was not affected, and the other type was the reverse pattern. In general, these studies have shown that the ANS deficit in dyscalculia is invariant across cultures.

16.3.2 Domain-General Ability

The domain-generality hypothesis proposes that the deficits underlying developmental dyscalculia are dysfunctions in one or more general cognitive systems necessary for mathematical learning: working memory, attention, spatial processing, inhibitory control, visual perception, or others. For example, Szűcs et al. (2013) provided evidence for impaired visual working memory and inhibitory control in UK children with dyscalculia. Another example is an attention deficit in dyscalculia which might also result in a diagnosis of attention deficit hyperactivity disorder (ADHD) (e.g., Mayes and Calhoun 2006). In this context, it must be noted that the number of studies in non-WEIRD (western-educated-industrialized-rich-democratic) countries is still insufficient for making comparisons.

According to the triple code model (Dehaene 1992), language is also important for number processing. In line with this hypothesis, impaired verbal ability in dyscalculia has also been observed across cultures. Fuchs et al. (2005) showed that rapid naming and phonological awareness tasks predicted calculation fluency. Similarly, multiplication depends on phonological processing (Zhou et al. 2007). Thus, children with dyscalculia can also have difficulties in language-related tasks. Although some cognitive mechanisms underlying dyscalculia and dyslexia can be dissociated (e.g., Butterworth and Kovas 2013), they also have many aspects in common (Moll et al. 2019) and dyscalculia often co-occurs with dyslexia (see Chapter 4, Banfi, Landerl, and Moll 2022) while the prevalence of this co-occurrence varies across cultures (Table 16.1). For example, Koponen et al. (2018) conducted a longitudinal study (grades 2–4) focusing on maths and reading ability of 1,928 Finnish students. They found that the co-occurrence rate of dyscalculia and dyslexia was 40–60%. In contrast, Cheng et al. (2018) investigated 1,142 Chinese children, finding that only 18 out of 66 children (27%) who met the criteria for dyscalculia were also severely impaired in reading performance.

Deficits in visual form perception have also been considered as an underlying cause of dyscalculia in Chinese children (e.g., Cheng et al. 2018; Zhou et al. 2015). Indeed, several studies have shown that visual form perception partly explains the relationship between the ANS and arithmetic (Cui et al. 2019; Zhou et al. 2015). In these studies, visual form perception was measured using a figure-matching task that required participants to rapidly judge whether a picture on the left matched any of three pictures on the right (Zhou et al. 2015). Cheng et al. (2018) found impaired visual form perception and impaired ANS processing in children with dyscalculia. They recruited 1,142 primary school students (aged 8–11 years) in Beijing and measured simple arithmetic and cognitive skills. Thirty-nine children who performed between 1.5 and 0.67 SDs below the mean (between the 6.7th and 25th percentile) on arithmetic were classified as having dyscalculia. After controlling for three cognitive variables (choice reaction time, mental rotation score, and visual tracking score), performance on the ANS task still differed significantly between children with dyscalculia compared to children with dyslexia and control groups. However, after controlling for figure-matching performance but not after controlling for other variables, the difference in ANS ability between controls and children with dyscalculia disappeared. These results indicated an impairment in visual perception underlying dyscalculia in Chinese students. There is further evidence that this effect is robust as visual perception training also may facilitate ANS processing and arithmetic performance in children with dyscalculia (Cheng et al. 2020) (for more details, see Section 16.5). Visual form perception deficits have not been reported so far in other cultures, but we believe it could be a common deficit leading to dyscalculia.

16.4 Neuroimaging Studies

To our knowledge, there are currently no published neuroimaging studies of dyscalculia in non-WEIRD cultures. Nevertheless, given the cross-cultural commonalities between the underlying cognitive deficits, we expect that the neural correlates should follow the same pattern across the world. In Table 16.2, we summarize seventeen functional studies in eight countries that compared brain responses in participants with developmental dyscalculia to typically developing controls during basic numerical processing, arithmetic, or both.

Non-symbolic magnitude was examined using fMRI in samples in Finland (Price et al. 2007), the USA (Simos et al. 2008), Austria (Kaufmann et al. 2009), Switzerland (Kucian et al. 2011; McCaskey et al. 2017), Germany (Dinkel et al. 2013), and Belgium (Bulthé et al. 2019; Mussolin et al. 2010). As the domain-specificity hypothesis suggests, neural dysfunction in magnitude processing was observed consistently across studies in the intraparietal sulcus (IPS). However, the direction of these results is mixed, with some studies reporting hypoactivation (Bulthé et al. 2019; Dinkel et al. 2013; Mussolin et al. 2010; Price et al. 2007) while others found hyper-activation in the IPS (Kaufmann et al. 2009; Simos et al. 2008). Additionally, two studies did not detect any altered activation in the parietal lobe (Kucian et al. 2011; McCaskey et al. 2017).

In addition to symbolic and non-symbolic number magnitude tasks, other studies employed number line and number ordering tasks. The number line task requires mapping between symbolic numbers and their relative location on a number line. Two studies conducted in Switzerland suggested that the corresponding differences in activity in the parietal lobe can go in opposing directions. Specifically, the parietal lobe displayed hypoactivation in Kucian et al. (2011), while Michels et al. (2018) reported the opposite results. Number ordering tasks revealed increased activation in the right parietal lobe (Kaufmann et al. 2009) and the left IPS (McCaskey et al. 2017) in individuals with dyscalculia. However, a study in the UK (Cappelletti and Price 2014) did not show impaired parietal lobe functioning, but impaired frontal lobe functioning including the right superior frontal cortex (SFC) and the left inferior frontal sulcus (IFS). Thus, while the behavioural results converged on the same number processing deficits, it is still far from clear whether they relate to neural activity in the IPS.

In addition to basic number processing, studies carried out in Germany (Kucian et al. 2006) and the USA (Ashkenazi et al. 2012; Rosenberg-Lee et al. 2015; Simos et al. 2008) suggest that deficits in arithmetic found in dyscalculia are related to altered activation in the parietal lobe. However, again, the direction of activation differences varies across studies. Ashkenazi et al. (2012) found hypoactivation in the right IPS, right SPL, right supramarginal gyri (SMG), and bilateral dorsolateral prefrontal cortex (DLPFC) using simple and complex arithmetic. In contrast, Rosenberg-Lee et al. (2015) and Simos et al. (2008) found hyper-activation in the right IPL, right SPL, and bilateral

Table 16.2 *Summary of functional imaging studies of dyscalculia across different cultures*

Study	Country	Sample[1]	Age[2]	Task	Altered activation[3]
Kucian et al. (2006)	Germany	18:20	9–12	Approximate arithmetic	−bilateral IPS −bilateral IFG −bilateral MFG
Price et al. (2007)	Finland	8:8	11	Non-symbolic magnitude	−right IPS
Simos et al. (2008)	USA	14:25	8–12	Exact arithmetic Non-symbolic magnitude	+right inferior PL +right superior PL
Kaufmann et al. (2009)	Austria	6:6	8–13	Number ordinality	+right SPL
Kaufmann et al. (2009)	Austria	9:9	8–10	Non-symbolic magnitude	+left IPL
Mussolin et al. (2010)	Belgium	15:15	9–11	Symbolic magnitude	+right PCG +right SMG +left THA −right MFG −left SPL −right IPS −left MCG
Kucian et al. (2011)	Switzerland	16:16	8–10	Number line	−bilateral PL
Kucian et al. (2011)	Switzerland	15:15	10–11	Non-symbolic magnitude	+SMA +right FFG
Ashkenazi et al. (2012)	USA	17:17	7–9	Exact arithmetic	−right IPS −right SPL +right SMG +bilateral DLPFC
Dinkel et al. (2013)	Germany	16:16	6–10	Non-symbolic magnitude Non-symbolic exact arithmetic	−VC
Cappelletti and Price (2014)	UK	11:22	24–70	Number semantic	+right SFC +left IFS
Rosenberg-Lee et al. (2015)	USA	19:21	7–9	Exact arithmetic	+bilateral IPS
McCaskey et al. (2017)	Switzerland	16:14	14	Non-symbolic magnitude	+left IFG
McCaskey et al. (2017)	Switzerland	17:11	8–11	Number ordinality	+left IPS +bilateral MFG +left IFG +bilateral AG

Table 16.2 (*cont.*)

Study	Country	Sample[1]	Age[2]	Task	Altered activation[3]
Michels et al. (2018)	Switzerland	15:16	7–12	Number line	+bilateral IPL +right SFG +bilateral IFG +bilateral TL
Bulthé et al. (2019)	Belgium	24:24	18–27	Non-symbolic magnitude	−right IPS −right IFG −right SFG

[1] dyscalculia:control [2]years [3]+ increased activation; − reduced activation; IPS, inferior parietal sulcus; IFG, inferior frontal gyrus; MFG, middle frontal gyrus; IPL, inferior parietal lobe; SPL, superior parietal lobe; POG, postcentral gyrus; SMG, supramarginal gyri; THA, thalamus; MCG, middle cingulate gyrus; PL, parietal lobe; SMA, supplementary motor area; FFG, fusiform gyrus; DLPFC, dorsolateral prefrontal cortex; AG, angular gyrus; POS, parieto-occipital sulcus; V1, primary visual cortex; SFC, superior frontal cortex; IFS, inferior frontal sulcus; SFG, superior frontal gyrus; TL, temporal lobe.

IPS using simple arithmetic. Kucian et al. (2006) also found that deficits in approximate arithmetic were related to hypoactivation, but in the frontal lobe (including bilateral IFG and bilateral MFG) not the parietal lobe. These findings support the alternative domain-generality hypothesis that working memory may be disrupted in dyscalculia (for a review, see Menon 2016).

In structural MRI studies, voxel-based and surface-based morphometry (VBM and SBM) has been used to compare grey and white matter volume between individuals with dyscalculia and healthy controls. Moreover, diffusion tensor imaging (DTI) was applied to examine differences in structural connectivity. Table 16.3 summarizes eight structural imaging studies across four countries (the USA, Switzerland, New Zealand, and the United Kingdom) that investigated brain structure in dyscalculia.

The available studies showed that compared to typically developing children, those with developmental dyscalculia had reduced grey matter volume in the parietal cortex (including right IPS, right IPL, left SPL and bilateral SMG; McCaskey et al. 2020; Ranpura et al. 2013; Rotzer et al. 2008; Rykhlevskaia et al. 2009), in the frontal lobe (left IFG, bilateral MFG) (Rotzer et al. 2008), in the parahippocampal gyrus (Ranpura et al. 2013; Rykhlevskaia et al. 2009; Skeide et al. 2018), and in the occipital lobe (including left MOG, right SOG) (McCaskey et al. 2020). White matter volume has also been observed to be reduced in cases of dyscalculia. Reportedly affected regions include the frontal lobe and parahippocampal gyrus (Rotzer et al. 2008), right temporal and parietal areas (Ranpura et al. 2013; Rykhlevskaia et al. 2009), and the bilateral inferior and superior longitudinal fasciculus (ILF, SLF), inferior fronto-occipital fasciculus (IFOF), corticospinal tracts, and right anterior thalamic radiation (ATR) (McCaskey et al. 2020). Studies using DTI (to measure

Table 16.3 *Summary of structural imaging studies of dyscalculia across different cultures*

Study	Country	Sample	Age[2]	Task	Method	Altered measure[3]
Rotzer et al. (2008)	Switzerland	12:12	9	Number processing Calculation	VBM	*GM volume:* right IPS bilateral AC left IFG bilateral MFG *WM volume:* left FL right PHG
Rykhlevskaia et al. (2009)	USA	23:24	7–9	WIAT-II Numerical operation	VBM DTI	*GM volume:* right IPS left SPL bilateral PHG bilateral FFG right ATC *WM volume:* right TPC right ILF right IFOF bilateral FM bilateral SLF
Ranpura et al. (2013)	UK	11:11	8–14	N/A	VBM	*GM surface:* bilateral SCG *GM thickness:* left TL right IFL *GM volume:* right PHG right IPL *WM volume:* right IPL right TP right TTG right ORB
Cappelletti and Price (2014)	UK	11:29	24–70	Number semantics	VBM	*GM volume:* right PL
Kucian et al. (2014)	Switzerland	15:15	8–11	ZAREKI-R WISC-III	DTI	*WM fractional anisotropy:* SLF
Skeide et al. (2018)	USA	42:29	7–12	WASI Working memory WIAT-II	SBM	*GM cortical folding:* right PHG
Moreau et al. (2018)	New Zealand	11:11	26–34	None	DTI	no effect

Table 16.3 (*cont.*)

Study	Country	Sample[1]	Age[2]	Task	Method	Altered measure[3]
Moreau et al. (2019)	New Zealand	12:12	22–37	None	VBM	no effect
McCaskey et al. (2020)	Switzerland	13:10	8–10	Arithmetic Numerical skills Quantity comparison Number line	VBM	*GM volume:* bilateral IPS bilateral SMG left PCUN left PCG right PCL left CG/CUN left MOG right SOG *WM volume:* bilateral SLF/ILF bilateral IFOF right ATR

[1]dyscalculia:control [2]years [3]all measures are reduced in dyscalculia; IPS, inferior parietal sulcus; ACC, anterior cingulate cortex; IFG, inferior frontal gyrus; MFG, middle frontal gyri; FL, frontal lobe; PHG, parahippocampal gyrus; SPL: superior parietal lobule; FFG, fusiform gyrus; ATC, anterior temporal cortex; TPC, temporo-parietal cortex; FA, fractional anisotropy; ILF, inferior longitudinal fasciculus; FM, forceps majors; IFOF, inferior fronto-occipital fasciculus; FA, Fractional anisotropy; SLF, superior longitudinal fasciculus; ATR, anterior thalamic radiation; SCeG, subcentral gyrus; TL, temporal lobe; IFL, inferior frontal lobe; IPL: inferior parietal lobe; TP, temporal pole; TTG, transverse temporal gyrus; IFGOr, IFG orbital part; SMG, supramarginal gyrus; PCUN, precuneus; POG, postcentral gyrus; PCL, paracentral lobule; CG, calcarine gyrus; CUN, cuneus; MOG, middle occipital gyrus; SOG, superior occipital gyrus; ATR, anterior thalamic radiation.

fractional anisotropy) in the USA (Rykhlevskaia et al. 2009) and in Switzerland (Kucian et al. 2014) have consistently shown that white matter connectivity was reduced in the SLF, ILF, IFOF, and forceps majors (FM) in children with dyscalculia. However, two studies focusing on adults with developmental dyscalculia did not find any differences using VBM or DTI analysis in samples from New Zealand (Moreau et al. 2019; Moreau et al. 2018). The reasons for the conflicting results across studies remain unclear, with potential factors being the participant age, culture or experimental design. Nevertheless, overall, abnormal brain structure has been consistently detected in the parietal cortex, in agreement with the available functional neuroimaging results.

In general, the neuroimaging studies conducted across cultures converge in the observation that individuals with developmental dyscalculia can be identified based on brain systems related to performing number and arithmetic tasks. Although the IPS is typically affected, results are mixed across studies, so the specific neural foundations of dyscalculia remain unclear. We have mainly reviewed neuroimaging studies from western cultures due to the lack of literature on non-WEIRD cultures.

In the final part of this section, we discuss potentially universal brain-functional patterns for dyscalculia with respect to event-related potential (ERPs). The ERP underlying non-symbolic magnitude representation is characterized as a positivity within a 500-ms window over the parietal lobes known as the late parietal positivity (Hyde and Spelke 2012). Converging evidence indicates that dyscalculia, particularly deficits in non-symbolic magnitude representation, is associated with a reduced late parietal positivity amplitude (Heine et al. 2013; Soltész et al. 2007; Wang et al. 2015). Heine et al. (2013) studied Belgian children with dyscalculia at an age of around 8 years using a dot-array comparison task. In general, children suffering from dyscalculia performed slower and less accurately only when the numerical distance between two dot arrays was small (known as distance effect). This distance effect was related to a reduced late parietal activity amplitude which was more prominent in the right hemisphere (Soltész et al. 2007; Heine et al. 2013). Similarly, Wang et al. (2015) recruited twenty Chinese children with dyscalculia (11.5–13.5 years) and healthy controls and asked them to remember both Chinese numerals and Arabic numbers using a digit memory task. They found that the children with dyscalculia displayed a significantly smaller amplitude at 500–600 ms than controls during the encoding of numbers. These findings corroborate the notion of a universal parietal cortex deficit hampering number processing in dyscalculia.

16.5 Intervention

We will now return to the question posed at the beginning of this chapter: why do researchers across the globe study dyscalculia? We argue that one of the main motivations is to find the most effective and adaptive interventions that can help remediate or prevent maths difficulties. Specific intervention approaches depend on numerous factors, including but not limited to, the characteristics of dyscalculia (which can vary in severity and type of impairment), the group size, intervention duration (several days or months), the role of the instructor (researchers, clinicians, or classroom teachers), assessment types, and methods of instruction. Here we review intervention studies that focused on dyscalculia diagnostically defined as an impairment in basic number processing or arithmetic skills despite at least average intelligence.

16.5.1 Intervention Targets

Intervention programmes for dyscalculia can be classified into two types based on the training content: numerical processing abilities (e.g., Wilson et al. 2006) or domain-general cognitive abilities (e.g., Faramarzi et al. 2016; Layes et al. 2018). The majority of the currently available interventions have focused on the former. Currently available dyscalculia intervention studies are summarized in Table 16.4.

Table 16.4 *Summary of dyscalculia intervention studies across different cultures*

Study	Country	Sample[1]	Grade	Intervention	Tests	Duration	Follow-up	Effect size[9]
Kaufmann et al. (2003)	Austria	6:18[2]	3	Organized modules	Basic numerical knowledge	6 months	–	1.41
					Arithmetical fact knowledge			0.93
					Procedural knowledge			0.69
					Conceptual knowledge			0.39
Wilson et al. (2006)	French	9:0[2]	7–9y	'The Number Race'	Symbolic magnitude	10 weeks	–	–
					Non-symbolic magnitude			
					Arithmetic			
Räsänen et al. (2009)	Finland	15:30[2]	K[5]	'Graphogame-Math'	Number comparison	3 weeks	3 weeks	0.11, −0.53[10]
		15:30[2]		'The Number Race'	Arithmetic			−0.11, −0.22[10]
					Number comparison			−0.36
					Arithmetic			−0.39[10]
								0.22, −0.64[10]
Bryant et al. (2011)	USA	139:64[2]	1	Instructions	TEMI-PM[6]	8 months	–	0.50
Kucian et al. (2011)	Switzerland	16:16[2]	3	'Rescue Calcularis'	Number line	5 weeks	–	−0.38
					Arithmetic			0.31
Swanson (2011)	USA	20:20[2]	2–3	Strategy training	Maths problem solving	10 weeks	–	0.41
					Arithmetic			0.11
de Castro et al. (2014)	Brazil	13:13[3]	2	'Tom's Rescue'	Maths performance[7]	5 weeks	–	1.43
Faramarzi et al. (2016)	Iran	15:15[3]	2	Neuropsychological interventions	Maths performance[7]	2 months	–	3.72
Re et al. (2014)	Italy	10:9[2]	2–5	Individualized training	Mental calculation	32 weeks	4 months	−0.87
					Arithmetic fact			−0.88

Study	Country			Intervention	Outcome measure	Duration	Follow-up	Effect size
Mohd Syah et al. (2016)	Malaysia	25:25[2]	7	Computer game	Numerical knowledge	7 days	–	0.55
Layes et al. (2018)	Algeria	14:14[2]	4	Working memory training	Maths achievement	8 weeks	–	1.14
					ZAREKI-R[8]			3.33
Cheng et al. (2020)	China	38:40[2]	3–5	'Collecting apples'	Numerosity	8 days	–	0.34
					Arithmetic			0.80
Lu et al. (2021)	China	245:234[4]	1	Abacus course	Maths performance	2–3 years	–	–
Kohn et al. (2020)	Germany	34:33[2]	2–5	'Calcularis 2.0'	Number line	13 weeks	3 months	−0.39
					Arithmetic			0.49
					Number comparison			−0.26
					Numerosity			−0.44
Ribeiro and Santos (2019)	Brazil	22:22[2]	3	Music training	ZAREKI-R[8]	14 weeks	10 weeks	1.18 1.78[10]

1 Experimental group : control group [2] dyscalculia : typically developing [3] dyscalculia : dyscalculia

4 typically developing : typically developing [5] kindergarten

6 Texas Early Mathematics Inventories Progress Monitoring

7 Maths concepts, arithmetic and maths problem solving

8 ZAREKI-R battery for maths performance (von Aster et al. 2006)

9 Hedge's g (Hedges and Olkin 1985; Chodura, Kuhn and Holling 2015); comparing performance (pre vs. post test) between the experimental group and control group.

10 additional effect sizes for the follow-up tests

Interventions aiming to improve numerical processing ability in children with dyscalculia mostly focus on one or several of the following three aspects: (1) non-symbolic number sense, (2) mapping between non-symbolic quantity and symbolic number (e.g., Arabic numerals; termed 'mapping skills'), and (3) numerical cognition. In France and Finland, researchers utilized the 'Number Race' game, which targets both non-symbolic number sense and mapping skills, to train children with dyscalculia (Räsänen et al. 2009; Wilson et al. 2006). French children showed improvements in number sense tasks and subtraction, but no improvements were found in their comprehension of the base-10 system (Wilson et al. 2006). Finnish children with dyscalculia were compared with age-matched typical children, and showed significant improvement in number comparison but not in any other number skills, including verbal counting, object counting, and arithmetic (Räsänen et al. 2009). In Switzerland (Kucian et al. 2011) and Germany (Kohn et al. 2020), intervention programmes using a mental number line task improved mapping skills and arithmetic performance in children with dyscalculia. Until recently, most interventions have been based on counting, ordering, comparing, calculating, comprehending of base-10 comprehension, and building numerical knowledge in samples from the USA (e.g., Bryant et al. 2011), Italy (e.g., Re et al. 2014), Brazil (e.g., de Castro et al. 2014), Austria (e.g., Kaufmann et al. 2003), China (e.g., Zhang and Zhou 2016), and Malaysia (e.g., Mohd Syah et al. 2016). Across these countries, children with dyscalculia showed an improved conceptual understanding of arithmetic calculation and demonstrated improved arithmetic performance. However, in the USA, Bryant et al. (2011) found that numerical intervention only improved performance on whole-number computation, but not in problem solving.

Some intervention studies have also targeted deficits in domain-general cognitive abilities, including working memory, executive function, attention, and basic perception. In Iran, an intervention programme targeted visual and auditory short-term memory, executive functions, visuospatial perception, and skills related to speech and language (Faramarzi and Sadri 2014). This comprehensive intervention significantly improved the mathematics achievement of students with dyscalculia (including sub-scores in basic concepts, operations, and applications, and the total test score). A study in Algeria (Layes et al. 2018) focused on visual and auditory working memory of numbers and found that both working memory and mathematical performance were significantly improved in children with dyscalculia.

A new trend in dyscalculia intervention studies is to target basic perception (e.g., music perception, Brazil: Ribeiro and Santos 2019; visual perception, China: Cheng et al. 2020). Cheng et al. (2020) designed a computerized 'apple collecting' game to improve visual perception. In this game, participants have to control an animated pig character to collect as many apples as possible, while neglecting the physical size of the apples. To get a higher score, participants have to catch bunches that contain more apples rather than physically larger apples. Meanwhile, participants have to avoid collecting bombs that deduct points. While no improvement in spatial or verbal abilities was observed (measured in mental rotation and sentence completion), this 8-day training significantly improved visual form perception, arithmetic performance, and non-symbolic number sense in children with dyscalculia. Indeed, their improvements in arithmetic performance were fully mediated by the improvements in visual form perception.

Taken together, studies in different countries have used various intervention designs leading to improvements in the specific training-related ability transfer effects on mathematical performance. Moreover, studies in Italy (Re et al. 2014), Germany (Kohn et al. 2020), and Brazil (Ribeiro and Santos 2020) showed that the improvements were stable in later follow-up tests (three to four months after training). Given that there is currently no clear evidence showing that one intervention method is superior to the others, we believe that intervention methods for dyscalculia can be effective via multiple pathways.

16.5.2 Intervention Methods

In recent years, technological devices including personal computers, laptops, online tools, smartphones, and tablets (known as Information and Communication Technologies [ICT]) have been used for dyscalculia intervention in Finland (the 'Number Race' game that targets non-symbolic and approximate number sense, the 'Graphogame-Math' game that targets exact numerosities and number symbols; Räsänen et al. 2009), Brazil (a virtual environment named 'Tom's Rescue' that incorporates eighteen games targeting foundational mathematical skills; de Castro et al. 2014), France ('Number Race' game; Wilson et al. 2006), Switzerland (a mental number line game called 'Rescue Calcularis'; Kucian et al. 2011), Germany (a training programme named 'Calcularis' that included adaptive games tapping into non-symbolic comparison and calculation; Kohn et al. 2020), China (an 'apple collecting' game; Cheng et al. 2020; the web-based curriculum learning system; Zhang and Zhou 2016), and Malaysia (software named 'Maths ACE' for improving numerical concepts and capacities; Syah et al. 2016). To our knowledge, in the USA, ICT intervention effects have thus far only been examined in students without dyscalculia (e.g., Kiger et al. 2012) or in students with learning difficulties that were not number- or arithmetic-specific (O'Malley et al. 2013). Overall, we observed consistent effectiveness of ICT-based intervention in improving number comparison skills, arithmetic calculation ability, and mathematical achievement (see Table 16.4). Moreover, the study in Brazil showed that the ICT-based intervention not only improved mathematical performance, but also improved the motivation of children with dyscalculia because these interventions are entertaining and adaptable to individual performance levels (de Castro et al. 2014).

Apart from ICT, there is evidence that abacus training could be used to eradicate developmental dyscalculia (see also Chapter 12, Iuculano 2022). Lu et al. (2021) examined the effect of a Chinese abacus ('suanpan') course on dyscalculia prevalence in Chinese school settings. In their study, 1st grade students were randomly assigned to the abacus classes or to control classes. After two to three years, the prevalence of dyscalculia in the control classes was in line with previous studies (6.4%). In contrast, no students met the criteria for dyscalculia in the abacus classes. Thus, the authors proposed that abacus training courses could be an effective method for preventing and eradicating dyscalculia. It remains unclear, however, whether or not such abacus courses can be successfully employed in other cultures and also have a remediation effect.

16.6 Conclusion

In this chapter, we outlined cultural similarities and differences with respect to the cognitive and neural manifestation and the remediation of dyscalculia. Even though the average mathematical performance of East Asian students is superior to other countries, the percentage of people affected by dyscalculia does not differ from other cultures. In fact, with some exceptions, dyscalculia is mostly related to common cognitive deficits and universal signatures of altered brain activity. Building on these insights from basic research, promising software-based programmes for intervention, targeting problems in numerical processing and general cognitive functions, have become available in many countries.

Internationally, dyscalculia is much less studied than other developmental learning disorders such as dyslexia (Butterworth and Kovas 2013). Recent studies in different regions have shown common trends in dyscalculia, but the cross-cultural perspective is still very new and a number of questions remain to be answered. What are the commonalities and differences in genetic origin (see Chapter 8, Skeide 2022)? To what extent do different educational and social contexts contribute to developmental learning difficulties (see Chapter 6, Malanchini and Gidziela 2022; Chapter 7, Hoeft and Bouhali 2022; Chapter 13, Cantlon 2022; Chapter 14, Fish 2022) Educational resources are the most important predictor for mathematical achievement when controlling for genetic origin in the normal population (Rodic et al. 2015), but would this hold for dyscalculia as well? In terms of intervention, is the effectiveness of current training approaches universal or constrained by cultural contexts? Together, these questions can direct future research towards a better understanding of both culturally universal and culturally diverse dimensions of dyscalculia.

Suggestions for Further Reading

Cheng, D. , Q. Xiao, Q. Chen, J. Cui, and X. Zhou. 2018. 'Dyslexia and Dyscalculia Are Characterized by Common Visual Perception Deficits'. *Developmental Neuropsychology* 43 (6): 497–507.

Devine, A., F. Soltész, A. Nobes, U. Goswami, and D. Szűcs. 2013. 'Gender Differences in Developmental Dyscalculia Depend on Diagnostic Criteria'. *Learning and Instruction* 27 (October): 31–9.

Lu, Y., M. Mei, G. Chen, and X. Zhou. 2021. 'Can Abacus Course Eradicate Developmental Dyscalculia'. *Psychology in the Schools* 58 (2): 235–51. https://doi.org/10.1002/pits.22441.

Miller, K. F., M. Kelly, and X. Zhou. 2005. 'Learning Mathematics in China and the United States'. *Handbook of Mathematical Cognition* 8 (35): 163–78.

Rodic, M., X. Zhou, T. Tikhomirova, et al. 2015. 'Cross-Cultural Investigation into Cognitive Underpinnings of Individual Differences in Early Arithmetic'. *Developmental Science* 18 (1): 165–74. https://doi.org/10.1111/desc.12204.

Summary: Cultural Unity and Diversity

(1) **Learning challenges of alphabetic scripts:** Learning English is most difficult since it is least transparent in terms of print-to-speech conversion (and vice versa) and most complex in terms of syllable structure, while Italian shows one of the most extreme opposite patterns.

(2) **Prevalence in alphabetic learning contexts:** In line with (1), dyslexia is typically diagnosed twice as often in English-speaking countries (about 7%) compared to Italy (about 3.5%), although, in (diagnostic) theory, prevalence rates should be similar by definition (see Chapter 22, Lachmann, Bergström, Huber, and Nürk 2022).

(3) **Difficulty profiles in alphabetic learning contexts:** In Italian and other writing systems with transparent print-to-speech conversion (e.g., Arabic, Finnish, German, Korean, and Turkish) individuals with dyslexia typically show more pronounced difficulties in reading fluency than in reading accuracy.

(4) **Learning challenges of logographic scripts:** In Chinese and other logographic systems, print-to-speech conversion does not involve phonemes, but only larger linguistic units – that is, syllables, morphemes, and words. Moreover, logographic characters have a much more complex visual configuration (ordered strokes in a squared space) than alphabetic letters. Accordingly, children typically need about 6 years to acquire around 2,500–3,000 Chinese characters, while they have to master about 6,500 characters to fully understand modern Chinese texts.

(5) **Difficulty profiles in logographic learning contexts:** Similar to alphabetic learners with dyslexia, who have reduced letter knowledge, logographic learners suffering from dyslexia have reduced character knowledge (both of which relate to hampered print-to-speech conversion). Moreover, rapid automatized (object and symbol) naming skills predict dyslexia across these writing systems. However, in alphabetic learners, phonological awareness seems to be a stronger predictor of dyslexia than morphological awareness while logographic learners might show the opposite pattern. There is mixed evidence that logographic learners with dyslexia might also have a visuospatial deficit (long-term and working memory), but it is currently unclear whether this is a cause or a consequence of developing dyslexia in a logographic learning context.

(6) **Dyslexia in multilingual contexts:** There is preliminary evidence that, with some exceptions, dyslexia usually affects learning across multiple scripts with

hampered print-to-speech conversion as a putative common source of the learning difficulties.

(7) **Cultural unity of dyscalculia:** Children in Asian Pacific countries (e.g., China, Japan, Korea, Singapore) typically show the highest average maths performance worldwide. Nevertheless, prevalence rates of dyscalculia are similar across all cultures studied so far (about 5%). Whether co-occurrence rates of dyscalculia and dyslexia are lower in China than in Europe and the USA (as suggested by a single study so far) remains to be verified.

In all cultures studied so far, children suffering from dyscalculia reveal faulty (non-)symbolic quantity representations, while hardly anything is known about the unity and diversity of potential additional deficits in attention, executive functioning, working memory, and long-term memory.

PART VII

Early Prediction

17 Early Prediction of Learning Outcomes in Reading

Arne Lervåg and Monica Melby-Lervåg

17.1 Introduction

This chapter focuses on the processes involved in the development of children's decoding skills: the ability to translate printed words into a speech code, typically assessed by the accuracy and speed of reading aloud. If children struggle in developing this ability, they are often characterized as having dyslexia, but since decoding skills are normally distributed in the population, the cut-off for this diagnosis is somewhat arbitrary (Melby-Lervåg et al. 2012). During the first two years of school, the main aim for children is to develop accurate and fluent early reading abilities that will lay the foundation for the main goal of reading – to be able to extract meaning from text. Thus, though insufficient by itself, efficient word reading is, in turn, a necessary condition for the development of reading comprehension. Research on the foundations of learning to read has burgeoned in the last twenty-five years, with important theoretical and practical consequences.

For children in primary school, the most frequently used overarching framework to understand reading development is the simple view of reading. The simple view of reading suggests that reading comprehension is the product of decoding and linguistic comprehension (Gough and Tunmer 1986). The component we focus on in this chapter is decoding (i.e. the ability to read accurately and fluently). Thus, here the term 'reading' is restricted to decoding skills. We will take a closer look at predictors of decoding and also discuss other factors that possibly influence the development of early reading. The second component in the simple view of reading, linguistic comprehension, is the process of deriving semantic information at a word level – that is, deriving meaning from sentences and discourse interpretation (Gough and Tunmer 1986). As we will see, it has been argued that linguistic comprehension is the starting point for the development of early reading skills.

17.2 Phonological Awareness and Letter Knowledge As Predictors of Early Reading Skills

17.2.1 Phonological Awareness and Prediction of Early Reading: Rhymes, Phonemes, or Both?

Phonological awareness refers to an individual's ability to reflect upon and manipulate the sound structure of spoken words. This ability has repeatedly been shown to be uniquely related to the development of early reading skills in longitudinal latent variable studies (De Jong and Van der Leij 1999; Lervåg et al. 2009; Wagner et al. 1994; Dutch, Norwegian, and US-American samples). The hypothetical reason for this is that phonological awareness tasks tap into how the sound structures of words are represented in the brain (Melby-Lervåg et al. 2012; meta-analysis with a focus on European and US samples). It is not clear, however, when it comes to the particular phonological representations (e.g., whether it is encoding, storage, or retrieval) that are most important for developing accurate and fluent reading. The reason is that such representations can never be directly observed, only indirectly inferred. What does seem clear, though, is that a lack of phonemically structured phonological representations makes phoneme awareness tasks difficult or impossible to perform. Moreover, since early reading is dependent on this awareness, early reading will be difficult as well (Melby-Lervåg et al. 2012).

A large set of different tasks has been used to assess phonological awareness. These tasks differ in at least two main aspects: First, they vary when it comes to the size of the phonological units that are manipulated: these are either syllables, rhymes, or phonemes (Melby-Lervåg et al. 2012). This choice between tasks can be explained by the observation that the development of phonological awareness progresses in a hierarchical fashion throughout childhood. Specifically, a child typically first becomes aware of large sound units such as syllables, then moves on to intermediate units (onsets and rimes), and finally reaches the stage where phoneme awareness is mastered (Carrol et al. 2003; English sample). Second, the tasks also differ concerning the type of problem to be solved (Melby-Lervåg et al. 2012). Some include more forced-choice tasks (e.g., 'Do these two words rhyme?'), while others have more explicit tasks (e.g., 'Which word do we create if we remove the /h/ in /hat/?'). This large variety has often led to low correlations between the tasks, and it can be difficult to find out whether different studies actually measure the same underlying construct.

The two most common tasks concerning the size of phonological units have been rhyme awareness tasks and phonemic awareness tasks. These two tasks are rather different in nature and difficulty. Unfortunately, many earlier studies merged these two tasks and labelled them 'phonological awareness tasks'. However, a considerable controversy in the field has centred on the question of whether one of them is more important than the other in predicting early reading skills (Bryant 2002; Hulme et al. 1998; Hulme et al. 2002). One prominent theory in this context is grain size theory (Goswami and Bryant 2016; Ziegler and Goswami 2005). This theory postulates that children learn to read by becoming aware of the letters that correspond with onsets and rhymes in language. According to this theory, awareness of phonemes comes later, possibly as a consequence of and in reciprocity with learning to read. Further, it should also be noted that there is an alternative view suggesting that phonological awareness is best considered as a unitary construct and that the skills are so strongly interrelated and correlated that it is not meaningful to separate them into different constructs (Anthony et al. 2002; Anthony and Lonigan 2004). Thus, according to this unitary theory, the division between phonemes and rhymes is artificial, since both are a part of the same construct.

Grain size theory and the theory of phonological awareness as a unitary construct are, however, challenged by studies that have shown that phoneme awareness is a stronger predictor of reading than rhyme awareness, both cross-sectionally and longitudinally, at least from the age range of 6–7 years (Muter et al. 1998; Muter et al. 2004; English samples). A review also showed that the mean bivariate correlation between phoneme awareness and early reading was larger than that for rhyme awareness and early reading ($r = 0.57$ and $r = 0.43$) and that children with dyslexia had significantly more problems with phoneme awareness than with rhyme awareness ($d = -1.73$ and $d = -0.93$, respectively) (Melby-Lervåg et al. 2012). It seems that there is now a consensus that phoneme awareness is critical for learning to read, and rhyme awareness is an important precursor ability, but it has little or no influence on early reading beyond phoneme awareness.

17.2.2 Is Letter Knowledge Separable from Phoneme Awareness?

Letter knowledge is perhaps a more obvious predictor of early reading ability than phoneme awareness because children need to know letters to be able to decode at all. Indeed, it has been repeatedly shown that letter knowledge is a strong and unique predictor of early reading ability (De Jong and Van der Leij 1999; Lervåg et al. 2009; Wagner et al. 1994; Dutch, Norwegian, and US-American samples). While studies vary regarding their separation of letter–name and letter–sound knowledge, most of them find that these two dimensions are best conceptualized as a unitary construct (Lervåg et al. 2009; Muter et al. 2004). Out of the few studies to have reported separate measures of letter–name and letter–sound knowledge obtained from the same children, most show that both name and sound knowledge are correlates of reading ability (Caravolas et al. 2001; McBride-Chang 1999: English samples).

Still, even if it may seem obvious that letter knowledge is a predictor of early reading, the explanation for this association might not be straightforward. Most obvious, of course, is that knowledge of letter–sound links is pivotal to the child's discovery of the alphabetic principle (i.e. how individual speech sounds (phonemes) in oral words are represented by letters in printed words (graphemes)). However, it is also plausible that letter knowledge taps into the visual-phonological learning that is critical for early reading (Lervåg et al. 2009; Norwegian sample). This hypothesis has been tested in studies focusing on paired-associate learning (i.e., associating figures with a nonsense word). The results of these studies vary, but some have shown that visual-phonological learning is a concurrent predictor of early reading (Hulme et al. 2007). From a longitudinal perspective, however, there seems to be little support that visual-phonological learning is a longitudinal unique predictor of early reading (Lervåg et al. 2009).

Another issue that has been debated in the field is whether phoneme awareness contributes independently to letter knowledge. Castles and Coltheart (2004) claimed that studies did not unequivocally show this. One of the reasons for the failure to demonstrate a causal link was that studies were not able to reveal separate contributions of phoneme awareness and letter knowledge to reading ability. However, several studies now demonstrate an independent contribution of phoneme awareness over and above letter knowledge (and vice versa). For example, Lervåg et al. (2009) report standardized path coefficients of 0.34 for the relation between early reading and letter knowledge, and of 0.32 for the relation between early reading and phoneme awareness. Similarly, in the study by Muter et al. (2004) standardized path coefficients to early reading were 0.25 for letter knowledge and 0.15 for phoneme awareness. Still, it is important to note that phoneme awareness does not come into play until right before the child is able to decode. Moreover, phoneme awareness is also enhanced in reciprocity with early reading skills, such that learning letters refines phoneme awareness (Wagner et al. 1994). Further, there is also a study that found no independent contribution of phonological awareness beyond letter knowledge (De Jong and Van der Leij 1999). It should be mentioned, however, that in this study phonological awareness comprised measures of both phoneme and rhyme awareness.

Altogether, research on phonological awareness, letter knowledge, and early reading is a mature research field, and there are a number of studies and reviews to support the main findings in this area. Of course, observational prediction studies cannot draw a conclusion about causality. It is therefore important to note that there are also a number of training studies that support the main issues discussed here (for reviews, see National Early Literacy Panel (US) 2008; National Reading Panel (US) 2000). Notably, it also seems clear that there is a strong coherence between the findings in studies of children with dyslexia and prediction studies of typically developing children (Melby-Lervåg et al. 2012; Snowling and Melby-Lervåg 2016): The strongest predictors of individual differences in reading abilities of typically developing children belong to those domains in which children with dyslexia struggle most, namely phoneme awareness and letter knowledge.

17.3 Rapid Automatized Naming and Beginning Reading Skills

Beyond phoneme awareness and letter knowledge, rapid automatized naming (RAN) has been a consistent predictor of beginning reading skills (Lervåg et al. 2009; Lervåg and Hulme 2009; Norwegian and English samples). Typical RAN tasks include a sheet with either colours, objects, digits, or letters that are (semi-)randomly repeated across several lines. The task is to say aloud all items as quickly as possible, beginning at the upper left corner and ending at the bottom right corner of the sheet. The time it takes to finish naming all items predicts beginning reading skills both concurrently and longitudinally, also across different orthographies (Araújo et al. 2015; Caravolas et al. 2012; European and US samples). Furthermore, RAN is able to predictively differentiate between people who are diagnosed with dyslexia and people who are not (Araújo and Faísca 2019; meta-analysis with a focus on European and US samples). RAN is correlated with phoneme awareness, letter knowledge, and verbal short-term memory, but it is able to predict the development of beginning reading skills beyond these other predictors (De Jong and Van der Leij 1999; Lervåg et al. 2009).

Several theories have been proposed to explain the relationship between RAN and beginning reading skills. There seems to be consensus that RAN taps into a basic mechanism that is causally relevant for learning to read. It is less clear, however, what this mechanism actually is. One popular suggestion is that RAN reflects the speed at which phonological representations can be retrieved from long-term memory (Wagner and Torgesen 1987; Wimmer et al. 2000). However, this is not to say that RAN taps into phonological representations in the same way as phonological awareness does since the correlations between typical tasks related to these domains are only low to moderate. In addition, RAN has been consistently shown to explain variations in reading development beyond phoneme awareness and verbal short-term memory tasks. For instance, Lervåg and Hulme (2009) found that non-alphanumeric RAN (colours and objects) measured before the start of formal reading instruction explained reading development one year later after formal reading instruction had started (English sample). Additionally, alphanumeric RAN (letters and digits) explained further growth in text-reading efficiency between the 2nd and 4th grade beyond earlier reading skills, phoneme awareness, and IQ. Findings such as these have led researchers to the conclusion that RAN taps into the integrity of the neural circuits involved in object identification and naming and that these neural circuits are recruited as critical components of the children's developing visual word recognition system (Lervåg & Hulme 2009).

Studies have shown that serial RAN seems to be a better predictor than discrete naming, particularly amongst more experienced readers. While both serial RAN and discrete naming seem to predict beginning reading beyond each other, only serial RAN seems to predict reading among older children and adults beyond discrete naming and not vice versa (Altani et al. 2018; Georgiou and Parrila 2020; van den Boer and de Jong 2015; Greek, English and Dutch samples). According to Altani et al. (2020), this difference reflects a shift from dealing with words at a micro level (word-by-word reading), as beginning readers do, to dealing with words at a macro level (multi-word reading), as more experienced readers do. Reading at a macro level is thought to be partially determined by the ability to simultaneously deal with several items in a cascaded fashion (Altani et al. 2020). The ability to deal with several items simultaneously in cascades is also assumed to be an ability taxed by serial RAN but not by discrete naming (Altani et al. 2020; Protopapas et al. 2018). Thus, both serial and discrete RAN predict beginning reading presumably because they reflect fast access to and retrieval of phonological representations. Serial RAN, in addition, reflects word processing in readers who read serially at a macro level.

Several studies have also searched for a reciprocal relationship by addressing the question of whether reading also predicts the development of RAN. There could be several reasons why reading might be able to predict RAN. One is that the automaticity of letter and digit recognition could promote the development of good alphanumeric skills. Another is that left-to-right visual scanning skills and visual attention, both of which are presumably refined by reading experience, could make the RAN tasks more familiar and thereby easier to execute. While there are studies supporting the first idea, showing that letter knowledge can predict the development of alphanumeric RAN skills (Lervåg and Hulme 2009; Peterson et al. 2018), the second idea is not empirically supported. For instance, Protopapas et al. (2013) showed that reversing the RAN task from left-to-right to right-to-left did not change RAN's predictive value for reading skills (Greek sample). There is also a study indicating that early reading skills predict the development of non-alphanumeric RAN (Powell and Atkinson 2020; English sample), but this link currently seems rather uncertain since this study was based on observed variables. It is well known that the measurement error embedded in observed variables can affect the results of these cross-lagged panel models (Little 2013). Thus, the potential issue of a reciprocal relationship seems unresolved. However, one should not yet fully discard the idea that reading experience can modulate the ability to simultaneously deal with several items in a cascaded fashion, or that, in turn, this may promote the development of RAN skills. Still, additional empirical evidence is needed to support this hypothesis.

One problem with all the studies examining reciprocal relationships between RAN and reading is that none of them has attempted to separate within-subject from between-subject variance in their statistical models. It is expected that much of the correlation between RAN and reading originates from correlations at the between-subject level (i.e., stable trait-like between-person variance). Therefore, these models do not tell us if reading actually affects the development of RAN or if the reading–RAN association is only a product of the stable parts of reading and RAN. Some more recent statistical models, such as the random intercept–cross lagged model (RI-CLM), allow us to look at the predictors of change within an individual (i.e., the individual serves as their own control) (Usami et al. 2019). These models might be preferred when addressing questions about reciprocal relationships.

17.4 Are There Other Cognitive Predictors of Early Reading Than 'the Big Three'?

As we have seen, there are three predictors that have been repeatedly demonstrated to be most influential for early reading skills: phonological awareness, letter knowledge, and RAN. How much variation in early reading skills they explain together, however, varies between studies. In latent variable analyses, the explained variance in early reading based on measures taken in pre-readers ranges from 40% (Näslund and Schneider 1991; German sample), 45% (De Jong and Van der Leij 1999; Dutch sample) 52% (Lervåg et al. 2009; Norwegian sample) to 56% (Wagner et al. 1994; US sample). Accordingly, there is still variance left to be explained by other predictors; we will now examine some of the potential candidates.

17.4.1 Verbal Short-term Memory

It has long been suggested that verbal short-term memory plays an important role for developing early reading skills. In particular, this notion has been linked to Baddeley and Hitch's 1974 working memory model. According to Gathercole and Baddeley (2014), verbal short-term memory is important for early reading because early reading involves holding sounds in memory while deciphering letters. A poor verbal short-term memory could therefore restrain the development of a phonological early reading strategy based on letter-by-letter decoding (Gathercole and Baddeley 2014). Thus, in earlier studies, verbal short-term memory was typically included in a broader phonological processing construct, for instance, in Wagner and Torgesens' (1987) seminal review.

Prior studies, however, provide little support for a unique relationship between verbal short-term memory and early reading. Specifically, the review by Melby-Lervåg et al. (2012) supports the idea that verbal short-term memory measures can also be seen as an index for the quality of phonological representations. Accordingly, the tight link to phonological representations might underlie the importance of verbal short-term memory for early reading rather than the memory part in itself. Finally, there are also several longitudinal studies indicating that verbal short-term memory (as measured by various span measures, e.g. words, digits, and non-words) does not uniquely explain early reading development on top of the 'big three' predictors (Lervåg et al. 2009; Näslund and Schneider 1991; Wagner et al. 1994). Cunningham et al. (2021), however, found that verbal short-term memory predicted later early reading beyond phoneme awareness, with the limitation that this study did not include rapid naming (English sample).

17.4.2 Vocabulary and Language Comprehension

It has also been suggested that vocabulary explains variation in reading ability in addition to phoneme awareness, letter knowledge, and rapid naming. Theoretically, this can be explained with the lexical quality hypothesis (Perfetti 2007), which claims that high-quality word representations (including not only phonology, but also morphology and semantics) are mutually supportive and critical for early reading development. Thus, the better and broader the representation of a word, the easier it is to decode it. This theory is in line with the observation that non-words are much more difficult to decode than real words.

The empirical evidence supporting this view is mixed. In studies using latent variables, vocabulary hardly explains any variance in early reading development beyond the 'big three'. In a study by Lervåg et al. (2009), which traced reading development in 1st and 2nd grade, vocabulary did not show a direct influence on top of the other predictors. A similar finding was also reported in a cross-linguistic longitudinal study by Furnes and Samuelsson (2011) and in a study by Muter et al. (2004). However, a longitudinal latent variable study by Hecht et al. (2000) showed significant unique contributions of kindergarten vocabulary skills to the prediction of early reading in 1st, 2nd, and 3rd grade (between 4% and 13% of explained variance), but this work was based on a sample with a low socioeconomic status (in England).

Still, even if vocabulary and language comprehension are not directly important for the development of early reading skills, they might play an indirect role as a foundation for the precursor skills of early reading. Language comprehension and the precursors for early reading are highly related, but studies using confirmatory factor analyses have shown that they are different constructs (Hjetland et al. 2020;

Hulme et al. 2015; Storch and Whitehurst 2002; Torppa et al. 2016). According to the lexical restructuring hypothesis (Walley et al. 2003), vocabulary growth enhances the development of clearer representations for phonological units in childhood. This enables the child to develop awareness for increasingly smaller linguistic units (syllables, rhymes), with phoneme awareness forming the endpoint. An alternative view is proposed by segmentation theory (Boada and Pennington 2006). This theory postulates that auditory perception and speech processing, rather than vocabulary growth, form the starting point of phonological skills and word reading ability. According to this hypothesis, vocabulary growth can be a consequence of the development of more fine-grained phonological representations. Thus, in line with segmentation theory, phonological representations become more detailed because segmentation of speech sounds drives the emergence of phonological awareness, and this also enables vocabulary growth.

Based on the currently available literature (Hjetland et al. 2020; Hulme et al. 2015; Snowling et al. 2019; Storch and Whitehurst 2002; Torppa et al. 2016), it is difficult to draw conclusions about the direction of the relationship between the precursors of early reading and linguistic comprehension. An important part of this problem is that it is difficult to find autoregressors (i.e., previous skills related to the same construct) for phonological skills in young children. What is clear, however, is that language comprehension and the precursors for early reading are highly intertwined and closely related. We currently consider it to be more likely that there is a reciprocal rather than a unidirectional relationship between them.

17.4.3 Executive Functions

Executive functioning has also been suggested to be important for early reading, and several authors have argued that early reading problems cannot be fully understood in terms of phonology. According to this view, executive functioning influences early reading because early reading involves parallel activation of lexical and phono-logical routes, which places cognitive demands on executive functions (Ober et al. 2020; meta-analysis with a focus on European and US samples).

Evidence in support of this view was provided in a meta-analysis which found a moderate correlation between early reading and executive functions, and which also showed that this link was rather stable across different moderators (Ober et al. 2020). However, a concurrent correlation alone does not necessarily imply that executive functioning is important for the development of early reading. When it comes to longitudinal associations, results are scarce. A study with latent variables has shown that a general working memory factor predicts early reading in 1st grade, but this association is not specific since this study does not include measures of rapid naming or phonological awareness (Preßler et al. 2014; German sample). Another study comprising observed variables showed that executive functions (measured by atten-tional control) in kindergarten predict 1st grade reading ability, but this work did not include rapid naming (Segers et al. 2016; Dutch sample). Similarly, other work supporting a predictive role of executive functioning for early reading also lacks all or some of the 'big three' (Colé et al. 2014; Foy and Mann 2013; French and US-American samples).

17.4.4 Non-Word Repetition

A number of studies indicate that children with dyslexia experience problems with non-word repetition. Non-word repetition is widely used as a cognitive marker of dyslexia and as a predictor of early word reading skills (Goulandris et al. 2000; English sample). The main explanation for why non-word repetition should be related to early reading is that it reflects how efficiently a person can process phonological information (Melby-Lervåg & Lervåg 2012). Non-word repetition is considered to be highly dependent on output phonology (Snowling and Hulme 1989), and may therefore be a marker of dyslexia. However, if non-word repetition is an important marker of dyslexia, it should also be a strong predictor of early reading, since individuals with dyslexia typically have problems in the domains that explain individual differences in early reading (Melby-Lervåg et al. 2012).

A meta-analysis of studies that have examined non-word repetition skills confirms that individuals with dyslexia struggle particularly with non-word repetition (mean differences in d = −0.82), which is also moderately correlated with early reading (R = 0.33) (Melby-Lervåg and Lervåg 2012). However, the severity of the non-word repetition problem varies significantly between studies, and the most important predictor of this variability is linguistic comprehension. While non-word repetition has been used mainly as a marker of dyslexia, there are few longitudinal prediction studies with typically developing children. One of the few available studies found that non-word repetition goes together with measures of verbal short-term memory in a latent construct but does not predict variation in early reading beyond the 'big three' (De Jong and Van der Leij 1999). In a recent study, however, a latent variable capturing non-word repetition at 5 years was shown to predict early word reading at 6 years beyond phoneme awareness and an autoregressor variable for early reading (Cunningham et al. 2021). Still, in the latent variable study of Hulme et.al. (2015; English sample) it was shown that it was the variance that non-word repetition had in common with broader language skills such as vocabulary, sentence structure, etc., and not the unique variance that it shared with word repetition and articulation at 3.5 years beyond broader language skills that predicted later decoding skills indirectly through the big three (phoneme awareness, letter knowledge, and RAN), and reading comprehension directly.

17.4.5 Non-Verbal IQ

Non-verbal IQ of one standard deviation below the population average was traditionally used as an exclusion criterion for dyslexia following the assumption that early decoding was related to non-verbal IQ (Stuebing et al. 2002). However, a meta-analysis of forty-six studies addressing the validity of this diagnostic classification showed considerable decoding performance overlap between the IQ-discrepant and IQ-consistent poor readers, indicating that non-verbal IQ is not strongly related to early reading (Stuebing et al. 2002). Furthermore, longitudinal studies have also shown that non-verbal IQ cannot explain development in early reading beyond the 'big three' (De Jong and Van der Leij 1999; Lervåg et al. 2009).

17.5 Prediction of Early Reading Skills in Different Orthographies

As alphabetic orthographies differ in how consistently letters (graphemes) represent sounds (phonemes), it is important to ask what impact this has on early reading development. One major difference between orthographies is how quickly children master fluent and accurate reading skills. Comparing fourteen European orthographies, Seymour et al. (2003) found that in relatively consistent orthographies (like Finnish), children had fluent and accurate reading skills (> 80%) at the end of grade 1, while in English – which is seen as a less consistent orthography – children had much lower reading accuracy levels (34%). A study by Caravolas et al. (2013) confirmed this result in a longitudinal sample comparing early reading development in three different orthographies: two relatively consistent (Spanish and Czech) and one inconsistent orthography (English). While the children in relatively consistent orthographies revealed a similar growth pattern with a clear acceleration after the onset of formal reading instruction, the children learning an inconsistent orthography revealed a more even and slower growth in their reading skills.

As the growth pattern of emerging reading skills seems to differ as a function of how consistent an orthography is, it is also important to ask whether predictors of reading development differ as a function of orthographic consistency. In other words, do the same predictors predict reading development in consistent and in inconsistent orthographies? This has been a controversially discussed issue (Caravolas et al. 2012; Share 2008). Some authors have, for example, suggested that phoneme awareness is less important and RAN is more important in consistent compared to inconsistent orthographies (Wimmer et al. 2000).

In the last decade, a handful of studies have addressed this issue. First, the concurrent studies of Vaessen et al. (2010) and Ziegler et al. (2010) concluded that to a large extent the same predictors are important in both consistent and inconsistent orthographies. In their longitudinal study, Caravolas and colleagues (2012, 2013) went even further, claiming that there are universal cognitive prerequisites for learning to read in all alphabetic orthographies, even though the rate of learning differs between consistent and inconsistent orthographies. This claim was based on the observation that letter knowledge, phoneme awareness, and RAN predicted growth in all three orthographies. Interestingly, Caravolas et al. (2013) found that these three predictors were associated with growth in reading at different stages in the developmental process. While letter knowledge and phoneme awareness were associated with reading at the very beginning of the developmental process, RAN was associated with the later acceleration of reading growth.

Still, not all longitudinal results are so clear cut. For example, Furnes and Samuelson (2009) found that phoneme awareness predicted reading only at the end of grade 1 in the relatively consistent Norwegian and Swedish orthographies but continued to predict reading in the more inconsistent English orthography in grade 2. In contrast, RAN was a consistent predictor in all three orthographies. The finding that phoneme awareness only predicted reading very early in the consistent orthographies and longer in the inconsistent English orthography fits well with the work of Caravolas et al. (2013). They found that learning to read takes longer in inconsistent orthographies and that phoneme awareness was associated only with early reading development. As it takes longer to develop fluent and accurate reading skills in inconsistent orthographies, it is to be expected that phoneme awareness will predict reading development for a longer time as well.

Compared to the studies discussed here, the data of Landerl and colleagues (Landerl et al. 2019) draw a less consistent picture. While RAN turned out to be a reliable predictor of reading development in both consistent and inconsistent orthographies, phoneme awareness predicted later reading skills in French and German (inconsistent and consistent, respectively) but not in English, Dutch, and Greek (inconsistent, consistent, and consistent, respectively). On the basis of these results, they concluded that while RAN seems to be a consistent and universal predictor of reading development, the predictive power of phoneme awareness might have been overstated in the literature. It should be noted, however, that the study by Landerl et al. (2019) started after the onset of formal reading instruction, whereas the studies by Caravolas et al. (2012, 2013) started before formal reading onset. As phoneme awareness is most strongly associated with very early reading development, this discrepancy might explain why Landerl et al. (2019) did not find an association with reading development in all of these orthographies. Nevertheless, the finding that phoneme awareness did not predict reading development in English is not in line with a large body of literature reporting the opposite effect.

17.6 Prediction of Early Reading Skills Based on Socioeconomic Background

It is well known that there is a moderate to high positive correlation between socioeconomic status (SES) and reading (Sirin 2005: meta-analysis with a focus on European and US samples; see also Chapter 14, Fish 2022). This is the case not only for reading comprehension, but also for basic early reading skills (Buckingham et al. 2014). Hence, children living in poverty have been found to achieve a considerably lower level of literacy than their peers with higher SES (Buckingham et al. 2014). Indicators of SES typically include income, educational level, employment, and living conditions (Buckingham et al. 2014).

An important issue is whether there is a causal relationship between SES and early reading or whether there is only a correlation. To disentangle this, three issues need to be clarified. The first is whether SES can explain development or growth in early reading beyond the autoregressor (i.e., early reading ability itself). The second is whether SES also explains development in early reading beyond the 'big three' predictors. Third, it remains to be specified what it would mean if SES explains growth beyond the autoregressor and the 'big three' predictors. Possible interpretations are complicated by the fact that SES has often been called a fuzzy construct because it comprises a large range of factors, including genes and environments. Presumably around 50% of the relationship between SES and academic achievement can be explained by genetic factors (Krapohl and Plomin 2015; English sample) (see also Chapter 6, Malanchini and Gidziela 2022). What the rest can be attributed to is not clear. Potential candidates could be stress of poverty, parental home literacy practices, early diet and nutrition that are important for brain development, and instructional quality in schools (see Chapter 14, Fish 2022).

SES is typically not able to explain development in early reading when the autoregressor and the 'big three' predictors are controlled for (Buckingham et al. 2014). Thus, in general, a causal relationship between SES and early reading development does not seem likely. However, there are exceptions in the literature. One study of children in Romania (Dolean et al. 2019) provided evidence that SES explained actual growth in early reading beyond rapid naming, letter knowledge, and phoneme awareness. Variation in SES was large in this sample, ranging from children living in severe poverty to children from affluent families. Thus, poverty alone does not explain why SES was related to growth in early reading skills. Notably, SES was modelled as a latent construct consisting of family income, mother's education, parents' employment, and living conditions. This is a more differentiated model of SES compared to most other studies, which might have given SES greater predictive strength. Interestingly, the relationship between SES and early reading was mediated through school absence. Similar findings have also been demonstrated in other studies in the context of high levels of poverty (Herbers et al. 2012; US-American sample).

17.7 Conclusion

In this chapter, we have looked at various potential predictors of beginning reading development by reviewing longitudinal observational studies. Although the title of this overview refers to prediction, we have gone beyond prediction in our descriptions and discussions. With prediction, we typically refer to merely foreseeing a future outcome. Thus, when we are concerned with pure prediction, we are not interested in why certain factors predict something. Instead, we are merely interested in finding a set of variables that predicts as much variation in an outcome variable as possible (Pedhazur 1997; Shmueli 2010). When predicting reading development, however, we are not only interested in identifying a set of predictors associated with later reading skills, we are also interested in explaining why they predict reading skills. To this end, we need to apply theories and see to what degree they fit the empirical evidence. These theories can explain how the predictors reflect causes for the ease or the learning experience of a particular child (e.g., less distinct phonological representations will cause difficulties in learning to read).

If a variable measured before a child can read is able to predict variation in later reading development, we often say it fits with a causal theory of reading development. The same is the case if a variable predicts later reading skills beyond earlier reading skills or actual growth in reading skills. In this way, longitudinal observational studies can help us to test theories about reading development and thereby inform us about why certain skills are important for learning to read. It should be noted, however, that observational studies cannot prove empirically that the predictors are causally related to reading development. Nevertheless, they can help us to generate theories that can be used as a framework for designing randomized control trials (see Chapter 19, Galuschka and Schulte-Körne 2022). In turn, such intervention studies can help us to test causal theories and understand how we can support children on their way to becoming literate (Lervåg 2020). It should also be noted that there are more theories about predictors of reading development than only those we describe here (see Chapter 1, Goswami 2022). We describe and discuss only those theories that we consider as most debated and/or best supported by the recent literature.

Our overview indicates that phoneme awareness, letter knowledge, and RAN, measured just before the children start learning to read, are the most reliable predictors of reading across several studies and across consistent and inconsistent orthographies. While letter knowledge and phoneme awareness seem most important at the very beginning of learning to read, RAN continues to be associated with growth in reading skills, probably as a function of the serial information processing aspects inherent to both RAN and reading. In addition, some studies indicate that SES might have a direct impact on reading development, at least in samples including children living in poverty (Dolean et al. 2019). That being said, there are several other variables that are associated with beginning reading skills, but they do not seem to predict reading beyond the 'big three'. Nevertheless, these variables can have indirect effects on reading, and this is demonstrated, for instance, for measures related to vocabulary and linguistic comprehension (Hjetland et al. 2020; Hulme et al. 2015).

Suggestions for Further Reading

Castles, A., K. Rastle, and K. Nation. 2018. 'Ending the Reading Wars: Reading Acquisition from Novice to Expert'. *Psychological Science in the Public Interest* 19 (1), 5–51. https://doi.org/10.1177/1529100618772271.

Hulme, Charles, Hannah M. Nash, Debbie Gooch, Arne Lervåg, and Margaret J. Snowling. 2015. 'The Foundations of Literacy Development in Children at Familial Risk of Dyslexia'. *Psychological Science* 26 (12): 1877–86.

Lervåg, A., I. Bråten, and C. Hulme. 2009. 'The Cognitive and Linguistic Foundations of Early Reading Development: A Norwegian Latent Variable Longitudinal Study'. *Developmental Psychology* 45 (3): 764–81.

Melby-Lervåg, M., S. A. H. Lyster, and C. Hulme. 2012. 'Phonological Skills and Their Role in Learning to Read: A Meta-Analytic Review'. *Psychological Bulletin* 138 (2): 322–52.

18 Early Prediction of Learning Outcomes in Mathematics

Elizabeth A. Gunderson

18.1 Introduction

Why do some children arrive in kindergarten already knowing how to add, while others struggle to count? Why do some students avoid challenging maths problems, while others embrace them? Given the importance of maths learning for academic success and future earning potential (e.g., Ritchie and Bates 2013), and the strong relation between school-entry maths skills and later maths achievement (Watts et al. 2014), it is critical to understand the sources of variability in maths knowledge in early childhood. Researchers have identified several broad factors present before or at the start of schooling (US preschool or kindergarten, ages 3 to 6 years) that robustly relate to later maths achievement. These include early cognitive skills (numeracy, spatial skills, executive functioning, and language and literacy skills) and early environmental factors (interactions at home and in preschool settings). Building on these initial findings, more recent work has begun to (1) test longer-term relations between early factors and later maths achievement, and (2) elaborate on the specific relations between early predictors and later mathematical outcomes by treating both as multidimensional. In this chapter, I review the evidence supporting the predictive effects of each preschool factor on later maths achievement, with a focus on longitudinal studies that begin in the preschool or kindergarten years. Although most studies are from children in the United States, this review incorporates evidence from a variety of other countries, including Canada, Chile, China, Germany, Greece, Iceland, and the Netherlands. Many studies have also intentionally sampled children from low-socioeconomic-status (low-SES) families, who are more at risk of low maths achievement than their higher-SES peers (Jordan et al. 1992). I conclude by discussing the relative strengths and limitations of the evidence, theoretical and practical implications, and suggestions for future research.

18.2 Cognitive Predictors of Later Math Achievement

18.2.1 Numeracy Skills

It is well-established, and perhaps unsurprising, that early numeracy skills predict later maths achievement (e.g., Claessens et al. 2009; Jordan et al. 2009; Watts et al. 2014). For example, in a nationally representative sample of US children, maths skills in kindergarten strongly predicted later maths skills in 5th grade: a 1 standard deviation (SD) increase in kindergarten maths skills predicted a 0.35 SD increase in 5th grade maths achievement (Claessens et al. 2009). Similarly, a recent large-scale study of German children found that children's maths skills at the start of kindergarten significantly predicted their later calculation skills at the end of 1st grade (Kucian, in press). Another large-scale US study found that a 1 SD increase in preschool maths skills (measured at age 4.5 years) predicted a 0.24-SD increase in maths achievement at age 15 years (Watts et al. 2014). In both studies, early maths skills were compared to other potential predictors, including early literacy, attention, and social–emotional skills, and early maths skills emerged as the largest predictor of later maths achievement.

These broad relations between early maths – even before school entry – and later maths achievement through high school have inspired researchers to delve into the specific early maths skills that are most predictive of later achievement. Further specificity is necessary for identifying children at risk of maths difficulties and for developing interventions targeting the most important skills. Several competencies have emerged as key components of early numeracy: counting and cardinality, symbolic number sense, and non-symbolic number sense.

Counting and cardinality. Counting and cardinality skills undergo major developmental change in the preschool years (e.g., Carey and Barner 2019; Wynn 1990). Before age 3 years, most US children can recite the count words from 1 to 10 and point to items following the principle of one-to-one correspondence (Wynn 1990). However, it takes substantially longer for children to understand the *cardinal principle* – that the last word reached when counting a set represents the size of the whole set (Geary and vanMarle 2018; Wynn 1992b). Understanding of the cardinal principle is typically assessed using the Give-a-Number task, in which children are asked to produce set sizes from a collection of objects (e.g., 'Can you put six fish in the pond?') (Wynn 1992b). Children who understand the cardinal principle can reliably produce set sizes of six or more, and use counting to correct their answers (Le Corre and Carey 2007). Cardinal principle knowledge is a major milestone in preschool numerical development, which accelerates children's learning of further numerical concepts (Davidson et al. 2012; Geary and vanMarle 2018; Spaepen et al. 2018).

Large individual differences exist in the age at which children first understand the cardinal principle. A particularly thorough longitudinal study assessed US children's cardinal principle knowledge twice per year during two preschool years (Geary and vanMarle 2018). Illustrating these individual differences, 29% of the children already understood the cardinal principal at the first assessment (age 3 years, 10 months), whereas 10% had not yet achieved this milestone by the last assessment in preschool (age 5 years, 2 months). In other words, there was already at least a gap of at least 1.5 years in cardinal principle knowledge by age 5 between higher- and lower-achieving children in this typically developing sample. The same study followed these children through the start of 1st grade and found that children who had learnt the cardinal principle at an earlier age had significantly better number systems knowledge in 1st grade (Geary and van Marle 2018). Another, longer-term study compared specific aspects of preschool numeracy to determine which were most predictive of 5th grade maths achievement (Nguyen et al. 2016). Conducted in primarily low-income schools in the United States, this study identified four domains of early numeracy: counting and cardinality, patterning, geometry, and measurement and data. Preschool counting and cardinality skills – especially advanced skills, such as counting with cardinality and counting forwards and backwards from a given number – were the strongest predictor of 5th grade maths achievement (Nguyen et al. 2016). Thus, cardinality knowledge – a conceptual understanding of how counting allows us to represent exact set sizes – is a critical foundation that sets the stage for later maths learning.

Symbolic number sense. Children's symbolic number sense refers to the fluency with which children can understand and compare the magnitudes represented by Arabic numerals (Siegler and Lortie-Forgues 2014; Smedt et al. 2013). Symbolic number comparison skill – the ability to rapidly and accurately compare single-digit numerals (e.g., which is more: 7 or 5) – is robustly related to maths achievement in both childhood and adulthood (Holloway and Ansari 2009; Lyons and Beilock 2011; Nosworthy et al. 2013). A recent study found that symbolic number comparison skill in a sample of Canadian kindergarteners predicted their 1st grade maths achievement even after accounting for potential confounds such as language skills and processing speed (Hawes et al. 2019).

This 'sense of numbers' is also frequently assessed through the number line estimation task (Siegler and Opfer 2003). In preschool, a typical number line estimation task involves showing children a horizontal line labelled 0 at one end and 10 at the other, and asking them to make a hatch-mark where a particular Arabic numeral goes (Ramani and Siegler 2008). The accuracy of children's estimates increases with age (Siegler and Booth 2004); is better on smaller, more-familiar number line ranges (e.g., 0 to 10) than on larger, less-familiar ranges (e.g., 0 to 100 or 0 to 1,000) (Siegler and Booth 2004); and is robustly related to concurrent maths achievement across ages (Schneider et al. 2018). Several studies have established that preschool and kindergarten number line estimation skills predict later maths skills. Among US children, number line estimation skills at age 6 years predicted approximate calculation skills at age 8 years (Gunderson et al. 2012). In a larger-scale study assessing children in the Netherlands twice per year from kindergarten to 2nd grade, children's number line estimation skills predicted later standardized tests of maths achievement, and this relation was reciprocal, with earlier maths achieve-ment also predicting later number line estimation skill (Friso-van den Bos et al. 2015).

Importantly, randomized training studies have shown that children's symbolic number sense can be improved, and that these improvements transfer to untrained numerical skills (Ramani et al. 2020; Ramani and Siegler 2008; Scalise et al. 2020; Siegler and Ramani 2009). Playing a simple, 1 to 10 linear number board game led to broad improvements in numeracy skills among low-income US preschoolers, includ-ing symbolic magnitude comparison, number line estimation, counting, and identi-fying Arabic numerals, compared to a non-numerical control game (Ramani and Siegler 2008). Among kindergartners, playing a 1 to 100 board game (implemented as a tablet game) improved children's maths knowledge, and these gains persisted at least one month later (Ramani et al. 2020). These studies establish that symbolic number sense in preschool and kindergarten is not only correlated with maths achievement, but that improving this number sense can directly improve children's maths skills in a durable manner.

Non-symbolic number sense. Another key area of preschool numeracy is children's non-symbolic number sense (also referred to as 'approximate number system acuity' and 'analogue magnitude system acuity') (e.g., Halberda and Feigenson 2008; Odic and Starr 2018; Wagner and Johnson 2011). Non-symbolic number sense involves discriminating between two quantities of items without counting (Dehaene 1992). This ability is present in human infants as well as non-human animals (Feigenson et al. 2004), and improves with age from infancy through young adulthood (Halberda et al. 2008). Non-symbolic number sense obeys Weber's law, such that it is more difficult to discriminate items with a smaller ratio (e.g., 8 vs. 12) than items with a larger ratio (e.g., 8 vs. 16), regardless of their actual magnitude (Nieder and Miller 2003). Researchers have proposed that this non-symbolic number sense serves as the cognitive foundation on which our understanding of symbolic mathematics is built (Feigenson et al. 2004; Halberda et al. 2008). Consistent with this, individual differences in the acuity of the non-symbolic number sense correlate with concurrent maths achievement across the lifespan (for a meta-analysis, see Chen and Li 2014). Most relevant to this chapter, several studies have found evidence that non-symbolic number sense in preschool predicts later maths achievement 6 months to 2 years later (e.g., Libertus et al. 2013; Mazzocco et al. 2011).

However, the directionality of the association between non-symbolic number sense and maths achievement has been the subject of much debate. On the one hand, there is evidence that formal schooling may increase the acuity of non-symbolic number sense (Portuguese sample: Nys et al. 2013; indigenous Brazilian sample [Mundurucú]: Piazza et al. 2013). On the other hand, experimental evidence from US preschoolers suggests that practicing a non-symbolic number sense task can transfer to symbolic maths skills, at least in the short term (Park et al. 2016). A recent longitudinal study followed children at three time-points from ages 3 to 5 years, and found evidence for bidirectional relations between non-symbolic number sense and maths achievement (Elliott et al. 2019). In other words, children's non-symbolic number sense may serve as an early foundation for symbolic maths skills, and, at the same time, the process of learning about and manipulating number symbols may help to 'tune up' and increase the precision of the non-symbolic system.

Another salient point of debate is the extent to which the non-symbolic number sense relates to maths achievement after accounting for symbolic number sense (Smedt et al. 2013). Whereas symbolic number sense robustly relates to maths achievement across ages, task formats, and populations, the relation between non-symbolic number sense and maths achievement is weaker and less consistent (Schneider et al. 2017; Smedt et al. 2013). Additionally, one's non-symbolic number sense is more strongly related to maths achievement at early developmental stages (i.e., at young ages or among children with lower maths skills) than at later ones (e.g., Schneider et al. 2017). One theoretical proposal is that non-symbolic number sense may ground the meaning of the Arabic numerals' magnitudes in early learning. Supporting this, the relation between children's non-symbolic number sense and maths achievement is mediated by their understanding of the cardinal principle (Chu et al.2015) and by their ability to map between number symbols and non-symbolic quantities (e.g., to see a group of 8 dots and say 'nine' without counting) (Libertus et al. 2016). In sum, non-symbolic number sense may serve as an important foundation on which young children build their understanding of the magnitudes of number symbols.

18.2.2 Spatial Skills

Children's spatial skills have also emerged as robust predictors of maths achievement (Mix 2019). Spatial skills involve holding in mind and mentally manipulating spatial information, and include skills such as mental rotation, mental transformation, visual form perception, proportional reasoning, and visuo-motor integration. Early research with older students and adults found that spatial skills were strong predictors of maths achievement; majoring in a science, technology, engineering, or maths (STEM) field; and pursuing a career in STEM (Wai et al. 2009). The robust relation between spatial skills and maths achievement has since been confirmed in younger students, including children as young as preschool (Pritulsky et al. 2020).

Recently, a number of studies have attempted to identify specific mechanisms connecting spatial skills to early maths achievement (e.g., Hawes and Ansari 2020; Mix 2019). One line of work has identified number line estimation skill – a key aspect of children's non-symbolic number sense – as a potential mediator of the relation between early spatial skills and later maths achievement (Gunderson et al. 2012). Number line estimation appears to draw on children's spatial skills, likely because it requires children to coordinate spatial magnitudes (line lengths) and numerical magnitudes (Lefevre et al. 2013; Simms et al. 2016). For example, one longitudinal study found that mental rotation skill at age 5 significantly predicted number line estimation skill at age 6, which in turn predicted performance on a symbolic approximate calculation task at age 8 (Gunderson et al. 2012). A second potential mechanism connecting early spatial skills to early numeracy is mental modelling (Mix 2019). According to this hypothesis, learners use their spatial skills to construct visuospatial models as a means of understanding new mathematical concepts at all ages, from a preschooler learning simple addition to a college student learning calculus (Uttal and Cohen 2012). Supporting this, a large cross-sectional study of US students in kindergarten, 3rd, and 6th grades found that, across all age groups, students' spatial visualization skill was more related to novel maths content than to familiar maths content (Mix et al. 2016). It is important to note that these potential mechanisms are not mutually exclusive, and it is quite possible that children's spatial skills may enhance their maths achievement through number line estimation, spatial mental modelling, and other routes.

Building on this theoretical and empirical work, which had previously been conducted primarily with older students, recent work has established the predictive relation between preschoolers' and kindergartners' spatial skills and their later maths achievement. For example, among kindergartners in Luxembourg, children's spatial orientation skills predicted both arithmetic and number line estimation skills four months later (Cornu et al. 2017). Similarly, in a sample of Chinese 4-year-olds in Hong Kong, children's initial spatial skills predicted their performance on both symbolic and non-symbolic arithmetic problems one year later (Zhang and Lin 2015). An even longer-term study in Switzerland found that kindergartners' spatial transformation skills in kindergarten predicted their 2nd grade arithmetic and numerical-logical relations skills, with standardized path coefficients of 0.31 to 0.46, even after accounting for verbal IQ and kindergarten basic calculation skills (Frick 2019). Examining this relation among very young children, a recent study assessed spatial skills at age 3 using a novel measure which required children to copy 2D and 3D block figures (Verdine et al. 2017). In this study, US 3-year-olds' spatial skills significantly predicted their maths achievement two years later, even after accounting for their earlier vocabulary, executive functioning, and symbolic numeracy skills. Taken together, these studies show that preschoolers' and kindergartners' spatial skills serve as an important predictor of later mathematics skills.

Importantly, several studies have demonstrated causal effects of spatial skills on maths achievement by showing that spatial training not only increases young children's spatial skills, but also improves maths skills that were not directly trained (Bower et al. 2020; Cheung et al. 2020; Hawes et al. 2017). In a study of US 6–7-year-olds, one week of online mental rotation training led to large improvements in spatial skills and, importantly, also increased children's arithmetic calculation skills compared to an active control group (literacy training) (Cheung et al. 2020). Among low-income US preschoolers, 5 weeks of one-on-one spatial assembly training led to gains in children's spatial skills and maths achievement, compared to a business-as-usual control group (Bower et al. 2020). A 32-week preschool classroom intervention in Canada which involved a variety of whole-class and small-group activities aimed at practicing mental visualization led to improvements in spatial skills and transfer to symbolic numeracy compared to an active control group (Hawes et al. 2017). These studies show that spatial skills are not just associated with maths achievement, and that enhancing spatial skills can cause improvements in maths achievement in preschool.

18.2.3 Executive Functioning

Executive functioning (EF) skills, which involve working memory capacity, inhibitory control, and task switching skills, strongly relate to maths achievement across ages and maths domains (e.g., Fuhs et al. 2014; Peng et al. 2016; Cragg and Gilmore 2014). This relation is present in preschool: longitudinal studies in the United States have found that EF measured at age 3 (Clark et al. 2013) or at age 4 (Fuhs et al. 2014; Schmitt et al. 2017) was a consistent and strong predictor of maths achievement at the end of kindergarten. Similarly, among Icelandic children, EF at age 4 (based on teacher report) predicted children's maths achievement in 1st grade (Birgisdottir et al. 2020).

To better understand the mechanisms underlying these robust links, recent studies have begun to disentangle relations between specific components of preschool EF and specific aspects of mathematics. One longitudinal study of children in Italy found that EF at age 5 was best described using two components: inhibition and working memory/flexibility (Viterbori et al. 2015). The working memory/flexibility component of EF at age 5 (a latent variable composed of four tasks measuring verbal working memory, spatial working memory, semantic fluency, and task switching) significantly predicted 3rd grade maths achievement, whereas the inhibition component did not. A similar study examined components of EF among German 5-year-olds (Simanowski and Krajewski 2019). This study also concluded that EF consisted of two components: updating and shifting/inhibition. The updating component of EF directly predicted number-word sequence knowledge at age 6, but did not directly predict more advanced, later-developing maths skills. In contrast, the shifting/inhibition component of EF directly predicted later-developing quantity-to-number word linkages at the beginning of 1st grade. In addition, both aspects of EF indirectly predicted overall maths achievement in 2nd grade via their links to prior maths skills. Although these studies support the notion that specific aspects of EF have distinct relations to different aspects of maths learning, each found different factor structures of EF (inhibition and working memory/flexibility versus updating and shifting/inhibition), illustrating the challenges of examining components of EF in preschool.

Researchers have also proposed a variety of theories regarding why EF in preschool predicts maths achievement. Working memory and updating may support children's ability to recall number words in order, and therefore aid in learning the number-word sequence (Simanowski and Krajewski 2019). Strong working memory skills may also aid in children's ability to memorize maths facts, and to hold in mind parts of multi-step calculations (Viterbori et al. 2017). Moreover, working memory may have a cumulative effect on learning, as children with lower working memory may struggle to hold in mind all relevant information while attempting to learn new concepts in the classroom (Alloway et al. 2009). Inhibitory control may aid in learning by helping children to avoid general distractions (such as other children talking), and by helping them to inhibit irrelevant information and incorrect strategies on specific types of maths problems (Ren et al. 2019; Ren and Gunderson 2021). In addition, developing a strong number sense may require inhibiting irrelevant dimensions of sets, such as their size or shape, in order to focus on their numerosity (Clayton and Gilmore 2015; Fuhs and McNeil 2013). Preschoolers have particular difficulty choosing which set has more items when the number of items conflicts with the items' size (e.g., comparing 3 large stars to 6 tiny stars). Recent work indicates that preschoolers' ability to flexibly switch between focusing on numerosity or size while inhibiting the other dimension predicts their later maths achievement over and above general EF (Fuhs et al. 2021). In sum, the longitudinal relations between preschool executive functioning and later maths achievement are large and robust, and researchers have identified many potential pathways connecting EF to early maths achievement.

Building on these robust longitudinal relations, researchers have moved towards intervention designs to test whether improving preschoolers' EF has a causal impact on their maths achievement. However, although EF interventions in preschool and kindergarten are effective in improving the specific EF skills trained, most studies show little to no evidence for transfer to mathematics (Diamond and Ling 2016; Ramani et al. 2020). A promising exception is the kindergarten *Tools of the Mind* curriculum, which incorporates a number of supports for executive function, emotion regulation, and metacognition embedded in all parts of the school day (Blair and Raver 2014) One year of using *Tools of the Mind* led to gains in US kindergarteners' maths achievement as well as other subject areas compared to a business-as-usual control group (Blair and Raver 2014). It should be noted that the *Tools of the Mind* curriculum has not shown the same benefits when implemented in US preschool settings (ages 3 to 4 years), suggesting that kindergarten (ages 5 to 6 years) may be a more optimal time for this type of intervention (Barnett et al. 2008). In sum, EF is a strong correlate of early maths achievement. However, given these mixed intervention results, more research is needed to determine the dosage and timing of EF interventions for effectively improving early maths learning. It may be the case that embedding EF challenges within maths content is most likely to lead to improvements in both EF and maths.

18.2.4 Language and Literacy Skills

Students' achievement in maths and literacy tends to be positively correlated (e.g., Fuchs et al. 2006; Marsh et al. 2015), and recent research has begun to examine the contributions of language and literacy skills to mathematics in early childhood. In a US longitudinal study, letter identification and word reading skills at the start of kindergarten predicted children's maths skills at the end of the year (Schmitt et al. 2017). Similarly, Chinese 4-year-olds' language skills predicted their performance one year later on maths word problems and written arithmetic (Zhang and Lin 2015). A ten-year longitudinal study of Icelandic children found that preschool language skills (phonological awareness and receptive oral language including vocabulary and grammar) explained 20% of the variance in maths achievement in 10th grade (Einarsdóttir et al. 2016). These studies indicate that early language and literacy skills predict both short-term and long-term maths outcomes.

Further, language and literacy skills are multidimensional and can predict maths outcomes through several pathways. In preschool, early literacy skills include oral language skills (e.g., vocabulary knowledge), phonological awareness (the ability to consciously reflect on the sounds in one's language), and print knowledge (e.g., naming letters and letter–sound correspondences) (Whitehurst and Lonigan 1998). Phonological awareness may help children to isolate individual number words in the counting sequence, facilitating early counting knowledge. Supporting this, German kindergartners' phonological awareness predicted their early symbolic numeracy skills, such as counting and naming Arabic numerals, but did not predict other skills, such as mapping number words to quantities (Krajewski and Schneider 2009). Children's print knowledge, especially recognizing letters, may require similar cognitive processes and experiences as learning to recognize and name Arabic numerals, and children's general vocabulary skills may foster the ability to understand maths language (e.g., words such as 'more', 'taller', 'plus') and to comprehend word problems in mathematics. Supporting this, US preschoolers' print knowledge and vocabulary both significantly predicted maths achievement on a standardized test involving maths word problems and symbolic number concepts one year later (Purpura et al. 2011). A subsequent study more directly investigated the mediating role of maths language and found that the relation between preschoolers' general language skills and their numeracy skills was fully mediated by their maths language skills (Purpura and Reid 2016). Further, a recent randomized training study established that improving preschoolers' maths language via a dialogic reading intervention had a causal impact on their numeracy skills (Purpura et al. 2017). Thus, children's developing literacy skills, especially those that contribute to their understanding of mathematical language, may play an important role in their early mathematical development.

18.3 Environmental Predictors of Later Math Achievement

It is clear that individual differences in maths skills are rooted in variations in children's home, childcare, and preschool environments well before school entry (LeFevre et al. 2009; Levine et al. 2010). Children's environments can support each of the cognitive predictors of maths learning reviewed herein (i.e., numeracy skills, spatial skills, EF, and language and literacy skills). The roles of children's early environments on the development of language and literacy skills (e.g., Goldin-Meadow et al. 2014; Golinkoff et al. 2015; Sénéchal and LeFevre 2002) and on EF (e.g., Bindman et al. 2013, 2015; Deater-Deckard 2014; Korucu et al. 2019) are substantial and well-studied, but are beyond the scope of this chapter. Here, I will focus on the most direct predictors of children's mathematical development, namely the home numeracy and home spatial environments and early childcare qualities and practices.

18.3.1 Home Numeracy Environment

Typical home numeracy practices in preschool and kindergarten include formal and informal activities, such as counting objects, identifying written numerals, measuring ingredients while cooking, reading number books, and playing board games or card games (LeFevre et al. 2009). By assessing the frequency of these activities based on parental report, researchers have established that the home numeracy environment varies greatly across families and positively correlates with children's concurrent maths skills (Blevins-Knabe and Musun-Miller 1996; Kleemans et al. 2012; LeFevre et al. 2009). Further, several studies using parental reports have found that early home numeracy activities predict children's later maths skills. For example, in a Canadian sample, parents' advanced formal home numeracy practices (e.g., teaching children simple sums) at the start of kindergarten predicted children's symbolic number knowledge one year later (Skwarchuk et al. 2014). Another study conducted in Greece found that parents' home numeracy practices at the beginning of kindergarten predicted children's 1st grade maths achievement indirectly, via earlier counting and maths concepts in kindergarten (Manolitsis et al. 2013). In a similar study of German children, the home numeracy environment at the beginning of kindergarten predicted children's maths achievement at the end of 1st grade, both directly and indirectly via earlier-developing numeracy skills (Niklas and Schneider 2014).

The relation between the early home numeracy environment and children's maths development is further supported by studies that directly observe parent–child interactions and record instances of mathematically relevant talk (e.g., Gunderson and Levine 2011; Levine et al. 2010; Ramani et al. 2015). In a longitudinal study of US children, parents' use of the number words 'one' to 'ten' at home when children were 1–2.5 years old predicted children's cardinality knowledge at age 4 years (Levine et al. 2010). These studies have also advanced our understanding of the specific types of interactions that are most predictive of numerical development. One key factor is contextualization: parents' number talk that involved counting or labelling visible objects or pictures robustly predicted children's later cardinality knowledge, whereas rote counting and other decontextualized uses of number words did not (Gunderson and Levine 2011). There is also evidence that labelling set sizes, which is critical for understanding the cardinal principle, is a more robust predictor of later maths achievement than counting. Mothers' labelling of set sizes (e.g., 'there are three pennies') during a videotaped interaction when children were 3 years old predicted children's 1st grade maths achievement; in contrast, there was no relation between mothers' counting or labelling of Arabic numerals and children's later maths skills (Casey et al. 2018).

Building on this work, a recent experimental intervention has established a causal relation between home numeracy and children's maths skills. This study used researcher-designed number books to increase parent number talk at home, focusing on 2–4-year-olds in the United States who had not yet learnt the cardinal principle (Gibson et al. 2020). Children and their parents were randomly assigned to one of three conditions: reading number books about the numbers 4, 5, and 6 (large-number books), reading number books about the numbers 1, 2, and 3 (small-number books), and an active control condition (adjective books). Parents were asked to read the books with their child every day for 4 weeks, and reported actually reading the books about 4 times per week. Children in the small-number books condition gained substantially in their cardinal number knowledge compared to the non-numerical control, and children with somewhat more advanced number skills also learnt from the large-number book. This study clearly shows that the home numeracy environment exerts a causal effect on children's numerical development, and that this effect can be enhanced through targeted interventions.

18.3.2 Home Spatial Environment

More recently, researchers have expanded their conceptualization of the home maths environment to include the home spatial environment – that is, home activities that develop children's spatial skills, such as playing with puzzles and building with construction toys (Zippert and Rittle-Johnson 2020). Concurrent and longitudinal studies support the positive relation between the home spatial environment and young children's spatial skills. In a large, representative sample of US 4–7-year-olds, parent-reported frequency of engagement with puzzles, blocks, and board games significantly related to children's concurrent spatial skills (Jirout and Newcombe 2015). Further, a longitudinal study examined 9 hours of videotaped home observations of US children from ages 2 to 4 years, and found that children who played with a puzzle at least once during these observations had significantly higher mental transformation skills at age 4.5 years than children who did not (Levine et al. 2012). In the same naturalistic longitudinal study, parents' use of spatial language (e.g., 'straight', 'edge', and 'triangle') when children were 1 to 3 years old predicted children's later spatial skills (Pruden et al. 2011). Given the robust relations between spatial skills and later maths achievement, these findings indicate that home support for spatial skill development may be an important precursor to later maths achievement.

18.3.3 Childcare and Preschool Environments

In addition to the home environment, researchers have found that both broad indices of childcare quality and specific measures of preschool maths teaching predict children's maths achievement (e.g., Klibanoff et al. 2006; Miller et al. 2014). In one large-scale study that used broad measures of preschool quality (e.g., individuality of care and quality of social interactions), children who attended high-quality preschools in Northern Ireland were three times more likely to attain the highest levels of maths achievement by age 11 years than children who did not attend preschool (Melhuish et al. 2013). Similarly, another large-scale longitudinal study examined US mothers' and childcare providers' general stimulating and responsive caregiving (i.e., not specific to the maths domain) from the time children were 6 months to 3 years old. To measure stimulating-responsive caregiving, mothers completed four 15-minute toy play interactions with their child, and these interactions were coded by trained researchers for overall levels of maternal sensitivity, positivity, stimulation, and (lack of) intrusiveness. In addition, researchers visited the childcare setting on 8 occasions and used a live observational coding procedure to record the frequency of specific behaviours by the non-parental childcare provider (e.g., asking questions, positive talk, responding to the child's vocalizations, and cognitive and social stimulation). Results showed that both mothers' and caregivers' stimulating-responsive caregiving at ages 6 months to 3 years predicted children's maths achievement through 3rd grade (Duncan et al. 2019). This study also found an interactive effect, such that children with low-quality interactions from both mothers and childcare providers were especially at risk for low maths achievement. This effect indicates that high-quality interactions from one source (i.e., parent or childcare provider) can compensate for lower-quality interactions from the other. Further evidence for this compensatory effect comes from research on Head Start, a federally funded, high-quality preschool programme for low-income US children (Miller et al. 2014). By the end of one academic year, children who were randomly assigned to attend Head Start had maths achievement that was 0.17 SD higher than control children, and this effect was largest (0.47 SD) among children whose parents had reported infrequently engaging in home numeracy and literacy activities. Thus, high-quality childcare and preschool environments appear to have positive effects on later maths achievement, especially among children experiencing less cognitively stimulating home environments.

In addition to these effects of general childcare and preschool quality on maths achievement, several studies have specifically investigated the impact of the preschool maths learning environment. One study observed US preschool teachers' maths talk (e.g., mentioning cardinality, counting, number symbols, and simple calculations) during whole-group 'circle time' (Klibanoff et al. 2006). This study found large amounts of variability in the amount of teacher maths talk, from 1 to 104 instances in one hour of observation, reflecting the large amount of discretion that US preschool teachers have in their maths teaching. Further, the amount of preschool teacher maths talk significantly predicted children's growth in maths achievement over the school year, controlling for overall classroom quality and children's socioeconomic status. Importantly, the preschool maths learning environment can be substantially enhanced via research-based maths curricula, with corresponding maths achievement gains among students. A large-scale randomized trial investigated the scaled-up implementation of the research-based pre-kindergarten maths curriculum, *Building Blocks*, in forty-two schools in low-income communities in the United States (Clements et al. 2013). Students who received the curriculum in pre-kindergarten continued to outperform control students in maths two years later at the end of 1st grade. Further, the effect on 1st grade maths achievement was even larger in schools where kindergarten and 1st grade teachers also received follow-up professional development related to the *Building Blocks* curriculum. In sum, consistent with the role of the home learning environment, children's maths learning is clearly influenced by the quality and frequency of the maths learning opportunities they encounter in childcare and preschool settings (see Chapter 22, Lachmann, Bergström, Huber, and Nürk 2022).

18.4 Conclusion

Researchers have established multiple cognitive skills present in preschool and kindergarten that are predictive of later maths achievement, including numeracy, spatial, EF, and literacy skills. Early numeracy skills, especially counting, cardinality, and symbolic number sense, tend to be the largest and most robust predictors. A particularly thorough study investigated the extent to which late-elementary maths achievement was predicted by multiple school-entry factors measured at ages 5 to 6 years, including early maths skills, early reading skills, and attention skills (which are tightly linked to EF) (Duncan et al. 2007). Using six longitudinal datasets from the United States, Britain, and Canada, the results showed that school-entry maths skills were the strongest predictor of later maths achievement, with a standardized meta-analytic regression coefficient of 0.42. Early reading and attention were also consistently predictive of later maths, but with smaller standardized regression coefficients of 0.10 and 0.11, respectively. However, this study did not investigate spatial skills, which have also emerged in recent years as particularly consistent predictors of later maths achievement (Mix 2019; Pritulsky et al. 2020). Importantly, children's early environments – the frequency and quality of numerically and spatially relevant interactions at home and in childcare and preschool settings – also shape their numerical and spatial skills (e.g., Klibanoff et al. 2006; Zippert and Rittle-Johnson 2020).

Although correlational studies are sufficient to identify factors that place children at risk for later maths difficulties, it remains possible that early predictors of later maths achievement are merely correlates rather than drivers of maths learning. Indeed, longitudinal associations between cognitive skills and later maths achievement may reflect stably correlated individual differences (e.g., some children are higher achieving across academic areas) and environments (e.g., some parents provide both maths and literacy supports) rather than causal effects. For this reason, designs that allow for causal inferences, such as randomized training studies, are necessary for establishing mechanistic relations and for developing targeted interventions to improve early maths learning (see Chapter 19, Galuschka and Schulte-Körne 2022). Among the cognitive factors reviewed here, randomized intervention designs have been most successful at improving maths learning when they target early counting, cardinality, symbolic number sense, and spatial skills (e.g., Clements et al. 2013; Hawes et al. 2017; Ramani et al. 2020; Ramani and Siegler 2008). In contrast, interventions targeted towards non-symbolic number sense and EF have shown weaker evidence for transfer to mathematics (Diamond and Ling 2016; Park et al. 2016), and the potential causal effect of early language and literacy skills on later maths is less well-studied (Purpura et al. 2017). More research is needed to understand whether non-symbolic number sense, EF, and language and literacy may be effective targets for early interventions on maths learning. A potentially impactful way forward may be to integrate support for multiple cognitive skills within a single intervention, such as embedding executive function training within a symbolic numeracy intervention. It is worth noting that early educational interventions often yield moderate effect sizes (see Chapter 19, Galuschka and Schulte-Körne 2022), and even when interventions yield positive short-term effects, like the ones reviewed here, those effects often fade after a few months (see Chapter 21, Sokolowski and Peters 2022). Thus, achieving long-term improvements may require finding the appropriate timing for each intervention and ensuring that children continue to experience high-quality educational environments well past the intervention period.

Another important future direction will be for researchers to investigate the roles of affective and motivational factors in maths learning in preschool and kindergarten. Among elementary school students, these factors have already been found to relate to maths achievement, including maths anxiety (a negative emotional reaction to mathematics; see Chapter 5, Szűcs 2022; see also Ramirez et al. 2013), incremental motivational frameworks (the belief that ability is malleable and preference for challenging tasks) (Gunderson et al. 2018), and maths self-concepts (believing that one is good at math) (Arens and Preckel 2018). Recent work has begun to show that children develop meaningful individual differences in these factors at even younger ages. For instance, preschoolers' maths self-concepts are stable over time and relate to their concurrent maths skills (Arens et al. 2016). In a longitudinal study of Hungarian children, preschoolers' negative responses to failure (which are closely related to motivational frameworks) significantly predicted lower 1st grade maths achievement, while controlling for children's socioeconomic status and IQ (Józsa and Barrett 2018). Relatedly, among Finnish children, teacher-reported task avoidance (e.g., giving up easily and avoiding challenges) in kindergarten predicted slower growth in maths achievement through 4th grade (Hirvonen et al. 2012). Although only a few studies to date have investigated these relations, they suggest that affective and motivational responses to maths begin to develop prior to school entry, in the preschool and kindergarten years. More research is needed to understand the development of these responses and how children's views of maths can be improved via targeted interventions.

In sum, preschoolers' and kindergartners' numeracy skills, spatial skills, EF skills, and language and literacy skills are consistent predictors of their later maths achievement. Variations in all of these skills can be traced, at least in part, to children's experiences at home and in childcare and preschool environments. Environmental supports for numeracy and spatial skills, such as counting objects, reading number books, playing board games, building with blocks, and playing with puzzles, have the most direct relation to children's maths learning. Going forward, children's emotional and motivational reactions to maths are a promising area for future research in early childhood mathematics. Given the potential for reciprocal relations between maths skills and motivation (Gunderson et al. 2018), it is important to understand and support the cognitive skills, attitudes, and environments that will set young children onto positive trajectories in mathematics.

Suggestions for Further Reading

Bailey, D. H., G. J. Duncan, T. Watts, D. H. Clements, and J. Sarama. 2018. 'Risky Business: Correlation and Causation in Longitudinal Studies of Skill Development'. *The American Psychologist* 73 (1): 81–94. doi:10.1037/amp0000146, 10.1037/amp0000146.

De Smedt, B., M.-P. Noël, C. Gilmore, and D. Ansari. 2013. 'How Do Symbolic and Non-Symbolic Numerical Magnitude Processing Skills Relate to Individual Differences in Children's Mathematical Skills? A Review of Evidence from Brain and Behavior'. *Trends in Neuroscience and Education*. 2 (2), 48–55. https://doi.org/10.1016/j.tine.2013.06.001.

Gunderson, E. A., G. Ramirez, S. L. Beilock, and S. C. Levine. 2012. 'The Relation between Spatial Skill and Early Number Knowledge: The Role of the Linear Number Line'. *Developmental Psychology* 48 (5): 1229–41. https://doi.org/10.1037/a0027433.

Schmitt, S. A., G. John Geldhof, D. J. Purpura, R. Duncan, and M. M. McClelland. 2017. 'Examining the Relations between Executive Function, Math, and Literacy during the Transition to Kindergarten: A Multi-Analytic Approach'. *Journal of Educational Psychology* 109 (8): 1120–40. https://doi.org/10.1037/edu0000193.

Skwarchuk, S.-L., C. Sowinski, and J.-A. LeFevre. 2014. 'Formal and Informal Home Learning Activities in Relation to Children's Early Numeracy and Literacy Skills: The Development of a Home Numeracy Model'. *Journal of Experimental Child Psychology* 121 (May): 63–84. http://dx.doi.org/10.1016/j.jecp.2013.11.006.

Summary: Early Prediction

(1) **The 'big three' predictors of dyslexia in alphabetic learning contexts:** Phonological awareness, letter knowledge, and rapid automatized (object and symbol) naming most strongly predict reading outcomes and dyslexia (explaining 40–60% of the behavioural variance). In scripts with transparent print-to-speech conversion, phonological awareness most strongly predicts reading outcomes during early stages of learning (but remains a reliable predictor in later grades for spelling).

(2) **The 'big three' vs. competing constructs:** The 'big three' predict reading and dyslexia over and above each other, early reading ability itself (the autoregressor), and other related constructs (e.g., non-word repetition, verbal short-term memory, vocabulary, and intelligence). Whether socioeconomic status (modelled as a latent construct consisting of family income, mother's education, parents' employment, and living conditions) predicts early reading trajectories beyond the 'big three' (as suggested by a single study so far) remains to be verified.

(3) **The nature of phonological awareness difficulties:** The currently available evidence suggests that difficulties in phonological awareness tasks (which tap into many processes, e.g. representation, storage, access, and manipulation of speech information) result from imprecise phonological representations emerging in early childhood (see Parts I and IV).

(4) **The nature of rapid automatized naming difficulties:** It is currently assumed (but not yet shown) that rapid automatized naming taps into converting visual objects to speech (sound and meaning) which is a critical foundation for word recognition (print-to-speech conversion).

(5) **Cognitive predictors of maths learning outcomes:** Maths learning outcomes in primary school are predicted by (non-)symbolic number comparison skills, cardinal counting skills, spatial skills (number line estimation, visuospatial mental modelling), executive functioning (switching/shifting, inhibition), and spoken and written language skills (vocabulary, letter knowledge). Non-symbolic number comparison skill most strongly predicts maths outcomes during early stages of learning. Counting most strongly predicts maths learning outcomes when also tapping into executive functioning (forwards and backwards counting from a given number).

(6) **Learning environments predict maths learning outcomes:** Maths learning outcomes are predicted by parents' number talk (e.g., counting or labelling

visible objects and set sizes); by the quality and quantity of playing with spatial puzzles, blocks, and board games; and by early educators' maths talk (e.g., mentioning cardinality, counting, number symbols, and simple calculations) and reading number books. The predictive power of these factors over and above the relevant cognitive skills remains to be investigated.

PART VIII

Intervention and Compensation

19 Randomized Controlled Trials in Dyslexia and Dyscalculia

Katharina Galuschka and Gerd Schulte-Körne

19.1 Introduction

Persistent, specific, and unexpected difficulties in the acquisition of efficient reading and/or spelling abilities (dyslexia) and mathematical abilities (dyscalculia) leads to marked impairment in school, at work, and in everyday life. Furthermore, years of academic frustration can have the effect that many affected children and adolescents encounter problems such as low self-esteem and symptoms of anxiety and depression (Carroll et al. 2005; Visser et al. 2020). The development, evaluation, and implementation of effective remedial interventions for children with dyslexia and dyscalculia is therefore of profound importance for mitigating the negative consequences for the life of affected children.

A wealth of research has been carried out to investigate interventions for dyslexia and dyscalculia. In intervention research, randomized controlled trials (RCT) are considered an important tool to derive an unbiased estimate of the causal effect of an intervention (Ginsburg and Smith 2016). The RCT is a study design in which subjects are randomly assigned to at least one experimental group (EG) and at least one control group (CG). The EG receives the target intervention while the CG receives an alternative treatment, no treatment, or treatment as usual. The groups are tested before and after the intervention to compare learning abilities and other outcome variables and to determine the effectiveness of the intervention.

If an adequate randomization technique is applied (e.g., computer-generated random numbers, table of random numbers), randomization counteracts bias during the selection process (selection bias). However, it does not protect against bias that may arise after allocation to the study groups. This means that a good intervention study needs more than just a randomized group allocation. In intervention research, *performance bias*, *treatment adherence bias*, *attrition bias*, and *reporting bias* are also common sources of bias that affect study results and conclusions.

Performance bias can occur due to knowledge of group allocation, in either the study personnel or the study subjects. This can lead to a difference in care received by the EG and CG. For example, parents or teachers of subjects in the CG might seek other treatment options or make extra efforts to support the child if they know he or she is affected by dyslexia or dyscalculia and is not receiving effective treatment. Moreover, in expectation of a treatment effect, study personnel might treat study subjects differently depending on which group they are in. Therefore, to counteract performance bias, participants, tutors, and parents should be kept blind to group allocation. Additionally, studies should comprise a (placebo) control intervention of equal duration and intensity and blinded study personnel for outcome assessment (Wood et al. 2008)(Kaufmann et al. 2008).

Treatment adherence bias occurs if failures in implementing the intervention affect the outcome. Regular supervision or the use of adherence ratings of recorded sessions can help to lower the risk for introducing a bias or at least render it possible to determine the influence of the quality of the implementation on the outcome (Storebø et al. 2018).

Systematic differences between participants who drop out of a study and those who continue can cause *attrition bias*. In order to keep the drop-out rate as low as possible, a lot of effort has to be put into binding the sample. This involves, for example, effective communication and incentives to continue. Intention-to-treat analyses can also be performed to counteract a distortion of the study results. In intention-to-treat analyses all participants who were randomized in a trial are included in the statistical analysis and analysed according to the group they were originally assigned, regardless of whether they received any treatment or received a different treatment (White et al. 2012). This method also renders it possible to draw conclusions regarding the practical applicability of an intervention.

Reporting bias arises from selective reporting of hypotheses, design, method, analyses, or results. An important method to prevent reporting bias is to preregister a study, make the protocol publicly available, and report all pre-specified outcomes. In addition, the dependent variables should be assessed with standardized, valid, and reliable tests because non-standardized tests involve the risk of overestimating intervention effects (Swanson 1999).

In research on cognitive interventions, it is extremely difficult to put these high methodological requirements into practice. There is often a lack of financial resources, (e.g., to enable a blind assessment of the outcomes). Also, not every researcher is aware of the various forms of bias or recognizes their importance. In addition, ethical concerns, (e.g., regarding a placebo intervention) must also be taken into account when designing the study. However, high methodological standards are essential to ensure that children with dyslexia and dyscalculia receive effective treatment.

The methodological standard of intervention research on dyslexia and dyscalculia has improved in recent years. There are more and more RCTs (e.g., Görgen et al. 2020), and more and more pre-registered studies (Giofrè et al. 2017) that blindly assess outcomes (e.g., Volkmer et al. 2019) and that report measures of treatment fidelity (Sanetti et al. 2020). The current chapter provides an overview of available treatment approaches for dyslexia and dyscalculia and reviews the evidence in support of these approaches. Whenever possible, we refer to evidence from RCTs and meta-analyses. We would like to highlight that this overview does not claim to be exhaustive and should therefore not be understood as an overview of the entire existing literature.

19.2 Treatment Approaches for Children With Dyslexia

19.2.1 Overview of Existing Interventional Approaches

A large number of interventions and therapies, following different treatment approaches, have been developed and evaluated to improve the reading and spelling performance of children with dyslexia.

Besides symptom-specific interventions that focus directly on reading and spelling processes, auditory and visual processing interventions, Irlen lenses (tinted spectacle lenses or coloured sheets of plastic overlays), attention training, as well as medical treatments were evaluated in RCTs.

Auditory interventions are based on a theory claiming that impairments in rapid auditory temporal processing skills are responsible for the symptoms of dyslexic children (e.g., Tallal 1980; see also Chapter 1, Goswami 2022). A logical prediction of this theory is that training auditory functions can lead to lasting improvements in children's reading skills. Interventions of this category mainly contain tasks with rapidly changing transitions in speech. Alternatively, participants are confronted with non-verbal and verbal stimuli, and are trained to identify and distinguish these stimuli.

Overall, there are only a few RCTs that examine the effectiveness of this training approach for improving reading and spelling performance in children with dyslexia. These studies generally do not show significant improvement in reading and spelling performance (e.g., Given et al. 2008). Moreover, RCTs that do find an effect reveal methodological flaws such as questionable data analysis techniques or no blind assessment of the outcomes (Törmänen and Takala 2009). Meta-analyses could not demonstrate a significant effect of auditory trainings on reading performance (Galuschka et al. 2014; Strong et al. 2011).

Visual processing interventions are based on the notion that dyslexics have dysfunctional magnocellular cells of the visual system, mainly in the corpus geniculatum laterale of the thalamus, which is important for processing high-contrast and low-spatial-frequency visual stimuli, visual search, and eye movement control. It is argued that a weakness in eye movement control may lead to unstable binocular fixation, which in turn may lead to the supposed tendency of dyslexic children to mirror-reverse or twist letters during reading.

It should be noted that this understanding of dyslexia as an impairment of controlling eye movements was refuted decades ago (Fischer et al. 1978). Accordingly, there is limited evidence for the efficacy of treatments of eye movement control on reading and spelling performance of dyslexic children. An RCT by Stein, Richardson, and Fowler (2000) showed a large effect on reading performance after monocular occlusion in a randomized placebo-controlled study. However, it was not reported whether the subjects participated in other reading programmes in addition to the visual intervention. Furthermore, the effectiveness of monocular occlusion compared to symptom-specific interventions has not been studied. Another RCT on oculomotor training in dyslexia showed no effect on reading performance (Peyre et al. 2018).

Irlen Lenses are coloured glasses or coloured overlays designed to compensate for the so-called Scotopic Sensitivity Syndrome (Irlen Syndrome), a perceptual dysfunction that causes visual distortions when reading text (Ritchie et al. 2011). The existence of the Irlen Syndrome and its diagnosis, as well as the efficacy of wearing coloured lenses or overlays, are controversially discussed in the scientific community. Studies on Irlen lenses can be methodologically questionable as they often include no control group and no standardized reading assessment (e.g., Robinson and Conway 1990; Evans et al. 2008). The few adequately conducted randomized placebo-controlled studies paint an inconsistent picture (e.g., Robinson and Foreman 1999; O'Connor et al. 1990; Ritchie et al. 2011) and fail to clearly demonstrate the efficacy of Irlen lenses. The majority of methodologically weak studies report an improvement in the subjective self-assessment of the subjects which might indicate a placebo effect (Döhnert and Englert 2003).

Attention trainings have been developed and investigated because the relationship between different domains of attentional performance and reading or spelling skills is well established (e.g., Savage et al. 2006). The specific research question asked was whether an improvement in the attention performance of children with dyslexia (but no co-occurring attention deficit hyperactivity disorder [ADHD]) could also lead to an improvement in reading and spelling skills. So far, however, no effects of *attention training* on reading accuracy, reading speed, and reading comprehension of children with dyslexia has been demonstrated (Chenault et al. 2006; Solan et al. 2003).

In *medical interventions* dyslexic children mainly receive the nootropic piracetam to enhance their reading and spelling performance. Piracetam is a cyclic derivative of gamma-aminobutyric acid (GABA) and is supposed to improve memory and learning. There are also studies on atomoxetine or methylphenidate for children with dyslexia and co-occurring ADHD, which are beyond the scope of this article (see Froehlich et al. 2018 for a review). Studies that tried to enhance reading and spelling skills of children and adolescents with reading difficulties by medication with the nootropic piracetam showed only minor treatment effects (Di Ianni et al. 1985; Wilsher et al. 1987). A meta-analysis was also unable to demonstrate a significant treatment effect (Galuschka et al. 2014). Wilsher and Taylor (1994) emphasized that taking medication can lead to side effects, so the risks of piracetam in remediation of dyslexic children seem to be higher than the benefits (Wilsher and Taylor 1994).

The empirical findings of recent decades of research suggest that a major source of the difficulties experienced by children with dyslexia is in the language domain and that the specific problems of children with dyslexia are best addressed with cognitive interventions that relate to reading and spelling development.

An important precursor of reading and spelling acquisition (Moll et al. 2014) in alphabetic languages is the ability to recognize, discriminate, and manipulate phonemes in words or word units (Moll et al. 2014). This ability is called phonological awareness. Therefore, *phonological awareness interventions* that implement oral tasks for recognizing phonemes within words, blending phonemes into words, segmenting a word into phonemes, deleting a phoneme from a word, or adding a phoneme to a word are often used to treat reading and spelling deficits.

It is currently adequate to conclude that interventions targeting solely phonological awareness skills are beneficial in preschool years and can facilitate reading during early stages of learning (Ehri et al. 2001; Pfost et al. 2019; see also Chapter 23, Hasselhorn and Schneider 2022). As soon as children master the phonemic structure of their language, the effectiveness in improving reading and spelling skills is reduced (Bus and van IJzendoorn 1999; Galuschka et al. 2014). Continuing phonological awareness instruction was found to be more effective when it was taught with letters than without letters (Ehri et al. 2001). Therefore, we argue that once the phonological structure of the language is understood, phonological awareness interventions should be replaced by or combined with phonics instruction.

Phonics instruction teaches children the relationship between graphemes and phonemes and between phonemes and graphemes. Phoneme–grapheme and grapheme–phoneme correspondence skills are fundamental for reading and spelling since this knowledge gives children the ability to decode most words in their language. Phonics instruction is currently the best-supported treatment approach. Twenty years ago, the US National Reading Panel demonstrated the effectiveness of phonics instruction in a meta-analysis of controlled trials (Ehri et al. 2001). Many other meta-analyses and RCTs (McArthur et al. 2018; Suggate 2016; Galuschka et al. 2014; Galuschka et al. 2020) have since confirmed these results. Despite the large body of evidence in favour of phonics, even this line of research is not without flaws. Some RCTs that evaluated the use of phonics lack a blind assessment of the outcomes (e.g., Bhattacharya and Ehri 2004), verification of treatment fidelity (e.g., Hughes et al. 2013), or standardized tests for reading and spelling assessment (e.g., Ferraz et al. 2018). Since meta-analyses can only be as good as the studies they contain, they naturally also have their methodological weaknesses. Meta-analyses on phonics instruction often contain only a few studies, show a high conceptual and technical heterogeneity and publication bias (see Bowers 2020) criticizing the evidence for the effectiveness of a phonics instruction derived from meta-analyses and (see Fletcher et al. 2020 for a response). In addition, study design and content aspects of interventions are inconsistent and difficult to summarize in meta-analyses. Nevertheless, even when conducting a critical and conservative review of the available research, the results of numerous RCTs and meta-analyses paint a relatively clear picture and show small to medium effects of phonics instruction on reading performance and medium to large effects on spelling performance (Galuschka et al. 2020; Galuschka et al. 2014; McArthur et al. 2018).

Representing phonemes with letters or sounding out words through grapheme–phoneme correspondences (alphabetic decoding) is not sufficient for skilled reading and spelling. Fluent word reading also involves gaining access to meaning directly from the spelling (sight word reading), without the requirement to do so via grapheme–phoneme conversions. According to Share (1995) the effortful process of alphabetic decoding also provides an opportunity to acquire orthographic knowledge and promotes sight word reading. Indeed, meta-analyses revealed effects of phonics training on reading fluency, reading comprehension, and spelling for children with dyslexia (e.g., McArthur et al. 2018; Galuschka et al. 2020).

There is also evidence that other treatment approaches following up on phonics interventions can further increase dyslexic children's reading and spelling performance. Positive results have been primarily reported for interventions focusing on morphological and orthographic knowledge. *Morphological knowledge* refers to the awareness of the smallest meaningful language units (Carlisle 2003; Nagy et al. 2003; Görgen et al. 2021). *Orthographic knowledge* enables an understanding of the orthographic system that forms the backbone of correct writing in terms of rules and patterns of written language (Rothe et al. 2014). In many orthographies, not all words can be read or spelled correctly based on simple grapheme-phoneme correspondences. One sound can have different spellings in different words (e.g., the phoneme /i/ in English may be spelled <ee> as in 'deep' or <ea> as in 'mean') and the same spelling patterns can have different pronunciations (e.g., 'heat', 'head', 'bear'). *Morphological and orthographic interventions* aim to help children with dyslexia deal with the deviations from one-to-one mappings between graphemes and phonemes (or vice versa), and provide explanations for these deviations.

Morphological interventions often include instructions centred on morpheme structure, repeated reading of frequent morphemes, practicing inflections and derivations, and training children to apply this knowledge to spelling. The underlying assumption is that once morphological regularities have been acquired, reading and spelling can be more efficient since the effortful process of alphabetical decoding is replaced by recognizing and reproducing morphemes and morphological components (e.g., reading and spelling of the word 'friendship' through the morphological components 'friend' and '-ship'). Especially in the last decade, morphological interventions have been increasingly evaluated. It was shown that they raise the reading and spelling performance of children with dyslexia and even have transfer effects on untrained word material (Goodwin and Ahn 2013; Berninger et al. 2008). *Orthographic interventions* mainly focus on the improvement of spelling skills and train the application of graphotactic (letter positioning) and phonological–orthographic regularities that govern the positions, combinations, and resulting pronunciations of letters within words. Squires and Wolter (2016) and Galuschka et al. (2020) synthesized intervention studies that evaluated orthographic interventions and demonstrated moderate effects on spelling skills.

Another option for improving reading and spelling are sight word reading and spelling memorization interventions. Such interventions use flash cards or word lists and try to foster sight word reading and spelling through word-specific memorization of letter sequences and the visual appearance of written words. Memorizing all words of a writing system is an inconceivable task (Castles et al. 2018) and those treatment approaches do not support the acquisition of strategies which lead to transfer effects (Berninger et al. 2008; Gray 2015). However, it is likely that memorization and sight word reading training can usefully complement phonics or morphological and orthographic interventions. Not every word's spelling or pronunciation can be reasonably inferred from morphological or orthographic knowledge. For exceptional words which are very difficult to decode or spell, these interventions could be useful (Galuschka et al. 2020; McArthur et al. 2015).

To summarize, it can be concluded that treatment of children with dyslexia should always concentrate on reading and writing activities. Phonics instruction as well as interventions that foster morphological and orthographic knowledge have been shown to be particularly effective in improving reading and spelling skills.

19.2.2 Combining Treatment Approaches

What is the best way to combine the different treatment approaches for a holistic remediation of reading and spelling skills? Although there are only a few studies that actually limit their intervention to one approach, there is a lack of studies that systematically combine different treatment approaches and compare different combinations. These studies are very difficult to conduct and only small effects can be expected, so a large sample size is required. Moderator analyses in meta-analyses have often been used to try to fill this research gap (Goodwin and Ahn 2010; Galuschka et al. 2020), but so far this approach has not revealed a clear picture. For example, meta-analyses obtained higher effect sizes if morphological training started in preschool and early elementary grades. Therefore, some researchers concluded that combining phonics and morphological instruction at the beginning of literacy instruction might be particularly helpful for remediating dyslexia (Goodwin and Ahn 2010; Bowers et al. 2010). Other researchers argued that focusing on these morphological regularities is likely to be more appropriate in the later years of primary school when the intervention is supported by the text experiences that students make in the early elementary grades (Rastle and Taylor 2018).

The few RCTs that exist indicate that even children in the first year of literacy instruction benefit more from interventions that are not limited to phonics instructions. An RCT by Morris et al. (2012) examined a sample of 1st and 2nd graders (N=297, about 60 per group) and demonstrated superior reading and spelling outcomes for multidimensional literacy interventions combining phonics with other decoding strategies (including morphological decoding) than for students who participated in a training that was limited to phonics instruction alone.

Abbott and Berninger (1999) tested the hypothesis that students with reading and spelling deficits in grades 4–7 would improve more rapidly in reading and spelling if a phonics training is combined with morphological instruction rather than phonics training alone. Individual growth curves displayed a trend towards a greater individual treatment response within the group receiving the combined treatment, but due to the small sample size (10 subjects in each group) no intervention effects could be observed at the group level.

Recently, McArthur et al. (2015). investigated a combination of phonics and sight word reading training. Results indicated that a combination of both treatment approaches (first phonics, then sight word reading training) is particularly helpful for remediating reading deficits.

Another study that combined multiple treatment approaches and explored different combinations was conducted by Calhoon et al. (2010), who varied the amount and combination of components within a reading programme to increase intervention effects for middle-school poor readers. It turned out that extensively strengthening linguistic knowledge (phonetics, phonology, syllable structure, morphology) in combination with orthographic spelling instruction and repeated sentence reading led to better spelling, reading fluency, and reading comprehension skills compared to a treatment of linguistic knowledge and reading comprehension alone.

The few studies that systematically combined treatment approaches allow us to cautiously assume that, across age groups, children with dyslexia need comprehensive interventions. In an optimal intervention, children with dyslexia would first be trained on the regular connections between phonemes and graphemes and graphemes and phonemes; once these are mastered they would receive help to deal with the deviations from these regular connections by explicitly building morphological or orthographic knowledge.

Nevertheless, we need more high-quality RCTs that systematically combine different treatment approaches and compare different combinations to be able to draw conclusions about which combination of approaches is particularly helpful for children at a particular age or literacy level.

19.3 Treatment Approaches for Children With Dyscalculia

To understand the rationale behind the design of interventions for dyscalculia it is important to understand how children acquire mathematical skills and which cognitive skills are involved in this process.

Studies on mathematical learning point to the existence of a basic number sense that allows infants to compare and discriminate between magnitudes. Another very basic skill, subitizing, refers to the ability to perceive small quantities (1–4) simultaneously without having to count them. Subitizing and the ability to compare and discriminate between magnitudes are basic numerical competencies and serve as a foundation for the development of more advanced numerical and arithmetic skills (see Chapter 18, Gunderson 2022). The acquisition of verbal symbolic representations (number words) and visual symbolic representations (arabic digits), as well as learning the association between numerals and quantities, follows in preschool and the early school years. This allows children to learn to count, to build a spatial representation of numerical magnitude ('mental number line'), to understand the place-value system, and finally to acquire basic arithmetic skills (calculation procedures and concepts such as addition, subtraction, multiplication, and division).

Dyscalculia is associated with a less pronounced number sense, a reduced subitizing range, problems with counting and transforming number words into digits (transcoding), limited understanding of the place-value system and impaired development of the mental number line, limited understanding of arithmetic procedures, and persistent use of ineffective finger-based arithmetic problem solving strategies. In addition to these number-specific deficits, children with dyscalculia also show more general cognitive deficits in visuospatial working memory and executive functions (e.g., inhibition) (see Haberstroh and Schulte-Körne 2019, and

Chapter 18, Gunderson 2022). Accordingly, the cognitive profiles can differ greatly between affected individuals.

Following the heterogeneous manifestations of dyscalculia (see Chapter 4, Banfi, Landerl, and Moll 2022) interventional approaches can be classified into *domain-specific interventions*, which include interventions that foster basic numerical competencies, train basic arithmetic skills, or train mathematical problem solving skills; and *domain-general interventions*, which target general cognitive abilities such as working memory to foster arithmetic skills. Although research on dyscalculia has caught up in recent years, there are still only a few methodologically sound RCTs. Thus, the following review is based only sporadically on RCTs but mainly on non-randomized-controlled studies.

Interventions that foster basic numerical competencies often concentrate on counting, counting principles, the cardinality principle, part-whole understanding, numerical magnitudes, number comparison, transcoding between non-symbolic quantities, digits, and number words. Controlled trials demonstrated an effect on basic numerical competencies (Sella et al. 2016; Van Luit and Schopman 2000; Lambert and Spinath 2014), and some studies also indicated transfer effects on basic arithmetic skills (Sella et al. 2016; Van Luit and Schopman 2000; Hellstrand et al. 2020). Basic numerical skills are fundamental for the development of basic arithmetic skills and have to be acquired before a training of basic arithmetic skills can bring about lasting effects (Moeller et al. 2012). Therefore, many interventions begin with basic numerical competencies and move on to basic arithmetic skills (e.g., Re et al. 2014; Bryant et al. 2016).

Basic arithmetic interventions involve calculation procedures and concepts such as addition, subtraction, multiplication, and division. Research based on this intervention approach has shown that children's arithmetic skills can strongly improve in the domain targeted with the training (Powell et al. 2009; Moran et al. 2014; Kroesbergen and van Luit 2002). In their meta-analyses, Kroesbergen and Van Luit (2003) and Chodura et al. (2015) reported large effects of this approach on mathematical achievement. While these specific effects are encouraging, transfer to related arithmetic competencies cannot be expected (Fuchs et al. 2008). This means that each individual arithmetic skill must also be targeted separately so that children can acquire age-appropriate competencies.

Simply teaching basic arithmetic skills is not enough to foster mathematical problem solving capacities. Children also need to know how and when to apply their knowledge in new and sometimes unfamiliar contexts. For this purpose, *problem solving interventions* have been developed. While these interventions have in common that they aim to provide children with strategies for applying their basic arithmetic knowledge in new and unfamiliar contexts, they differ greatly in content and instructional methods. Fuchs et al. (2010), for example, assessed the effects of a counting or decomposition strategy instruction on addition and subtraction within the framework of word-problem tutoring. Moran et al. (2014) evaluated a paraphrasing intervention for word problems, and Topping et al. (2011) evaluated a peer-tutoring programme encouraging dialogue about mathematical problems. All of the aforementioned interventions displayed an improvement in arithmetic performance in children with maths difficulties. Chodura et al. (2015) and Kroesbergen and van Luit (2003) also evaluated the effectiveness of problem solving interventions in their meta-analyses and demonstrated moderate mean effect sizes. So far, however, it is not clear which strategies are particularly suitable for specific cognitive profiles, age groups, and maths performance levels. That being said, problem solving skills are more advanced and more difficult to improve than basic arithmetic skills (Kroesbergen and Van Luit 2003). It is therefore reasonable not to implement problem solving interventions until basic numerical and arithmetic skills are already mastered.

As mentioned, children experiencing difficulties in mathematics frequently exhibit problems with respect to domain-general cognitive abilities, especially working memory and cognitive control (inhibition). It is also often reported that these difficulties influence treatment effects of domain-specific interventions (Swanson et al. 2014). Accordingly, numerous working-memory-based interventions have been developed to improve children's arithmetic skills. Results are inconsistent, however, with some studies demonstrating an improvement of mathematical skills through working memory training (e.g., Kuhn and Holling 2014) while others do not reveal any effects (e.g., Karbach et al. 2015; Kaufmann and Pixner 2012). Meta-analyses on this topic (Schwaighofer et al. 2015; Melby-Lervåg et al. 2016) consistently conclude that working memory training does not lead to transfer effects on mathematical skills. However, the importance of working memory for dyscalculia cannot be denied. Therefore, further research is needed to address working memory problems in interventions for children with dyscalculia.

In summary, it can be concluded that an effective treatment of dyscalculia requires targeting domain-specific mathematical skills. Moreover, remediation should gradually progress from basic numerical skills to basic arithmetical skills to problem solving.

19.4 Quality Criteria for Effective Interventions for Children With Dyslexia and Dyscalculia

Effective remediation should build on evidence-based training content, but content alone does not make an intervention effective. Snowling and Hulme (2011) reviewed quality criteria of evidence-based interventions and concluded that interventions should be systematic, well structured, and multisensory, and should include time for consolidation and frequent revisions. Moeller et al. (2012) emphasized that intervention programmes should involve different modules comprehensively covering the potentially impaired domains. These modules should be self-contained and able to be used independently of each other so that the programme can be customized according to the individual child's needs.

Going beyond Snowling and Hulme and Moeller et al. we propose the following criteria to enhance intervention effects for children with dyslexia and dyscalculia.

First, interventions should be individualized since there is evidence that they are more successful if the instruction is adjusted to the student's individual demands than to the grade curriculum (Re et al. 2014; Lee Swanson and Sachse-Lee 2000). Accordingly, we recommend assessing the student's individual needs, providing tailored interventions, and monitoring performance. This is also essential since it can be assumed that there are different deficiencies in dyslexia and dyscalculia based on impairments in different areas (see Chapter 4, Banfi, Landerl, and Moll 2022).

Second, *interventions should be adapted to the cognitive profile and possible co-occurring difficulties* of the individual child. It could be demonstrated repeatedly that cognitive abilities and co-occurring learning difficulties of children with dyslexia influence treatment effects (e.g., Swanson 2015).

Third, interventions should be implemented individually or in small groups. Considering meta-analyses on interventions for children with dyscalculia, it has been consistently shown that interventions are more effective in individual settings than in groups or in the classroom. Interestingly, meta-analyses of effective interventions for children with dyslexia found no differences between interventions administered in individual settings or in small group settings (Galuschka et al. 2014; Galuschka et al. 2020). However, meta-analyses explicitly excluded children with dyslexia and co-occurring difficulties, so that no recommendation regarding the setting can be made for this group so far.

Fourth, using computer-based interventions should be considered. In general, traditional interventions (with human tutors) show slightly higher effect sizes than computer-based interventions (Zaphiris and Ioannou 2016; Galuschka et al. 2020; Chodura et al. 2015). Nevertheless, the use of computers has some advantages as it places fewer demands on tutors and can have positive effects on the motivation of learners (Cohen Kadosh et al. 2013). Computer-based intervention could also be used to ensure widespread availability of evidence-based programmes and to provide early intervention (see Chapter 23, Hasselhorn and Schneider 2022).

Fifth, interventions should start as early as possible. It has been observed that children at risk of developing learning difficulties have minimal chances to overcome these risks via typical instruction (Shaywitz et al. 1999). Moreover, repeated experiences of school failure can precipitate, consolidate, and intensify co-occurring anxiety, depression, hyperactivity, and conduct disorders (Maughan and Carroll 2006). Crucially, interventions are more effective the earlier they begin (Chodura et al. 2015; Ehri et al. 2001).

Recapitulating the body of research we summarized in this chapter, we conclude that there are still gaps in some areas. In Europe, for example, there are still relatively few studies in which children's performance is monitored during the intervention and in which the intervention is adapted accordingly. Furthermore, apart from studies focusing on the combination of medication and cognitive interventions for dyslexia and ADHD (Shaywitz et al. 2017), there are hardly any studies that consider co-occurring dyslexia and dyscalculia (about 5% of the population; Willcutt et al. 2013). We currently cannot make any evidence-based recommendations on how to deal with these and other constellations.

Many children with dyslexia and dyscalculia suffer from emotional problems (e.g., maths or reading anxiety [see Chapter 5, Szűcs 2022] and depression; see also Visser et al. 2020). A few attempts to address these co-occurring problems during intervention have been made (e.g., Boyes et al. 2020), but currently there are not enough studies to derive concrete conclusions. Thus, at present hardly anything is known about how to address these problems during intervention.

19.5 Conclusion

In this chapter, we have described the existing treatment approaches for dyslexia and dyscalculia, referring preferably to RCTs and meta-analyses. The available evidence suggests that effective intervention in dyslexia requires working on the specific symptoms of the disorder (inaccurate or slow and effortful word reading; difficulties in reading comprehension; difficulties with spelling, such as adding, omitting, or substitute letters and graphemes).

Similarly, effective dyscalculia intervention requires addressing domain-specific difficulties in numerical and arithmetic skills. We also established quality criteria for effective interventions: interventions should be individualized and consider cognitive profiles and co-occurring difficulties, should be implemented individually or in small groups, should start as early as possible, and may be computer-based to maximize the outreach.

Here we have focused on RCTs and meta-analyses centred on poor reading, spelling, or maths abilities in general education. Given the evidence that children with below-average intelligence also respond to interventions for dyslexia and dyscalculia (e.g., Jiménez et al. 2003) and studies that indicate that children with mild mental disabilities also benefit from similar support (e.g., explicit and direct instruction, systematic instruction; Scruggs et al. 2010; Alnahdi 2015), we believe that our conclusions might apply to children in special education. However, further research is needed to draw clear conclusions about this topic.

Our conclusions for dyslexia intervention can be applied to all languages with an alphabetic writing system. Alphabetic orthographies have certain variations in orthographic depth (see Chapter 15, Siok 2022) which affects the time it takes to learn the grapheme–phoneme and phoneme–grapheme mappings, but the general framework of literacy development and the cognitive factors underlying reading and spelling performance is valid across alphabetic orthographies (Caravolas 2004; Caravolas et al. 2012). In addition, similar treatment approaches developed in different alphabetic orthographies do not differ significantly in their effectiveness (Galuschka et al. 2020).

The causal factors and cognitive profiles of children with dyscalculia appear to be largely similar across languages and cultures (see Chapter 16, Lyu and Zhou 2022). Nevertheless, given the lack of empirical evidence for non-WEIRD (western-educated-industrialized-rich-democratic) populations, we cannot safely assume that our conclusions are culturally unrestricted.

We have also highlighted some research gaps. In particular, we pointed to the lack of studies that systematically combine different treatment approaches and compare different combinations. We also emphasized that more studies are needed to evaluate how certain co-occurring difficulties can be addressed during intervention.

Neurobiologically driven research might help to understand the brain functions that are altered during reading, spelling, number processing, and maths problem solving. Thus, intervention research integrating neurobiological and behavioural outcomes can help us to understand treatment processes and to identify predictors of individual treatment effectiveness. To return to the introduction of this chapter, we would like to emphasize that research on dyslexia and dyscalculia is constantly growing and improving, and we see research on computer-based support as particularly promising. These technical tools promise that evidence-based support can soon be offered to every child with initial difficulties in reading, spelling, or arithmetic.

Suggestions for Further Reading

Haberstroh, S., and G. Schulte-Körne. 2019. 'The Diagnosis and Treatment of Dyscalculia'. *Deutsches Arzteblatt International* 116 (7): 107–14.

Galuschka, K., R. Görgen, J. et al. 2020. 'Effectiveness of Spelling Interventions for Learners with Dyslexia: A Meta-Analysis and Systematic Review'. *Educational Psychologist* 55 (1): 1–20.

Castles, A., K. Rastle, and K. Nation. 2018. 'Ending the Reading Wars: Reading Acquisition from Novice to Expert'.*Psychological Science in the Public Interest* 19 (1), 5–51. https://doi.org/10.1177/1529100618772271.

Benavides-Varela, S., Callegher, C. Z., Fagiolini, B., Leo, I., Altoè, G., and Lucangeli, D. (2020). Effectiveness of digital-based interventions for children with mathematical learning difficulties: A meta-analysis. Computers & Education 157, 103953. https://doi.org/10.1016/j.compedu.2020.103953.

20 Cognitive Enhancement and Brain Stimulation in Dyslexia and Dyscalculia

Nienke E. R. van Bueren, Evelyn H. Kroesbergen, and Roi Cohen Kadosh

20.1 Introduction

In this chapter, we provide an overview of different types of cognitive enhancement techniques that target key neural regions related to dyslexia and dyscalculia. The main emphasis is on non-invasive brain stimulation (NIBS), such as transcranial magnetic stimulation (TMS) and transcranial electrical stimulation (tES). The former sends a pulse of current through a coil to evoke a magnetic field that penetrates the skull and enters the brain. The direction of neuromodulation by TMS is controlled by the stimulation frequency. Specifically, high-frequency stimulation increases neural excitability whereas low-frequency stimulation decreases it (Peterchev et al. 2008). Transcranial electrical stimulation directly applies a small electrical current through electrodes attached to a target area on the head. Several types of tES can be distinguished: transcranial direct current stimulation (tDCS), transcranial random noise stimulation (tRNS), and transcranial alternating current stimulation (tACS). All these techniques make use of one or more surface electrode-(s) that are fixed over brain areas of interest on the scalp and that apply a weak current, usually between 1 mA and 2 mA. It is thought that NIBS alters cortical excitability by promoting neural plasticity and modulating behaviour (Cirillo et al. 2017). During tDCS, a constant current flows between a cathode and an anode with the putative effect that stimulated neurons targeted by the anode are depolarized and thereby excited, while neurons targeted by the cathode are hyperpolarized and thereby inhibited (Jacobson et al. 2012). By contrast, tRNS makes use of an alternating current with random frequencies so that cortical excitation is induced under both surface electrodes (Terney et al. 2008). The effect of tRNS is assumed to be via stochastic resonance – that is, stimulation with an optimal amount of noise can enhance performance whereas suboptimal amounts decrease performance (van der Groen and Wenderoth 2016). Transcranial alternating current differs from tRNS because it uses stimulation at a particular fixed frequency, and this is thought to lead to neuronal entrainment of cortical oscillations and phase locking (Battleday et al. 2014; Witkowski et al. 2016). Neuronal entrainment takes place when the endogenous neuronal oscillations (i.e., brain waves) are entrained to the exogenous stimulation frequency of tACS (Battleday et al. 2014). Neuronal entrainment is achieved by influencing the transmembrane potential of the targeted neurons. Phase locking takes place when the endogenous and exogenous oscillations are synchronized in phase. To observe neurophysiological changes induced by NIBS these techniques are combined with imaging methods such as electroencephalography (EEG) or functional magnetic resonance imaging (fMRI).

NIBS research faces some important challenges. In particular, the specific short- and long-term effects are unknown (Cohen Kadosh et al. 2012), replication studies are scarce, replicability of results is limited, and there is a good deal of variability in effects between studies (Huang et al. 2017; Ziemann and Siebner 2015). This variability is explained by individual differences at the neural and behavioural levels. For example, a study by Krause and Cohen Kadosh (2014) suggested that tES responsiveness depends on the age, gender, brain state, hormonal levels, and pre-existing regional excitability of the subjects. Thus, brain stimulation results are heterogeneous and should be interpreted with caution. Nevertheless, there have been promising results in terms of modulating cognitive processing such as working memory (Brunoni and Vanderhasselt 2014), learning (Simonsmeier et al. 2018), and numerical and mathematical skills (Schroeder et al. 2017; van Bueren et al. 2021). NIBS has even been advocated as a reliable intervention for clinical disorders such as depression (Brunoni et al. 2019), drug addiction (Song et al. 2019), migraines (Brighina et al. 2019), schizophrenia (Kennedy et al. 2018), and Alzheimer's and Parkinson's diseases (Kekic et al. 2016). Additionally, the popularity of tES as a possible therapeutic intervention is rising due to its ease of applicability, negligible side effects during stimulation, and low cost (Nitsche et al. 2003; Rossi et al. 2009). Nevertheless, implications for practice raise several ethical questions (Cohen Kadosh et al. 2012), even though NIBS has been proven safe for adults and minors (Palm et al. 2016). Importantly, NIBS could reveal a causal link between brain activity and behaviour. It is therefore a promising method by which to investigate potentially causal neurocognitive mechanisms underlying learning difficulties and to improve educational interventions. Accordingly, the main aim of this chapter is to review studies that use NIBS to improve behavioural performance in dyscalculia and dyslexia.

It is generally accepted that poor reading skills have a bigger impact on functioning in daily life and in the classroom than poor mathematical skills, though this is not necessarily the case (Parsons et al. 2005). It is therefore not surprising that studies on poor literacy skills are overrepresented in the current literature on possible interventions for dyslexia and dyscalculia (Bishop 2010). As we outline in the following sections, this imbalance is also found with respect to studies using NIBS as an intervention for dyslexia and dyscalculia. As a consequence, this chapter contains substantially more information about the efficacy of NIBS as an intervention for dyslexia than for dyscalculia.

Even though learning difficulties are thought to have a neural foundation, the diagnostic label given to children and adults is based solely on behavioural traits (e.g., performance in reading and mathematics). To understand the efficacy of NIBS as a cognitive enhancement (i.e., rehabilitation) technique, it is nevertheless crucial to understand which brain mechanisms are targeted to improve cognition. Therefore, ideally, NIBS studies should first investigate by means of neuroimaging whether the labelled individuals show any neural signs of processing deficits. Additionally, the severity of neural and behavioural deficits differs between individuals and should therefore also be considered (see Chapter 4, Banfi, Landerl, and Moll 2022).

20.2 Neuroanatomical Correlates

20.2.1 Dyslexia

The neural deficits that are thought to be associated with dyslexia are related to structural deficits in the temporal lobe. In particular, the inferior and superior posterior temporal cortex (pTC) in the left hemisphere becomes more specialized when children learn to read. Additionally, activation of this area in the right hemisphere becomes less specialized either due to decreased right hemispheric activation or to increased left-hemispheric activation (Simos et al. 2001; Turkeltaub et al. 2003). Hemispheric lateralization differences have therefore been proposed as an underlying cause of dyslexia in children and adults (Kershner 2019; Richlan et al. 2009; Shaywitz and Shaywitz 2008). Children with dyslexia showed reduced activation in the left temporo-parietal junction (TPJ) and higher activation in the right TPJ in a magnetic source imaging study (Simos et al. 2002). To further support the notion of this hemispheric lateralization deficit, a recent network analysis study identified which neural networks based on fMRI data were involved in fluent reading. Abnormal connectivity was found in the left inferior frontal gyrus and the TPJs, which implies that atypical development underlies hemispheric differences in domain-general areas that subserve attention, memory, and executive functions (Bailey et al. 2018; for further details, see Chapter 9, Fraga González, Jednoróg, and Brem 2022).

20.2.2 Dyscalculia

Anatomical abnormalities in the right parietal lobe have been related to low numerical competencies or dyscalculia. Hereby, abnormal functioning of the intraparietal sulcus (IPS) is pointed out as the main reason because of the important role that the IPS plays both in numerical processing and in attentional processing (Fan et al. 2005). In addition, dysfunction in the prefrontal cortex is also related to an executive attention deficit in affected children (Peters and De Smedt 2018). However, imaging studies have shown that adults and children with dyscalculia display increased frontal activation, and this has been suggested as a possible compensatory mechanism for the hypoactivation shown in the parietal areas (Cappelletti and Price 2014; Peters and De Smedt 2018). Voxel-based morphometry also related reduced grey matter volumes in the right parietal region to dyscalculia (Cappelletti and Price 2014). Another recent imaging study assessed the fMRI activation of individuals with dyscalculia and controls while they performed a non-symbolic and symbolic magnitude comparison task (Bulthé et al. 2019). The individuals with dyscalculia performed worse in both tasks in terms of slower response times. With regard to non-symbolic processing, individuals with dyscalculia showed abnormal activity in the parietal regions, including the IPS (domain-specific processing), the frontal gyri, and the temporal regions (domain-general processing). No structural brain deficiencies were found, but functional connectivity analysis showed a hyperconnectivity in the temporo-occipital cortex that was related to compensatory mechanisms for processing complex visual objects. It is worth mentioning that previous structural imaging studies have shown structural abnormalities in the arcuate fasciculus (e.g., the white matter bundle connecting frontal, parietal, and temporal areas) related to mathematical skills (Matejko and Ansari 2015; van Eimeren et al. 2008).

20.3 Cognitive Rehabilitation for Learning Disorders by Means of Transcranial Magnetic Stimulation

For the following part of the chapter, we reviewed (in chronological order) existing TMS studies that have focused on cognitive rehabilitation for dyslexia and dyscalculia or their underlying mechanisms. The national origin of the samples used in the research articles were as follows: United States (1), Italy (1), and the Netherlands (1). The adults in these studies were between 19 and 57 years of age. Figure 20.1 provides an overview of the studies: their design, montage, behavioural tasks, outcomes, and a visualization of the stimulation sites.

20.3.1 Dyslexia

Several studies investigating TMS as an intervention tool for dyslexia have reported promising results. They have shown that reading can be positively influenced at both the word and the sentence levels (for a review, see Noort et al. 2015).

One of the first studies that used TMS as a possible cognitive rehabilitation technique stimulated both the left and the right brain hemisphere in one patient with acquired dyslexia (Coslett and Monsul 1994; see Figure 20.1). Unlike developmental dyslexia, acquired dyslexia usually results from a head trauma or a stroke and can change in severity over time. In this study, single-pulse TMS was applied over either the left or the right posterior temporal lobe 45 ms after a written word appeared on a screen. The patient was then asked to read the word aloud; the number of words that were read aloud correctly were counted. Interestingly, only stimulation of the right hemisphere resulted in disrupted (oral) reading, which contradicted the discovery of hypoactivation of the left hemisphere in dyslexia (see Chapter 9, Fraga González, Jednoróg, and Brem 2022). This discrepancy may, however, be explained by the difference between acquired and developmental dyslexia and the low power of a single-case study.

Building on Coslett and Monsul's (1994) seminal work, the main focus of a later TMS study (Costanzo et al. 2013) involved upregulating the right hemisphere to induce compensatory mechanisms and normalizing the hypoactivation of the left hemisphere. A compensatory mechanism of the right hemisphere, which resulted in

Study	Design (type, current, durration, sample)	Montage	Task(s)	Outcome	Visualization of the stimulation sites
			Dyslexia		
Coslett & Monsul, 1994	TMS; within – subjects, 1 session, N=1 adult with acquired dyslexia	Left and right posterior temporal lobe	List of reading words aloud	Disrupted reading after right hemisphere stimulation	
Costanzo et al., 2013	rTMS; between-subjects, 5 Hz, 1 session, N=10 adults with dyslexia	Left and right IPL and the STG (over P3 and P4 & P5 and P6)	Reading word, nonword, and text aloud	Left IPL: less errors for nonword reading, Left STG: faster word reading and less errors for text reading, Right IPL: less errors for nonword reading	
Turkeltaub et al., 2012	tDCS; within-subjects, 1.5 mA, 2 sessions for 20 min, N=25 adults with no learning disability	Anode: left pTC (between T7 & TP7) Cathode: right pTC (between T8 & TP8)	Word and nonword reading tests	Left pTC: anodal stimulation improved word reading in below average readers	
Heth & Lavidor, 2015	tDCS; between-subjects, 1.5 mA, 5 sessions for 20 min over 2 weeks, N=19 adults with dyslexia	Anode: left V5/MT area Cathode: right orbitofrontal cortex	Oral reading test, Rapid automatized naming (RAN), and the symbol search subtest of the Wechsler Adult Intelligence test	Improved oral text reading, letter-naming, and number-naming speed up to one week	
Costanzo et al., 2016a	tDCS; between-subjects, 1 mA, 1 session for 20 min, N=19 children and adolescents with dyslexia	Left anodal/right cathodal parieto-temporal and right anodal/left cathodal parieto-temporal (between P7 and TP7 & between P8 and TP8)	Reading words aloud, non-words, and text, lexical decision, phoneme blending, verbal N-back, and rapid, automatized naming tasks	Left anodal tDCS induced an error reduction for reading, Right anodal tDCS increased errors for text reading accuracy	
Costanzo et al., 2016b	tDCS; between-subjects, 1 mA, 18 sessions for 20 min over 6 weeks, N=18 children and adolescents with dyslexia	Left anodal/right cathodal parieto-temporal (between P7 and TP7 & between P8 and TP8)	Reading tasks of text, high- and low-frequency words, and non-words	Lower error score for the low-frequency word reading, Shorter delay in non-word reading after left anodal tDCS, Present up to 1 month	
Rios et al., 2018	tDCS; between-subjects, 2 mA, 5 sessions for 30 min over 5 days, N=12 children and adolescents with dyslexia	Left anodal/right cathodal parieto-temporal (between T3 & T5 and FP2)	Identification and reading of letters, syllables, words, non-words, and text	Diminished error rate for non-word and reading tasks after stimulation	

Figure 20.1 *Overview of brain stimulation studies of dyslexia and dyscalculia.*

Costanzo et al., 2019	tDCS; between-subjects, 1 mA, 18 sessions for 20 min over 6 weeks, N=26 children and adolescents with dyslexia	Left anodal/right cathodal parieto-temporal (between P7 and TP7 & between P8 and TP8)	Reading tasks of text, high- and low-frequency words, and non-words	Non-word reading and low-frequency word reading improved, Present up to 6 months	
Rufener et al., 2019	tACS, within-subjects, 1 mA, 40 Hz, 1 session of 20 min, tRNS; 1.5 mA, 100-640 Hz, 1 session of 20 min, N=15 adolescents with dyslexia, N=15 adults with dyslexia	The bilateral auditory cortex (over T7 and T8)	Phoneme-categorization task	Improved acuity after tACS for adolescents and adults related to increased P50-N1-complex amplitudes, More pronounced effect of tRNS in adults	
Marchesotti et al., 2020	tACS: between/within-subjects, 2 mA, 30 Hz or 60 Hz, 1 session for 20 min, N=15 adults with dyslexia, N=15 healthy adults	Left auditory cortex (4x1 ring configuration, at TTP7h, FTT9h, FCC5h, CPP5h, TPP9h)	Pseudo-word repetition, spoonerism, and text reading	30 Hz tACS improved phonological processing and text reading accuracy	
Lazzaro et al., 2020	tDCS: between-subjects, 1 mA, 3 sessions per week over 6 weeks for 20 min, N=26 children and adolescents with dyslexia	Left anodal/right cathodal parieto-temporal (between P7 and TP7 & between P8 and TP8)	Reading training tasks of words and nonwords (word reading acceleration task and a spelling task)	Percentage of responders for word reading fluency was higher for active tDCS than for sham, Word reading fluency was improved as a function of baseline performance, age and IQ	

Dyscalculia

Cohen Kadosh et al., 2007	TMS; between/within-subjects, 10 Hz, 4 sessions over 2 days, N=5 healthy adults, N=5 adults with dyscalculia	Left and right IPS (fMRI-guided TMS Neuronavigation)	Numerical and physical comparison task	Disrupt right IPS: impaired automatic magnitude processing	
Cohen Kadosh et al., 2010	tDCS; between-subjects, 1 mA, 6 sessions over 6 days for 20 min, N=15 healthy adults	Left anodal and right cathodal parietal lobe (over P3 and P4)	Numerical Stroop task and a number-to-space task Learning task,	Right parietal lobe: anodal stimulation increased performance in both tasks and cathodal stimulation led to underperformance	
Iuculano & Cohen Kadosh, 2014	tDCS; between-subjects, 1 mA, 6 sessions over 7 days for 20 min, N=2 adults with dyscalculia	Left anodal/right cathodal parietal lobe and right anodal/left cathodal parietal lobe (over P3 and P4)	numerical Stroop task, and number line task	Left parietal lobe: only anodal stimulation improved performance	
Looi et al., 2017	tRNS; between-subjects, 0.75 mA, 9 sessions over 5 weeks for 20 min, N=12 children with MLD	Bilateral DLPFC (over F3 and F4)	Digit span task, the Corsi blocks task, number line task in video-game format, and a mathematical test (MALT)	tRNS improved accuracy and steeper learning rates for arithmetic performance, No effect on working memory	

Figure 20.1 *(Cont.)*

increased accuracy of reading non-words, was induced when the right inferior parietal lobule (IPL) was stimulated with repetitive transcranial magnetic stimulation (rTMS) at 5 Hz (Costanzo et al. 2013; see Figure 20.1). Repetitive transcranial magnetic stimulation was used to stimulate repetitively in different frequencies (e.g., 5 Hz and 60 Hz). It allowed the experimenters to vary the frequency, duration, and intensity of the stimulation and thus inhibit or excite a specific brain area under the coil. Additionally, when the left superior temporal gyrus (STG) was stimulated, the adults with dyslexia performed faster and more accurately on a reading task in which they had to read a text out loud. When the left and right IPL were stimulated, the participants showed increased accuracy in non-word reading. This finding also suggested a difference in function between the left IPL and the left STG because of the differential roles in word, non-word, and text reading. In short, the findings demonstrated that TMS may facilitate neural activity that was previously associated with hypoactivity in individuals with dyslexia, and that it may help to enhance reading performance. However, the studies discussed here did not combine TMS with an imaging method such as fMRI or EEG to shed more light on exactly how TMS modulated neural activity. Also, participants who underwent the rTMS protocol used by Costanzo et al. (2013) reported pain and uncomfortable sensations over the prefrontal cortex (Borckardt et al. 2013). Accordingly, this intervention may not be optimal for individuals with dyslexia, especially since more sessions would be needed to improve reading over the long term. Therefore, tES might offer a better solution because of its less undesirable side effects (Fertonani et al. 2015).

20.3.2 Dyscalculia

To the best of our knowledge, no published studies have explored the potential of TMS as a cognitive rehabilitation technique for children or adults with dyscalculia. That being said, the authors of one study were able to induce temporary virtual dyscalculia by applying fMRI-guided inhibitory TMS over the right IPS in a sample of five healthy adults (Cohen Kadosh et al. 2007; see Figure 20.1). The performance of the five healthy participants after TMS was compared with five individuals suffering from dyscalculia. Numerical performance was measured by a magnitude task in which the participants had to attend to 2 digits that varied in their physical size. They were instructed to focus on one dimension (e.g., numerical value or physical size) while ignoring the other dimension, and they had to decide which stimulus was numerically or physically larger. The healthy participants showed a similarly poor processing of magnitude as the developmental dyscalculia group after right IPS disruption. Since this resulted in similar impairments of quantitative and spatial magnitude processing, the finding supported the ATOM theory of dyscalculia (see Chapter 2, Menon and Chang 2022). Although Cohen Kadosh et al. (2007) did not focus on cognitive enhancement, their study corroborated the causal importance of the right parietal lobe for automatic magnitude processing. Future studies should explore the possibility of enhancing magnitude processing by applying TMS to the right IPS to increase cortical excitability. Furthermore, TMS might also contribute to the discovery of compensatory mechanisms, for example by upregulating frontal cortex activity (Cappelletti and Price 2014; Peters and De Smedt 2018).

20.4 Cognitive Rehabilitation for Learning Disorders by Means of Electrical Stimulation

We reviewed all existing tES studies (in chronological order) that have focused on cognitive rehabilitation for dyslexia and dyscalculia, or their underlying mechanisms. The national origin of the samples used in the research articles were as follows: United States (1), Israel (1), Italy (4), Brazil (1), Germany (1), Switzerland (1), and the United Kingdom (3). Children and adolescents between 8–17.8 years of age and adults between 18–50 years of age were included. Figure 20.1 again provides an overview of the studies: their design, montage, behavioural tasks, outcomes, and a visualization of the stimulation sites.

20.4.1 Dyslexia

As with the TMS studies discussed here, earlier tES studies investigated the hemisphere-specific effects of tES on reading accuracy and speed. For example, Turkeltaub et al. (2012) showed that 20 minute anodal tDCS of 1.5 mA over the left pTC improved word reading efficiency in slow readers (without a formal diagnosis of dyslexia; see Figure 20.1). During this study, the anodal electrode was placed over the left pTC and the cathodal electrode over the right pTC. Modelling the effects of tDCS revealed an increase in left pTC excitability and a decrease in right pTC excitability, which was related to word reading efficiency. There may therefore be a relationship between reading ability and pTC lateralization that could be explored in a sample of dyslexic individuals. It should be noted, however, that the improvements in reading were only shown directly after stimulation (i.e., the effects were short term), and subject blinding of the stimulation was not assessed.

Heth and Lavidor (2015) focused on the magnocellular deficit theory of dyslexia (see Chapter 1, Goswami 2022). They were the first to study the effects of tDCS on adults with dyslexia (see Figure 20.1). The authors based their design on the possible role of the middle temporal visual area V5 for attention during word recognition (Laycock et al. 2009). Stimulation was applied offline over the left V5 over five sessions and compared with sham stimulation in adults with dyslexia. The tDCS group and the sham group did not differ in vocabulary scores, intelligence, or baseline reading levels. Stimulation of 1.5 mA for 20 minutes over the left V5 improved both reading speed and fluency after one week. The authors mentioned that the results offered evidence in favour of the magnocellular deficit, but other theories such as the phonological deficit theory, the rapid auditory processing theory, and the cerebellar theory of dyslexia cannot be ruled out. The authors' findings were in keeping with a previous study which suggested that anodal tDCS over a targeted brain area can increase performance in semantic and phonemic fluency tasks when

Broca's area is targeted (Cattaneo et al. 2011), and picture naming when Wernicke is targeted (Fiori et al. 2011). However, up until then it was unclear whether the same protocol could be applied to developmental groups with dyslexia.

In a later study by Costanzo et al. (2016a) children and adolescents with dyslexia were included if they showed 1.5 SD scores below the mean for performance on reading tasks in terms of accuracy and speed. Twenty minutes of 1 mA anodal tDCS over the left parietotemporal area induced an error reduction (i.e., increased performance) for reading, but right anodal tDCS increased errors for text reading accuracy. Costanzo et al. (Costanzo et al. 2016a) also examined the effect of multi-session tDCS (18 sessions for 6 weeks) on children and adolescents with dyslexia using similar stimulation parameters. After left anodal tDCS, participants made fewer mistakes when reading low-frequency words and exhibited increased non-word reading fluency. These effects were still present 1 month after the end of the study. Similarly, another recent study using left anodal temporo-parietal tDCS of 2 mA for 30 minutes for 5 consecutive days revealed reduced error rates for (non-)word reading in children and adolescents with dyslexia (Rios et al. 2018). More evidence of long-term effects was provided by Costanzo et al. (2019), who combined left anodal tDCS with a training paradigm for reading. The beneficial effects of tDCS on reading in children and adolescents with dyslexia were still present up to six months after the study. This has recently been confirmed by a study from Lazzaro et al. (2020), who showed that left anodal/right cathodal tDCS over parietotemporal regions for six weeks improved word reading fluency in children and adolescents with dyslexia. This ameliorative effect corroborated the results of Costanzo et al. (Costanzo et al. 2019; Costanzo et al. 2016a; Costanzo et al. 2016b) and Turkeltaub et al. (2012). The authors stated that active tDCS over the parietotemporal regions accelerated letter-to-sound mapping and in turn positively influenced word reading fluency.

What set Lazzaro et al.'s (2020) study apart from previous studies (Costanzo et al. 2019; Costanzo et al. 2016a; Costanzo et al. 2016b), was that the authors assessed different reading stimuli and the impact of individual differences on the effect of stimulation. Namely, they combined low- and high-frequency stimuli that are frequently used in clinical settings. More interestingly, the authors showed that the effect of tDCS on word reading fluency depended on individual differences such as reading level at baseline, age, and IQ. Strong and long-lasting effects (i.e., six months after training) were found especially among slower readers with dyslexia, which indicated the importance of inter-individual variability in baseline performance.

While tDCS is the most frequently used tES technique for dyslexia, several studies have also investigated the effects of transcranial random noise stimulation (tRNS) and transcranial alternating current stimulation (tACS). The human brain is capable of entraining its endogenous oscillation signal at the spectro-temporal oscillation rate of speech to facilitate efficient communication (Buzsáki et al. 2012). Neural oscillations in the low gamma range (25–35 Hz) have been associated with the rate at which speech is normally sampled (Giraud and Poeppel 2012). Therefore, brain stimulation targeting this specific frequency range (around 40 Hz) might improve speech processing. Building on these findings, Rufener et al. (2019) showed that 20 minutes of 40 Hz tACS over bilateral auditory cortices improved phoneme categorization of children and adolescents with dyslexia. Similarly, high-frequency tRNS improved phoneme categorization performance in a sample of adults. In this study, participants were instructed to indicate via a button press if the presented stimulus contained the syllable /da/ or /ta/. The authors focused on disrupted auditory processing as a well-known deficit in dyslexia that can be captured by the P50-N1 complex of the auditory event-related potential (ERP). Increased amplitudes of the P50-N1-complex were related to more accurate phoneme categorization acuity for both tACS and tRNS.

It should be mentioned, however, that the anatomical specificity of the effect (i.e., the bilateral auditory cortex) remained unclear because an active control paradigm was lacking. Including an active control paradigm targeting an unrelated brain area would have enabled the authors to study site-specific effects. Nevertheless, a beneficial effect of low gamma tACS stimulation on phonological processing was also recently reported by Marchesotti et al. (2020). Twenty minutes of 30 Hz tACS over the left auditory cortex in adults with dyslexia boosted phonemic processing and reading accuracy. The authors suggested that this enhancement was due to restored left lateralization of 30 Hz activity in the left temporal cortex which underlies phonemic processing.

What can be concluded from the current literature is that tACS and tRNS are promising methods for restoring left-lateralized phonemic processing in dyslexia. Most of the available studies were limited in their specificity, however, since they did not include an active control condition.

20.4.2 Dyscalculia

To date, tES has rarely been used as a possible intervention for dyscalculia. Cohen Kadosh et al. (2010) combined a numerical learning paradigm with tDCS to investigate a causal link between parietal activity and numerical competencies in typical adults (see Figure 20.1). In this experiment, participants had to learn an association between nine arbitrary symbols with no known quantity relation over a period of six days. Twenty minutes of 1 mA tDCS was applied to either the left or right parietal lobe at the beginning of the learning paradigm. Number skills were measured after tDCS with a numerical Stroop task and a number-to-space task with the learnt symbols. During the numerical Stroop task, participants had to indicate which numeral out of two was physically larger in size. During the number-to-space task participants had to map a number on a physical line. Participants performed better when receiving right anodal/left cathodal parietal stimulation, whereas the opposite right cathodal/left anodal parietal stimulation led to underperformance on both numerical tasks. A later study by Iuculano and Cohen Kadosh (2014) employed a similar design: two adult subjects with dyscalculia had to associate artificial symbols with numerical quantities (see Figure 20.1). This was the first study to show the potential remediation effect of tES in dyscalculia for the improvement of both automatic number processing and mapping numbers in space. Interestingly, in contrast with Cohen Kadosh et al. (2010), Iuculano and Cohen Kadosh (2014) observed enhanced numerical learning when administering left anodal/right cathodal parietal stimulation (see Figure 20.1). The contrasting results indicated that tES can have different effects on typical and atypical populations. In particular, the typically developing individuals may have relied more heavily on a quantity system that is located in the right parietal area, while the atypical individuals may have used verbal compensation strategies to perform the task. More specifically, the effect of tES might have been dependent on the brain state (i.e., neural activation state) of the subject (Krause and Cohen Kadosh 2014).

Looi et al. (2017) focused on rehabilitation effects in children with dyscalculia. They applied 20 minutes of 0.75 mA tRNS over the dorsolateral prefrontal cortex to 12 children in 9 sessions over 5 weeks. Participants underwent the mathematical assessment for learning and teaching (MALT) and performed number line training in a video game format that integrated bodily movements by moving side to side. It turned out that children who received tRNS were more accurate and had steeper learning rates across the sessions for the number line training than the children who did not receive tRNS. Moreover, the children who received tDCS showed a positive transfer effect on mathematical assessment scores. It should be noted that this study contained a small sample size and was not double-blinded. Although the results should therefore be interpreted with caution, they suggest promising rehabilitation effects in a developing population with dyscalculia.

A later study in juvenile mice that used the same stimulation protocol, albeit without the number line training, found that this stimulation protocol was associated with a reduction of GAD 65/67 immunoreactivity levels in the region directly beneath the electrode. These results suggest an excitatory effect associated with a decrease in GABA levels (Sánchez-León et al. 2021).

20.5 Conclusion

Our review of the scarce literature suggests that TMS and tES might be useful for restoring left-hemispheric phonological processing in dyslexia and disrupted parietal quantity processing in dyscalculia. Nevertheless, a number of substantial limitations currently make it difficult to draw reliable conclusions from the available data. First, most of the studies conducted thus far have been based on small samples and therefore present a substantial power problem. Accordingly, the results reported herein should be interpreted as initial results that remain to be replicated under the guidance of a priori power calculations. Second, most of the studies have been based on a behavioural diagnosis of dyslexia or dyscalculia without taking neural deficits into account. We argue that it is important to investigate the effects of brain stimulation on different neural subtypes. This may reveal individual differences in response to the intervention (Krause and Cohen Kadosh 2014). In particular, recent studies have shown that tES efficacy depends on both behavioural and neural moderators in a healthy adult population (Lazzaro et al. 2020; Sheffield et al. 2022; van Bueren et al. 2022). Finally, little research in the field has focused on the developmental trajectory of the specific learning disorder. The coping mechanisms adopted by affected individuals to compensate for their behavioural deficits may have been undetected, so further longitudinal studies are needed to disentangle these from faulty processing.

A promising future line of research in the field would be to focus on personalized brain stimulation approaches. For example, Van Bueren et al. (2022) recently introduced a machine-learning-based technique that could help tailor interventions for individual ability profiles and thus allow more efficient searches for optimal stimulation parameters.

Suggestions for Further Reading

Finisguerra, A., R. Borgatti, and C. Urgesi. 2019. 'Non-Invasive Brain Stimulation for the Rehabilitation of Children and Adolescents With Neurodevelopmental Disorders: A Systematic Review'. *Frontiers in Psychology* 10 (February): 135.

Schroeder, P. A., T. Dresler, J. Bahnmueller, C. Artemenko, R. Cohen Kadosh, and H-C Nuerk. 2017. 'Cognitive Enhancement of Numerical and Arithmetic Capabilities: A Mini-Review of Available Transcranial Electric Stimulation Studies'. *Journal of Cognitive Enhancement* 1 (1), 39–47. https://doi.org/10.1007/s41465-016-0006-z.

Simonsmeier, B. A., R. H. Grabner, J. Hein, U. Krenz, and M. Schneider. 2018. 'Electrical Brain Stimulation (tES) Improves Learning More than Performance: A Meta-Analysis'. *Neuroscience and Biobehavioral Reviews* 84 (January): 171–81.

Van Bueren, N. E. R., Reed, T. L., Nguyen, V., Sheffield, J. G., van der Ven, S. H., Osborne, M. A., Kroesbergen, E. H, and Cohen Kadosh, R. 2021. Personalized brain stimulation for effective neurointervention across participants. *PLoS Computational Biology*, 17(9), e1008886. https://doi.org/10.1371/journal.pcbi.1008886.

21 Persistence and Fade-Out of Responses to Reading and Mathematical Interventions

H. Moriah Sokolowski and Lien Peters

21.1 Introduction

Education is a major pillar of contemporary society. Educating children provides them with stability, purpose, and financial security at an individual level and bolsters economic growth at a societal level (Hanushek and Kimko 2000; Jamison et al. 2007). Nonetheless, in the developing world, more than 200 million children under 5 years of age live in poverty, with poor nutrition, limited access to healthcare, and either inadequate or no education (Engle et al. 2007). Universal education provides a key pathway towards societal equality. UNICEF Canada suggests that education is 'a powerful tool for breaking the cycle of poverty; supporting child survival, growth, development and well-being; and closing the gap in social inequality' (Unicef Canada 2016).

For decades, researchers, educators, and policymakers have worked towards the goal of worldwide educational equality. Recently, it has been suggested that to reduce poverty and achieve societal equality, we must shift our focus from enhancing educational equality to increasing educational equity (Espinoza 2007; Mann 2014; Sokolowski and Ansari 2018). Equality in education refers to sharing resources and opportunities equally among students. Although this seems fair, different students require different resources to attain the same achievements. Equity in education refers to the redistribution of resources to reduce the inequality of particular outcome measures. It is educational equity that is needed to reduce achievement gaps, even if this means that students receive unequal resources (e.g., providing students who have fallen behind, such as children with learning difficulties, with access to additional educational resources). Enhancing educational equity is also beneficial to support children from similar backgrounds with different strengths, weaknesses, and educational needs (Sokolowski and Ansari 2018). In view of this, researchers are beginning to advocate for the development and implementation of policy changes that will improve equity within our education systems both nationally and internationally (Ainscow 2016; Education Equity Research Initiative 2017; Whitley and Hollweck 2020).

Early educational interventions have been recommended as a means to address the achievement gap and improve equity in our education systems (Heckman 2012). An educational intervention is a programme that is implemented with the goal of helping children by providing them with the additional support needed to acquire the skills being taught within the educational system. Typically, educational interventions are intended for children who find learning exceptionally challenging and consequently are falling behind their peers (i.e., children with learning difficulties). For more than fifty years, a wide range of educational intervention programmes have been implemented and tested. These programmes typically fall into one of two categories: (1) community-based intervention programmes, which are large-scale publicly funded programmes often aimed at reducing the impacts of poverty (e.g., Campbell et al. 2002; Mughal et al. 2016), or (2) skill-based interventions focusing on either general cognitive skills (for review, see Simons et al. 2016) or specific subjects (e.g., Kroeger and Brown 2018; Lovett et al. 2014; Park et al. 2014; Supekar et al. 2013; see also Chapter 11, Yeatman 2022; Chapter 12, Iuculano 2022; Chapter 19, Galuschka and Schulte-Körne 2022; Chapter 20, van Bueren, Kroesbergen, and Cohen Kadosh 2022). The majority of subject-specific, skill-based educational intervention programmes focus on reading and maths, as these subjects are basic building blocks for higher-level concepts and are predictive of later life outcomes (Duncan et al. 2007). Additionally, reading and maths are key academic domains in which children with learning difficulties exhibit challenges (American Psychiatric Association 2013). Despite the wide use of educational interventions, their effectiveness continues to be debated (Bailey et al. 2017; Barnett 2011; Nores and Barnett 2010; Simons et al. 2016).

In this chapter, we discuss how the effectiveness of educational interventions is evaluated and concurrently review a subset of educational interventions aimed at remediating or supporting reading and mathematics, with a focus on children with learning difficulties. Following this, we consider, from methodological and biological perspectives, whether we should expect educational interventions to be effective, and why positive effects immediately following an intervention often fade-out over time. We conclude with a discussion on how to foster long-term change, and provide recommendations on how to improve the methodology of studies assessing the effectiveness of educational interventions.

Here, we review data from educational interventions and biological research based on a wide range of nationalities and educational backgrounds. We focus on specific interventions from the USA, Canada, and Sweden, as well as large-scale reviews and meta-analyses reporting data from many countries (e.g., 62 countries over 10-year intervals: Jamison et al. 2007; 23 non-US countries: Nores and Barnett 2010). Most of the studies discussed include samples with elementary-school-aged children. The biological (behavioural genetic) research presented is based on large samples from the USA, the United Kingdom, Australia, New Zealand, Scotland, China, and, in one case, on an extended cohort of individuals of European descent.

21.2 Evaluating the Effectiveness of Educational Interventions

The effectiveness of educational interventions is typically evaluated through children's scores on educational outcome measures (e.g., achievements on standardized tests of reading and math). Researchers typically evaluate whether the average scores of a group of children improve immediately following an intervention. In general, when using this group metric to evaluate the effectiveness of educational interventions, results reveal that children exhibit substantive improvements in a range of educational outcome measures, but particularly in cognitive outcomes (Camilli et al. 2010).

Overall, most published interventions aimed at remediating children with learning difficulties in reading or maths report improvement following completion of a targeted intervention programme (see, e.g., Bus and van IJzendoorn 1999; Ehri et al. 2001; Goodwin and Ahn 2010; Solis et al. 2012). In the reading domain, intervention programmes that focus on promoting phonological awareness and phonics, or a combination of phonological processing and other skills associated with reading (e.g., reading comprehension or morphological skills), lead to improvements in reading abilities in struggling readers (e.g., Bus and van IJzendoorn 1999; Ehri et al. 2001; Goodwin and Ahn 2010; Solis et al. 2012). Similarly, in the mathematical domain, intervention programmes that focus on explicit instruction and encourage children to explain their mathematical reasoning (i.e., verbalizing strategies) have been linked to improvements in mathematical abilities in struggling learners (e.g., Gersten et al. 2009; Stevens et al. 2018). Across the domains of learning, programmes implemented in small groups of children, as compared to larger groups, seem to lead to the greatest remediation of learning difficulties (e.g., Monei and Pedro 2017).

There are substantial differences between studies that evaluate educational interventions. More specifically, there is wide variation in the characterization of participant samples that is driven by differences in the strictness of the criteria used to categorize students as having a learning difficulty and the age groups included in the intervention study (for an in-depth discussion, see Peters and Ansari 2019). Additionally, the content and duration of intervention programmes themselves differs greatly between studies (e.g., Stevens et al. 2018). These striking differences between studies that evaluate the effectiveness of educational interventions likely contribute to the large differences in reported effect sizes of the intervention gains between studies. Additionally, due to publication bias (i.e., a type of bias in academic research that occurs when the outcome of the research influences whether a study gets published), research revealing very minimal or no effects directly following educational interventions is less likely to be published (Franco et al. 2014). Consequently, studies with minimal or no effects are less likely to be included in meta-analyses, which could skew the overall effects of interventions, making them appear stronger and more positive than they actually are. These methodological challenges complicate the summarizing and synthesizing of findings from research exploring the effects of educational interventions.

Improvements following interventions are typically reported when assessments occur immediately or shortly after an intervention is completed (see, e.g., Gersten et al. 2009; Solis et al. 2012; Stevens et al. 2018). However, in order to characterize an intervention as 'effective', improvements following an educational intervention should persist over time, thereby driving long-lasting change. The few studies that have assessed the persistence of the effects of educational interventions suggest that

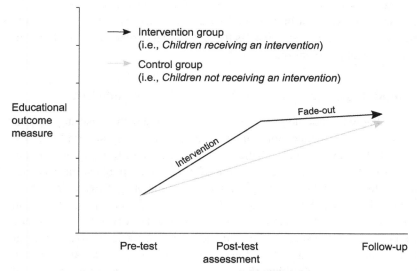

Figure 21.1 *Schematic illustration of fade-out following an intervention. This graph depicts one possible trajectory of fade-out following an intervention, but there are many alternative trajectories that would also be considered fade-out. This figure was inspired by Figure 1 in (Bailey et al. 2020).*

the improvements seen following educational interventions tend to 'fade-out' over time (for reviews, see Bailey et al. 2017; Bailey et al. 2020; Sokolowski and Ansari 2018). A schematic depiction of a 'fade-out effect' is shown in Figure 21.1. For example, a one-year follow-up of an intervention that improved reading in struggling readers revealed that growth in reading achievement stabilized for some measures (e.g., passage comprehension) but reduced for other measures (e.g., word reading; Lovett et al. 2012). Fade-out has also been reported for long-term follow-up effects following interventions aimed at improving children's maths skills (Bailey et al. 2016). Specifically, the considerable treatment effect of a well-known maths intervention called the Building Blocks mathematics curriculum (reported in Clements et al. 2013) diminished over time. Children who did not participate in the intervention eventually performed at the same level as children who received the intervention (Bailey et al. 2016). Taken together, the above-reviewed literature suggests that many educational interventions lead to immediate improvements in children's academic abilities. However, we cannot conclude that educational interventions 'work', as positive effects following educational interventions exhibited by some (but not all) children typically diminish or even disappear over time.

21.3 Why Do We See Fade-out?

Why do the initial treatment effects of educational interventions fade-out over time? Explanations for fade-out range from non-substantive methodological explanations suggesting that fade-out is a result of methodological issues, to substantive explanations based in biology and specifically neuroscience, psychology, and genetics. Here, we review and discuss these potential explanations for fade-out following educational interventions.

21.3.1 Methodological and Statistical Explanations of Fade-out

There are a number of methodological challenges associated with measuring patterns of fade-out in response to educational interventions (for review, see Bailey 2019; Bailey et al. 2020). Some of these challenges include scaling test scores, tracking effect sizes across time, misleading reporting of effect sizes, publication bias, and unwarranted differences between groups either at baseline or post-treatment. These challenges have led researchers to suggest that fade-out effects may simply be an artefact of measurement rather than a substantive finding. However, leading experts in the field report that these statistical explanations are not sufficient to account for reports of fade-out (Bailey et al. 2020). Specifically, these authors explain that such methodological explanations are insufficient to explain the finding that the rate of fade-out in the first year following an intervention is considerably more rapid than typical fluctuations in ability observed across developmental time. Moreover, they argue that fade-out is unlikely to be simply a methodological artefact because fade-out effects are observed across a variety of measurements, including some that are not vulnerable to such methodological issues, such as different cognitive constructs, methods of scaling, and age groups (e.g., Bailey et al. 2020; Roberts et al. 2016). Bailey and colleagues (2020) also challenge the notion that fade-out effects are simply artefacts of publication bias by highlighting that some observed instances of fade-out emerge in conditions that make publication bias unlikely, such as from randomized control trials with prespecified outcome measures (e.g., Clements et al. 2013) and retrospective quasi-experimental studies for which the entire dataset had been collected prior to analysis (e.g., Deming 2009). Finally, it has been suggested that fade-out is a consequence of overly strong correspondence between the treatment and initial short-term outcome measures (often referred to as 'teaching to test', as in Protzko 2016). However, over-alignment is unlikely, as fade-out has been observed for a wide range of outcome measures, both specific and broad (Bailey et al. 2020). Although these methodological explanations of fade-out effects certainly deserve consideration and discussion, it is clear that they cannot fully account for the fade-out effects. Indeed, these methodological constraints are not present in all cases in which fade-out effects post-intervention have been reported.

21.3.2 Psychological and Biological Explanations of Fade-Out

As the methodological issues described cannot fully explain the finding of fade-out across a wide range of educational interventions, we turn to research from the biological sciences. The importance of the biological sciences for understanding human development has been highlighted for decades (Bjorklund and Pellegrini 2000; Geary et al. 2014; Scarr and McCartney 1983). In this section, we review findings from neuroscience, psychology, and genetics to uncover why the effects of early educational interventions fade-out over time.

Neurobiology of forgetting. An area of biological research that can provide insights into why treatment effects following educational interventions fade-out over time is research into the neuroscience of memory, and specifically research on forgetting. Forgetting is an all-encompassing term that refers to the loss or modification of information that has been stored in an individual's memory system. More than a century ago, early investigations into the rate of forgetting lead to the derivation of a 'forgetting curve' (Ebbinghaus 1885). The shape of forgetting curves resembles the curve of fade-out effects following educational interventions, making the neurobiology of memory an important area of research in addressing fade-out effects (Bailey et al. 2020; Kang et al. 2019).

The development of high-level memory systems, and particularly memory for events (i.e., episodic memory), is greatly protracted in children. This developmental period is referred to as childhood (or infantile) amnesia (Alberini and Travaglia 2017; Freud 1924; Miles 1895; Newcombe et al. 2007). While there are several social and cognitive psychological theories arguing that childhood amnesia is a consequence of underdeveloped language abilities, social interactions, or self-identity (Fivush and Nelson 2004; Nelson and Fivush 2004), the most compelling explanation for childhood amnesia comes from biology. The biological account of childhood amnesia is that children have greater rates of forgetting than adults because the biological mechanisms, and particularly the hippocampal memory system needed to store memories, are not mature enough to store memories in a way that can be recalled later (Bauer 2006; Newcombe et al. 2007). Broadly, childhood amnesia is thought to reflect a critical developmental period during which the memory system is 'learning how to learn and remember' (Alberini and Travaglia 2017, p. 1). More specifically, the developing brain exhibits heightened growth and development of nervous tissue within the hippocampus during this period of childhood amnesia, relative to later childhood and adulthood. This process is referred to as hippocampal neurogenesis. It has been suggested that this enhanced hippocampal neurogenesis in childhood drives a continuous remodelling of the brain systems that support memory, thereby disrupting children's ability to remember (Akers et al. 2014; Frankland et al. 2013; Josselyn and Frankland 2012; Richards and Frankland 2017). Although it may seem maladaptive for children to have high rates of forgetting, infants and young children are born into chaotic, complex environments from which they must extract meaningful information to make sense of their new world. Therefore, forgetting details that are not needed for building knowledge structures may in fact be biologically adaptive for children as it might enhance openness and cognitive flexibility when facing novel situations (Richards and Frankland 2017).

Forgetting is a compelling explanation for fade-out effects. Moreover, the one study to date that examined the role of forgetting in fade-out revealed that children who received a pre-K maths intervention were more likely to answer a maths question incorrectly than children who did not receive the intervention, despite having previously answered correctly (Kang et al. 2019). This study provides some support for the idea that forgetting explains fade-out. However, this difference between the groups only explained 25% of the fade-out effect observed in this sample. Additionally, forgetting does not explain the common finding that fade-out effects are often a consequence of children who did not receive an intervention catching-up to the children who did receive the intervention (Bailey et al. 2016). Therefore, we conclude that forgetting may be one of *several* key neurobiological mechanisms that explains fade-out effects following educational interventions.

State–trait framework. The field of psychology has long made the distinction between the effect of state compared to trait variables (e.g., Steyer et al. 1989). A state variable represents a temporary way of being, while a trait variable is a characteristic or pattern of behaviour that tends to be more stable and enduring. Individual differences in trait abilities are biologically based and reliable across the lifespan of the individual (Andellini et al. 2015; Seitzman et al. 2019), whereas differences in state variables depend on the context. This state–trait framework has been applied to theories of learning and fade-out to consider the degree to which prior knowledge (i.e., states), compared to stable characteristics such as IQ or working memory skills (i.e., traits), influence learning over time (Bailey et al. 2014). Bailey and colleagues (2014) compared the relative influence of trait effects (i.e., stable characteristics associated with learning across time, such as attention and processing speed) and state effects (e.g., prior knowledge) on children's mathematics achievement over time. They discovered that latent trait effects have a substantially larger effect on children's mathematical development than state effects. A related study also supports the idea that stable pre-existing individual differences in children and the environment in which they are raised (i.e., trait effects) explain fade-out effects better than the mathematical content learnt in school (i.e., state effects; Bailey et al. 2016). Together, these findings suggest that state effects have a relatively smaller influence than trait effects on later maths achievement, thereby providing insights into why the brief treatment effects following educational interventions diminish over time.

Heritability of educational attainment. Understanding the biological underpinnings of these pre-existing stable individual differences holds promise for uncovering why effects of educational interventions fade-out over time. A long standing, now defunct argument between and within fields that study human behaviour is the nature–nurture debate (e.g., Hollingworth 1926; Leahy 1961; Pastore 1949). The nature perspective of this debate argued that genes drive variations in behaviour, while the nurture perspective argued that humans are blank slates, with variations in behaviour being purely a consequence of experiences. The fields of education and psychology have traditionally been strongly biased towards the 'nurture' side of this debate and consequently have been hesitant to consider 'nature' or genetics. This bias may be a consequence of the common and persistent misconception that considering biological factors associated with behaviour implies that behaviour is determined. It is often assumed that the term 'heritability' means 'genetic inheritance'. However, heritability is a population measure that refers to the amount of variability of a trait in a population that arises from genetic variation, not a causal process within a single individual. Counterintuitively, as heritability is calculated by examining whether variance associated with a behaviour within a population can be explained by genetic variability (compared to environmental variability), a higher estimate of heritability inherently means a more equal environment (Moore and Shenk 2017). Educational achievement, including measures of numeracy and literacy, are highly heritable, particularly in countries with more equitable education systems (Kovas et al. 2013; Krapohl et al. 2014; Shakeshaft et al. 2013; Tucker-Drob and Bates 2016). This replicable finding – that educational attainment has high heritability – has led researchers to consider whether variability within the human genome relates to educational outcome measures (Belsky et al. 2016; Chen et al. 2017; David Hill et al. 2016; Luciano et al. 2013; Rietveld et al. 2013; Sniekers et al. 2017). Genome-wide association studies (GWAS) have been used to examine millions of linked genetic-variants samples from hundreds of thousands of individuals to identify genetic variants that correlate with particular outcome measures (for a concise description of GWAS, see Anreiter et al. 2018; see also Chapter 6, Malanchini and Gidziela 2022). While GWAS has primarily been used to identify individuals with genetic risks for developing complex diseases (Visscher et al. 2012), it has also been used to link genetic variants to educational attainment measures, including years of schooling (e.g., Okbay et al. 2016), intelligence (e.g., Marioni et al. 2014), reading (e.g., Luciano et al. 2013), and maths ability (e.g., Chen et al. 2017). Recently, it was reported that parents' genetic variants that are *not* passed on to the child (i.e., non-transmitted genetic variants) account for variance (approximately 30%) in their children's educational achievement, a phenomenon referred to as 'genetic nurture' (Kong et al. 2018). Together, these results highlight that genetic variability is associated with variability in educational achievement. This can be taken to suggest that children's academic abilities are not entirely attributable to their environments, as biological factors are tightly linked to individual differences in academic achievement. Additionally, children's environments themselves might be influenced by their parents' genetics. Exposure to a brief environments such as a short-term educational intervention hence occurs within the context of a life-long set of experiences, and is one of many factors influencing behaviour, including biological factors. In other words, biological factors and constant environmental exposures continue to influence a child even after an intervention concludes. This idea is helpful for understanding why a short-term experience such as an educational intervention may not produce a long-lasting effect.

Gene–environment interplay. When considering the link between genetics and educational attainment, it is critical to remember that genes do *not* operate independently from environmental influences. For decades, scientists have noted that while these two concepts may seem like independent components that uniquely affect behaviour, neither genetics nor the environment alone, or even the additive effect of genes plus environments (G+E), can sufficiently explain individual differences in complex behaviours. Individual differences in behaviour across development emerge as a consequence of a complex, dynamic interplay between genetic predispositions and environmental exposure (gene–environment interplay) (Anreiter et al. 2018; Boyce et al. 2012; Boyce et al. 2020; Rutter et al. 2006; Sokolowski and Wahlsten 2001). From the perspective of education, this means that each child enters an educational intervention with a unique genetic make-up that has been in constant interplay with their ongoing experiences since the child was in the prenatal environment. Consequently, children have different strengths, weaknesses, tolerances to stressors, and preferences for particular academic subjects.

Consideration of the different components of gene–environment interplay, such as gene–environment correlations (G-E correlations) and gene–environment interactions (GxE), holds promise for understanding why results reveal that stable individual differences diminish initial treatment effects following educational interventions (Scarr and McCartney 1983). G-E correlations and GxE are population-based statistical measures, but the idea behind the relationship can be discussed here for illustrative purposes by comparing two children: Child A and Child B.

An individual's genetic make-up and environment correlate across the life span, with passive, evocative, and active G-E correlations being more prevalent at particular points in development. Passive G-E correlations refer to a child's genotype correlating with the environment created by parents with similar genotypes, and is most prevalent in infancy. For example, if Child A has parents with a genetic predisposition to enjoy reading, Child A is more likely to have that same genetic predisposition, and also to be read to more often by her parents. Evocative G-E correlations are an individual's genetics evoking particular responses from the environment and are most prevalent in early childhood. For instance, Child A, who is predisposed to enjoy reading, might be unusually excited to be read to, thereby encouraging adults to want to read to them more often. Finally, active G-E correlations refer to the idea that individuals select environmental niches that relate to their genetic propensities, and is most common in later childhood and adolescence, once a child is older and able to select their own environment. An example of this is Child A, with their genetic predisposition to enjoy reading, choosing to read during free time. The way in which G-E correlations change across time from passive to active might, in part, explain why the effects of educational interventions fade-out over time (Sokolowski and Ansari 2018). Specifically, environmental inputs, such as educational interventions, might have greater influence on behaviour for young children, who are more likely to experience passive than active G-E correlations, resulting in short-term gains immediately following an educational intervention. However, as children get older and are presented with the opportunity to select their own environments, they are likely to select environments that align more closely with their genotypes. This shift possibly results in children selecting environments that are associated with their intrinsic strengths, which are not necessarily the skills targeted in the educational intervention, thus leading to fade-out. In other words, the shift from passive to active G-E correlations across development may be useful in understanding why children's improvements following educational interventions fade-out over time (for more details, see Sokolowski and Ansari 2018). While this idea is in its infancy, correlations between genetics and environments have already been reported for broad educational outcome measures (e.g., Belsky et al. 2016). Future research is needed to assess the prediction that G-E correlations across developmental time help explain fade-out effects following educational interventions.

The relationship between genetics and environment goes beyond individuals having a set of genes and a set of experiences that correlate. In addition to an individual's genetic make-up correlating with their environment, genetic predispositions interact with environmental exposure to affect behavioural outcomes (for reviews, see Meaney 2010; Rutter 2010; Sokolowski and Wahlsten 2001). An example of a GxE interaction requires comparing Child A, the child with a genetic predisposition to enjoy reading, to Child B, a child who has a genetic predisposition to dislike reading. If Child A and Child B are reared in an environment where they both have access to countless books and reading opportunities (i.e., an enriched reading environment), we might predict that Child A will be a stronger reader than Child B. However, if both Child A and Child B are raised in an environment with no access to books or reading opportunities (i.e., an impoverished reading environment), the difference in their reading abilities would be considerably smaller, perhaps even non-existent. While this is a simplified, hypothetical example of a GxE interaction (a population-based statistical measure), research has revealed that a wide variety of genetic predispositions interact with environmental factors to predict behavioural outcome measures, including measures that are relevant to education (Anreiter et al. 2018). Notably, there are many other aspects of gene–environment interplay, beyond G-E correlations and GxE interactions, that may be relevant for understanding the effects of educational interventions. For example, in addition to genes predisposing individuals to respond to certain environments, experience can also become embedded in our biology through a mechanism that is referred to as epigenetics (Boyce and Kobor 2015; Meaney 2010; Moore 2017; Rutter et al. 2006). However, these additional examples of gene–environment interplay are beyond the scope of this chapter as it remains too early to make direct predictions of what biological mechanisms specifically are driving fade-out effects.

Gene–environment interplay is a dynamic, ongoing process across the entire lifespan, not a static event. Behavioural and neural development has temporal constraints, often referred to as 'critical' or 'sensitive' periods (Hensch 2004). During a critical period, an organism becomes more sensitive to specific experiences. Critical periods have primarily been documented for low-level processing such as visual perception (Morishita and Hensch 2008), but some data suggests they exist for complex aspects of behaviour such as learning language as well (Werker and Hensch 2014). This idea of critical periods is important as it shows that experience influences individuals differently depending on when the experience occurs during development. Therefore, an educational intervention might be more or less effective depending on the developmental stage a child is in when the intervention is administered. Critical periods are regulated by gene–environment interplay, with molecular events regulating the timing of when critical periods open and close within an individual (Boyce et al. 2020). Considerations of critical periods in development as an important component of gene–environment interplay highlight, from a biological perspective, why identifying optimal timing for implementing an intervention is likely crucial for instigating long-term change.

Understanding how something as multifaceted as gene–environment interplay relates to the equally complex construct of fade-out of educational interventions is a major undertaking. However, we know that children enter formal schooling and educational interventions with their genes having interacted with countless experiences throughout prenatal and postnatal life. An intervention is one type of experience typically implemented during a small, potentially inopportune window of time during development. It should come as no surprise that the long-term effectiveness of such interventions may be influenced by biology during development. Therefore, we believe that future research on how genetic prepositions interact with children's early experiences before, during, and after an educational intervention will be fruitful for uncovering why the effects of educational interventions tend to fade-out over time.

21.4 How Can We Foster Long-Term Change?

The effects of educational interventions which aim to strengthen children's academic skills in general and remediate those with learning disorders (LDs) tend to fade-out over time. In other words, educational interventions typically do not lead to long-term change. Herein, we leveraged theory and empirical data from the biological sciences to understand why fade-out occurs following educational interventions. We argue that fade-out following interventions is expected. This leads us to two questions: How can fade-out after intervention be mitigated? And how can educational interventions and curricula be designed to promote long-lasting effects?

As discussed, children differ in their genetic predispositions, life-long experiences, and, consequently, profiles of academic strengths and weaknesses. The dynamic interplay between the child's biological predispositions and a lifetime of experiences influences how children respond to new experiences, such as educational interventions (Anreiter et al. 2018; Boyce et al. 2020). Indeed, certain students may respond more strongly than others to an intervention programme (for a comprehensive discussion of individual differences in response to and following interventions, see Sokolowski and Ansari 2018). Consequently, investigations of individual responses rather than average responses of a group of individuals to an intervention are critical.

Children with and without LD diagnoses exhibit substantial variation in educational outcomes measures. Groups of children with the same LD diagnosis are substantially heterogeneous, both with respect to their specific difficulties and range of academic skills (for a review, see Peters and Ansari 2019). In view of this, a 'one size fits all' approach to remedial teaching or educational interventions might not be the most effective: What works for one child might not be effective for another. Instead, individualized intervention programmes hold promise for supporting each unique learner. Partanen et al. (2019), for example, designed and implemented individually tailored reading interventions to children with reading difficulties. Specifically, children's profiles of strengths and weaknesses were carefully mapped, and individual remedial programmes were designed to target weakness of each individual child. Results revealed that children who received such an individualized intervention improved in subcomponents of reading ability, and that these improvements were maintained in a follow-up assessment one year later.

Similarly, as documented by Gustafson et al. (2007), children with reading challenges who exhibited relatively more weaknesses in either orthography or phonology showed greater improvements after receiving an intervention that targeted their specific weakness. Specifically, children with orthography impairments improved more from an orthographic intervention, whereas children with phonology impairments improved more from a phonographic intervention. Together, these data suggest that interventions that are tailored to the individual's needs rather than general, 'one size fits all' remedial programmes might be more effective, particularly in the long term.

Although interventions tailored to individual students' needs might be more effective than non-tailored educational interventions, they are more time-consuming and costly to design than a standard intervention programme that is applied to all students who struggle with a learning difficulty. Such traditional educational interventions (i.e., not tailored to individual student needs) often focus on a single subcomponent of an academic skill (e.g., reading skills are often enhanced through training on phonological awareness; see, e.g., Bus and van IJzendoorn 1999). The multiple deficit model of learning disorders (Pennington 2006), however, posits that academic difficulties cannot be traced back to a single cognitive deficit, such as a phonological awareness deficit in poor readers (Wagner and Torgesen 1987). Rather, multiple interacting factors lie at the basis of learning difficulties (i.e., a combination of multiple cognitive skills, including phonological awareness, play a role in reading achievement). Therefore, educational interventions that focus on multiple components of an academic skill (e.g., interventions that comprise phonology *and* reading comprehension training) might be more effective compared to programmes that hone in on only one specific subcomponent of a skill (e.g., phonology only; see Gustafson et al. 2011; Lovett et al. 2000; Morris et al. 2012; see also Chapter 19, Galuschka and Schulte-Körne 2022).

Optimizing the content of an educational intervention is unquestionably important for the success of that intervention. However, findings from biological research indicate that the timing of interventions is also a key contributor to an intervention's success. For instance, interventions are more effective when the recipients of the intervention are younger children, rather than older children (see, e.g., Stevens et al. 2018). Biological explanations for this phenomenon include that the developing brain has greater plasticity than the adult brain and undergoes critical or sensitive periods, as discussed earlier. In view of this, it may be possible to leverage understanding of the timing of critical or sensitive periods in brain plasticity to enhance the effectiveness of educational interventions. More specifically, aligning targeted interventions within the opening and closing of critical periods for specific skills holds promise to increase the long-term effectiveness of educational interventions. In addition to considering biological timing, we must also consider timing within educational systems and society in general. Indeed, there are specific time periods during which the performance of a child may be more or less likely to enhance or diminish subsequent academic opportunities. For example, the opportunity to enter specific schools and programmes or to access additional resources may be dependent on a child's performance on a particular test at a specific time point. Timing educational interventions to align with such key moments might provide children with more access to enriched environments or additional support, thereby enhancing educational equity (see, e.g., Bailey et al. 2020). Notably, ensuring optimal timing of an educational intervention still does not guarantee that the effects of that specific intervention will be long lasting. However, it might bolster the chance that children will benefit from societally implemented opportunities, environments, and/or support programmes.

We predict that optimizing both the subject matter and the timing of specific interventions may not be enough to ensure long-term intervention gains. Findings of educational interventions not producing long-term change should not come as a surprise. Results of physical diets intended to help overweight individuals lose weight consistently indicate that weight lost is gained back quickly if the individual does not change his or her lifestyle following an initially effective diet. In line with this, perhaps researchers, educators, policymakers, and parents should actually expect the gains of an educational intervention to diminish quickly if students return to 'business as usual' following the implementation of an intervention programme. The 'sustaining environment hypothesis' suggests that the long-term success of educational interventions is dependent on the quality of the succeeding learning environment (Bailey et al. 2017; Bailey et al. 2020). A recent study explicitly tested this hypothesis by assessing students' maths and language achievements three years after they had completed a successful Pre-K intervention programme (Pearman et al. 2020). The results of this study showed that *either* attending a high-quality school *or* having highly effective teachers after the intervention programme was not sufficient to foster long-term change. However, the combination of both attending a high-quality school *and* having highly effective teachers was associated with a persistent positive advantage for students who had completed the Pre-K programme (Pearman et al. 2020). This suggests that after an intervention, there is a cumulative advantage for children who were provided with an enriched educational environment (i.e., high-quality school and teachers). Indeed, large-scale educational intervention programmes that appear to have a lasting positive impact on participants' later-life outcomes, such as the Abecedarian Project (see, e.g., Campbell et al. 2014), actively involved teachers and parents during the intervention, and encouraged educators and parents to continue to foster children's learning and development even after the programme had concluded (Campbell and Ramey 1994). In view of this, we argue that a high-quality environment after the completion of a programme is critical to sustain gains and foster long-term change post-intervention. Figure 21.2 illustrates predicted trajectories for relevant educational outcome measures following an intervention if (1) the intervention is tailored to promote long-term change, as discussed earlier, and (2) if the quality of the subsequent educational environment is enriched as recommended by the sustaining environment hypothesis. As a first step towards increasing the long-term effectiveness of educational interventions, it is pivotal to ensure that teachers and educators are continually educated on how to enrich their students' educational environment, for both typically developing children and children with LDs.

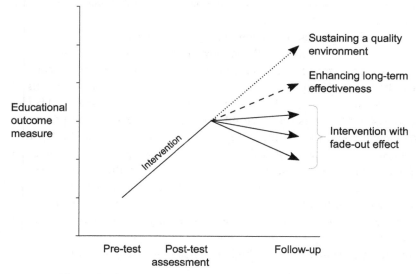

Figure 21.2 *Schematic illustration of examples of fade-out following an intervention (solid black lines), as well as predicted trajectories of relevant educational outcome measures following an intervention when the intervention is designed with the goal of invoking long-term change (dashed line), and sustaining a quality environment (dotted line).*

To adequately evaluate the long-term effects of interventions and remediation programmes, the methodology and evaluation metrics used in research can and should be optimized. Too often, research studies assess only the short-term efficiency of intervention programmes (i.e., assessments occur for only a few months following an intervention program; see, e.g., Gustafson et al. 2007; Solis et al. 2012; Stevens et al. 2018). Research uncovering how to foster long-term change should include multiple assessment time-points post-intervention, in order to evaluate both short-term and long-term effects. Long-term assessments in particular are necessary to identify when and whether effects of individual intervention programmes are maintained. There are obvious logistic and financial difficulties associated with studies with multiple assessment time-points. However, the possible gain in our understanding of the long-term effectiveness of programmes that are often expensive and government-funded would have a high rate of return (as shown with economic assessments of investing in early childhood development; Heckman 2012). When setting up longitudinal studies with multiple time-points that extend over multiple years, it is important to consider the inevitable high rates of attrition; students will drop out of the study over time. It is therefore pivotal to recruit a very large sample of children pre-intervention. Psychological and educational research is often statistically underpowered due to small sample sizes (VanVoorhis et al. 2007), leading to unreliable results that do not necessarily generalize over studies or replicate in new studies. It is only once we have optimized the empirical methodology needed to evaluate the long-term effectiveness of educational interventions that we can make progress in fostering long-term change.

Although an in-depth discussion of community-based interventions is beyond the scope of this chapter, it is worth briefly acknowledging the success of large-scale, community-based programmes. Enriching a child's environment is crucial, particularly for children growing up in adverse environments. Research on the effects of socioeconomic status, poverty, and stress on children's cognitive, social, and health outcomes consistently reveals that early-life adversity has detrimental effects on child development (Bunea et al. 2017; Lopez´ et al. 2021; Luby et al. 2020). It is therefore not surprising that large-scale, community-based programmes aimed at reducing poverty and providing support and resources for families with low socioeconomic status (e.g., free lunch programmes) have long-lasting, positive effects on children's academic skills and life outcomes (see, e.g., Gordanier et al. 2020). Therefore, we underscore that implementing community-based interventions that reduce the impact of poverty and stress in a child's environment is a fundamental step towards enhancing educational equity, both nationally and internationally.

21.5 Conclusion

Academic interventions programmes aim to help improve academic abilities for all children, remediate learning difficulties in some children, and improve equity in our education systems. Given the impact of early maths and reading skills on later life outcomes (Duncan et al. 2007), supporting all children to attain a sufficient level of academic proficiency to succeed in the workforce is pivotal in our increasingly technological society. Nonetheless, effects of intervention programmes designed to boost children's academic skills do not impact all children equally, and the treatment effects exhibited by some children immediately after interventions tend to fade-out over time. In other words, skill-based educational interventions lack persistent impact. In the previous sections we considered why the effects of educational interventions seem to fade-out over time and how to overcome these fade-out effects and foster long-term change. We reject the idea that fade-out is solely a consequence of non-substantive methodological artefacts and instead draw on biological research to argue that fade-out effects might be a natural consequence of biological mechanisms that constrain development. In terms of how to foster long-term change, we suggest tailoring the content and timing to individual student needs, and enhancing the quality of the subsequent learning environment following an educational intervention (as recommended by the sustaining environments hypothesis). Critically, more research with long-term follow-up assessments is needed to investigate the effects of implementing these suggestions.

Research is continuing to unveil more about the complexity and heterogeneity of academic learning difficulties in children (see, e.g., Peters and Ansari 2019). These individual differences in children are driven by the dynamic interplay between each child's genetic predisposition and their environmental history (Anreiter et al. 2018; Thomas Boyce et al. 2020; Rutter et al. 2006; Sokolowski and Ansari 2018).

Although the goal of education continues to be to increase equity and to support the development of academic skills in both typical and struggling learners, it is simultaneously important to acknowledge that there are substantial individual differences between children. Indeed, while educational attainment scores immediately following an intervention improve across children (i.e., on average), interventions do not eliminate individual differences in educational attainment measures in a population (Sokolowski and Ansari 2018). Relatedly, there are individual differences in the degree to which children respond to educational interventions (e.g., Fuchs et al. 2006; Torgesen 2000). These differences will remain even after effective and potentially long-lasting effects of intervention programmes. Struggling learners can improve after interventions, but academic performance will continue to be distributed on a spectrum, with some children outperforming others. It is therefore pivotal to embrace individual differences between learners and to acknowledge that different children have different profiles of academic strengths and weaknesses. Educational interventions and education more broadly are not always suitable for a 'one size fits all' approach. As a society, we should continue to strive to enrich environments, at home, at school, and in the community that optimally support growth and development in all children.

Suggestions for Further Reading

Bailey, D. H., G. J. Duncan, F. Cunha, B. R. Foorman, and D. S. Yeager. 2020. 'Persistence and Fade-Out of Educational-Intervention Effects: Mechanisms and Potential Solutions'. *Psychological Science in the Public Interest: A Journal of the American Psychological Society* 21 (2): 55–97. https://doi.org/10.1177/1529100620915848.

Bailey, D., G. J. Duncan, C. L. Odgers, and W. Yu. 2017. 'Persistence and Fadeout in the Impacts of Child and Adolescent Interventions'. *Journal of Research on Educational Effectiveness* 10 (1): 7–39. https://doi.org/10.1080/19345747.2016.1232459.

Barnett, W. S. 2011. 'Effectiveness of Early Educational Intervention'. *Science* 333 (6045): 975–78.

Moore, D. S., and D. Shenk. 2017. 'The Heritability Fallacy'. *Wiley Interdisciplinary Reviews. Cognitive Science* 8 (1–2): e1400.

Sokolowski, H. M., and D. Ansari (2018). Understanding the Effects of Education through the Lens of Biology'. *NPJ Science of Learning* 3 (1) (October): 17. https://doi.org/10.1038/s41539-018-0032-y.

Summary: Intervention and Compensation

(1) **Quality criteria for effective intervention:** There is evidence that interventions are most effective when they are individualized, adaptive, embedded into 1:1 or small group settings, focused on multiple domains, and start as early as possible. The slightly lower effect size of computer (vs. in-person interventions) should be balanced against their potentially wider applicability.

(2) **Transient effectiveness of phonological awareness interventions:** Interventions targeting only phonological awareness skills have a moderate positive transfer effect on reading during early stages of alphabetic learning. The effectiveness of these interventions becomes small as soon as children have acquired basic phonemic print-to-speech conversion skills (which happens earlier when learning transparent scripts vs. intransparent scripts such as English).

(3) **Persistent effectiveness of print-to-speech conversion interventions:** Interventions targeting print-to-speech conversion (and vice versa) at the phoneme and morpheme levels have a small to moderate positive effect on reading and a moderate to large effect on spelling. A moderate positive effect on spelling has also been reported for orthographic interventions based on practicing positions, combinations, and resulting pronunciations of letters within words. There is preliminary evidence that a combination of all these approaches (possibly also with a preceding phonological awareness intervention) might yield the largest positive treatment effect, but this hypothesis needs to be confirmed by follow-up studies.

(4) **Effectiveness of basic number interventions:** Interventions targeting basic number skills (e.g., number comparison; converting quantities, digits, and number words; counting; cardinality) have a moderate to large positive transfer effect on basic arithmetic skills.

(5) **Effectiveness of basic arithmetic interventions:** Interventions targeting basic arithmetic skills have a large effect on the particular skill trained (e.g., subtraction training improves subtraction skills).

(6) **Effectiveness of mathematical problem solving interventions:** Interventions targeting mathematical problem solving (applying basic arithmetic knowledge in new and unfamiliar contexts) have a moderate positive effect on arithmetic skills.

(7) **Effectiveness of non-invasive brain stimulation for treating dyslexia:** Transcranial direct current stimulation over the left superior temporal and inferior parietal cortices (parts of the auditory-phonological system) might

transiently increase reading accuracy in children with dyslexia immediately after the intervention. Given that the persistence of this effect strongly increases to six months when combined with a behavioural reading intervention, the specific contributions of brain stimulation are unclear. Moreover, the large effect sizes reported should be treated with caution given the few small-sample studies currently available.

(8) **Effectiveness of non-invasive brain stimulation for treating dyscalculia**: Transcranial direct current stimulation over the dorsolateral prefrontal cortex (parts of the executive functioning and working memory systems) might transiently increase mathematical problem solving skills in children with dyscalculia immediately after the intervention. This effect was obtained in a single study based on a small sample and should be treated with the utmost caution until independent replication studies become available.

(9) **Fade-out of intervention effects:** Positive effects immediately following an intervention often diminish or disappear within a year. Methodological issues cannot fully explain this finding. Additional explanations are forgetting (e.g., childhood amnesia), state effects induced by an intervention that have a relatively smaller influence than trait effects (stable individual differences, e.g., in attention or processing speed), and long-term environmental experiences and genetic effects (including their different forms of interaction) which diminish the effect of the short-term intervention experience. Key factors for overcoming fade-out are: individualizing contents and covering multiple domains, optimizing timing, and providing enriched learning environments after the intervention.

(10) **Optimizing the timing of an intervention:** An optimal timing for implementing an intervention is likely crucial for instigating long-term change due to (yet to be understood) sensitive periods during which a child responds most strongly to specific experiences. In addition to considering biological timing, timing within educational systems and society in general should also be taken into consideration (e.g., school entry test at a specific time point).

(11) **Optimizing the post-intervention environment:** A high-quality enriched learning environment after the completion of a programme (e.g., psychoeducational programmes for parents and teachers, community-based programmes in adverse environments) is critical to sustain gains and foster long-term change after the intervention.

PART IX

Best Practice – Diagnostics and Prevention

22 Diagnosis of Dyslexia and Dyscalculia: Challenges and Controversies

Thomas Lachmann, Kirstin Bergström, Julia Huber, and Hans-Christoph Nuerk

22.1 Introduction

Reading, writing, and arithmetic skills are key cultural techniques in most societies. These *academic skills* must be acquired at a symbolic level – that is, enable us to produce and comprehend text and to perform more than very basic numerical operations, judgements, and calculations. These skills must be taught and learnt. During this procedural learning process (Nicolson and Fawcett 2007; Nicolson and Fawcett 2018), pre-existing functions – amongst them visual, auditory, memory, language, spatial, or quantity processing – are modified and coordinated to form novel cognitive procedures (Lachmann 2002; Lachmann 2008; Lachmann 2018; Lachmann and van Leeuwen 2014) which are then automatized after prolonged intensive training (Froyen et al. 2009; Lachmann and Van Leeuwen 2008; Barrouillet and Fayol 1998). This leads to structural and functional changes in the brain (Dehaene and Cohen 2007) – for example, the formation of specific cortical networks which are automatically activated if required (Dehaene et al. 2010; Rueckl et al. 2015). The acquisition of academic skills can thus be considered an *acculturation of the brain* (Huettig et al. 2018a; see also Posner and Rothbart 2017). Recent research suggests that it is not only the modules of the neural networks which develop over time but also the connectivity between the involved brain regions (Carreiras et al. 2007; Klein et al. 2016; Peters and De Smedt 2018; Pugh et al. 2000; Skeide et al. 2015; Skeide et al. 2017). Following the principles of a feedback loop, acquiring more advanced literacy and numeracy skills has a reciprocal impact on the pre-existing functions involved. For instance, learning to read and write has an impact on phonological (Wimmer et al. 1991; Goswami and Bryant 2016; see Huettig et al. 2018b for a review) and visual processing (Ventura et al. 2008), memory (Kolinsky et al. 2020), and oral language abilities (Konerding et al. 2020, Tarone and Bigelow 2005). In numerical cognition, it has been suggested that calculation ability improves basic spatial-numerical processing as indexed by the number line estimation task (Barth and Paladino 2011; Cipora et al. 2015; Dackermann et al. 2015). Even with respect to the approximate number system, which is assumed to be the most basic precursor of advanced numerical processing already present in infants (McCrink and Wynn 2004), there is evidence that formal mathematical education improves performance (Nys et al. 2013). When interpreting assessments of literacy and numeracy skills, it is essential to consider these recipro-cal connections between pre-existing functions and advanced academic skills (Huettig et al. 2018b).

In most countries, academic skills are acquired by formal education in school. For alphabetic reading and writing systems, for instance, abstract conversions between graphemes and phonemes and orthographic skills are learnt and trained (Frith 1985) and later form distinct routes for skilled reading and writing (Coltheart et al. 2001). In arithmetic, symbols such as Arabic numerals and operators have to be acquired. Moreover, mathematical operations and arithmetic fact retrieval have to be automatized (e.g., multiplication fact retrieval) to enable fluent calculation. How fast and how well academic skills are acquired, however, depends not only on the quality and quantity of the formal education, but also on cultural factors (e.g., differences in the orthographic system or the number word system; Paulesu et al. 2000) and on individual factors (e.g., learning-relevant personality traits). Even with equal instruction, there is great variation in how fast and how well children learn reading, writing, and arithmetic during the first years of education. While the majority of children learn these skills eventually without greater problems, some show persistent serious difficulties despite having no general learning problems. If these difficulties are specific to reading and/or spelling, the learning disorder is termed 'developmental dyslexia'; if they are related to arithmetic skills, the learning disorder is termed 'developmental dyscalculia'. Both are defined as *neuro-developmental* disorders, implying a specific causal deficit in brain devel-opment during early childhood. Compared to a reference population, this deficit is assumed to later lead to severe and specific difficulties while learning the related academic skills. The specificity of the deficit must be confirmed by an unimpaired general cognitive development. Additionally, the difficulties must be unexpected due to adequate instruction and psychosocial conditions, as well as individual factors such as proficiency in language of instruction, normal or corrected-to normal vision and hearing, and the absence of neurological disorders. Furthermore, these difficulties must manifest themselves as poor academic achievement in subjects of the respective domain while other subjects are less affected, except as secondary symptoms or in terms of comorbidities.

The term 'developmental' is intended to distinguish learning disorders from acquired dyslexia and dyscalculia resulting from brain damage, stroke, or other degenerative processes and affecting academic skills which were previously typic-ally developed (e.g., Coltheart 1996; Willmes et al. 2013). A simple analogue assumption (i.e., assuming that the damaged brain areas identified to be causative for the loss of academic skills in patients are the same as those responsible for developmental deficits) is considered obsolete (Lachmann 2002). In this chapter, we will use the terms 'dyslexia' and 'dyscalculia' to refer to developmental learning disorders.

The articles referenced in this chapter sampled populations from the following countries (number of articles): Australia (1), Austria (8), Belgium (3), Brazil (2), Canada (1), China (8), Czech Republic (2), Finland (1), France (2), Germany (32), Greece (1), Hungary (1), India (1), Israel (3), Italy (4), Japan (2), Netherlands (3),

Norway (1), Palestine (1), Poland (1), Portugal (3), Norway (1), Spain (3), Switzerland (2), Thailand (1), United Kingdom (15), United States (11), and Vietnam (1). Ages ranged from 2 to 76 years of age (2–3 years old: 5%; 4–12 years old: 68%; 13–17 years old: 9%; 18 years old or older: 17%). In addition, 11 cross-national studies and 73 meta-analyses/reviews with data from multiple countries were reviewed.

22.2 Multilevel Framework for the Diagnosis of Dyslexia and Dyscalculia

What does the definition introduced here imply for the diagnosis of these specific learning disorders? Since the assumed origin at the *neurobiological level* cannot be assessed directly, in practice the focus is on the *skill level* (see Figure 22.1) – that is, the measurement of the performance in the related skills. In particular, based on the introduced definition, the following five *diagnostic features* focus on the evaluation of whether difficulties in the affected skill performance are:

(1) severe in comparison to the reference population (*severity*);
(2) persistent (i.e., distinct from performance fluctuations and a delayed but adequate acquisition), starting in childhood with a certain assumed pattern of trajectory across the lifespan (*persistence*);
(3) specific to the related academic skills (i.e., contrasting a general cognitive impairment; *specificity*);
(4) unexpected due to adequate environmental and individual learning conditions (*unexpectedness*);
(5) manifested in terms of specific poor school performance and possible secondary problems (*manifestation*).

Following this logic, a valid diagnosis can be given only after a certain level of skill proficiency with decreased variance has been reached in the reference population and individual compensation strategies are less sufficient, typically in the second half of primary school. This is unfortunate because by then the automatization of suboptimal procedures has already started, which makes intervention more difficult (Lachmann 2018). One opportunity for earlier intervention is to identify possibly deficient pre-existing perceptual, cognitive, and motor functions at the *information processing level* that are required for learning academic skills (see Figure 22.1). These functions include visual, auditory, phonological, and speech processing, and the representation of ordinality and cardinality for numbers. The variance in task performances based on some of these precursor skills in young children (e.g., phonological processing: Badian 1994; Bradley and Bryant 1983; Melby-Lervåg et al. 2012; Wimmer et al. 1991; Grube and Hasselhorn 2006) was shown to predict later academic learning outcomes. Hence, identifying deficits at the information processing level, for instance with efficient diagnostic screenings, offers a chance for prevention at the beginning of primary school and even before instruction starts.

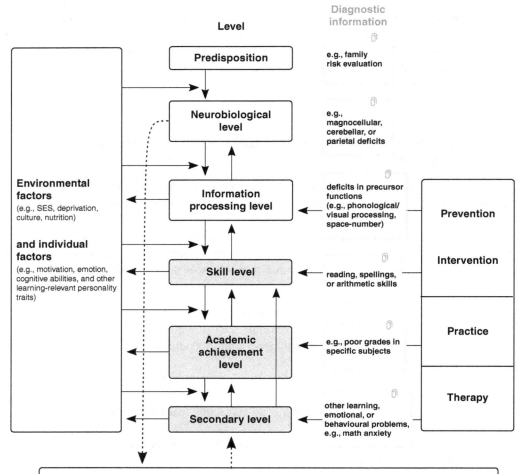

Figure 22.1 *Multiple-level framework for developmental learning disorders. Whether a genetic predisposition has an impact on the pre- or postnatal development of specific neurobiological structures and functions depends on both environmental and individual factors (Frith 1999; Galaburda 1993). The exact mechanisms of the transition from genotype to the neurobiological level and further to the information processing level are still debated (e.g.,Skeide et al. 2015; Skeide et al. 2016; Sokolowski et al. 2017). One assumption is the neuronal migration abnormality hypothesis (Galaburda et al. 1985); for a critical discussion see Guidi et al. (2018); see also Chapter 8 (Skeide 2022), for instance of magno cells in the cortex (Stein 2018a; Stein 2018b). Others proposed neurodevelopmental deficits, for instance concerning the cerebellum (Fawcett 2002), the insula (Steinbrink et al. 2009), parietal regions (Kucian et al. 2006), or deficits in connectivity of the relevant brain network (Rosenberg-Lee et al. 2015; Michels et al. 2018). Deficits at the neurobiological level may lead to selective mild impairments of information*

Another possible approach for prevention is the consideration of *genetic predispositions*: the family risk (see Figure 22.1). Children whose parents were diagnosed with a neurodevelopmental disorder are at higher risk of showing similar problems (McBride-Chang et al. 2011; Gallagher et al. 2000, Snowling et al. 2003; van Bergen et al. 2014) and may thus benefit from prevention programmes targeting the affected precursor functions. Note, however, that even though an early diagnosis on the basis of precursor abilities or genetic predisposition is important, it can only identify a *risk* of developing a learning disorder (see Pennington 2006; see also Chapter 4, Banfi, Landerl, and Moll 2022). Not all children with a family risk and/or deficient precursor abilities later show deficits in learning academic skills (e.g., Catts 1993) and, vice versa, some children with developmental dyslexia or dyscalculia do not have a family risk and were not found to show abnormalities in the functioning of precursors before instruction started (e.g., Steinbrink et al. 2010). This may be due to individual factors (e.g., motivation, cognitive abilities, and other learning-relevant personality traits) and environmental factors (e.g., culture, deprivation, socioeconomic status; Frith 1985; Frith 1999; Steinbrink and Lachmann 2014), which influence the transition of the assumed causal deficit at the *neurobiological level* to the development of cognitive functions (precursor abilities) at the *information processing level* and further to the phenotype (reading, spelling, and arithmetic) at *the skill level* (see Figure 22.1).

Caption for Figure 22.1   *(cont.)*

processing, for instance in the temporal processing of auditory and/or visual information (e.g., Farmer and Klein 1995; Tallal 1980; but see also Ramus et al. 2003). Such deficits may then affect cognitive functions required for building up the cognitive procedure for acquiring the academic skill, such as phonological processing, speech perception (e.g., Catts 1993), the interaction of transient and sustained visual channels (e.g., Stein 2018a; Stein 2018b), visual recognition, and others. The skill level starts with formal instruction (marked grey) and involves the recruitment of relevant pre-existing functions and their modification and coordination to create the skill-specific procedures which form the basis of subsequent automatization (Lachmann and van Leeuwen 2014; Nicolson and Fawcett 2018; Soltanlou et al. 2018; Koshmider and Ashcraft 1991). A failure in coordination may, depending on individual and environmental factors (e.g., socioeconomic status [SES], see Chapter 17, Lervåg and Melby-Lervåg 2022, or noise in classroom: Calcus et al. 2018; Klatte et al. 2017), lead to an automatization of abnormally developed functional coordination. This can then lead further to specific learning deficits (Lachmann 2018), and thus the manifestation of academic failures specific to the affected skill(s), and to further secondary problems (e.g., Schulte-Körne 2010; Soltanlou et al. 2019). Transmission of deficits to the skill level can be minimized through professional and targeted prevention and intervention (Dackermann et al. 2017; Klatte et al. 2018). This requires valid diagnostics which, in practice, are mainly focused on performance at the skill and achievement levels in formal school settings (marked grey). However, pure enlargement in terms of more practice at skill level may be suboptimal and has a positive effect only if optimal coordination (enrichment) has been achieved (Lachmann 2018).

22.3 Dimensional Versus Categorical Approaches Towards Diagnosis

A fundamental controversy regarding the diagnosis of dyslexia and dyscalculia deals with the question of whether these really represent distinct clinical categories of qualitatively different individuals whose problems are caused by a specific neurobiological origin. The definition we introduced here is an example of such a *categorical* diagnostic approach, as opposed to a *dimensional* view proposing that specific learning problems are only an extreme expression of a dimensional variation of skill performances within the population, without the necessity of causal brain abnormalities and without clear-cut boundaries such as performance score thresholds. Note, however, that assuming dyslexia and dyscalculia simply represent the lower tail of a normal distribution of abilities in the related academic skill(s) in the population (e.g., Peters and Ansari 2019; Shaywitz et al. 1992; Stanovich 1994; for discussion, see Elliott and Grigorenko 2014; Stein 2018a) does not automatically mean that a diagnosis, and thus at least some fuzzy categorization, is not needed. At the same time, using categories for diagnosis does not violate the assumption that skills are normally distributed in the population and that members of any category are part of this distribution. At least in practice, applying a categorical approach would not mean assuming independent distributions in different categories. Methodologically, it could be argued that the categorical view is more nomothetic.

In the end, the main dispute between these diagnostic approaches is about the need for thresholds or quantitative criteria that clearly define distinct classes of causes, symptoms, and trajectories to form a universally valid clinical category to which any individual either does or does not belong. Within the categorical approach, however, there are controversies about the criteria required to guarantee such an unambiguous assignment of an individual to a category. These contain questions such as (1) which symptoms (measured at skill level) and which levels of *severity*, progress, and consistency (*persistence*) qualify for the assignment to the category; (2) how to prove the *specificity* and the *unexpectedness* of the learning problems; and (3) the *manifestation* of the problems at the achievement level (see Figure 22.1). In the following, we discuss some of these controversies in more detail after introducing the diagnostic criteria defined in the most established clinical classification systems (related to the test features introduced earlier). However, it is important to emphasize that strictly quantitatively defined criteria in categorical classification systems do not mean that these necessarily lead to the diagnosis of any individual in a real-world setting. Categorical systems must be logical and unambiguous in themselves, but, in the end, they are only tools of the diagnostician who ultimately decides on the diagnostic assignment of a person on the basis of various diagnostic sources.

22.4 Diagnostic Criteria of the Clinical Classification Systems

The most widely used clinical classification systems are the International Classification of Diseases and Related Health Problems (ICD), published by the World Health Organization (ergänzt 2019; see also Dilling and Freyberger 2019) and the Diagnostic and Statistical Manual of Mental Diseases (DSM), published by the American Psychiatric Association (2013). In most countries, national adaptations of the ICD and ICD-derived national clinical guidelines are officially used for any clinical diagnosis. Moreover, these guidelines are also commonly adopted outside the clinical context and often serve as a basis for educational and psychological guidelines for the diagnosis of dyslexia and dyscalculia. The DSM is widely used by researchers to define samples in their studies. New versions of the DSM usually influence the development of new volumes of the ICD. The tenth volume (ICD-10) is the current version of the ICD at the time of writing this chapter, but in most countries a new version (ICD-11) has come into effect in 2022. Here we describe the categories and criteria defined in the ICD-10, since these have built a broadly accepted basis for diagnosis and research (including critique) over the past decades and will probably influence the practice and the scientific discussion in the future. We compare the categories and criteria of the ICD-10 with those of the current version of the DSM (DSM-5) and, as far as is available in 2020, with those planned for the ICD-11 (World Health Organization 2020).

The ICD-10 uses alpha-numerical codes whereas the DSM-5 uses numerical codes to classify diseases. While the US-developed DSM-5 categorizes only mental disorders, the ICD-10 contains all diseases and addresses *Mental and Behavioral Disorders* in a separate chapter (chapter 5, Code F). This chapter also includes the criteria for the diagnosis of dyslexia and dyscalculia as part of the category *Specific Developmental Disorders* (F81) within the block *Disorders of Psychological Development* (F8). In this block, the affected academic skill(s) are assigned to one of three sub-categories: *Specific Reading Disorder* (F81.0), *Specific Spelling Disorder* (F81.1), and *Specific Disorder of Arithmetic Skills* (F81.2). A further category comprises mixed disorders of arithmetic with reading and/or spelling disorder (F81.3). The ICD-10 is strictly hierarchical and thus criteria at all levels must be considered for the diagnosis. The ICD-11 is also hierarchical, but the coding system has been modified to a so-called cluster coding. In the ICD-11, chapter 6, *Mental, Behavioral and Neurodevelopmental Disorders* contains the block *Neurodevelopmental Disorders*, which includes the category *Developmental Learning Disorders* (6A03). This category comprises three separate sub-categories pertaining to different learning domains: *Developmental Learning Disorder with Impairment in Reading* (6A03.0), *with Impairment in Written Expression* (6A03.1), and *with Impairment in Mathematics* (6A03.2), without a sub-category for mixed disorders. In the DSM-5, the diagnostic criteria for developmental dyslexia and dyscalculia are provided together within the overarching category *Specific Learning Disorder* as part of the diagnostic class *Neurodevelopmental Disorders*. The coding specifies the impaired academic domains: *Specific Learning Disorder with Impairment in Reading* (315.00), *with Impairment in Written Expression*

(315.2), and *with Impairments in Mathematics* (315.1), without a single coding for mixed disorders. In addition to this coding, the DSM-5 requires the specification of affected sub-skill(s) using the term *with Impairment in . . .* (e.g., '315.00, Specific Learning Disorder with Impairment in Reading, with Impairment in Word Reading Accuracy and with Impairment in Reading Rate or Fluency') and their severity (mild, moderate, severe).

Even though the ICD and the DSM assume that the basis of the cognitive abnormalities affecting skill acquisition are neurobiological, both classification systems only describe the deficits at skill, achievement, and secondary levels (see Figure 22.1). In particular, they focus on their *severity, specificity, persistence*, and developmental course (including symptoms before skill acquisition and after, across lifespan), their *manifestation* in school performance, their *unexpectedness*, and on exclusion criteria and symptoms that define another category. In the following, some of these criteria are described in detail.

Regarding the description of symptoms and their *severity* (diagnostic feature 1), both the ICD and DSM require a discrepancy in skill performance, individually measured by specific and standardized tests. This discrepancy is defined by a statistical criterion in terms of standard deviations (SD) below the mean (M) of the norms of the reference population (population discrepancy). In the ICD-10 (Criterion A) the cut-off criterion for the population discrepancy is set at 2 SD below M of the age group. Assuming normal distribution of scores, this means that 2–3% of the age group fulfil this criterion. The DSM-5 (Criterion B) defines 1.5 SD as a norm-oriented cut-off but emphasizes that, in practice, this threshold may be less strictly considered within the context of other diagnostic information or alternative criterion-oriented testing (see Section 22.5.3). The ICD-11 requires a 'significant' discrepancy, but cut-offs have not yet been provided at the time of writing (2020). Note that, in all classification systems, the reference population is the age group, which can be seen as contradictory to the definition of dyslexia and dyscalculia as learning disorders. We argue that the reference should be the grade level – as is actually the case for most achievement tests.

Which sub-skills should be measured for the evaluation of the population discrepancy? For the ICD-10, this is specified at the level of the specific sub-category. For the sub-category *Specific Reading Disorder*, the discrepancy must be evident for measures derived from tests of reading accuracy, reading comprehension, or both (Criterion A; Dilling and Freyberger 2019). Which measures are appropriate, however, strongly depends on the orthographic system (e.g., Goswami et al. 2005; Landerl and Wimmer 2008). For instance, in alphabetic writing systems with a relatively transparent grapheme–phoneme relation, reading speed was shown to be a more sensitive measure than accuracy. In contrast, for alphabets with relatively opaque orthographies and a relatively high number of irregular words, accuracy is a sensitive measure. The DSM-5 (Criterion A) and ICD-11 address these cultural differences and give a much broader definition of possible symptoms at skill level than the ICD-10, including word reading accuracy, reading fluency, and comprehension. Note, however, that even though some researchers consider comprehension problems as secondary to dyslexia (for a discussion, see Nation 2007) and more as a problem of functional illiteracy (Bulajić et al. 2019; Vágvölgyi et al. 2016; Vágvölgyi et al. 2021), a population discrepancy in reading comprehension alone would be a criterion for dyslexia in both the ICD and DSM. In contrast to the ICD-11 and the DSM-5, in the ICD-10 for Specific Reading Disorders (Criterion A2), a population discrepancy for spelling performance can also justify this categorization if reading problems, as described earlier, are also evident or were evident in the past. For this reason, in some countries this sub-category is termed *Reading and Spelling Disorder* (e.g., *Lese- und Rechtschreibstörung* in Germany; Dilling and Freyberger 2019) in the national adaptations of the ICD-10. Regarding the use of the term 'dyslexia', the DSM-5 explicitly refers to a specific pattern of difficulties in accurate and fluent word recognition, poor decoding, and poor spelling abilities, as well as possible other symptoms to be specified, while the ICD-10 and ICD-11 mention dyslexia as a synonym for reading disorder.

For the ICD-10 sub-category *Specific Spelling Disorder*, the population discrepancy must be evident for spelling test performance while reading skills must be at least at an average level. In the DSM-5 and the ICD-11, (specific/developmental) learning disorder with impairment in written expression (ICD-11: 6A03.1; DSM-5: 315.2) is described as deficits in spelling, grammar, and punctuation accuracy, or clarity and organization of written expression. None of the categorization systems uses the term 'dyslexia' for this sub-category. The controversy in the literature on how reading and spelling impairments are related to each other becomes obsolete in the DSM-5. The reason for this is that the diagnostic criteria are defined independently from the affected academic skill for the category *Developmental/Specific Learning Disorders* and must only be specified for the coding.

For the ICD-10 sub-category *Specific Disorder of Arithmetic Skills*, the population discrepancy must be evident for mathematical test performance, while reading and spelling skills must be in the average range. The assessment of population discrepancy in the ICD-10 requires testing the basic mathematical skills of addition, subtraction, and multiplication rather than more abstract mathematical skills involved in algebra, trigonometry, geometry, or calculus. The DSM-5 and ICD-11 are less strict in this respect. For the sub-category *Developmental/Specific Learning Disorder with Impairment in Mathematics*, the ICD-11 lists possible impairments in mastering number sense, in memorization of number facts, in (accurate and fluent) calculation, or in difficulties with mathematical reasoning. According to the DSM-5, the term 'dyscalculia' refers to a specific pattern of difficulties in processing numerical information, learning arithmetic facts, and performing accurate or fluent calculations, while the ICD-11 mentions dyscalculia as a synonym for an impairment in mathematics (ICD-10 uses the term 'acalculia').

According to both classification systems, the specific deficits at the skill level must be *persistent* (ICD block F81: without remissions and relapses; DSM-5 Criterion A: at least six months despite targeted interventions) and must emerge early during formal schooling (diagnostic feature 2). In most cases, deficits at the cognitive level can be present before skill acquisition, such as language processing, visual–spatial processing, and motor functions. The skill-related problems remain across the lifespan, while the pattern of symptoms and their severity may change with age, intervention, and reading experience. Due to the assumed impairment or delay in neurobiological maturation, the symptoms must be shown to be present developmentally and thus not caused by acquired disorders. Therefore, the higher-order criteria for the ICD and DSM require that skill deficits emerge during childhood ('developmental phase' – i.e., before age 18 in the ICD or age 17 in the DSM). This implies (1) that everyone has received educational instruction in childhood (which is not the case for all children in some countries; see Chapter 24, Nag 2022) and (2) that development is restricted to childhood. This makes a later diagnosis problematic: documented symptoms in childhood are, for many, not possible. In any case, the diagnosis requires the consideration of a longer developmental period than just the moment of testing and should include an exploration of the learning history and other developmental abnormalities to validate the diagnosis and exclude other diagnostic categories.

The *specificity* of the deficits at the skill level (diagnostic feature 3) must be confirmed by an at least average general cognitive development. Traditionally, before the ICD-11 and the DSM-5, this was defined as a statistically evident discrepancy between the individual performance in a standardized test of the affected academic skill and the performance in an individually conducted standardized test of general intelligence. Since intelligence tests usually provide norm values as Intelligence Quotient (IQ), this criterion is often termed *IQ-discrepancy* and is set to 2 SD in the ICD-10 (Criterion A; Dilling and Freyberger 2019). A consequence of this so-called *double discrepancy* (population and IQ-discrepancy combined) would be that the prevalence of developmental dyslexia and dyscalculia is far less than 2% because individuals with below-average IQ must perform extremely poorly in the tests of the affected academic skill(s) to fulfil this criterion (see examples in Steinbrink and Lachmann 2014). The double discrepancy criterion was criticized by many researchers for reasons we will discuss in greater detail in Section 22.5.2. Therefore, IQ-discrepancy is not explicitly required anymore in the ICD-11 and the DSM-5. Besides the structure of coding, this change can be considered as the main modification in the most recent versions of the classification systems regarding the diagnostic criteria for dyslexia and dyscalculia. Note, however, that both systems still require (the DSM-5 explicitly, the ICD-11 implicitly by age norms) a discrepancy between tested skill performance and expected skill performance. Importantly, the expected skill performance is now based on more general measures of typical cognitive development and not a strict IQ threshold.

Regarding the evaluation of the *unexpectedness* of the specific learning problems (diagnostic feature 4), all diagnostic systems require proof of adequate education, intact vision and hearing, and the absence of mental or neurological disorders which may affect the learning of academic skills (ICD-10 Criterion C and D; DSM-5 Criterion D). The DSM-5 additionally refers to adequate individual learning conditions, including psychosocial adversity and a sufficient proficiency in the language of instruction.

Evidence for the *manifestation* of the disorder in terms of skill-related poor school achievements (diagnostic feature 5) or daily life situations is required by both systems. The DSM-5 (Criterion B) explicitly requires confirmation by standardized achievement tests, presupposing that the person has received formal and adequate instruction.

As is typical for categorical systems, exclusion criteria are explicitly defined. Most importantly, in all systems, general intellectual impairment (ICD-10: mental retardation) must be excluded on the basis of an individually conducted standardized IQ test. Note that in the most recent versions of the classification systems, an intelligence test is only required for exclusion, not for the proof of *unexpectedness* (as in the ICD-10). Regarding the course of development, possible early developmental delays, such as a delay in language acquisition, are mentioned and should not be considered as an exclusion criterion.

As for problems at the secondary level (see Figure 22.1), all systems refer to possible emotional and behavioural problems resulting from specific learning disabilities. Furthermore, the DSM-5 also includes daily living and occupational success (Criterion B).

In summary, clinical classification systems such as the ICD and DSM provide a helpful tool for diagnosing developmental dyslexia and dyscalculia based on criteria that are internationally known and accepted at the time of publication. A main advantage of these systems is that they provide rules that enhance the reliability of communication between clinicians, psychologists, teachers, and decision-makers, and also between and among practitioners and scientists. The price that has to be paid for increased 'objectivity' in these classification systems is a relatively inflexible set of criteria. This includes fixed presumptions of aetiology, narrowly specified syndrome descriptions and the associated measures, strictly defined cut-offs, and predefined developmental trajectories. An inherent problem is that the systems are based on the assumption of neurobiological origins, while the testable criteria mainly refer to the description of the syndromes. Moreover, a major criticism related to the nature of nosological classification systems is the assumed universality of criteria across cultures and individuals. It is often argued that classification systems neglect the complexity and uniqueness of individuals in favour of generating labels to pigeonhole them. Another problem is that the design and implementation of such classification systems is a difficult process that possibly takes decades and thus results in some criteria not reflecting the most recent research. The new version of the DSM and the upcoming version of the ICD better address some of these critical issues, in particular the rigidity of cut-offs and strictly defined measures, but they still remain predominantly syndromatological, universal, and rule based. However, despite the justified criticism, the criteria in the classification systems are not carved in stone; nobody would claim that they must be used like an assembly manual from IKEA. As pointed out earlier, and as is explicitly stated in the introductions of the classification systems, they should be considered as a tool for the diagnostician who, in the end, makes the diagnostic decision.

The diagnosis of specific learning disorders using the recent ICD/DSM classification systems requires a multimethod approach and is based on the synthesis of the information obtained from a variety of sources. In addition to the necessary psychological/cognitive assessment of non-verbal, fluid intelligence and the affected academic skills, anamnesis should take into account the developmental, educational, and medical history; family conditions; previous manifestation of the affected skills; and the functional (academic, occupational, social) impairments. For example, the developmental history and the persistence of difficulties can be assessed by means of observation, clinical interviews, standardized educational or psychological tests, rating scales, and the consideration of school reports and evaluated work samples. The assessment should always take into account the language competencies in the test language and the linguistic and cultural background (see culture-related diagnostic issues in DSM-5; see also Section 22.6). Furthermore, a physical and neurological examination should be carried out to assess if certain exclusion criteria are met. Concrete criteria may also be adapted depending on cultural specificities in the national guidelines. These adaptations often consider cultural aspects and typically result in recommending specific tests to be used for the diagnosis.

22.5 Controversies Regarding the Diagnosis of Dyslexia and Dyscalculia

22.5.1 Controversies About Cut-Off Criteria for the Evaluation of the Population Discrepancy

The categorical diagnosis of dyslexia and dyscalculia requires a clear determination of discrepancy between individual skill performance and the mean performance of the reference population (population discrepancy). This requires deciding which population serves as the reference and how the cut-off should be determined. ICD and DSM both define the age group as the reference population. While this may be an appropriate reference population for evaluating general cognitive development through IQ tests, performance at the skill level is more of an outcome of education than of age (see Section 22.5.3).

Cut-offs are mainly criticized for being arbitrary. Academic skills are distributed along a continuum and there is no scientifically grounded threshold that distinguishes between individuals with versus without a specific neurodevelopmental disorder. The following thought experiment may illustrate the issue of such a purely statistical criterion: Suppose we have a perfect test and a perfect training programme. If we set the cut-off for identifying children with specific learning disorders to 2 SD below the average performance of the reference population, then 2–3% of the children would be diagnosed and therefore benefit from the perfect training. This would then lead to these children showing average performance in the relevant domain after training. How many children with specific learning disorders would then exist in the population according to this criterion? The same number of children! Since the achievements are still normally distributed, other children that show the same performance as before would now fall below the 2 SD cut-off and would be classified as qualitatively distinct due to having a neurodevelopmental learning disorder (Steinbrink and Lachmann 2014).

Being aware that thresholds are artificially set, various cut-offs are used in the classification systems and guidelines, both in research and practice. The ICD uses a 2 SD criterion (with varying cut-offs in different national ICD-based guidelines) while the DSM uses a 1.5 SD criterion and allows for substantial flexibility (1–2.5 SD). It must be emphasized again, however, that all systems and guidelines recommend that cut-offs are to be used only in conjunction with the other available diagnostic information (see Section 22.2). A wide range of cut-offs is also used in scientific studies (see Chapter 11, Yeatman 2022), making it difficult to compare research results and the reported prevalence estimates of developmental learning disorders (5–15%; American Psychiatric Association 2013; see also Chapter 15, Kucian and McCaskey 2022, and 16 Chapter 11, Yeatman 2022) across and within orthographies (see Peters and Ansari 2019).

A further point of criticism regarding cut-offs is that they ignore the measurement error. In psychological diagnostics, a confidence interval is usually calculated to take into account the inaccuracy of psychometric measurements (Ehlert et al. 2012). Furthermore, the psychometric approach of forming groups by applying cut-offs to identify learning difficulties is questionable. For example, Francis et al. (2005) found that subdividing a normal distribution by arbitrary cut-offs leads to unstable group memberships. Several authors systematically compared the use of cut-off criteria in studies on developmental dyscalculia (Devine et al. 2013; Murphy et al. 2007) and found an enormous range of results in the literature. Some studies showed, for instance, that gender differences in dyslexia and dyscalculia depend on the cut-off chosen for group definition (Devine et al. 2013, Fischbach et al. 2013; also see Chapter 13, Cantlon 2022). Furthermore, the population discrepancy required for diagnosing neurodevelopmental disorders is the same for each affected academic skill. Assuming normal distribution, this means that the prevalence rates for these disorders should be the same in the population. However, dyslexia is diagnosed more frequently than dyscalculia (e.g., Dirks et al. 2008; Wyschkon et al. 2009).

Many researchers also question the general validity of a population discrepancy to separate poor readers with and without a neurodevelopmental disorder (for review, see Peters and Ansari 2019). Even the ICD and DSM do not assume that the population discrepancy clearly differentiates between children with and without specific learning disorders but require additional criteria (see next section). Despite the assumed neurobiological basis, none of the classification systems require testing at the neurobiological level.

22.5.2 Controversies About the Double Discrepancy Criterion

For the diagnosis of dyslexia and dyscalculia, the ICD-10 (see Section 22.4) requires a *combination* of the 2 SD population discrepancy and a 2 SD discrepancy between the individual performance in the affected skill and the individual's general intelligence (IQ-discrepancy). Many practitioners and researchers have been using this so-called *double discrepancy* as a standard criterion to confirm the specificity of a learning deficit with varying cut-off values for one or both of these discrepancies (see Wyschkon et al. 2009; Fischbach et al. 2013, for discussion). The rationale behind the IQ-discrepancy criterion was to differentiate dyslexia and dyscalculia as specific learning disorders caused by a neurodevelopmental impairment from a general delay in cognitive development. On the one hand, this implies that a test of intelligence measures the status of general cognitive development independent from the neurodevelopmental status of the pre-existing functions needed for the skill acquisition (information processing level, see next paragraph). On the other hand, this implies that, as long as learning conditions are adequate, IQ and skill performance are systematically related to each other and thus the IQ of a person tells us something about the expected performance in academic skills. For instance, according to the ICD-10, to meet the double discrepancy criterion, a person with an IQ of 85 must perform much worse (3 SD below M of the reference population) in a test of the affected academic skill(s) compared to a person with an IQ of 100 (2 SD below), because the first is expected to have poorly developed academic skills anyway. Finally, the logic of the double discrepancy criterion implies that general cognitive abilities and the independent pre-existing functions required for skill acquisition both develop continuously in a linear fashion; whereas the former has no influence on skill acquisition (skill level), the latter has a continuous influence which is measurable by achievement tests. All these assumptions are partially contradictory and have been debated for decades (Stanovich 1991), and many authors have argued against the need for the IQ discrepancy (e.g., Fletcher and Miciak 2019; Restori et al. 2009; Toth and Siegel 1994; Toth and Siegel 2020). We will discuss some of these issues in further detail in the subsequent sections.

To apply the double discrepancy criterion in practice, it is necessary to conduct an intelligence test as well as a test to assess skill achievement. Comparing these test procedures, however, reveals a problematic overlap. For example, many intelligence tests contain numerical-mathematical tasks, which in turn partly overlap with the testing procedures for measuring mathematical competence. In addition, intelligence tests often use written text for instructions and tasks, and therefore also measure reading comprehension to some extent. The issue of overlapping domains is problematic since individuals with deficits in specific academic skills are disadvantaged in typical IQ tests, resulting in an underestimation of their IQ (Ise and Schulte-Körne 2013; Lambert and Spinath 2018). The higher the overlap in the tasks, the less likely it is that a discrepancy between intelligence and academic competence can be identified (Ehlert et al. 2012). It is therefore recommended to use a non-verbal testing procedure (Ehlert et al. 2012; Lewis et al. 1994). This will reduce the overlap in content, but the IQ assessment is then limited in both choice and domain.

As mentioned, psychological measurements are always subject to measurement error. Calculating the IQ discrepancy by means of a difference score thus leads to the problem that measurement errors add up (Cotton et al. 2005). According to the classical test theory, the observed score X results from the true score T and the measurement error E (Novick 1966). This applies to both the intelligence test ($X_{IQ} = T_{IQ} + E_{IQ}$) and the achievement test ($X_{Ach} = T_{Ach} + E_{Ach}$).

Thus, the IQ-achievement discrepancy scores have twice as much error as a single test score (Schulte and Borich 1984), which increases the chance of wrong diagnostic decisions (Cotton et al. 2005).

Another methodological problem of the discrepancy criterion concerns the concrete method for determining the discrepancy between IQ and skill achievement. Probably the most common method is the simple standard score difference (Van den Broeck 2002). However, this method has been criticized for the statistical effect of regression towards the mean, which leads to an overestimation of discrepancies for above-average intelligence and underestimation of discrepancies for below-average intelligence (Ehlert et al. 2012; Hasselhorn and Mähler 2006; Van den Broeck 2002). To avoid such a systematic over- or underidentification of learning difficulties depending on the IQ, the regression-based discrepancy method has been proposed. However, the validity of this method has been questioned (Van den Broeck 2002). Simulations revealed that the regression-based discrepancy method overidentifies persons with low IQ as underachievers and underidentifies persons with high IQ as underachievers. Thus, it shifts the probability of meeting the discrepancy criterion in favour of individuals with low performance scores, resulting in an overcorrection (Hasselhorn and Mähler 2006). Another point of criticism is that the calculation of the threshold depends on the correlation between IQ and achievement. For example, for IQ and mathematical achievement, the correlations vary depending on the measuring instruments used (Ehlert et al. 2012). This can lead to a situation where, depending on which correlation is used to calculate the threshold, the person is diagnosed as having a learning disorder in one case but not in the other, just because a different correlation was chosen and not because their skills or IQ differed. Apart from these methodological problems, the main criticism concerns the general validity of the IQ discrepancy criterion. Specifically, this criterion has difficulty distinguishing between individuals with a neurodevelopmentally caused learning problem and individuals with learning problems due to other causes (garden variety poor readers). Many researchers argue that affected children with and without an IQ discrepancy do not differ in their specific deficits, neither at the information processing level nor at the skill level (e.g., Busch et al. 2015; González and Espínel 1999; Flowers et al. 2001; O'Malley et al. 2002; Share 1996, Siegel 1992; see Aaron 1997 for a review) and also show the same response to intervention (Aaron 1997; Chodura et al. 2015; Klatte et al. 2018; Stanovich 1991; Stanovich 2005). Moreover, many studies reveal a high degree of heterogeneity regarding the deficits at the information processing level within the group of individuals diagnosed with dyslexia or dyscalculia (e.g., Fias et al. 2013; Kaufmann et al. 2013; Steinbrink et al. 2014). This applies regardless of whether the double discrepancy or only the population discrepancy was used in the diagnosis. These findings were put forward by deniers of cut-offs as valid criteria to distinguish between children with qualitatively different causes for their learning problems. Others, in contrast, argue in favour of a causal distinction between the groups (e.g., Rutter and Yule 1975; Stein 2018a; see Nicolson and Fawcett 2007 for a discussion). The within-category heterogeneity, for instance, could be explained by subgroups with different phenotypes (e.g., Burgess et al. 2018; Heim et al. 2008; Lachmann and Van Leeuwen 2008; Siegel and Ryan 1989) all having a neurodevelopmental origin (e.g., Lachmann et al. 2005). The classification systems assume that the proposed criteria can identify those with neurobiologically caused specific learning disorders. The ICD-10 even expects a biologically based difference in sex prevalence (see also Galaburda 2018) within the group diagnosed by the double discrepancy criterion (Dilling & Freyberger 2019). Altogether, however, the problems with the reliability and validity of the double discrepancy criterion ultimately contributed to the disappearance of the IQ-discrepancy from the DSM-5 and the ICD-11, whereas the population discrepancy remains a main criterion for classification. In practice, the double-discrepancy criterion is being used less and less.

22.5.3 The Controversy About Criterion-Oriented vs. Norm-Oriented Diagnostics of Academic Skills

A particular difficulty with respect to the diagnosis of developmental dyslexia and dyscalculia arises from the mix of criterion- and norm-oriented diagnostics. Specifically, the interpretation of the learning disorder is usually criterion-oriented (i.e., suggesting that somebody has insufficiently functioning reading, spelling, or arithmetic skills). In this context, 'insufficient' seems to imply that there is a common criterion for sufficient academic skills. However, this is not how impairments of academic skills are diagnosed. Such impairments are usually diagnosed in a norm-oriented way (i.e., in comparison to a reference group of the same age, grade, curriculum, or culture). This discrepancy between a criterion-oriented interpretation and a norm-oriented diagnosis of a disorder can lead to huge imbalances in practical settings. Consider, for instance, international differences in academic achievement. In the Trends in International Mathematics and Science Study (TIMMS; Mullis et al. 2020; Fishbein et al. 2018), many Asian countries are almost 1 SD ahead of many European countries in mathematical abilities (see Chapter 16, Lyu and Zhou 2022). At the same time, the DSM-5 proposes to diagnose a specific learning disorder if a student performs 1.5 SD below the reference sample in the affected academic skill. Accordingly, if the TIMMS was a diagnostic test, this would imply that an Asian student who is diagnosed with dyscalculia would be in the normal range if compared to European students in the same grade. The Asian student would be at the 31st percentile, which corresponds to 0.5 SD below the mean. Basically, the same child with the same arithmetic skills would be defined as dyscalculic in Asia while being well within the normal range in Europe.

   Similar problems may arise not only between but also within cultures. For instance, the current DSM-5 and ICD-11 criteria both suggest that performance should be measured in comparison to children of the same age. However, the progress of academic skills depends heavily on the progress in school. This creates problems in diagnostics if the age of the child does not match the typical age in their grade. For instance, children who are typically developed compared to their peers in the same grade, but are one year older, may receive a false diagnosis if their performance is compared to the same-aged children of a higher grade. Therefore, we argue that the age-oriented criteria in the ICD-11 and the DSM-5 are not suitable for diagnosing academic skills. We recommend reserving age norms for those cognitive functions which are more dependent on general (cognitive) maturation (e.g., attention, memory, IQ).

Another critical point relates to differences in curricula. In the UK curriculum, for instance, the learning goals for 5-year-olds in reading, spelling, and arithmetic (and their precursor abilities) are higher than the learning goals for 6-year-olds in Germany. Even within countries, curricula might differ between states, regions, school districts, or even schools and teachers. For instance, in Germany, each of the sixteen federal states has its own curriculum. If the expectations, goals, and tests differ between these states, diagnostic results in reading and arithmetic, especially in the earlier years, might then not be comparable. Children might be (falsely) diagnosed as dyscalculic or dyslexic not because their individual development is deviant, but because the curriculum they are exposed to is deviant.

A further problem of reference-group-oriented norms is the relatively wide age range of the reference group. Some diagnostic assessments use norms which cover either a full year of age or an entire school year. However, especially in the early grades, learning progress is substantial and skills improve considerably during a full year. Thus, testing a child at the beginning of the year might falsely lead to a diagnosis of dyscalculia or dyslexia because the child is compared to more educated children. At the same time, testing a child at the end of the year might lead to a false-negative diagnosis of dyscalculia or dyslexia because they are being compared to less educated children. Some diagnostic tests use age- or grade-related linear interpolation of scores to deal with that problem. A linear interpolation means that the performance at a particular point is estimated by a linear approximation of the time-points between two measurement points. For instance, if a child is assessed midway through grade 2, but norms only exist for end of grade 1 and end of grade 2, the child's performance might be compared to the mean of end of grade 1 and end of grade 2 norms. While a linear interpolation might be better than no interpolation, it does not reflect the empirical reality of learning. For instance, in the German dyscalculia test Tedi-Math (Kaufmann et al. 2009), which uses half-year norms, one can observe a huge, non-linear jump in multiplication skills from the first half of 2nd grade to the second half of 2nd grade. Between these two measurement points, multiplication tables were usually introduced in school in the norm sample. Luckily, children seem to have learnt at least something in school which subsequently improved their test results. However, for the proper interpretation of test results against the norms of a full grade (or, even worse, age), this poses a major problem. To consider non-linear developments in school performance during a school year, some tests specify an administration period that corresponds to the assessment period of the norm sample (e.g., the end of the school year: i.e., June or July in the German silent reading test WLLP-R; Schneider et al. 2011).

All these problems can be traced back to commingling criterion-oriented interpretations and norm-oriented testing of specific learning disorders. The DSM and ICD try to categorize children's deviant abilities as being qualitatively distinct. In the tests, we diagnose children in comparison to reference groups, which differ according to culture, age, curriculum, and many other factors not discussed here (e.g., socioeconomic status). As long as these factors are not equalized across the world, or even within a country, there is no straightforward assessment of academic abilities given that they depend so heavily on formal education. Comprehensive individual diagnostics should carefully consider these factors and not just blindly follow the test outcomes independent of such norm-oriented reference group effects.

22.6 Cultural Influences on Diagnostics

Academic skills do not exist in an abstract vacuum; they are deeply embedded in the culture and history of a country. In our view, at least three types of cultural influences can be distinguished: (1) cultural features of the language and the symbol systems used for reading, spelling, and arithmetic; (2) formal curricular differences; and (3) informal differences regarding academic skills (e.g., family environment). We will mostly focus on (1), but do not wish to neglect the fact that differences in schooling and other extracurricular differences in a society (such as the value of education) have an important influence as well. Note, however, that cultural differences are, at least to some extent, acknowledged in the diagnostic classification systems. In the following, we will discuss the consequences of cultural factors for diagnosing dyscalculia and dyslexia.

22.6.1 Cultural Influences on the Diagnosis of Developmental Dyslexia

Language and orthography are crucial cultural factors affecting reading acquisition and the manifestation of dyslexia (e.g., Seymour et al. 2003; for reviews, see Ziegler and Goswami 2005; Verhoeven et al. 2019; see also Chapter 15, Siok 2022, and Figure 22.1). In alphabetic orthographies, the smallest written units (graphemes) are certain letters or letter combinations that are mapped to phonemes (specific sounds). In contrast, in a syllabic writing system (e.g., kana in Japanese) graphemes are linked to syllables and in morpho-syllabic writing systems (e.g., Chinese) graphemes are mostly linked to morphemes (smallest, undividable, meaningful units).

Alphabetic orthographies vary in how consistently graphemes are mapped to phonemes (grapheme–phoneme correspondence). In transparent orthographies, there are consistent one-to-one relationships between graphemes and phonemes so that the pronunciation is the same across different words. In opaque orthographies, in contrast, the phonemes corresponding to the same grapheme are pronounced differently in different words (e.g., in English: *a* in *car*, *hat*, *late*, *want*). Orthographic transparency can be considered as a continuum from the predominantly transparent orthographies (e.g., Finnish) to predominantly opaque orthographies (English; Borleffs et al. 2017). In more transparent orthographies (e.g., Greek, Finnish, Italian, German), grapheme–phoneme mappings are easy to learn due to their regularity, and word reading accuracy typically reaches skill ceiling by the end of the first school year. As languages become less transparent, word reading accuracy decreases continually (e.g., Seymour et al. 2003). Therefore, in transparent orthographies, reading accuracy is not a good measure and reading speed should be used instead (e.g., Diamanti et al. 2018; Wimmer

1993). In opaque orthographies, both reading accuracy and reading speed are good indicators.

The orthography-specific differences in typical reading development are also accompanied by different manifestations of dyslexia and must, therefore, be taken into account in the diagnosis. Children with dyslexia have less impaired reading accuracy in languages with transparent orthographies when compared to languages with opaque orthographies (e.g., Diamanti et al. 2018; Landerl et al. 1997). Furthermore, within transparent languages (e.g., German), reading speed is more impaired than reading accuracy. In contrast, both reading accuracy (particularly for low-frequency words and non-words) and reading speed were impaired in English children with dyslexia (Landerl et al. 1997). Other cross-orthography studies (e.g., Diamanti et al. 2018) also show that English-speaking children with dyslexia are more impaired in reading accuracy, but equally impaired in reading speed, when compared to children who learn more transparent orthographies. Thus, dyslexic reading in transparent orthographies is slow but mostly accurate, while dyslexic reading in opaque orthographies is both slow and less accurate. Therefore, the diagnosis of dyslexia should be based on different sub-skills depending on the orthography.

Another relevant issue relates to the question of whether characteristics of typical and impaired reading are specific to individual languages or are shared across languages and orthographies (universality vs. language specificity: see Joshi 2018; Landerl et al. 2013; Landerl et al. 2019; Pugh and Verhoeven 2018). With respect to alphabetic orthographies, various studies have shown that the relevance of pre-existing cognitive functions involved in dyslexia, such as phonological awareness and rapid automatized naming (RAN), vary depending on the transparency of the orthography (e.g., Landerl et al. 2019; Moll et al. 2014; Ziegler et al. 2010; see also Chapter 15, Siok 2022). For example, the impact of phonological awareness on reading is more important in opaque orthographies than in transparent orthographies (Ziegler et al. 2010). Studies in German children revealed that the variance explained by phonological awareness declines rapidly after the first school year for reading, but remains reliable in later grades for spelling (Ennemoser et al. 2012; Landerl and Wimmer 2008; Wimmer and Mayringer 2002). In contrast, RAN was found to explain the variance in reading speed and reading comprehension independent of orthographic transparency (e.g., Araújo et al. 2015; Landerl et al. 2019; Moll et al. 2014). Similarly, a meta-analysis of adult data (Reis et al. 2020) revealed the effect of orthographic transparency on the manifestation of dyslexia. Specifically, the deficits in reading accuracy, reading speed, reading comprehension, spelling, and phonological awareness are weaker in transparent (Spanish, Icelandic, Norwegian, Italian, Finnish, Polish) than in intermediate (Dutch, German, European-Portuguese, Swedish) and opaque orthographies (Danish, English, French, and Hebrew). Moreover, the deficits were (1) more severe in measures of reading and spelling than in measures of cognitive functions (e.g., phonological awareness) and (2) more severe in measures of speed (word and pseudoword reading, phonological awareness and orthographic knowledge) than in measures of accuracy. Thus, when diagnosing dyslexia in adults, reading and writing skills should be assessed using measures of speed. This is especially the case in transparent orthographies in which the dissociation between accuracy and speed is greater.

Theoretical models of dyslexia are often based on findings in alphabetic writing systems (for reviews about dyslexia in languages not considered in this chapter, see, e.g., Hebrew: Share et al. 2019; Russian: Zhukova and Grigorenko 2019). However, there is an increasing number of findings from non-alphabetic writing systems (e.g., Chinese: Hung et al. 2018; Ho and Bryant 1997; Tzeng et al. 2018; Japanese: Wydell 2019) and cross-orthography comparison studies that seek to test the applicability of existing reading-related and dyslexia-related models in non-alphabetic languages (e.g., Joshi 2018; Peng et al. 2021). In the following, findings relevant to the diagnosis of dyslexia in the Chinese morpho-syllabic writing system are considered (for a review, see also Xu et al. 2019).

Chinese characters represent monosyllabic morphemes and most of them are ideophonetic (semantic-phonetic) compounds with both semantic radicals (giving information about the meaning) and phonetic radicals (indicating the pronunciation; for further explanations, see Shu et al. 2003). A recent meta-analysis by Peng et al. (2017) revealed that Chinese children with reading difficulties have deficits in various cognitive functions (phonological awareness, RAN, working memory, morphological awareness, orthographic knowledge, visual skills, and motor skills) compared to age-matched children. Compared to reading-level matched children, however, they only have deficits in RAN and orthographic knowledge (see also Chapter 15, Siok 2022). That being said, unlike in alphabetic orthographies in which phoneme awareness is a strong predictor of reading skills, morphological awareness may be more important in Chinese (McBride-Chang et al. 2005). A recent study by Song et al. (2020) showed that deficits in phonological awareness and RAN were strong predictors of dyslexia in Chinese children, but the strongest predictor was morphological awareness. The less important role of phonological awareness for reading is expected, since the Chinese orthography, in contrast to alphabetic orthographies, does not correspond to the segmental structure of the language, and only 39% of the Chinese characters that are taught in school are regular and contain reliable information about their pronunciation (Shu et al. 2003). Peng et al. (2017) suggest that assessing cognitive skills in addition to reading measures (character recognition or character recognition combined with reading comprehension) could improve diagnostic accuracy. In fact, in Hong Kong, a diagnosis of dyslexia requires evidence of a deficit (population discrepancy of 1 SD) in at least one of the cognitive-linguistic skills (phonological, morphological, visual-orthographic, or RAN) in addition to below-average performance in three different standardized literacy tasks (timed word recognition, untimed word recognition, and dictation) and average intelligence (see McBride et al. 2018). However, the required diagnostic criteria vary across the regions of China. In Beijing, for example, a diagnosis of dyslexia requires evidence of below-average reading accuracy (population discrepancy of 1.5 SD in word recognition), below-average reading speed, and average intelligence; however, unlike Hong Kong, a diagnosis in Beijing does not require evidence of below-average performance in cognitive skills (see McBride et al. 2018).

Similar to dyslexic children from alphabetic orthographies, there is a large variability in cognitive skill deficits among Chinese children with dyslexia (e.g., Song et al. 2020; for a review, see McBride-Chang et al. 2005) and thus different subgroups could be identified (Song et al. 2020). For example, Song et al. (2020) identified four different deficit groups of Chinese children with dyslexia: a phonological deficit group, a RAN deficit group, a morphological deficit group, and a global deficit group with impairments in all three functions. Since not all individuals with dyslexia have cognitive deficits, however, it is not recommended to use such cognitive deficits as an additional criterion for the diagnosis (see Jong and van Bergen 2017). Nevertheless, certain deficits in cognitive functions can be used to validate the diagnosis of dyslexia (Pennington et al. 2012) and can be informative regarding intervention.

22.6.2 Cultural Influences on the Diagnosis of Developmental Dyscalculia

The Arabic numeral system has a unique advantage as its place-value system allows for more externalization of the intermediate steps of calculation and makes number processing both easier and more transparent than symbol number systems (such as, e.g., Roman numbers; see Zhang and Norman 1995 for a taxonomy). Since the Arabic numeral system is almost universally used, there are few cultural differences affecting dyscalculia diagnosis around the world. That being said, it has been repeatedly shown that linguistic properties such as grammar or number word structure affect numerical and arithmetic performance from the beginning of number processing. Dowker and Nuerk (2016) provide a comprehensive overview of seven types of potential language differences, which we cannot fully elaborate upon here. Therefore, we will focus on two important examples: grammatical attributes of language and lexical attributes of number words. Grammatical attributes in a language have a major influence on early number word acquisition preceding early numerical skills. Research suggests that the grammatical structure of language extends even to early numerical skills, which are precursors of later arithmetic functioning. For instance, in a recent study (Haman et al. 2020), Polish and German kindergarten children were compared. In Polish, the grammatical structure is different than in German or English. The numbers 1–4 function similarly in all three languages (e.g., 'there is one car' with a singular verb, and 'there are four cars' with a plural verb), but the numbers 5–9 have a rather complex grammatical structure in Polish as they are used with a singular verb (e.g., 'there is five of cars'). In the Give-a-number task (Wynn 1990), in which children are asked to give a specified number of tokens to the experimenter, Polish children, but not German children, showed particular problems with exactly those numbers 5-9 (i.e., to give 5 to 9 tokens to the experimenter) that are associated with the more difficult grammar. This holds when a couple of other capabilities, both non-verbal numerical and domain-general, are controlled (Haman et al. 2020). Furthermore, the grammatical number properties of a language (i.e., if there is singular [for the number 1] and plural [for numbers >=2 in English]), affects the ease of acquisition of numbers. While to English readers the aforementioned structure may seem universal, this is not the case. Some languages, such as Arabic, also have a dual case (a special grammatical case devoted to the number 2), while others use the singular case for all numbers (e.g., Japanese; for an overview, see Sarnecka 2014). Such simple differences may affect early number acquisition and also subsequent numerical and arithmetic abilities.

Another major influence, perhaps even more relevant for diagnostics, is number inversion. Some languages, such as many Germanic languages and Arabic, have an inversion for the units and decade (e.g., German 'einundzwanzig' = 'one-and-twenty'). This leads to a major decrease in performance in many tasks used for diagnosing dyscalculia in children. For instance, almost 50% of transcoding (writing down a number to dictation) errors in 1st grade are related to inversion (Zuber et al. 2009), while such errors are rarely observed in languages without inversion (e.g., Moeller et al. 2015a, for a comparison of German and Japanese in 1st graders; see also Imbo et al. 2014, for 2nd graders, and Macizo et al. 2011, for bilingual adults). Other cultural attributes are unlikely to explain these major performance differences, because (1) they are quite specifically tailored to the language structure and (2) they can be shown even in within-participants designs in a language in which both forms exist (e.g., Pixner et al. 2011b). Given the high prevalence of such errors in certain age groups, it is clear that error frequencies of transparent and intransparent number word systems are not comparable for a diagnosis of dyscalculia and that language-specific norms are needed.

Importantly, the influence of inversion on children's mathematical learning goes beyond transcoding, where the number word structure is an explicit part of the task. Number line estimation tasks (Helmreich et al. 2011), number comparison (Pixner et al. 2011a; Nuerk et al. 2015), and addition (especially with carry-overs; cf. Göbel et al. 2014) are all negatively affected by inversion: Children respond more slowly and are more error-prone, especially in conditions with more complex place-value processing. Furthermore, inversion effects are also modulated by reading/writing direction, both in transcoding, where it can be enhanced (Hayek et al. 2019), and in magnitude comparison, where it can be reduced (Moeller et al. 2015b). All these tasks are used in some diagnostic tests and clearly need to be considered in the interpretation of diagnostic test results for dyscalculia. Norms or tasks established in one country might not be transferable to another country and may be insensitive for diagnosing dyscalculia if the number word system is more transparent in a country.

That being said, we would also like to highlight the caveat that not all cultural differences attributed to language differences may in fact be due to language differences. Mark and Dowker (2015) compared basic numerical performance in English-speaking children from the United Kingdom, English-speaking children from Hong Kong, and Chinese-speaking children from Hong Kong. The Chinese number word system is more transparent because it explicitly denotes the power for all place-value positions (i.e., 327 –> three-hundred-two-ten-seven). Interestingly, the authors observed that for some tasks, language structure indeed seems to determine performance (i.e., English-speaking children performed worse than Chinese-speaking children), while for other tasks, non-lingual cultural attributes seem to be most relevant (i.e., English children performed worse than both groups of children from Hong Kong). Similarly, Lê and Noël (2020) found only a limited advantage of transparent number systems over intransparent systems.

It is important to keep in mind that every cross-cultural study is a quasi-experimental study. This implies that the principle of isolated variation does not apply. Many attributes other than language may differ between cultures and contribute to the profound cultural influences we observe. Therefore, cultural differences other than language must also be considered for diagnostics.

22.6.3 Formal and Informal Schooling Differences

Different countries have different school entry ages and cut-off dates. For example, the starting age of primary education, and thus of formal literacy instruction, varies from 4/5 years (United Kingdom) to 7 years (Estonia, Croatia) across Europe, with many countries also requiring compulsory preschool attendance (earliest start at age 3 in France and Hungary; European Commission/EACEA/Eurydice (2020). Similarly, within Chinese societies, onsets of formal reading instruction differ considerably (for an overview of differences in script, language, and literacy instructions across Chinese societies, see McBride et al. 2018). Formal reading instruction in Mainland China and Taiwan begins with school entry at about age 6, while in Hong Kong, Macau, and Singapore children often receive Chinese literacy instruction in preschool from age 3 onwards. Therefore, age norms are usually not comparable between most cultures and countries.

Grade norms, however, are also not comparable due to the fact that age-related maturation in cognitive processes (e.g., working memory, sustained attention) may also contribute to academic performance. However, even if school was to start at exactly the same age for all children, this still would not mean that grade norms are comparable. Countries may differ with respect to teaching methods (e.g., McBride et al. 2018), the intensity with which precursor abilities are trained in preschool, the progression speed in school, and the achievement goals within a grade (e.g., different countries cover different number ranges in grades 1 and 2). Furthermore, the amount of time spent in school per day can vary greatly, with some countries having half-day schooling (like in Germany), some having full-day schooling (like in United Kingdom, USA), and some having full-day schooling with additional private lessons afterwards or on the weekend (like in some Asian countries). This does not only affect general performance. Different items may be differentially difficult for different cultures – that is, some items are easier for one culture, while others are easier for another culture. Indeed, a recent Rasch analysis (Kuratli Geeler et al. 2021) shows that even for the same language and the same test, differential item functions may differ between related cultures. The authors suggest that this may depend on formal learning goals, in which different cultures focus on different task types. In sum, formal curricula influence academic progress differentially and interfere with diagnostic comparability across cultures.

Besides those formal curricular differences, there are many more important informal differences which may affect diagnostics. Societal differences, such as the social value of education or whether education is an effective tool for the advancement of disadvantaged groups (e.g., women or minorities), may play a major role in learning. Furthermore, an immigrant background and speaking another native language may interfere with academic development in reading, spelling, and arithmetic, especially when children are tested in their second language dominant in the society to which they immigrated. Severe underestimation of their skills may be a dramatic consequence if these cultural attributes are not appropriately considered.

Altogether, formal and informal differences may influence performance in diagnostic tests and may make meaningful cross-cultural comparisons of dyscalculia or dyslexia difficult or in some cases even impossible.

22.7 Implications for Practice

We have discussed several difficulties and controversies to be considered in diagnosing dyslexia and dyscalculia. A fundamental problem that we have outlined is distinguishing between neurodevelopmentally caused specific learning disorders and problems in learning academic skills that may have other causes. We argued that this distinction is, in practice, hardly possible to make and that the criteria proposed in the classification systems are not suitable for this purpose. The reason is that these classification systems essentially refer to skill level and thus only indirectly test for neurobiological causes. As long as there is no general agreement on a measurable origin of specific learning disorders at the neurobiological level, a valid and reliable diagnostic differentiation is not possible.

Given all the inconsistencies we have discussed in this chapter, can we just disregard clearly defined criteria for classification? Our answer is 'no'. What diagnosticians are ultimately interested in is how to help children with specific learning problems catch up with their peers and not in which particular brain region is involved in that problem. This requires a valid identification of the affected children – that is, a diagnosis that identifies those children who need help. We argue that such a diagnosis should never be the end result but should instead lead to an optimized intervention plan which includes repeated diagnostic testing. In principle, this assessment and intervention strategy is independent from the neurobiological origins of the deficits. Accordingly, agreed-upon criteria, including arbitrary cut-offs, are helpful in deciding which child is most likely to benefit from a particular intervention (hits) and also which child would benefit less, given the effort required (correct rejections). Explicitly defined criteria also lead to better communication between practitioners (teachers, therapists, authorities, healthcare systems, etc.) and to a diagnostic justification of special treatments (e.g., dyslexia classes in some parts of Germany). Misses (children who would benefit from the intervention but were not identified) and false alarms (children who would waste time and effort with an intervention they do not need) cannot be completely avoided but should be minimized by thorough assessment (see also Chapter 23, Hasselhorn and Schneider 2022). This is not easy because diagnosing a specific learning disorder is not like categorizing a set of blue and yellow marbles into two different boxes according to a colour criterion. Assessing a complex personality interacting with a complex environment is more similar to trying to categorize infinite shades of green. Every single person is like a big, standalone humanities research project, in which complex hypotheses are tested but an infallible solution may never be found.

Objective criteria and test cut-offs may be problematic, but they are more reliable, comparable, and valid than subjective opinions. However, we argue that such criteria alone are not sufficient. They must be integrated with other diagnostic information from across the lifespan and different learning periods, which may include subjective opinions of teachers and parents as well. If this is done in a proper way, there is a good chance of a valid diagnosis and an optimal intervention. The response to this intervention should then also be used as diagnostic information.

22.8 Conclusion

In the following, we summarize some of the issues discussed in this chapter and mention some further points we believe are necessary to consider for a proper diagnostic process.

(1) *Neurobiological origin:* Research at the neurobiological level is important for furthering the understanding of dyslexia and dyscalculia. However, at the moment, we are not aware of any tailored intervention programme for dyslexia or dyscalculia that relies on a particular individual neurobiological marker. Therefore, individual neurobiological differences should not be taken into account in the diagnosis of dyslexia and dyscalculia at this moment.

(2) *The individual matters:* Cut-off values should be based on tests with a high standard of objectivity, reliability, and validity. However, even with the best tests, diagnosing an individual is a complex ordeal. Test outcomes are only one source of diagnostic information within a multidimensional approach centred around an individual.

(3) *Minimum performance principle:* When a child performs significantly below the average of the reference population in an achievement test, this finding cannot immediately be interpreted as evidence for a specific learning disorder. Test results should be interpreted as the minimum performance, instead of the maximum performance, that the child could exhibit. It cannot be excluded that other factors (e.g., motivation, emotion, noise, fatigue, or attempted fraud) led to poor results and thus further diagnostic information is required to justify the diagnosis. In contrast, if a child performs at or above the mean on an achievement test, a specific learning disorder in that domain is unlikely. Note, however, that a child may overperform in achievement tests if their items are specifically trained ('training to the test').

(4) *Repeated testing:* Measuring academic skills is an inherently imperfect process. Academic skills may vary at the time of assessment due to acute factors such as fatigue or motivation, but may also vary over time due to differential

individual development. Therefore, those children that are reasonably close to the threshold of a learning disorder diagnosis should be regularly retested. Repeated testing is especially advisable for screening approaches, since screening tests are usually shorter and less reliable. However, again, note that repeated assessment with the same test may lead to test-specific learning effects.

(5) *Multicomponentiality approach – identify the specific impairments:* Reading, spelling, and solving complex arithmetic problems build upon many different domain-specific and domain-general components. Simply categorizing a child as having dyslexia or dyscalculia may not be sufficient to plan an optimal and effective intervention. Knowledge of the sub-skill-specific impairments unique to each individual is necessary to plan a tailored, adaptive intervention targeting the largest difficulties, instead of applying a one-size-fits-all programme.

(6) *Componential dimensional vs. typological subgroup analysis:* While different components of reading/spelling/arithmetic should be distinguished at the individual level, as yet there is no comprehensive agreement on if and how many distinct subgroups exist, or what they are. Subgroups are of interest for research purposes, but for diagnostics we recommend avoiding subgroups in terms of distinct categories for distinct interventions at this point in time. Instead, we argue in favour of tailoring the treatment on an individual basis.

(7) *Continuous remediation:* In practice, people are often treated once and are not expected to return. Particularly in dyscalculia, in the course of some developmental trajectories and during certain learning periods an intervention may help to overcome one specific hurdle, but when the next hurdle appears the child may once again have problems. Generally, process diagnosis and follow-up diagnostics are necessary to see whether the learning problems have actually been resolved by the intervention or whether additional support for newly emerging problems is required.

(8) *Gender differences:* While some achievement tests used in the diagnosis of specific learning disorders contain gender-specific norms, there are no gender-specific interventions. Since everyone typically receives the same education regardless of gender, the diagnostics should therefore also be gender neutral.

(9) *Cultural differences:* Cultural differences (e.g., language and learning environment) need to be considered. For example, diagnostics with tests or norms from another culture, even if they share a language, may be misleading.

(10) *Consideration of relevant personality traits and secondary consequences:* Emotional, cognitive, motivational, and other aspects (e.g., self-concept) must be considered for diagnostics and intervention of specific learning disorders. For instance, maths anxiety is related to mathematical performance, mathematical learning, and math avoidance. Accordingly, maths anxiety can thus be both a consequence and a cause of bad maths performance (see Figure 22.1).

(11) *Comorbidity:* Co-occurrence of dyslexia, dyscalculia, and other neurodevelopmental disorders has been found to be higher than chance, with wide variation in comorbidity rates. In addition, dyslexia and dyscalculia may co-occur with other behavioural (e.g., attention deficit hyperactivity disorder) and emotional (e.g., depression and anxiety) disorders. This significantly complicates the proof of the

criterion of specificity. A symptom (e.g., attention problems) that does not fit a certain diagnosis (e.g., dyslexia) is not necessarily evidence against this diagnosis, but may instead be a symptom of another co-occurring disorder (e.g., ADHD).

In summary, although much progress has been made in understanding learning disorders, there is no simple recipe for such a complex diagnostic process. A proper diagnosis requires deep and sophisticated knowledge of both the learning disorder itself and how it can be affected by both individual factors and the environment.

Acknowledgement

The authors would like to thank Christopher Allison, as well as our reviewers (including Michael A. Skeide), for comments and remarks throughout this chapter.

Suggestions for Further Reading

Butterworth, B., S. Varma, and D. Laurillard. 2011. 'Dyscalculia: From Brain to Education'. *Science*, 27, 1049–53. https://doi.org/10.1126/science.1201536.

Kaufmann, L., M. M. Mazzocco, A. Dowker, et al. 2013. 'Dyscalculia from a Developmental and Differential Perspective'. *Frontiers in Psychology* 4 (August): 516. http://dx.doi.org/10.3389/fpsyg.2013.00516.

Lachmann, T., and T. Weis (Eds.) 2018. *Reading and Dyslexia: From Basic Functions to Higher Order Cognition*. Cham: Springer International Publishing. https://doi.org/10.1007/978-3-319-90805-2.

Washington, J. A., D. L. Compton, and P. D. McCardle (Eds.). 2020. *Dyslexia: Revisiting Etiology, Diagnosis, Treatment, and Policy*. Baltimore: Paul H. Brookes Publishing Co.

23 Prevention of Dyslexia and Dyscalculia: Best Practice and Policy in Early Education

Marcus Hasselhorn and Wolfgang Schneider

23.1 Introduction

Social and educational policy expectations regarding pre-primary education and care have changed in a fundamental way. For a long time, the main purpose of attending kindergarten was to foster the social, emotional, motor-related, and moral development of children. Nowadays, fostering children's school-relevant skills in the domains of language, literacy, and mathematics are among the expectations of parents with regard to the educational mission of kindergartens (Roßbach and Hasselhorn 2014). As a consequence, a significant change in official guiding principles can be observed throughout the past decades (OECD 2011). Remarkably, up until the 1960s the prevailing opinion was that early learning achievement is mainly predisposed by innate skills. This view has been supplanted, however, by the idea that special support in early education can reduce children's risk of only insufficiently acquiring basic academic skills during the primary school years.

23.2 Problems With Dyslexia and Dyscalculia in School: Why Is Early Prevention Necessary?

There is no doubt that reading and spelling are essential to social participation and personal and professional success throughout the world. Moreover, the ability to read and spell is highly valued and important for social, academic, and economic advancement. While most children learn to read fairly well during the first years of elementary school, some children, despite parental support and adequate instruction, show extreme reading and spelling learning difficulties from the very beginning of schooling onwards. Similar findings have been reported for the development of maths competencies and related difficulties leading to dyscalculia. In both cases, it seems puzzling that many children developing reading or maths problems in school are inconspicuous with regard to general intelligence and come from families with at least average socioeconomic backgrounds. Given that developmental dyslexia and dyscalculia are typically not diagnosed before the end of 2nd grade, intervention efforts traditionally begin rather late – often too late for correcting undesirable developmental trends.

In the case of dyslexia, numerous theories have been developed over the course of the last 150 years to describe and explain children's reading and spelling difficulties (see Chapter 1, Goswami 2022). For instance, while some theories suggested a predominantly visual deficit, others focused on working memory capacity or an automatization deficit, or emphasized the causal role of a phonological processing deficit. In particular, the question of whether precursors of reading and spelling can already be identified in kindergarten and preschool attracted much interest by researchers from the early 1980s on (see reviews by Goswami and Bryant 2016; Schneider and Stengard 2000). As a consequence, several longitudinal studies have been carried out to explore the impact of early precursors of reading and spelling for subsequent development. For instance, various measures assessing different aspects of phonological information processing (phonological awareness, memory, verbal information processing speed) as well as IQ during the kindergarten period were used to predict a variety of reading and spelling assessments in the Munich Longitudinal Study of the Genesis of Individual Competencies (LOGIC). This project started with a sample of 200 kindergarten children in 1984 and ended when participants were young adults (Schneider 2009). Kindergarten measures did predict performance at the beginning of elementary school. The battery of predictor variables accounted for significant amounts of variance (about 27% to 35%) in reading speed and reading comprehension both at the beginning and at the end of grade 2. At the end of grade 2, phonological awareness and information processing speed contributed significantly to the prediction of both reading speed and reading comprehension. In addition, early letter knowledge and listening span also turned out to be important for the prediction of reading speed, particularly at the beginning of grade 2. Similar results were obtained for the spelling measures. Analyses focusing on further reading and spelling development revealed that the impact of early phonological information processing and letter knowledge was only important for the initial literacy acquisition period, with its effect diminishing over time. Similar findings were obtained for a variety of different languages (see reviews by Muter and Snowling 1998, Schneider and Stengard 2000; Wagner and Torgesen 1987). For a comprehensive review of recent developments in the field, see Chapter 17, Lervåg and Melby-Lervåg 2022.

While these findings suggest that early phonological processing generally affects reading and spelling in school, the phonological deficit hypothesis also found the strongest support in dyslexia research (e.g.,Catts et al. 2017; Rack 2017; see also Chapter 1, Goswami 2022; Chapter 4, Banfi, Landerl, and Moll 2022; Chapter 17, Lervåg and Melby-Lervåg 2022). Thus, the most effective interventions designed to tackle possible problems in this area focus on phonological processing and include phonological awareness, phonological coding in verbal short-term memory, naming speed, speech perception, and speech production (Brady and Shankweiler 2013).

As regards the issue of dyscalculia, there is consensus that several components such as basic knowledge of number, counting principles, memory for mathematical facts, understanding of mathematical concepts, and cognitive strategies all contribute to maths performance (e.g., Dowker 2019; Siegler and Braithwaite 2017). Although there is no single cause for developmental dyscalculia, children struggling with maths in school often indicate a deficient number sense and show deficits in working memory and a reduced speed of processing (Bjorklund and Causey 2017; Geary 2011; see also Chapter 17, Lervåg and Melby-Lervåg 2022).

Several subtypes of dyscalculia have been identified (e.g., Geary 1993; Koponen et al. 2007; Landerl and Moll 2010). In fact, there is considerable overlap and co-occurrence among the populations of dyslexic and dyscalculic children (see Chapter 4, Banfi, Landerl, and Moll 2022). According to Fischbach et al. (2013), almost 45% of children with maths difficulties also show reading or spelling problems. Apparently, one problem of children with both maths and reading problems is that they are not able to retrieve semantic information from long-term memory efficiently (Bjorklund and Causey 2017; Geary 1993). This overarching deficit could lead to fact retrieval problems in simple arithmetic tasks and to word recognition problems in reading.

Reading and maths intervention programmes carried out in schools can help to improve children's reading and maths competencies. Nevertheless, it must be noted that children who begin school behind their peers with respect to their reading or spelling skills or their ability to understand numbers, counting, and simple arithmetic are at high risk of staying behind throughout their school career (Aunola et al. 2004; Duncan et al. 2007; Schneider and Bullock 2009). Moreover, affected children are more often rejected by their peer group (Krull et al. 2014). As a consequence, they are prone to experience stigmatization (Geiger and Brewster 2018) and social exclusion (Daley and Rappolt-Schlichtmann 2018). Furthermore, children with severe learning difficulties are reported to suffer from symptoms of anxiety and depression twice as often as their non-affected peers (Visser et al. 2020). It is thus desirable to remediate their most relevant learning difficulties even before school entry.

23.3 Implementation of Intervention Programmes Designed to Strengthen Relevant Precursor Skills

23.3.1 Training Studies Focusing on Phonological Awareness

Based on longitudinal studies confirming the important role of phonological awareness as a predictor of later reading and spelling skills, systematic phonological awareness training was assumed to yield positive effects on children's literacy learning outcomes. The notion behind this approach was that such training should not only substantially improve phonological awareness but also show a significant transfer effect by facilitating literacy learning in school. Several phonological awareness training studies were carried out in different countries so that the impact of such interventions is known for a variety of orthographies. Most of these studies were designed as follows: The sample consisted of kindergarten children who were tested for their phonological skills in a pretest session. Next, training and control groups were established that did not differ in their phonological awareness level and were also comparable with respect to several other demographic and behavioural test variables. The intervention periods for the training group lasted for about 10–20 weeks in most cases. Control groups participated in the normal kindergarten programme during this time period. Immediately thereafter, a post-test identical with the pretest assessed changes in children's phonological awareness at the end of the kindergarten year. Several studies also included a phonological awareness follow-up test at school entry. This test consisted of more difficult items serving the purpose of assessing delayed training effects. The assumption was that the training effect was still observable, and that the training group would again outperform the control group. Standardized tests of reading and spelling were then administered at the end of 1st grade. The expectation was that the phonological awareness advantage of the trained children would transfer to literacy learning, leading to better reading and spelling scores in the training group.

A seminal early training study focusing on a subcomponent of phonological awareness (sound categorization) was carried out by Bradley and Bryant (1983). Sixty-five preschool children were selected from a larger longitudinal study and divided into four groups: two training groups and two control groups. Whereas the first training group received intensive training focusing on sound categorization, the second group was not only trained on sound categorization but was also taught how each sound was represented by a letter of the alphabet. The first control group learnt how to categorize pictures in semantic groups, and the second control group received no training at all. Bradley and Bryant (1983) were able to demonstrate that the two training groups outperformed the control groups on standardized reading and spelling tests presented four years later. Although performance on the reading test was comparable for the two training groups, the second group outperformed the first on the spelling test. Given that their intervention study was embedded in a more comprehensive correlational longitudinal study on the same topic that yielded similar results, the researchers concluded that the link between early sound categorization and subsequent literacy development is causal.

A now classic training study focusing on phonological awareness was conducted by Lundberg et al. (1988) in Denmark. Lundberg and colleagues assumed that metalinguistic games would help children in developing their sensitivity to phonemes in words and enable them to understand the alphabetic principle more quickly as they learn to read and spell. The training programme targeted oral language activities embedded in a set of games and was carried out during the last year of kindergarten for about eight months. A control group did not receive any specific instruction, but participated in the regular kindergarten programme. The authors ensured that kindergarten teachers of the control group were not aware of training activities in the intervention group. Pre- and post-test measures were taken immediately before and after the training and various metalinguistic abilities revealed significant treatment effects. Even more importantly, significant effects of the programme on subsequent spelling skills were demonstrated from the first grades of elementary school onwards, lasting until the end of 4th grade. Given that the connection between phonemes and letters was not explicitly taught in the training programme, this longitudinal intervention study thus showed that phonological awareness can be trained effectively in kindergarteners without providing any knowledge on letters or written language skills.

Another study was carried out by Kjeldsen et al. (2003) in a sample of Swedish children who were followed up until the end of grade 9 (Kjeldsen et al. 2014). One unique aspect of this longitudinal study was that the attrition rate observed over a period of about ten years was very small, which is probably due to the fact that the study took place in the autonomous archipelago district of Aland where mobility was extremely low. The sample consisted of about 200 children, half of whom received phonological awareness training according to the guidelines set by Lundberg and colleagues. Positive training effects were found for children's letter and word decoding skills in grades 1 to 6, and for reading comprehension assessed in grade 9. The difference between trained and untrained students was in place already in grade 1 and remained stable through the elementary school years. Reading progress was comparable for training and control groups from grade 3 onwards, leading to highly stable learning trajectories (indicated by high test–retest correlations) in both groups over time. It seems important to note that significant training effects were observed despite the fact that phonological competencies were also occasionally trained in the control group, due to the broad attention that Lundberg's programme attracted in Scandinavian countries.

The programme was also translated into other languages. An English version that was adapted for US classrooms and field-tested with US-American kindergarten students and teachers (Adams et al. 1998) yielded similarly positive results. At about the same time, Schneider and colleagues (e.g., Schneider et al. 1997; Schneider et al. 2000) developed a German version of the programme which was labelled 'Hearing, Listening, Learning' (HLL), also known as the 'Würzburg training program' in German-speaking countries. The German version of the programme consisted of fifty-seven different 'language games' in six consecutive training units that tapped into phonological awareness in the broad and narrow sense. Phonological awareness in the broad sense refers to large linguistic units such as words, syllables, and rhymes, while phonological awareness in the narrow sense refers to small units such as phonemes within words. Kindergarten teachers were asked to carry out the programme over the course of 20 weeks during the last year of kindergarten, spending about 10–15 minutes per day with the training units. Like Lundberg and colleagues, Schneider et al. (1997) were able to show that the training was success-ful. There were substantial immediate and long-term training effects on phonological awareness, indicated by an effect size of about 1 standard deviation. Furthermore, there were significant (but smaller) short- and long-term effects on reading and spelling which lasted until the end of German elementary school (i.e., grade 4).

A subsequent training study by Schneider et al. (2000) focused on children at risk for dyslexia, defined as kindergarten children with very low levels of phonological awareness. In addition to the Lundberg version, a second training component ('Hearing, Listening, Learning 2' – HLL 2) was used to improve children's knowledge of the relationship between sounds and letters. The idea behind this approach was that children who are already able to distinguish between different sounds in words (a major goal of HLL) should be ready for a next step – that is, for linking sounds to letters. The children at risk were assigned to three training versions. One group received HLL, another one HLL 2, and a third group received a combination of HLL and HLL 2. The combined training programme was shortened to ensure that training duration was comparable across groups. As a main result, it was found that the combination of HLL and HLL2 was particularly effective in improving at-risk children's phonological awareness. This result is in line with the 'phonological linkage hypothesis' (Hatcher et al. 1994), which is based on the assumption that a training approach systematically linking a phonological awareness training with a training component focusing on knowledge about letter–sound correspondences should yield larger effects than training these components in isolation. Children's development during the early school years was also compared with that of a randomly selected control group. Findings obtained at the end of 3rd grade indicated that the combined training procedure turned out to be most effective in the long run. Children at risk who were given this combined training performed at about the same level as the normal controls. Moreover, a large percentage of trained children at risk for dyslexia did not show any problems in respect of reading or spelling in elementary school.

Several meta-analyses have demonstrated that increases in phonological awareness are related to improved reading and spelling ability (e.g., Bus and van IJzendoorn 1999; Ehri et al. 2001). For instance, in the quantitative meta-analysis carried out by Bus and van IJzendoorn (1999), the effects of phonological awareness training on reading were investigated for a homogeneous set of US studies with a randomized or matched design. The combined effect sizes were d = 0.73 for randomized control trials and d = 0.70 for matched designs. Thus, experimentally manipulated phonological awareness explained about 12% of the variance in subsequent reading skills. Programmes combining phonological and letter training were more effective than a purely phonological training. The authors concluded from their findings that phonological awareness is an important but not a sufficient condition for early reading.

Another quantitative meta-analysis evaluating the effects of phonological awareness instruction on learning to read and spell was conducted by Ehri et al. (2001). This analysis was based on fifty-two studies comparing the outcomes of treatment and control groups. Analysis of effect sizes revealed that the impact of phonological awareness instruction on helping children acquire phonological awareness was large (d = 0.86). In comparison, phonological awareness instruction exerted a moderate but statistically significant impact on reading (d = 0.53), including reading comprehension, and spelling (d = 0.59). The meta-analysis also revealed that phonological awareness instruction was more effective when it was taught in combination with letters than without letters. Moreover, typically developing readers, at-risk children, and children with dyslexia all benefitted from this kind of instruction. A recent meta-analysis basically confirmed these findings but also highlighted the fact that phonological awareness intervention programmes are particularly helpful for children at risk for developing dyslexia (Suggate 2016).

Several longitudinal studies addressed the impact of phonological awareness training on the further development of children at risk for dyslexia (e.g., Elbro and Petersen 2004; Kjeldsen et al. 2014; Partanen and Siegel 2014; Snowling and Hulme

2011; Weber et al. 2007). Overall, training-related gains in at-risk readers were found in all studies, not only for letter and word decoding but also for reading comprehension and spelling. For instance, Elbro and Petersen (2004) found that the at-risk training group significantly outperformed the at-risk control group when follow-up tests on word and non-word reading were conducted in grades 2 and 3. In addition, Snowling and Hulme (2011) asked how well an early intervention can raise at-risk children's performance to a more typical range of reading skills. As predicted, substantial gains in word reading were found immediately after the intervention and were sustained after almost a year. Interestingly, a reading comprehension test showed that the average performance of the training group was close to the population mean. Similarly positive findings were reported by Kjeldsen et al. (2014), who found strong positive training effects on reading in school for the whole sample, but also for an at-risk group composed of the lowest quartile of the sample.

Using a somewhat different approach, Weber et al. (2007) explored the effects of a training programme combining phonological awareness and letter knowledge for other risk groups. In this study, children with specific language impairment as well as children with a migration background and suboptimal proficiency in the German language were compared with 'typical' kindergarten children and a control group of children with specific language impairment. Although the 'typical' group outperformed the three groups of children at risk in most aspects of language-related abilities at pretest, substantial training effects were found for all groups. Interestingly, trained children with specific language impairment clearly outperformed control children with specific language impairment at post-test (but not at pretest) even though the control children's teachers claimed that the content of the training programme was part of their standard curriculum. Thus, children with specific language impairment and children with a migration background can substantially benefit from a combined training approach. Subsequent German training studies focusing on training children with a migration background confirmed this finding (Pröscholdt et al. 2013).

Despite the generally positive findings summarized here, the effectiveness of phonological awareness training programmes for literacy learning has been controversially discussed in German-speaking countries. Intervention effects of the 'Hearing, Listening, Learning' programme have been evaluated several times by different authors (Fischer and Pfost 2015; Wolf et al. 2016). Across all training studies, participants showed significant improvements in phonological awareness with an at least medium effect size. Contrary to the findings of the international meta-analyses described here, however, more recent German studies focusing on random samples of kindergarten children reported only small intervention effects on reading at the beginning of school, which tended to vanish after a post-test interval of more than one year. Pfost et al. (2019) did not find lasting intervention effects for a random sample of kindergarten children. One possible explanation for these null findings is that children in the control groups are now confronted with more language-related input (including phonological training) during their kindergarten routine compared to several decades ago. Another reason could be that the training programmes were not always implemented as carefully as the first-generation of intervention procedures. One aspect supporting this assumption is that in several studies, immediate training effects of phonological awareness did not exceed half a standard deviation, which may limit positive transfer effects on subsequent reading or spelling (Schneider 2019).

23.3.2 Training Studies Focusing on Early Math Competencies

The development of preschool training programmes focusing on mathematical competencies lagged behind the development of training programmes for basic literacy competencies. This is mainly due to the fact that comprehensive theoretical models were not developed before the end of the last century (e.g., Krajewski et al. 2008; Resnick 1989), and that most longitudinal studies testing these models and exploring the impact of a variety of numerical skills on subsequent maths development were not completed before the beginning of this century. There is now plenty of empirical evidence that early quantity–number competencies predict later mathematical school achievement (e.g., Aunola et al. 2004; Koponen et al. 2007; Krajewski and Schneider 2009a; Krajewski and Schneider 2009b). More specifically, counting ability at preschool age turned out to be a reliable predictor of mathematical achievement in 1st grade (see also Passolunghi et al. 2007). Also, individual differences in counting speed explained a considerable amount of variance in subsequent maths performance. Preschool number concepts were strongly related to children's procedural calculation skills in grade 4 (Koponen et al. 2007). Moreover, as emphasized by Jordan and colleagues (Jordan et al. 2007; Jordan et al. 2009), preschool children's non-symbolic counting abilities, number comparisons, and non-verbal calculation procedures not only accounted for a large percentage (about 66%) of the variance in 1st grade maths achievement, but also for variance at the end of grade 3. Similarly, Krajewski and Schneider (2009a) showed that basic numerical skills and the ability to link quantity to number words predicted mathematical fact retrieval as well as performance on standardized maths tests conducted in grades 1 and 4. Thus, the available longitudinal evidence clearly illustrates the importance of early quantity–number competencies for mathematical achievement in school (see Chapter 18, Gunderson 2022 for a more comprehensive overview).

Training programmes focusing on early maths competencies that were based on this empirical evidence as well as first reports on the effects of such programmes date back to the early 2000s. In the United States, several preschool intervention programmes have been shown to improve student mathematical skills in the preschool years. The degree to which these effects last or fade-out in elementary school, however, has been the subject of substantial research and debate. As a consequence, differences in scholarly viewpoints have prevented researchers from making clear and consistent policy recommendations to educational decision-makers and stakeholders (see Dumas et al. 2019).

There is evidence that some early interventions can be successful. For instance, research assessing the impact of the preschool programme Building Blocks (Clements and Sarama 2007; Clements et al. 2013) has demonstrated significantly improved mathematical outcomes in the training group, with particularly promising findings for groups of students with low socioeconomic status. Clements et al. (2013) examined the effects of a mathematics intervention, administered during preschool, on the student-specific growth trajectories of mathematical ability through elementary school. Mathematical ability of the sample was assessed in kindergarten, 1st, 3rd, 4th, and 5th grade. The authors found that the Building Blocks intervention significantly reduced the time it took students to develop half of their predicted elementary mathematical skill. This finding implies that the learning trajectories of students in the treatment group were significantly steeper, indicating that their growth early in elementary school was more rapidly approaching their asymptotic capacity. Accordingly, while Building Blocks did not significantly alter the capacity of the students in the treatment group to develop mathematical skill, it did improve the rate at which students approached their asymptotic capacity. The authors concluded from their findings that by shifting the focus of investigation from eventual skill level to the shape of the learning trajectory over time (i.e., by comparing the learning rates), they detected a positive effect of the preschool intervention through elementary school.

Nonetheless, as noted by Bailey et al. (2016), the fading-out of early intervention effects is a serious problem (see also Chapter 21, Sokolowski and Peters 2022) robustly encountered in US-American research on early childhood education. In this context, fading-out means that the treatment effect diminishes over time, with children who did not receive the intervention eventually catching up to children who did. One popular explanation for the fade-out of early mathematics interventions is that elementary school teachers may not teach the kind of advanced content that children are prepared for after receiving the intervention. Thus, lower-achieving children in the control groups of early mathematics interventions can catch up to the higher-achieving children in the treatment groups. An alternative explanation is that persistent individual differences in children's long-term mathematical development result from relatively stable pre-existing differences in their skills, genes, and environments, rather than from the direct effects of previous knowledge on later knowledge (Sokolowski 2018; Snowling and Hulme 2011). In line with this notion, Bailey et al. (2016) found that approximately 70% of the fade-out effect can be attributed to pre-existing differences between children in treatment and control groups with the same level of achievement at post-test.

To explore the effects of preschool intervention on subsequent maths performance in school, Dumas et al. (2019) used a relatively novel statistical framework (Dynamic Measurement Modelling) that takes both intra- and inter-individual student differences across time into account. Using this approach, they were able to demonstrate that students who receive a short-term intervention in preschool may not differ from a control group in terms of their long-term mathematics outcomes at the end of elementary school. Nevertheless, they do exhibit significantly steeper growth curves as they approach their eventual skill level. In addition, an important finding was that this significant improvement of the learning rate in elementary school benefitted minority students most, thus highlighting the critical societal need for research-based mathematics curricula in preschool.

In Germany, several kindergarten maths intervention programmes have been developed over the past two decades. The most frequently evaluated programme 'Quantities, Counting, Numbers' (Quantities, counting, numbers (MZZ) n.d.) is based on Krajewski's three-level model of basic mathematical development. According to this model, children progress from the level of number sense to a level at which they link numbers to number words and then to a level at which they link quantity relations to number words (Krajewski et al. 2008). This programme is guided by the general idea that an effective early maths intervention should follow natural numerical development as closely as possible. An evaluation study of the programme that also included other programmes was carried out during the last year of kindergarten (Krajewski et al. 2008). While one group of children participated in the programme, another group participated in training focused on inductive reasoning. A third group of children took part in another mathematical training programme (Zahlenland) in an uncontrolled setting, while the control group did not receive any specific maths training. Unspecific and specific predictors were assessed immediately before training and subsequently twice – that is, about 8 and 2 months before children entered school. The children in the group participating in the 'Quantities, Counting, Numbers' programme showed the largest short-term and long-term progress with respect to basic number and quantity competencies.

Gerlach et al. (2013) developed the intervention programme MARKO-T, which is based on an adaptive individual training approach designed for 5- to 8-year-old children with maths problems in kindergarten and elementary school. The training programme aims at improving children's basic arithmetic concepts and maths problem solving strategies. The selection of training units is adaptive in the sense that it first assesses a child's competence level and then uses this information to introduce appropriate training content. The specific content comprises tasks dealing with counting skills, number line processing, cardinality, and class inclusion. The training programme revealed short-term effects of the intervention four months after completion, even for children with learning difficulties (Ehlert and Fritz 2013; Gerlach et al. 2013).

23.4 Successful Prevention Strategies in Different Countries

Across the world, educational policymakers aspire to implement prevention measures to reduce the prevalence of learning difficulties in reading, spelling, and mathematics. The proposed measures differ, however, with regard to the specificity of the preferred prevention approach. According to Caplan (1974) it is helpful in this context to differentiate between three levels of prevention measures: a universal level (primary prevention), a selected level (secondary prevention), and an indicated level (tertiary prevention).

Universal prevention approaches refer to educational offerings for all children, irrespective of their social background or whether they are at risk for dyslexia or dyscalculia. While tertiary prevention refers to measures that are applied when the horse has already left the barn and learning deficits have been diagnosed, secondary prevention is provided early to selected groups of children to reduce the probability that they will develop learning deficits later in school. Thus, secondary prevention approaches seem to be most promising for prevention of dyslexia and dyscalculia in early education settings. The intervention programmes described here that are designed to strengthen relevant precursor skills are suitable educational offerings within this targeted framework.

In most European countries, state-based regulations for early education with regard to the prevention of dyslexia and dyscalculia are rather weak. For instance, the German-speaking countries mostly rely on the universal variant of prevention since the responsible Early Childhood Education and Care associations set great value on non-selective approaches integrated into everyday kindergarten activities. As a consequence of this strategy, related Early Childhood Education and Care measures are not targeted precisely at children's individual developmental needs. Moreover, the effectiveness of the specific prevention strategy depends on the process quality within the individual Early Childhood Education and Care centres. As reported by Ulferts et al. (2019) in a recent meta-analysis, the process quality with regard to academic outcomes generally seems to be rather fragile in most European countries.

To our knowledge, the approach taken by the Finnish Ministry of Education and Culture is one of the most appropriate prevention policies worldwide regarding dyslexia and dyscalculia. The National Board of Education, a subsection of the Finnish Ministry, provides general guidelines for prevention measures. Since about the early 2000s, the National Board has issued recommendations to include phonological awareness training in kindergarten activities. Recently, Kjeldsen et al. (2019) provided longitudinal evidence for long-lasting positive effects of this policy, especially for children at risk for reading difficulties.

The Finnish policy, however, is not restricted to the prevention of dyslexia. The Finnish Ministry of Education has also supported the implementation of innovative maths training programmes. For instance, Mononen, Aunio, and Koponen (2014) explored the effects of the RightStart Mathematics instruction (originally developed in the USA) on Finnish kindergartner's mathematics performance. A control group received the mathematics instruction typically provided during the last kindergarten year. It was shown that both approaches helped in improving children's counting, number comparison, and addition skills. One especially positive aspect of both programmes was that initially low-performing children gained the most.

In 2006, the Ministry started a programme called LukiMat (ReadMath) with the aim of having an internet-based environment promoting and evaluating basic skills relevant for reading and maths. During 2007–15, the development and maintenance of LukiMat was supported with the goal of making the tools and the service freely available to the kindergartens and preschools. One component of the LukiMat environment is GraphoLearn (previously known as GraphoGame), which includes digital learning games to prevent dyslexia. Similar tools were also developed for basic maths skills.

The LukiMat initiative was launched by the Niilo Mäki Institute at the University of Jyväskylä, which promotes the concept of an evidence-based learning game via partnerships with universities, NGOs, and companies all over the world. Parts of the learning games are now available in more than ten European countries, four African countries, five American countries (including several US states), as well as five Asian countries. The beneficial prevention effects in at-risk children that had been reported in many controlled field trials (see https://info.grapholearn.com/research/publications/), however, are only achievable by continuous and intensive practice.

23.5 Conclusion

There is strong agreement among policymakers and the general public that reading, spelling, and arithmetic are essential to educational and professional success, and to life in general. Accordingly, in many countries, early childhood education and care associations recommend integrating books and quantity games into everyday preschool education activities.

In this chapter, we argue that this is not a sufficiently effective strategy for prevention of dyslexia and dyscalculia, although it might be helpful for young children to become familiar with materials related to the contents of literacy and mathematics. Given the evidence that there are trainable specific preschool skills relevant for successful learning in the domains of reading, spelling, and maths, we consider universal prevention measures as a non-sufficient early intervention concept.

We outlined the current state of the art with regard to the impact of preschool children's specific foundational skills on school achievement in reading, spelling, and mathematics. Given that most of the relevant preschool skills also are suited to identify children at risk for dyslexia and dyscalculia, targeted attempts to provide appropriate remedial kindergarten programmes should be evaluated as a necessary supplement for a successful early education strategy, with the ultimate goal of preventing the emergence of dyslexia and dyscalculia during primary school years.

We also provided evidence that the idea of preventing dyslexia and dyscalculia via training programmes aimed at improving the relevant preschool skills does work. Many of these programmes do provide exercises that are embedded in computer-based learning games that can be flexibly used even in distance learning settings.

Although appropriate measures to prevent dyslexia and dyscalculia are available in several countries, policymakers in the field of early education are often hesitant to implement them, with positive exceptions in Scandinavia. As outlined, the Finnish Ministry of Education and Culture supports the evidence-based development of a set of learning games with great potential to reduce the prevalence of dyslexia and dyscalculia. These learning games targeting phonological processing and basic maths skills, are used daily in schools and homes across Finland by thousands of children. One might speculate whether these measures will lead to larger decreases in the percentage of children with dyslexia and/or dyscalculia in Finland as compared to other countries. From our point of view, this can indeed be expected, provided that the responsible preschool teachers will become more and more open to selective prevention strategies (but see Chapter 22, Lachmann, Bergström, Huber, and Nürk 2022). If this vision becomes reality, we are confident that the enduring and intense usage of appropriate prevention programmes, particularly by children at risk for dyslexia and/or dyscalculia, will increase dramatically, such that the number of affected children will decrease substantially.

Suggestions for Further Reading

Geary, D. C. 2011. 'Cognitive Predictors of Achievement Growth in Mathematics: A 5-Year Longitudinal Study'. *Developmental Psychology* 47 (6): 1539–52

Hulme, C., and M. J. Snowling. 2013. 'Learning to Read: What We Know and What We Need to Understand Better'. *Child Development Perspectives*, 7: 1–5.

Kjeldsen, A.-C., L., Educ, S., Saarento-Zaprudin, and P. Niemi. 2019. 'Kindergarten Training in Phonological Awareness: Fluency and Comprehension Gains are Greatest for Readers at Risk in Grades 1 Through 9. *Journal of Learning Disabilities*, 52: 366–82.

Mononen, R., P. Aunio, T. Koponen, and M. Aro. 2015. 'A Review of Early Numeracy Interventions for Children at Risk in Mathematics'. *International Journal of Early Childhood Special Education*, 6: 25–54.

Siegler, R. S., and H. Lortie-Forgues. 2014. 'An Integrative Theory of Numerical Development'. *Child Development Perspectives*, 8: 144–50.

Summary: Best Practice – Diagnostics and Prevention

(1) **Diagnostic criteria for specific learning disorders:** (a) severity (1.5–2 standard deviations below the average grade-level (not age-level) performance); (b) persistence (a history of difficulties confirmed by repeated assessments and by response to intervention); (c) specificity (typical general cognitive development, but not an IQ discrepancy threshold); (d) unexpectedness (adequate education; sufficient language proficiency; no sensory, neural, or mental disorders; no severe psychosocial adversity); (e) manifestation (confirmed by standardized achievement tests with a high standard of objectivity, reliability, and validity). These criteria need to be tailored to the specific script/number (language) system and cultural educational setting (see Parts VI and X; Chapter 24, Nag 2022) while also taking individual circumstances into account (e.g., motivation, emotions, self-concept, noise, fatigue).

(2) **Overcoming the wait-to-fail approach by implementing an early risk assessment:** A valid diagnosis can usually only be given after about two years of instruction when children typically reach a stable basic proficiency level. As a consequence, a *wait-to-fail* approach is still common in practice. This approach impedes intervention (e.g., due to the automatization of sub-optimal processing, negative learning experiences (e.g., educators: Matthew effect; peers: bullying), emerging mental health issues) and should therefore be replaced by a comprehensive early risk assessment focusing on early predictors (see Part VII), but also considering familial predispositions, social-environmental backgrounds (see Part III) and cross-cultural differences (see Part VI).

(3) **Being aware of the limitations of diagnostic practice:** Despite being based on classification systems (ICD, DSM), diagnoses leave room for subjectivity and bias and are prone to measurement error. Diagnoses are not generalizable since they are based on comparisons to specific reference samples which may differ according to culture, age, curriculum, language, and many other factors (see Chapter 24, Nag 2022).

(4) **Effective prevention strategies:** Effective prevention strategies are based on established early predictors (see Part VII) and centred on early childhood education and care measures that selectively target children at risk due to their individual needs (see points 1 and 2). An example is the LukiMat programme supported by the Finnish Ministry of Education and Culture,

which comprises digital learning games that are freely available to kindergartens and preschools and can be flexibly used even in distance learning settings. The effectiveness of such programmes depends on a number of factors, such as the quality management within the early childhood education and care institutions and the continuity and intensity of participation.

PART X

Best Practice – Schooling and Educational Policy

24 Dyslexia and the Dyslexia-Like Picture: Supporting All Children in Primary School

Sonali Nag

24.1 Introduction

Children typically record dramatic growth in reading skills in primary school. This is not surprising since reading instruction has been placed at the heart of primary school curricula. Irrespective of country, learning outcomes in primary schools everywhere articulate the expectation that children will read, comprehend, and write to express themselves well. This chapter focuses on children who fall behind these stated literacy expectations within their school system, arguing that, while some will qualify for the diagnosis of dyslexia, all those who struggle will need a measured response from the primary school system. A cursory look at the decision-making framework that primary schools follow for those who fall behind shows variation across countries and also within countries, including those that have a well-articulated protocol of referral and response. Given this, it is useful to think of school systems as placed at different points on a continuum of support, with schools that have no discernable provisions and schools with multilayered provisions put at either extreme. This variety may reflect differences in access to resources for screening, diagnostic testing, and tiers of targeted interventions. The variety may also reflect macro-systemic issues such as education policies and the state of science related to atypical development in the languages of the region.

A response by school systems to children who fall behind triggers several questions: what to label poor readers? how to support them? and what to do when response to intervention is variable? Arguably, one reason for asking these questions is that the profile of visible difficulties that characterize a child with dyslexia looks remarkably similar to the profile of difficulties when a child has reduced access to high-quality and contextually appropriate literacy learning opportunities. The behavioural characteristics of children with dyslexia are not just varied but also similar, at least in part, to children who struggle due to, for example, ineffective teaching or a lack of books for practice (Nag and Snowling 2012). The proximal and distal causes for the manifest difficulty with reading in dyslexia and the *dyslexia-like picture* are, however, different, even if sometimes overlapping. In dyslexia, although there is no one causal factor, a proximal cause for the poor reading is a phonological processing deficit and also, for example, difficulties with higher-order visual processing and unresolved early difficulties with vocabulary learning and grammar knowledge (see Chapter 4, Banfi, Landerl, and Moll 2022). Co-occurring problems may also occur with the child's pattern of difficulties attracting an additional diagnosis of, for example, attention deficit disorder (ADD), developmental language disorder (DLD), dyscalculia, and dyspraxia. In contrast, the causes for other forms of poor reading are more distal and located in the absence of explicit instruction, few opportunities to practice, reduced quality of inputs, and the child not knowing the language of instruction well because it is a new language or a new dialect. Importantly, unless carefully assessed, the manifest difficulties with, for example, word decoding (as needed in word recognition but also spelling) may not be qualitatively or quantitatively different in the two groups. Even established assessment systems may falter and show a 'built in' bias against some children due to, for example, their language histories and differences from the cultural mainstream (e.g., Seidenberg 2018; Verpalen et al. 2018).

Thus, more than a century after 'congenital word-blindness' entered the imagination of the European medical fraternity to describe the child who struggles with reading (e.g., Hinshelwood 1900), there still remain instances of uncertainty about differential diagnosis between dyslexia and the dyslexia-like picture. In this chapter, the term dyslexia is taken as a diagnostic category as defined by, for example, the American Psychiatric Association's (2013) Diagnostic and Statistical Manual of Mental Disorders (5th ed.; DSM-5), and the World Health Organization's (2019) (ICD-11) International Statistical Classification of Diseases and Related Health Problems (11th ed.; ICD-11). Both systems of classification ask for substantial evidence prior to diagnosis, and it is recognized that not all children who struggle with reading are children with dyslexia. Yet, all struggling children will require an equal response from the primary school system. For this reason, the focus necessarily needs to be on both children who reach the criteria for a diagnosis of dyslexia (or 'specific learning disorder', 'developmental learning disorder') and those whose difficulties are subclinical but who struggle with reading and reading-related skills (or the 'garden variety' poor reader, 'otherwise caused specific learning failures'; see Chapter 22, Lachmann, Bergström, Huber, and Nürk 2022).

24.2 Multiple Risks and Multiple Manifestations

24.2.1 Varieties of Risk Factors

The agreed view in the field of dyslexia, as with other developmental disorders, is that several factors together explain why a child struggles to read. These are risk factors that act in a probabilistic manner, interacting with each other and together triggering exceptional variety at the level of individual differences in cognitive skills and behavioural manifestation of literacy and language attainment (Hulme and Snowling 2013). The probabilistic nature of the associations between risk and outcome adds complexity to the task of developing an explanatory model for what causes dyslexia. As a start, characterizing the child who is a poor reader is the focus of several lines of research. Prenatal incidents and vulnerabilities due to exposure to toxins, for example, have been shown to impact later reading attainments in primary school (see Chapter 7, Hoeft and Bouhali 2022). There is also more information available now on the neurodevelopmental correlates of poor reading and, using evidence from US samples, for example, genetic studies show that genetic vulnerability may be more generalized than previously appreciated and can manifest via one or more of the multiple cognitive and linguistic skills that underpin a reading difficulty (Erbeli et al. 2018). fMRI studies show that less skilled readers show lower neurocognitive integration of information from the print and spoken language 'streams', and this is assumed to account for their lower reading comprehension (Shankweiler et al. 2008). In addition, longitudinal observational surveys, such as a six-year study in the United Kingdom, show that children with a family history of reading problems are at substantial risk of showing early reading and/or language difficulties and reduced reading comprehension in primary school, albeit with a slightly different profile of difficulties in component skills (Snowling et al. 2020). Such advances in our understanding of the brain-bases of reading difficulty and the genetic mechanisms that underpin dyslexia hold promise for differential diagnosis, although the field remains far from ready to deploy insights on the biology of dyslexia into primary school settings. But there is one line of evidence that is important to note since primary school systems are tasked with providing learning support: educational interventions dynamically change multiple neuroanatomical parameters in the brain (see Chapter 11, Yeatman 2022, and Chapter 12, Iuculano 2022).

In parallel, advances in our understanding of the environmental bases of literacy development are helping specify the correlates of educational inequality. Environmental risk factors include sociodemographic characteristics related to gender, geography, and socioeconomic status (e.g., Nag et al. 2014; see also Chapter 13, Cantlon 2022, and Chapter 14, Fish 2022). In high poverty contexts, for example, associations are present between children's language and literacy attainments in primary school and dimensions of the home such as availability of books, home tutoring, and presence of adults who also engage in literacy activities (Nag et al. 2018). Importantly, even when any or all of these resources are limited, the evidence suggests that families differ in how they harness what is available. For example, even when families have comparable levels of limited resources, there are differences in the extent to which individual families connect with the school and the wider community to support the child's literacy development. Within such a capabilities characterization of significant individuals in the child's life (Sen et al. 1979), risk factors could be linked to situations where resources are withheld from the family, institutional responses are alienating, or there is an absence of social networks for the child and family to turn to or trust for a timely and effective intervention. Repeated disruption in learning is another class of risk. This could be due to school closures, absent teachers, or reduced school attendance by the child due to poor health or pressing duties such as sibling care, household chores, or income-generation (for review, see Verhoeven et al. in press). Amongst all of these risk factors, the issue of absenteeism is particularly difficult to reconcile when considering a diagnosis of dyslexia, and confusion is seen across professionals as well as country contexts (teachers and school psychologists, USA and India: Al Otaiba et al. 2019; Sprick et al. 2020; Nag 2013).

24.2.2 Varieties of School Underachievement

Diagnostic systems typically set a cut-off of 1.5 or 2 standard deviations below an expected norm to consider a diagnosis of dyslexia and mark the level of severity of deficits. These are arbitrary cut-off points on an attainment continuum, although the cut-off points are derived through consensus building within the research and practitioner fraternity (see Chapter 22, Lachmann, Bergström, Huber, and Nürk 2022). It is assumed that the cut-off provides information for important decisions about treatment and learning support. For example, a diagnosis based on the cut-off triggers institutionalized support. Within the primary school setting, support materializes by way of access to programmes for assisted learning and professionals such as specialist teachers, speech and language therapists, and psychologists. Usually, those who are clinically identified go on to gain access to the support that is mandated in the said education system. However, the same diagnostic protocols that open services to children in need may become instruments to deny specialist help to other children because they do not meet the diagnostic criteria. These may be the children whose difficulties, even though educationally noteworthy for intervention (e.g., to reduce attainment gaps, to stop gaps from widening), are on the margins of cut-off points and therefore judged as subclinical.

The application of cut-off criteria becomes especially contentious in educational settings where there is large-scale underattainment. Settings with unusually high numbers of children struggling to read are not rare. They are, for example, widespread in some low- and middle-income countries and concentrated in pockets of deprivation in some high-income countries (Nag, et al. 2014; Strand et al. 2010). Interpretation of diagnostic criteria requires particular caution when referrals are from within such school systems since even if the large-scale underattainment implies that many children will fall below the 1.5 or 2 standard deviations on standardized tests, a diagnosis of dyslexia is obviously not valid. However, it is clear that these school systems will also need evidence-informed intervention planning.

24.3 Learning Support

24.3.1 Risks and Resources

Within a multifactorial view of reading difficulties, a good point to start planning interventions is to identify the precursor skills that support the reading development specifically expected during the primary school years. A point of learning support would be to target the profile of difficulties on these precursor skills. The extant literature has identified multiple precursor skills, including symbol knowledge, phonological processing skills, morphological knowledge, verbal memory, and visuo-motor skills (see Chapter 17, Lervåg and Melby-Lervåg 2022). Although the importance of each to primary school reading depends on the characteristics of the language (for multiple languages, see Verhoeven and Perfetti 2017; see also Chapter 15, Siok 2022), the defining characteristics are at the phonological, orthographic, and morphological levels.

Alongside skill development for all relevant cognitive-linguistic foundation skills, there is a need to consider how children cope with a reading difficulty. Helpful coping resources may compensate for specific difficulties and build resilience in the child, and these may also interact with each other and potential risk factors. Impressive vocabulary knowledge and grammar knowledge could, for example, come to the aid of word recognition when decoding skills are poor. Similarly, resilience could aid decoding accuracy in the form of persistence on a task, and this is despite the experience of repeated failure when reading. Resilience may also be associated with other affective-motivational factors, such as self-efficacy for literacy-related tasks. It is therefore reasonable to propose that what manifests as poor reading depends on a constellation of risk factors, both biological and environmental, and this is in interaction with compensatory resources and the quality of resilience. Schools become central in this account of reading difficulty because learning support is intended to address children's cognitive-linguistic difficulties and also support growth of resilience, self-efficacy, and compensatory cognitive-linguistic skills (e.g., a strong oral language foundation; Snowling et al. 2020).

24.3.2 Test–Teach–Test

Learning support can play an important role in informing the diagnosis process. Teach-and-then-test is an approach to diagnosis that stands on the insight that the association between risk factors and children's learning outcomes is moderated by instruction. Teach-and-test, or more accurately, test–teach–test, is a blended framework that accounts for both within-child risk factors and the nature of persistent difficulties after learning support has been offered. The framework intends to disambiguate poor performance due to a lack of instruction from a 'pure' difficulty by first offering quality teaching. Such a 'hybrid model' incorporates low response to intervention as an indicator for the diagnosis of dyslexia alongside cognitive-linguistic indicators such as deficits in phonological processing, speed of performance, and reading-related skills. Preliminary evidence (e.g., Spencer et al. 2014; Erbeli et al. 2018, using US samples) suggests this particular variety of a multifactorial view of reading difficulties is better than a model that is solely about within-child factors or response to intervention, particularly if the interest is for individual differences in learning trajectories at the lower end of the attainment continuum. The framework has found application in the field of childhood disabilities and developmental disorders and is seen as a promising 'prevention-based system' (Miller et al. 2019).

Nag (2013) followed this approach when working with widespread under-attainment in a resource poor public school in south India where many children's home language was different from the school language. Absenteeism and irregular teaching due to school closures and teacher deployment to other tasks also characterized the setting. Business-as-usual teaching was not always effective and did not build bridges for school language learning. The test–teach–test approach in this context aimed for 'an orientation to quality first' in what children received in school before considering diagnosis. Assessment of learning was across component skills that were informed by the small research base available for the local school languages (e.g., Nag and Snowling 2011). The process approach was examined through a case series of ten children who were reading two years behind their class level at the start of the intervention. A two-tiered intervention was used. The intervention ran over two academic years, with Tier 1 when children were in grade 3 and, six months later, Tier 2 when they were in grade 4. Children's *change score* following each round of intervention was computed using each child's narrative writing, which arguably provides rich information on multiple component skills of literacy learning. Outcome measures included number of sentences in narrative writing, words per sentence, spelling accuracy in the narrative production, and accuracy of inflections on nouns and verbs. Three children continued to show persistent difficulties with language measures and three with spelling. Their muted growth in target skills despite two tiers of evidence-informed interventions was taken as a signal to initiate clinical assessment. The working hypothesis from the learning support process was that some children may have a developmental language disorder (or language impairment) and some, dyslexia. Importantly, four children had caught up with the class average. It can be argued that what was done over the two years in this particular class is in line with what effective and thoughtful teachers everywhere do: when a child falls behind, teachers look to fine-tune their teaching methods, increase the intensity of their teaching, and, after many iterations of this, then consider a referral if concerns remain. Such an approach may seem at odds with an early identification and early intervention model, but is meaningful when intervention begins early without waiting for a diagnosis. Learning support in primary schools in this instance plays the important role of also avoiding over-diagnosis (false positives), a danger in programmes of early identification.

In conclusion, learning support may be thought of as more than the targeted teaching that addresses specific cognitive-linguistic weaknesses in children's profiles of attainments. Instead, learning support may be conceived to be more comprehensive, with the aim to additionally build resilience, self-efficacy, and sound compensatory skills. A multidimensional view of risk and resilience is a useful framework for such an approach to learning support. Such provisions in primary schools look beyond diagnostic protocols and the labels they offer. Instead, the learning support is sensitive to all three potential circumstances: when dyslexia is formally stated, when difficulties are identified but considered subclinical, and when underattainment is widespread in school. Further, such an approach to learning support may also help scaffold the diagnostic process by ensuring tiers of well-conceived instruction are first offered to a struggling reader before decisions are made about the presence of dyslexia (or another developmental disorder).

24.4 Decision-Making and the Evidence-Base

For schools to be principled in their response to all children along the attainments continuum, an extensive evidence base is needed. Synthesis reports, meta-analyses, and 'what works' clearing houses such as those found in a small selection of countries (e.g., the USA, the United Kingdom) provide useful guidance in this regard. The evidence base is, however, currently maturing at an uneven pace, with more details becoming available about the universals in literacy development and less about equally important particularities related to specific languages, orthographies, and contexts. This impacts decision-making within many primary schools around the world. Two issues are highlighted here: the developing nature of the evidence-base in well-researched school languages and what needs attention when working with under-researched school languages.

24.4.1 Decision-Making in Much-Researched School Languages

A central question for decision-making is whether the core principles of instruction for children with dyslexia are different from the core principles of instruction for those with a dyslexia-like picture. Recent systematic reviews in well-researched languages such as English (e.g., National Reading Panel (US) 2000) show that as yet there are too few studies in most sub-domains of literacy instruction to suggest that dyslexia-friendly interventions should be different from the robust support needed to counter all manifestations of poor reading. Not enough is known about the specificities of teaching for the two groups for oral language, reading fluency, reading comprehension, narrative writing, and metalinguistic awareness. The one exception is the teaching of 'alphabetics' covering phonemic awareness and phonics instruction, with the research synthesis allowing for a clear conclusion: the same methods of instruction work well for both groups: those with dyslexia and those with a dyslexia-like picture (National Reading Panel (US) 2000). For phonemic awareness instruction, for example, this meta-analysis suggests that the effect sizes are largest for 'at-risk readers' compared to those with a diagnosis and those considered typically developing, although studies comparing these groups in grades 2 and above are still too few to make a definitive statement. In addition, phonemic awareness instruction is effective across the SES continuum, with higher effects for children from mid- and high-SES homes compared to low-SES homes. Finally, instruction with a small set of phonological activities returns higher effect sizes than instruction that is 'multi-skill'. Two further insights from the 2020 Report of the National Reading Panel can help develop an evidence-informed school response for all children. Experimental, researcher-delivered alphabetic instruction produces higher gains but, more importantly, teacher-delivered instruction also shows high effect sizes ($d = 0.94$ for researchers vs. $d = 0.78$ for teachers). In other words, teachers know and can deliver effective learning support, although other research has recorded the challenge of low skill and poor content knowledge for literacy instruction in many teachers (e.g., Joshi and Wijekumar 2020). In addition, all lengths of intervention made a difference, with higher effect sizes seen for interventions of medium length (5–9.3 hrs: $d = 1.37$; 10–18 hrs: $d = 1.14$)

compared to the very brief (< 5 hrs: $d = 0.61$) and the longer lengths (>18 hrs: $d = 0.65$). This finding suggests that a modular approach embedded within an ongoing programme could be a structure of choice when planning learning support in primary school systems.

Another question is related to the decision-making framework implicit in the Response to Intervention (RTI) approach. This approach may be considered as a Multi-Tiered System of Supports (MTSS). In RTI or MTSS, multiple tiers of support are offered, starting with improved mainstream programmes to more and more intensive and individualized programmes. In this approach, the priority in decision-making is related to matching the child to the right level of intervention within a multi-tiered system; the focus is less on diagnostic protocols (e.g., Toste et al. 2014). Within this system, the implications of decisions are not always clear: what are the criteria to decide who is a non-responder, or which type of measure is ideal for identifying non-responders: school-level norms versus national norms, single test results versus composites, cross-sectional data versus change over time, who gets how many tiers of intervention, what are the implications when some continue to need more and more intensive levels of intervention, and what has fallen short in the offered intervention? These and related questions are captured in the following excerpt on the RTI system in the United States:

> Despite the promise of RTI, and the hard work of many research and school teams, there remains ongoing concern . . . For example, how do we ensure that other exclusionary criteria are not responsible for a lack of response (e.g., language minority status, a lack of opportunity to learn due to poor or inadequate instruction or due to intervention implemented without fidelity)? (Al Otaiba et al. 2019, pp. 129–130)

Clearly, more research is needed, since the confusions that persist also link back to issues related to the diagnosis of dyslexia and the response from the primary school system for those with a dyslexia-like picture.

24.4.2 Decision-Making in Under-researched School Languages

Turning to under-researched areas, the Asian orthographies stand out. It is not uncommon to find an uncritical application of insights from the European languages across Asia. This is problematic for several reasons. First, the component skills critical for early literacy in the non-alphabetic orthographies of Asia do not entirely mirror those for the European alphabetic systems (for reviews of a selection of Asia's school languages, see Verhoeven and Perfetti 2017; see also Chapter 15, Siok 2022). Second, assumptions in models from European languages are based on a certain architectural design of the writing system and this is not inclusive of design elements found in Asian systems. For instance, the orthographic unit is *a symbol block* in Korean, Japanese, Chinese, and Indic orthographies. A task demand of decoding symbol blocks is intra-symbol processing and being analytic of elements within each symbol. These are learning demands that are at variance with most (but not all) symbol sets in the European languages since the alphabet typically does not decompose further into smaller sound or meaning elements. Third, there is a difference in the mapping principle that links the Asian orthographic units to the language. The differences are both at the level of mapping to phonology (e.g., the alphasyllabic units of south and south-east Asia map to syllable, body-coda, and phoneme) and its realization in morpho-semantics (e.g., the Chinese systems of east Asia map to meaning-bearing information). All of these differences have implications for primary school decision-making: When there is poor word decoding – arguably the most manifest of difficulties in dyslexia and the dyslexia-like picture – then it is useful to assess symbol block knowledge and mapping principles specific to the particular Asian writing system. Writing systems differences also define pedagogical decisions. Most obviously, since Asian writing systems are well specified at the level of syllables and/or morphemes, it is unclear what value is provided by borrowing methods related to alphabetics (phoneme awareness and phonics instruction). Instead, the indications in the literature are for activities that support morphological awareness, visuo-motor practice, and an analytic approach to intra-symbol processing.

Extrapolations from research in the European orthographies to the Latin-based orthographies of Latin America, Africa, Asia, and the Asia-Pacific are arguably less problematic. This is because they each share the alphabetic principle making letter knowledge and phonemic processing candidate skills to prioritize in a primary school programme. Here too, however, there are challenges to a simple extension of instructions on the alphabetic principle because languages differ in orthographic transparency, phonological complexity, and morphological features, which suggests each may need teaching components weighted differently. Consider, for example, the syllabic teaching approaches of the languages of Africa that use the Latin alphabet (e.g., Asfaha et al. 2009): their focus is on the syllable, a clear departure from the phoneme-focused interventions, for example, in English. However, such an alertness to the psycholinguistic characteristics of the language of instruction is yet to be found in synthesis documents such as the Report of the National Reading Panel (2020).

24.4.3 Other Practical Challenges: Fairness and Experience History

One practical challenge is to identify what would comprise a fair test for all test takers. It is reasonably clear that the potential to develop a test with good psychometric properties is high when the test is restricted to children whose home language is the same as the language of assessment. Similarly, it may be easier to interpret test results when children come from the same cultural group that informed test construction and the standardization norms. Such close match also increases the likelihood of achieving both sensitivity and specificity to detect dyslexia. However, when the test is taken to diverse populations, issues of test fairness surface, and have a knock-on effect on interpretation of results: questions arise as to whether the profiles of difficulty are due to contextual factors such as opportunity history and home language–school language differences or due to within-child factors of a neurolinguistic origin. Language and literacy tests are particularly dependent on opportunities that support the development of the skills they test. In contrast, a test of working memory, where new information must be stored and processed, has been forwarded as a less experience-driven candidate test with the potential to be less unequal between those who have and those who do not have the prior knowledge implicit in the task (de Abreu et al. 2013). However, even working memory tasks draw on prior knowledge such as knowledge about the linguistic items used to capture working memory (Schwering and MacDonald 2020). Moreover, children who differ on sociodemographic variables such as book exposure or preschool attendance can perform differently on specific test items, including in tests usually considered as least dependent on prior knowledge, such as the backward digit span task with its closed class items (e.g., Verpalen et al. 2018).

Related to the role of contextual factors in explanations of test performance is the second practical challenge of identifying test items that aren't too sensitive to children's experience histories. Practical solutions for language and literacy tasks appear to be linked to a careful monitoring of words in children's worlds. For example, if the assessment is in the home language, and when working with multilingual children with not as yet enough exposure to the school language, de Abreu et al. (2013) argued for an overrepresentation of words from the home language. On the other hand, for assessment in the school language, Bialystok et al. (2010) picked words from the school context and ignored words from the home context because a word survey found that differences in vocabulary knowledge between native speakers of the school language and second language learners of that language were most pronounced for words that were rarely used in school. According to this study, items related to food, the household, and items that are unlikely to occur in the classroom context were classified as home items. Professions, animals, plants, shapes, musical instruments, and items reflecting school experiences were classified as school items. Early acquired lexical items, closed class items like number names, and picking words that are less sensitive to dialect effects have also been considered (e.g. Nag 2016). Given below are innovations in language-specific item generation for tests in understudied school languages:

For a vocabulary test:

(1) selection of phonologically close, semantically close and semantically unrelated words as distracters (Kiswahili, Alcock, Ngorosho, Deus, and Jukes 2010).
(2) selection of words that are similar/identical and very different in the home dialect and the language of assessment (Standard and Moroccan Arabic, Rochdi 2010).
(3) selection of words for their prefixes and suffixes (Bahasa Indonesia, Winskel and Widjaja 2007).

For a word reading test:

(1) words taken from [school] primers (early grades: Kiswahili: Alcock et al. 2000; Bahasa Indonesia: Winskel and Widjaja, 2007; later grades: Herero: Veii and Everett 2005).

(2) words randomly selected from a dictionary list of all words in the textbook or a selection of children's literature (e.g., Eritrean languages: Asfaha et al. 2009; Kannada: Nag 2007).

(3) words with the highest token frequency within a textbook (e.g., Most Used Words (MUW) in Zambia: Friedlander et al. 2014; and Zimbabwe: Chinyama et al. 2012).

(4) words that reflect the psycholinguistic properties of a language (e.g., words with digraph accents, stop sounds in Filipino: Ledesma 2002; an affixed word in Malay: Lee and Wheldall 2011).

(5) words that reflect the orthographic properties of the written language (e.g., 2 and 3 letter words in Turkish, Oktay and Aktan 2002; 4 and 5 letter words in Albanian, Hoxhallari, Van Daal, and Ellis 2004; words with 'joint symbols' in Bengali, Chowdhury et al. 1994; words with various symbol types in Kannada, Nag 2007).

(Excerpt from Nag 2016, p. 30)

24.5 The Social Cognitive Environment

A further issue complicates any attempt at a synthesis of the literature on dyslexia and decision-making in primary school: matters related to dyslexia have a deeply sociocultural aspect to them. This section uses recent commentaries from the United Kingdom and the USA – two countries with arguably the most influential research agendas in the field of dyslexia – to illustrate how shared ways of thinking mark the process of identification and support. The first excerpt is related to help-seeking on behalf of the child, the second to the attitude of those who respond to the child. Inherent in both are deeply embedded social processes, suggesting the role of prestige and privilege in garnering of resources on the one hand, and implicit biases in the offer of resources on the other.

> [D]iagnosis may prove to be a means to gain additional resources, albeit operating via differing routes in the US and the UK. However, in both nations, two parallel systems operate with all children having equal opportunity for RTI [response to intervention] procedures, but with more socially advantaged children dominating the dyslexia route. (Gibbs and Elliott 2020, p. 495)

> Finally, with the help of policy makers, the current 'failure' model of dyslexia must be replaced with a 'support' model that enables school-, clinic-, and community-based early screenings and subsequent evidence-based response to screening through empowered and well-trained teachers within the general education framework. (Sanfilippo et al. 2020, p. 6)

Implicit in these excerpts is the multilayered and dynamically interconnected matrix of home–community–institutions (Nag 2011), and how established patterns of thought mark the use of protocols of practice. Arulmani (2004), reviewing communities in India, labelled such widespread patterns of thought within communities as a social cognitive environment and theorized that their impact is insidious and far reaching. An analysis of such social cognitive processes is important to consider when examining the learning support and decision-making processes within a primary school system.

25.6 Education Policies and Primary Schools

Another powerful factor that shapes the provisions made available within a primary school setting is education policy. The policy formulations for the primary school years, such as the Individuals With Disabilities Act (2004) from the USA and the Rose Report (Rose 2006) from the United Kingdom, and language-in-education policies from high-income countries have received considerable research attention (e.g., Pesco et al. 2016; Agrawal et al. 2019) and critical responses (e.g., Wyse and Goswami 2008). This section will instead focus on lesser-known policy documents that nonetheless are influential within their contexts.

The term dyslexia finds specific mention in policies of some countries, paving the way for a targeted school response. For example, Bhutan's Guidelines on Assessment, Examination, Promotion and Transition for Students with Disabilities (2018) lists dyslexia and dysgraphia, while the National Policy on Special Needs Education in Nigeria (2015) spells out a policy focus not just for those with a diagnosis ('including dyscalculia, dyslexia, auditory processing disorder, visual processing disorder, attention deficit disorders etc.': pp. 11–12) but also those 'at risk'. Documents in some other countries use a catch-all phrase and it is assumed that children with dyslexia are also served by these policy instruments. For example, Afghanistan's National Early Grade Reading Policy (2018) refers to students with 'disability and learning challenges' (p. 6), (the Vanuatu Inclusive Education (IE) Policy (2011) refers to 'children with impairments', and Thailand's Education for Persons with Disabilities Act, B.E. 2551 (2008) takes 'People with Disability' to cover 'the impairment in sight, hearing, moving, communicating, mental health, emotion, behaviour, intellect, learning, or other impairment, or having other obstructions' (p. 2). India's National Education Policy (2020) carries the term 'specific disabilities'.

A policy document requires action points, and it is at this level of policy implementation that the diversity in response from primary schools becomes more obvious. Specifically, countries have a distinct policy response to children who struggle to read. Countries also differ in the extent of local research available to inform assessment and intervention development in the school language(s) and the challenges for children whose home language is different from these school languages. A contrast between one high-income country and one upper-middle-income country serves to show this contrast.

24.6.1 Norway

Primary schools in Norway are from grade 1 to 7, with school entry at age 6. While preschooling is not compulsory, early childhood care and education is a statutory right. Norway's education system appears to offer a robust buffer against the negative effects of socioeconomic status on children's reading attainment, although gaps remain. For example, even after accounting for students' socioeconomic status and language spoken at home (two factors that are known to explain underachievement), the difference in scores attained by immigrant students is substantially lower than the scores of non-immigrant students in the Programme for International Student Assessment (PISA) conducted in 2018 (OECD 2020; TALIS 2018). This pattern of different levels of attainment among native and immigrant children is to be understood against the background of three defining features of Norwegian schools: children from immigrant backgrounds have more than doubled in the last decade, Norway's indices of immigrant inclusion (less segregation, more self-report of not feeling like an outsider in school) are higher than the OECD average, and only 15.3% of Norwegian teachers (compared to the OECD average of 25.5%) report feeling prepared to teach in the increasingly multicultural and multilingual Norwegian classroom (OECD 2018; Education Policy Outlook in Norway 2020).

Home language and school language variations are found in different configurations across Norway. Northern Norway is particularly multilingual, with the Sami languages, Norwegian, and Finnish. There are multiple home languages reflecting the historical patterns of immigration into Norway. Apart from Norwegian, children in grade 1 also study English. Approximately one-third of children enter grade 1 with some degree of letter knowledge and phoneme awareness, skills that are necessary to learn the alphabetic principle of the Norwegian orthography (Lervåg 2005). Sound and letter games, and interventions with a large and consistent body of evidence of positive effects for children at risk for or with dyslexia are a common part of a mainstream grade 1 programme. Together, these appear to provide the required foundation for most children when formal reading instruction begins in grade 2. An active programme of research has ensured a growing evidence-base on Norwegian literacy acquisition, development of assessment tools, and interventions both for native speakers and vulnerable second language learners (e.g., Rogde et al. 2016; Karlsen et al. 2017; Lervåg and Aukrust 2010). These are important milestones for a country with persistent educational inequality, although this is clearly concentrated around specific sociodemographic groups. Among Norway's policy responses are an investment in teacher professional development, appropriate assisted learning resources, and tools to track learning. Tiers of testing are available and evidence-informed practice is encouraged. Decision-making regarding what to offer to whom appears to be driven by learning outcomes rather than being triggered only upon diagnosis. In many ways, Norway's primary school system may be seen as an exemplar of what institutionalization of special needs education, evidence-informed decision-making, and a dyslexia response might look like within a general education setting.

24.6.2 Republic of Botswana

Primary schools in Botswana span seven grades with entry into grade 1 usually at the age of 6. Botswana has the highest human development index among the forty-six Sub-Saharan African countries. It is also one of the world's most thinly populated countries, and schooling for children in remote communities is a challenge that is receiving policy attention through, for example, introduction of mobile schools to reduce distance-to-school as a barrier to education. In contrast to the earlier absence of a differentiated curriculum for primary schools (Abosi 2007), current education policies expressly state a preference for a differentiated curriculum tailored to specific risk profiles. This is useful in the context of widespread low attainment due to historic disadvantage and recent deprivation.

Over the years, Botswana has adopted several initiatives to improve learning outcomes for diverse learners. Notable among these is the Child Friendly Schools initiative that draws upon UNICEF's framework that was first introduced in 1999, and further distilled for replication as a model that is heuristic and changeable rather than a fixed 'blueprint' (Osher et al. 2009). Child Friendly Schools aim to institutionalize inclusiveness, child centredness, and democratic participation – all principles necessary for a primary school system to be responsive to children with varied profiles, including those with dyslexia and a dyslexia-like picture. In addition, Botswana has a policy for free diagnostic services for learners with special educational needs. This is planned to be delivered through regional education centres, and data are awaited on the coverage and relevance of the services offered through these centres. Two further points are relevant for this discussion: Policy actions aim to improve literacy in the mainstream, establish specialized reading centres, and introduce a remediation programme in all primary school grades to attain irreversible literacy and numeracy skills. This focus on 'irreversible' skills is a reminder that for many children the absence of resources to practice and use their literacy skills leads to fade-out effects, and hence a slippage along the attainments continuum. Botswana's action plan also includes the introduction of early screening in grade 1, coaching clinics and learning camps, and special classes for learners with extreme learning difficulties. Below is a list of activities that has relevance to a discussion on dyslexia and primary schools:

(1) Identify and redeploy one remediation programme officer per region.
(2) Develop remediation guidelines.
(3) Train public primary school teachers in remediation methods and techniques.
(4) Develop a differentiated curriculum for learners with diverse needs.
(5) Develop tools to identify children with special educational needs.
(6) Develop teaching and learning materials for compulsory remediation programmes.
(7) Implement compulsory remediation programmes in every region.
(8) Carry out advocacy campaigns for compulsory remediation programmes.
(9) Develop monitoring and evaluation strategies and tools.
(10) Develop inspection and supervision strategies and tools.
(11) Review remediation programmes based on an analysis of the percentage of students meeting their remediation goals.
(12) Develop training on action research on the causes of declining performance.
(13) Introduce action research for teachers.

Excerpt from Programme 2, Primary Education, Botswana Education
and Training Sector Strategic Plan (ETSSP 2015–2020),
p. 60 (Botswana 2015)

Two key points stand out from Botswana's stated country response: (a) the mandated 'compulsory' status that is given to learning support for children who struggle, and (b) the multi-pronged approach needed for a developing school system to respond to children with special educational needs. This action plan has to be read against the background of a ten-country review of responses to children with 'visible' and 'invisible' disabilities that included Botswana: 'Even when schools did provide screening, it was not clear if the results were used to provide services or simply to "label"' (Osher et al. 2009). The first challenge for Botswana was therefore to move away from a system that did little more than label children to a system that had an intervention plan at its core. The second challenge was and remains the absence of established local research about the cognitive bases of learning to read in the languages spoken in Botswana's schools. Setswana is the first taught language in school, children learn English in grade 2, and, similar to other multilingual countries such as India, a third language is also taught towards the end of primary school. Setswana is the home language for most children, although there is a substantial number with other home languages. Setswana uses the Latin alphabet and is learnt alongside English. Initial research suggests complex cross-language transfer between English and Setswana (Lekgoko and Winskel 2008) that has implications for a primary school's response at the levels of screening, clinical assessment, and intervention planning for children who struggle. Botswana, in direct contrast to Norway, is at a point where building of local evidence is yet to be established and there is thus a disproportionate dependence on evidence-bases from elsewhere to develop a dyslexia response.

The two contrasting country sketches show some similarities as well: a policy commitment to inclusive education within mainstream primary school systems, equity in services is a stated aim, and action is expected when there is the double disadvantage of poor reading and deprivation. Both countries aim to be responsive to all children along the attainments continuum. In addition, points of confusion are likely present in both countries regarding a differential diagnosis between dyslexia and the 'dyslexia-like-picture'. Finally, a sensitivity to multiple dimensions of disadvantage is necessary, and both countries address this. Taken together, the document analysis of the two case study countries, alongside other education policies such as those cited at the start of this section, confirms that the child who struggles to read is recognized in several countries, and policy action is likely becoming more the norm worldwide, rather than the exception.

24.7 Conclusion

In recent decades, great progress has been made in developing a multifactorial understanding of the child who struggles with reading and writing. Risk profiles have been defined alongside the resources that aid resilience and ameliorate the effects of core deficits and co-occurring difficulties. Within the risk-and-resources perspective described in this chapter, targeted teaching is conceptualized to focus on both difficulties and strengths. The field has also advanced in the conceptualization of fairness in testing, when is it compromised, and how children's experience history impacts item-level functioning in most tests (including the tests adopted for dyslexia screening and diagnostics by most school systems). This has prompted the suggestion in this chapter for a test–teach–test approach when a child struggles in primary school. Another advance in the field is that more and more interventions are being more robustly assessed (see Chapter 19, Galuschka and Schulte-Körne 2022). Yet, several gaps in the evidence-base remain. In parallel, there is the substantial evidence-base to show that learning to read and spell is shaped by the psycholinguistic properties of the language of literacy and its writing system and that teaching programmes must be responsive to these properties. The implication for school systems delivering instruction in understudied languages is to follow a bottom-up approach, exploring thoroughly the morphological and phonological characteristics of the language and its writing system. A further aspect considered is that protocols of practice are often driven by entrenched patterns of thought within a community of practitioners and their research collaborators. This chapter has attempted to show that periodic reflection is warranted even in, or perhaps especially in, primary school systems with established protocols because the assumptions that inform decision-making may need reconsideration – as, for example, when formerly monolingual classrooms become multilingual due to a change in student intake.

Finally, indications in the literature suggest the study of dyslexia has reached a critical milestone. Synthesis of the neuroscientific, genetic, cognitive-behavioural, and educational literature has allowed for recommendations to practitioners to be more specific, although the certainty in recommendations is greater for those tasked with diagnosis (e.g., paediatricians; Sanfilippo et al. 2020) than for educators (e.g., Report of the National Reading Panel 2020). A historical analysis of the term 'dyslexia' has added to our understanding. One influential analysis suggests a 'loosening of criteria for dyslexia' (Snowling et al. 2020, p. 501). The same authors go on to state that 'In the longer term, the use of the term may need to change' (p. 501), showing once again that the very idea of who has 'dyslexia' remains a topic of debate. What is clear, however, is that throughout the decades of research, policy action, and individual activism, primary schools have remained at the heart of a coherent response to the child with dyslexia. There is no reason to expect any of this to change. What remains to be achieved is an assurance that all children entering primary school, including those with dyslexia and those with a dyslexia-like picture, will be supported in their learning. Importantly, this support should be irrespective of the manner and scope of diagnostic protocols that will enter the next generation of classrooms.

Suggestions for Further Reading

Brown, M., D. Sibley, J. Washington, et al. 2015. 'Impact of Dialect Use on a Basic Component of Learning to Read'. *Frontiers in Psychology*, 6, 196.

Gibbs, S. J., and J. G. Elliott. 2020. 'The Dyslexia Debate: Life without the Label'. *Oxford Review of Education* 46 (4): 487–500.

Nag, S. 2013. 'Low Literacy Attainments in School and Approaches to Diagnosis: An Exploratory Study'. *Contemporary Education Dialogue* 10 (2): 197–221. https://doi.org/10.1177/0973184913484997.

Snowling, M. J. 2019. *Dyslexia: A Very Short Introduction*. Oxford University Press.

Wyse, D. and U. Goswami. 2008. 'Synthetic Phonics and the Teaching of Reading'. *British Educational Research Journal*, 34 (6): 691–710.

25 Best Practice and Policy in Maths Education in School

Antje Ehlert and Luisa Wagner

25.1 Introduction

In the international school context, pupils with learning disabilities are educated differently. There are many countries in which the common practice is the combined teaching of children with and without disabilities, as is the case in the United Kingdom. There are also countries, however, that have just begun to adapt their separate school systems step by step to allow for combined teaching, as is the case in Germany. There are still other countries that keep to a dual system or offer both inclusive and separate teaching formats in parallel. School systems practicing inclusive education have already gathered many experiences and insights in dealing with the high degree of heterogeneity in terms of pupils' learning performance at school. They have adapted their school systems to this heterogeneity, tested supportive measures, and trained or retrained their teaching staff.

Even without consideration of specific learning disabilities or learning difficulties in general, classrooms are heterogeneous. This means that pupils perform at different levels in their learning, often representing a difference of multiple years of development. Traditional instruction usually focuses on teaching to the average performance level of the class. Even without pupils with specific disabilities, this is not conducive to a high-quality education. Nevertheless, this orientation is all too common at the present time.

The increased heterogeneity of inclusive classrooms cannot be approached with this style of instruction. In particular, pupils with maths disability, who will be the focus of this chapter, do not profit from this as they become overwhelmed in such an environment. These pupils often require specific interventions beyond regular instruction. Mathematical skills are taught and acquired primarily in school. Therefore, it is important to focus on specific support mechanisms and interventions for mathematics education, also taking into account existing school structures.

For this reason, the present chapter will examine various ways of supporting pupils' existing maths disabilities. A number of empirical findings show that interventions with a proven effectiveness in the research community are often not effective in the school context, or only to a limited extent (Sabatier 1986; Hasselhorn et al. 2014; Petermann 2014). The first step here is to examine the existing implementation research. This research approach seeks to analyse why the effectiveness of these interventions is so low and how, after scientific evaluation, supportive measures and interventions can be successfully implemented in practice.

This research approach thus focuses on the practicalities of the school context with all its actors, framework conditions, and internal and external effect mechanisms and, thus, the educational reality of children and adolescents in this system. This pertains especially to practices of inclusive education, which rely on effective support measures and intervention as described here. Providing instruction and learning environments at various developmental and comprehension levels is only one feature of a supportive school system. Thus, the next step is to study the different models for implementing inclusive education. The necessary conditions for a successful mathematics intervention programme are outlined. These apply only to scientifically evaluated interventions that are both effective and efficient for training mathematical skills. In addition, conditions necessary for implementing specific support measures and intervention in mathematics education will also be discussed. Finally, academic best-practices that successfully meet maths disabilities and support learning development effectively will be presented. The core focus will be on dealing with maths disabilities and the factors that lead to successful interventions from an international perspective.

25.2 Practical Challenges in Implementing Interventions

Great differences exist between the results of a scientifically developed and evaluated intervention and the results in everyday practice after the intervention has been implemented. Specifically, these two contexts show different degrees of effectiveness (Scheirer et al. 1995). Claims about the effectiveness and success of an intervention depend on the scope of its implementation (McCoy and Reynolds 1998). Studies that examine these differences and test the influence of various factors on the successful implementation of an intervention in practice originate from a field known as implementation research. Because this field is relevant for successfully supporting learning disabilities of all kinds in schools, implementation research and related findings shall be briefly presented in Sections 25.2.1–25.2.3.

25.2.1 Implementation Research

Implementation research is dedicated to describing and analysing processes affecting the implementation of concepts or programmes. The different actors involved play a special role here, as they affect the implementation with their perceptions, actions, and decision logics.

Implementation research has its origins in the United States and has been conducted since the mid-1960s, especially to examine the lack of success of social reform programmes (Petermann 2014). Thus, early studies on implementation came primarily from the USA and were mostly analyses of single cases (Sabatier 1986). The results showed that the government did not succeed in effectively implementing its programmes (Pressman and Wildavsky 1973; Murphy 1973; Bardach 1974). The subsequent generation of studies was conducted in Western Europe (for a general overview, see Yin 1980; Barrett and Fudge 1981; Alexander 1982; Sabatier and

Mazmanian 1983). These studies also took a 'top down' approach, but tried to explain through a conceptual framework the different degrees of implementation success based on specific factors, such as clear and consistent objectives, an adequate causal theory or legally structured implementation processes to enhance compliance, committed and skillful implementing officials, support from interest groups and sovereigns, changes in socioeconomic conditions that did not substantially undermine political support, and a causal theory that 'select[ed] implementing institutions supportive of the new programme and suggested creating new agencies as a specific strategy' (Sabatier 1986, p. 27). In the late 1970s and early 1980s the perspective changed, and implementations were developed from the 'bottom up'. Implementations then began with an analysis at the operational level focusing on the actors and the strategies they use to pursue certain goals. The findings of these studies suggested that local actors frequently redirect centrally mandated programmes to suit their own purposes (Lipsky 1971; Berman and McLaughlin 1976; Hanf and Scharpf 1978; Ingram 1978; Elmore 1979; Browning et al. 1981; Barrett and Fudge 1981; Hjern and Hull 1982; Hanf 1982; Lipsky 1971; Berman and McLaughlin 1974; Hanf and Scharpf 1978; Ingram 1978; Barrett and Fudge 1981; Hull and Hjern 1982).

Although implementation research is increasingly gaining attention, the number of empirical studies is growing, and a broad conceptual and methodological debate is taking place, there is still a divide between research, policy, and praxis. This can be seen in the results of empirical studies as well as reported experiences. Schrader et al. (2020) summarized thirty-three publications on implementation research in a review. They showed that there is still a lack of theoretically grounded insights regarding the institutional, organizational, and personal conditions necessary for effective implementation studies. Cultural differences between countries as well as institutional differences between educational fields were found. (Evidence-based) treatment is frequently focused on and empirically evaluated, but rarely theoretically reflected on. In the Anglo-American context, broad interest has been established regarding the forms (polity), content (policy), and processes (politics) of educational policy and its effects on the education system (Odden 1991; Honig 2006). Implementation processes are seen here as highly relevant for instituting reforms (Young and Lewis 2015).

25.2.2 Practical Challenges in Implementing Interventions in Schools

Implementing interventions in the day-to-day school reality poses particular challenges for science. First, in the school context there are a number of variables and factors at play. In order to draw conclusions about the effectiveness of an intervention under real conditions, it has to be tested in an implementation study – and precisely therein lies the second greatest challenge for the research community, namely the methodological implementation. This can only be approved after it has been tested. These circumstances are surely one of the reasons why evidence is still generally lacking regarding the extent to which an intervention is effective in the area for which it was originally conceived (Hasselhorn et al. 2014). A third challenge is posed with the question of how the success of an implementation can be operationalized. Here, differentiating between the effectiveness of the implementation and that of the intervention itself appears particularly problematic. If the implementation fails, researchers must carefully determine whether the intervention was unsuitable (intervention error) or whether a suitable intervention was incorrectly implemented (implementation error). Knowledge in this area is limited as the processes involved are often not yet fully understood (Michie et al. 2009).

25.2.3 Conditions Necessary for a Successful Implementation

To determine the success of an implementation, Coburn (2003) suggests four evaluation criteria: depth, sustainability, spread, and ownership. The criterion of *depth* describes the extent of the change, for example with respect to the action principles of the actors involved or the institutional guiding principles. *Sustainability* describes its permanence over time – that is, how long an implementation can be maintained. *Spread* examines the norms, principles, and convictions that are adopted by a large number of people, how widespread the implementation is, and who benefits from it. The criterion of *ownership* evaluates to what extent the actors live the day-to-day implementation and put it into practice, and thus feel co-responsible for helping it succeed and continue in the future.

To answer the question of what exactly makes for a successful implementation, both the process and the result of the implementation themselves must be examined. A basic prerequisite is understanding the quality of the intervention or aspect to be implemented. This includes obtaining evidence of its fundamental effectiveness and scientific merit as well as the robustness of the research findings. In a comprehensive research overview of more than 17,700 publications, Schrader et al. (2020) outlined the necessary conditions for successful implementation of an evidence-based intervention. They identified 194 supportive and inhibitory factors grouped into 86 different categories of influencing factors. *Context factors* have already been intensively researched and can basically be seen as supportive influencing factors. These include ideational support of the implementing actors by the organizational management, support in the form of financial-material resources, and a positive institutional environment, as well as training sessions for the implementers. Influencing factors in connection with the *addressees* of the interventions, on the other hand, appear to still lack adequate theoretical grounds or be empirically proven. One reason for this could be that an evaluation may prove the effectiveness of an intervention only under controlled conditions. Also, *context variables on the micro-level* (referring to the individual school, e.g. school climate, instructor cooperation, financial, temporal, and equipment resources, as well as didactic and curricular school practices) *and the macro-level* (referring to the school administration and the context of each school, e.g. support from the school administration and the community, the quality of the implementation, and the subject knowledge of the programme coordinators) currently lack sufficient empirical attention. There are significantly fewer findings on inhibitory factors. Worth mentioning here is the *degree of fidelity* – that is, how closely the implementation follows the original design. This is shown to be supportive only to a certain extent. Too much fidelity to the original plan can become an inhibitory factor, because in that case the implementation can no longer be successfully adapted to the local conditions. This functions similarly to the factor of *time investment*, where implementers must determine the right amount for a successful implementation.

Schrader et al. (2020) come to the final conclusion that meaningful findings are still lacking, but urgently needed. Only a few researchers at this point have dedicated quasi-experimental studies to determining the most efficient amount of adaptation, time investment, etc. Usually, the general recommendation is to find a balance. The question of which conditions are necessary for an implementation to succeed cannot be answered conclusively at this time.

25.3 Modelling the Implementation of Inclusive Education from an International Perspective

As shown in the research outlined here, implementing different concepts in a real school setting presents significant challenges (Hasselhorn et al. 2014). Putting an evidence-based intervention into practice in the everyday reality of the school environment is not enough to guarantee a lasting effect on pupils' learning success. Rather, the entire educational institution, with all its structures and actors, competences and attitudes, must be considered in the implementation process (Takala et al. 2020; Hasselhorn et al. 2014). These challenges should not discourage from changing traditional instructional settings, not least because it has been deemed urgently necessary by the UN Convention on Rights of Persons with Disabilities that established the right to inclusive education for all children (United Nations 2007). In the international context, therefore, a number of approaches have already emerged to increase the heterogeneity of the student body in the classroom and support every child in the best way possible.

25.3.1 The Response-to-Intervention Model

In the US school system, the response-to-intervention approach (RTI) has been an established component for some time now (Deno 1985; Fuchs and Fuchs 1986; Voss et al. 2016). For years, this approach has been used as a framework for inclusive education in heterogeneous classrooms (Berkeley et al. 2009; Hasselhorn et al. 2014). In 2004 it was established as a means to legally identify impaired learners (Individuals with Disabilities Education Improvement Act (IDEIA); Castle 2004). The overarching goal of the approach is to design instruction in such a way that every child can be optimally supported, thus preventing long-term learning difficulties (NCRTI 2012). The wait-to-fail strategy (Huber and Grosche 2012; Vaughn and Fuchs 2003), which means ignoring learning difficulties until a full-blown disability manifests, should be avoided in all cases. The RTI uses a multilevel system to ascertain whether positive learning progress can be observed in children as a response to a given pedagogical intervention (NCRTI 2010; Reschley and Bergström 2009; Gutkin and

Reynolds 2008). The RTI approach is conceptualized by a three-tier system (Caplan 1964; NCRTI 2010):

(1) Primary level of prevention (Tier 1): high-quality evidence-based instruction for all children, regular screenings to identify children at risk of developing learning difficulties.
(2) Secondary level of prevention (Tier 2): additional small-group intensive support for pupils with learning difficulties (approx. 20% of children; Johnson et al. 2006; Kivirauma and Ruoho 2007) with detailed progress monitoring.
(3) Tertiary level of prevention (Tier 3): for around 1–5% of children, high-intensity individual instruction combined with specific disability identification (Reschley and Bergström 2009; Gutkin and Reynolds 2008).

This multilevel system makes up one of the four core components of the RTI approach. In order to provide pupils with the needed level of support, two other key ingredients of RTI are indispensable: screenings and progress monitoring (Blumenthal et al. 2019; (NCRTI 2010). These are likewise accomplished in multiple steps: at least once per school year, all pupils go through screening to assess their current achievement level and identify pupils with learning difficulties or learning deficits in a particular subject as early as possible (Blumenthal et al. 2019). Children who demonstrate results under a certain 'cut-off point' receive a specific diagnostic and their development is closely observed through short-term progress monitoring with the help of, for example, curriculum-based measurements (CBM) (Blumenthal et al. 2019; NCRTI 2010; NCRTI 2012).

The fourth and overarching component of the RTI approach consists of data-based decision-making (NCRTI 2010). On the one hand, data from the screenings and progress monitoring are used to assign each child to a prevention level and individually adapt the support to his or her needs. On the other hand, evidence-based interventions and research-based curricula should be used for 'normal' instruction and additional support (NCLB 2001; NCRTI 2010) to ensure a high quality of instruction and the best possible support (Björn et al. 2016; Blumenthal et al. 2019; NCRTI 2010).

An approach very similar to the RTI model introduced in the United Kingdom is the National Numeracy Strategy (NNS) (DfEE 1999). The NNS suggests dividing mathematics instruction into three 'waves' (DfEE 1999; Dowker 2004): the first wave contains maths instruction for the entire class, which should take between 45 and 60 minutes every day. Wave 2 provides additional support for pupils with slight difficulties in a particular area (Dowker 2004). This usually takes about 30 minutes twice a week and helps pupils work through the daily mathematics lesson. The third wave is intended for pupils who demonstrate serious difficulties learning maths, where they can benefit from individualized diagnoses and scientifically evaluated materials (Dowker 2004). As we can see, the core elements of the RTI approach are also used here.

25.3.2 The Student Welfare Group

In Finland, another system that is similar to the RTI approach builds the foundation for inclusive education in schools, in which general teaching staff and special education teachers work together (Takala et al. 2020). Since 2010, three legally anchored forms of support for pupils have been developed: general support, intensified support, and special support (Finnish Basic Education Act 2010; Finnish Ministry of Education 2007). The first and second forms of support usually take place in regular lessons, while special support is given in separate classes at the same school by special education teachers (Takala et al. 2020). In order to receive special support, an individualized educational plan (IEP) is required, which is drafted in collaboration with the child and the parents and describes the child's current level of education and the needed support (Finnish Basic Education Act 2010).

Beyond this basic support, a Student Welfare Group (SWG) was formed in almost every school as a key element in the support and monitoring of children with learning difficulties (Sabel 2012). The particular feature of these groups is that they were not created based on state mandates, but rather emerged out of daily cooperation between teachers and other actors (Sabel 2012). These SWGs consist of various actors in the school (principal, special education teachers, school nurses, school psychologists), and when necessary can also be complemented by external resources, such as municipal social-welfare services (Sabel 2012; Takala et al. 2020). The tasks of the SWGs are described as follows:

> In the normal case, the SWG reviews the performance of each class (and sometimes each student) in the school at least once a year. This allows identification and tracking of students in need of remedial, part-time special education. When a student is identified as requiring full-time special education, the SWG checks that the individualized study plans ... guiding the development of each pupil [who] needs support are being followed to good effect, and if not, what corrections are necessary. (Sabel 2012, pp. 12–13)

To carry out these tasks, SWGs usually meet once or twice a month. Their work focusses on pupils in need of special support (Sabel 2012). They create individual IEPs for these pupils and/or monitor subsequent learning processes. Moreover, through SWGs it is ensured that all the necessary resources are available to support teachers and special education instructors as well (Sabel 2012).

Both the regular and special education teachers therefore work closely with the SWGs and can thereby prevent learning difficulties or, if they already exist, address them in a focused and timely manner (Finnish National Agency for Education 2017). Further, through the SWGs a kind of peer review was established in schools (Sabel 2012). This interlinked system leads to optimal support of pupils and, not least, also yields excellent results in international comparative studies (PISA 2018; TIMSS 2019).

25.4 Necessary Conditions for the Successful Implementation of Mathematics Interventions

The development and implementation of intervention programmes for school settings share a common driver: professional engagement with heterogeneous learning groups. Heterogeneity in the school context addressed here primarily refers to pupils' achievement levels. Levels of reading and maths proficiency are given particular attention in schools. This section takes a closer look at supporting maths proficiency acquisition. There is an absolute consensus among educators that maths proficiency plays an essential role in a successful life. It is one of the prerequisites for solving everyday problems (Ramaa and Gowramma 2002). Impairments in the development of maths proficiency have a negative effect on a child's formal education (Schulz et al. 2018), professional career (Kucian and von Aster 2015; Butterworth et al. 2011; Dowker 2019), and participation in an education-based society. Although the prevalence and consequences in terms of their importance for an individual's development of specific learning disability in mathematics are comparable to those of reading disabilities, children with these learning disabilities are still not yet correctly diagnosed or supported (Dowker 2004). This is explained by the lack of knowledge in educational praxis.

25.4.1 Findings of Math Proficiency Assessments

International comparisons of pupils' mathematical skills reveal alarming score distributions and severities of maths difficulties worldwide. In the following sections, the reference group to identify children with difficulties in mathematics is no longer determined by national norm sampling, but rather through international school score comparisons such as the PISA or TIMSS (Trends in International Mathematics and Science Study). (Sandefur 2016) found in a sample of thirteen participating countries in sub-Saharan Africa that the pupils scored on average more than two standard deviations under the sample mean of the TIMSS and thus fell below the 5th percentile of most industrial countries (Conn 2017). This means that depending on where children grow up and attend school, they could potentially show very weak maths proficiency as defined by the ICD-10 or DSM-5 even without being diagnosed with a learning disability. Other findings show that between 70% and 80% of South African primary school children acquire only very rudimentary mathematical skills. Here, the consequences of social disadvantages and less well-equipped primary schools contribute to the immense difference in achievement scores between children from low socioeconomic class and those from the middle class (Kay and Yeo 2012). In an Indian study, Ramaa and Gowramma (2001) examined the arithmetical difficulties of 5th graders taught in state primary schools, albeit from families with low socioeconomic status. Teachers were asked to create a list of pupils with average reading and writing skills. They identified 43.53% as average performers. However, all of these children demonstrated serious difficulties in arithmetic in a standardized mathematical test for 1st–4th grades. Although the severity of learning difficulties in mathematics is lower in industrial countries, there are also findings showing that even pupils far from being diagnosed with a specific learning disability in mathematics may not acquire sufficient maths proficiency during school. This can be seen in the TIMSS results from 2015, for example. Almost a quarter of pupils in Germany (23%) achieved maths scores that fell below proficiency level III. These children demonstrate only very basic mathematical skills and abilities. It can be assumed that these children will have significant difficulties mastering mathematics in secondary school (Wendt et al. 2016). Still, 4% of pupils score at the lowest proficiency level (I). These pupils possess only rudimentary mathematical knowledge. All participating countries that scored better than Germany in the TIMSS 2015 on the combined mathematics scale counted fewer pupils in this performance range, except for the USA (5%) and Hungary (8%).

In this light, the following findings on the effectiveness of mathematics intervention and training programmes and corresponding support measures applied directly in the classroom become even more relevant. It is thus important for various people involved in education to understand which educational measures are most effective in supporting maths proficiency and improving learning results. This pertains especially to developing countries that have limited financial resources at their disposal (see Chapter 24, Nag 2022).

25.4.2 Effectiveness of Maths Interventions at School

Comparable to the findings on the effectiveness of mathematics intervention and training programmes (see Chapter 19, Galuschka and Schulte-Körne 2022), direct instructional methods are rated as highly effective in regular maths classes as well (Hattie 2008; Kirschner et al. 2006). Lazonder and Harmsen (2016) conducted a meta-analysis in which they found that a direct instructional approach is preferable to an unguided or minimally instructional approach (effect sizes for teenagers, $d = 3.62$, for adolescents, $d = 0.70$). They explain that children's working memory can become overwhelmed in self-directed learning. In contrast, direct instruction can show learners exactly how to deal with this when acquiring new content. This is done by providing appropriate learning strategies and useful information which help to acquire mathematical concepts and understand solution approaches in depth. Unguided or minimal instruction includes teaching methods focused on discovery, research, and problem-based, experimental, and constructivist learning. For pupils with learning difficulties, there is a significant difference between teacher-supported self-directed learning and direct instruction from the teachers (Blum and Schukajlow 2018). Providing specific guidance has a greater effect size, whereby explanations ($d = 1.45$; large effect) differ significantly from all other kinds of assistance. Furthermore, heuristics ($d = 1.17$; large effect) proved to be more effective than less-specific guidance (Lazonder and Harmsen 2016), although more specific assistance seems to lead to greater short-term success. For long-term learning, however, specific assistance does not necessarily result in greater success. Interventions with insufficient group-work diagnostics and a lack of coordination with the solution process show lower situational awareness (low orientation and low task awareness). Such interventions are contraindicated and do not raise pupils' achievement levels (Dann et al. 1999). With an experimental intervention control group design, Kramarski et al. (2002) examined the effectiveness of metacognitive questions used in different interventions in general maths instruction to teach selection, justification, and reflection on the strategies deployed. For high-performing and weak-performing pupils, utilizing the following instructional guidance was proven most effectively in a collaborative work to solve mathematical tasks: comprehension questions aimed at understanding the problem ('What is the problem?'), questions that draw analogies to tasks that have already been solved ('What does this task have in common with problems you have already solved?'), questions that require the selection of a suitable strategy ('What strategy can you use?'; 'Why is this strategy the most suitable?'; 'How can the strategy be used?'), and questions that prompt reflection on the solution process ('What am I doing right now?'; 'Can I solve the task another way?'). However, it must be mentioned that intra-group processes and metacognitive assistance cannot eliminate problems of understanding the content. Effects for pupils suffering from mathematics comprehension deficits should not be expected.

Findings on interventional measures in mathematics classrooms also reveal, however (for an overview, see Klock 2020), that teachers rarely explicitly diagnose difficulties in group work or problem-solving processes (Fürst 1999; Krammer 2009; Leiss 2007; Webb et al. 2006). Many of the measures used are invasive and show detrimental aspects, such as low orientation to learners' difficulties and solution processes, as well as a high degree of controlling (Fürst 1999) (Dann et al. 1999). Instructors often intervene to control and direct the solution process. These interventions usually do not meet pupils' needs and are often simply too easy (Webb et al. 2006). They often focus on content, where the teachers give direct or indirect explanations (Krammer 2009; Leiss 2007). Accordingly, learners' abilities to find their own solutions and high-level discussions among pupils were rarely supported. Instead, self-regulating activities were taken over by the teachers. For this reason, the acquisition of cognitive, metacognitive, and social skills in mathematics instruction currently used at school can be seen as problematic with respect to supporting cooperative modelling processes (Klock 2020). It can be assumed that children with difficulties and learning disabilities in mathematics rarely profit from this type of mathematics instruction.

25.5 Best Practices for Implementing Maths Interventions in Inclusive Instruction

Based on the presented findings on effectiveness of different interventions supporting mathematics proficiency, specific best-practice examples can be identified in a number of countries that try to provide the best possible support for pupils with difficulties acquiring mathematical skills. Some examples are presented in this section.

25.5.1 The Rügen Inclusion Model

The Rügen Inclusion Model (RIM) represents the first attempt to implement the RTI approach in an entire German region (the island of Rügen). Since the 2010/11 school year, all children with difficulties in learning, emotional and social development, and language skills are taught in inclusive settings (Voss et al. 2016). During this period, instruction was completely adapted to the RTI support principles, including mathematics instruction.

The primary level of prevention still needed to provide high-quality instruction to the entire class, so a suitable textbook first had to be chosen. As described in the previous section, direct instruction, cooperative work, and reflection on used strategies have a positive effect on the learning success of all pupils (Kroesbergen and Van Luit 2003; Chodura et al. 2015); to achieve this, the German-language maths textbook *Das Zahlenbuch* (Wittman and Müller 2012) was chosen. This textbook contains tasks and exercises that pupils can work on at various proficiency levels and also offers open tasks that can be tackled with different strategies by each child. The effectiveness of this textbook in class has already been proven in a few studies (Hess 2003), which meets the RTI model's requirement for the use of evidence-based materials (Blumenthal et al. 2019). Pupils' learning success was evaluated with screenings twice a year for the entire class, and with curriculum-based measurements (CBMs). Pupils who scored below the 25th percentile were supported more intensively at the secondary level of prevention (Blumenthal et al. 2019).

The secondary level of prevention took place in groups of 4–6 pupils in addition to 'normal' lessons and focused on both the lesson material and developing basic maths skills and arithmetic strategies (Blumenthal et al. 2019). Additional supportive materials besides the *Zahlenbuch* textbook included the support programme Kalkulie (Gerlach et al. 2007) and the computer-based learning programme Rechenspiele mit Elfe und Mathis (Lenhard et al. 2011). CBMs were used to measure the success of the intervention on this level as well. If pupils' scores were still in the below-average range (< 10th percentile), they received further support in Tier III (Blumenthal et al. 2019).

At the highest level of prevention, pupils were supported by special education teachers one-on-one or in very small groups (max. three pupils) and the content was adjusted to the learning disabilities of each child individually (Blumenthal et al. 2019). Here again, knowledge of implementation research as well as direct instructions and adaptive procedures were applied. If a child still showed no learning progress despite the intensive support at this level, an individual diagnosis was made to determine what special education support was needed (Blumenthal et al. 2019).

The model's implementation was scientifically evaluated in various studies. The development of the children's mathematics competencies was examined in one study in a pre- and post-test experimental design with two groups (treatment group and control group; Blumenthal et al. 2019). From the experimental and control groups, $N = 283$ statistical twins were created, as well as $N = 16$ twins from so-called 'diagnostic intervention classes' (DIC) (Blumenthal et al. 2019), which were held in regular primary schools for pupils with learning and behavioural problems. An assessment of the scientific findings on the mathematics support at the end of the primary school period in the RIM showed that both the experimental and control groups developed over the measurement period, but pupils with learning difficulties (DIC) in the RIM did significantly better (large effect size of $d = 0.84$) than those in the control group (Blumenthal et al. 2019). In addition, more pupils (89%) attending schools in the RIM reached minimum standards in mathematics compared to the control group (82%) (Blumenthal et al. 2019). From this, the RIM researchers conclude that this model 'seems to be an emerging alternative for an inclusive school system in Germany' (Blumenthal et al. 2019, p. 143; but see also Summary: Best Practice – Schooling and Educational Policy).

25.5.2 Learning Support for Mathematics

In Singapore, the Learning Support for Mathematics (LSM) programme was introduced to identify and support pupils with difficulties in learning mathematics as early as possible. The aim was to recognize and thus prevent risks of learning deficits at the beginning of school through different forms of individual support (Cheam and Jocelyn 2009). Three main components of this programme can be identified:

(1) Systematic screening and identification of pupils early in the first year of school;
(2) Provision of additional resources for schools to provide early intervention for identified pupils;
(3) Teaching by specially trained LSM teachers.

                                        (Cheam and Jocelyn 2009, p. 371)

In this system, pupils with learning difficulties in mathematics are identified by School-Readiness Tests (SRT) at each school (Toh and Kaur 2019). These tests evaluate basic maths skills such as counting and the first addition and subtraction tasks with and without pictures (Cheam and Jocelyn 2009). In addition, there are various assessments during the school year that determine pupils' learning progress (Toh and Kaur 2019).

Pupils are then supported not only by specially trained LSM teachers, but also by a number of other resources. Each school offers a buddy or peer programme in which pupils can support one another (Cheam and Jocelyn 2009). External resources – so-called stakeholders – are involved as well (Khong and Ng 2005). Particular focus is placed on parents, however, so that a supportive learning environment is created at home and parents are helped in supporting their children (Khong and Ng 2005). The result is an increasing number of home–school partnerships, and communication between teachers and parents increases as well (Khong and Ng 2005).

The LSM approach from Singapore thus connects various elements of the model for implementing inclusive instruction presented in Section 25.3. A wide range of school support is offered for pupils experiencing difficulties in mathematics alongside collaboration with external resources and parental home (like in the Finnish Welfare Groups). The result is a broad basis of support for the pupils.

25.5.3 QuickSmart Numeracy

With the research programme QuickSmart (SiMERR National Research Centre 2021), Australia implemented an intervention programme to support basic mathematical competencies. The QuickSmart programme was developed for both numeracy and literacy. Only QuickSmart Numeracy will be considered here.

The programme was developed via a collaboration between the National Centre for Science, Information and Communication Technology, and Mathematics Education for Rural and Regional Australia (SiMERR National Research Centre) and the University of New England (SiMERR National Research Centre 2021). The implementation began in 2001 and was systematically evaluated scientifically. More than

1,200 schools across the country are now participating. Effectiveness has already been proven for a very large number of pupils (SiMERR National Research Centre 2021).

QuickSmart Numeracy particularly addresses pupils with difficulties in basic maths who therefore have increasing deficits in relation to their classmates (Graham and Pegg 2010). The programme is based on five principles (SiMERR National Research Centre 2021, p. 3):

(1) Research evidence should inform policy positions and systemic approaches to addressing the needs of low-achieving middle-school students.
(2) Programmes designed to address the learning needs of low-achieving middle-school students should be intense, of significant duration, and conducted in small class instructional settings.
(3) An extensive professional learning programme for teachers, teacher aides, and executive members of schools and education jurisdictions should be an important component of any sustainable instructional intervention.
(4) Improving the skill base of teacher aides should be a focus of attention for all support programmes, especially those in rural and remote areas or difficult-to-staff schools where teaching staff mobility is a significant factor.
(5) To ensure sustainability, national-, state-, regional-, and school-level stakeholders need to coordinate their efforts and collaborate to ensure the fidelity of the programme, and the viability of its implementation and scaling-up processes.

In order to support the learning development of pupils with difficulties, in the QuickSmart programme they participate in half-hour lessons three times a week over a period of thirty weeks (Graham and Pegg 2011). They attend in teams of two pupils with a similar learning status, led by a trained instructor. As the name of the programme states, the goal is to recall number facts and simple calculations more quickly and use smarter arithmetic strategies. This is achieved through the use of methods such as explicit instruction, discussions, and feedback.

Instructors are supported as well. They attend workshops before and during their work in the QuickSmart programme. In addition, the programme uses 'a nested model of implementation' (Pegg and Graham 2012, p. 7), which means that there are different groups that communicate with one another: 1. groups of teachers within a school who work with the pupils; 2. multiple schools within a cluster that promote the professionalization of teachers in the programme; 3. multiple clusters within a region that monitor the implementation of the programme; and, finally, 4. multiple regions within a federal state that evaluate the programme (Pegg and Graham 2012). A large network and all levels of educational landscape are included in the programme's implementation and evaluation.

The programme was evaluated in a large-scale longitudinal study from 2001 to 2008. A quasi-experimental research design was set up with an experimental group (consisting of $N = 2,100$ pupils who took part in the QuickSmart programme) and a control group ($N = 830$ non-participating pupils of the same age from the same schools; Graham and Pegg 2011). Both groups took part in all achievement tests. For all sub-tests with exception of the very elementary test of numerical identification accuracy, significant effects were found in favour of experimental groups with moderate to large effect sizes between $d = 0.49$ and $d = 0.80$ (Graham and Pegg 2011; see also https://simerr.une.edu.au/quicksmart-pdf/qs_annual_numeracy_re port_2009.pdf). This programme also shows that individual and evidence-based support in connection with cooperation of all involved actors represents an effective possibility to deal with maths learning difficulties and thus enable inclusive education in schools.

25.6 Conclusion

The diverse empirical findings show that it may be possible to successfully support children with maths difficulties. However, any attempt must consider the specific conditions necessary for success. These are summarized and discussed below.

Promising school programmes supporting heterogeneous learning groups are primarily characterized by their implementation of *high-quality instruction in mathematics*. This type of instruction entails detailed assessment of mathematical skills, as well as coordination between teaching and specific interventions. The diagnosis is used to identify pupils at risk of developing learning disabilities. It is also used, however, to evaluate the intervention both in class and beyond. Recognizing a mismatch between a pupil's learning needs and the teaching strategy then triggers an adjustment of the strategy. A multi-stage support system may be beneficial, in which the individualization and intensity of the intervention increases with each stage. This way, high-quality instruction can be achieved that takes into consideration the pupil's initial achievement level and learning trajectory over time.

Related decisions regarding the allocation and adaptation of intervention are data-based and guided by *multiprofessional cooperation*. Different actors meet regularly and jointly make plans and decisions together. Further, the involvement of additional resources, such as the parents, is shown to be effective for creating expanded learning-supportive structures.

The conditions necessary for success are based on *data-based procedures*. All support measures share a core aim of strengthening maths proficiency in a systematic manner. This must be accomplished in small steps through direct instruction and be accompanied by both cognitive and metacognitive learning strategies.

As the problem of learning difficulties in mathematics is still underestimated in the international context due to either lack of knowledge (Dowker 2004) or miscalculated relevance, it is all the more important to train maths teachers not only in different ways to develop pupils' proficiency, but also in diagnostics and intervention-related skills. Especially in countries with lacking or insufficient development of inclusive education approaches, it would be helpful to increase teachers' awareness of inclusive school systems and teaching formats in addition to subject-related knowledge. An understanding of how to develop support structures in school, maths instruction, and multiprofessional cooperation is fundamental to initiating change processes. This is crucial, because pupils with learning disorders cannot – or, at least, not easily – acquire proficiency in traditional school structures and lesson formats.

Suggestions for Further Reading

Breznitz, Z., O. Rubinsten, V. Molfese, and D. Molfese. 2012. *In Reading, Writing, Mathematics and the Developing Brain: Listening to Many Voices*. Heidelberg, New York, London: Springer, Dordrecht.

Deno, S. L. 1985. 'Curriculum-based Measurement: The Emerging Alternative'. *Exceptional Children*, 52, 219–232. https://doi.org/10.1177/001440298505200303.

Dowker, A. (2004). 'What Works for Children with Mathematical Difficulties?' *Research Report*, 554. University of Oxford. www.researchgate.net/publication/253032270_What_Works_for_Children_with_Mathematical_Difficulties.

Fuchs, L. S. and D. Fuchs. 1986. 'Effects of Systematic Formative Evaluation: A Meta-analysis'. *Exceptional Children* 53, 19–208.

Kollosche, D., R. Marcone, M. Knigge, M. Godoy Penteado, and O. Skovsmose. 2019. *Inclusive Mathematics Education. State-of-the-Art Research from Brazil and Germany*. Cham: Springer.

Summary: Best Practice – Schooling and Educational Policy

(1) **Fostering learning beyond learning disorders:** All children who struggle with learning (including children with underattainment or subclinical difficulties, but without a dyslexia or dyscalculia diagnosis) need measured support from the education system following an explicit protocol of referral and response (e.g., primary school systems in Norway and Botswana). This is particularly important in global contexts given that many children worldwide have limited or even no access to high-quality and contextually appropriate learning opportunities, and also in heterogeneous contexts in which children, for example, do not know the language of instruction well because it is a new language or a new dialect.

(2) **Overcoming obstacles to receiving educational support:** Obstacles to be overcome are linked to situations where resources are withheld from or not used by the family (e.g., absenteeism); institutional responses are alienating; trusted social networks to turn to are missing; and/or learning is repeatedly disrupted due to school closures, missing teachers, or reduced school attendance by the child due to poor health or socioeconomic duties such as sibling care, household chores, or income generation.

(3) **Affective-motivational dimensions of educational support:** Future studies should evaluate the plausible hypothesis that support measures are most effective when they offer not only cognitive resources (see Part VIII) but also coping resources that boost self-efficacy and build resilience in the form of persistence on a task despite the experience of repeated failure.

(4) **Response to intervention:** The response-to-intervention support framework is based on a three-level prevention system designed to enable data-based and multiprofessional educational decision-making (primary: high-quality instruction and screening; secondary: small-group support and progress monitoring (curriculum-based measurements); tertiary: individual instruction and diagnosis). The largest currently available studies suggest that response-to-intervention-based programmes might have moderate positive effects on basic learning outcomes.

(5) **Test-teach-test:** The test–teach–test support framework is based on the objective to disambiguate poor performance due to a lack of quality instruction from a specific learning disorder. Whether test–teach–test is an effective complementary support framework remains to be confirmed by controlled studies.

(6) **Evidence for the effectiveness of educational support:** Given the limited quasi-experimental accessibility of educational settings such as schools and kindergartens, current positive evidence for the effectiveness of institutional support programmes should be treated with utmost caution. Most existing studies are not explicit in terms of statistical power, await independent replication, do not include long-term follow-up data capturing possible fade-out effects (see Chapter 21, Sokolowski and Peters 2022), and are prone to a number of biases due to insufficient or missing blinding, randomization, and active control (see Chapter 19, Galuschka and Schulte-Körne 2022).

General Summary

Michael A. Skeide

1 Current State of the Art

Dyslexia and dyscalculia originate from the joint effects of multiple genetic and environmental factors on the developing brain in the first years of life, including the prenatal phase. While many candidate genes have been reported in the literature (e.g., *DCDC2*, *DYX1C1*, *KIAA0319*, and *ROBO1*), so far no DNA variants have revealed reliable associations across the whole genome. Moreover, potential early environmental influences (e.g., preterm birth, prenatal substance exposure, breast-feeding, maternal psychosocial stress, developmental toxicants) currently preclude specific interpretations since they also have a genetic basis that is typically not controlled in existing studies. Correspondingly, the question of how gene–environment correlation and interaction lead to learning difficulties can only be answered at a very general level at present.

In all cultures studied so far, individuals with dyslexia universally show reduced letter or character knowledge (hampered print-to-speech conversion) while individuals with dyscalculia universally show faulty (non-)symbolic quantity representations. Nevertheless, dyslexia also involves cultural differences dependent on print-to-speech conversion differences between scripts. Specifically, dyslexia is diagnosed less often the more transparent the particular script is that children learn (prevalence in transparent Italian about 3.5% vs. 7% in intransparent English). Moreover, individuals with dyslexia who learn a transparent alphabetic script typically show more pronounced difficulties in reading fluency than in reading accuracy.

Learning disorders manifest themselves heterogeneously in a number of behavioural domains (dyslexia: e.g., reading, spelling, audition, language, attention; dyscalculia: e.g., numbers, counting, transcoding, calculation, fact retrieval, working memory, executive functioning). Additionally, they can co-occur with each other and with language disorder, coordination disorder, internalizing disorders (depression and anxiety), and externalizing disorders (ADHD and conduct disorder). At the same time, thus far there are few early deficits that have been consistently found to play a potentially causal role. For dyslexia, these are rapid automatized naming deficits and auditory-phonological deficits related to the auditory cortex and downstream phonological processing regions in superior temporal, inferior parietal, and inferior frontal cortices connected via the arcuate fasciculus. For dyscalculia, these are faulty (non-)symbolic quantity representations related to parietal and prefrontal cortices. In a similar vein, there are only a few currently known causally relevant early predictors of dyslexia (the 'big three': phonological awareness, letter knowledge, and rapid automatized naming) and dyscalculia (number comparison, cardinal counting, spatial skills, vocabulary, and letter knowledge).

We recommend that, based on these predictors, children should undergo an early risk assessment and take part in a prevention programme to overcome the traditional wait-to-fail approach (see, for example, LukiMat in Finland). Such programmes are most effective when they are individualized, adaptive, carried out in small groups, focused on all relevant domains, and start as early as possible. Yet, while prevention/intervention programmes are very valuable tools they typically yield moderate effect sizes and their positive effects often fade-out within a year. One potential key factor for overcoming fade-out is an optimal biological time window during which a child responds most strongly to an intervention (yet-to-be-understood sensitive periods). In addition, a high-quality, enriched learning environment after the completion of a programme (e.g., psychoeducational programmes for parents and teachers, community-based programmes in adverse environments) can be assumed to be critical to sustain gains and foster long-term change after an intervention.

While it is clear that learning disorders have a biological basis, children's individual personal states (e.g., motivation, emotions, self-concept, noise, fatigue) and their embeddings in social contexts are often overlooked. How social actors (parents, peers, educators) deal with affected children is prone to a number of biases, such as gender bias (e.g., boys are diagnosed with dyslexia about twice as often as girls), and to stereotyping (e.g., performance constructs related to ethnic background and social status). This also means that diagnoses leave ample room for subjectivity, despite being based on classification systems. Furthermore, diagnoses are typically not generalizable across social learning contexts due to differences in culture, age, curriculum, language, and many other factors. Finally, given the limited quasi-experimental accessibility of social settings such as schools and kindergartens, it is currently hard to say how effective educational support programmes are (e.g., response to intervention or test–teach–test).

2 Future Challenges

2.1 Theoretical Challenges

Progress in research on dyslexia and dyscalculia depends on the progress of many other fields dealing with human cognitive development. For example, as long as there is no theory that is able to explain the intergenerational transmission of cognitive abilities in detail, there is no genetic theory of learning disorders. The same applies to social-environmental theory building, which currently seems too complex to go beyond existing toy models such as ecological systems theory. Tracing how gene–environment interplay dynamically shapes human learning in the first years of life is currently out of reach, or at least very challenging, especially when also trying to take genetic nurture and epigenetic effects into account.

Another prominent example for at best rudimentary theoretical understanding is the large gap between psychological models of reading and maths and their neuro-biological foundation. Existing models are either too simple to capture how learning works in the developing brain (e.g., based on supervised learning algorithms built into single-layer neural networks) or they are based on deep learning algorithms that are not fully explicit in terms of the actual computations carried out to solve particular learning tasks. Accordingly, advances in understanding atypical learning will go hand-in-hand with new insights into the computational architecture of learning algorithms. At the same time, existing methods used in human neuroscience are often not suitable for the biological validation of a cognitive process. These measures are usually not quantitative (not measured in physical units and not robust to differences in hardware, physiology, or experimental tasks), so little is known about the relationship between (changing) brain measures and (atypical) learning behaviour. Quantitative neuroscience will thus be a crucial experimental approach for developing biologically valid theories of dyslexia and dyscalculia.

2.2 Sampling Challenges

The vast majority of currently available data has been collected in European and US samples that are WEIRD (western-educated-industrialized-rich-democratic). Comprehensive additional work is thus needed to determine the degree to which the currently available findings generalize to other samples. Other forms of heterogeneity (e.g., in terms of socioeconomic background) also remain strongly understudied (but also ill-defined) with respect to dyslexia and dyscalculia. This kind of research is critical for developing culturally valid models of typical and atypical learning.

2.3 Statistical Challenges

One of the most severe limitations of research on learning disorders is that the statistical standards of the field are comparably low. Studies that are based on a priori power calculations are rarely seen in the literature. While this issue applies to virtually all types of studies (including behavioural and brain studies) it is particularly problematic in the context of genetic and environmental research, given the very small effect sizes of single genetic variants and environmental factors. As a consequence, it is likely that much of the work published so far is underpowered and not (fully) replicable. A first step to overcome this replication crisis could be to set stricter publication standards making it mandatory to conduct an a priori power calculation based on which authors can determine adequate sample sizes needed for obtaining a predefined effect following prespecified hypotheses.

2.4 Measurement Challenges

Given the effort of conducting human-subject research, the results reported in the literature are typically just cross-sectional observational snapshots of individuals with dyslexia and dyscalculia. Such correlative data, while certainly informative, cannot tell us what causes learning disorders and how to treat them. This calls for a major commitment of the community and research funding agencies for more long-term longitudinal work in which children are followed as early as possible for several years, ideally using an intervention design. Another obstacle that is often overlooked is that virtually all existing data are group data that do not translate to an individual person and thus have no straightforward real-world application. Accordingly, there is an urgent need for single-subject studies that make it possible to draw conclusions about individual learners.

2.5 Practical Challenges

Difficulties that ultimately result in dyslexia and dyscalculia can emerge well before children enter educational institutions and may persist over the entire lifespan. It is well-known, for example, that a substantial proportion of children who go on to develop dyslexia or dyscalculia have early language acquisition difficulties that may lead to developmental language disorder. This means that many at-risk children may benefit from language support in their first years of life. It remains to be seen whether existing psychoeducation programmes for parents (such as the Heidelberger Elterntraining in Germany; Buschmann et al. 2009) fulfil this expectation.

At the institutional level, there are promising examples of how an early education policy for dyslexia and dyscalculia may look (e.g., in Scandinavia). Given that it is barely possible to get educational institutions under quasi-experimental control, however, it remains a major challenge for the educational sciences to determine empirically which factors are most relevant for the effective implementation of such a policy.

References

Part I – Part XI

71st World Health Assembly. 2018. 21–26 May 2018. https://ec.europa.eu/info/events/sustain able-development-goals/71st-world-health-assembly-2018-may-21_de.

Aarnoudse-Moens, C. S. H., N. Weisglas-Kuperus, J. B. van Goudoever, and J. Oosterlaan. 2009. 'Meta-Analysis of Neurobehavioral Outcomes in Very Preterm and/or Very Low Birth Weight Children'. *Pediatrics* 124 (2): 717–28.

Abreu-Villaça, Y., F. J. Seidler, C. A. Tate, M. M. Cousins, and T. A. Slotkin. 2004. 'Prenatal Nicotine Exposure Alters the Response to Nicotine Administration in Adolescence: Effects on Cholinergic Systems during Exposure and Withdrawal'. *Neuropsychopharmacology: Official Publication of the American College of Neuropsychopharmacology* 29 (5): 879–90.

Ackerman, J. P., T. Riggins, and M. M. Black. 2010. 'A Review of the Effects of Prenatal Cocaine Exposure among School-Aged Children'. *Pediatrics* 125 (3): 554–65.

Ahmad, K., M. Casey, and T. Bale. 2002. 'Connectionist Simulation of Quantification Skills'. *Connection Science* 14 (3): 165–201.

Ahmed, W. 2018. 'Developmental Trajectories of Math Anxiety during Adolescence: Associations with STEM Career Choice'. *Journal of Adolescence* 67 (August): 158–66.

Alarcón, M., J. C. DeFries, J. G. Light, and B. F. Pennington. 1997. 'A Twin Study of Mathematics Disability'. *Journal of Learning Disabilities* 30 (6): 617–23.

Alexander, R. 1982. 'Implementation: Does a Literature Add Up to a Theory?' *Journal of the American Planning Association* 48 (1): 132–55.

Allik, J., and T. Tuulmets. 1991. 'Occupancy Model of Perceived Numerosity'. *Perception & Psychophysics* 49 (4): 303–14.

Al-Saleh, I., N. Shinwari, M. Nester, et al. 2008. 'Longitudinal Study of Prenatal and Postnatal Lead Exposure and Early Cognitive Development in Al-Kharj, Saudi Arabia: A Preliminary Results of Cord Blood Lead Levels'. *Journal of Tropical Pediatrics* 54 (5): 300–7.

American College of Obstetricians and Gynecologists (ACOG). 2004. 'Neonatal Encephalopathy and Cerebral Palsy: Executive Summary'. *Obstetrics and Gynecology* 103 (4): 780–1.

American Psychiatric Association. 2013. *Diagnostic and Statistical Manual of Mental Disorders (DSM-5®)*. American Psychiatric Publishing.

Amin-Zaki, L., S. Elhassani, M. A. Majeed, et al. 1976. 'Perinatal Methylmercury Poisoning in Iraq'. *American Journal of Diseases of Children* 130 (10): 1070–6.

Amin-Zaki, L., M. A. Majeed, M. R. Greenwood, et al. 1981. 'Methylmercury Poisoning in the Iraqi Suckling Infant: A Longitudinal Study over Five Years'. *Journal of Applied Toxicology: JAT* 1 (4): 210–14.

Anderson, J. R., S. Betts, J. L. Ferris, and J. M. Fincham. 2011. 'Cognitive and Metacognitive Activity in Mathematical Problem Solving: Prefrontal and Parietal Patterns'. *Cognitive, Affective & Behavioral Neuroscience* 11 (1): 52–67.

Anderson, J. W., B. M. Johnstone, and D. T. Remley. 1999. 'Breast-Feeding and Cognitive Development: A Meta-Analysis'. *The American Journal of Clinical Nutrition* 70 (4): 525–35.

Anjari, M., L. Srinivasan, J. M. Allsop, et al. 2007. 'Diffusion Tensor Imaging with Tract-Based Spatial Statistics Reveals Local White Matter Abnormalities in Preterm Infants'. *NeuroImage* 35 (3): 1021–7.

Anobile, G., P. Stievano, and D. C. Burr. 2013. 'Visual Sustained Attention and Numerosity Sensitivity Correlate with Math Achievement in Children'. *Journal of Experimental Child Psychology* 116 (2): 380–91.

Ansari, D. 2007. 'Does the Parietal Cortex Distinguish between "10," "Ten," and Ten Dots?' *Neuron* 53 (2): 165–7. https://doi.org/10.1016/j.neuron.2007.01.001.

——— 2008. 'Effects of Development and Enculturation on Number Representation in the Brain'. *Nature Reviews. Neuroscience* 9 (4): 278–91.

——— 2010. 'Neurocognitive Approaches to Developmental Disorders of Numerical and Mathematical Cognition: The Perils of Neglecting the Role of Development'. *Learning and Individual Differences* 20 (2): 123–9.

Ansari, D. and B. Dhital. 2006. 'Age-Related Changes in the Activation of the Intraparietal Sulcus during Nonsymbolic Magnitude Processing: An Event-Related Functional Magnetic Resonance Imaging Study'. *Journal of Cognitive Neuroscience* 18 (11): 1820–8. https://doi.org/10.1162/jocn.2006.18.11.1820.

Ansari, D., N. Garcia, E. Lucas, K. Hamon, and B. Dhital. 2005. 'Neural Correlates of Symbolic Number Processing in Children and Adults'. *Neuroreport* 16 (16): 1769–73.

Araki, M., K. Nagata, Y. Satoh, et al. 2002. 'Developmentally Regulated Expression of Neuro-p24 and Its Possible Function in Neurite Extension'. *Neuroscience Research* 44 (4): 379–89. https://doi.org/10.1016/s0168-0102(02)00156-6.

Araújo, S., A. Reis, K. M. Petersson, and L. Faísca. 2015. 'Rapid Automatized Naming and Reading Performance: A Meta-Analysis'. *Journal of Educational Psychology* 107 (3): 868–83. https://doi.org/10.1037/edu0000006.

Archer, K., K. Pammer, and T. R. Vidyasagar. 2020. 'A Temporal Sampling Basis for Visual Processing in Developmental Dyslexia'. *Frontiers in Human Neuroscience* 14 (July): 213.

Arciuli, J., and I. C. Simpson. 2012. 'Statistical Learning Is Related to Reading Ability in Children and Adults'. *Cognitive Science* 36 (2): 286–304.

Arnold, E. M., D. B. Goldston, A. K. Walsh, et al. 2005. 'Severity of Emotional and Behavioral Problems among Poor and Typical Readers'. *Journal of Abnormal Child Psychology* 33 (2): 205–17.

Arsalidou, M., M. Pawliw-Levac, M. Sadeghi, and J. Pascual-Leone. 2018. 'Brain Areas Associated with Numbers and Calculations in Children: Meta-Analyses of fMRI Studies'. *Developmental Cognitive Neuroscience* 30: 239–50. https://doi.org/10.1016/j.dcn.2017.08.002.

Arsalidou, M., and M. J. Taylor. 2011. 'Is 2+2=4? Meta-Analyses of Brain Areas Needed for Numbers and Calculations'. *NeuroImage* 54 (3): 2382–93.

Artemenko, C., M. Soltanlou, A.-C. Ehlis, H.-C. Nuerk, and T. Dresler. 2018. 'The Neural Correlates of Mental Arithmetic in Adolescents: A Longitudinal fNIRS Study'. *Behavioral and Brain Functions: BBF* 14 (1): 5.

Aschard, H., J. Chen, M. C. Cornelis, et al. 2012. 'Inclusion of Gene-Gene and Gene-Environment Interactions Unlikely to Dramatically Improve Risk Prediction for Complex Diseases'. *American Journal of Human Genetics* 90 (6): 962–72.

Ashcraft, M. H. 2002. 'Math Anxiety: Personal, Educational, and Cognitive Consequences'. *Current Directions in Psychological Science* 11 (5): 181–85.

Ashcraft, M. H., and M. W. Faust. 1994. 'Mathematics Anxiety and Mental Arithmetic Performance: An Exploratory Investigation'. *Cognition and Emotion* 8 (2): 97–125.

Ashcraft, M. H., and E. P. Kirk. 2001. 'The Relationships among Working Memory, Math Anxiety, and Performance'. *Journal of Experimental Psychology: General* 130 (2): 224–37.

Ashcraft, M. H., and J. A. Krause. 2007. 'Working Memory, Math Performance, and Math Anxiety'. *Psychonomic Bulletin & Review* 14 (2): 243–8.

Ashcraft, M. H., and A. M. Moore. 2009. 'Mathematics Anxiety and the Affective Drop in Performance'. *Journal of Psychoeducational Assessment* 27 (3): 197–205.

Ashcraft, M. H., and K. S. Ridley. 2005. 'Math Anxiety and Its Cognitive Consequences'. In D. Campbell (ed.) *Handbook of Mathematical Cognition*, 315–27. Psychology Press.

Ashkenazi, S., J. M. Black, D. A. Abrams, F. Hoeft, and V. Menon. 2013a. 'Neurobiological Underpinnings of Math and Reading Learning Disabilities'. *Journal of Learning Disabilities* 46 (6). https://doi.org/10.1177/0022219413483174.

Ashkenazi, S., N. Mark-Zigdon, and A. Henik. 2009. 'Numerical Distance Effect in Developmental Dyscalculia'. *Cognitive Development* 24 (4): 387–400.

Ashkenazi, S., M. Rosenberg-Lee, A. W. S. Metcalfe, A. G. Swigart, and V. Menon. 2013b. 'Visuo-Spatial Working Memory is an Important Source of Domain-General Vulnerability in the Development of Arithmetic Cognition'. *Neuropsychologia* 51 (11): 2305–17.

Ashkenazi, S., M. Rosenberg-Lee, C. Tenison, and V. Menon. 2012. 'Weak Task-Related Modulation and Stimulus Representations during Arithmetic Problem Solving in Children with Developmental Dyscalculia'. *Developmental Cognitive Neuroscience* 2 Suppl 1 (February): S152–66.

Askenazi, S., and A. Henik. 2010. 'Attentional Networks in Developmental Dyscalculia'. *Behavioral and Brain Functions: BBF* 6 (January): 2.

Ask, H., M. Idstad, B. Engdahl, and K. Tambs. 2013. 'Non-Random Mating and Convergence over Time for Mental Health, Life Satisfaction, and Personality: The Nord-Trøndelag Health Study'. *Behavior Genetics* 43 (2): 108–19.

Assaf, Y., and O. Pasternak. 2008. 'Diffusion Tensor Imaging (DTI)-Based White Matter Mapping in Brain Research: A Review'. *Journal of Molecular Neuroscience: MN* 34 (1): 51–61.

Aster, M. G. von, and R. S. Shalev. 2007. 'Number Development and Developmental Dyscalculia'. *Developmental Medicine & Child Neurology.* 49 (11): 868–73. https://doi.org/10.1111/j.1469-8749.2007.00868.x.

Aster, M. von, K. Kucian, M. Schweiter, and E. Martin. 2005. 'Rechenstörungen Im Kindesalter'. *Monatsschrift Kinderheilkunde: Organ Der Deutschen Gesellschaft Fur Kinderheilkunde* 153 (7): 614–22.

Aster, M. von, Z. M. Weinhold, and R. Horn. 2006. Neuro-psychologische Testbatterie für Zahlenverarbeitung und Rechnen bei Kindern (ZAREKI-R). Har-court Test Services.

Astle, D. E., and S. Fletcher-Watson. 2020. 'Beyond the Core-Deficit Hypothesis in Developmental Disorders'. *Current Directions in Psychological Science* 29 (5): 431–7.

Astley, S. J., E. H. Aylward, H. C. Olson, et al. 2009. 'Functional Magnetic Resonance Imaging Outcomes from a Comprehensive Magnetic Resonance Study of Children with Fetal Alcohol Spectrum Disorders'. *Journal of Neurodevelopmental Disorders* 1 (1): 61–80.

Atkinson, J., J. King, O. Braddick, et al. 1997. 'A Specific Deficit of Dorsal Stream Function in Williams' Syndrome'. *Neuroreport* 8 (8): 1919–22.

Attout, L., and S. Majerus. 2015a. 'Working Memory Deficits in Developmental Dyscalculia: The Importance of Serial Order'. *Child Neuropsychology* 21 (4): 432–50. https://doi.org/10.1080/09297049.2014.922170.

——— 2015b. 'Working Memory Deficits in Developmental Dyscalculia: The Importance of Serial Order'. *Child Neuropsychology: A Journal on Normal and Abnormal Development in Childhood and Adolescence* 21 (4): 432–50.

——— 2018. 'Serial Order Working Memory and Numerical Ordinal Processing Share Common Processes and Predict Arithmetic Abilities'. *British Journal of Developmental Psychology* 36 (2): 285–98. https://doi.org/10.1111/bjdp.12211.

Avancini, C., and D. Szűcs. 2019. 'Psychophysiological Correlates of Mathematics Anxiety'. In *Mathematics Anxiety*. Routledge. https://doi.org/10.4324/9780429199981-3.

Axelrad, D. A., D. C. Bellinger, L. M. Ryan, and T. J. Woodruff. 2007. 'Dose-Response Relationship of Prenatal Mercury Exposure and IQ: An Integrative Analysis of Epidemiologic Data'. *Environmental Health Perspectives* 115 (4): 609–15.

Bach, S., U. Richardson, D. Brandeis, E. Martin, and S. Brem. 2013. 'Print-Specific Multimodal Brain Activation in Kindergarten Improves Prediction of Reading Skills in Second Grade'. *NeuroImage* 82 (November): 605–15.

Back, S. A., A. Riddle, and M. M. McClure. 2007. 'Maturation-Dependent Vulnerability of Perinatal White Matter in Premature Birth'. *Stroke: A Journal of Cerebral Circulation* 38 (2 Suppl): 724–30.

Badawi, N., J. J. Kurinczuk, J. M. Keogh, et al. 1998. 'Antepartum Risk Factors for Newborn Encephalopathy: The Western Australian Case-Control Study'. *BMJ* 317 (7172): 1549–53.

Bajic, D., K. G. Commons, and S. G. Soriano. 2013. 'Morphine-Enhanced Apoptosis in Selective Brain Regions of Neonatal Rats'. *International Journal of Developmental Neuroscience: The Official Journal of the International Society for Developmental Neuroscience* 31 (4): 258–66.

Baker, L., and A. Wigfield. 1999. 'Dimensions of Children's Motivation for Reading and Their Relations to Reading Activity and Reading Achievement'. *Reading Research Quarterly* 34 (4): 452–77.

Ballard, O., and A. L. Morrow. 2013. 'Human Milk Composition: Nutrients and Bioactive Factors'. *Pediatric Clinics of North America* 60 (1): 49–74.

Bander, R. S., and N. E. Betz. 1981. 'The Relationship of Sex and Sex Role to Trait and Situationally Specific Anxiety Types'. *Journal of Research in Personality* 15 (3): 312–22.

Banfi, C., F. Kemény, M. Gangl, et al. 2018. 'Visual Attention Span Performance in German-Speaking Children with Differential Reading and Spelling Profiles: No Evidence of Group Differences'. *PloS One* 13 (6): e0198903.

Bar, S., R. Milanaik, and A. Adesman. 2016. 'Long-Term Neurodevelopmental Benefits of Breastfeeding'. *Current Opinion in Pediatrics* 28 (4): 559–66.

Barbosa, F., Jr, J. E. Tanus-Santos, R. F. Gerlach, and P. J. Parsons. 2005. 'A Critical Review of Biomarkers Used for Monitoring Human Exposure to Lead: Advantages, Limitations, and Future Needs'. *Environmental Health Perspectives* 113 (12): 1669–74.

Bardach, E. 1974. The Implementation Game. MIT Press.

Bardach, E. 1978. *The Implementation Game*. MIT Press. https://mitpress.mit.edu/books/implementation-game.

Bar-Kochva, I., and M. Amiel. 2016. 'The Relations between Reading and Spelling: An Examination of Subtypes of Reading Disability'. *Annals of Dyslexia* 66 (2): 219–34.

Barquero, L. A., N. Davis, and L. E. Cutting. 2014. 'Neuroimaging of Reading Intervention: A Systematic Review and Activation Likelihood Estimate Meta-Analysis'. *PloS One* 9 (1): e83668.

Barres, B. A., and M. C. C. Raff. 1993. 'Proliferation of Oligodendrocyte Precursor Cells Depends on Electrical Activity in Axons'. *Nature* 361 (21): 258–60.

Barroso, C., C. M. Ganley, A. L. McGraw, et al. 2020. 'A Meta-Analysis of the Relation between Math Anxiety and Math Achievement'. *Psychological Bulletin*, 147 (2): 134–68. https://doi.org/10.1037/bul0000307.

Barrouillet, P., M. Mignon, and C. Thevenot. 2008. 'Strategies in Subtraction Problem Solving in Children'. *Journal of Experimental Child Psychology* 99 (4): 233–51.

Basten, M., J. Jaekel, S. Johnson, C. Gilmore, and D. Wolke. 2015. 'Preterm Birth and Adult Wealth: Mathematics Skills Count'. *Psychological Science* 26 (10): 1608–19.

Batista-García-Ramó, Karla, and Caridad Ivette Fernández-Verdecia. 2018. 'What We Know About the Brain Structure-Function Relationship'. *Behavioral Sciences* 8 (4). https://doi.org/10.3390/bs8040039.

Bauer, A.-K. R., S. Debener, and A. C. Nobre. 2020. 'Synchronisation of Neural Oscillations and Cross-Modal Influences'. *Trends in Cognitive Sciences* 24 (6): 481–95.

Beaulieu, C., C. Plewes, L. A. Paulson, et al. 2005. 'Imaging Brain Connectivity in Children with Diverse Reading Ability'. *NeuroImage* 25 (4): 1266–71.

Beilock, S. L. 2008. 'Math Performance in Stressful Situations'. *Current Directions in Psychological Science* 17 (5): 339–43.

Beilock, S. L., E. A. Gunderson, G. Ramirez, and S. C. Levine. 2010. 'Female Teachers' Math Anxiety Affects Girls' Math Achievement'. *Proceedings of the National Academy of Sciences of the United States of America* 107 (5): 1860–63.

Bellato, A., I. Arora, C. Hollis, and M. J. Groom. 2020. 'Is Autonomic Nervous System Function Atypical in Attention Deficit Hyperactivity Disorder (ADHD)? A Systematic Review of the Evidence'. *Neuroscience and Biobehavioral Reviews* 108 (January): 182–206.

Bellinger, D. C., K. O'Leary, H. Rainis, and H. J. Gibb. 2016. 'Country-Specific Estimates of the Incidence of Intellectual Disability Associated with Prenatal Exposure to Methylmercury'. *Environmental Research* 147 (May): 159–63.

Beltrán-Campos, V., M. Silva-Vera, M. L. García-Campos, and S. Díaz-Cintra. 2015. 'Effects of Morphine on Brain Plasticity'. *Neurología (English Edition)* 30 (3): 176–80.

Ben-Shachar, M., R. F. Dougherty, G. K. Deutsch, and B. A. Wandell. 2011. 'The Development of Cortical Sensitivity to Visual Word Forms'. *Journal of Cognitive Neuroscience* 23 (9): 2387–99.

Ben-Shachar, M., R. F. Dougherty, and B. A. Wandell. 2007. 'White Matter Pathways in Reading'. *Current Opinion in Neurobiology* 17 (2): 258–70.

Bentley, J. P., C. L. Roberts, J. R. Bowen, et al. 2016. 'Planned Birth Before 39 Weeks and Child Development: A Population-Based Study'. *Pediatrics* 138 (6). https://doi.org /10.1542/peds.2016-2002.

Berghuis, P., M. B. Dobszay, X. Wang, et al. 2005. 'Endocannabinoids Regulate Interneuron Migration and Morphogenesis by Transactivating the TrkB Receptor'. *Proceedings of the National Academy of Sciences of the United States of America* 102 (52): 19115–20.

Berglundh, S., M. Vollrath, A. L. Brantsæter, et al. 2021. 'Maternal Caffeine Intake during Pregnancy and Child Neurodevelopment up to Eight Years of Age: Results from the Norwegian Mother, Father and Child Cohort Study'. *European Journal of Nutrition* 60 (2): 791–805.

Berman,P. and M. W. McLaughlin. 1976. 'Implementation of Educational Innovation'. The Educational Forum 40 (3): 345–70.

Bernard-Bonnin, A. C., Canadian Paediatric Society, Mental Health and Developmental Disabilities Committee. 'Maternal Depression and Child Development'. 2004. *Paediatrics & Child Health* 9 (8): 575–83.

Berteletti, I., J. Prado, and J. R. Booth. 2014. 'Children with Mathematical Learning Disability Fail in Recruiting Verbal and Numerical Brain Regions When Solving Simple Multiplication Problems'. *Cortex: A Journal Devoted to the Study of the Nervous System and Behavior* 57 (August): 143–55.

Betz, N. E. 1978. 'Prevalence, Distribution, and Correlates of Math Anxiety in College Students'. *Journal of Counseling Psychology* 25 (5): 441–48.

Bhide, A., A. Power, and U. Goswami. 2013. 'A Rhythmic Musical Intervention for Poor Readers: A Comparison of Efficacy with a Letter-Based Intervention'. *Mind, Brain and Education: The Official Journal of the International Mind, Brain, and Education Society* 7 (2): 113–23.

Bieg, M., T. Goetz, and A. A. Lipnevich. 2014. 'What Students Think They Feel Differs from What They Really Feel: Academic Self-Concept Moderates the Discrepancy between Students' Trait and State Emotional Self-Reports'. *PloS One* 9 (3): e92563.

'Biomonitoring Summary'. 2019a. May 6, 2019. www.cdc.gov/biomonitoring/Benzene_ BiomonitoringSummary.html.

2019b. May 6, 2019. www.cdc.gov/biomonitoring/Benzene_BiomonitoringSummary.html.

Bishop, D. V., and C. Adams. 1990. 'A Prospective Study of the Relationship between Specific Language Impairment, Phonological Disorders and Reading Retardation'. *Journal of Child Psychology and Psychiatry, and Allied Disciplines* 31 (7): 1027–50.

Black, J. M., Z. Xia, and F. Hoeft. 2017. 'Neurobiological Bases of Reading Disorder Part II: The Importance of Developmental Considerations in Typical and Atypical Reading'. *Language and Linguistics Compass* 11 (10): 1–26.

Blau, V., J. Reithler, N. van Atteveldt, et al. 2010. 'Deviant Processing of Letters and Speech Sounds as Proximate Cause of Reading Failure: A Functional Magnetic Resonance Imaging Study of Dyslexic Children'. *Brain: A Journal of Neurology* 133 (Pt 3): 868–79.

Bleker, L. S., S. R. de Rooij, and T. J. Roseboom. 2019. 'Prenatal Psychological Stress Exposure and Neurodevelopment and Health of Children'. *International Journal of Environmental Research and Public Health* 16 (19): 3657. https://doi.org/10 .3390/ijerph16193657.

Blencowe, H., S. Cousens, M. Z. Oestergaard, et al. 2012. 'National, Regional, and Worldwide Estimates of Preterm Birth Rates in the Year 2010 with Time Trends since 1990 for Selected Countries: A Systematic Analysis and Implications'. *The Lancet* 379 (9832): 2162–72.

Bloechle, J., S. Huber, J. Bahnmueller, et al. 2016. 'Fact Learning in Complex Arithmetic-the Role of the Angular Gyrus Revisited'. *Human Brain Mapping* 37 (9): 3061–79.

Boets, B., and B. De Smedt. 2010. 'Single-Digit Arithmetic in Children with Dyslexia'. *Dyslexia* 16 (2): 183–91.

Boets, B., H. P. Op de Beeck, M. Vandermosten, et al. 2013. 'Intact but Less Accessible Phonetic Representations in Adults with Dyslexia'. *Science* 342 (6163): 1251–4.

Boets, B., M. Vandermosten, H. Poelmans, et al. 2011. 'Preschool Impairments in Auditory Processing and Speech Perception Uniquely Predict Future Reading Problems'. *Research in Developmental Disabilities* 32 (2): 560–70.

Borchers, L R., L.Bruckert, C. K. Dodson, et al. 2019. 'Microstructural Properties of White Matter Pathways in Relation to Subsequent Reading Abilities in Children: A Longitudinal Analysis'. *Brain Structure & Function* 224 (2): 891–905.

Bortolato, M., V. Bini, R. Frau, et al. 2014. 'Juvenile Cannabinoid Treatment Induces Frontostriatal Gliogenesis in Lewis Rats'. *European Neuropsychopharmacology: The Journal of the European College of Neuropsychopharmacology* 24 (6): 974–85.

Bosse, M.-L., M. J. Tainturier, and S. Valdois. 2007. 'Developmental Dyslexia: The Visual Attention Span Deficit Hypothesis'. *Cognition* 104 (2): 198–230.

Bosse, M.-L., and S. Valdois. 2009. 'Influence of the Visual Attention Span on Child Reading Performance: A Cross-Sectional Study'. *Journal of Research in Reading* 32 (2): 230–53.

Boucher, O., G. Muckle, J. L. Jacobson, et al. 2014. 'Domain-Specific Effects of Prenatal Exposure to PCBs, Mercury, and Lead on Infant Cognition: Results from the Environmental Contaminants and Child Development Study in Nunavik'. *Environmental Health Perspectives* 122 (3): 310–16.

Boulet-Craig, A., P. Robaey, K. Lacourse, et al. 2017. 'Visual Short Term Memory Related Brain Activity Predicts Mathematical Abilities'. *Neuropsychology* 31 (5): 535–45.

Bowman, C. R., and D. Zeithamova. 2018. 'Abstract Memory Representations in the Ventromedial Prefrontal Cortex and Hippocampus Support Concept Generalization'. *The Journal of Neuroscience: The Official Journal of the Society for Neuroscience* 38 (10): 2605–14.

Brady, S. A., D. Braze, and C. A. Fowler. 2011. *Explaining Individual Differences in Reading: Theory and Evidence*. Psychology Press.

Brain Development Cooperative Group. 2012. 'Total and Regional Brain Volumes in a Population-Based Normative Sample from 4 to 18 Years: The NIH MRI Study of Normal Brain Development'. *Cerebral Cortex* 22 (1): 1–12.

Braun, J. M., R. S. Kahn, T. Froehlich, P. Auinger, and B. P. Lanphear. 2006. 'Exposures to Environmental Toxicants and Attention Deficit Hyperactivity Disorder in US Children'. *Environmental Health Perspectives* 114 (12): 1904–9.

Brem, S., S. Bach, K. Kucian, et al. 2010. 'Brain Sensitivity to Print Emerges When Children Learn Letter-Speech Sound Correspondences'. *Proceedings of the National Academy of Sciences of the United States of America* 107 (17): 7939–44.

Brem, S., P. Halder, K. Bucher, et al. 2009. 'Tuning of the Visual Word Processing System: Distinct Developmental ERP and fMRI Effects'. *Human Brain Mapping* 30 (6): 1833–44.

Brem, S., U. Maurer, M. Kronbichler, et al. 2020. 'Visual Word Form Processing Deficits Driven by Severity of Reading Impairments in Children with Developmental Dyslexia'. *Scientific Reports* 10 (1): 18728.

Brennan, A. R., and A. F. T. Arnsten. 2008. 'Neuronal Mechanisms Underlying Attention Deficit Hyperactivity Disorder: The Influence of Arousal on Prefrontal Cortical Function'. *Annals of the New York Academy of Sciences* 1129: 236–45.

Bressler, J. P., and G. W. Goldstein. 1991. 'Mechanisms of Lead Neurotoxicity'. *Biochemical Pharmacology* 41 (4): 479–84.

'Brominated Flame Retardants'. n.d. Accessed July 21, 2021. www.efsa.europa.eu/en/topics/topic/brominated-flame-retardants.

Brossard-Racine, M., A. J. du Plessis, and C. Limperopoulos. 2015. 'Developmental Cerebellar Cognitive Affective Syndrome in Ex-Preterm Survivors Following Cerebellar Injury'. *Cerebellum* 14 (2): 151–64.

Browning, R., D. Marshall, and D. Tabb. 1981. 'Implementation and Political Change: Sources of Local Variation in Federal Social Programs'. In Effective Policy Implementation, edited by D. Mazmanian and P. Sabatier. D. C. Heath.

Brubaker, C. J., K. N. Dietrich, B. P. Lanphear, and K. M. Cecil. 2010. 'The Influence of Age of Lead Exposure on Adult Gray Matter Volume'. *Neurotoxicology* 31 (3): 259–66.

Brubaker, C. J., V. J. Schmithorst, E. N. Haynes, et al. 2009. 'Altered Myelination and Axonal Integrity in Adults with Childhood Lead Exposure: A Diffusion Tensor Imaging Study'. *Neurotoxicology* 30 (6): 867–75.

Bruckert, L., L. R. Borchers, C. K. Dodson, et al. 2019. 'White Matter Plasticity in Reading-Related Pathways Differs in Children Born Preterm and at Term: A Longitudinal Analysis'. *Frontiers in Human Neuroscience* 13 (May): 139.

Bublitz, M. H., and L. R. Stroud. 2012. 'Maternal Smoking during Pregnancy and Offspring Brain Structure and Function: Review and Agenda for Future Research'. *Nicotine & Tobacco Research: Official Journal of the Society for Research on Nicotine and Tobacco* 14 (4): 388–97.

Bugden, S., and D. Ansari. 2016. 'Probing the Nature of Deficits in the "Approximate Number System" in Children with Persistent Developmental Dyscalculia'. *Developmental Science* 19 (5): 817–33. https://doi.org/10.1111/desc.12324.

Bulik-Sullivan, B., H. K. Finucane, V. Anttila, et al. 2015. 'An Atlas of Genetic Correlations across Human Diseases and Traits'. *Nature Genetics* 47 (11): 1236–41.

Bullock, T. H., M. V. L. Bennett, D. Johnston, et al. 2005. 'The Neuron Doctrine, Redux'. *Science* 310 (5749): 791–93.

Bulthé, J., J. Prinsen, J. Vanderauwera, et al. 2019. 'Multi-Method Brain Imaging Reveals Impaired Representations of Number as Well as Altered Connectivity in Adults with Dyscalculia'. *NeuroImage* 190: 289–302. https://doi.org/10.1016/j.neuroimage.2018.06.012.

Burbacher, T. M., P. M. Rodier, and B. Weiss. 1990. 'Methylmercury Developmental Neurotoxicity: A Comparison of Effects in Humans and Animals'. *Neurotoxicology and Teratology* 12 (3): 191–202.

Burr, D., and J. Ross. 2008. 'A Visual Sense of Number'. *Current Biology: CB* 18 (6): 425–28.

Butterworth, Brian. 2011. 'Chapter 16 – Foundational Numerical Capacities and the Origins of Dyscalculia**Reprinted from Trends in Cognitive Sciences, Vol 14, Brian Butterworth, Foundational Numerical Capacities and the Origins of Dyscalculia, Pg 534–541, 2010, with Permission from Elsevier.' In *Space, Time and Number in the Brain*, edited by S. Dehaene and E. M. Brannon, 249–65. Academic Press.

Butterworth, Brian, and Vincent Walsh. 2011. 'Neural Basis of Mathematical Cognition'. *Current Biology* 21 (16): PR618–R621. https://doi.org/10.1016/j.cub.2011.07.005.

Butterworth, B., S. Varma, and D. Laurillard. 2011. 'Dyscalculia: From Brain to Education'. *Science*, 27, 1049–53. https://doi.org/10.1126/science.1201536.

Buzsáki, G., and X. J. Wang. 2012. 'Mechanisms of Gamma Oscillations'. Annu Rev Neurosci. 35: 203–25. doi: 10.1146/annurev-neuro-062111-150444.

Cabrera, O. H., S. D. O'Connor, B. S. Swiney, et al. 2017. 'Caffeine Combined with Sedative/Anesthetic Drugs Triggers Widespread Neuroapoptosis in a Mouse Model of Prematurity'. *The Journal of Maternal-Fetal & Neonatal Medicine: The Official Journal of the European Association of Perinatal Medicine, the Federation of Asia and Oceania Perinatal Societies, the International Society of Perinatal Obstetricians* 30 (22): 2734–41.

Cai, K., Q. Song, W. Yuan, et al. 2020. 'Human Exposure to PBDEs in E-Waste Areas: A Review'. *Environmental Pollution* 267 (December): 115634.

Cannizzaro, C., F. Plescia, M. Martire, et al. 2006. 'Single, Intense Prenatal Stress Decreases Emotionality and Enhances Learning Performance in the Adolescent Rat Offspring: Interaction with a Brief, Daily Maternal Separation'. *Behavioural Brain Research* 169 (1): 128–36.

Cantlon, J. F., E. M. Brannon, E. J. Carter, and K. A. Pelphrey. 2006. 'Functional Imaging of Numerical Processing in Adults and 4-y-Old Children'. *PLoS Biology* 4 (5): e125.

Cantlon, J. F., and R. Li. 2013. 'Neural Activity During Natural Viewing of Sesame Street Statistically Predicts Test Scores in Early Childhood'. *PLoS Biology* 11 (1): e1001462.

Cappelletti, M., D. Didino, I. Stoianov, and M. Zorzi. 2014. 'Number Skills Are Maintained in Healthy Ageing'. *Cognitive Psychology* 69 (March): 25–45.

Carey, E., A. Devine, F. Hill, et al. 2019. 'Understanding Mathematics Anxiety: Investigating the Experiences of UK Primary and Secondary School Students'. *Apollo – University of Cambridge Repository*. https://doi.org/10.17863/CAM.37744.

Carey, E., A. Devine, F. Hill, and D. Szűcs. 2017. 'Differentiating Anxiety Forms and Their Role in Academic Performance from Primary to Secondary School'. *PloS One* 12 (3): e0174418.

Carey, E., F. Hill, A. Devine, and D. Szücs. 2015. 'The Chicken or the Egg? The Direction of the Relationship between Mathematics Anxiety and Mathematics Performance'. *Frontiers in Psychology* 6: 1987.

Carey, E., F. Hill, A. Devine, and D. Szűcs. 2017. 'The Modified Abbreviated Math Anxiety Scale: A Valid and Reliable Instrument for Use with Children'. *Frontiers in Psychology* 8 (January): 11.

Carrillo-Reid, L., W. Yang, Y. Bando, D. S. Peterka, and R. Yuste. 2016. 'Imprinting and Recalling Cortical Ensembles'. *Science* 353 (6300): 691–4.

Casad, B. J., P. Hale, and F. L. Wachs. 2015. 'Parent-Child Math Anxiety and Math-Gender Stereotypes Predict Adolescents' Math Education Outcomes'. *Frontiers in Psychology* 6 (November): 1597.

Cascio, C. J., G. Gerig, and J. Piven. 2007. 'Diffusion Tensor Imaging: Application to the Study of the Developing Brain'. *Journal of the American Academy of Child and Adolescent Psychiatry* 46 (2): 213–23.

Casey, R., S. E. Levy, K. Brown, and J. Brooks-Gunn. 1992. 'Impaired Emotional Health in Children with Mild Reading Disability'. *Journal of Developmental and Behavioral Pediatrics: JDBP* 13 (4): 256–60.

Caspi, A., B. Williams, J. Kim-Cohen, et al. 2007. 'Moderation of Breastfeeding Effects on the IQ by Genetic Variation in Fatty Acid Metabolism'. *Proceedings of the National Academy of Sciences of the United States of America* 104 (47): 18860–65.

Castaldi, E., M. Piazza, and T. Iuculano. 2020. 'Learning Disabilities: Developmental Dyscalculia'. *Handbook of Clinical Neurology* 174: 61–75.

Castles, A., and M. Coltheart. 1993. 'Varieties of Developmental Dyslexia'. *Cognition* 47 (2): 149–80.

Castoldi, A. F., T. Coccini, and L. Manzo. 2003. 'Neurotoxic and Molecular Effects of Methylmercury in Humans'. *Reviews on Environmental Health* 18 (1): 19–31.

Caviola, S., L. J. Colling, I. C. Mammarella, and D. Szűcs. 2020. 'Predictors of Mathematics in Primary School: Magnitude Comparison, Verbal and Spatial Working Memory Measures'. *Developmental Science* 23 (6): e12957.

Caviola, S., C. Primi, F. Chiesi, and I. C. Mammarella. 2017. 'Psychometric Properties of the Abbreviated Math Anxiety Scale (AMAS) in Italian Primary School Children'. *Learning and Individual Differences* 55 (April): 174–82.

Cecil, K. M., C. J. Brubaker, C. M. Adler, et al. 2008. 'Decreased Brain Volume in Adults with Childhood Lead Exposure'. *PLoS Medicine* 5 (5): e112.

Cecil, K. M., K. N. Dietrich, Mekibib Altaye, et al. 2011. 'Proton Magnetic Resonance Spectroscopy in Adults with Childhood Lead Exposure'. *Environmental Health Perspectives* 119 (3): 403–8.

Centanni, T. M., E. S. Norton, O. Ozernov-Palchik, et al. 2019. 'Disrupted Left Fusiform Response to Print in Beginning Kindergartners Is Associated with Subsequent Reading'. *NeuroImage. Clinical* 22 (November 2018): 101715.

Center for Food Safety, and Applied Nutrition. 2020. 'Advice about Eating Fish'. www.fda.gov/food/consumers/advice-about-eating-fish.

Cernerud, L., M. Eriksson, B. Jonsson, G. Steneroth, and R. Zetterström. 1996. 'Amphetamine Addiction during Pregnancy: 14-Year Follow-up of Growth and School Performance'. *Acta Paediatrica* 85 (2): 204–8.

Chandramouli, K., C. D. Steer, M. Ellis, and A. M. Emond. 2009. 'Effects of Early Childhood Lead Exposure on Academic Performance and Behaviour of School Age Children'. *Archives of Disease in Childhood* 94 (11): 844–48.

Chang, H., and S. L. Beilock. 2016. 'The Math Anxiety-Math Performance Link and Its Relation to Individual and Environmental Factors: A Review of Current Behavioral and Psychophysiological Research'. *Current Opinion in Behavioral Sciences* 10 (August): 33–38.

Chang, H., M. Rosenberg-Lee, S. Qin, and V. Menon. 2019. 'Faster Learners Transfer Their Knowledge Better: Behavioral, Mnemonic, and Neural Mechanisms of Individual Differences in Children's Learning'. *Developmental Cognitive Neuroscience* 40 (December): 100719.

Chang, S., C. Chen, Z. Yang, and A. David Rodrigues. 2009. 'Further Assessment of 17alpha-Ethinyl Estradiol as an Inhibitor of Different Human Cytochrome P450 Forms in Vitro'. *Drug Metabolism and Disposition: The Biological Fate of Chemicals* 37 (8): 1667–75.

Chang, T.-T., Arron W. S. Metcalfe, A. Padmanabhan, T. Chen, and V. Menon. 2016. 'Heterogeneous and Nonlinear Development of Human Posterior Parietal Cortex Function'. *NeuroImage* 126 (February): 184–95.

Charleston, J. S., R. L. Body, R. P. Bolender, et al. 1996. 'Changes in the Number of Astrocytes and Microglia in the Thalamus of the Monkey Macaca Fascicularis Following Long-Term Subclinical Methylmercury Exposure'. *Neurotoxicology* 17 (1): 127–38.

Chen, A., K.Yolton, S. A. Rauch, et al. 2014. 'Prenatal Polybrominated Diphenyl Ether Exposures and Neurodevelopment in US Children through 5 Years of Age: The HOME Study'. *Environmental Health Perspectives* 122 (8): 856–62.

Chen, C. L., T. H. Wu, M. C. Cheng, et al. 2006. 'Prospective Demonstration of Brain Plasticity after Intensive Abacus-Based Mental Calculation Training: An fMRI Study'. *Nuclear Instruments & Methods in Physics Research. Section A, Accelerators, Spectrometers, Detectors and Associated Equipment* 569 (2): 567–71.

Cheng, D., Q. Xiao, Q. Chen, J. Cui, and X. Zhou. 2018. 'Dyslexia and Dyscalculia Are Characterized by Common Visual Perception Deficits'. *Developmental Neuropsychology* 43 (6): 497–507.

Chen, N. T., M. Zheng, and C. Suk-Han Ho. 2019. 'Examining the Visual Attention Span Deficit Hypothesis in Chinese Developmental Dyslexia'. *Reading and Writing* 32 (3): 639–62.

Chen, S., Z. Zhou, M. Fang and J. L. McClelland. 2018. 'Can Generic Neural Networks Estimate Numerosity Like Humans?' *Cognitive Science.* https://stanford.edu /~jlmcc/papers/ChenZhouFangMcC18Estimation.pdf

Child, A. E., P. T. Cirino, J. M. Fletcher, E. G. Willcutt, and L. S. Fuchs. 2019. 'A Cognitive Dimensional Approach to Understanding Shared and Unique Contributions to Reading, Math, and Attention Skills'. *Journal of Learning Disabilities* 52 (1): 15–30.

Choe, K. W., J. B. Jenifer, C. S. Rozek, M. G. Berman, and S. L. Beilock. 2019. 'Calculated Avoidance: Math Anxiety Predicts Math Avoidance in Effort-Based Decision-Making'. *Science Advances* 5 (11): eaay1062.

Cho, K., J. C. Frijters, H. Zhang, L. L. Miller, and J. R. Gruen. 2013. 'Prenatal Exposure to Nicotine and Impaired Reading Performance'. *The Journal of Pediatrics* 162 (4): 713–18.

Cho, S., A. W. S. Metcalfe, C. B. Young, et al. 2012. 'Hippocampal-Prefrontal Engagement and Dynamic Causal Interactions in the Maturation of Children's Fact Retrieval'. *Journal of Cognitive Neuroscience* 24 (9): 1849–66.

Chung, K. K. H., C. McBride-Chang, S. W. L. Wong, et al. 2008. 'The Role of Visual and Auditory Temporal Processing for Chinese Children with Developmental Dyslexia'. *Annals of Dyslexia* 58 (1): 15–35.

Chyl, K., G. Fraga-González, S. Brem, and K. Jednoróg. 2021. 'Brain Dynamics of (a)Typical Reading Development-a Review of Longitudinal Studies'. *NPJ Science of Learning* 6 (1): 4.

Chyl, K., B. Kossowski, A. Dębska, et al. 2019. 'Reading Acquisition in Children: Developmental Processes and Dyslexia-Specific Effects'. *Journal of the American Academy of Child and Adolescent Psychiatry* 58 (10): 948–60.

Cicchini, G. M., G. Anobile, and D. C. Burr. 2016. 'Spontaneous Perception of Numerosity in Humans'. *Nature Communications* 7 (August): 12536.

Cicero, T. J., M. S. Ellis, and Z. A. Kasper. 2020. 'Polysubstance Use: A Broader Understanding of Substance Use During the Opioid Crisis'. *American Journal of Public Health* 110 (2): 244–50.

Cipolotti, L., B. Butterworth, and G. Denes. 1991. 'A Specific Deficit For Numbers In A Case Of Dense Acalculia'. *Brain* 114 (6): 2619–37. https://doi.org/10.1093/brain/114 .6.2619.

Cipora, K., M. Szczygieł, K. Willmes, and H.-C. Nuerk. 2015. 'Math Anxiety Assessment with the Abbreviated Math Anxiety Scale: Applicability and Usefulness: Insights from the Polish Adaptation'. *Frontiers in Psychology* 6 (November): 1833.

Cirino, P. T., L. S. Fuchs, J. T. Elias, S. R. Powell, and R. F. Schumacher. 2015. 'Cognitive and Mathematical Profiles for Different Forms of Learning Difficulties'. *Journal of Learning Disabilities* 48 (2): 156–75.

Clark, K. A., T. Helland, K.Specht, et al. 2014. 'Neuroanatomical Precursors of Dyslexia Identified from Pre-Reading through to Age 11'. *Brain: A Journal of Neurology* 137 (Pt 12): 3136–41.

Cleveland, L. M., M. L. Minter, K. A. Cobb, A. A. Scott, and V. F. German. 2008. 'Lead Hazards for Pregnant Women and Children: Part 1: Immigrants and the Poor Shoulder Most of the Burden of Lead Exposure in This Country. Part 1 of a Two-Part Article Details How Exposure Happens, Whom It Affects, and the Harm It Can Do'. *The American Journal of Nursing* 108 (10): 40–49; quiz 50.

Cohen, J. T., D. C. Bellinger, W. E. Connor, et al. 2005. 'A Quantitative Risk-Benefit Analysis of Changes in Population Fish Consumption'. *American Journal of Preventive Medicine* 29 (4): 325–34.

Cohen Kadosh, R., K. C. Kadosh, A. Kaas, A. Henik, and R. Goebel. 2007. 'Notation-Dependent and -Independent Representations of Numbers in the Parietal Lobes'. *Neuron* 53 (2): 307–14.

Coles, C. D., K. A. Platzman, C. L. Raskind-Hood, et al. 1997. 'A Comparison of Children Affected by Prenatal Alcohol Exposure and Attention Deficit, Hyperactivity Disorder'. *Alcoholism, Clinical and Experimental Research* 21 (1): 150–61.

Collet, G., C. Colin, W. Serniclaes, et al. 2012. 'Effect of Phonological Training in French Children with SLI: Perspectives on Voicing Identification, Discrimination and Categorical Perception'. *Research in Developmental Disabilities* 33 (6): 1805–18.

Collin, S. H. P., B. Milivojevic, and C. F. Doeller. 2015. 'Memory Hierarchies Map onto the Hippocampal Long Axis in Humans'. *Nature Neuroscience* 18 (11): 1562–64.

Coltheart, M. 1978. 'Lexical Access in Simple Reading Tasks'. *Strategies of Information Processing*, 151–216.

Coltheart, M., K. Rastle, C. Perry, R. Langdon, and J. Ziegler. 2001. 'DRC: A Dual Route Cascaded Model of Visual Word Recognition and Reading Aloud'. *Psychological Review* 108 (1): 204–56.

Conley, D., E. Rauscher, C. Dawes, P. K.E. Magnusson, and M. L. Siegal. 2013. 'Heritability and the Equal Environments Assumption: Evidence from Multiple Samples of Misclassified Twins'. *Behavior Genetics* 43 (5): 415–26.

Conradt, E., T. Flannery, J. L. Aschner, et al. 2019. 'Prenatal Opioid Exposure: Neurodevelopmental Consequences and Future Research Priorities'. *Pediatrics* 144 (3). https://doi.org/10.1542/peds.2019-0128.

Constantinidis, C., and T. Klingberg. 2016. 'The Neuroscience of Working Memory Capacity and Training'. *Nature Reviews Neuroscience* 17: 438–49. https://doi.org/10.1038/nrn .2016.43.

Cope, N., J. D. Eicher, H.Meng, et al. 2012. 'Variants in the DYX2 Locus Are Associated with Altered Brain Activation in Reading-Related Brain Regions in Subjects with Reading Disability'. *NeuroImage* 63 (1): 148–56. https://doi.org/10.1016/j .neuroimage.2012.06.037.

Cornelissen, P., A. Richardson, A. Mason, S. Fowler, and J. Stein. 1995. 'Contrast Sensitivity and Coherent Motion Detection Measured at Photopic Luminance Levels in Dyslexics and Controls'. *Vision Research* 35 (10): 1483–94.

Corriveau, K., E. Pasquini, and U. Goswami. 2007. 'Basic Auditory Processing Skills and Specific Language Impairment: A New Look at an Old Hypothesis'. *Journal of Speech, Language, and Hearing Research: JSLHR* 50 (3): 647–66.

Corsi, D. J., H.Hsu, D. B. Fell, S. W. Wen, and M. Walker. 2020. 'Association of Maternal Opioid Use in Pregnancy With Adverse Perinatal Outcomes in Ontario, Canada, From 2012 to 2018'. *JAMA Network Open* 3 (7): e208256.

Costa, L. G., and G. Giordano. 2014. 'Polybrominated Diphenyl Ethers'. In *Encyclopedia of Toxicology* (3rd ed.), edited by P. Wexler, 1032–4. Academic Press.

Costa, L. G., R. de Laat, S. Tagliaferri, and C. Pellacani. 2014. 'A Mechanistic View of Polybrominated Diphenyl Ether (PBDE) Developmental Neurotoxicity'. *Toxicology Letters* 230 (2): 282–94.

Cragg, L. and C. Gilmore. 2014. 'Skills Underlying Mathematics: The Role of Executive Function in the Development of Mathematics Proficiency'. *Trends in Neuroscience and Education* 3 (2): 63–8.

Crocker, N.,E. P. Riley, and S. N. Mattson. 2015. 'Visual-Spatial Abilities Relate to Mathematics Achievement in Children with Heavy Prenatal Alcohol Exposure'. *Neuropsychology* 29 (1): 108–16.

Crump, K. S., T. Kjellström, A. M. Shipp, A. Silvers, and A. Stewart. 1998. 'Influence of Prenatal Mercury Exposure upon Scholastic and Psychological Test Performance: Benchmark Analysis of a New Zealand Cohort'. *Risk Analysis: An Official Publication of the Society for Risk Analysis* 18 (6): 701–13.

Cumming, R., A. Wilson, and U. Goswami. 2015. 'Basic Auditory Processing and Sensitivity to Prosodic Structure in Children with Specific Language Impairments: A New Look at a Perceptual Hypothesis'. *Frontiers in Psychology* 6 (July): 972.

Curran, E. A., G. W. O'Keeffe, A. M. Looney, et al. 2018. 'Exposure to Hypertensive Disorders of Pregnancy Increases the Risk of Autism Spectrum Disorder in Affected Offspring'. *Molecular Neurobiology* 55 (7): 5557–64.

Darki, F., M. Peyrard-Janvid, H. Matsson, J. Kere, and T. Klingberg. 2012. 'Three Dyslexia Susceptibility Genes, DYX1C1, DCDC2, and KIAA0319, Affect Temporo-Parietal White Matter Structure'. *Biological Psychiatry* 72 (8): P671–6. https://doi.org/10.1016/j.biopsych.2012.05.008.

——— 2014. 'DCDC2 Polymorphism Is Associated with Left Temporoparietal Gray and White Matter Structures during Development'. *The Journal of Neuroscience: The Official Journal of the Society for Neuroscience* 34 (43): 14455–62.

Daskalakis, N. P., R. C. Bagot, K. J. Parker, C. H. Vinkers, and E. R. de Kloet. 2013. 'The Three-Hit Concept of Vulnerability and Resilience: Toward Understanding Adaptation to Early-Life Adversity Outcome'. *Psychoneuroendocrinology* 38 (9): 1858–73.

Davidson, P. W., A. Leste, E.Benstrong, et al. 2010. 'Fish Consumption, Mercury Exposure, and Their Associations with Scholastic Achievement in the Seychelles Child Development Study'. *Neurotoxicology* 31 (5): 439–47.

Davis, C. J., J. Gayán, V. S. Knopik, et al. 2001. 'Etiology of Reading Difficulties and Rapid Naming: The Colorado Twin Study of Reading Disability'. *Behavior Genetics* 31 (6): 625–35.

Davis, N., C. J. Cannistraci, B. P. Rogers, et al. 2009. 'Aberrant Functional Activation in School Age Children at-Risk for Mathematical Disability: A Functional Imaging

Study of Simple Arithmetic Skill'. *Neuropsychologia* 47 (12): 2470–9. https://doi.org/10.1016/j.neuropsychologia.2009.04.024.

Davis, O. S. P., G. Band, M. Pirinen, et al. 2014. 'The Correlation between Reading and Mathematics Ability at Age Twelve Has a Substantial Genetic Component'. *Nature Communications* 5 (July): 4204.

Day, N. L., G. A. Richardson, L. Goldschmidt, et al. 1994. 'Effect of Prenatal Marijuana Exposure on the Cognitive Development of Offspring at Age Three'. *Neurotoxicology and Teratology* 16 (2): 169–75.

Dean, J., G. S. Corrado, R. Monga, et al. 2012. 'Large Scale Distributed Deep Networks'. http://research.google/pubs/pub40565/.

Dehaene-Lambertz, G., K. Monzalvo, and S. Dehaene. 2018. 'The Emergence of the Visual Word Form: Longitudinal Evolution of Category-Specific Ventral Visual Areas during Reading Acquisition'. *PLoS Biology* 16 (3): e2004103.

Dehaene, S., and L. Cohen. 1997. 'Cerebral Pathways for Calculation: Double Dissociation between Rote Verbal and Quantitative Knowledge of Arithmetic'. *Cortex: A Journal Devoted to the Study of the Nervous System and Behavior* 33 (2): 219–50.

Dehaene, S., and L. Cohen. 2011. 'The Unique Role of the Visual Word Form Area in Reading'. *Trends in Cognitive Sciences* 15 (6): 254–62.

Dehaene, S. 2001. 'Precis of The Number Sense'. *Mind and Language* 16 (1): 16–36. https://doi.org/10.1111/1468-0017.00154.

——— 2011. *The Number Sense: How the Mind Creates Mathematics, Revised and Updated Edition*. Oxford University Press.

Dehaene, S., and J.-P. Changeux. 1993. 'Development of Elementary Numerical Abilities: A Neuronal Model'. *Journal of Cognitive Neuroscience* 5 (4): 390–407. https://doi.org/10.1162/jocn.1993.5.4.390.

Dehaene, S., L. Cohen, J. Morais, and R. Kolinsky. 2015. 'Illiterate to Literate: Behavioural and Cerebral Changes Induced by Reading Acquisition'. *Nature Reviews. Neuroscience* 16 (4): 234–44.

Dehaene, S., M. Piazza, P. Pinel, and L. Cohen. 2003. 'Three Parietal Circuits for Number Processing'. *Cognitive Neuropsychology* 20 (3): 487–506.

De La Cruz, V. M., A. Di Nuovo, S. Di Nuovo, and A. Cangelosi. 2014. 'Making Fingers and Words Count in a Cognitive Robot'. *Frontiers in Behavioral Neuroscience* 8 (February): 13.

Delazer, M., F. Domahs, A. Lochy, et al. 2004. 'Number Processing and Basal Ganglia Dysfunction: A Single Case Study'. *Neuropsychologia* 42 (8): 1050–62.

Delazer, M., F. Domahs, L. Bartha, et al. 2003. 'Learning Complex Arithmetic: An fMRI Study'. *Brain Research. Cognitive Brain Research* 18 (1): 76–88.

Delazer, M., A. Ischebeck, F. Domahs, et al. 2005. 'Learning by Strategies and Learning by Drill: Evidence from an fMRI Study'. *NeuroImage* 25 (3): 838–49.

Demeyere, N., P. Rotshtein, and G. W. Humphreys. 2012. 'The Neuroanatomy of Visual Enumeration: Differentiating Necessary Neural Correlates for Subitizing versus Counting in a Neuropsychological Voxel-Based Morphometry Study'. *Journal of Cognitive Neuroscience* 24 (4): 948–64. https://doi.org/10.1162/jocn_a_00188.

Denes, G., L. Cipolotti, and M. Zorzi. 2020. 'Acquired Dyslexias and Dysgraphias'. In *Handbook of Clinical and Experimental Neuropsychology*, 289–318. Psychology Press.

Denes, G., and L. Pizzamiglio. 1999. Handbook of Clinical and Experimental Neuropsychology (1st ed.). Psychology Press. https://doi.org/10.4324/9781315791272

Dennis, C.-L., K. Falah-Hassani, and R. Shiri. 2017. 'Prevalence of Antenatal and Postnatal Anxiety: Systematic Review and Meta-Analysis'. *The British Journal of Psychiatry: The Journal of Mental Science* 210 (5): 315–23.

Denny, C. H., C. S. Acero, T. S. Naimi, and S. Y. Kim. 2019. 'Consumption of Alcohol Beverages and Binge Drinking Among Pregnant Women Aged 18–44 Years – United States, 2015–2017'. *MMWR. Morbidity and Mortality Weekly Report* 68 (16): 365–8.

Deoni, S., D. Dean 3rd, S. Joelson, J. O'Regan, and N. Schneider. 2018. 'Early Nutrition Influences Developmental Myelination and Cognition in Infants and Young Children'. *NeuroImage* 178 (September): 649–59.

Department for Education and Employment. 1999. The National Numeracy Strategy: Framework for Teaching Mathematics from Reception to Year 6. London: DfEE.

Der, G., G. D. Batty, and I. J. Deary. 2006. 'Effect of Breast Feeding on Intelligence in Children: Prospective Study, Sibling Pairs Analysis, and Meta-Analysis'. *BMJ* 333 (7575): 945.

De Smedt, B., and B. Boets. 2010. 'Phonological Processing and Arithmetic Fact Retrieval: Evidence from Developmental Dyslexia'. Neuropsychologia 48 (14): 3973–81. doi: 10.1016/j.neuropsychologia.2010.10.018.

De Smedt, B., and C. K. Gilmore. 2011. 'Defective Number Module or Impaired Access? Numerical Magnitude Processing in First Graders with Mathematical Difficulties'. *Journal of Experimental Child Psychology* 108 (2): 278–92.

De Smedt, B., I. D. Holloway, and D. Ansari. 2011. 'Effects of Problem Size and Arithmetic Operation on Brain Activation during Calculation in Children with Varying Levels of Arithmetical Fluency'. *NeuroImage* 57 (3): 771–81.

Deutsch, G. K., R. F. Dougherty, R. Bammer, et al. 2005. 'Children's Reading Performance Is Correlated with White Matter Structure Measured by Diffusion Tensor Imaging'. *Cortex: A Journal Devoted to the Study of the Nervous System and Behavior* 41 (3): 354–63.

Devine, A., K. Fawcett, D. Szűcs, and A. Dowker. 2012. 'Gender Differences in Mathematics Anxiety and the Relation to Mathematics Performance While Controlling for Test Anxiety'. *Behavioral and Brain Functions: BBF* 8 (July): 33.

Devine, A., F. Hill, E. Carey, and D. Szűcs. 2018. 'Cognitive and Emotional Math Problems Largely Dissociate: Prevalence of Developmental Dyscalculia and Mathematics Anxiety'. *Journal of Educational Psychology* 110 (3): 431–44.

De Visscher, A., and M.-P. Noël. 2013. 'A Case Study of Arithmetic Facts Dyscalculia Caused by a Hypersensitivity-to-Interference in Memory'. *Cortex: A Journal Devoted to the Study of the Nervous System and Behavior* 49 (1): 50–70.

De Vos, A., S. Vanvooren, P. Ghesquière, and J. Wouters. 2020. 'Subcortical Auditory Neural Synchronization Is Deficient in Pre-Reading Children Who Develop Dyslexia'. *Developmental Science* 23 (6): e12945.

De Vos, A., S. Vanvooren, J. Vanderauwera, P. Ghesquière, and J. Wouters. 2017a. 'Atypical Neural Synchronization to Speech Envelope Modulations in Dyslexia'. *Brain and Language* 164 (January): 106–17.

2017b. 'A Longitudinal Study Investigating Neural Processing of Speech Envelope Modulation Rates in Children with (a Family Risk For) Dyslexia'. *Cortex: A Journal Devoted to the Study of the Nervous System and Behavior* 93 (August): 206–19.

Dew, K. H., and J. P. Galassi. 1983. 'Mathematics Anxiety: Some Basic Issues'. *Journal of Counseling Psychology* 30 (3): 443–6.

Di Bono, M. G., and M. Zorzi. 2013. 'Deep Generative Learning of Location-Invariant Visual Word Recognition'. *Frontiers in Psychology* 4 (September): 635.

DiCarlo, J. J., D. Zoccolan, and N. C. Rust. 2012. 'How Does the Brain Solve Visual Object Recognition?' *Neuron Perspective* 73 (3): 415–34.

Di Liberto, G. M., P. Varghese, M. Kalashnikova, et al. 2018. 'Atypical Çortical Entrainment to Speech in the Right Hemisphere Underpins Phonemic Deficits in Dyslexia'. *NeuroImage* 175 (July): 70–9.

Dingemans, M. M. L., M. van den Berg, and R. H. S. Westerink. 2011. 'Neurotoxicity of Brominated Flame Retardants: (In)direct Effects of Parent and Hydroxylated Polybrominated Diphenyl Ethers on the (Developing) Nervous System'. *Environmental Health Perspectives* 119 (7). https://doi.org/10.1289/ehp.1003035.

Dingemans, M. M. L., M. Kock, and M. van den Berg. 2016. 'Mechanisms of Action Point Towards Combined PBDE/NDL-PCB Risk Assessment'. *Toxicological Sciences: An Official Journal of the Society of Toxicology* 153 (2): 215–24.

Di Nuovo, A., and T. Jay. 2019. 'Development of Numerical Cognition in Children and Artificial Systems: A Review of the Current Knowledge and Proposals for Multi-disciplinary Research'. *Cognitive Computation and Systems* 1 (1): 2–11.

Dirks, E., G.Spyer, E. C. D. M. van Lieshout, and L. de Sonneville. 2008. 'Prevalence of Combined Reading and Arithmetic Disabilities'. *Journal of Learning Disabilities* 41 (5): 460–73.

Dodson, C. K., K. E. Travis, L. R. Borchers, et al. 2018. 'White Matter Properties Associated with Pre-Reading Skills in 6-Year-Old Children Born Preterm and at Term'. *Developmental Medicine and Child Neurology* 60 (7): 695–702.

Doelling, K. B., L. H. Arnal, O. Ghitza, and D. Poeppel. 2014. 'Acoustic Landmarks Drive Delta-Theta Oscillations to Enable Speech Comprehension by Facilitating Perceptual Parsing'. *NeuroImage* 85 Pt 2 (January): 761–8.

Donald, K. A., E. Eastman, F. M. Howells, et al. 2015. 'Neuroimaging Effects of Prenatal Alcohol Exposure on the Developing Human Brain: A Magnetic Resonance Imaging Review'. *Acta Neuropsychiatrica* 27 (5): 251–69.

D'Onofrio, B. M., Q. A. Class, M. E. Rickert, et al. 2016. 'Translational Epidemiologic Approaches to Understanding the Consequences of Early-Life Exposures'. *Behavior Genetics* 46 (3): 315–28.

D'Onofrio, B. M., A. L. Singh, A. Iliadou, et al. 2010. 'A Quasi-Experimental Study of Maternal Smoking during Pregnancy and Offspring Academic Achievement'. *Child Development* 81 (1): 80–100.

Donolato, E., E. Toffalini, D. Giofrè, S. Caviola, and I. C. Mammarella. 2020. 'Going beyond Mathematics Anxiety in Primary and Middle School Students: The Role of Ego-resiliency in Mathematics'. *Mind, Brain and Education: The Official Journal of the International Mind, Brain, and Education Society* 14 (3): 255–66.

Dowker, A., A. Sarkar, and C. Y. Looi. 2016. 'Mathematics Anxiety: What Have We Learned in 60 Years?' *Frontiers in Psychology* 7 (April): 508.

Downing, C., and M. Caravolas. 2020. 'Prevalence and Cognitive Profiles of Children With Comorbid Literacy and Motor Disorders'. *Frontiers in Psychology* 11 (December): 573580.

Dreger, R. M., and L. R. Aiken Jr. 1957. 'The Identification of Number Anxiety in a College Population'. *Journal of Educational Psychology* 48 (6): 344–51.

Dreier, J. W., G. Berg-Beckhoff, P. K. Andersen, and A.-M. N. Andersen. 2017. 'Prenatal Exposure to Fever and Infections and Academic Performance: A Multilevel Analysis'. *American Journal of Epidemiology* 186 (1): 29–37.

Ducharme, S., M. D. Albaugh, T.-V.Nguyen, et al. 2016. 'Trajectories of Cortical Thickness Maturation in Normal Brain Development: The Importance of Quality Control Procedures'. *NeuroImage* 125 (January): 267–79.

Dumontheil, I., and T. Klingberg. 2012. 'Brain Activity during a Visuospatial Working Memory Task Predicts Arithmetical Performance 2 Years Later'. *Cerebral Cortex* 22 (5): 1078–85.

Duncan, L. E., and M. C. Keller. 2011. 'A Critical Review of the First 10 Years of Candidate Gene-by-Environment Interaction Research in Psychiatry'. *The American Journal of Psychiatry* 168 (10): 1041–9.

Dunkel Schetter, C. 2011. 'Psychological Science on Pregnancy: Stress Processes, Biopsychosocial Models, and Emerging Research Issues'. *Annual Review of Psychology* 62: 531–58.

Durston, S., and B. J. Casey. 2006. 'What Have We Learned about Cognitive Development from Neuroimaging?' *Neuropsychologia* 44 (11): 2149–57.

Eckert, M. A., V. W. Berninger, K. I. Vaden Jr, M. Gebregziabher, and L. Tsu. 2016. 'Gray Matter Features of Reading Disability: A Combined Meta-Analytic and Direct Analysis Approach(1,2,3,4)'. *eNeuro* 3 (1). https://doi.org/10.1523/ENEURO.0103-15.2015.

Eddins, D., A. Petro, N. Pollard, J. H. Freedman, and E. D. Levin. 2008. 'Mercury-Induced Cognitive Impairment in Metallothionein-1/2 Null Mice'. *Neurotoxicology and Teratology* 30 (2): 88–95.

Eden, G. F., K. M. Jones, K. Cappell, et al. 2004. 'Neural Changes Following Remediation in Adult Developmental Dyslexia'. *Neuron* 44 (3): 411–22.

'Education at a Glance 2018: OECD Indicators'. n.d. Accessed February 17, 2021. www.oecd -ilibrary.org/education/education-at-a-glance-2018_eag-2018-en.

EFSA n.d. 'EFSA Provides Advice on the Safety and Nutritional Contribution of Wild and Farmed Fish'. n.d. Accessed July 16, 2021. www.efsa.europa.eu/en/news/efsa-provides-advice-safety-and-nutritional-contribution-wild-and-farmed-fish.

Ehrhart, F., S. Roozen, J. Verbeek, et al. 2019. 'Review and Gap Analysis: Molecular Pathways Leading to Fetal Alcohol Spectrum Disorders'. *Molecular Psychiatry* 24 (1): 10–17.

Ehri, L. C. 2008. 'Development of Sight Word Reading: Phases and Findings'. In M. J Snowling and C. Hulme (eds.), *The Science of Reading: A Handbook*, 135–54. Blackwell Publishing Ltd.

Eicher, J. D., N. R. Powers, K. Cho, et al. 2013. 'Associations of Prenatal Nicotine Exposure and the Dopamine Related Genes ANKK1 and DRD2 to Verbal Language'. *PloS One* 8 (5): e63762.

Elman, J. L., E. A. Bates, M. H. Johnson, A. Parisi Karmiloff-Smith, D. Parisi, and K. Plunkett. 1996. *Rethinking Innateness: A Connectionist Perspective on Development*. MIT Press.

Elmore, R. F. 1979. Backward Mapping: Implementation Research and Policy Decisions. Political Science Quarterly 94 (4): 601–16.

Emerson, Robert W., and Jessica F. Cantlon. 2012. 'Early Math Achievement and Functional Connectivity in the Fronto-Parietal Network'. *Developmental Cognitive Neuroscience* 2 (1) (February): S139–51.

2015. 'Continuity and Change in Children's Longitudinal Neural Responses to Numbers'. *Developmental Science* 18 (2): 314–26.

EPA, US and OCSPP. 2015. 'Polybromated Diphenylethers (PBDEs) Significant New Use Rules (SNUR)', September. www.epa.gov/assessing-and-managing-chemicals-under-tsca/polybrominated-diphenylethers-pbdes-significant-new-use.

EPA, US, and OLEM. 2013. 'Technical Fact Sheet – Polybrominated Diphenyl Ethers (PBDEs) and Polybrominated Biphenyls (PBBs)', July. www.epa.gov/fedfac/technical-fact-sheet-polybrominated-diphenyl-ethers-pbdes-and-polybrominated-biphenyls-pbbs.

2015. 'Learn about Polychlorinated Biphenyls (PCBs),' August. www.epa.gov/pcbs/learn-about-polychlorinated-biphenyls-pcbs.

EPA, US, and OP. 2016. 'Biomonitoring: PBDEs – Report Contents,' November. www.epa.gov/americaschildrenenvironment/biomonitoring-pbdes-report-contents.

Eskenazi, B., J. Chevrier, S. Rauch, et al. 2015. 'In Utero and Childhood Polybrominated Diphenyl Ether (Pbde) Exposures and Neurodevelopment In The Chamacos Study'. *Environmental Hazards and Neurodevelopment* 121 (2): 257–62. https://doi.org/10.1201/b18030-18.

Evans, T. M., D. L.Flowers, M. M. Luetje, E. Napoliello, and G. F. Eden. 2016. 'Functional Neuroanatomy of Arithmetic and Word Reading and Its Relationship to Age'. *NeuroImage* 143 (December): 304–15.

Evans, T. M., D. L.Flowers, E. M. Napoliello, O. A. Olulade, and G. F. Eden. 2014. 'The Functional Anatomy of Single-Digit Arithmetic in Children with Developmental Dyslexia'. *NeuroImage* 101 (November): 644–52.

Evans, T. M., J.Kochalka, T. J. Ngoon, et al. 2015. 'Brain Structural Integrity and Intrinsic Functional Connectivity Forecast 6 Year Longitudinal Growth in Children's Numerical Abilities'. *The Journal of Neuroscience: The Official Journal of the Society for Neuroscience* 35 (33): 11743–50.

Evenhouse, E., and S. Reilly. 2005. 'Improved Estimates of the Benefits of Breastfeeding Using Sibling Comparisons to Reduce Selection Bias'. *Health Services Research* 40 (6 Pt 1): 1781–802.

Evens, A., D. Hryhorczuk, B. P. Lanphear, et al. 2015. 'The Impact of Low-Level Lead Toxicity on School Performance among Children in the Chicago Public Schools: A Population-Based Retrospective Cohort Study'. *Environmental Health: A Global Access Science Source* 14 (April): 21.

Eysenck, M. W., and M. G. Calvo. 1992. 'Anxiety and Performance: The Processing Efficiency Theory'. *Cognition and Emotion* 6 (6): 409–34.

Eysenck, M. W., N. Derakshan, R. Santos, and M. G. Calvo. 2007. 'Anxiety and Cognitive Performance: Attentional Control Theory'. *Emotion* 7 (2): 336–53.

Facoetti, A., N. Corradi, M. Ruffino, S. Gori, and M. Zorzi. 2010. 'Visual Spatial Attention and Speech Segmentation Are Both Impaired in Preschoolers at Familial Risk for Developmental Dyslexia'. *Dyslexia* 16 (3): 226–39.

Facoetti, A., A. N. Trussardi, M. Ruffino, et al. 2010. 'Multisensory Spatial Attention Deficits Are Predictive of Phonological Decoding Skills in Developmental Dyslexia'. *Journal of Cognitive Neuroscience* 22 (5): 1011–25.

Fang, W.-Q., and R. Yuste. 2017. 'Overproduction of Neurons Is Correlated with Enhanced Cortical Ensembles and Increased Perceptual Discrimination'. *Cell Reports* 21 (2): 381–92.

Fang, M., Z. Zhou, S. Chen, and J. McClelland. 2018. Can a Recurrent Neural Network Learn to Count Things? In Proceedings of the 40th Annual Meeting of the Cognitive Science Society, https://stanford.edu/~jlmcc/papers/FangZhouChenMcC18Count.pdf

Faramarzi, S. and S. Sadri. 2014. The Effect of Basic Neuropsychological Interventions on Performance of Students with Dyscalculia. Neuropsychiatria i Neuropsychologia. 9. 48–54.

Farina, M., J. B. T. Rocha, and M. Aschner. 2011. 'Mechanisms of Methylmercury-Induced Neurotoxicity: Evidence from Experimental Studies'. *Life Sciences* 89 (15-16): 555–63.

Fawcett, A. J., R. I. Nicolson, and P. Dean. 1996. 'Impaired Performance of Children with Dyslexia on a Range of Cerebellar Tasks'. *Annals of Dyslexia* 46 (1): 259–83.

Fayol, M., M. Zorman, and Bernard L. 2009. 'Associations and Dissociations in Reading and Spelling French: Unexpectedly Poor and Good Spellers'. *British Journal of Educational Psychology* 2: 63–75. https://doi.org/10.1348/000709909x421973.

Feigenson, L., S. Dehaene, and E. Spelke. 2004. 'Core Systems of Number'. *Trends in Cognitive Sciences* 8 (7): 307–14.

Felleman, D. J., and D. C. Van Essen. 1991. 'Distributed Hierarchical Processing in the Primate Cerebral Cortex'. *Cerebral Cortex* 1 (1): 1–47.

Feng, X., I. Altarelli, K. Monzalvo, et al. 2020. 'A Universal Reading Network and Its Modulation by Writing System and Reading Ability in French and Chinese Children'. *eLife* 9 (October). https://doi.org/10.7554/eLife.54591.

Fergusson, D. M., A. L. Beautrais, and P. A. Silva. 1982. 'Breast-Feeding and Cognitive Development in the First Seven Years of Life'. *Social Science & Medicine* 16 (19): 1705–8.

Ferrer, E., J. J. McArdle, B. A. Shaywitz, et al. 2007. 'Longitudinal Models of Developmental Dynamics between Reading and Cognition from Childhood to Adolescence'. *Developmental Psychology* 43 (6): 1460–73.

Fias, W., V. Menon, and D. Szűcs. 2013. 'Multiple Components of Developmental Dyscalculia'. *Trends in Neuroscience and Education* 2 (2): 43–7.

Fields, R. D. 2015. 'A New Mechanism of Nervous System Plasticity: Activity-Dependent Myelination'. *Nature Reviews. Neuroscience* 16 (12): 756–67.

Figueiró-Filho, E. A., B. A. Croy, J. N. Reynolds, et al. 2017. 'Diffusion Tensor Imaging of White Matter in Children Born from Preeclamptic Gestations'. *AJNR. American Journal of Neuroradiology* 38 (4): 801–6.

Finnish Basic Education Act (2010). Perusopetuslain muutokset 642/2010 [Amendments to the Finnish Basic Education Act].

Finnish National Agency for Education (2017). Support in Basic Education.

Flak, A. L., S. Su, J. Bertrand, et al. 2014. 'The Association of Mild, Moderate, and Binge Prenatal Alcohol Exposure and Child Neuropsychological Outcomes: A Meta-Analysis'. *Alcoholism, Clinical and Experimental Research* 38 (1): 214–26.

Flanagan, S., and U. Goswami. 2018. 'The Role of Phase Synchronisation between Low Frequency Amplitude Modulations in Child Phonology and Morphology Speech Tasks'. *The Journal of the Acoustical Society of America* 143 (3): 1366.

Flaugnacco, E., L. Lopez, C. Terribili, et al. 2015. 'Music Training Increases Phonological Awareness and Reading Skills in Developmental Dyslexia: A Randomized Control Trial'. *PloS One* 10 (9): e0138715.

Fleming, R. W., and K. R. Storrs. 2019. 'Learning to See Stuff'. *Current Opinion in Behavioral Sciences* 30 (December): 100–8.

Fletcher, J. M., and J. MiciakJ. 2019. The Identification of Specific Learning Disabilities: A Summary of Research on Best Practices. Meadows Center for Preventing Educational Risk.

Flore, P. C., and J. M. Wicherts. 2015. 'Does Stereotype Threat Influence Performance of Girls in Stereotyped Domains? A Meta-Analysis'. *Journal of School Psychology* 53 (1): 25–44.

Formisano, E., and N. Kriegeskorte. 2012. 'Seeing Patterns through the Hemodynamic Veil – The Future of Pattern-Information fMRI'. *NeuroImage* 62 (2): 1249–56. https://doi .org/10.1016/j.neuroimage.2012.02.078.

Forray, A. 2016. 'Substance Use during Pregnancy'. *F1000Research* 5 (May). https://doi.org /10.12688/f1000research.7645.1.

Fraga G., Gorka, G. Zarić, J. Tijms, et al. 2014. 'Brain-Potential Analysis of Visual Word Recognition in Dyslexics and Typically Reading Children'. *Frontiers in Human Neuroscience* 8 (June): 474.

Franceschini, S., and S. Bertoni. 2019. 'Improving Action Video Games Abilities Increases the Phonological Decoding Speed and Phonological Short-Term Memory in Children with Developmental Dyslexia'. *Neuropsychologia* 130 (July): 100–6.

Franceschini, S., S. Bertoni, L. Ronconi, et al. 2015. "Shall We Play a Game?": Improving Reading Through Action Video Games in Developmental Dyslexia'. *Current Developmental Disorders Reports* 2 (4): 318–29.

Franceschini, S., P. Trevisan, L. Ronconi, et al. 2017. 'Action Video Games Improve Reading Abilities and Visual-to-Auditory Attentional Shifting in English-Speaking Children with Dyslexia'. *Scientific Reports* 7 (1): 5863.

Franke, K., B. R. H. Van den Bergh, et al. 2020. 'Effects of Maternal Stress and Nutrient Restriction during Gestation on Offspring Neuroanatomy in Humans'. *Neuroscience and Biobehavioral Reviews* 117 (October): 5–25.

Frankland, P. W., and B. Bontempi. 2005. 'The Organization of Recent and Remote Memories'. *Nature Reviews. Neuroscience* 6 (2): 119–30.

Frederiksen, M., K. Vorkamp, M. Thomsen, and L. E. Knudsen. 2009. 'Human Internal and External Exposure to PBDEs–a Review of Levels and Sources'. *International Journal of Hygiene and Environmental Health* 212 (2): 109–34.

Fried, P. A., and A. M. Smith. 2001. 'A Literature Review of the Consequences of Prenatal Marihuana Exposure. An Emerging Theme of a Deficiency in Aspects of Executive Function'. *Neurotoxicology and Teratology* 23 (1): 1–11.

Fried, P. A., B. Watkinson, and L. S. Siegel. 1997. 'Reading and Language in 9- to 12-Year Olds Prenatally Exposed to Cigarettes and Marijuana'. *Neurotoxicology and Teratology* 19 (3): 171–83.

Fried, P. A., B. Watkinson, and R. Gray. 2003. 'Differential Effects on Cognitive Functioning in 13- to 16-Year-Olds Prenatally Exposed to Cigarettes and Marihuana'. *Neurotoxicology and Teratology* 25 (4): 427–36.

Friguls, B., X. Joya, J. Garcia-Serra, et al. 2012. 'Assessment of Exposure to Drugs of Abuse during Pregnancy by Hair Analysis in a Mediterranean Island'. *Addiction* 107 (8): 1471–9.

Frith, U. 1985. Beneath the Surface of Developmental Dyslexia. Developmental Dyslexia. 13.

Frith, U. 1998. 'Literally Changing the Brain'. *Brain: A Journal of Neurology* 121 (Pt 6) (June): 1011–12.

Froyen, D. J. W., M. L. Bonte, N. van Atteveldt, and L. Blomert. 2009. 'The Long Road to Automation: Neurocognitive Development of Letter-Speech Sound Processing'. *Journal of Cognitive Neuroscience* 21 (3): 567–80.

Frye, R. E., K. Hasan, B. Malmberg, et al. 2010. 'Superior Longitudinal Fasciculus and Cognitive Dysfunction in Adolescents Born Preterm and at Term'. *Developmental Medicine and Child Neurology* 52 (8): 760–6.

Fryer, S. L., S. N. Mattson, T. L. Jernigan, et al. 2012. 'Caudate Volume Predicts Neurocognitive Performance in Youth with Heavy Prenatal Alcohol Exposure'. *Alcoholism, Clinical and Experimental Research* 36 (11): 1932–41.

Fryer, S. L., S. F. Tapert, S. N. Mattson, et al. 2007. 'Prenatal Alcohol Exposure Affects Frontal-Striatal BOLD Response during Inhibitory Control'. *Alcoholism, Clinical and Experimental Research* 31 (8): 1415–24.

Fuchs, E., and G. Flügge. 2014. 'Adult Neuroplasticity: More than 40 Years of Research'. *Neural Plasticity* 2014 (May): 541870.

Fuchs, L. S., D. C. Geary, D. L. Compton, et al. 2013. 'Effects of First-Grade Number Knowledge Tutoring With Contrasting Forms of Practice'. *Journal of Educational Psychology* 105 (1): 58–77.

Fuchs, L. S., S. R. Powell, C. L. Hamlett, et al. 2008. 'Remediating Computational Deficits at Third Grade: A Randomized Field Trial'. *Journal of Research on Educational Effectiveness* 1 (1): 2–32.

Fuchs, L. S., S. R. Powell, P. M. Seethaler, et al. 2009. 'Remediating Number Combination and Word Problem Deficits Among Students With Mathematics Difficulties: A Randomized Control Trial'. *Journal of Educational Psychology* 101 (3): 561–76.

Fuchs, L. S., S. R. Powell, P. M. Seethaler, et al. 2010. 'A Framework for Remediating Number Combination Deficits'. *Exceptional Children* 76 (2): 135–65.

Fujioka, T., A. Fujioka, N. Tan, et al. 2001. 'Mild Prenatal Stress Enhances Learning Performance in the Non-Adopted Rat Offspring'. *Neuroscience* 103 (2): 301–7.

Fürst, C. 1999. Die Rolle der Lehrkraft im Gruppenunterricht. In H.-D. Dann, T. Diegritz, and H. S. Rosenbusch (eds.), Gruppenunterricht im Schulalltag. Realität und Chancen, 107–50. Universitätsbund Erlangen-Nürnberg e.V.

Gabel, L. A., C. J. Gibson, J. R. Gruen, and J. J. LoTurco. 2010. 'Progress towards a Cellular Neurobiology of Reading Disability'. *Neurobiology of Disease* 38 (2): 173–80. https://doi.org/10.1016/j.nbd.2009.06.019.

Gallit, F., A. Wyschkon, N. Poltz, et al. 2018. 'Henne Oder Ei: Reziprozität Mathematischer Vorläufer Und Vorhersage Des Rechnens'. *Lernen Und Lernstörungen* 7 (2): 81–92.

Gangl, M., K.Moll, M. W. Jones, et al. 2018. 'Lexical Reading in Dysfluent Readers of German'. *Scientific Studies of Reading: The Official Journal of the Society for the Scientific Study of Reading* 22 (1): 24–40.

Garnelo, M., and M. Shanahan. 2019. 'Reconciling Deep Learning with Symbolic Artificial Intelligence: Representing Objects and Relations'. *Current Opinion in Behavioral Sciences* 29 (October): 17–23.

Garry, A., V. Rigourd, A. Amirouche, et al. 2009. 'Cannabis and Breastfeeding'. *Journal of Toxicology* 2009 (April): 596149.

Gauthier, I., P. Skudlarski, J. C. Gore, and A. W. Anderson. 2000. 'Expertise for Cars and Birds Recruits Brain Areas Involved in Face Recognition'. *Nature Neuroscience* 3 (2): 191–7.

Geary, D. C., M. K. Hoard, J. Byrd-Craven, et al. 2007. 'Cognitive Mechanisms Underlying Achievement Deficits in Children with Mathematical Learning Disability'. *Child Development* 78 (4): 1343–59.

Geary, D. C., M. K. Hoard, L. Nugent, and D. H. Bailey. 2012. 'Mathematical Cognition Deficits in Children With Learning Disabilities and Persistent Low Achievement: A Five-Year Prospective Study'. *Journal of Educational Psychology* 104 (1): 206–23.

Geary, D. C., C. C. Bow-Thomas, and Y. Yao. 1992. 'Counting Knowledge and Skill in Cognitive Addition: A Comparison of Normal and Mathematically Disabled Children'. *Journal of Experimental Child Psychology* 54 (3): 372–91.

Geary, D. C., C. O. Hamson, and M. K. Hoard. 2000. 'Numerical and Arithmetical Cognition: A Longitudinal Study of Process and Concept Deficits in Children with Learning Disability'. *Journal of Experimental Child Psychology* 77 (3): 236–63.

Geary, D. C., M. K. Hoard, and C. O. Hamson. 1999. 'Numerical and Arithmetical Cognition: Patterns of Functions and Deficits in Children at Risk for a Mathematical Disability'. *Journal of Experimental Child Psychology* 74 (3): 213–39.

Gebauer, D., A. Fink, R. Kargl, et al. 2012. 'Differences in Brain Function and Changes with Intervention in Children with Poor Spelling and Reading Abilities'. *PloS One* 7 (5): e38201.

Gentle, S. J., C. P. Travers, and W. A. Carlo. 2018. 'Caffeine Controversies'. *Current Opinion in Pediatrics* 30 (2): 177–81.

Georgiou, G. K., A. Protopapas, T. C. Papadopoulos, C. Skaloumbakas, and R.Parrila. 2010. 'Auditory Temporal Processing and Dyslexia in an Orthographically Consistent Language'. *Cortex* 46 (10): 1330–44. https://doi.org/10.1016/j.cortex.2010.06.006.

Gerlach,M., A. Fritz, G. Ricken, S. Schmidt. 2007. Kalkulie. Diagnose- und Trainingsprogramm für rechenschwache Kinder. Cornelsen.

Germanò, E., A. Gagliano, and P.Curatolo. 2010. 'Comorbidity of ADHD and Dyslexia'. *Developmental Neuropsychology* 35 (5): 475–93.

Germano, G. D., C. Reilhac, S. A. Capellini, and S. Valdois. 2014. 'The Phonological and Visual Basis of Developmental Dyslexia in Brazilian Portuguese Reading Children'. *Frontiers in Psychology* 5 (October): 1169.

Gialluisi, A., T. F. M. Andlauer, Na. Mirza-Schreiber, et al. 2020. 'Genome-Wide Association Study Reveals New Insights into the Heritability and Genetic Correlates of Developmental Dyslexia'. *Molecular Psychiatry*, 26: 3004–17. https://doi.org/10.1038/s41380-020-00898-x.

Gibbons, L., J. M. Belizán, J. A. Lauer, et al. 2010. 'The Global Numbers and Costs of Additionally Needed and Unnecessary Caesarean Sections Performed per Year: Overuse as a Barrier to Universal Coverage'. *World Health Report* 30 (1): 1–31.

Gibson, E. M., D. Purger, C. W. Mount, et al. 2014. 'Neuronal Activity Promotes Oligodendrogenesis and Adaptive Myelination in the Mammalian Brain'. *Science* 344 (6183): 480–1.

Giménez, M., M. J. Miranda, A. P. Born, et al. 2008. 'Accelerated Cerebral White Matter Development in Preterm Infants: A Voxel-Based Morphometry Study with Diffusion Tensor MR Imaging'. *NeuroImage* 41 (3): 728–34.

Giofrè, D., E. Borella, and I. C. Mammarella. 2017. 'The Relationship between Intelligence, Working Memory, Academic Self-Esteem, and Academic Achievement'. *Journal of Cognitive Psychology* 29 (6): 731–47.

Giraud, A.-L., and D. Poeppel. 2012. 'Cortical Oscillations and Speech Processing: Emerging Computational Principles and Operations'. *Nature Neuroscience* 15 (4): 511–17.

Giraud, A.-L., and F. Ramus. 2013. 'Neurogenetics and Auditory Processing in Developmental Dyslexia'. *Current Opinion in Neurobiology* 23 (1): 37–42.

Glass, L., D. M. Graham, N. Akshoomoff, and S. N. Mattson. 2015. 'Cognitive Factors Contributing to Spelling Performance in Children with Prenatal Alcohol Exposure'. *Neuropsychology* 29 (6): 817–28.

Glass, L., E. M. Moore, N. Akshoomoff, et al. 2017. 'Academic Difficulties in Children with Prenatal Alcohol Exposure: Presence, Profile, and Neural Correlates'. *Alcoholism, Clinical and Experimental Research* 41 (5): 1024–34.

Glezer, L. S., X. Jiang, and M. Riesenhuber. 2009. 'Evidence for Highly Selective Neuronal Tuning to Whole Words in the "Visual Word Form Area."' *Neuron* 62 (2): 199–204.

Glezer, L. S., J. Kim, J. Rule, X. Jiang, and M. Riesenhuber. 2015. 'Adding Words to the Brain's Visual Dictionary: Novel Word Learning Selectively Sharpens Orthographic Representations in the VWFA'. *Journal of Neuroscience* 35 (12): 4965–72.

Glover, V. 2015. 'Prenatal Stress and Its Effects on the Fetus and the Child: Possible Underlying Biological Mechanisms'. *Advances in Neurobiology* 10: 269–83.

Gobel, S.M., and M.J. Snowling. 2010. 'Number-Processing Skills in Adults with Dyslexia'. *Quarterly Journal of Experimental Psychology* 63 (7): 1361–73.

Göbel, S. M., S. E. Watson, A. Lervåg, and C. Hulme. 2014. 'Children's Arithmetic Development'. *Psychological Science* 25 (3): 789–98. https://doi.org/10.1177/0956797613516471.

Goetz, T., M. Bieg, O. Lüdtke, R. Pekrun, and N. C. Hall. 2013. 'Do Girls Really Experience More Anxiety in Mathematics?' *Psychological Science* 24 (10): 2079–87.

Goffin, C., and D. Ansari. 2016. 'Beyond Magnitude: Judging Ordinality of Symbolic Number Is Unrelated to Magnitude Comparison and Independently Relates to Individual Differences in Arithmetic'. *Cognition* 150 (May): 68–76.

Goldenberg, R. L., J. F. Culhane, J. D. Iams, and R. Romero. 2008. 'Epidemiology and Causes of Preterm Birth'. *The Lancet* 371 (9606): 75–84.

Goldschmidt, L., G. A. Richardson, M. D. Cornelius, and N. L. Day. 2004. 'Prenatal Marijuana and Alcohol Exposure and Academic Achievement at Age 10'. *Neurotoxicology and Teratology* 26 (4): 521–32.

Goldschmidt, L., G. A. Richardson, J. A. Willford, S. G. Severtson, and N. L. Day. 2012. 'School Achievement in 14-Year-Old Youths Prenatally Exposed to Marijuana'. *Neurotoxicology and Teratology* 34 (1): 161–7.

Goldschmidt, L., G. A. Richardson, J. Willford, and N. L. Day. 2008. 'Prenatal Marijuana Exposure and Intelligence Test Performance at Age 6'. *Journal of the American Academy of Child and Adolescent Psychiatry* 47 (3): 254–63.

Gomez, J., M. Barnett, and K. Grill-Spector. 2019. 'Extensive Childhood Experience with Pokémon Suggests Eccentricity Drives Organization of Visual Cortex'. *Nature Human Behaviour* 3 (6): 611–24.

Gonda, Y., W. D. Andrews, H. Tabata, et al. 2013. 'Robo1 Regulates the Migration and Laminar Distribution of Upper-Layer Pyramidal Neurons of the Cerebral Cortex'. *Cerebral Cortex* 23 (6): 1495–508. https://doi.org/10.1093/cercor/bhs141.

Gonzalez, F. F., and S. P. Miller. 2006. 'Does Perinatal Asphyxia Impair Cognitive Function without Cerebral Palsy?' *Archives of Disease in Childhood. Fetal and Neonatal Edition* 91 (6): F454–9.

Goodfellow, I., Y. Bengio, and A. Courville. 2016. *Deep Learning*. MIT Press.

Goodlett, C. R., and K. H. Horn (2001). 'Mechanisms of Alcohol-Induced Damage to the Developing Nervous System'. *Alcohol Research and Health: The Journal of the*

National Institute on Alcohol Abuse and Alcoholism, 25 (3), 175–84. https://pubs
.niaaa.nih.gov/publications/arh25-3/175-184.htm.

Gori, S., P. Cecchini, A. Bigoni, M. Molteni, and A. Facoetti. 2014. 'Magnocellular-Dorsal
Pathway and Sub-Lexical Route in Developmental Dyslexia'. *Frontiers in Human
Neuroscience* 8 (June): 460.

Gori, S., S. Mascheretti, E. Giora, et al. 2015. 'The DCDC2 Intron 2 Deletion Impairs Illusory
Motion Perception Unveiling the Selective Role of Magnocellular-Dorsal Stream in
Reading (dis)ability'. *Cerebral Cortex* 25 (6): 1685–95.

Goswami, U. 2011. 'A Temporal Sampling Framework for Developmental Dyslexia'. *Trends
in Cognitive Sciences* 15 (1): 3–10.

2015a. 'Sensory Theories of Developmental Dyslexia: Three Challenges for Research'.
Nature Reviews. Neuroscience 16 (1): 43–54.

2015b. 'Visual Attention Span Deficits and Assessing Causality in Developmental
Dyslexia'. *Nature Reviews: Neuroscience* 16: 225–6.

2018. 'A Neural Basis for Phonological Awareness? An Oscillatory Temporal-Sampling
Perspective'. *Current Directions in Psychological Science* 27 (1): 56–63.

2019a. 'A Neural Oscillations Perspective on Phonological Development and Phonological
Processing in Developmental Dyslexia'. *Language and Linguistics Compass* 13 (5):
e12328.

2019b. 'Speech Rhythm and Language Acquisition: An Amplitude Modulation Phase
Hierarchy Perspective'. *Annals of the New York Academy of Sciences* 1453 (1):
67–78.

2020a. 'Reading Acquisition and Developmental Dyslexia: Educational Neuroscience and
Phonological Skills'. In M. S. C. Thomas, D. Mareschal, and I. Dumontheil (eds.),
Educational Neuroscience: Development across the Lifespan, pp. 144–68.
Routledge.

2020b. 'Toward Realizing the Promise of Educational Neuroscience: Improving
Experimental Design in Developmental Cognitive Neuroscience Studies'. *Annual
Review of Developmental Psychology* 2 (1): 133–55.

Goswami, U., M. Huss, N. Mead, and T. Fosker. 2021. 'Auditory Sensory Processing and
Phonological Development in High IQ and Exceptional Readers, Typically
Developing Readers, and Children With Dyslexia: A Longitudinal Study'. *Child
Development* 92 (3): 1083–98.

Goswami, U., M. Huss, N. Mead, T. Fosker, and J. P. Verney. 2013. 'Perception of Patterns of
Musical Beat Distribution in Phonological Developmental Dyslexia: Significant
Longitudinal Relations with Word Reading and Reading Comprehension'. *Cortex:
A Journal Devoted to the Study of the Nervous System and Behavior* 49 (5): 1363–76.

Goswami, U., N. Mead, T. Fosker, et al. 2013. 'Impaired Perception of Syllable Stress in
Children with Dyslexia: A Longitudinal Study'. *Journal of Memory and Language*
69 (1): 1–17.

Goswami, U., A. J. Power, M. Lallier, and A. Facoetti. 2014. 'Oscillatory 'Temporal
Sampling' and Developmental Dyslexia: Toward an Over-arching Theoretical
Framework'. *Frontiers in Human Neuroscience* 8 (November): 904.

Goswami, U., H-L Sharon Wang, A. Cruz, et al. 2011. 'Language-Universal Sensory Deficits
in Developmental Dyslexia: English, Spanish, and Chinese'. *Journal of Cognitive
Neuroscience* 23 (2): 325–37.

Grabner, R. H., D. Ansari, K. Koschutnig, et al. 2009. 'To Retrieve or to Calculate? Left Angular Gyrus Mediates the Retrieval of Arithmetic Facts during Problem Solving'. *Neuropsychologia* 47 (2): 604–8.

Grabner, R. H., D. Ansari, G. Reishofer, et al. 2007. 'Individual Differences in Mathematical Competence Predict Parietal Brain Activation during Mental Calculation'. *NeuroImage* 38 (2): 346–56.

Grabner, R. H., A. Ischebeck, G. Reishofer, et al. 2009. 'Fact Learning in Complex Arithmetic and Figural-Spatial Tasks: The Role of the Angular Gyrus and Its Relation to Mathematical Competence'. *Human Brain Mapping* 30 (9): 2936–52.

Graham, A. M., M. Marr, C.Buss, E. L. Sullivan, and D. A. Fair. 2021. 'Understanding Vulnerability and Adaptation in Early Brain Development Using Network Neuroscience'. *Trends in Neurosciences* 44 (4): 276–88.

Grandjean, P., and P. J. Landrigan. 2014. 'Neurobehavioural Effects of Developmental Toxicity'. *Lancet Neurology* 13 (3): 330–8.

Grandjean, P., P. Weihe, R. F. White, et al. 1997. 'Cognitive Deficit in 7-Year-Old Children with Prenatal Exposure to Methylmercury'. *Neurotoxicology and Teratology* 19 (6): 417–28.

Grant, J. G., L. S. Siegel, and A. D'Angiulli. 2020. 'From Schools to Scans: A Neuroeducational Approach to Comorbid Math and Reading Disabilities'. *Frontiers in Public Health* 8 (October): 469.

Grant, K. S., R. Petroff, N. Isoherranen, N. Stella, and T. M. Burbacher. 2018. 'Cannabis Use during Pregnancy: Pharmacokinetics and Effects on Child Development'. *Pharmacology & Therapeutics* 182 (February): 133–51.

Gray, S. (2015). The Effects of Morpho-Phonemic and Whole Word Instruction on the Literacy Skills of Adult Struggling Readers. City University of New York.

Gray, K. A., M. A. Klebanoff, J. W. Brock, et al. 2005. 'In Utero Exposure to Background Levels of Polychlorinated Biphenyls and Cognitive Functioning among School-Age Children'. *American Journal of Epidemiology* 162 (1): 17–26.

Grayson, D. S., and D. A. Fair. 2017. 'Development of Large-Scale Functional Networks from Birth to Adulthood: A Guide to the Neuroimaging Literature'. *NeuroImage* 160 (October): 15–31.

Greicius, M. D., B. Krasnow, A. L. Reiss, and V. Menon. 2003. 'Functional Connectivity in the Resting Brain: A Network Analysis of the Default Mode Hypothesis'. *Proceedings of the National Academy of Sciences* 100 (1): 253–8. https://doi.org/10.1073/pnas.0135058100.

Grills, A. E., J. M. Fletcher, S. Vaughn, et al. 2014. 'Anxiety and Response to Reading Intervention among First Grade Students'. *Child & Youth Care Forum* 43 (4): 417–31.

Grill-Spector, K., and K. S. Weiner. 2014. 'The Functional Architecture of the Ventral Temporal Cortex and Its Role in Categorization'. *Nature Reviews. Neuroscience* 15 (8): 536–48.

Grills-Taquechel, A. E., J. M. Fletcher, S. R. Vaughn, and K. K. Stuebing. 2012. 'Anxiety and Reading Difficulties in Early Elementary School: Evidence for Unidirectional- or Bi-Directional Relations?' *Child Psychiatry and Human Development* 43 (1): 35–47.

Groeschel, S., J.-D. Tournier, G. B. Northam, et al. 2014. 'Identification and Interpretation of Microstructural Abnormalities in Motor Pathways in Adolescents Born Preterm'. *NeuroImage* 87 (February): 209–19.

Gross, J., N. Hoogenboom, G. Thut, et al. 2013. 'Speech Rhythms and Multiplexed Oscillatory Sensory Coding in the Human Brain'. *PLoS Biology* 11 (12): e1001752.

Grump, K. S., T. Kjellstrom, A. M. Shipp, A.Silvers, and A. Stewart. 1998. 'Influence of Prenatal Mercury Exposure upon Scholastic and Psychologica Test Performance: Benchmark Analysis of a New Zealand Cohort'. *Risk Analysis: An Official Publication of the Society for Risk Analysis* 18 (6): 701–13.

Gu, S., T. D. Satterthwaite, J. D. Medaglia, et al. 2015. 'Emergence of System Roles in Normative Neurodevelopment'. *Proceedings of the National Academy of Sciences of the United States of America* 112 (44): 13681–6.

Gullick, M. M., and J. R. Booth. 2015. 'The Direct Segment of the Arcuate Fasciculus Is Predictive of Longitudinal Reading Change'. *Developmental Cognitive Neuroscience* 13 (June): 68–74.

Gulson, B. L., K. J. Mizon, M. J. Korsch, et al. 1996. 'Impact on Blood Lead in Children and Adults Following Relocation from Their Source of Exposure and Contribution of Skeletal Tissue to Blood Lead'. *Bulletin of Environmental Contamination and Toxicology* 56 (4): 543–50.

Gumusoglu, S. B., A. S. S. Chilukuri, D. A. Saantillan, et al. 2020. 'Neurodevelopmental Outcomes of Prenatal Preeclampsia Exposure'. *Trends in Neurosciences* 43 (4): 253–68.

Guttorm, T. K., P. H. T. Leppänen, J. A. Hämäläinen, et al. 2010. 'Newborn Event-Related Potentials Predict Poorer Pre-Reading Skills in Children at Risk for Dyslexia'. *Journal of Learning Disabilities* 43 (5): 391–401.

Habermann, S., C. Donlan, S. M. Göbel, and C. Hulme. 2020. 'The Critical Role of Arabic Numeral Knowledge as a Longitudinal Predictor of Arithmetic Development'. *Journal of Experimental Child Psychology* 193 (May): 104794.

Haberstroh, S., and G. Schulte-Körne. 2019. 'The Diagnosis and Treatment of Dyscalculia'. *Deutsches Arzteblatt International* 116 (7): 107–14.

Halberda, J., and L. Feigenson. 2008. 'Developmental Change in the Acuity of the 'Number Sense': The Approximate Number System in 3-, 4-, 5-, and 6-Year-Olds and Adults'. *Developmental Psychology* 44 (5): 1457–65.

Halberda, J., R. Ly, J. B. Wilmer, D. Q. Naiman, and L. Germine. 2012. 'Number Sense across the Lifespan as Revealed by a Massive Internet-Based Sample'. *Proceedings of the National Academy of Sciences of the United States of America* 109 (28): 11116–20.

Halberda, J., M. M. M. Mazzocco, and L. Feigenson. 2008. 'Individual Differences in Non-Verbal Number Acuity Correlate with Maths Achievement'. *Nature* 455 (7213): 665–8.

Halpern, D., A. Beninger, and C. Straight. 2011. 'Sex Differences in Intelligence'. In R. Sternberg and S. Kaufman (eds.), The Cambridge Handbook of Intelligence, 253–72). Cambridge University Press. doi:10.1017/CBO9780511977244.014

Hancock, R., K. R. Pugh, and F. Hoeft. 2017. 'Neural Noise Hypothesis of Developmental Dyslexia'. *Trends in Cognitive Sciences* 21 (6): 434–48.

Handel, M. van, H.Swaab, L. S. de Vries, and M. J. Jongmans. 2007. 'Long-Term Cognitive and Behavioral Consequences of Neonatal Encephalopathy Following Perinatal Asphyxia: A Review'. *European Journal of Pediatrics* 166 (7): 645–54.

Handler, S. M., W. M. Fierson, and the Section on Ophthalmology and Council on Children with Disabilities, American Academy of Ophthalmology, American Association for Pediatric Ophthalmology and Strabismus, and American Association of Certified

Orthoptists. 2011. 'Learning Disabilities, Dyslexia, and Vision'. *Pediatrics* 127 (3): e818–56.

Hanf, K. 1982. 'The Implementation of Regulatory Policy'. Journal of Political Research, 1982.

Hanich, L. B., N. C. Jordan, D. Kaplan, and J. Dick. 2001. 'Performance across Different Areas of Mathematical Cognition in Children with Learning Difficulties'. *Journal of Educational Psychology* 93 (3): 615–26. https://doi.org/10.1037/0022-0663 .93.3.615.

Hannagan, T., A. Amedi, L. Cohen, G. Dehaene-Lambertz, and S. Dehaene. 2015. 'Origins of the Specialization for Letters and Numbers in Ventral Occipitotemporal Cortex'. *Trends in Cognitive Sciences* 19 (7): 374–82.

Hannagan, T., J. C. Ziegler, S. Dufau, J. Fagot, and J. Grainger. 2014. 'Deep Learning of Orthographic Representations in Baboons'. *PLoS One* 9 (1): e84843.

Harada, M. 1995. 'Minamata Disease: Methylmercury Poisoning in Japan Caused by Environmental Pollution'. *Critical Reviews in Toxicology* 25 (1): 1–24.

Harlaar, N., P. S. Dale, and R. Plomin. 2007. 'From Learning to Read to Reading to Learn: Substantial and Stable Genetic Influence'. *Child Development* 78 (1): 116–31.

Harlaar, N., K. Deater-Deckard, L. A. Thompson, L. S. Dethorne, and S. A. Petrill. 2011. 'Associations between Reading Achievement and Independent Reading in Early Elementary School: A Genetically Informative Cross-Lagged Study'. *Child Development* 82 (6): 2123–37.

Harlaar, N., F. M. Spinath, P. S. Dale, and R. Plomin. 2005. 'Genetic Influences on Early Word Recognition Abilities and Disabilities: A Study of 7-Year-Old Twins'. *Journal of Child Psychology and Psychiatry, and Allied Disciplines* 46 (4): 373–84.

Harlaar, N., M. Trzaskowski, P. S. Dale, and R. Plomin. 2014. 'Word Reading Fluency: Role of Genome-Wide Single-Nucleotide Polymorphisms in Developmental Stability and Correlations with Print Exposure'. *Child Development* 85 (3): 1190–205.

Harm, M. W., and M. S. Seidenberg. 2004. 'Computing the Meanings of Words in Reading: Cooperative Division of Labor between Visual and Phonological Processes'. *Psychological Review* 111 (3): 662–720.

Harm, M. W., and M. S. Seidenberg. 1999. 'Phonology, Reading Acquisition, and Dyslexia: Insights from Connectionist Models'. *Psychological Review* 106 (3): 491–528.

Harris, J. J., C. Reynell, and D. Attwell. 2011. 'The Physiology of Developmental Changes in BOLD Functional Imaging Signals'. *Developmental Cognitive Neuroscience* 1 (3): 199–216.

Hart, S. A., C. Little, and E. van Bergen. 2021. 'Nurture Might Be Nature: Cautionary Tales and Proposed Solutions'. *NPJ Science of Learning* 6 (1): 2.

Hasko, S., K. Groth, J. Bruder, J. Bartling, and G. Schulte-Körne. 2013. 'The Time Course of Reading Processes in Children with and without Dyslexia: An ERP Study'. *Frontiers in Human Neuroscience* 7 (October): 570.

Haworth, C. M. A., Y. Kovas, N. Harlaar, et al. 2009. 'Generalist Genes and Learning Disabilities: A Multivariate Genetic Analysis of Low Performance in Reading, Mathematics, Language and General Cognitive Ability in a Sample of 8000 12-Year-Old Twins'. *Journal of Child Psychology and Psychiatry, and Allied Disciplines* 50 (10): 1318–25.

Hayatbakhsh, M. R., V. J. Flenady, K. S. Gibbons, et al. 2012. 'Birth Outcomes Associated with Cannabis Use before and during Pregnancy'. *Pediatric Research* 71 (2): 215–19.

Hay, D. F., S. Pawlby, C. S. Waters, and D. Sharp. 2008. 'Antepartum and Postpartum Exposure to Maternal Depression: Different Effects on Different Adolescent Outcomes'. *Journal of Child Psychology and Psychiatry, and Allied Disciplines* 49 (10): 1079–88.

Hay, D. F., S. Pawlby, D. Sharp, et al. 2001. 'Intellectual Problems Shown by 11-Year-Old Children Whose Mothers Had Postnatal Depression'. *Journal of Child Psychology and Psychiatry, and Allied Disciplines* 42 (7): 871–89.

Health Canada. 2009. 'Prenatal Nutrition Guidelines for Health Professionals – Fish and Omega-3 Fatty Acids'. April 28, 2009. www.canada.ca/en/health-canada/services/publications/food-nutrition/prenatal-nutrition-guidelines-health-professionals-fish-omega-3-fatty-acids-2009.html.

Hedges, L. V., and I. Olkin. 1985. Statistical Methods for Meta-Analysis. Academic Press

Heikkilä, K., Y. Kelly, M. J. Renfrew, A. Sacker, and M. A. Quigley. 2014. 'Breastfeeding and Educational Achievement at Age 5'. *Maternal & Child Nutrition* 10 (1): 92–101.

Heim, S., J. Pape-Neumann, M. van Ermingen-Marbach, M. Brinkhaus, and M. Grande. 2015. 'Shared vs. Specific Brain Activation Changes in Dyslexia after Training of Phonology, Attention, or Reading'. *Brain Structure & Function* 220 (4): 2191–207.

Heinonen, K., J. G. Eriksson, Eero Kajantie, et al. 2013. 'Late-Preterm Birth and Lifetime Socioeconomic Attainments: The Helsinki Birth Cohort Study'. *Pediatrics* 132 (4): 647–55.

Hembree, R. 1990. 'The Nature, Effects, and Relief of Mathematics Anxiety'. *Journal for Research in Mathematics Education* 21 (1): 33–46.

Hensler, B. S., C. Schatschneider, J. Taylor, and R. K. Wagner. 2010. 'Behavioral Genetic Approach to the Study of Dyslexia'. *Journal of Developmental and Behavioral Pediatrics: JDBP* 31 (7): 525–32.

Hernandez-Miranda, L. R., A. Cariboni, C. Faux, et al. 2011. 'Robo1 Regulates Semaphorin Signaling to Guide the Migration of Cortical Interneurons through the Ventral Forebrain'. *Journal of Neuroscience* 31 (16): 6174–87. https://doi.org/10.1523/jneurosci.5464-10.2011.

Herting, M. M., P. Gautam, Z. Chen, A. Mezher, and N. C. Vetter. 2018. 'Test-Retest Reliability of Longitudinal Task-Based fMRI: Implications for Developmental Studies'. *Developmental Cognitive Neuroscience* 33 (October): 17–26.

Hervais-Adelman, A., U. Kumar, R. K. Mishra, et al. 2019. 'Learning to Read Recycles Visual Cortical Networks without Destruction'. *Science Advances* 10.

Higginbotham, H., T.-Y. Eom, L. E. Mariani, et al. 2012. 'Arl13b in Primary Cilia Regulates the Migration and Placement of Interneurons in the Developing Cerebral Cortex'. *Developmental Cell* 23 (5): P925–38. https://doi.org/10.1016/j.devcel.2012.09.019.

Higuera-Matas, A., M. Ucha, and E. Ambrosio. 2015. 'Long-Term Consequences of Perinatal and Adolescent Cannabinoid Exposure on Neural and Psychological Processes'. *Neuroscience and Biobehavioral Reviews* 55 (August): 119–46.

Hill, F., I. C. Mammarella, A. Devine, et al. 2016. 'Maths Anxiety in Primary and Secondary School Students: Gender Differences, Developmental Changes and Anxiety Specificity'. *Learning and Individual Differences* 48 (May): 45–53.

Hill, S. Y., L. Lowers, J. Locke-Wellman, and S. A. Shen. 2000. 'Maternal Smoking and Drinking during Pregnancy and the Risk for Child and Adolescent Psychiatric Disorders'. *Journal of Studies on Alcohol* 61 (5): 661–8.

Hinshelwood, J. 1896. 'A Case Of Dyslexia: A Peculiar Form Of Word-Blindness.'. *The Lancet* 148 (3821): 1451–4.

Hinton, G., L. Deng, D. Yu, et al. 2012. 'Deep Neural Networks for Acoustic Modeling in Speech Recognition: The Shared Views of Four Research Groups'. *IEEE Signal Processing Magazine* 29 (6): 82–97.

Hinton, G. E. 2007. 'Learning Multiple Layers of Representation'. *Trends in Cognitive Sciences* 11 (10): 428–34.

Hinton, G. E., and T. J. Sejnowski. 1999. *Unsupervised Learning: Foundations of Neural Computation*. MIT Press.

Hoeft, F., B. D. McCandliss, J. M. Black, et al. 2011. 'Neural Systems Predicting Long-Term Outcome in Dyslexia'. *Proceedings of the National Academy of Sciences of the United States of America* 108 (1): 361–6.

Hoeft, F., A. Meyler, A. Hernandez, et al. 2007. 'Functional and Morphometric Brain Dissociation between Dyslexia and Reading Ability'. *Proceedings of the National Academy of Sciences of the United States of America* 104 (10): 4234–9.

Hohnen, B., and J. Stevenson. 1999. 'The Structure of Genetic Influences on General Cognitive, Language, Phonological, and Reading Abilities'. *Developmental Psychology* 35 (2): 590–603.

Hokkanen, L., J. Launes, and K. Michelsson. 2014. 'Adult Neurobehavioral Outcome of Hyperbilirubinemia in Full Term Neonates-a 30 Year Prospective Follow-up Study'. *PeerJ* 2 (March): e294.

Holland, E. B., J. V. Goldstone, I. N. Pessah, et al. 2017. 'Ryanodine Receptor and FK506 Binding Protein 1 in the Atlantic Killifish (Fundulus Heteroclitus): A Phylogenetic and Population-Based Comparison'. *Aquatic Toxicology* 192 (November): 105–15.

Holloway, I. D., and D. Ansari. 2009. 'Mapping Numerical Magnitudes onto Symbols: The Numerical Distance Effect and Individual Differences in Children's Mathematics Achievement'. *Journal of Experimental Child Psychology* 103 (1): 17–29. https://doi.org/10.1016/j.jecp.2008.04.001.

——— 2010. 'Developmental Specialization in the Right Intraparietal Sulcus for the Abstract Representation of Numerical Magnitude'. *Journal of Cognitive Neuroscience* 22 (11): 2627–37.

Hopko, D. R., R. Mahadevan, R. L. Bare, and M. K. Hunt. 2003. 'The Abbreviated Math Anxiety Scale (AMAS): Construction, Validity, and Reliability'. *Assessment* 10 (2): 178–82.

Hopko, D. R., M. H. Ashcraft, J. Gute, K. J. Ruggiero, and C. Lewis. 1998. 'Mathematics Anxiety and Working Memory: Support for the Existence of a Deficient Inhibition Mechanism'. *Journal of Anxiety Disorders* 12 (4): 343–55.

Horsfield, M. A., and D. K. Jones. 2002. 'Applications of Diffusion-Weighted and Diffusion Tensor MRI to White Matter Diseases: A Review'. *NMR in Biomedicine* 15 (7–8): 570–7.

Horta,B., L. Bahl, Rajiv, J. C. Martinés, C. G. Victora, Cesar and World Health Organization. 2007. Evidence on The Long-Term Effects of Breastfeeding: Systematic Review and Meta-Analyses. World Health Organization. https://apps.who.int/iris/handle/10665/43623.

Horta, B. L., C. L. de Mola, and C. G. Victora. 2015. 'Breastfeeding and Intelligence: A Systematic Review and Meta-Analysis'. *Acta Paediatrica* 104 (467): 14–19.

Horwitz, E. K. 1986. 'Preliminary Evidence for the Reliability and Validity of a Foreign Language Anxiety Scale'. *TESOL Quarterly* 20 (3): 559–62.

Horwitz, E. K., M. B. Horwitz, and J. Cope. 1986. 'Foreign Language Classroom Anxiety'. *The Modern Language Journal* 70 (2): 125–32.

Horwood, L. J., and D. M. Fergusson. 1998. 'Breastfeeding and Later Cognitive and Academic Outcomes'. *Pediatrics* 101 (1): E9.

Houdé, O., S. Rossi, A. Lubin, and M. Joliot. 2010. 'Mapping Numerical Processing, Reading, and Executive Functions in the Developing Brain: An fMRI Meta-Analysis of 52 Studies Including 842 Children'. *Developmental Science* 13 (6): 876–85.

Houston, S. M., C. Lebel, T. Katzir, et al. 2014. 'Reading Skill and Structural Brain Development'. *Neuroreport* 25 (5): 347–52.

Howell, K. K., M. E. Lynch, K. A. Platzman, G. H. Smith, and C. D. Coles. 2006. 'Prenatal Alcohol Exposure and Ability, Academic Achievement, and School Functioning in Adolescence: A Longitudinal Follow-Up'. *Journal of Pediatric Psychology* 31 (1): 116–26.

Hubbard, E. M., M. Piazza, P. Pinel, and S. Dehaene. 2005. 'Interactions between Number and Space in Parietal Cortex'. *Nature Reviews. Neuroscience* 6 (6): 435–48.

Huber, E., P. M. Donnelly, A. Rokem, and J. D. Yeatman. 2018. 'Rapid and Widespread White Matter Plasticity during an Intensive Reading Intervention'. *Nature Communications* 9 (1): 2260.

Huettig, F., R. Kolinsky, and T. Lachmann. 2018. 'The Culturally Co-Opted Brain: How Literacy Affects the Human Mind'. *Language, Cognition and Neuroscience* 33 (3): 275–7.

Huettig, F., T. Lachmann, A. Reis, and K. M. Petersson. 2018. 'Distinguishing Cause from Effect – Many Deficits Associated with Developmental Dyslexia May Be a Consequence of Reduced and Suboptimal Reading Experience'. *Language, Cognition and Neuroscience* 33 (3): 333–50.

Hughes, C. A., L. A. O'Gorman, Y. Shyr, et al. 1999. 'Cognitive Performance at School Age of Very Low Birth Weight Infants with Bronchopulmonary Dysplasia'. *Journal of Developmental and Behavioral Pediatrics: JDBP* 20 (1): 1–8.

Huizink, A. C., and E. J. H. Mulder. 2006. 'Maternal Smoking, Drinking or Cannabis Use during Pregnancy and Neurobehavioral and Cognitive Functioning in Human Offspring'. *Neuroscience and Biobehavioral Reviews* 30 (1): 24–41.

Hulme, C., H. M. Nash, D. Gooch, A. Lervåg, and M. J. Snowling. 2015. 'The Foundations of Literacy Development in Children at Familial Risk of Dyslexia'. *Psychological Science* 26 (12): 1877–86.

Hulme, C., and M. J. Snowling. 2016. 'Reading Disorders and Dyslexia'. *Current Opinion in Pediatrics* 28 (6): 731–5.

Huss, M., J. P. Verney, T. Fosker, N. Mead, and U. Goswami. 2011. 'Music, Rhythm, Rise Time Perception and Developmental Dyslexia: Perception of Musical Meter Predicts Reading and Phonology'. *Cortex: A Journal Devoted to the Study of the Nervous System and Behavior* 47 (6): 674–89.

Hutton, J. S., J. Dudley, T. Horowitz-Kraus, T. DeWitt, and S. K. Holland. 2020. 'Associations between Home Literacy Environment, Brain White Matter Integrity and Cognitive Abilities in Preschool-Age Children'. *Acta Paediatrica* 109 (7): 1376–86.

Hutton, J. S., T. Horowitz-Kraus, A. L. Mendelsohn, et al. 2015. 'Home Reading Environment and Brain Activation in Preschool Children Listening to Stories'. *Pediatrics* 136 (3): 466–78.

Hutton, J. S., K. Phelan, T. Horowitz-Kraus, et al. 2017. 'Shared Reading Quality and Brain Activation during Story Listening in Preschool-Age Children'. *The Journal of Pediatrics* 191 (December): 204–11.

Hu, Y., F. Geng, L. Tao, et al. 2011. 'Enhanced White Matter Tracts Integrity in Children with Abacus Training'. *Human Brain Mapping* 32 (1): 10–21.

Hyde, J. S., E. Fennema, M. Ryan, L. A. Frost, and C. Hopp. 1990. Gender Comparisons of Mathematics Attitudes and Affect: A Meta-Analysis. *Psychology of Women Quarterly* 14 (3): 299–324.

Ialongo, N., G. Edelsohn, L. Werthamer-Larsson, L. Crockett, and S. Kellam. 1994. 'The Significance of Self-Reported Anxious Symptoms in First-Grade Children'. *Journal of Abnormal Child Psychology* 22 (4): 441–55.

IDEA. 2019 Annual Report to Congress on the Individuals with Disabilities Education Act (IDEA). https://sites.ed.gov/idea/2019-annual-report-to-congress-IDEA/

Infant and Young Child Feeding. 2018. Seventy-First World Health Assembly Agenda item 12.6; 26 May: https://apps.who.int/iris/bitstream/handle/10665/279517/A71_R9-en.pdf.

Isaacs, E. B., C. J. Edmonds, A. Lucas, and D. G. Gadian. 2001. 'Calculation Difficulties in Children of Very Low Birthweight: A Neural Correlate'. *Brain: A Journal of Neurology* 124 (Pt 9): 1701–7.

Isaacs, E. B., B. R. Fischl, B. T. Quinn, et al. 2010. 'Impact of Breast Milk on Intelligence Quotient, Brain Size, and White Matter Development'. *Pediatric Research* 67 (4): 357–62.

Ischebeck, A., L. Zamarian, M. Schocke, and M. Delazer. 2009. 'Flexible Transfer of Knowledge in Mental Arithmetic–an fMRI Study'. *NeuroImage* 44 (3): 1103–12.

Ischebeck, A., L. Zamarian, C. Siedentopf, et al. 2006. 'How Specifically Do We Learn? Imaging the Learning of Multiplication and Subtraction'. *NeuroImage* 30 (4): 1365–75.

Ishibashi, T., K. A. Dakin, B. Stevens, et al. 2006. 'Astrocytes Promote Myelination in Response to Electrical Impulses'. *Neuron* 49 (6): 823–32.

Iuculano, T. 2016. 'Neurocognitive Accounts of Developmental Dyscalculia and Its Remediation'. In *Progress in Brain Research*, edited by M. Cappelletti and W. Fias, 227:305–33. Elsevier.

Iuculano, T., and V. Menon. 2018. 'Development of Mathematical Reasoning'. In *Stevens' Handbook of Experimental Psychology and Cognitive Neuroscience*, 1–40. John Wiley & Sons, Inc. https://doi.org/10.1002/9781119170174.epcn406.

Iuculano, T., A. Padmanabhan, and V. Menon. 2018. 'Systems Neuroscience of Mathematical Cognition and Learning: Basic Organization and Neural Sources of Heterogeneity in Typical and Atypical Development'. In *Heterogeneity of Function in Numerical Cognition*, edited by A. Henik and W. Fias, 287–336. Academic Press.

Iuculano,., M. Rosenberg-Lee, J. Richardson, et al. 2015. 'Cognitive Tutoring Induces Widespread Neuroplasticity and Remediates Brain Function in Children with Mathematical Learning Disabilities'. *Nature Communications* 6 (8453). https://doi.org/10.1038/ncomms9453.

Iuculano, T., J. Tang, C. W. B. Hall, and B. Butterworth. 2008. 'Core Information Processing Deficits in Developmental Dyscalculia and Low Numeracy'. *Developmental Science* 11 (5): 669–80.

Izard, V., C. Sann, E. S. Spelke, and A. Streri. 2009. 'Newborn Infants Perceive Abstract Numbers'. *Proceedings of the National Academy of Sciences of the United States of America* 106 (25): 10382–5.

Jacobson, J. L., N. C. Dodge, M. J. Burden, R. Klorman, and S. W. Jacobson. 2011. 'Number Processing in Adolescents with Prenatal Alcohol Exposure and ADHD: Differences in the Neurobehavioral Phenotype'. *Alcoholism, Clinical and Experimental Research* 35 (3): 431–42.

Jacobson, J. L., and S. W. Jacobson. 2002. 'Effects of Prenatal Alcohol Exposure on Child Development'. *Alcohol Research & Health: The Journal of the National Institute on Alcohol Abuse and Alcoholism* 26 (4): 282–6.

Jaekel, J., N. Baumann, and D. Wolke. 2013. 'Effects of Gestational Age at Birth on Cognitive Performance: A Function of Cognitive Workload Demands'. *PloS One* 8 (5): e65219.

Jalongo, M. R., and R. A. Hirsh. 2010. 'Understanding Reading Anxiety: New Insights from Neuroscience'. *Early Childhood Education Journal* 37 (6): 431–5.

James, K. H. 2010. 'Sensori-Motor Experience Leads to Changes in Visual Processing in the Developing Brain'. *Developmental Science* 13 (2): 279–88.

Jaques, S. C., A. Kingsbury, P. Henshcke, et al. 2014. 'Cannabis, the Pregnant Woman and Her Child: Weeding out the Myths'. *Journal of Perinatology: Official Journal of the California Perinatal Association* 34 (6): 417–24.

Jarlenski, M., C. L. Barry, S. Gollust, et al. 2017. 'Polysubstance Use Among US Women of Reproductive Age Who Use Opioids for Nonmedical Reasons'. *American Journal of Public Health* 107 (8): 1308–10.

Jensen, A. R. 1998. The G Factor: The Science of Mental Ability. Praeger Publishers/ Greenwood Publishing Group.

Jirikowic, T., D. Kartin, and H. Carmichael Olson. 2008. 'Children with Fetal Alcohol Spectrum Disorders: A Descriptive Profile of Adaptive Function'. *Canadian Journal of Occupational Therapy. Revue Canadienne D'ergotherapie* 75 (4): 238–48.

Johansen-Berg, H., and T. E. J. Behrens. 2006. 'Just Pretty Pictures? What Diffusion Tractography Can Add in Clinical Neuroscience'. *Current Opinion in Neurology* 19 (4): 379–85.

Jolles, D., S. Ashkenazi, J. Kochalka, et al. 2016. 'Parietal Hyper-Connectivity, Aberrant Brain Organization, and Circuit-Based Biomarkers in Children with Mathematical Disabilities'. *Developmental Science* 19 (4): 613–31.

Jolles, D., K. Supekar, J. Richardson, et al. 2016. 'Reconfiguration of Parietal Circuits with Cognitive Tutoring in Elementary School Children'. *Cortex: A Journal Devoted to the Study of the Nervous System and Behavior* 83 (October): 231–45.

Jolles, D., D. Wassermann, R. Chokhani, et al. 2016. 'Plasticity of Left Perisylvian White-Matter Tracts Is Associated with Individual Differences in Math Learning'. *Brain Structure & Function* 221 (3): 1337–51.

Joo, S. J., K. Tavabi, and J. D. Yeatman. 2019. 'Automaticity in the Reading Circuitry'. *Cold Spring Harbor Laboratory.* https://doi.org/10.1101/829937.

Jordan, N. C., L. B. Hanich, and D. Kaplan. 2003a. 'A Longitudinal Study of Mathematical Competencies in Children with Specific Mathematics Difficulties versus Children with Comorbid Mathematics and Reading Difficulties'. *Child Development* 74 (3): 834–50.

2003b. 'Arithmetic Fact Mastery in Young Children: A Longitudinal Investigation'. *Journal of Experimental Child Psychology* 85 (2): 103–19.

Jordan, N. C., D. Kaplan, C. Ramineni, and M. N. Locuniak. 2009. 'Early Math Matters: Kindergarten Number Competence and Later Mathematics Outcomes'. *Developmental Psychology* 45 (3): 850–67. https://doi.org/10.1037/a0014939.

Jordan, N. C., and T. O. Montani. 1997. 'Cognitive Arithmetic and Problem Solving'. *Journal of Learning Disabilities* 30 (6): 624–34. https://doi.org/10.1177/002221949703000606.

Joyner, R. E., and R. K. Wagner. 2020. 'Co-Occurrence of Reading Disabilities and Math Disabilities: A Meta-Analysis'. *Scientific Studies of Reading: The Official Journal of the Society for the Scientific Study of Reading* 24 (1): 14–22.

Kadosh, R. C., and V. Walsh. 2009. 'Numerical Representation in the Parietal Lobes: Abstract or Not Abstract?' *Behavioral and Brain Sciences* 32 (3-4): 313–28. https://doi.org /10.1017/s0140525x09990938.

Kalashnikova, M., D. Burnham, and U. Goswami. 2020. 'The Role of Paired Associate Learning in Acquiring Letter-Sound Correspondences: A Longitudinal Study of Children at Family Risk for Dyslexia'. *Scientific Studies of Reading: The Official Journal of the Society for the Scientific Study of Reading*, December, 1–15.

Kalashnikova, M., U. Goswami, and D. Burnham. 2018. 'Mothers Speak Differently to Infants at-Risk for Dyslexia'. *Developmental Science* 21 (1). https://doi.org/10 .1111/desc.12487.

2019a. 'Delayed Development of Phonological Constancy in Toddlers at Family Risk for Dyslexia'. *Infant Behavior & Development* 57 (November): 101327.

2019b. 'Sensitivity to Amplitude Envelope Rise Time in Infancy and Vocabulary Development at 3 Years: A Significant Relationship'. *Developmental Science* 22 (6): e12836.

2020. 'Novel Word Learning Deficits in Infants at Family Risk for Dyslexia'. *Dyslexia* 26 (1): 3–17.

Kamijo, S., Y. Ishii, S.-I. Horigane, et al. 2018. 'A Critical Neurodevelopmental Role for L-Type Voltage-Gated Calcium Channels in Neurite Extension and Radial Migration'. *The Journal of Neuroscience: The Official Journal of the Society for Neuroscience* 38 (24): 5551–66.

Karipidis, I. I., G. Pleisch, D. Brandeis, et al. 2018. 'Simulating Reading Acquisition: The Link between Reading Outcome and Multimodal Brain Signatures of Letter-Speech Sound Learning in Prereaders'. *Scientific Reports* 8 (1): 7121.

Kasala, S., S. Briyal, P. Prazad, et al. 2020. 'Exposure to Morphine and Caffeine Induces Apoptosis and Mitochondrial Dysfunction in a Neonatal Rat Brain'. *Frontiers in Pediatrics* 8 (September): 593.

Katzir, T., Y.-S. G. Kim, and S. Dotan. 2018. 'Reading Self-Concept and Reading Anxiety in Second Grade Children: The Roles of Word Reading, Emergent Literacy Skills, Working Memory and Gender'. *Frontiers in Psychology* 9 (July): 1180.

Kaufmann, L., G. Wood, O. Rubinsten, and A. Henik. 2011. 'Meta-Analyses of Developmental fMRI Studies Investigating Typical and Atypical Trajectories of Number Processing and Calculation'. *Developmental Neuropsychology* 36 (6): 763–87.

Kaufmann, L., M. M. Mazzocco, A. Dowker, et al. 2013. 'Dyscalculia from a Developmental and Differential Perspective'. *Frontiers in Psychology* 4 (August): 516.

Kaufmann, L. S. E. Vogel, M. Starke, et al. 2009. 'Developmental Dyscalculia: Compensatory Mechanisms in Left Intraparietal Regions in Response to Nonsymbolic Magnitudes'. *Behavioral and Brain Functions: BBF* 5 (August): 35.

Kaufmann, L., S. E. Vogel, G. Wood, et al. 2008. 'A Developmental fMRI Study of Nonsymbolic Numerical and Spatial Processing'. *Cortex: A Journal Devoted to the Study of the Nervous System and Behavior* 44 (4): 376–85.

Kaufmann, L., S. E. Vogel, M. Starke, C. Kremser, and M. Schocke. 2009. 'Numerical and Non-Numerical Ordinality Processing in Children with and without Developmental Dyscalculia: Evidence from fMRI'. *Cognitive Development* 24 (4): 486–94.

Kazemi, T., S.Huang, N. G. Avci, et al. 2020. 'Investigating the Influence of Perinatal Nicotine and Alcohol Exposure on the Genetic Profiles of Dopaminergic Neurons in the VTA Using miRNA-mRNA Analysis'. *Scientific Reports* 10 (1): 15016.

Keller, T. A., and Marcel Adam Just. 2009. 'Altering Cortical Connectivity: Remediation-Induced Changes in the White Matter of Poor Readers'. *Neuron* 64 (5): 624–31.

Kelly, C. E., J. L. Y. Cheong, L. G. Fam, et al. 2016. 'Moderate and Late Preterm Infants Exhibit Widespread Brain White Matter Microstructure Alterations at Term-Equivalent Age Relative to Term-Born Controls'. *Brain Imaging and Behavior* 10 (1): 41–9.

Kendler, K. S., M. Neale, R. Kessler, A. Heath, and L. Eaves. 1993. 'A Twin Study of Recent Life Events and Difficulties'. *Archives of General Psychiatry* 50 (10): 789–96.

Kermani, M., A. Verghese, and T. R. Vidyasagar. 2018. 'Attentional Asymmetry between Visual Hemifields Is Related to Habitual Direction of Reading and Its Implications for Debate on Cause and Effects of Dyslexia'. *Dyslexia* 24 (1): 33–43.

Kerper, L. E., N. Ballatori, and T. W. Clarkson. 1992. 'Methylmercury Transport across the Blood-Brain Barrier by an Amino Acid Carrier'. *The American Journal of Physiology* 262 (5 Pt 2): R761–5.

Kerr-Wilson, C. O., D. F. Mackay, G. C. S. Smith, and J. P. Pell. 2012. 'Meta-Analysis of the Association between Preterm Delivery and Intelligence'. *Journal of Public Health* 34 (2): 209–16.

Kersey, A. J., K.-.M. Wakim, R. Li, and J. F. Cantlon. 2019. 'Developing, Mature, and Unique Functions of the Child's Brain in Reading and Mathematics'. *Developmental Cognitive Neuroscience* 39 (October): 100684.

Kevan, A., and K. Pammer. 2008. 'Making the Link between Dorsal Stream Sensitivity and Reading'. *Neuroreport* 19 (4): 467–70.

——— 2009. 'Predicting Early Reading Skills from Pre-Reading Measures of Dorsal Stream Functioning'. *Neuropsychologia* 47 (14): 3174–81.

Khwaja, O., and J. J. Volpe. 2008. 'Pathogenesis of Cerebral White Matter Injury of Prematurity'. *Archives of Disease in Childhood. Fetal and Neonatal Edition* 93 (2): F153–61.

Kim, D., and S. A. Thayer. 2001. 'Cannabinoids Inhibit the Formation of New Synapses between Hippocampal Neurons in Culture'. *The Journal of Neuroscience: The Official Journal of the Society for Neuroscience* 21 (10): RC146.

Kim, G., J. Jang, S. Baek, M. Song, and S.-B. Paik. 2021. 'Visual Number Sense in Untrained Deep Neural Networks'. *Science Advances* 7 (1): eabd6127.

Kim, K. H., D. D. Bose, A. Ghogha, et al. 2011. 'Para- and Ortho -Substitutions Are Key Determinants of Polybrominated Diphenyl Ether Activity toward Ryanodine Receptors and Neurotoxicity'. *Environmental Health Perspectives* 119 (4). https://doi.org/10.1289/ehp.1002728.

King, K. M., A. K. Littlefield, C. J. McCabe, et al. 2018. 'Longitudinal Modeling in Developmental Neuroimaging Research: Common Challenges, and Solutions from Developmental Psychology'. *Developmental Cognitive Neuroscience* 33 (October): 54–72.

Klebanoff, M. A., and S.A. Keim. 2015. 'Maternal Caffeine Intake During Pregnancy and Child Cognition and Behavior at 4 and 7 Years of Age'. *American Journal of Epidemiology* 182 (12): 1023–32.

Klein, E., K.Willmes, S. M. Bieck, J. Bloechle, and K. Moeller. 2019. 'White Matter Neuro-Plasticity in Mental Arithmetic: Changes in Hippocampal Connectivity

Following Arithmetic Drill Training'. *Cortex: A Journal Devoted to the Study of the Nervous System and Behavior* 114 (May): 115–23.

Klingberg, T., M. Hedehus, E. Temple, et al. 2000. 'Microstructure of Temporo-Parietal White Matter as a Basis for Reading Ability: Evidence from Diffusion Tensor Magnetic Resonance Imaging'. *Neuron* 25 (2): 493–500.

Knight, M. J., A. Smith-Collins, S. Newell, M. Denbow, and R. A. Kauppinen. 2018. 'Cerebral White Matter Maturation Patterns in Preterm Infants: An MRI T2 Relaxation Anisotropy and Diffusion Tensor Imaging Study'. *Journal of Neuroimaging: Official Journal of the American Society of Neuroimaging* 28 (1): 86–94.

Knopik, V. S., J. M. Neiderhiser, J. C. DeFries, and R. Plomin. 2016. *Behavioral Genetics*. Macmillan Higher Education.

Kodavanti, P. R. S. 2017. 'Polychlorinated Biphenyls (PCBs)☆'. *Reference Module in Neuroscience and Biobehavioral Psychology*. Elsevier.

Kohonen, T. 1990. 'The Self-Organizing Map'. *Proceedings of the IEEE* 78 (9): 1464–80.

Koletzko, B., C. Agostoni, S. E. Carlson, et al. 2007. 'Long Chain Polyunsaturated Fatty Acids (LC-PUFA) and Perinatal Development'. *Acta Paediatrica* 90 (4): 460–4.

Kolkman, M. E., E. H. Kroesbergen, and P.P. M. Leseman. 2013. 'Early Numerical Development and the Role of Non-Symbolic and Symbolic Skills'. *Learning and Instruction* 25 (June): 95–103.

Kondracki, A. J. 2019. 'Prevalence and Patterns of Cigarette Smoking before and during Early and Late Pregnancy according to Maternal Characteristics: The First National Data Based on the 2003 Birth Certificate Revision, United States, 2016'. *Reproductive Health* 16 (1): 142.

Koponen, T., M. Aro, A.-M. Poikkeus, et al. 2018. 'Comorbid Fluency Difficulties in Reading and Math: Longitudinal Stability Across Early Grades'. *Exceptional Children*. https://doi.org/10.1177/0014402918756269.

Koponen, T., K. Eklund, R. Heikkilä, et al. 2020. 'Cognitive Correlates of the Covariance in Reading and Arithmetic Fluency: Importance of Serial Retrieval Fluency'. *Child Development* 91 (4): 1063–80.

Koren, G. 1995. 'Fetal Toxicology of Environmental Tobacco Smoke'. *Current Opinion in Pediatrics* 7 (2): 128–31.

Kotimäki, S., J. Härkönen, L. Karlsson, H. Karlsson, and N. M. Scheinin. 2020. 'Educational Differences in Prenatal Anxiety and Depressive Symptoms and the Role of Childhood Circumstances'. *SSM – Population Health* 12 (December): 100690.

Kovachy, V. N., J. N. Adams, J. S. Tamaresis, and H. M. Feldman. 2015. 'Reading Abilities in School-Aged Preterm Children: A Review and Meta-Analysis'. *Developmental Medicine and Child Neurology* 57 (5): 410–19.

Kovas, Y., C. M. A. Haworth, N. Harlaar, et al. 2007. 'Overlap and Specificity of Genetic and Environmental Influences on Mathematics and Reading Disability in 10-Year-Old Twins'. *Journal of Child Psychology and Psychiatry, and Allied Disciplines* 48 (9): 914–22.

Kovas, Y., V. Giampietro, E. Viding, et al. 2009. 'Brain Correlates of Non-Symbolic Numerosity Estimation in Low and High Mathematical Ability Children'. *PloS One* 4 (2): e4587.

Kovas, Y., Claire M. A. Haworth, P. S. Dale, and R. Plomin. 2007. 'The Genetic and Environmental Origins of Learning Abilities and Disabilities in the Early School

Years'. *Monographs of the Society for Research in Child Development* 72 (3): vii, 1–144.

Kovas, Y., C. M. A. Haworth, S.A. Petrill, and R. Plomin. 2007. 'Mathematical Ability of 10-Year-Old Boys and Girls: Genetic and Environmental Etiology of Typical and Low Performance'. *Journal of Learning Disabilities* 40 (6): 554–67.

Kovas, Y., and R. Plomin. 2006. 'Generalist Genes: Implications for the Cognitive Sciences'. *Trends in Cognitive Sciences* 10 (5): 198–203.

Kovelman, I., E. S. Norton, J. A. Christodoulou, et al. 2012. 'Brain Basis of Phonological Awareness for Spoken Language in Children and Its Disruption in Dyslexia'. *Cerebral Cortex* 22 (4): 754–64.

Krafnick, A. J., and T. M. Evans. 2018. 'Neurobiological Sex Differences in Developmental Dyslexia'. *Frontiers in Psychology* 9: 2669.

Krafnick, A. J., D. L.Flowers, M. M. Luetje, E. M. Napoliello, and G. F. Eden. 2014. 'An Investigation into the Origin of Anatomical Differences in Dyslexia'. *The Journal of Neuroscience: The Official Journal of the Society for Neuroscience* 34 (3): 901–8.

Krafnick, A. J., D. Lynn Flowers, E. M. Napoliello, and G. F. Eden. 2011. 'Gray Matter Volume Changes Following Reading Intervention in Dyslexic Children'. *NeuroImage* 57 (3): 733–41.

Kraft, I., J. Schreiber, R. Cafiero, et al. 2016. 'Predicting Early Signs of Dyslexia at a Preliterate Age by Combining Behavioral Assessment with Structural MRI'. *NeuroImage* 143 (December): 378–86.

Krajewski, K., and W. Schneider. 2009. 'Exploring the Impact of Phonological Awareness, Visual-Spatial Working Memory, and Preschool Quantity-Number Competencies on Mathematics Achievement in Elementary School: Findings from a 3-Year Longitudinal Study'. *Journal of Experimental Child Psychology* 103 (4): 516–31.

Kramer, M. S., F. Aboud, E. Mironova, et al. 2008. 'Breastfeeding and Child Cognitive Development: New Evidence from a Large Randomized Trial'. *Archives of General Psychiatry* 65 (5): 578–84.

Krapohl, E., L. J. Hannigan, J-B Pingault, et al. 2017. 'Widespread Covariation of Early Environmental Exposures and Trait-Associated Polygenic Variation'. *Proceedings of the National Academy of Sciences of the United States of America* 114 (44): 11727–32.

Krapohl, E., K. Rimfeld, N. G. Shakeshaft, et al. 2014. 'The High Heritability of Educational Achievement Reflects Many Genetically Influenced Traits, Not Just Intelligence'. *Proceedings of the National Academy of Sciences of the United States of America* 111 (42): 15273–8.

Krinzinger, H., L. Kaufmann, A. Dowker, et al. 2007. 'Deutschsprachige Version Des Fragebogens Für Rechenangst (FRA) Für 6- Bis 9-Jährige Kinder'. *Zeitschrift Fur Kinder- Und Jugendpsychiatrie Und Psychotherapie* 35 (5): 341–51.

Krinzinger, H., L. Kaufmann, and K. Willmes. 2009. 'Math Anxiety and Math Ability in Early Primary School Years'. *Journal of Psychoeducational Assessment* 27 (3): 206–25.

Krinzinger, H., J. W. Koten, H. Horoufchin, et al. 2011. 'The Role of Finger Representations and Saccades for Number Processing: An FMRI Study in Children'. *Frontiers in Psychology* 2 (December): 373.

Kristjansson, A. L., S. Thomas, C. L. Lilly, et al. 2018. 'Maternal Smoking during Pregnancy and Academic Achievement of Offspring over Time: A Registry Data-Based Cohort Study'. *Preventive Medicine* 113 (August): 74–9.

Krizhevsky, Alex, Ilya Sutskever, and Geoffrey E. Hinton. 2017. 'ImageNet Classification with Deep Convolutional Neural Networks'. *Communications of the ACM*. https://doi.org/10.1145/3065386.

Krueger, R. F., and K.E. Markon. 2014. 'The Role of the DSM-5 Personality Trait Model in Moving toward a Quantitative and Empirically Based Approach to Classifying Personality and Psychopathology'. *Annual Review of Clinical Psychology* 10: 477–501.

Kubilius, J., S. Bracci, and H. P. Op de Beeck. 2016. 'Deep Neural Networks as a Computational Model for Human Shape Sensitivity'. *PLoS Computational Biology* 12 (4): e1004896.

Kubota, E. C., S. J. Joo, E. Huber, and J. D. Yeatman. 2019. 'Word Selectivity in High-Level Visual Cortex and Reading Skill'. *Developmental Cognitive Neuroscience* 36 (September 2018): 100593.

Kucian, K. 2016. 'Developmental Dyscalculia and the Brain'. In D. Berch, D. Geary, and K. Mann Koepke (eds.), *Development of Mathematical Cognition*, 165–93. Elsevier.

Kucian, K. 2021. 'Chapter 10 - Developmental Course of Numerical Learning Problems in Children and How to Prevent Dyscalculia: A Summary of the Longitudinal Examination of Children from Kindergarten to Secondary School'. In W. Fias and A. Henik (eds.), Heterogeneous Contributions to Numerical Cognition, 229–51. Academic Press.

Kucian, K., S. S. Ashkenazi, J. Hänggi, et al. 2014. 'Developmental Dyscalculia: A Dysconnection Syndrome?' *Brain Structure & Function* 219 (5): 1721–33.

Kucian, K., and M. von Aster. 2015. 'Developmental Dyscalculia'. *European Journal of Pediatrics* 174 (1): 1–13.

Kucian, K., M. von Aster, T. Loenneker, T. Dietrich, and E. Martin. 2008. 'Development of Neural Networks for Exact and Approximate Calculation: A FMRI Study'. *Developmental Neuropsychology* 33 (4): 447–73.

Kucian, K., T. Loenneker, T. Dietrich, et al. 2006. 'Impaired Neural Networks for Approximate Calculation in Dyscalculic Children: A Functional MRI Study'. *Behavioral and Brain Functions: BBF* 2 (September): 31.

Kucian, K., T. Loenneker, E. Martin, and M. von Aster. 2011. 'Non-Symbolic Numerical Distance Effect in Children With and Without Developmental Dyscalculia: A Parametric fMRI Study'. *Developmental Neuropsychology* 36 (6): 741–62. https://doi.org/10.1080/87565641.2010.549867.

Kucian, K., U. McCaskey, R. O'Gorman Tuura, and M. von Aster. 2018. 'Neurostructural Correlate of Math Anxiety in the Brain of Children'. *Translational Psychiatry* 8 (1): 273.

Kucian, K., U. Grond, S. Rotzer, et al. 2011. 'Mental Number Line Training in Children with Developmental Dyscalculia'. *NeuroImage* 57 (3): 782–95.

Kuhl, P. K. 2004. 'Early Language Acquisition: Cracking the Speech Code'. *Nature Reviews. Neuroscience* 5 (11): 831–43.

Kuhl, U., A. D. Friederici, LEGASCREEN Consortium, and M. A. Skeide. 2020a. 'Early Cortical Surface Plasticity Relates to Basic Mathematical Learning'. *NeuroImage* 204 (January): 116235.

Kuhl, U., N. E. Neef, I. Kraft, et al. 2020b. 'The Emergence of Dyslexia in the Developing Brain'. *NeuroImage* 211 (May): 116633.

Kuhl,U., S. Sobotta, Legascreen Consortium, and M. A. Skeide. (in press) Mathematical learning deficits originate in early childhood from atypical development of a frontoparietal brain network. PLoS Biol. 2021 Sep 30;19(9):e3001407. doi: 10.1371/journal.pbio.3001407.

Kuja-Halkola, R., B. M. D'Onofrio, H. Larsson, and P. Lichtenstein. 2014. 'Maternal Smoking during Pregnancy and Adverse Outcomes in Offspring: Genetic and Environmental Sources of Covariance'. *Behavior Genetics* 44 (5): 456–67.

Kussmaul, A. 1877. *Die Storungen Der Sprache [A Disorder of Speech]*. FCW Vogel.

Kyttälä, M., and P. M. Björn. 2010. 'Prior Mathematics Achievement, Cognitive Appraisals and Anxiety as Predictors of Finnish Students' Later Mathematics Performance and Career Orientation'. *Educational Psychology Review* 30 (4): 431–48.

Labouesse, M. A., W. Langhans, and U. Meyer. 2015. 'Long-Term Pathological Consequences of Prenatal Infection: Beyond Brain Disorders'. *American Journal of Physiology. Regulatory, Integrative and Comparative Physiology* 309 (1): R1–12.

Landerl, K., S. M. Göbel, and K. Moll. 2013. 'Core Deficit and Individual Manifestations of Developmental Dyscalculia (DD): The Role of Comorbidity'. *Trends in Neuroscience and Education* 2 (2): 38–42.

Landerl, K. 2013. 'Development of Numerical Processing in Children with Typical and Dyscalculic Arithmetic Skills – a Longitudinal Study'. *Frontiers in Psychology* 4: 459.

Landerl, K., A. Bevan, and B. Butterworth. 2004. 'Developmental Dyscalculia and Basic Numerical Capacities: A Study of 8-9-Year-Old Students'. *Cognition* 93 (2): 99–125.

Landerl, K., B. Fussenegger, K. Moll, and E. Willburger. 2009. 'Dyslexia and Dyscalculia: Two Learning Disorders with Different Cognitive Profiles'. *Journal of Experimental Child Psychology* 103 (3): 309–24.

Landerl, K., H. H. Freudenthaler, M. Heene, et al. 2019. 'Phonological Awareness and Rapid Automatized Naming as Longitudinal Predictors of Reading in Five Alphabetic Orthographies with Varying Degrees of Consistency'. *Scientific Studies of Reading* 23 (3): 220–34. https://doi.org/10.1080/10888438.2018.1510936.

Landerl, K., and C. Kölle. 2009. 'Typical and Atypical Development of Basic Numerical Skills in Elementary School'. *Journal of Experimental Child Psychology* 103 (4): 546–65.

Landerl, K., and K. Moll. 2010. 'Comorbidity of Learning Disorders: Prevalence and Familial Transmission'. *Journal of Child Psychology and Psychiatry, and Allied Disciplines* 51 (3): 287–94.

Landerl, K., F. Ramus, K. Moll, et al. 2013. 'Predictors of Developmental Dyslexia in European Orthographies with Varying Complexity'. *Journal of Child Psychology and Psychiatry, and Allied Disciplines* 54 (6): 686–94.

Landerl, K. S. E. Vogel, R. H. Grabner, Chapter 15 – Early neurocognitive development of dyscalculia, ed. W. Fias and A. Henik, Heterogeneous Contributions to Numerical Cognition, Academic Press, 2021, pp. 359–82. https://doi.org/10.1016/B978-0-12-817414-2.00011-7.

Landerl, K., and E. Willburger. 2010. 'Temporal Processing, Attention, and Learning Disorders'. *Learning and Individual Differences* 20 (5): 393–401. https://doi.org/10.1016/j.lindif.2010.03.008.

Landerl, K., and H. Wimmer. 2000. 'Deficits in Phoneme Segmentation Are Not the Core Problem of Dyslexia: Evidence from German and English Children'. *Applied Psycholinguistics* 21 (2): 243–62.

Landi, N., A. Trey, M. J. Crowley, J. Wu, and L. Mayes. 2017. 'Prenatal Cocaine Exposure Impacts Language and Reading Into Late Adolescence: Behavioral and ERP Evidence'. *Developmental Neuropsychology* 42 (6): 369–86.

Langer, N., B. Peysakhovich, J. Zuk, et al. 2015. 'White Matter Alterations in Infants at Risk for Developmental Dyslexia'. *Cerebral Cortex* 27 (2), 1027–36.

Lange, S., C. Probst, J. Rehm, and S. Popova. 2018. 'National, Regional, and Global Prevalence of Smoking during Pregnancy in the General Population: A Systematic Review and Meta-Analysis'. *The Lancet: Global Health* 6 (7): e769–76.

Lanphear, B. P., R. Hornung, J. Khoury, et al. 2005. 'Low-Level Environmental Lead Exposure and Children's Intellectual Function: An International Pooled Analysis'. *Environmental Health Perspectives* 113 (7). https://doi.org/10.1289/ehp.7688.

Lauermann, F., J. S. Eccles, and R. Pekrun. 2017. 'Why Do Children Worry about Their Academic Achievement? An Expectancy-Value Perspective on Elementary Students' Worries about Their Mathematics and Reading Performance'. *ZDM: The International Journal on Mathematics Education* 49 (3): 339–54.

Lauritzen, L., H. S. Hansen, M. H. Jørgensen, and K. F. Michaelsen. 2001. 'The Essentiality of Long Chain N-3 Fatty Acids in Relation to Development and Function of the Brain and Retina'. *Progress in Lipid Research* 40 (1–2): 1–94.

Law, J., J. Charlton, J. Dockrell, et al. 2017. 'Early Language Development: Needs, Provision, and Intervention for Preschool Children from Socio-Economically Disadvantage Backgrounds: A Report for the Education Endowment Foundation: October 2017'. www.research.manchester.ac.uk/portal/en/publications/early-language-develop ment-needs-provision-and-intervention-for-preschool-children-from-socioeconom ically-disadvantage-backgrounds(2429d543-cb90-4381-bf9b-6e83f06991f5)/ export.html.

Lawton, T. 2016. 'Improving Dorsal Stream Function in Dyslexics by Training Figure/ Ground Motion Discrimination Improves Attention, Reading Fluency, and Working Memory'. *Frontiers in Human Neuroscience* 10 (August): 397.

Lebel, C., A. Benischek, B. Geeraert, et al. 2019. 'Developmental Trajectories of White Matter Structure in Children with and without Reading Impairments'. *Developmental Cognitive Neuroscience* 36 (April): 100633.

Lebel, C., L. Walker, A. Leemans, L. Phillips, and C. Beaulieu. 2008. 'Microstructural Maturation of the Human Brain from Childhood to Adulthood'. *NeuroImage* 40 (3): 1044–55.

Lee, S. J., L. J. Woodward, and J. M. T. Henderson. 2019. 'Educational Achievement at Age 9.5 Years of Children Born to Mothers Maintained on Methadone during Pregnancy'. *PloS One* 14 (10): e0223685.

Lehongre, K., F. Ramus, N. Villiermet, D. Schwartz, and A.-L. Giraud. 2011. 'Altered Low-γ Sampling in Auditory Cortex Accounts for the Three Main Facets of Dyslexia'. *Neuron* 72 (6): 1080–90.

Leiss, D. (2007). '*Hilf mir es selbst zu tun'. Lehrerinterventionen beim mathematischen Modellieren.* Franzbecker.

Leng, Y. and Y. Wei. 1994. Zhonghua zihai [China's sea of characters]. Beijing, China: Zhongguo youyi chuban gongsi.

Leong, V., and U. Goswami. 2015. 'Acoustic-Emergent Phonology in the Amplitude Envelope of Child-Directed Speech'. *PloS One* 10 (12): e0144411.

Leong, V., M. Kalashnikova, D. Burnham, and U. Goswami. 2017. 'The Temporal Modulation Structure of Infant-Directed Speech'. *Open Mind* 1 (2): 78–90.

Leong, V., M. A. Stone, R. E. Turner, and U. Goswami. 2014. 'A Role for Amplitude Modulation Phase Relationships in Speech Rhythm Perception'. *The Journal of the Acoustical Society of America* 136 (1): 366–81.

Leppänen, P. H. T., J. A. Hämäläinen, H. K. Salminen, et al. 2010. 'Newborn Brain Event-Related Potentials Revealing Atypical Processing of Sound Frequency and the Subsequent Association with Later Literacy Skills in Children with Familial Dyslexia'. *Cortex: A Journal Devoted to the Study of the Nervous System and Behavior* 46 (10): 1362–76.

Levy, L. M., I. L. Reis, and J. Grafman. 1999. 'Metabolic Abnormalities Detected by 1H-MRS in Dyscalculia and Dysgraphia'. *Neurology* 53 (3): 639–41.

Liang, H., A. M. Vuong, C. Xie, et al. 2019. 'Childhood Polybrominated Diphenyl Ether (PBDE) Serum Concentration and Reading Ability at Ages 5 and 8 Years: The HOME Study'. *Environment International* 122 (January): 330–9.

Libertus, M. E., L. Feigenson, and J. Halberda. 2011. 'Preschool Acuity of the Approximate Number System Correlates with School Math Ability'. *Developmental Science* 14 (6): 1292–1300.

Liebig, J., A. D. Friederici, N. E. Neef, and LEGASCREEN Consortium. 2020. 'TEMPORARY REMOVAL: Auditory Brainstem Measures and Genotyping Boost the Prediction of Literacy: A Longitudinal Study on Early Markers of Dyslexia'. *Developmental Cognitive Neuroscience* 46 (December): 100869.

Li, J., M. Robinson, E. Malacova, et al. 2013. 'Maternal Life Stress Events in Pregnancy Link to Children's School Achievement at Age 10 Years'. *The Journal of Pediatrics* 162 (3): 483–9.

Li, J., L. Na, H. Ma, et al. 2015. 'Multigenerational Effects of Parental Prenatal Exposure to Famine on Adult Offspring Cognitive Function'. *Scientific Reports* 5 (September): 13792.

Lillicrap, T. P., A. Santoro, L.Marris, C.J. Akerman, and G. Hinton. 2020. 'Backpropagation and the Brain'. *Nature Reviews: Neuroscience* 21 (6): 335–46.

Limperopoulos, C., H. Bassan, K. Gauvreau, et al. 2007. 'Does Cerebellar Injury in Premature Infants Contribute to the High Prevalence of Long-Term Cognitive, Learning, and Behavioral Disability in Survivors?' *Pediatrics* 120 (3): 584–93.

Linkersdörfer, J., A. Jurcoane, S. Lindberg, et al. 2015. 'The Association between Gray Matter Volume and Reading Proficiency: A Longitudinal Study of Beginning Readers'. *Journal of Cognitive Neuroscience* 27 (2): 308–18.

Linkersdörfer, J., J. Lonnemann, S. Lindberg, M. Hasselhorn, and C. J. Fiebach. 2012. 'Grey Matter Alterations Co-Localize with Functional Abnormalities in Developmental Dyslexia: An ALE Meta-Analysis'. *PloS One* 7 (8): e43122.

Liu, L., J. Wang, S. Shao, et al. 2016. 'Descriptive Epidemiology of Prenatal and Perinatal Risk Factors in a Chinese Population with Reading Disorder'. *Scientific Reports* 6 (November): 36697.

Li, Y., F. Chen, and W. Huang. 2016. 'Neural Plasticity Following Abacus Training in Humans: A Review and Future Directions'. *Neural Plasticity* 2016 (January): 1213723.

Li, Y., Y. Hu, M. Zhao, et al. 2013. 'The Neural Pathway Underlying a Numerical Working Memory Task in Abacus-Trained Children and Associated Functional Connectivity in the Resting Brain'. *Brain Research* 1539 (November): 24–33.

Li, Y., Y. Wang, Y. Hu, Y. Liang, and F. Chen. 2013. 'Structural Changes in Left Fusiform Areas and Associated Fiber Connections in Children with Abacus Training: Evidence from Morphometry and Tractography'. *Frontiers in Human Neuroscience* 7 (July): 335.

Lizarazu, M., M. Lallier, N. Molinaro, et al. 2015. 'Developmental Evaluation of Atypical Auditory Sampling in Dyslexia: Functional and Structural Evidence'. *Human Brain Mapping* 36 (12): 4986–5002.

Lizarazu, M., L. Scotto di Covella, V. van Wassenhove, et al. 2021. 'Neural Entrainment to Speech and Nonspeech in Dyslexia: Conceptual Replication and Extension of Previous Investigations'. *Cortex: A Journal Devoted to the Study of the Nervous System and Behavior* 137 (April): 160–78.

Li, Z., X. Ma, S. Peltier, et al. 2008. 'Occipital-Temporal Reduction and Sustained Visual Attention Deficit in Prenatal Alcohol Exposed Adults'. *Brain Imaging and Behavior* 2 (1): 39–48.

Lohvansuu, K., J. A. Hämäläinen, L. Ervast, H. Lyytinen, and P. H. T. Leppänen. 2018. 'Longitudinal Interactions between Brain and Cognitive Measures on Reading Development from 6 Months to 14 Years'. *Neuropsychologia* 108 (January): 6–12.

Low, J. A., R. S. Galbraith, D. W. Muir, et al. 1988. 'Motor and Cognitive Deficits after Intrapartum Asphyxia in the Mature Fetus'. *American Journal of Obstetrics and Gynecology* 158 (2): 356–61.

Lozano, J., O. García-Algar, E. Marchei, et al. 2007. 'Prevalence of Gestational Exposure to Cannabis in a Mediterranean City by Meconium Analysis'. *Acta Paediatrica* 96 (12): 1734–7.

Lubman, D. I., A. Cheetham, and M. Yücel. 2015. 'Cannabis and Adolescent Brain Development'. *Pharmacology & Therapeutics* 148 (April): 1–16.

Ludwig, K. U., P. Sämann, M. Alexander, et al. 2013. 'A Common Variant in Myosin-18B Contributes to Mathematical Abilities in Children with Dyslexia and Intraparietal Sulcus Variability in Adults'. *Translational Psychiatry* 3 (February): e229.

Łuniewska, M., K. Chyl, A. Dębska, et al. 2019. 'Children With Dyslexia and Familial Risk for Dyslexia Present Atypical Development of the Neuronal Phonological Network'. *Frontiers in Neuroscience* 13 (November): 1287.

Łuniewska, M., K. Chyl, A. Dębska, et al. 2018. 'Neither Action nor Phonological Video Games Make Dyslexic Children Read Better'. *Scientific Reports* 8 (1): 549.

Lutchmaya, S., S. Baron-Cohen, and P. Raggatt. 2001. 'Foetal Testosterone and Vocabulary Size in 18- and 24-Month-Old Infants'. *Infant Behavior & Development* 24 (4): 418–24.

Lyon, G. R., S. E. Shaywitz, and B. A. Shaywitz. 2003. 'A Definition of Dyslexia'. *Annals of Dyslexia* 53 (1): 1–14.

Lyons, I. M., D. Ansari, and S. L. Beilock. 2012. 'Symbolic Estrangement: Evidence against a Strong Association between Numerical Symbols and the Quantities They Represent'. *Journal of Experimental Psychology: General* 141 (4): 635–41. https://doi.org/10.1037/a0027248.

Lyons, I. M., G. R. Price, A. Vaessen, L. Blomert, and D. Ansari. 2014. 'Numerical Predictors of Arithmetic Success in Grades 1-6'. *Developmental Science* 17 (5): 714–26.

Lyons, I. M., S. E. Vogel, and D. Ansari. 2016. 'On the Ordinality of Numbers: A Review of Neural and Behavioral Studies'. *Progress in Brain Research* 227 (May): 187–221.

Maher, B. 2008. 'Personal Genomes: The Case of the Missing Heritability'. *Nature* 456 (7218): 18–21.

Maisog, J. M., E. R. Einbinder, D. L. Flowers, P. E, Turkeltaub, and G. F. Eden. 2008. 'A Meta-Analysis of Functional Neuroimaging Studies of Dyslexia'. *Annals of the New York Academy of Sciences* 1145 (December): 237–59.

Majerus, S. 2019. 'Verbal Working Memory and the Phonological Buffer: The Question of Serial Order'. *Cortex: A Journal Devoted to the Study of the Nervous System and Behavior* 112 (March): 122–33.

Mak, L. E., B. A. Croy, V. Kay, et al. 2018. 'Resting-State Functional Connectivity in Children Born from Gestations Complicated by Preeclampsia: A Pilot Study Cohort'. *Pregnancy Hypertension* 12 (April): 23–8.

Makrides, M., M. A. Neumann, R. W. Byard, K. Simmer, and R. A. Gibson. 1994. 'Fatty Acid Composition of Brain, Retina, and Erythrocytes in Breast- and Formula-Fed Infants'. *The American Journal of Clinical Nutrition* 60 (2): 189–94.

Malanchini, M., L. E. Engelhardt, A. D. Grotzinger, K. Paige Harden, and E. M. Tucker-Drob. 2019. '"Same but Different": Associations between Multiple Aspects of Self-Regulation, Cognition, and Academic Abilities'. *Journal of Personality and Social Psychology* 117 (6): 1164–88.

Malanchini, M., K. Rimfeld, A. G. Allegrini, S. J. Ritchie, and R. Plomin. 2020. 'Cognitive Ability and Education: How Behavioural Genetic Research Has Advanced Our Knowledge and Understanding of Their Association'. *Neuroscience and Biobehavioral Reviews* 111 (April): 229–45.

Malanchini, M., K. Rimfeld, Z. Wang et al. 2020. 'Genetic Factors Underlie the Association between Anxiety, Attitudes and Performance in Mathematics'. *Translational Psychiatry* 10 (1): 12.

Malanchini, M., Z. Wang, I. Voronin, et al. 2017. 'Reading Self-Perceived Ability, Enjoyment and Achievement: A Genetically Informative Study of Their Reciprocal Links over Time'. *Developmental Psychology* 53 (4): 698–712.

Malisza, K. L., A.-A. Allman, D.H Shiloff, et al. 2005. 'Evaluation of Spatial Working Memory Function in Children and Adults with Fetal Alcohol Spectrum Disorders: A Functional Magnetic Resonance Imaging Study'. *Pediatric Research* 58 (6): 1150–7.

Maloney, E. A., G. Ramirez, E. A. Gunderson, S. C. Levine, and S. L. Beilock. 2015. 'Intergenerational Effects of Parents' Math Anxiety on Children's Math Achievement and Anxiety'. *Psychological Science* 26 (9): 1480–8.

Maloney, E. A., M. W. Schaeffer, and S. L. Beilock. 2013. 'Mathematics Anxiety and Stereotype Threat: Shared Mechanisms, Negative Consequences and Promising Interventions'. *Research in Mathematics Education* 15 (2): 115–28.

Mammarella, I. C., S. Caviola, and A. Dowker. 2019. *Mathematics Anxiety: What Is Known and What Is Still to Be Understood*. Routledge, Taylor & Francis Group.

Mammarella, I. C., S. Caviola, D. Giofrè, and D. Szűcs. 2018. 'The Underlying Structure of Visuospatial Working Memory in Children with Mathematical Learning Disability'. *The British Journal of Developmental Psychology* 36 (2): 220–35.

Mammarella, I. C., F. Hill, A. Devine, S. Caviola, and D. Szűcs. 2015. 'Math Anxiety and Developmental Dyscalculia: A Study on Working Memory Processes'. *Journal of Clinical and Experimental Neuropsychology* 37 (8): 878–87.

Mañeru, C., J. M. Serra-Grabulosa, C. Junqué, et al. 2003. 'Residual Hippocampal Atrophy in Asphyxiated Term Neonates'. *Journal of Neuroimaging: Official Journal of the American Society of Neuroimaging* 13 (1): 68–74.

Manis, F. R., M. S. Seidenberg, L. M. Doi, C. McBride-Chang, and A. Petersen. 1996. 'On the Bases of Two Subtypes of Development Dyslexia'. *Cognition* 58 (2): 157–95. https://doi.org/10.1016/0010-0277(95)00679-6.

Manolio, T. A., F. S. Collins, N. J. Cox, et al. 2009. 'Finding the Missing Heritability of Complex Diseases'. *Nature* 461 (7265): 747–53.

Manolitsis, G., and G. K. Georgiou. 2015. 'The Cognitive Profiles of Poor Readers/Good Spellers and Good Readers/Poor Spellers in a Consistent Orthography: A Retrospective Analysis'. *Preschool and Primary Education* 3 (2): 103. https://doi.org/10.12681/ppej.178.

Marcus, G. F. 2003. *The Algebraic Mind: Integrating Connectionism and Cognitive Science.* MIT Press.

Mareschal, D., and M. S. C. Thomas. 2007. 'Computational Modeling in Developmental Psychology'. *IEEE Transactions on Evolutionary Computation* 11 (2): 137–50.

Marino, C., P. Scifo, P. A. Della Rosa, et al. 2014. 'The DCDC2/intron 2 Deletion and White Matter Disorganization: Focus on Developmental Dyslexia'. *Cortex* 57: 227–243. https://doi.org/10.1016/j.cortex.2014.04.016.

Markowitz, G. 2018. 'From Industrial Toxins to Worldwide Pollutants: A Brief History of Polychlorinated Biphenyls'. *Public Health Reports* 133 (6): 721–5.

Marks, R. A., I. Kovelman, O. Kepinska, et al. 2019. 'Spoken Language Proficiency Predicts Print-Speech Convergence in Beginning Readers'. *NeuroImage* 201 (November): 116021.

Martin, A., M. Kronbichler, and F. Richlan. 2016. 'Dyslexic Brain Activation Abnormalities in Deep and Shallow Orthographies: A Meta-analysis of 28 Functional Neuroimaging Studies'. *Human Brain Mapping* 37 (7): 2676–99. https://doi.org/10.1002/hbm.23202.

Martin, M. M., D.L. Graham, D. M. McCarthy, P. G. Bhide, and G. D. Stanwood. 2016. 'Cocaine-Induced Neurodevelopmental Deficits and Underlying Mechanisms'. *Birth Defects Research. Part C, Embryo Today: Reviews* 108 (2): 147–73.

Martin, N., D. Boomsma, and G. Machin. 1997. 'A Twin-Pronged Attack on Complex Traits'. *Nature Genetics* 17 (4): 387–92.

Martin, N. G., and L. J. Eaves. 1977. 'Stages: The First to Determine the Genetical and Environmental Model'. *Most* 38: 79–95.

Martín-Puga, M. E., M. J. Justicia-Galiano, M. Mar Gómez-Pérez, and S. Pelegrina. 2020. 'Psychometric Properties, Factor Structure, and Gender and Educational Level Invariance of the Abbreviated Math Anxiety Scale (AMAS) in Spanish Children and Adolescents'. *Assessment* 29 (3): 425–40.

Mascheretti, S., A. De Luca, V. Trezzi, et al. 2017. 'Neurogenetics of Developmental Dyslexia: From Genes to Behavior through Brain Neuroimaging and Cognitive and Sensorial Mechanisms'. *Translational Psychiatry* 7: e987. https://doi.org/10.1038/tp.2016.240.

Mason, L. H., J. P. Harp, and D. Y. Han. 2014. 'Pb Neurotoxicity: Neuropsychological Effects of Lead Toxicity'. *BioMed Research International* 2014 (January): 840547.

Matas-Blanco, C., and R. A. Caparros-Gonzalez. 2020. 'Influence of Maternal Stress during Pregnancy on Child's Neurodevelopment'. *Psych* 2 (4): 186–97.

Matejko, A. A., and D. Ansari. 2015. 'Drawing Connections between White Matter and Numerical and Mathematical Cognition: A Literature Review'. *Neuroscience and Biobehavioral Reviews* 48 (January): 35–52.

——— 2019. 'The Neural Association between Arithmetic and Basic Numerical Processing Depends on Arithmetic Problem Size and Not Chronological Age'. *Developmental Cognitive Neuroscience* 37 (June): 100653.

Matejko, A. A., J. E. Hutchison, and D. Ansari. 2019. 'Developmental Specialization of the Left Intraparietal Sulcus for Symbolic Ordinal Processing'. *Cortex: A Journal Devoted to the Study of the Nervous System and Behavior* 114 (May): 41–53.

Matejko, A. A., G. R. Price, M. M. M. Mazzocco, and D. Ansari. 2013. 'Individual Differences in Left Parietal White Matter Predict Math Scores on the Preliminary Scholastic Aptitude Test'. *NeuroImage* 66 (February): 604–10.

Mattson, S. N., G. A. Bernes, and L. R. Doyle. 2019. 'Fetal Alcohol Spectrum Disorders: A Review of the Neurobehavioral Deficits Associated with Prenatal Alcohol Exposure'. *Alcoholism, Clinical and Experimental Research* 43 (6): 1046–62.

Matuszewski, Jacek, Bartosz Kossowski, Łukasz Bola, et al. 2020. 'Brain Plasticity Dynamics during Tactile Braille Learning in Sighted Subjects: Multi-Contrast MRI Approach'. *NeuroImage* 227: 117613.

Maurer, Urs, Vera C. Blau, Yuliya N. Yoncheva, and Bruce D. McCandliss. 2010. 'Development of Visual Expertise for Reading: Rapid Emergence of Visual Familiarity for an Artificial Script'. *Developmental Neuropsychology* 35 (4): 404–22.

Maurer, U., S. Brem, K. Bucher, et al. 2007. Impaired Tuning of a Fast Occipito-Temporal Response for Print in Dyslexic Children Learning to Read. Brain 130 (12): 3200–10. https://doi.org/10.1093/brain/awm193.

Maurer, U., S. Brem, K. Bucher, and D. Brandeis. 2005. 'Emerging Neurophysiological Specialization for Letter Strings'. *Journal of Cognitive Neuroscience* 17 (10): 1532–52.

Maurer, U., S. Brem, F. Kranz, et al. 2006. 'Coarse Neural Tuning for Print Peaks When Children Learn to Read'. *NeuroImage* 33 (2): 749–58.

Maurer, U., K. Bucher, S. Brem, et al. 2009. 'Neurophysiology in Preschool Improves Behavioral Prediction of Reading Ability Throughout Primary School'. *Biological Psychiatry* 66 (4): P341–8. https://doi.org/10.1016/j.biopsych.2009.02.031.

Maurer, U., E. Schulz, S. Brem, et al. 2011. 'The Development of Print Tuning in Children with Dyslexia: Evidence from Longitudinal ERP Data Supported by fMRI'. *NeuroImage* 57 (3): 714–22.

Ma, X. 1999. 'A Meta-Analysis of the Relationship between Anxiety toward Mathematics and Achievement in Mathematics'. *Journal for Research in Mathematics Education* 30 (5): 520–40.

Ma, X., and J. Xu. 2004. 'The Causal Ordering of Mathematics Anxiety and Mathematics Achievement: A Longitudinal Panel Analysis'. *Journal of Adolescence* 27 (2): 165–79.

Mazzocco, M. M. M., L. Feigenson, and J. Halberda. 2011. 'Impaired Acuity of the Approximate Number System Underlies Mathematical Learning Disability (Dyscalculia)'. *Child Development* 82 (4): 1224–37.

Mazzocco, M. M. M., and G. F. Myers. 2003. 'Complexities in Identifying and Defining Mathematics Learning Disability in the Primary School-Age Years'. *Annals of Dyslexia* 53 (1): 218–53.

McBryde, M., G. C. Fitzallen, H. G. Liley, H. G. Taylor, and S. Bora. 2020. 'Academic Outcomes of School-Aged Children Born Preterm: A Systematic Review and Meta-Analysis'. *JAMA Network Open* 3 (4): e202027.

McCandliss, B. D., L. Cohen, and S. Dehaene. 2003. 'The Visual Word Form Area: Expertise for Reading in the Fusiform Gyrus'. *Trends in Cognitive Sciences* 7 (7): 293–9.

McCaskey, U., M. von Aster, U. Maurer, et al. (2018). 'Longitudinal Brain Development of Numerical Skills in Typically Developing Children and Children with Developmental Dyscalculia'. *Frontiers in Human Neuroscience* 11, 629.

McCaskey, U., M. von Aster, R. O'Gorman, and K. Kucian. 2020. 'Persistent Differences in Brain Structure in Developmental Dyscalculia: A Longitudinal Morphometry Study'. *Frontiers in Human Neuroscience* 14 (July): 272.

McClelland, J. L. 2009. 'The Place of Modeling in Cognitive Science'. *Topics in Cognitive Science* 1 (1): 11–38.

McClelland, J. L., and D. E. Rumelhart. 1981. 'An Interactive Activation Model of Context Effects in Letter Perception: I. An Account of Basic Findings'. *Psychological Review* 88 (5): 375–407.

McCloskey, M., and A. M. Lindemann. 1992. 'MATHNET: Preliminary Results from a Distributed Model of Arithmetic Fact Retrieval'. *The Nature and Origins of Mathematical Skills*. 569: 365–409.

McCoy, A. R., and A. J. Reynolds. 1998. 'Evaluating Implementation'. In A. J. Reynolds and H. J. Walberg (eEds.), Advances in Educational Productivity, 117–33. JAI Press.

McCrory, C., and R. Layte. 2011. 'The Effect of Breastfeeding on Children's Educational Test Scores at Nine Years of Age: Results of an Irish Cohort Study'. *Social Science & Medicine* 72 (9): 1515–21.

McGaugh, J. L., L. Cahill, and B. Roozendaal. 1996. 'Involvement of the Amygdala in Memory Storage: Interaction with Other Brain Systems'. *Proceedings of the National Academy of Sciences of the United States of America* 93 (24): 13508–14.

McGrath, L. M., R. L. Peterson, and B. F. Pennington. 2020. 'The Multiple Deficit Model: Progress, Problems, and Prospects'. *Scientific Studies of Reading: The Official Journal of the Society for the Scientific Study of Reading* 24 (1): 7–13.

McKenzie, I. A., D. Ohayon, H. Li, et al. 2014. 'Motor Skill Learning Requires Active Central Myelination'. *Science* 346 (6207): 318–22.

Meda, S. A., J. Gelernter, J. R. Gruen, et al. 2008. 'Polymorphism of DCDC2 Reveals Differences in Cortical Morphology of Healthy Individuals – A Preliminary Voxel Based Morphometry Study'. *Brain Imaging and Behavior* 2: 21–6. https://doi.org/10.1007/s11682-007-9012-1.

Meintjes, E. M., J. L. Jacobson, C. D. Molteno, et al. 2010. 'An FMRI Study of Number Processing in Children with Fetal Alcohol Syndrome'. *Alcoholism, Clinical and Experimental Research* 34 (8): 1450–64.

Melby-Lervåg, M., S. A. H. Lyster, and C. Hulme. 2012. 'Phonological Skills and Their Role in Learning to Read: A Meta-Analytic Review'. *Psychological Bulletin* 138 (2): 322–52.

Menghini, D., A. Finzi, M. Benassi, et al. 2010. 'Different Underlying Neurocognitive Deficits in Developmental Dyslexia: A Comparative Study'. *Neuropsychologia* 48 (4): 863–72.

Menon, V. 2016. 'Memory and Cognitive Control Circuits in Mathematical Cognition and Learning'. *Progress in Brain Research* 227 (June): 159–86.

Menon, V. 2015. 'Arithmetic in the Child and Adult Brain'. *The Oxford Handbook of Numerical Cognition*, edited by K. Cohen Kadosh and A. Dowker, 502–30. . Oxford University Press.

Menon, V., A. Padmanabhan, and F. Schwartz. 2020. 'Cognitive Neuroscience of Dyscalculia and Math Learning Disabilities'. In *The Oxford Handbook of Developmental Cognitive Neuroscience*, edited by K. Cohen Kadosh. Oxford University Press.

Mensch, S., M. Baraban, R. Almeida, et al. 2015. 'Synaptic Vesicle Release Regulates Myelin Sheath Number of Individual Oligodendrocytes in Vivo'. *Nature Neuroscience* 18 (5): 628–30.

Micalizzi, L., K. Marceau, A. S. Evans, et al. 2021. 'A Sibling-Comparison Study of Smoking during Pregnancy and Risk for Reading-Related Problems'. *Neurotoxicology and Teratology* 84 (March): 106961.

Michels, L., R. O'Gorman, and K. Kucian. 2018. 'Functional Hyperconnectivity Vanishes in Children with Developmental Dyscalculia after Numerical Intervention'. *Developmental Cognitive Neuroscience* 30 (April): 291–303.

Miller, E. C., L. Zhang, B. W. Dummer, et al. 2012. 'Differential Modulation of Drug-Induced Structural and Functional Plasticity of Dendritic Spines'. *Molecular Pharmacology* 82 (2): 333–43.

Miller, S. P., V. Ramaswamy, D. Michelson, et al. 2005. 'Patterns of Brain Injury in Term Neonatal Encephalopathy'. *The Journal of Pediatrics* 146 (4): 453–60.

Mills, K. L., A.-L. Goddings, M. M. Herting, et al. 2016. 'Structural Brain Development between Childhood and Adulthood: Convergence across Four Longitudinal Samples'. *NeuroImage* 141 (November): 273–81.

Missall, K. N., S. H. Mercer, R. S. Martínez, and D. Casebeer. 2012. 'Concurrent and Longitudinal Patterns and Trends in Performance on Early Numeracy Curriculum-Based Measures in Kindergarten Through Third Grade'. *Assessment for Effective Intervention: Official Journal of the Council for Educational Diagnostic Services* 37 (2): 95–106.

Miyake, A., N. P. Friedman, M. J. Emerson, A. H. Witzki, A. Howerter, and T. D. Wager. 2000. 'The Unity and Diversity of Executive Functions and Their Contributions to Complex "Frontal Lobe" Tasks: A Latent Variable Analysis'. *Cognitive Psychology* 41 (1): 49–100.

Molfese, D. L. 2000. 'Predicting Dyslexia at 8 Years of Age Using Neonatal Brain Responses'. *Brain and Language* 72 (3): 238–45.

Molinaro, N., M. Lizarazu, M. Lallier, M. Bourguignon, and M. Carreiras. 2016. 'Out-of-Synchrony Speech Entrainment in Developmental Dyslexia'. *Human Brain Mapping* 37 (8): 2767–83.

Moll, K., B. Fussenegger, E. Willburger, and K. Landerl. 2009. 'RAN Is Not a Measure of Orthographic Processing. Evidence From the Asymmetric German Orthography'. *Scientific Studies of Reading* 13 (1): 1–25. https://doi.org/10.1080/10888430802631684.

Moll, K., S. M. Göbel, D. Gooch, K. Landerl, and M. J. Snowling. 2016a. 'Cognitive Risk Factors for Specific Learning Disorder'. *Journal of Learning Disabilities* 49 (3): 272–81. https://doi.org/10.1177/0022219414547221.

2016b. 'Cognitive Risk Factors for Specific Learning Disorder: Processing Speed, Temporal Processing, and Working Memory'. *Journal of Learning Disabilities* 49 (3): 272–81.

Moll, K., S. M. Göbel, and M. J. Snowling. 2015. 'Basic Number Processing in Children with Specific Learning Disorders: Comorbidity of Reading and Mathematics Disorders'.

Child Neuropsychology: A Journal on Normal and Abnormal Development in Childhood and Adolescence 21 (3): 399–417.

Moll, K., S. Kunze, N. Neuhoff, J. Bruder, and G. Schulte-Körne. 2014. 'Specific Learning Disorder: Prevalence and Gender Differences'. *PloS One* 9 (7): e103537.

Moll, K., and K. Landerl. 2009. 'Double Dissociation between Reading and Spelling Deficits'. *Scientific Studies of Reading* 13 (5): 359–82. https://doi.org/10.1080/10888430903162878.

Moll, K., K. Landerl, M. J. Snowling, and G. Schulte-Körne. 2019. 'Understanding Comorbidity of Learning Disorders: Task-Dependent Estimates of Prevalence'. *Journal of Child Psychology and Psychiatry, and Allied Disciplines* 60 (3): 286–94.

Moll, K., F. Ramus, J. Bartling, et al. 2014. 'Cognitive Mechanisms Underlying Reading and Spelling Development in Five European Orthographies'. *Learning and Instruction* 29: 65–77. https://doi.org/10.1016/j.learninstruc.2013.09.003.

Monnelly, V. J., D. Anblagan, A. Quigley, et al. 2018. 'Prenatal Methadone Exposure Is Associated with Altered Neonatal Brain Development'. *NeuroImage. Clinical* 18: 9–14.

Monzalvo, K., J. Fluss, C. Billard, S. Dehaene, and G. Dehaene-Lambertz. 2012. 'Cortical Networks for Vision and Language in Dyslexic and Normal Children of Variable Socio-Economic Status'. *NeuroImage* 61 (1): 258–74.

Moore, E. M., R. Migliorini, M. A. Infante, and E. P. Riley. 2014. 'Fetal Alcohol Spectrum Disorders: Recent Neuroimaging Findings'. *Current Developmental Disorders Reports* 1 (3): 161–72.

Moreau, D., K. Wiebels, A. J. Wilson, and K. E. Waldie. 2019. 'Volumetric and Surface Characteristics of Gray Matter in Adult Dyslexia and Dyscalculia'. *Neuropsychologia* 127 (April): 204–10.

Morie, K. P., M. J. Crowley, L. C. Mayes, and M. N. Potenza. 2019. 'Prenatal Drug Exposure from Infancy through Emerging Adulthood: Results from Neuroimaging'. *Drug and Alcohol Dependence* 198 (May): 39–53.

Morken, F., T. Helland, K. Hugdahl, and K. Specht. 2017. 'Reading in Dyslexia across Literacy Development: A Longitudinal Study of Effective Connectivity'. *NeuroImage* 144 (Pt A): 92–100.

Morsanyi, K., B. M. C. W. van Bers, P. A. O'Connor, and T. McCormack. 2018. 'Developmental Dyscalculia Is Characterized by Order Processing Deficits: Evidence from Numerical and Non-Numerical Ordering Tasks'. *Developmental Neuropsychology* 43 (7): 595–621.

Moulton, E., F. Bouhali, K. Monzalvo, et al. 2019. 'Connectivity between the Visual Word Form Area and the Parietal Lobe Improves after the First Year of Reading Instruction: A Longitudinal MRI Study in Children'. *Brain Structure & Function* 224 (4): 1519–36.

Mount, C. W., and M. Monje. 2017. 'Wrapped to Adapt: Experience-Dependent Myelination'. *Neuron* 95 (4): 743–56.

Moura, R., G. Wood, P. Pinheiro-Chagas, et al. 2013. 'Transcoding Abilities in Typical and Atypical Mathematics Achievers: The Role of Working Memory and Procedural and Lexical Competencies'. *Journal of Experimental Child Psychology* 116 (3): 707–27.

Moura, R., J. B. Lopes-Silva, and L. R. Vieira. 2015. 'From 'five' to 5 for 5 Minutes: Arabic Number Transcoding as a Short, Specific, and Sensitive Screening Tool for

Mathematics Learning Difficulties'. *Archives of Clinical Neuropsychology* 30 (1): 88–98. https://doi.org/10.1093/arclin/acu071.

Moyer, R. S., and T. K. Landauer. 1967. 'Time Required for Judgements of Numerical Inequality'. *Nature* 215 (5109): 1519–20.

Mullen, K. M., B. R. Vohr, K. H. Katz, et al. 2011. 'Preterm Birth Results in Alterations in Neural Connectivity at Age 16 Years'. *NeuroImage* 54 (4): 2563–70.

Mullis, I. V. S., M. O. Martin, P. Foy, D. l. Kelly, and B. Fishbein. 2020. TIMSS 2019 International Results in Mathematics and Science. https://timss2019.org/reports/wp-content/themes/timssandpirls/download-center/TIMSS-2019-International-Results-in-Mathematics-and-Science.pdf

Murray, L., A. Arteche, P. Fearon, et al. 2010. 'The Effects of Maternal Postnatal Depression and Child Sex on Academic Performance at Age 16 Years: A Developmental Approach'. *Journal of Child Psychology and Psychiatry, and Allied Disciplines* 51 (10): 1150–9.

Murphy, J. 1973. 'The Education Bureaucracies Implement Novel Policy: The Politics of Title I of ESEA'. In Allan Sindler (ed.), Policy and Politics in America, 160–99. Little, Brown.

Mushak, P. 1991. 'Gastro-Intestinal Absorption of Lead in Children and Adults: Overview of Biological and Biophysico-Chemical Aspects'. *Chemical Speciation and Bioavailability* 3 (3–4): 87–104.

Mussolin, C., A. De Volder, C. Grandin, et al. 2010. 'Neural Correlates of Symbolic Number Comparison in Developmental Dyscalculia'. *Journal of Cognitive Neuroscience* 22 (5): 860–74.

Mussolin, C., S. Mejias, and M.-P. Noël. 2010. 'Symbolic and Nonsymbolic Number Comparison in Children with and without Dyscalculia'. *Cognition* 115 (1): 10–25.

Myers, G. J., P. W. Davidson, C. Cox, et al. 2003. 'Prenatal Methylmercury Exposure from Ocean Fish Consumption in the Seychelles Child Development Study'. *The Lancet* 361 (9370): 1686–92.

Myers, G. J., P. W. Davidson, and B. Weiss. 2020. 'Methyl Mercury Exposure and Poisoning at Niigata, Japan'. *Neurotoxicology* 81 (December): 358–9.

Myers, R. E. 1972. 'Two Patterns of Perinatal Brain Damage and Their Conditions of Occurrence'. *American Journal of Obstetrics and Gynecology* 112 (2): 246–76.

1975. 'Fetal Asphyxia due to Umbilical Cord Compression. Metabolic and Brain Pathologic Consequences'. *Biology of the Neonate* 26 (1–2): 21–43.

Nag, S. 2016. Assessment Of Literacy And Foundational Learning In Developing Countries: www.heart-resources.org/wp-content/uploads/2017/06/Assessment-of-literacy-and-foundational-learning-in-developing-countries.pdf.

Nagy, Z., H. Westerberg, S. Skare, et al. 2003. 'Preterm Children Have Disturbances of White Matter at 11 Years of Age as Shown by Diffusion Tensor Imaging'. *Pediatric Research* 54 (5): 672–9.

Namkung, J. M., P. Peng, and X. Lin. 2019. 'The Relation between Mathematics Anxiety and Mathematics Performance Among School-Aged Students: A Meta-Analysis'. *Review of Educational Research* 89 (3): 459–96.

Naranjo, V. I., M. Hendricks, and K. S. Jones. 2020. 'Lead Toxicity in Children: An Unremitting Public Health Problem'. *Pediatric Neurology* 113 (December): 51–5.

Nation, K. 2019. Children's Reading Difficulties, Language, and Reflections on the Simple View of Reading, Australian Journal of Learning Difficulties, 24:1, 47–73.

Nation, K. (2007). Children's reading comprehension difficulties. In M. J. Snowling, & C. Hulme (Hrsg), The science of reading (S. 248–265). Malden, MA: Blackwell.

National Center on Response to Intervention (NCRTI). 2010. Essential Components of RTI – A Closer Look at Response to Intervention. National Center on Response to Intervention (NCRTI) (2012). Progress Monitoring Tools.

Nava-Ruiz, C., M. Méndez-Armenta, and C. Ríos. 2012. 'Lead Neurotoxicity: Effects on Brain Nitric Oxide Synthase'. *Journal of Molecular Histology* 43 (5): 553–63.

Nelson, G., and S. R. Powell. 2018. 'A Systematic Review of Longitudinal Studies of Mathematics Difficulty'. *Journal of Learning Disabilities* 51 (6): 523–39.

Nguyen, L. 2019. 'Cell Migration Promotes Dynamic Cellular Interactions to Control Cerebral Cortex Morphogenesis'. *IBRO Reports* 6: S8. https://doi.org/10.1016/j.ibror.2019.07.009.

Nicolson, R. I., and A. J. Fawcett. 1990. 'Automaticity: A New Framework for Dyslexia Research?' *Cognition* 35 (2): 159–82.

Nicolson, R. I., A. J. Fawcett, and P. Dean. 2001. 'Developmental Dyslexia: The Cerebellar Deficit Hypothesis'. *Trends in Neurosciences* 24 (9): 508–11.

Nicolson, R. I., and A. J. Fawcett. 2018. 'Procedural Learning, Dyslexia and Delayed Neural Commitment'. In *Reading and Dyslexia: From Basic Functions to Higher Order Cognition*, edited by T. Lachmann and T. Weis, 235–69. Springer International Publishing.

Nieder, A. 2016. 'The Neuronal Code for Number'. *Nature Reviews Neuroscience* 17: 366–82. https://doi.org/10.1038/nrn.2016.40.

Nieder, A., and S. Dehaene. 2009. 'Representation of Number in the Brain'. *Annual Review of Neuroscience* 32: 185–208.

Nieder, A., D. J. Freedman, and E. K. Miller. 2002. 'Representation of the Quantity of Visual Items in the Primate Prefrontal Cortex'. *Science* 297 (5587): 1708–11.

Niederhofer, H., and A. Reiter. 2004. 'Prenatal Maternal Stress, Prenatal Fetal Movements and Perinatal Temperament Factors Influence Behavior and School Marks at the Age of 6 Years'. *Fetal Diagnosis and Therapy* 19 (2): 160–2.

Ni, M., X. Li, J. B. T. Rocha, M. Farina, and M. Aschner. 2012. 'Glia and Methylmercury Neurotoxicity'. *Journal of Toxicology and Environmental Health. Part A* 75 (16–17): 1091–101.

Niogi, S. N., and B. D. McCandliss. 2006. 'Left Lateralized White Matter Microstructure Accounts for Individual Differences in Reading Ability and Disability'. *Neuropsychologia* 44 (11): 2178–88.

No Child Left Behind Act of 2001 (NCLB), Public Law 107-110. 20 USC 6301.

Noble, K. G., M. F. Norman, and Ma. J. Farah. 2005. 'Neurocognitive Correlates of Socioeconomic Status in Kindergarten Children'. *Developmental Science* 8 (1): 74–87.

Norton, E. S., and M. Wolf. 2012. 'Rapid Automatized Naming (RAN) and Reading Fluency: Implications for Understanding and Treatment of Reading Disabilities'. *Annual Review of Psychology* 63: 427–52.

Notebaert, K., S. Nelis, and B. Reynvoet. 2011. 'The Magnitude Representation of Small and Large Symbolic Numbers in the Left and Right Hemisphere: An Event-Related fMRI Study'. *Journal of Cognitive Neuroscience* 23 (3): 622–30. https://doi.org/10.1162/jocn.2010.21445.

Novita, S. 2016. 'Secondary Symptoms of Dyslexia: A Comparison of Self-Esteem and Anxiety Profiles of Children with and without Dyslexia'. *European Journal of Special Needs Education* 31 (2): 279–88.

Núñez, R. E. 2017. 'Is There Really an Evolved Capacity for Number?' *Trends in Cognitive Sciences* 21 (6): 409–24.

Nyaradi, A., W. H. Oddy, S. Hickling, J. Li, and J. K. Foster. 2015. 'The Relationship between Nutrition in Infancy and Cognitive Performance during Adolescence'. *Frontiers in Nutrition* 2 (February): 2.

O'Brien, G., and J. D. Yeatman. 2021. 'Bridging Sensory and Language Theories of Dyslexia: Toward a Multifactorial Model'. *Developmental Science* 24 (3): e13039. https://doi.org/10.1111/desc.13039.

Oddy, W. H., J. Li, A. J. O. Whitehouse, S. R. Zubrick, and E. Malacova. 2011. 'Breastfeeding Duration and Academic Achievement at 10 Years'. *Pediatrics* 127 (1): e137–45.

OECD. 2013. *PISA 2012 Results: Ready to Learn (Volume III) Students' Engagement, Drive and Self-Beliefs: Students' Engagement, Drive and Self-Beliefs.* OECD Publishing.

OECD. 2016. *PISA 2015 Results.* OECD.

OECD. 2018. PISA 2018 results. www.oecd.org/pisa/publications/pisa-2018-results.htm.

OECD. 2020, PISA 2018 results. www.oecd-ilibrary.org/education/talis-2018-results-volume-i_1d0bc92a-en.

OECD, and The World Bank. 2020. 'Infant and Young Child Feeding'. Organisation for Economic Co-Operation and Development (OECD). https://doi.org/10.1787/67fe62a3-en.

Oei, J. L., E. Melhuish, H. Uebel, et al. 2017. 'Neonatal Abstinence Syndrome and High School Performance'. *Pediatrics* 139 (2). https://doi.org/10.1542/peds.2016-2651.

Ogundimu, E. O., D. G. Altman, and G. S. Collins. 2016. 'Adequate Sample Size for Developing Prediction Models Is Not Simply Related to Events per Variable'. *Journal of Clinical Epidemiology* 76 (August): 175–82.

O'Hare, E. D., E. Kan, J. Yoshii, et al. 2005. 'Mapping Cerebellar Vermal Morphology and Cognitive Correlates in Prenatal Alcohol Exposure'. *Neuroreport* 16 (12): 1285–90.

Oken, E., R. O. Wright, K. P. Kleinman, et al. 2005. 'Maternal Fish Consumption, Hair Mercury, and Infant Cognition in a US Cohort'. *Environmental Health Perspectives* 113 (10): 1376–80.

Oliver, A., M. H. Johnson, A. Karmiloff-Smith, and B. Pennington. 2000. 'Deviations in the Emergence of Representations: A Neuroconstructivist Framework for Analysing Developmental Disorders'. *Developmental Science* 3 (1): 1–23.

Oliver, B., N. Harlaar, M. E. H. Thomas, et al. 2004. 'A Twin Study of Teacher-Reported Mathematics Performance and Low Performance in 7-Year-Olds'. *Journal of Educational Psychology* 96 (3): 504–17.

Olson, H. C., J. J. Feldman, A. P. Streissguth, P. D. Sampson, and F. L. Bookstein. 1998. 'Neuropsychological Deficits in Adolescents with Fetal Alcohol Syndrome: Clinical Findings'. *Alcoholism, Clinical and Experimental Research* 22 (9): 1998–2012.

Olulade, O. A., D. L. Flowers, E. M. Napoliello, and G. F. Eden. 2015. 'Dyslexic Children Lack Word Selectivity Gradients in Occipito-Temporal and Inferior Frontal Cortex'. *NeuroImage: Clinical* 7: 742–54.

Olulade, O. A., E. M. Napoliello, and G. F. Eden. 2013. 'Abnormal Visual Motion Processing Is Not a Cause of Dyslexia'. *Neuron* 79 (1): 180–90.

O'Reilly, R. C. 1998. 'Six Principles for Biologically Based Computational Models of Cortical Cognition'. *Trends in Cognitive Sciences* 2 (11): 455–62.

Osmon, D. C., J. M. Smerz, M. M. Braun, and E. Plambeck. 2006. 'Processing Abilities Associated with Math Skills in Adult Learning Disability'. *Journal of Clinical and Experimental Neuropsychology* 28 (1): 84–95.

Ostad, S. A. 1997. 'Developmental Differences in Addition Strategies: A Comparison of Mathematically Disabled and Mathematically Normal Children'. *British Journal of Educational Psychology* 67 (Pt 3) (September): 345–57.

Ostad, S. A. 1998. 'Developmental Differences in Solving Simple Arithmetic Word Problems and Simple Number-Fact Problems: A Comparison of Mathematically Normal and Mathematically Disabled Children'. *Mathematical Cognition* 4 (1): 1–19. https://doi.org/10.1080/135467998387389.

Ou, X., A. Andres, R. T. Pivik, et al. 2016. 'Voxel-Based Morphometry and fMRI Revealed Differences in Brain Gray Matter in Breastfed and Milk Formula-Fed Children'. *AJNR. American Journal of Neuroradiology* 37 (4): 713–19.

Ozernov-Palchik, O., and N. Gaab. 2016. 'Tackling the 'Dyslexia Paradox': Reading Brain and Behavior for Early Markers of Developmental Dyslexia'. *Wiley Interdisciplinary Reviews. Cognitive Science* 7 (2): 156–76.

Pagliarini, E., M. T. Guasti, C. Toneatto, et al. 2015. 'Dyslexic Children Fail to Comply with the Rhythmic Constraints of Handwriting'. *Human Movement Science* 42 (August): 161–82.

Pantoja, N., M. W. Schaeffer, C. S. Rozek, S. L. Beilock, and S. C. Levine. 2020. 'Children's Math Anxiety Predicts Their Math Achievement Over and Above a Key Foundational Math Skill'. *Journal of Cognition and Development: Official Journal of the Cognitive Development Society* 21 (5): 709–28.

Papanikolaou, N. C., E. G. Hatzidaki, S. Belivanis, G. N. Tzanakakis, and A. M. Tsatsakis. 2005. 'Lead Toxicity Update. A Brief Review'. *Medical Science Monitor: International Medical Journal of Experimental and Clinical Research* 11 (10): RA329–36.

Park, D., G. Ramirez, and S. L. Beilock. 2014. 'The Role of Expressive Writing in Math Anxiety'. *Journal of Experimental Psychology. Applied* 20 (2): 103–11.

Park, J. 2018. 'A Neural Basis for the Visual Sense of Number and Its Development: A Steady-State Visual Evoked Potential Study in Children and Adults'. *Developmental Cognitive Neuroscience* 30 (April): 333–43.

Park, J., R. Li, and E. M. Brannon. 2014. 'Neural Connectivity Patterns Underlying Symbolic Number Processing Indicate Mathematical Achievement in Children'. *Developmental Science* 17 (2): 187–202.

Pasquini, E. S., K. H. Corriveau, and U. Goswami. 2007. 'Auditory Processing of Amplitude Envelope Rise Time in Adults Diagnosed With Developmental Dyslexia'. *Scientific Studies of Reading: The Official Journal of the Society for the Scientific Study of Reading* 11 (3): 259–86.

Passolunghi, M. C., C. De Vita, and S. Pellizzoni. 2020. 'Math Anxiety and Math Achievement: The Effects of Emotional and Math Strategy Training'. *Developmental Science* 23 (6): e12964.

Patandin, S., C. I. Lanting, P. G. H. Mulder, et al. 1999. 'Effects of Environmental Exposure to Polychlorinated Biphenyls and Dioxins on Cognitive Abilities in Dutch Children at 42 Months of Age'. *The Journal of Pediatrics* 134 (1): 33–41.

Paterson, S. J., J. Parish-Morris, K. Hirsh-Pasek, and R. Michnick Golinkoff. 2016. 'Considering Development in Developmental Disorders'. *Journal of Cognition and Development: Official Journal of the Cognitive Development Society* 17 (4): 568–83.

Patra, K., D. Wilson-Costello, H. G. Taylor, N. Mercuri-Minich, and M. Hack. 2006. 'Grades I–II Intraventricular Hemorrhage in Extremely Low Birth Weight Infants: Effects on Neurodevelopment'. *The Journal of Pediatrics* 149 (2): 169–73.

Paulesu, E., J. F. Démonet, F. Fazio, et al. 2001. 'Dyslexia: Cultural Diversity and Biological Unity'. *Science* 291 (5511): 2165–7.

Paulesu, E., R. Bonandrini, L. Zapparoli, et al. 2021. 'Effects of Orthographic Consistency on Bilingual Reading: Human and Computer Simulation Data'. *Brain Sciences* 11 (7). https://doi.org/10.3390/brainsci11070878.

Paulson, J. A., and M. J. Brown. 2019. 'The CDC Blood Lead Reference Value for Children: Time for a Change'. *Environmental Health* 18 (16). https://doi.org/10.1186/s12940-019-0457-7.

Paus, T. 2005. 'Mapping Brain Maturation and Cognitive Development during Adolescence'. *Trends in Cognitive Sciences* 9 (2): 60–8.

Peacock, A., J. Leung, S. Larney, et al. 2018. 'Global Statistics on Alcohol, Tobacco and Illicit Drug Use: 2017 Status Report'. *Addiction* 113 (10): 1905–26.

Pearson, R. M., M. H. Bornstein, M. Cordero, et al. 2016. 'Maternal Perinatal Mental Health and Offspring Academic Achievement at Age 16: The Mediating Role of Childhood Executive Function'. *Journal of Child Psychology and Psychiatry, and Allied Disciplines* 57 (4): 491–501.

Pegg, J. and L. Graham. 2013. 'A Three-Level Intervention Pedagogy to Enhance the Academic Achievement of Indigenous Students: Evidence From QuickSmart'. In R. Jorgenson, P. Sullivan and P. Grootenboer (eds.), Pedagogies to Enhance Learning for Indigenous Students, 123–38). Springer.

Pekrun, R., A. J. Elliot, and M. A. Maier. 2006. 'Achievement Goals and Discrete Achievement Emotions: A Theoretical Model and Prospective Test'. *Journal of Educational Psychology* 98 (3): 583–97.

Peng, P., and D. Fuchs. 2016. 'A Meta-Analysis of Working Memory Deficits in Children With Learning Difficulties: Is There a Difference between Verbal Domain and Numerical Domain?' *Journal of Learning Disabilities* 49 (1): 3–20.

Pennington, B. 2006. 'From Single to Multiple Deficit Models of Developmental Disorders'. *Cognition.* https://doi.org/10.1016/j.cognition.2006.04.008.

Pennington, B. F., L. M. McGrath, and R. L. Peterson. 2019. *Diagnosing Learning Disorders, Third Edition: From Science to Practice.* Guilford Publications.

Perry, C., J. C. Ziegler, M. Braun, and M. Zorzi. 2010. 'Rules versus Statistics in Reading Aloud: New Evidence on an Old Debate'. *The European Journal of Cognitive Psychology* 22 (5): 798–812.

Perry, C., J. C. Ziegler, and M. Zorzi. 2007. 'Nested Incremental Modeling in the Development of Computational Theories: The CDP+ Model of Reading Aloud'. *Psychological Review* 114 (2): 273–315.

———. 2010. 'Beyond Single Syllables: Large-Scale Modeling of Reading Aloud with the Connectionist Dual Process (CDP++) Model'. *Cognitive Psychology* 61 (2): 106–51.

———. 2014a. 'When Silent Letters Say More than a Thousand Words: An Implementation and Evaluation of CDP++ in French'. *Journal of Memory and Language* 72 (April): 98–115.

———. 2014b. 'CDP++.Italian: Modelling Sublexical and Supralexical Inconsistency in a Shallow Orthography'. *PloS One* 9 (4): e94291.

Perry, C., M. Zorzi, and J. C. Ziegler. 2019. 'Understanding Dyslexia Through Personalized Large-Scale Computational Models'. *Psychological Science* 30 (3): 386–95.

Peters, L., and D. Ansari. 2019. 'Are Specific Learning Disorders Truly Specific, and Are They Disorders?' *Trends in Neuroscience and Education* 17 (December): 100115.

Peters, L., J. Bulthé, N. Daniels, H. Op de Beeck, and B. De Smedt. 2018. 'Dyscalculia and Dyslexia: Different Behavioral, yet Similar Brain Activity Profiles during Arithmetic'. *NeuroImage: Clinical* 18: 663–74. https://doi.org/10.1016/j.nicl.2018.03.003.

Peters, L., and B. De Smedt. 2018. 'Arithmetic in the Developing Brain: A Review of Brain Imaging Studies'. *Developmental Cognitive Neuroscience* 30: 265–79. https://doi.org/10.1016/j.dcn.2017.05.002.

Peters, L., H. Op de Beeck, and B. De Smedt. 2020. 'Cognitive Correlates of Dyslexia, Dyscalculia and Comorbid Dyslexia/dyscalculia: Effects of Numerical Magnitude Processing and Phonological Processing'. *Research in Developmental Disabilities* 107: 103806. https://doi.org/10.1016/j.ridd.2020.103806.

Peters, L. L., C. Thornton, A. de Jonge, et al. 2018. 'The Effect of Medical and Operative Birth Interventions on Child Health Outcomes in the First 28 Days and up to 5 Years of Age: A Linked Data Population-Based Cohort Study'. *Birth* 45 (4): 347–57.

Peterson, R. L., R. Boada, L. M. McGrath, et al. 2017. 'Cognitive Prediction of Reading, Math, and Attention: Shared and Unique Influences'. *Journal of Learning Disabilities* 50 (4): 408–21.

Peterson, R.L., and B. F. Pennington. 2012. 'Developmental Dyslexia'. *The Lancet* 379 (9830): 1997–2007.

——— 2015. 'Developmental Dyslexia'. *Annual Review of Clinical Psychology* 11 (January): 283–307.

Peterson, R. L., B. F. Pennington, and R. K. Olson. 2013. 'Subtypes of Developmental Dyslexia: Testing the Predictions of the Dual-Route and Connectionist Frameworks'. *Cognition* 126 (1): 20–38.

Petryk, A., S. R. Harris, and L. Jongbloed. 2007. 'Breastfeeding and Neurodevelopment'. *Infants and Young Children* 20 (2): 120–34.

Pezzulo, G., M. Zorzi, and M. Corbetta. 2021. 'The Secret Life of Predictive Brains: What's Spontaneous Activity For?' *Trends in Cognitive Sciences*, 25 (9): P730–43. https://doi.org/10.1016/j.tics.2021.05.007.

Piazza, M., A. Facoetti, A. N. Trussardi, et al. 2010. 'Developmental Trajectory of Number Acuity Reveals a Severe Impairment in Developmental Dyscalculia'. *Cognition* 116 (1): 33–41.

Piazza, M., E. Giacomini, D. Le Bihan, and S. Dehaene. 2003. 'Single-Trial Classification of Parallel Pre-Attentive and Serial Attentive Processes Using Functional Magnetic Resonance Imaging'. *Proceedings. Biological Sciences / The Royal Society* 270 (1521): 1237–45.

Piazza, M., V. Izard, P. Pinel, D. Le Bihan, and S. Dehaene. 2004. 'Tuning Curves for Approximate Numerosity in the Human Intraparietal Sulcus'. *Neuron* 7: e1109. https://doi.org/10.1016/j.neuron.2004.10.014.

Piazza, M., P. Pinel, D. Le Bihan, and S. Dehaene. 2007. 'A Magnitude Code Common to Numerosities and Number Symbols in Human Intraparietal Cortex'. *Neuron* 53 (2): 293–305.

Piccolo, L. R., C. H. Giacomoni, A. Julio-Costa, et al. 2017. 'Reading Anxiety in L1: Reviewing the Concept'. *Early Childhood Education Journal* 45 (4): 537–43.

Pieper, I., C. A. Wehe, J. Bornhorst, et al. 2014. 'Mechanisms of Hg Species Induced Toxicity in Cultured Human Astrocytes: Genotoxicity and DNA-Damage Response'. *Metallomics: Integrated Biometal Science* 6 (3): 662–71.

Pietron, W., M. Pajurek, S. Mikolajczyk, et al. 2019. 'Exposure to PBDEs Associated with Farm Animal Meat Consumption'. *Chemosphere* 224 (June): 58–64.

Pievsky, M. A., and R. E. McGrath. 2018. 'The Neurocognitive Profile of Attention-Deficit/ Hyperactivity Disorder: A Review of Meta-Analyses'. *Archives of Clinical Neuropsychology: The Official Journal of the National Academy of Neuropsychologists* 33 (2): 143–57.

Pitsia, V., A. Biggart, and A. Karakolidis. 2017. 'The Role of Students' Self-Beliefs, Motivation and Attitudes in Predicting Mathematics Achievement: A Multilevel Analysis of the Programme for International Student Assessment Data'. *Learning and Individual Differences* 55 (April): 163–73.

Pixner, S., Moeller, K., Hermanova, V., Nuerk, H.-C., & Kaufmann, L. (2011a). Whorf reloaded: Language effects on nonverbal number processing in first grade – A trilingual study. Journal of Experimental Child Psychology, 108, 371–382. http://dx.doi.org/10.1016/j.jecp.2010.09.002.

Plaut, D. C., J. L. McClelland, M. S. Seidenberg, and K. Patterson. 1996. 'Understanding Normal and Impaired Word Reading: Computational Principles in Quasi-Regular Domains'. *Psychological Review* 103 (1): 56–115.

Pleisch, G., I. I. Karipidis, C. Brauchli, et al. 2019. 'Emerging Neural Specialization of the Ventral Occipitotemporal Cortex to Characters through Phonological Association Learning in Preschool Children'. *NeuroImage* 189 (April): 813–31.

Plomin, R., J. C. DeFries, and J. C. Loehlin. 1977. 'Genotype-Environment Interaction and Correlation in the Analysis of Human Behavior'. *Psychological Bulletin* 84 (2): 309–22.

Plomin, R. 2014. 'Genotype-Environment Correlation in the Era of DNA'. *Behavior Genetics* 44 (6): 629–38.

Plomin, R, and Y Kovas. 2005. 'Generalist Genes and Learning Disabilities'. *Psychological Bulletin* 131 (4): 592–617.

Pocock, S. J., M. Smith, and P. Baghurst. 1994. 'Environmental Lead and Children's Intelligence: A Systematic Review of the Epidemiological Evidence'. *BMJ* 309 (6963): 1189–97.

Poelmans, H., H. Luts, M. Vandermosten, et al. 2011. 'Reduced Sensitivity to Slow-Rate Dynamic Auditory Information in Children with Dyslexia'. *Research in Developmental Disabilities* 32 (6): 2810–19.

Poldrack, R. A. 2000. 'Imaging Brain Plasticity: Conceptual and Methodological Issues–a Theoretical Review'. *NeuroImage* 12 (1): 1–13.

Polidano, C., A. Zhu, and J. C. Bornstein. 2017. 'The Relation between Cesarean Birth and Child Cognitive Development'. *Scientific Reports* 7 (1): 11483.

Pong, K. M., M. E. Abdel-Latif, K. Lui, et al. 2010. 'The Temporal Influence of a Heroin Shortage on Pregnant Drug Users and Their Newborn Infants in Sydney, Australia'. *The Australian & New Zealand Journal of Obstetrics & Gynaecology* 50 (3): 230–6.

Powell, S. R., L. S. Fuchs, D. Fuchs, P. T. Cirino, and J. M. Fletcher. 2009a. 'Effects of Fact Retrieval Tutoring on Third-Grade Students with Math Difficulties with and without Reading Difficulties'. *Learning Disabilities Research & Practice: A Publication of the Division for Learning Disabilities, Council for Exceptional Children* 24 (1): 1–11.

2009b. 'Do Word-Problem Features Differentially Affect Problem Difficulty as a Function of Students' Mathematics Difficulty with and without Reading Difficulty?' *Journal of Learning Disabilities* 42 (2): 99–110.

Power, A. J., L. J. Colling, N. Mead, L. Barnes, and U. Goswami. 2016. 'Neural Encoding of the Speech Envelope by Children with Developmental Dyslexia'. *Brain and Language* 160 (September): 1–10.

Power, A. J., N. Mead, L. Barnes, and U. Goswami. 2013. 'Neural Entrainment to Rhythmic Speech in Children with Developmental Dyslexia'. *Frontiers in Human Neuroscience* 7 (November): 777.

Power, J. D., A. L. Cohen, S. M. Nelson, et al. 2011. 'Functional Network Organization of the Human Brain'. *Neuron* 72 (4): 665–78.

Prado, J., R. Mutreja, and J. R. Booth. 2014. 'Developmental Dissociation in the Neural Responses to Simple Multiplication and Subtraction Problems'. *Developmental Science* 17 (4): 537–52.

Pressman, J. and A. Wildavsky. 1973. Implementation. University of California Press.

Preston, J. L., P. J. Molfese, S. J. Frost, et al. 2016. 'Print-Speech Convergence Predicts Future Reading Outcomes in Early Readers'. *Psychological Science* 27 (1): 75–84.

Price, C. J., and J. T. Devlin. 2011. 'The Interactive Account of Ventral Occipitotemporal Contributions to Reading'. *Trends in Cognitive Sciences* 15 (6): 246–53.

Price, C. J. 2000. 'The Anatomy of Language: Contributions from Functional Neuroimaging'. *Journal of Anatomy* 197 Pt 3 (October): 335–59.

Price, G. R., I. Holloway, P. Räsänen, M. Vesterinen, and D. Ansari. 2007. 'Impaired Parietal Magnitude Processing in Developmental Dyscalculia'. *Current Biology* 17 (24): PR1042–R1043. https://doi.org/10.1016/j.cub.2007.10.013.

Price, G. R., D. J. Yeo, E. D. Wilkey, and L. E. Cutting. 2018. 'Prospective Relations between Resting-State Connectivity of Parietal Subdivisions and Arithmetic Competence'. *Developmental Cognitive Neuroscience* 30 (April): 280–90.

Primi, C., C. Busdraghi, C. Tomasetto, K. Morsanyi, and F. Chiesi. 2014. 'Measuring Math Anxiety in Italian College and High School Students: Validity, Reliability and Gender Invariance of the Abbreviated Math Anxiety Scale (AMAS)'. *Learning and Individual Differences* 34 (August): 51–56.

Pritchard, V. E., Malone, S. A., & Hulme, C. (2021). Early handwriting ability predicts the growth of children's spelling, but not reading, skills. *Scientific Studies of Reading*, 25(4), 304–318. https://doi.org/10.1080/10888438.2020.1778705.

Pugh, K. R., S. J. Frost, D. L. Rothman, et al. 2014. 'Glutamate and Choline Levels Predict Individual Differences in Reading Ability in Emergent Readers'. *The Journal of Neuroscience: The Official Journal of the Society for Neuroscience* 34 (11): 4082–9.

Pugh, K. R., S. J. Frost, R. Sandak, et al. 2012. 'Mapping the Word Reading Circuitry in Skilled and Disabled Readers'. In *The Neural Basis of Reading*, 281–305. Psychology Press.

Pulli, E. P., V. Kumpulainen, J. H. Kasurinen, et al. 2019. 'Prenatal Exposures and Infant Brain: Review of Magnetic Resonance Imaging Studies and a Population Description Analysis'. *Human Brain Mapping* 40 (6): 1987–2000.

Punaro, L., and R. Reeve. 2012. 'Relationships between 9-Year-Olds' Math and Literacy Worries and Academic Abilities'. *Child Development Research* 2012 (October). https://doi.org/10.1155/2012/359089.

Purpura, D. J., and C. M. Ganley. 2014. 'Working Memory and Language: Skill-Specific or Domain-General Relations to Mathematics?' *Journal of Experimental Child Psychology* 122 (June): 104–21.

Qin, S., S. Cho, T. Chen, et al. 2014. 'Hippocampal-Neocortical Functional Reorganization Underlies Children's Cognitive Development'. *Nature Neuroscience* 17: 1263–9. https://doi.org/10.1038/nn.3788.

Quantities, Counting, Numbers (MZZ). n.d. Understanding the World of Mathematics. Support Boxes for Day-Care Centres and Initial Lessons: www.cornelsen.de/pro dukte/foerderboxen-fuer-kita-und-anfangsunterricht-mengen-zaehlen-zahlen-mzz-die-welt-der-mathematik-verstehen-koffer-mit-foerdermaterialien-und-handrei chungen-80-s-9783060800155.

Raddatz, J., J.-T. Kuhn, H. Holling, K. Moll, and C. Dobel. 2017. 'Comorbidity of Arithmetic and Reading Disorder: Basic Number Processing and Calculation in Children With Learning Impairments'. *Journal of Learning Disabilities* 50 (3): 298–308.

Rafferty, J., G. Mattson, M. F. Earls, M. W. Yogman, and Committee on Psychosocial Aspects of Child and Family Health. 2019. 'Incorporating Recognition and Management of Perinatal Depression Into Pediatric Practice'. *Pediatrics* 143 (1): e20183260. https://doi.org/10.1542/peds.2018-3260.

Ragnarsdottir, L. D., A. L. Kristjansson, I. E. Thorisdottir, et al. 2017. 'Cumulative Risk over the Early Life Course and Its Relation to Academic Achievement in Childhood and Early Adolescence'. *Preventive Medicine* 96 (March): 36–41.

Ramaa, S., and I. P. Gowramma. 2002. A Systematic Procedure for Identifying and Classifying Children with Dyscalculia Among Primary School. Dyslexia 8: 67–85.

Raman, D. V., A. P. Rotondo, and T. O'Leary. 2019. 'Fundamental Bounds on Learning Performance in Neural Circuits'. *Proceedings of the National Academy of Sciences of the United States of America* 116 (21): 10537–46.

Ramirez, G., and S. L. Beilock. 2011. 'Writing about Testing Worries Boosts Exam Performance in the Classroom'. *Science* 331 (6014): 211–13.

Ramirez, G., H. Chang, E. A. Maloney, S. C. Levine, and S. L. Beilock. 2016. 'On the Relationship between Math Anxiety and Math Achievement in Early Elementary School: The Role of Problem Solving Strategies'. *Journal of Experimental Child Psychology* 141 (January): 83–100.

Ramirez, G., S. T. Shaw, and E. A. Maloney. 2018. 'Math Anxiety: Past Research, Promising Interventions, and a New Interpretation Framework'. *Educational Psychologist* 53 (3): 145–64.

Ranasinghe, S., G. Or, E. Y. Wang, et al. 2015. 'Reduced Cortical Activity Impairs Development and Plasticity after Neonatal Hypoxia Ischemia'. *The Journal of Neuroscience: The Official Journal of the Society for Neuroscience* 35 (34): 11946–59.

Ranpura, A., E. Isaacs, C. Edmonds, et al. 2013. 'Developmental Trajectories of Grey and White Matter in Dyscalculia'. *Trends in Neuroscience and Education* 2 (2): 56–64.

Rantalainen, V., J. Lahti, M. Henriksson, et al. 2018. 'Association between Breastfeeding and Better Preserved Cognitive Ability in an Elderly Cohort of Finnish Men'. *Psychological Medicine* 48 (6): 939–51.

Raschle, N. M., P. L. Stering, S. N. Meissner, and N. Gaab. 2014. 'Altered Neuronal Response during Rapid Auditory Processing and Its Relation to Phonological Processing in Prereading Children at Familial Risk for Dyslexia'. *Cerebral Cortex* 24 (9): 2489–501.

Rasmussen, C., and J. Bisanz. 2011. 'The Relation between Mathematics and Working Memory in Young Children With Fetal Alcohol Spectrum Disorders'. *The Journal of Special Education* 45 (3): 184–91.

Rätsep, M. T., A. Paolozza, A. F. Hickman, et al. 2016. 'Brain Structural and Vascular Anatomy Is Altered in Offspring of Pre-Eclamptic Pregnancies: A Pilot Study'. *AJNR. American Journal of Neuroradiology* 37 (5): 939–45.

Read, Charles. 1986. *Children's Creative Spelling*. Routledge.

Remer, J., E. Croteau-Chonka, D. C. Dean 3rd, et al. 2017. 'Quantifying Cortical Development in Typically Developing Toddlers and Young Children, 1–6 Years of Age'. *NeuroImage* 153 (June): 246–61.

Reynolds, C. A., J. K. Hewitt, M. T. Erickson, et al. 1996. 'The Genetics of Children's Oral Reading Performance'. *Journal of Child Psychology and Psychiatry, and Allied Disciplines* 37 (4): 425–34.

Reynolds, J. E., X. Long, M. N. Grohs, D. Dewey, and C. Lebel. 2019. 'Structural and Functional Asymmetry of the Language Network Emerge in Early Childhood'. *Developmental Cognitive Neuroscience* 39 (October): 100682.

Rice, D. C., R. Schoeny, and K. Mahaffey. 2003. 'Methods and Rationale for Derivation of a Reference Dose for Methylmercury by the US EPA'. *Risk Analysis: An Official Publication of the Society for Risk Analysis* 23 (1): 107–15.

Richards, M., R. Hardy, and M. E. J. Wadsworth. 2002. 'Long-Term Effects of Breast-Feeding in a National Birth Cohort: Educational Attainment and Midlife Cognitive Function'. *Public Health Nutrition* 5 (5): 631–5.

Richardson, F. C., and R. M. Suinn. 1972. 'The Mathematics Anxiety Rating Scale: Psychometric Data'. *Journal of Counseling Psychology* 19 (6): 551–4.

Richlan, F. 2020. 'The Functional Neuroanatomy of Developmental Dyslexia Across Languages and Writing Systems'. *Frontiers in Psychology* 11 (February): 155.

Richlan, F., M. Kronbichler, and H. Wimmer. 2009. 'Functional Abnormalities in the Dyslexic Brain: A Quantitative Meta-Analysis of Neuroimaging Studies'. *Human Brain Mapping* 30 (10): 3299–308.

——— 2011. 'Meta-Analyzing Brain Dysfunctions in Dyslexic Children and Adults'. *NeuroImage* 56 (3): 1735–42.

——— 2013. 'Structural Abnormalities in the Dyslexic Brain: A Meta-Analysis of Voxel-Based Morphometry Studies'. *Human Brain Mapping* 34 (11): 3055–65.

Rickard, T. C. 1997. 'Bending the Power Law: A CMPL Theory of Strategy Shifts and the Automatization of Cognitive Skills'. *Journal of Experimental Psychology. General* 126 (3): 288–311.

Riesenhuber, M., and L. S. Glezer. 2017. 'Evidence for Rapid Localist Plasticity in the Ventral Visual Stream: The Example of Words'. *Language, Cognition and Neuroscience* 32 (3): 286–94.

Riesenhuber, M., and T. Poggio. 1999. 'Hierarchical Models of Object Recognition in Cortex'. *Nature Neuroscience* 2 (11): 1019–25.

Rimfeld, K., M. Malanchini, T. Spargo, et al. 2019. 'Twins Early Development Study: A Genetically Sensitive Investigation into Behavioral and Cognitive Development from Infancy to Emerging Adulthood'. *Twin Research and Human Genetics: The Official Journal of the International Society for Twin Studies* 22 (6): 508–13.

Ríos-López, P., N. Molinaro, and M. Lallier. 2019. 'Tapping to a Beat in Synchrony Predicts Brain Print Sensitivity in Pre-Readers'. *Brain and Language* 199 (December): 104693.

Rivera, S. M., A. L. Reiss, M. A. Eckert, and V. Menon. 2005. 'Developmental Changes in Mental Arithmetic: Evidence for Increased Functional Specialization in the Left Inferior Parietal Cortex'. *Cerebral Cortex* 15 (11): 1779–90.

Robertson, C. M. T. 2003. 'Long-Term Follow-up of Term Infants with Perinatal Asphyxia'. In D. Stevenson, W. Benitz and P. Sunshine (eds.), *Fetal and Neonatal Brain Injury: Mechanisms, Management and the Risks of Practice*, 829–58. Cambridge University Press.

Robinson, C. S., B. M. Menchetti, and J. K. Torgesen. 2002. 'Toward a Two-Factor Theory of One Type of Mathematics Disabilities'. *Learning Disabilities Research and Practice* 17 (2): 81–9. https://doi.org/10.1111/1540-5826.00035.

Rochelle, K. S. H., and J. B. Talcott. 2006. 'Impaired Balance in Developmental Dyslexia? A Meta-Analysis of the Contending Evidence'. *Journal of Child Psychology and Psychiatry, and Allied Disciplines* 47 (11): 1159–66.

Rodríguez-Martínez, E. I., F. J. Ruiz-Martínez, C. I. Barriga Paulino, and C. M. Gómez. 2017. 'Frequency Shift in Topography of Spontaneous Brain Rhythms from Childhood to Adulthood'. *Cognitive Neurodynamics* 11 (1): 23–33.

Roeske, D., K. U. Ludwig, N. Neuhoff, et al. 2011. 'First Genome-Wide Association Scan on Neurophysiological Endophenotypes Points to Trans-Regulation Effects on SLC2A3 in Dyslexic Children'. *Molecular Psychiatry* 16: 97–107. https://doi.org/10.1038/mp.2009.102.

Rogers, A., S. Obst, S. J. Teague, et al. 2020. 'Association between Maternal Perinatal Depression and Anxiety and Child and Adolescent Development: A Meta-Analysis'. *JAMA Pediatrics* 174 (11): 1082–92.

Romeo, R. R., J. A. Christodoulou, K. K. Halverson, et al. 2017. 'Socioeconomic Status and Reading Disability: Neuroanatomy and Plasticity in Response to Intervention'. *Cerebral Cortex* 91 (2): 1–16.

Roncero, C., I. Valriberas-Herrero, M. Mezzatesta-Gava, et al. 2020. 'Cannabis Use during Pregnancy and Its Relationship with Fetal Developmental Outcomes and Psychiatric Disorders. A Systematic Review'. *Reproductive Health* 17 (1): 25.

Roos, D. H., R. L. Puntel, T. H. Lugokenski, et al. 2010. 'Complex Methylmercury-Cysteine Alters Mercury Accumulation in Different Tissues of Mice'. *Basic & Clinical Pharmacology & Toxicology* 107 (4): 789–92.

Rosenberg-Lee, M., S. Ashkenazi, T. Chen, et al. 2015. 'Brain Hyper-Connectivity and Operation-Specific Deficits during Arithmetic Problem Solving in Children with Developmental Dyscalculia'. *Developmental Science* 18 (3): 351–72. https://doi.org/10.1111/desc.12216.

Rosenberg-Lee, M., M. Barth, and V. Menon. 2011. 'What Difference Does a Year of Schooling Make? Maturation of Brain Response and Connectivity between 2nd and 3rd Grades during Arithmetic Problem Solving'. *NeuroImage* 57 (3): 796–808.

Rosenberg-Lee, M., T. Iuculano, S. R. Bae, et al. 2018. 'Short-Term Cognitive Training Recapitulates Hippocampal Functional Changes Associated with One Year of Longitudinal Skill Development'. *Trends in Neuroscience and Education* 10 (March): 19–29.

Rosen, M. G., S. M. Debanne, K. Thompson, and J. C. Dickinson. 1992. 'Abnormal Labor and Infant Brain Damage'. *Obstetrics and Gynecology* 80 (6): 961–5.

Ross, E. J., D. L. Graham, K. M. Money, and G. D. Stanwood. 2015. 'Developmental Consequences of Fetal Exposure to Drugs: What We Know and What We Still

Must Learn'. *Neuropsychopharmacology: Official Publication of the American College of Neuropsychopharmacology* 40 (1): 61–87.

Rotzer, S., K. Kucian, E. Martin, et al. 2008. 'Optimized Voxel-Based Morphometry in Children with Developmental Dyscalculia'. *NeuroImage* 39 (1): 417–22.

Rotzer, S., T. Loenneker, K. Kucian, et al. 2009. 'Dysfunctional Neural Network of Spatial Working Memory Contributes to Developmental Dyscalculia'. *Neuropsychologia* 47 (13): 2859–65.

Rourke, B. P., and M. A. Finlayson. 1978. 'Neuropsychological Significance of Variations in Patterns of Academic Performance: Verbal and Visual-Spatial Abilities'. *Journal of Abnormal Child Psychology* 6 (1): 121–33.

Rourke, B. P., and J. Strang. 1978. Neuropsychological Significance of Variations in Patterns of Academic Performance: Motor, Psychomotor, and Tactile-Perceptual Abilities. Journal of Pediatric Psychology 3: 62–6.

Rousselle, L., and M.-P. Noël. 2007. 'Basic Numerical Skills in Children with Mathematics Learning Disabilities: A Comparison of Symbolic vs Non-Symbolic Number Magnitude Processing'. *Cognition* 102 (3): 361–95.

Roussotte, F. F., K. K. Sulik, S. N. Mattson, et al. 2012. 'Regional Brain Volume Reductions Relate to Facial Dysmorphology and Neurocognitive Function in Fetal Alcohol Spectrum Disorders'. *Human Brain Mapping* 33 (4): 920–37.

Roux, F., and P. J. Uhlhaas. 2014. 'Working Memory and Neural Oscillations: α-γ versus θ-γ Codes for Distinct WM Information?' *Trends in Cognitive Sciences* 18 (1): 16–25.

Røysamb, E., and K. Tambs. 2016. 'The Beauty, Logic and Limitations of Twin Studies'. *Norsk Epidemiologi* 26 (1–2). https://doi.org/10.5324/nje.v26i1-2.2014.

Roze, E., L. Meijer, A. Bakker, et al. 2009. 'Prenatal Exposure to Organohalogens, Including Brominated Flame Retardants, Influences Motor, Cognitive, and Behavioral Performance at School Age'. *Environmental Health Perspectives* 117 (12): 1953–8.

Rozisky, J. R., G. Laste, I. C. de Macedo, et al. 2013. 'Neonatal Morphine Administration Leads to Changes in Hippocampal BDNF Levels and Antioxidant Enzyme Activity in the Adult Life of Rats'. *Neurochemical Research* 38 (3): 494–503.

Rubenstein, J. L. R., and M. M. Merzenich. 2003. 'Model of Autism: Increased Ratio of Excitation/inhibition in Key Neural Systems'. *Genes, Brain, and Behavior* 2 (5): 255–67.

Rubinsten, O., and A. Henik. 2005. 'Automatic Activation of Internal Magnitudes: A Study of Developmental Dyscalculia'. *Neuropsychology* 19 (5): 641–8.

——— 2006. 'Double Dissociation of Functions in Developmental Dyslexia and Dyscalculia'. *Journal of Educational Psychology* 98 (4): 854–67. https://doi.org/10.1037/0022-0663.98.4.854.

——— 2009. 'Developmental Dyscalculia: Heterogeneity Might Not Mean Different Mechanisms'. *Trends in Cognitive Sciences* 13 (2): P92–9. https://doi.org/10.1016/j.tics.2008.11.002.

Rucinski, M., A. Cangelosi, and T. Belpaeme. 2012. 'Robotic Model of the Contribution of Gesture to Learning to Count'. *2012 IEEE International Conference on Development and Learning and Epigenetic Robotics (ICDL)*. https://doi.org/10.1109/devlrn.2012.6400579.

Rückinger, S., P. Rzehak, C.-M. Chen, et al. 2010. 'Prenatal and Postnatal Tobacco Exposure and Behavioral Problems in 10-Year-Old Children: Results from the GINI-plus Prospective Birth Cohort Study'. *Environmental Health Perspectives* 118 (1): 150–4.

Rule, M. E., A. R. Loback, D. V. Raman, et al. 'Stable Task Information from an Unstable Neural Population'. *eLife* 9 (July). https://doi.org/10.7554/eLife.51121.

Rumelhart, D. E., and McClelland, J. L. (1986). *Parallel Distributed Processing: Explorations in the Microstructure of Cognition. Volume 1: Foundations* (Vol. 1; D. E. Rumelhart & J. L. McClelland, eds.). Cambridge, MA: MIT Press.

Rumelhart, D. E., G. E. Hinton, and R. J. Williams. 1986. 'Learning Representations by Back-Propagating Errors'. *Nature* 323 (6088): 533–6.

Rüsseler, J., S. Probst, S. Johannes, and T. Münte. 2003. 'Recognition Memory for High- and Low-Frequency Words in Adult Normal and Dyslexic Readers: An Event-Related Brain Potential Study'. *Journal of Clinical and Experimental Neuropsychology* 25 (6): 815–29.

Rykhlevskaia, E., L. Q. Uddin, L. Kondos, and V. Menon. 2009. 'Neuroanatomical Correlates of Developmental Dyscalculia: Combined Evidence from Morphometry and Tractography'. *Frontiers in Human Neuroscience* 3 (November): 51.

Sabatier, P. A. and D. Mazmanian. 1983. 'Policy Implementation'. In M. Dekker (ed.), Encyclopedia of Policy Studies, 43–69. Start Nagel.

Saez, T. M. M., M. P. Aronne, L. Caltana, and A. H. Brusco. 2014. 'Prenatal Exposure to the CB1 and CB2 Cannabinoid Receptor Agonist WIN 55,212-2 Alters Migration of Early-Born Glutamatergic Neurons and GABAergic Interneurons in the Rat Cerebral Cortex'. *Journal of Neurochemistry* 129 (4): 637–48.

Saffran, J. R. 2001. 'Words in a Sea of Sounds: The Output of Infant Statistical Learning'. *Cognition* 81 (2): 149–69.

Sahu, J. K., S. Sharma, M. Kamate, et al. 2010. 'Lead Encephalopathy in an Infant Mimicking a Neurometabolic Disorder'. *Journal of Child Neurology* 25 (3): 390–2.

Saigal, S., and L. W. Doyle. 2008. 'An Overview of Mortality and Sequelae of Preterm Birth from Infancy to Adulthood'. *The Lancet* 371 (9608): 261–9.

Saksida, A., S. Iannuzzi, C. Bogliotti, et al. 2016. 'Phonological Skills, Visual Attention Span, and Visual Stress in Developmental Dyslexia'. *Developmental Psychology* 52 (10): 1503–16.

Sampaio-Baptista, C., and H. Johansen-Berg. 2017. 'White Matter Plasticity in the Adult Brain'. *Neuron* 96 (6): 1239–51.

Santhanam, P., Z. Li, X. Hu, M. E. Lynch, and C. D. Coles. 2009. 'Effects of Prenatal Alcohol Exposure on Brain Activation during an Arithmetic Task: An fMRI Study'. *Alcoholism, Clinical and Experimental Research* 33 (11): 1901–8.

Sarason, I. G. 1984. 'Stress, Anxiety, and Cognitive Interference: Reactions to Tests'. *Journal of Personality and Social Psychology* 46 (4): 929–38.

——— 1988. 'Anxiety, Self-Preoccupation and Attention'. *Anxiety Research* 1 (1): 3–7.

Sasanguie, D., and H. Vos. 2018. 'About Why There Is a Shift from Cardinal to Ordinal Processing in the Association with Arithmetic between First and Second Grade'. *Developmental Science* 21 (5): e12653.

Sathian, K., T. J. Simon, S. Peterson, et al. 1999. 'Neural Evidence Linking Visual Object Enumeration and Attention'. *Journal of Cognitive Neuroscience* 11 (1): 36–51.

Saygin, Z. M., D. E. Osher, E. S. Norton, et al. 2016. 'Connectivity Precedes Function in the Development of the Visual Word Form Area'. *Nature Neuroscience* 19 (9): 1250–5.

Scheinost, D., R. Sinha, S. N. Cross, et al. 2017. 'Does Prenatal Stress Alter the Developing Connectome?' *Pediatric Research* 81 (1-2): 214–26.

Schel, M. A., and T. Klingberg. 2017. 'Specialization of the Right Intraparietal Sulcus for Processing Mathematics During Development'. *Cerebral Cortex* 27 (9): 4436–46.

Schiavone, G., K. Linkenkaer-Hansen, N. M. Maurits, et al. 2014. 'Preliteracy Signatures of Poor-Reading Abilities in Resting-State EEG'. *Frontiers in Human Neuroscience* 8 (September): 735.

Schillinger, F. L., S. E. Vogel, J. Diedrich, and R. H. Grabner. 2018. 'Math Anxiety, Intelligence, and Performance in Mathematics: Insights from the German Adaptation of the Abbreviated Math Anxiety Scale (AMAS-G)'. *Learning and Individual Differences* 61 (January): 109–19.

Schleifer, P., and K. Landerl. 2011. 'Subitizing and Counting in Typical and Atypical Development'. *Developmental Science* 14 (2): 280–91.

Schlichting, M. L., J. A. Mumford, and A. R. Preston. 2015. 'Learning-Related Representational Changes Reveal Dissociable Integration and Separation Signatures in the Hippocampus and Prefrontal Cortex'. *Nature Communications* 6 (August): 8151.

Schmalz, X., G. Altoè, and C. Mulatti. 2017. 'Statistical Learning and Dyslexia: A Systematic Review'. *Annals of Dyslexia* 67 (2): 147–62.

Schneider, W. 2009. 'The Development of Reading and Spelling: Relevant Precursors, Developmental Changes, and Individual Differences'. In W. Schneider and M. Bullock (eds.), *Human development from early childhood to early adulthood: Findings from a 20 year longitudinal study*, 199–220. Psychology Press.

Schneider, M., K. Beeres, L. Coban, et al. 2017. 'Associations of Non-Symbolic and Symbolic Numerical Magnitude Processing with Mathematical Competence: A Meta-Analysis'. *Developmental Science* 20 (3): e12372. https://doi.org/10.1111/desc.12372.

Schneider, M., S. Merz, J. Stricker, et al. 2018. 'Associations of Number Line Estimation with Mathematical Competence: A Meta-Analysis'. *Child Development* 89 (5): 1467–84.

Schneider, W., E. Roth, and M. Ennemoser. 2000. 'Training Phonological Skills and Letter Knowledge in Children at Risk for Dyslexia: A Comparison of Three Kindergarten Intervention Programs'. *Journal of Educational Psychology* 92 (2): 284–95. https://doi.org/10.1037/0022-0663.92.2.284.

Schneider, W., Blanke, I., Faust, V., Küspert, P. (2011). Würzburger Leise Leseprobe-Revision (WLLP-R). Hogrefe, Göttingen

Steinbrink, C., Klatte, M., & Lachmann, T. (2014). Phonological, temporal and spectral processing in vowel length discrimination is impaired in German primary school children with developmental dyslexia. *Research in Developmental Disabilities*, 35 (11), 3034–3045. https://doi.org/10.1016/j.ridd.2014.07.049.

Schneps, M. H., J. R. Brockmole, G. Sonnert, and M. Pomplun. 2012. 'History of Reading Struggles Linked to Enhanced Learning in Low Spatial Frequency Scenes'. *PloS One* 7 (4): e35724.

Schneps, M. H., J. M. Thomson, G. Sonnert, et al. 2013. 'Shorter Lines Facilitate Reading in Those Who Struggle'. *PloS One* 8 (8): e71161.

Schöneich, S., K. Kostarakos, and B. Hedwig. 2015. 'An Auditory Feature Detection Circuit for Sound Pattern Recognition'. *Science Advances* 1 (8): e1500325.

Schulte-Körne, G., J. Bartling, W. Deimel, and H. Remschmidt. 2004. 'Motion-Onset VEPs in Dyslexia. Evidence for Visual Perceptual Deficit'. *Neuroreport* 15 (6): 1075–8.

Schwartz, F., J. Epinat-Duclos, J. Léone, A. Poisson, and J. Prado. 2018. 'Impaired Neural Processing of Transitive Relations in Children with Math Learning Difficulty'. *NeuroImage. Clinical* 20 (October): 1255–65.

2020. 'Neural Representations of Transitive Relations Predict Current and Future Math Calculation Skills in Children'. *Neuropsychologia* 141 (April): 107410.

Schwartzman, A., R. F. Dougherty, and J. E. Taylor. 2005. 'Cross-Subject Comparison of Principal Diffusion Direction Maps'. *Magnetic Resonance in Medicine: Official Journal of the Society of Magnetic Resonance in Medicine / Society of Magnetic Resonance in Medicine* 53 (6): 1423–31.

Scientific Studies of Reading. 2020. 24 (1). www.tandfonline.com/toc/hssr20/24/1?nav=tocList.

Scott, J. A., C. W. Binns, W. H. Oddy, and K. I. Graham. 2006. 'Predictors of Breastfeeding Duration: Evidence from a Cohort Study'. *Pediatrics* 117 (4): e646–55.

Seidenberg, M. S., and J. L. McClelland. 1989. 'A Distributed, Developmental Model of Word Recognition and Naming'. *Psychological Review* 96 (4): 523–68.

Seipp, B. 1991. 'Anxiety and Academic Performance: A Meta-Analysis of Findings'. *Anxiety Research* 4 (1): 27–41.

Sella, F., I. Berteletti, D. Lucangeli, and M. Zorzi. 2016. 'Spontaneous Non-Verbal Counting in Toddlers'. *Developmental Science* 19 (2): 329–37.

Semeraro, C., D. Giofrè, G. Coppola, D. Lucangeli, and R. Cassibba. 2020. 'The Role of Cognitive and Non-Cognitive Factors in Mathematics Achievement: The Importance of the Quality of the Student-Teacher Relationship in Middle School'. *PloS One* 15 (4): e0231381.

Serniclaes, W., S. Van Heghe, P. Mousty, R. Carré, and L. Sprenger-Charolles. 2004. 'Allophonic Mode of Speech Perception in Dyslexia'. *Journal of Experimental Child Psychology* 87 (4): 336–61.

Shafrir, U., and L. S. Siegel. 1994. 'Subtypes of Learning Disabilities in Adolescents and Adults'. *Journal of Learning Disabilities.* 27 (2): 123–4 https://doi.org/10.1177/002221949402700207.

Shalev, R. S., O. Manor, B. Kerem, et al. 2001. 'Developmental Dyscalculia Is a Familial Learning Disability'. *Journal of Learning Disabilities* 34 (1): 59–65.

Share, D. L. 1995. 'Phonological Recoding and Self-Teaching: Sine qua Non of Reading Acquisition'. *Cognition* 55 (2): 151–218; discussion 219–26.

Sharma, A., and A. L. Brody. 2009. 'In Vivo Brain Imaging of Human Exposure to Nicotine and Tobacco'. *Handbook of Experimental Pharmacology*, 192: 145–71.

Shaywitz, S. E., and B. A. Shaywitz. 2008. Paying Attention to Reading: The Neurobiology of Reading and Dyslexia. Dev. Psychopathol. 20, 1329–49.

Shaywitz, B. A., S. E. Shaywitz, B. A. Blachman, et al. 2004. 'Development of Left Occipitotemporal Systems for Skilled Reading in Children after a Phonologically-Based Intervention'. *Biological Psychiatry* 55 (9): 926–33.

Shaywitz, B. A., S. E. Shaywitz, K. R. Pugh, et al. 2002. 'Disruption of Posterior Brain Systems for Reading in Children with Developmental Dyslexia'. *Biological Psychiatry* 52 (2): 101–10.

Sheffield, J. G., G. Raz, F. Sella, and R. Cohen Kadosh. 2022. How Can Noise Alter Neurophysiology in Order to Improve Human Behaviour? A Combined Transcranial Random Noise Stimulation and Electroencephalography Study. bioRxiv 2020.01.09.900118; https://doi.org/10.1101/2020.01.09.900118.

Sheehan, M. C., T. A. Burke, A. Navas-Acien, et al. 2014. 'Global Methylmercury Exposure from Seafood Consumption and Risk of Developmental Neurotoxicity: A Systematic Review'. *Bulletin of the World Health Organization* 92 (4): 254–69F.

Shohamy, D., and A. D. Wagner. 2008. 'Integrating Memories in the Human Brain: Hippocampal-Midbrain Encoding of Overlapping Events'. *Neuron* 60 (2): 378–89.

Shuey, E. A., & Kankaraš, M. 2018. 'The Power and Promise of Early Learning'. *OECD Education Working Papers*, (186), 0_1-100.

Siddiqi, M. A.l, R. H. Laessig, and K. D. Reed. 2003. 'Polybrominated Diphenyl Ethers (PBDEs): New Pollutants-Old Diseases'. *Clinical Medicine & Research* 1 (4): 281–90.

Sie, L. T., M. S. van der Knaap, J. Oosting, et al. 2000. 'MR Patterns of Hypoxic-Ischemic Brain Damage after Prenatal, Perinatal or Postnatal Asphyxia'. *Neuropediatrics* 31 (3): 128–36.

Siegler, R. S., and J. Shrager. 1984. Strategy Choice in Addition and Subtraction: How do Children Know What to Do? In C. Sophian (ed.), Origins of Cognitive Skills, 229–93. Erlbaum.

Silva, A. M., P. B. Júdice, C. N. Matias, et al. 2013. 'Total Body Water and Its Compartments Are Not Affected by Ingesting a Moderate Dose of Caffeine in Healthy Young Adult Males'. *Applied Physiology, Nutrition, and Metabolism = Physiologie Appliquee, Nutrition et Metabolisme* 38 (6): 626–32.

SiMERR National Research Centre. 2021. QuickSmart - Narrowing the Achievement Gap. QuickSmart Overview 2021.

Simmons, F. R., and C. Singleton. 2006. 'The Mental and Written Arithmetic Abilities of Adults with Dyslexia'. *Dyslexia* 12 (2): 96–114.

Simms, V., L. Cragg, C. Gilmore, N. Marlow, and S. Johnson. 2013. 'Mathematics Difficulties in Children Born Very Preterm: Current Research and Future Directions'. *Archives of Disease in Childhood: Fetal and Neonatal Edition* 98 (5): F457–63.

Simms, V., C. Gilmore, L. Cragg, et al. 2015. 'Nature and Origins of Mathematics Difficulties in Very Preterm Children: A Different Etiology than Developmental Dyscalculia'. *Pediatric Research* 77 (2): 389–95.

Simos, P. G., J. M. Fletcher, S. Sarkari, et al. 2007. 'Intensive Instruction Affects Brain Magnetic Activity Associated with Oral Word Reading in Children with Persistent Reading Disabilities'. *Journal of Learning Disabilities* 40 (1): 37–48.

Siok, W. T., C. A. Perfetti, Z. Jin, and L. H. Tan. 2004. 'Biological Abnormality of Impaired Reading Is Constrained by Culture'. *Nature* 431 (7004): 71–6.

Sireteanu, R., C. Goebel, R. Goertz, et al. 2008. 'Impaired Serial Visual Search in Children with Developmental Dyslexia'. *Annals of the New York Academy of Sciences* 1145 (December): 199–211.

Sirnes, E., L. Oltedal, H. Bartsch, et al. 2017. 'Brain Morphology in School-Aged Children with Prenatal Opioid Exposure: A Structural MRI Study'. *Early Human Development* 106–7 (March): 33–9.

Sister Mary Fides Gough, O. P. 1954. 'Why Failures in Mathematics? Mathemaphobia: Causes and Treatments'. *The Clearing House: A Journal of Educational Strategies, Issues and Ideas* 28 (5): 290–4.

Skagerlund, K., T. Bolt, J. S. Nomi, et al. 2019. 'Disentangling Mathematics from Executive Functions by Investigating Unique Functional Connectivity Patterns Predictive of Mathematics Ability'. *Journal of Cognitive Neuroscience* 31 (4): 560–73.

Skagerlund, Kenny, and Ulf Träff. 2016a. 'Number Processing and Heterogeneity of Developmental Dyscalculia'. *Journal of Learning Disabilities* 49 (1): 36–50. https://doi.org/10.1177/0022219414522707.

   2016b. 'Number Processing and Heterogeneity of Developmental Dyscalculia: Subtypes With Different Cognitive Profiles and Deficits'. *Journal of Learning Disabilities* 49 (1): 36–50.

Skeide, M. A., T. M. Evans, E. Z. Mei, D. A. Abrams, and V. Menon. 2018. 'Neural Signatures of Co-Occurring Reading and Mathematical Difficulties'. *Developmental Science* 21 (6): e12680.

Skeide, M. A., and A. D. Friederici. 2016. 'The Ontogeny of the Cortical Language Network'. *Nature Reviews. Neuroscience* 17 (5): 323–32.

Skeide, M. A., H. Kirsten, I. Kraft, et al. 2015. 'Genetic Dyslexia Risk Variant Is Related to Neural Connectivity Patterns Underlying Phonological Awareness in Children'. *NeuroImage* 118: 414–21. https://doi.org/10.1016/j.neuroimage.2015.06.024.

Skeide, M. A., I. Kraft, B. Muller, et al. 2016. 'NRSN1 Associated Grey Matter Volume Profiles in the Visual Word Form Area Reveal Dyslexia before It Manifests Itself in School'. *Brain: A Journal of Neurology* 39 (10): 2792–803. https://doi.org/10.1093/brain/aww153.

Skeide, M. A., U. Kumar, R. K. Mishra, et al. 2017. 'Learning to Read Alters Cortico-subcortical Cross-talk in the Visual System of Illiterates'. *Science Advances* 3 (5): e1602612.

Skeide, M. A., K. Wehrmann, Z. Emami, et al. 2020. 'Neurobiological Origins of Individual Differences in Mathematical Ability'. *PLOS Biology* 18 (10): 24 (4): 387–400. https://doi.org/10.1371/journal.pbio.3000871.

Slot, E. M., S. van Viersen, E. H. de Bree, and E. H. Kroesbergen. 2016. 'Shared and Unique Risk Factors Underlying Mathematical Disability and Reading and Spelling Disability'. *Frontiers in Psychology* 7 (June): 803.

Smedt, B. De, M.-P. Noël, C. Gilmore, and D. Ansari. 2013. 'How Do Symbolic and Non-Symbolic Numerical Magnitude Processing Skills Relate to Individual Differences in Children's Mathematical Skills? A Review of Evidence from Brain and Behavior'. *Trends in Neuroscience and Education* 2 (2): 48–55. https://doi.org/10.1016/j.tine.2013.06.001.

Smedt, B. De, J. Taylor, L. Archibald, and D. Ansari. 2010. 'How Is Phonological Processing Related to Individual Differences in Children's Arithmetic Skills?' *Developmental Science* 13 (3): 508–20. https://doi.org/10.1111/j.1467-7687.2009.00897.x.

Smit, D. J. A., D. I. Boomsma, H. G. Schnack, H. E. Hulshoff Pol, and E. J. C. de Geus. 2012. 'Individual Differences in EEG Spectral Power Reflect Genetic Variance in Gray and White Matter Volumes'. *Twin Research and Human Genetics: The Official Journal of the International Society for Twin Studies* 15 (3): 384–92.

Smith, C. N., and L. R. Squire. 2009. 'Medial Temporal Lobe Activity during Retrieval of Semantic Memory Is Related to the Age of the Memory'. *The Journal of Neuroscience: The Official Journal of the Society for Neuroscience* 29 (4): 930–8.

Smith, G. J., J. R. Booth, and C. McNorgan. 2018. 'Longitudinal Task-Related Functional Connectivity Changes Predict Reading Development'. *Frontiers in Psychology* 9 (September): 1754.

Snowling, M. J., and M. E. Hayiou-Thomas. 2006. 'The Dyslexia Spectrum: Continuities between Reading, Speech, and Language Impairments'. *Topics in Language Disorders* 26 (2): 110.

Snowling, M. J., and M. Melby-Lervåg. 2016. 'Oral Language Deficits in Familial Dyslexia: A Meta-Analysis and Review'. *Psychological Bulletin* 142 (5): 498–545.

Sokolowski, H. M., W. Fias, A. Mousa, and D. Ansari. 2017. 'Common and Distinct Brain Regions in Both Parietal and Frontal Cortex Support Symbolic and Nonsymbolic Number Processing in Humans: A Functional Neuroimaging Meta-Analysis'. *NeuroImage* 146 (February): 376–94.

Solon, O., T. J. Riddell, S. A. Quimbo, et al. 2008. 'Associations between Cognitive Function, Blood Lead Concentration, and Nutrition among Children in the Central Philippines'. *The Journal of Pediatrics* 152 (2): 237–43.

Soltanlou, M., C. Artemenko, A.-C. Ehlis, et al. 2018. 'Reduction but No Shift in Brain Activation after Arithmetic Learning in Children: A Simultaneous fNIRS-EEG Study'. *Scientific Reports* 8: 1707. https://doi.org/10.1038/s41598-018-20007-x.

Soltész, F., D. Szűcs, J. Dékány, A. Márkus, and V. Csépe. 2007. 'A Combined Event-Related Potential and Neuropsychological Investigation of Developmental Dyscalculia'. *Neuroscience Letters* 417 (2): 181–6.

Song, S., Y. Zhang, H. Shu, M. Su, C. McBride. 2020. 'Universal and Specific Predictors of Chinese Children With Dyslexia: Exploring the Cognitive Deficits and Subtypes'. Front Psychol. 10: 2904. doi: 10.3389/fpsyg.2019.02904.

Soni, A., and S. Kumari. 2017. 'The Role of Parental Math Anxiety and Math Attitude in Their Children's Math Achievement'. *International Journal of Science and Mathematics Education* 15 (2): 331–47.

Sonuga-Barke, E. J. S., J. A. Sergeant, J. Nigg, and E. Willcutt. 2008. 'Executive Dysfunction and Delay Aversion in Attention Deficit Hyperactivity Disorder: Nosologic and Diagnostic Implications'. *Child and Adolescent Psychiatric Clinics of North America* 17 (2): 367–84.

Sood, B., V. Delaney-Black, C. Covington, et al. 2001. 'Prenatal Alcohol Exposure and Childhood Behavior at Age 6 to 7 Years: I. Dose-Response Effect'. *Pediatrics* 108 (2): E34.

Sowell, E. R., L. H. Lu, E. D. O'Hare, et al. 2007. 'Functional Magnetic Resonance Imaging of Verbal Learning in Children with Heavy Prenatal Alcohol Exposure'. *Neuroreport* 18 (7): 635–9.

Spadoni, A. D., A. D. Bazinet, S. L. Fryer, et al. 2009. 'BOLD Response during Spatial Working Memory in Youth with Heavy Prenatal Alcohol Exposure'. *Alcoholism, Clinical and Experimental Research* 33 (12): 2067–76.

Spencer, S. J., C. M. Steele, and D. M. Quinn. 1999. 'Stereotype Threat and Women's Math Performance'. *Journal of Experimental Social Psychology* 35 (1): 4–28.

Sperling, A. J., Z.-L. Lu, F. R. Manis, and M. S. Seidenberg. 2005. 'Deficits in Perceptual Noise Exclusion in Developmental Dyslexia'. *Nature Neuroscience* 8 (7): 862–3.

Starr, A., N. K. DeWind, and E. M. Brannon. 2017. 'The Contributions of Numerical Acuity and Non-Numerical Stimulus Features to the Development of the Number Sense and Symbolic Math Achievement'. *Cognition* 168 (November): 222–33.

Starr, A., M. E. Libertus, and E. M. Brannon. 2013. 'Number Sense in Infancy Predicts Mathematical Abilities in Childhood'. *Proceedings of the National Academy of Sciences of the United States of America* 110 (45): 18116–20.

Staskal, D. F., J. J. Diliberto, and L. S. Birnbaum. 2006. 'Disposition of BDE 47 in Developing Mice'. *Toxicological Sciences: An Official Journal of the Society of Toxicology* 90 (2): 309–16.

Steckler, T., and A. Sahgal. 1995. 'The Role of Serotonergic-Cholinergic Interactions in the Mediation of Cognitive Behaviour'. *Behavioural Brain Research* 67 (2): 165–99.

Stein, John. 2014. 'Dyslexia: The Role of Vision and Visual Attention'. *Current Developmental Disorders Reports* 1 (4): 267–80.

⸻ 2019. 'The Current Status of the Magnocellular Theory of Developmental Dyslexia'. *Neuropsychologia* 130 (July): 66–77.

Stein, J., and V. Walsh. 1997. 'To See but Not to Read; the Magnocellular Theory of Dyslexia'. *Trends in Neurosciences* 20 (4): 147–52.

Stewart, P., S. Fitzgerald, J. Reihman, et al. 2003. 'Prenatal PCB Exposure, the Corpus Callosum, and Response Inhibition'. *Environmental Health Perspectives* 111 (13): 1670–7.

Stewart, P. W., E. Lonky, J. Reihman, et al. 2008. 'The Relationship between Prenatal PCB Exposure and Intelligence (IQ) in 9-Year-Old Children'. *Environmental Health Perspectives* 116 (10): 1416–22.

Stigler, J. W. 1984. '"Mental Abacus": The Effect of Abacus Training on Chinese Children's Mental Calculation'. *Cognitive Psychology* 16 (2): 145–76.

Stinson, L. F., M. S. Payne, and J. A. Keelan. 2018. 'A Critical Review of the Bacterial Baptism Hypothesis and the Impact of Cesarean Delivery on the Infant Microbiome'. *Frontiers of Medicine* 5 (May): 135.

Stockholm Convention. n.d. 'Guidance for the Inventory of PBDEs'. Accessed July 21, 2021a. http://chm.pops.int/Implementation/NIPs/Guidance/Guidanceforthe inventoryofPBDEs/tabid/3171/Default.aspx.

——— n.d. 'Stockholm Convention > Implementation > Industrial POPs > PCB > PCB Elimination Network > PEN Overview > Related Articles and Links > PCBs Info Exchange Platform'. Accessed July 21, 2021b. http://chm.pops.int/Default.aspx?tabid=3016.

Stoet, G., and D. C. Geary. 2015. 'Sex Differences in Academic Achievement Are Not Related to Political, Economic, or Social Equality'. *Intelligence* 48 (January): 137–51.

Stoianov, I. P., and M. Zorzi. 2017. 'Computational Foundations of the Visual Number Sense'. *Behavioral and Brain Sciences* 40: e191. https://doi.org/10.1017/s0140525x16002326.

Stoianov, I., and M. Zorzi. 2012. 'Emergence of a "Visual Number Sense" in Hierarchical Generative Models'. *Nature Neuroscience* 15 (2): 194–6.

Stoianov, I., M. Zorzi, and C. Umiltà. 2004. 'The Role of Semantic and Symbolic Representations in Arithmetic Processing: Insights from Simulated Dyscalculia in a Connectionist Model'. *Cortex; a Journal Devoted to the Study of the Nervous System and Behavior* 40 (1): 194–6.

Stoll, B. J., N. I. Hansen, I. Adams-Chapman, et al. 2004. 'Neurodevelopmental and Growth Impairment among Extremely Low-Birth-Weight Infants with Neonatal Infection'. *JAMA: The Journal of the American Medical Association* 292 (19): 2357–65.

Strand, S., A. De Coulon, E. Meschi, et al. 2010. Drivers and Challenges in Raising the Achievement of Pupils from Bangladeshi, Somali and Turkish Backgrounds. Research Report DCSF-RR226. Department for Children School and Families.

Stromswold, K. 2001. 'The Heritability of Language: A Review and Metaanalysis of Twin, Adoption, and Linkage Studies'. *Language* 77 (4): 647–723.

Strong, G. K., C. J. Torgerson, D. Torgerson, and C. Hulme. 2011. 'A Systematic Meta-Analytic Review of Evidence for the Effectiveness of the "Fast ForWord" Language Intervention Program'. *Journal of Child Psychology and Psychiatry, and Allied Disciplines* 52 (3): 224–35.

Suinn, R. M., and E. H. Winston. 2003. 'The Mathematics Anxiety Rating Scale, a Brief Version: Psychometric Data'. *Psychological Reports* 92 (1): 167–73.

Suinn, R. M., C. A. Edie, J. Nicoletti, and P. R. Spinelli. 1972. 'The MARS, a Measure of Mathematics Anxiety: Psychometric Data'. *Journal of Clinical Psychology* 28 (3): 373–5.

Supekar, K., T. Iuculano, L. Chen, and V. Menon. 2015. 'Remediation of Childhood Math Anxiety and Associated Neural Circuits through Cognitive Tutoring'. *The Journal of Neuroscience: The Official Journal of the Society for Neuroscience* 35 (36): 12574–83.

Supekar, K., A. G. Swigart, C. Tenison, et al. 2013. 'Neural Predictors of Individual Differences in Response to Math Tutoring in Primary-Grade School Children'. *Proceedings of the National Academy of Sciences of the United States of America* 110 (20): 8230–5.

Sutskever, I., O. Vinyals, and Q. V. Le. 2014. 'Sequence to Sequence Learning with Neural Networks'. In *Advances in Neural Information Processing Systems*, edited by Z. Ghahramani, M. Welling, C. Cortes, N. Lawrence, and K. Q. Weinberger. Vol. 27. Curran Associates, Inc. https://proceedings.neurips.cc/paper/2014/file/a14ac55a4f27472c5d894ec1c3c743d2-Paper.pdf.

Suttie, M., L. Wetherill, S. W. Jacobson, et al. 2017. 'Facial Curvature Detects and Explicates Ethnic Differences in Effects of Prenatal Alcohol Exposure'. *Alcoholism, Clinical and Experimental Research* 41 (8): 1471–83.

Sutton, E. F., L. A. Gilmore, D. B. Dunger, et al. 2016. 'Developmental Programming: State-of-the-Science and Future Directions-Summary from a Pennington Biomedical Symposium'. *Obesity* 24 (5): 1018–26.

Sutton, R. S., and A. G. Barto. 1998. 'Reinforcement Learning: An Introduction'. *IEEE Transactions on Neural Networks*. https://doi.org/10.1109/tnn.1998.712192.

Sverrisson, F. A., B. T. Bateman, T. Aspelund, S. Skulason, and H. Zoega. 2018. 'Preeclampsia and Academic Performance in Children: A Nationwide Study from Iceland'. *PloS One* 13 (11): e0207884.

Swanson, H. L., H. Lee Swanson, and O. Jerman. 2006. 'Math Disabilities: A Selective Meta-Analysis of the Literature'. *Review of Educational Research* 76 (2): 249–74. https://doi.org/10.3102/00346543076002249.

Szczygieł, M. 2020. 'When Does Math Anxiety in Parents and Teachers Predict Math Anxiety and Math Achievement in Elementary School Children? The Role of Gender and Grade Year'. *Social Psychology of Education: An International Journal* 23 (4): 1023–54.

Szkudlarek, E., and E. M. Brannon. 2017. 'Does the Approximate Number System Serve as a Foundation for Symbolic Mathematics?' *Language Learning and Development: The Official Journal of the Society for Language Development* 13 (2): 171–90.

Szűcs, D. 2016. 'Subtypes and Comorbidity in Mathematical Learning Disabilities'. *Progress in Brain Research*. 227: 277–304. https://doi.org/10.1016/bs.pbr.2016.04.027.

Szűcs, D., A. Devine, F. Soltesz, A. Nobes, and F. Gabriel. 2013. 'Developmental Dyscalculia Is Related to Visuo-Spatial Memory and Inhibition Impairment'. *Cortex; a Journal Devoted to the Study of the Nervous System and Behavior* 49 (10): 2674–88.

Szűcs, D., A. Devine, F. Soltesz, A. Nobes, and F. Gabriel. 2014. 'Cognitive Components of a Mathematical Processing Network in 9-Year-Old Children'. *Developmental Science* 17 (4): 506–24.

Szűcs, D., and U. Goswami. 2013. 'Developmental Dyscalculia: Fresh Perspectives'. *Trends in Neuroscience and Education* 2 (2): 33–7.

Szűcs, D., and J. P. A. Ioannidis. 2017. 'When Null Hypothesis Significance Testing Is Unsuitable for Research: A Reassessment'. *Frontiers in Human Neuroscience* 11 (August): 390.

Szűcs, D., and I. C. Mammarella. 2020. 'Math Anxiety. Educational Practices Series 31'. *UNESCO International Bureau of Education*. www.ibe.unesco.org/sites/default/files/resources/31_math_anxiety_web.pdf.

Takashima, A., I. L. C. Nieuwenhuis, O. Jensen, et al. 2009. 'Shift from Hippocampal to Neocortical Centered Retrieval Network with Consolidation'. *The Journal of Neuroscience: The Official Journal of the Society for Neuroscience* 29 (32): 10087–93.

Takeuchi, H., Y. Taki, Y. Sassa, et al. 2011. 'Working Memory Training Using Mental Calculation Impacts Regional Gray Matter of the Frontal and Parietal Regions'. *PloS One* 6 (8): e23175.

Tallal, P. 1980. 'Auditory Temporal Perception, Phonics, and Reading Disabilities in Children'. *Brain and Language* 9 (2): 182–98. https://doi.org/10.1016/0093-934x (80)90139-x.

———. 2004. 'Improving Language and Literacy Is a Matter of Time'. *Nature Reviews. Neuroscience* 5 (9): 721–8.

Tallal, P., and M. Piercy. 1973. 'Defects of Non-Verbal Auditory Perception in Children with Developmental Aphasia'. *Nature* 241 (5390): 468–9.

Tanaka, J. W., and T. Curran. 2001. 'A Neural Basis for Expert Object Recognition'. *Psychological Science* 12 (1): 43–7.

Tanda, R., P. J. Salsberry, P. B. Reagan, and M. Z. Fang. 2013. 'The Impact of Prepregnancy Obesity on Children's Cognitive Test Scores'. *Maternal and Child Health Journal* 17 (2): 222–9.

Taylor, J., A. D. Roehrig, B. Soden Hensler, C. M. Connor, and C. Schatschneider. 2010. 'Teacher Quality Moderates the Genetic Effects on Early Reading'. *Science* 328 (5977): 512–14.

Taylor, J. S. H., M. H. Davis, and Kathleen Rastle. 2019. 'Mapping Visual Symbols onto Spoken Language along the Ventral Visual Stream'. *Proceedings of the National Academy of Sciences of the United States of America* 116 (36): 17723–8.

Temple, E., G. K. Deutsch, R. A. Poldrack, et al. 2003. 'Neural Deficits in Children with Dyslexia Ameliorated by Behavioral Remediation: Evidence from Functional MRI'. *Proceedings of the National Academy of Sciences of the United States of America* 100 (5): 2860–5.

Temple, J. L., C. Bernard, S. E. Lipshultz, et al. 2017. 'The Safety of Ingested Caffeine: A Comprehensive Review'. *Frontiers in Psychiatry/Frontiers Research Foundation* 8 (May): 80.

Tenison, C., J. M. Fincham, and J. R. Anderson. 2014. 'Detecting Math Problem Solving Strategies: An Investigation into the Use of Retrospective Self-Reports, Latency and fMRI Data'. *Neuropsychologia* 54 (February): 41–52.

Terplan, M., E. J. Smith, M. J. Kozloski, and H. A. Pollack. 2009. 'Methamphetamine Use among Pregnant Women'. *Obstetrics and Gynecology* 113 (6): 1285–91.

Testolin, A. 2020. 'The Challenge of Modeling the Acquisition of Mathematical Concepts'. *Frontiers in Human Neuroscience* 14 (March): 100.

Testolin, A., Dolfi, S., Rochus, M., and Zorzi, M. (2020a). 'Visual sense of number vs. sense of magnitude in humans and machines'. *Scientific Reports, 10*(1), 1 –13.

Testolin, A., I. Stoianov, M. De Filippo De Grazia, and M. Zorzi. 2013. 'Deep Unsupervised Learning on a Desktop PC: A Primer for Cognitive Scientists'. *Frontiers in Psychology* 4 (May): 251.

Testolin, A., I. Stoianov, A. Sperduti, and M. Zorzi. 2016. 'Learning Orthographic Structure With Sequential Generative Neural Networks'. *Cognitive Science* 40 (3): 579–606.

Testolin, A., I. Stoianov, and M. Zorzi. 2017. 'Letter Perception Emerges from Unsupervised Deep Learning and Recycling of Natural Image Features'. *Nature Human Behaviour* 1 (9): 657–64.

Testolin, A., and M. Zorzi. 2016. 'Probabilistic Models and Generative Neural Networks: Towards an Unified Framework for Modeling Normal and Impaired Neurocognitive Functions'. *Frontiers in Computational Neuroscience* 10 (July): 73.

Testolin, A., W. Y. Zou, and J. L. McClelland. 2020b. 'Numerosity Discrimination in Deep Neural Networks: Initial Competence, Developmental Refinement and Experience Statistics'. *Developmental Science* 23 (5): e12940.

Thomas, M. S. C., A. Fedor, R. Davis, et al. 2019. 'Computational Modeling of Interventions for Developmental Disorders'. *Psychological Review* 126 (5): 693–726.

Thomas, M. S. C., and A. Karmiloff-Smith. 2003. 'Modeling Language Acquisition in Atypical Phenotypes'. *Psychological Review* 110 (4): 647–82.

Thompson, Paul A., Charles Hulme, Hannah M. Nash, et al. 2015. 'Developmental Dyslexia: Predicting Individual Risk'. *Journal of Child Psychology and Psychiatry, and Allied Disciplines* 56 (9): 976–87.

Tiffany-Castiglioni, E. 1993. 'Cell Culture Models for Lead Toxicity in Neuronal and Glial Cells'. *Neurotoxicology* 14 (4): 513–36.

Toll, S. W. M., E. H. Kroesbergen, and J. E. H. Van Luit. 2016. 'Visual Working Memory and Number Sense: Testing the Double Deficit Hypothesis in Mathematics'. *The British Journal of Educational Psychology* 86 (3): 429–45.

Toll, S. W. M., S. H. G. Van der Ven, E. H. Kroesbergen, and J. E. H. Van Luit. 2011. 'Executive Functions as Predictors of Math Learning Disabilities'. *Journal of Learning Disabilities* 44 (6): 521–32.

Tompary, A., and L. Davachi. 2017. 'Consolidation Promotes the Emergence of Representational Overlap in the Hippocampus and Medial Prefrontal Cortex'. *Neuron* 96 (1): 228–41.

Torppa, M., G. K. Georgiou, P. Niemi, M.-K. Lerkkanen, and A.-M. Poikkeus. 2017. 'The Precursors of Double Dissociation between Reading and Spelling in a Transparent Orthography'. *Annals of Dyslexia* 67: 42–62. https://doi.org/10.1007/s11881-016-0131-5.

Torre, G. A., A. A. Matejko, and G. F. Eden. 2020. 'The Relationship between Brain Structure and Proficiency in Reading and Mathematics in Children, Adolescents, and Emerging Adults'. *Developmental Cognitive Neuroscience* 45 (October): 100856.

Toth, G., and L. S. Siegel. 1994. 'A Critical Evaluation of the IQ-Achievement Discrepancy Based Definition of Dyslexia'. In K. P. van den Bos, L. S. Siegel, D. J. Bakker, and D. L. Share (eds.), Current Directions in Dyslexia Research, 45–70. Swets & Zeitlinger Publishers.

Traccis, F., R. Frau, and M. Melis. 2020. 'Gender Differences in the Outcome of Offspring Prenatally Exposed to Drugs of Abuse'. *Frontiers in Behavioral Neuroscience* 14 (June): 72.

Travis, K. E., J. N. Adams, M. Ben-Shachar, and H. M. Feldman. 2015. 'Decreased and Increased Anisotropy along Major Cerebral White Matter Tracts in Preterm Children and Adolescents'. *PloS One* 10 (11): e0142860.

Travis, K. E., M. Ben-Shachar, N. J. Myall, and H. M. Feldman. 2016. 'Variations in the Neurobiology of Reading in Children and Adolescents Born Full Term and Preterm'. *NeuroImage. Clinical* 11 (April): 555–65.

Trope, I., D. Lopez-Villegas, and R. E. Lenkinski. 1998. 'Magnetic Resonance Imaging and Spectroscopy of Regional Brain Structure in a 10-Year-Old Boy with Elevated Blood Lead Levels'. *Pediatrics* 101 (6): E7.

Tsai, C. L., T. H. Jang, and L. H. Wang. 1995. 'Effects of Mercury on Serotonin Concentration in the Brain of Tilapia, Oreochromis Mossambicus'. *Neuroscience Letters* 184 (3): 208–11.

Tschentscher, N., O. Hauk, M. H. Fischer, and F. Pulvermüller. 2012. 'You Can Count on the Motor Cortex: Finger Counting Habits Modulate Motor Cortex Activation Evoked by Numbers'. *NeuroImage* 59 (4): 3139–48.

Tsolaki, A., V. Kosmidou, L. Hadjileontiadis, I. Y. Kompatsiaris, and M. Tsolaki. 2015. 'Brain Source Localization of MMN, P300 and N400: Aging and Gender Differences'. *Brain Research* 1603 (April): 32–49.

Tucker-Drob, E. M. 2017. 'Motivational Factors as Mechanisms of Gene-Environment Transactions in Cognitive Development and Academic Achievement'. In A. J. Elliot, C. S. Dweck, and D. S. Yeager (eds.), *Handbook of Competence and Motivation: Theory and Application*, 471–86. Guilford Press.

Tucker-Drob, E. M., and K. Paige Harden. 2012. 'Intellectual Interest Mediates Gene × Socioeconomic Status Interaction on Adolescent Academic Achievement'. *Child Development* 83 (2): 743–57.

Twilhaar, E. S., J. F. de Kieviet, C. S. Aarnoudse-Moens, R. M. van Elburg, and J. Oosterlaan. 2018. 'Academic Performance of Children Born Preterm: A Meta-Analysis and Meta-Regression'. *Archives of Disease in Childhood. Fetal and Neonatal Edition* 103 (4): F322–30.

Ulfarsson, M. O., G. B. Walters, O. Gustafsson, et al. 2017. '15q11.2 CNV Affects Cognitive, Structural and Functional Correlates of Dyslexia and Dyscalculia'. *Translational Psychiatry* 7: e1109. https://doi.org/10.1038/tp.2017.77.

Undeman, E., T. N. Brown, M. S. McLachlan, and F. Wania. 2018. 'Who in the World Is Most Exposed to Polychlorinated Biphenyls? Using Models to Identify Highly Exposed Populations'. *Environmental Research Letters: ERL [Web Site]* 13 (6): 064036.

UNICEF Canada. 2016. Child Development & Education. www.unicef.ca/en/discover/education

United Nations (UN). 2007. Convention on the Rights of Persons with Disabilities.

United Nations Office on Drugs and Crime. 2013. 'World Drug Report 2013'. *World Drug Report*. www.unodc.org/doc/wdr2013/World_Drug_Report_2013.pdf. https://doi.org/10.18356/d30739c2-en.

Vaaga, C. E., S. T. Brown, and I. M. Raman. 2020. 'Cerebellar Modulation of Synaptic Input to Freezing-Related Neurons in the Periaqueductal Gray'. *eLife* 9 (March). https://doi.org/10.7554/eLife.54302.

Valdois, S., M.-L. Bosse, and M.-J. Tainturier. 2004. 'The Cognitive Deficits Responsible for Developmental Dyslexia: Review of Evidence for a Selective Visual Attentional Disorder'. *Dyslexia* 10 (4): 339–63.

Valdois, S., D. Lassus-Sangosse, and M. Lobier. 2012. 'Impaired Letter-String Processing in Developmental Dyslexia: What Visual-to-Phonology Code Mapping Disorder?' *Dyslexia* 18 (2): 77–93.

Vanbinst, K., E. Bellon, and A. Dowker. 2020. 'Mathematics Anxiety: An Intergenerational Approach'. *Frontiers in Psychology* 11 (July): 1648.

van Bergen, E., de Jong, P. F. de, Maassen, B., & van der Leij, A. (2014). The effect of parents' literacy skills and children's preliteracy skills on the risk of dyslexia. *Journal of Abnormal Child Psychology*, 42(7), 1187–1200. https://doi.org/10.1007/s10802-014-9858-9.

van Bueren, N. E. R., T. L. Reed, V. Nguyen, et al. 2021Personalized Brain Stimulation for Effective Neurointervention Across Participants. *PLOS Computational Biology* 17 (9): e1008886. https://doi.org/10.1371/journal.pcbi.1008886.

van Bueren, N. E. R., S. H. G. van der Ven, K. Roelofs, R. Cohen Kadosh, and E. H. Kroesbergen. 2022. Predicting Math Ability using Working Memory, Number Sense, and Neurophysiology in Children and Adults. bioRxiv 2022.02.10.479865; https://doi.org/10.1101/2022.02.10.479865.

Van den Bergh, B. R. H., M. I. van den Heuvel, M. Lahti, et al. 2020. 'Prenatal Developmental Origins of Behavior and Mental Health: The Influence of Maternal Stress in Pregnancy'. *Neuroscience and Biobehavioral Reviews* 117 (October): 26–64.

Vanderauwera, J., J. Wouters, M. Vandermosten, and P. Ghesquière. 2017. 'Early Dynamics of White Matter Deficits in Children Developing Dyslexia'. *Developmental Cognitive Neuroscience* 27 (October): 69–77.

Vandermosten, M., B. Boets, H. Luts, et al. 2010. 'Adults with Dyslexia Are Impaired in Categorizing Speech and Nonspeech Sounds on the Basis of Temporal Cues'. *Proceedings of the National Academy of Sciences of the United States of America* 107 (23): 10389–94.

Vandermosten, M., B. Boets, H. Poelmans, et al. 2012. 'A Tractography Study in Dyslexia: Neuroanatomic Correlates of Orthographic, Phonological and Speech Processing'. *Brain: A Journal of Neurology* 135 (3): 935–48.

Vandermosten, M., B. Boets, J. Wouters, and Pol G. 2012. 'A Qualitative and Quantitative Review of Diffusion Tensor Imaging Studies in Reading and Dyslexia'. *Neuroscience and Biobehavioral Reviews* 36 (6): 1532–52.

Vandermosten, M., J. Correia, J. Vanderauwera, et al. 2019. 'Brain Activity Patterns of Phonemic Representations Are Atypical in Beginning Readers with Family Risk for Dyslexia'. *Developmental Science*, April: e12857.

Vandermosten, M., J. Vanderauwera, C. Theys, et al. 2015. 'A DTI Tractography Study in Pre-Readers at Risk for Dyslexia'. *Developmental Cognitive Neuroscience* 14: 8–15.

Van Hirtum, T., P. Ghesquière, and J. Wouters. 2021. 'A Bridge over Troubled Listening: Improving Speech-in-Noise Perception by Children with Dyslexia'. *Journal of the Association for Research in Otolaryngology: JARO*, April. https://doi.org/10.1007/s10162-021-00793-4.

Van Hirtum, T., A. Moncada-Torres, P. Ghesquière, and J. Wouters. 2019. 'Speech Envelope Enhancement Instantaneously Effaces Atypical Speech Perception in Dyslexia'. *Ear and Hearing* 40 (5): 1242–52.

Vanvooren, S., H. Poelmans, M. Hofmann, P. Ghesquière, and J. Wouters. 2014. 'Hemispheric Asymmetry in Auditory Processing of Speech Envelope Modulations in Prereading Children'. *The Journal of Neuroscience: The Official Journal of the Society for Neuroscience* 34 (4): 1523–9.

Vatansever, G., S. Üstün, N. Ayyıldız, and M. Çiçek. 2020. 'Developmental Alterations of the Numerical Processing Networks in the Brain'. *Brain and Cognition* 141 (June): 105551.

Veena, S. R., C. R. Gale, G. V. Krishnaveni, et al. 2016. 'Association between Maternal Nutritional Status in Pregnancy and Offspring Cognitive Function during Childhood and Adolescence; a Systematic Review'. *BMC Pregnancy and Childbirth* 16 (August): 220.

Vellutino, F. R., J. M. Fletcher, M. J. Snowling, and D. M. Scanlon. 2004. 'Specific Reading Disability (Dyslexia): What Have We Learned in the Past Four Decades?' *Journal of Child Psychology and Psychiatry, and Allied Disciplines* 45 (1): 2–40.

Verguts, T., and W. Fias. 2004. 'Representation of Number in Animals and Humans: A Neural Model'. *Journal of Cognitive Neuroscience* 16 (9): 1493–504.

Verhoeven, L., C. Perfetti, and K. Pugh. 2019. *Developmental Dyslexia across Languages and Writing Systems.* Cambridge University Press.

Verhoeven, L., S. Nag, C. A. Perfetti, and K. Pugh (eds.). 2022. Global Variation of Literacy Development. Cambridge University Press.

Victora, C. G., R. Bahl, A. J. D. Barros, et al. 2016. 'Breastfeeding in the 21st Century: Epidemiology, Mechanisms, and Lifelong Effect'. *The Lancet* 387 (10017): 475–90.

Victora, C. G., F. C. Barros, B. L. Horta, and R. C. Lima. 2005. 'Breastfeeding and School Achievement in Brazilian Adolescents'. *Acta Paediatrica* 94 (11): 1656–60.

Vidyasagar, T. R., and K. Pammer. 2010. 'Dyslexia: A Deficit in Visuo-Spatial Attention, Not in Phonological Processing'. *Trends in Cognitive Sciences* 14 (2): 57–63.

Visscher, A. De, M.-P. Noël, M. Pesenti, and V. Dormal. 2018. 'Developmental Dyscalculia in Adults: Beyond Numerical Magnitude Impairment'. *Journal of Learning Disabilities* 51 (6): 600–11. https://doi.org/10.1177/0022219417732338.

Vogel, E. K., and S. J. Luck. 2000. 'The Visual N1 Component as an Index of a Discrimination Process'. *Psychophysiology* 37 (2): 190–203.

Vogel, S. E., C. Goffin, and D. Ansari. 2015. 'Developmental Specialization of the Left Parietal Cortex for the Semantic Representation of Arabic Numerals: An fMR-Adaptation Study'. *Developmental Cognitive Neuroscience* 12 (April): 61–73.

Volpe, J. J. 2009. 'Brain Injury in Premature Infants: A Complex Amalgam of Destructive and Developmental Disturbances'. *Lancet Neurology* 8 (1): 110–24.

von Aster, M., A. S. Kaufman, U. McCaskey and K. Kucian, K. (in press). Rechenstörungen im Kindes- und Jugendalter. In J. Fegert et al. (eds.), Psychiatrie und Psychotherapie des Kindes- und Jugendalters. Heidelberg: Springer.

Vukovic, R. K., and N. K. Lesaux. 2013. 'The Language of Mathematics: Investigating the Ways Language Counts for Children's Mathematical Development'. *Journal of Experimental Child Psychology* 115 (2): 227–44. https://doi.org/10.1016/j.jecp.2013.02.002.

Vuokko, E., M. Niemivirta, and P. Helenius. 2013. 'Cortical Activation Patterns during Subitizing and Counting'. *Brain Research* 1497 (February): 40–52.

Wachinger, C., S. Volkmer, K. Bublath, et al. 2018. 'Does the Late Positive Component Reflect Successful Reading Acquisition? A Longitudinal ERP Study'. *NeuroImage. Clinical* 17: 232–40.

Wakschlag, L. S., K. E. Pickett, E. Cook Jr, N. L. Benowitz, and B. L. Leventhal. 2002. 'Maternal Smoking during Pregnancy and Severe Antisocial Behavior in Offspring: A Review'. *American Journal of Public Health* 92 (6): 966–74.

Walfisch, A., C. Sermer, A. Cressman, and G. Koren. 2013. 'Breast Milk and Cognitive Development–the Role of Confounders: A Systematic Review'. *BMJ Open* 3 (8): e003259.

Walhovd, K. B., V. Moe, K. Slinning, et al. 2007. 'Volumetric Cerebral Characteristics of Children Exposed to Opiates and Other Substances in Utero'. *NeuroImage* 36 (4): 1331–44.

Walhovd, K. B., L. T. Westlye, V. Moe, et al. 2010. 'White Matter Characteristics and Cognition in Prenatally Opiate- and Polysubstance-Exposed Children: A Diffusion Tensor Imaging Study'. *AJNR. American Journal of Neuroradiology* 31 (5): 894–900.

Walhovd, K. B., R. Watts, I. Amlien, and L. J. Woodward. 2012. 'Neural Tract Development of Infants Born to Methadone-Maintained Mothers'. *Pediatric Neurology* 47 (1): 1–6.

Walker, A., M. Rosenberg, and K. Balaban-Gil. 1999. 'Neurodevelopmental and Neurobehavioral Sequelae of Selected Substances of Abuse and Psychiatric Medications in Utero'. *Child and Adolescent Psychiatric Clinics of North America* 8 (4): 845–67.

Walsh, V. 2003. 'A Theory of Magnitude: Common Cortical Metrics of Time, Space and Quantity'. *Trends in Cognitive Sciences* 7 (11): 483–8.

Wandell, B. A., A. M. Rauschecker, and J. D. Yeatman. 2012. 'Learning to See Words'. *Annual Review of Psychology* 63 (6): 31–53.

Wandell, B. A., and S. M. Smirnakis. 2009. 'Plasticity and Stability of Visual Field Maps in Adult Primary Visual Cortex'. *Nature Reviews. Neuroscience* 10 (12): 873–4.

Wandell, B. A., and J. D. Yeatman. 2013. 'Biological Development of Reading Circuits'. *Current Opinion in Neurobiology* 23 (2): 261–8.

Wang, F., I. I. Karipidis, G. Pleisch, G. Fraga-González, and S. Brem. 2020. 'Development of Print-Speech Integration in the Brain of Beginning Readers With Varying Reading Skills'. *Frontiers in Human Neuroscience* 14 (August): 289.

Wang, Y., M. V. Mauer, T. Raney, et al. 2016. 'Development of Tract-Specific White Matter Pathways During Early Reading Development in At-Risk Children and Typical Controls'. *Cerebral Cortex*, April: bhw095.

Wang, Y., M. V. Mauer, T. Raney, et al. 2017. Development of Tract-Specific White Matter Pathways During Early Reading Development in At-Risk Children and Typical Controls. Cereb Cortex. 27 (4): 2469–85.

Warner, T. D., D. Roussos-Ross, and M. Behnke. 2014. 'It's Not Your Mother's Marijuana: Effects on Maternal-Fetal Health and the Developing Child'. *Clinics in Perinatology* 41 (4): 877–94.

Water, E. de, P. Curtin, A. Zilverstand, et al. 2019. 'A Preliminary Study on Prenatal Polybrominated Diphenyl Ether Serum Concentrations and Intrinsic Functional Network Organization and Executive Functioning in Childhood'. *Journal of Child Psychology and Psychiatry, and Allied Disciplines* 60 (9): 1010–20.

Weiner, E. R. 2008. *Applications of Environmental Aquatic Chemistry: A Practical Guide, Second Edition*. 2nd ed. CRC Press. https://doi.org/10.1201/9781420008371.

Weinstock, M. 2005. 'The Potential Influence of Maternal Stress Hormones on Development and Mental Health of the Offspring'. *Brain, Behavior, and Immunity* 19 (4): 296–308.

Weiskopf, N., S. Mohammadi, A. Lutti, and M. F. Callaghan. 2015. 'Advances in MRI-Based Computational Neuroanatomy: From Morphometry to in-Vivo Histology'. *Current Opinion in Neurology* 28 (4): 313–22.

Wenger, E., C. Brozzoli, U. Lindenberger, and M. Lövdén. 2017. 'Expansion and Renormalization of Human Brain Structure During Skill Acquisition'. *Trends in Cognitive Sciences* 21 (12): 930–9.

Werker, J. F., and T. K. Hensch. 2014. 'Critical Periods in Speech Perception: New Directions'. *Annual Review of Psychology* 66 (September): 1–24.

Westmark, C. J. 2013. 'Soy Infant Formula May Be Associated with Autistic Behaviors'. *Autism-Open Access* 3 (November). https://doi.org/10.4172/2165-7890.1000120.

Wever, R., and T. F. H. Runia. 2018. 'Subitizing with Variational Autoencoders'. *arXiv [cs. CV]. arXiv.* http://arxiv.org/abs/1808.00257.

White, R. F., C. L. Palumbo, D. A. Yurgelun-Todd, et al. 2011. 'Functional MRI Approach to Developmental Methylmercury and Polychlorinated Biphenyl Neurotoxicity'. *Neurotoxicology* 32 (6): 975–80.

White, T., S. Su, M. Schmidt, C.-Y. Kao, and G. Sapiro. 2010. 'The Development of Gyrification in Childhood and Adolescence'. *Brain and Cognition* 72 (1): 36–45.

Whitney, D., and D. M. Levi. 2011. 'Visual Crowding: A Fundamental Limit on Conscious Perception and Object Recognition'. *Trends in Cognitive Sciences* 15 (4): 160–8.

Wigfield, A., J. S. Eccles, D. Mac Iver, D. A. Reuman, and Carol Midgley. 1991. 'Transitions during Early Adolescence: Changes in Children's Domain-Specific Self-Perceptions and General Self-Esteem across the Transition to Junior High School'. *Developmental Psychology* 27 (4): 552–65.

Wigfield, A., and J. L. Meece. 1988. 'Math Anxiety in Elementary and Secondary School Students'. *Journal of Educational Psychology* 80 (2): 210–16.

Wiggs, K. K., M. E. Rickert, S. Hernandez-Diaz, et al. 2017. 'A Family-Based Study of the Association between Labor Induction and Offspring Attention-Deficit Hyperactivity Disorder and Low Academic Achievement'. *Behavior Genetics* 47 (4): 383–93.

Wijngaarden, E. van, G. J. Myers, S. W. Thurston, C. F. Shamlaye, and P. W. Davidson. 2009. 'Interpreting Epidemiological Evidence in the Presence of Multiple Endpoints: An Alternative Analytic Approach Using the 9-Year Follow-up of the Seychelles Child Development Study'. *International Archives of Occupational and Environmental Health* 82 (8): 1031–41.

Wilcke, A., C. Ligges, J. Burkhardt, et al. 2012. 'Imaging Genetics of FOXP2 in Dyslexia'. *European Journal of Human Genetics: EJHG* 20 (2): 224–9.

Wilkey, E. D., L. E. Cutting, and G. R. Price. 2018. 'Neuroanatomical Correlates of Performance in a State-Wide Test of Math Achievement'. *Developmental Science* 21 (2): e12545. https://doi.org/10.1111/desc.12545.

Wilkey, E. D., C. Pollack, and G. R. Price. 2020. 'Dyscalculia and Typical Math Achievement Are Associated with Individual Differences in Number-Specific Executive Function'. *Child Development* 91 (2): 596–619.

Willburger, E., B. Fussenegger, K. Moll, G. Wood, and K. Landerl. 2008. 'Naming Speed in Dyslexia and Dyscalculia'. *Learning and Individual Differences* 18 (2): 224–36.

Willcutt, E. G., L. M. McGrath, B. F. Pennington, et al. 2019. 'Understanding Comorbidity between Specific Learning Disabilities'. *New Directions for Child and Adolescent Development* 2019 (165): 91–109.

Willcutt, E. G., B. F. Pennington, L. Duncan, et al. 2010. 'Understanding the Complex Etiologies of Developmental Disorders: Behavioral and Molecular Genetic Approaches'. *Journal of Developmental and Behavioral Pediatrics: JDBP* 31 (7): 533–44.

Willcutt, E. G., S. A. Petrill, S. Wu, et al. 2013. 'Comorbidity between Reading Disability and Math Disability: Concurrent Psychopathology, Functional Impairment, and

Neuropsychological Functioning'. *Journal of Learning Disabilities* 46 (6): 500–16.

Williams, G. R. 2008. 'Neurodevelopmental and Neurophysiological Actions of Thyroid Hormone'. *Journal of Neuroendocrinology* 20 (6): 784–94.

Willoughby, K. A., E. D. Sheard, K. Nash, and J. Rovet. 2008. 'Effects of Prenatal Alcohol Exposure on Hippocampal Volume, Verbal Learning, and Verbal and Spatial Recall in Late Childhood'. *Journal of the International Neuropsychological Society: JINS* 14 (6): 1022–33.

Wilson, A. J., S. G. Andrewes, H. Struthers, et al. 2015. 'Dyscalculia and Dyslexia in Adults: Cognitive Bases of Comorbidity'. *Learning and Individual Differences* 37 (January): 118–32.

Wimmer, H. 1993. 'Characteristics of Developmental Dyslexia in a Regular Writing System'. *Applied Psycholinguistics* 14 (1): 1–33.

Wimmer, H., and H. Mayringer. 2002. 'Dysfluent Reading in the Absence of Spelling Difficulties: A Specific Disability in Regular Orthographies'. *Journal of Educational Psychology* 94 (2): 227–77. https://doi.org/10.1037/0022-0663.94.2.272.

Wimmer, H., and M. Schurz. 2010. 'Dyslexia in Regular Orthographies: Manifestation and Causation'. *Dyslexia* 16 (4): 283–99.

Wise Younger, J., E. Tucker-Drob, and J. R. Booth. 2017. 'Longitudinal Changes in Reading Network Connectivity Related to Skill Improvement'. *NeuroImage* 158 (September): 90–8.

Wittmann, E., and G. Müller. 2012. Das Zahlenbuch. Klett.

Wong, P. W., W. R. Brackney, and I. N. Pessah. 1997. 'Ortho-Substituted Polychlorinated Biphenyls Alter Microsomal Calcium Transport by Direct Interaction with Ryanodine Receptors of Mammalian Brain'. *The Journal of Biological Chemistry* 272 (24): 15145–53.

Wood L, M. Egger, L. L. Gluud, et al. 2008. Empirical Evidence of Bias in Treatment Effect Estimates in Controlled Trials with Different Interventions and Outcomes: Meta-Epidemiological Study. BMJ 336 (7644): 601–5.

Woodruff Carr, K., T. White-Schwoch, A. T. Tierney, D. L. Strait, and N. Kraus. 2014. 'Beat Synchronization Predicts Neural Speech Encoding and Reading Readiness in Preschoolers'. *Proceedings of the National Academy of Sciences of the United States of America* 111 (40): 14559–64.

Woody, C. A., A. J. Ferrari, D. J. Siskind, H. A. Whiteford, and M. G. Harris. 2017. 'A Systematic Review and Meta-Regression of the Prevalence and Incidence of Perinatal Depression'. *Journal of Affective Disorders* 219 (September): 86–92.

World Health Organization. n.d. 'Breastfeeding'. n.d. Accessed July 13, 2021a. www.who.int/news-room/facts-in-pictures/detail/breastfeeding.

———. n.d. Accessed July 13, 2021. www.who.int/health-topics/breastfeeding.

———. 2015. *International Statistical Classification of Diseases and Related Health Problems: 10th Revision (ICD-10)*. World Health Organization.

———. 2019. International statistical classification of diseases and related health problems (10th ed.). Retrieved from https://icd.who.int/browse10/2019/en#/F80-F89.

———. 2019. ICD-11: International Classification of Diseases (11th revision). https://icd.who.int.

———. 2020. ICD-11: International Classification of Diseases (11th Revision). https://icd.who.int/.

Wren, D. G., and J. Benson. 2004. 'Measuring Test Anxiety in Children: Scale Development and Internal Construct Validation'. *Anxiety, Stress, and Coping* 17 (3): 227–40.

Wu, S. S., M. L. Meyer, U. Maeda, et al. 2008. 'Standardized Assessment of Strategy Use and Working Memory in Early Mental Arithmetic Performance'. *Developmental Neuropsychology* 33 (3): 365–93.

Wu, S. S., T. T. Chang, A. Majid, et al. 2009. 'Functional Heterogeneity of Inferior Parietal Cortex during Mathematical Cognition Assessed with Cytoarchitectonic Probability Maps'. *Cerebral Cortex* 19 (12): 2930–45.

Wu, Y., Y.-C. Lu, M. Jacobs, et al. 2020. 'Association of Prenatal Maternal Psychological Distress With Fetal Brain Growth, Metabolism, and Cortical Maturation'. *JAMA Network Open* 3 (1): e1919940.

Wynn, K. 1992a. 'Addition and Subtraction by Human Infants'. *Nature* 358 (6389): 749–50.

Xia, Z., R. Hancock, and F. Hoeft. 2017. 'Neurobiological Bases of Reading Disorder Part I: Etiological Investigations'. *Language and Linguistics Compass* 11 (4): 1–18.

Xie, Y., J. Weng, C. Wang, et al. 2018. 'The Impact of Long-Term Abacus Training on Modular Properties of Functional Brain Network'. *NeuroImage* 183 (December): 811–17.

Xu, F., and E. S. Spelke. 2000. 'Large Number Discrimination in 6-Month-Old Infants'. *Cognition* 74 (1): B1–11.

Yamada, Y., C. Stevens, M. Dow, et al. 2011. 'Emergence of the Neural Network for Reading in Five-Year-Old Beginning Readers of Different Levels of Pre-Literacy Abilities: An fMRI Study'. *NeuroImage* 57 (3): 704–13.

Yamins, D. L. K., and J. J. DiCarlo. 2016. 'Using Goal-Driven Deep Learning Models to Understand Sensory Cortex'. *Nature Neuroscience* 19 (3): 356–65.

Yang, J., B. D. McCandliss, H. Shu, and J. D. Zevin. 2009. 'Simulating Language-Specific and Language-General Effects in a Statistical Learning Model of Chinese Reading'. *Journal of Memory and Language* 61 (2): 238–57.

Yang, Y., Y. H. Yang, J. Li, M. Xu, and H.-Y. Bi. 2020. 'An Audiovisual Integration Deficit Underlies Reading Failure in Nontransparent Writing Systems: An fMRI Study of Chinese Children with Dyslexia'. *Journal of Neurolinguistics* 54: 100884. https://doi.org/10.1016/j.jneuroling.2019.100884.

Yeatman, J. D., R. F. Dougherty, M. Ben-Shachar, and B. A. Wandell. 2012. 'Development of White Matter and Reading Skills'. *Proceedings of the National Academy of Sciences of the United States of America* 109 (44): E3045–53.

Yeatman, J. D., R. F. Dougherty, E. Rykhlevskaia, et al. 2011. 'Anatomical Properties of the Arcuate Fasciculus Predict Phonological and Reading Skills in Children'. *Journal of Cognitive Neuroscience* 23 (11): 3304–17.

Yeatman, J. D., and A. L. White. 2021. 'Reading: The Confluence of Vision and Language'. *Annual Review of Vision Science* 7 (June): 487–517. https://doi.org/10.1146/annurev-vision-093019-113509.

Yeh, M. L., Y. Gonda, M. T. M. Mommersteeg, et al. 2014. 'Robo1 Modulates Proliferation and Neurogenesis in the Developing Neocortex'. *The Journal of Neuroscience: The Official Journal of the Society for Neuroscience* 34 (16): 5717–31.

Yeo, D.J., E. D. Wilkey, and G. R. Price. 2017. 'The Search for the Number Form Area: A Functional Neuroimaging Meta-Analysis'. *Neuroscience and Biobehavioral Reviews* 78 (July): 145–60.

Yin, R. 1980. Studying the Implementation of Public Programs. Boulder: Solar Energy Research Institute.

Yoncheva, Y. N., V. C. Blau, U. Maurer, and B. D. McCandliss. 2010. 'Attentional Focus during Learning Impacts N170 ERP Responses to an Artificial Script'. *Developmental Neuropsychology* 35 (4): 423–45.

Yoncheva, Y. N., J. Wise, and B. McCandliss. 2015. 'Hemispheric Specialization for Visual Words Is Shaped by Attention to Sublexical Units during Initial Learning'. *Brain and Language* 145–6 (June): 23–33.

Young, C. B., S. S. Wu, and V. Menon. 2012. 'The Neurodevelopmental Basis of Math Anxiety'. *Psychological Science* 23 (5): 492–501.

Yuan, Q., M. Rubic, J. Seah, et al. 2014. 'Do Maternal Opioids Reduce Neonatal Regional Brain Volumes? A Pilot Study'. *Journal of Perinatology: Official Journal of the California Perinatal Association* 34 (12): 909–13.

Yuan, W., S. K. Holland, K. M. Cecil, et al. 2006. 'The Impact of Early Childhood Lead Exposure on Brain Organization: A Functional Magnetic Resonance Imaging Study of Language Function'. *Pediatrics* 118 (3): 971–7.

Yu, X., T. Raney, M. V. Perdue, J. Zuk, et al. 2018. 'Emergence of the Neural Network Underlying Phonological Processing from the Prereading to the Emergent Reading Stage: A Longitudinal Study'. *Human Brain Mapping* 39 (5): 2047–63.

Yu, X., J. Zuk, M. V. Perdue, et al. 2020. 'Putative Protective Neural Mechanisms in Prereaders with a Family History of Dyslexia Who Subsequently Develop Typical Reading Skills'. *Human Brain Mapping* 41 (10): 2827–45.

Zacharopoulos, G., F. Sella, and R. Cohen Kadosh. 2021. 'The Impact of a Lack of Mathematical Education on Brain Development and Future Attainment'. *Proceedings of the National Academy of Sciences of the United States of America* 118 (24). https://doi.org/10.1073/pnas.2013155118.

Zago, L., L. Petit, E. Mellet, et al. 2010. 'Neural Correlates of Counting Large Numerosity'. *ZDM: The International Journal on Mathematics Education* 42 (6): 569–77.

Zagron, G., and M. Weinstock. 2006. 'Maternal Adrenal Hormone Secretion Mediates Behavioural Alterations Induced by Prenatal Stress in Male and Female Rats'. *Behavioural Brain Research* 175 (2): 323–8.

Zaigler, M., S. Rietbrock, J. Szymanski, et al. 2000. 'Variation of CYP1A2-Dependent Caffeine Metabolism during Menstrual Cycle in Healthy Women'. *International Journal of Clinical Pharmacology and Therapeutics* 38 (5): 235–44.

Zamarian, L., C. Scherfler, C. Kremser, et al. 2018. 'Arithmetic Learning in Advanced Age'. *PloS One* 13 (2): e0193529.

Zamarian, L., A. Ischebeck, and M. Delazer. 2009. 'Neuroscience of Learning Arithmetic: Evidence from Brain Imaging Studies'. *Neuroscience and Biobehavioral Reviews* 33 (6): 909–25.

Zatorre, R. J., R. Douglas Fields, and H. Johansen-berg. 2012. 'Plasticity in Gray and White: Neuroimaging Changes in Brain Structure during Learning'. *Nature Publishing Group* 15 (4): 528–36.

Zaunmüller, L., F. Domahs, K. Dressel, et al. 2009. 'Rehabilitation of Arithmetic Fact Retrieval via Extensive Practice: A Combined fMRI and Behavioural Case-Study'. *Neuropsychological Rehabilitation* 19 (3): 422–43.

Zbornik, J. J., and F. H. Wallbrown. 1991. 'The Development and Validation of a Scale to Measure Reading Anxiety'. *Chula Vista, Calif* 28 (1): 2.

Zebian, S., and D. Ansari. 2012. 'Differences between Literates and Illiterates on Symbolic but Not Nonsymbolic Numerical Magnitude Processing'. *Psychonomic Bulletin & Review* 19: 93–100. https://doi.org/10.3758/s13423-011-0175-9.

Zeitlin, J., M. J. Saurel-Cubizolles, J. De Mouzon et al. 2002. Fetal Sex and Preterm Birth: Are Males at Greater Risk? Hum Reprod. 17 (10): 2762–8.

Zhang, H., K. Yolton, G. M. Webster, et al. 2017. 'Prenatal PBDE and PCB Exposures and Reading, Cognition, and Externalizing Behavior in Children'. *Environmental Health Perspectives* 125 (4): 746–52.

Zhang, J., N. Zhao, and Q. P. Kong. 2019. 'The Relationship between Math Anxiety and Math Performance: A Meta-Analytic Investigation'. *Frontiers in Psychology* 10 (August): 1613.

Zhang, T., A. Sidorchuk, L. Sevilla-Cermeño, et al. 2019. 'Association of Cesarean Delivery With Risk of Neurodevelopmental and Psychiatric Disorders in the Offspring: A Systematic Review and Meta-Analysis'. *JAMA Network Open* 2 (8): e1910236.

Zhao, J., H. Liu, J. Li, et al. 2019. 'Improving Sentence Reading Performance in Chinese Children with Developmental Dyslexia by Training Based on Visual Attention Span'. *Scientific Reports* 9 (1): 18964.

Zhao, J., M. Liu, H. Liu, and C. Huang. 2018. 'Increased Deficit of Visual Attention Span with Development in Chinese Children with Developmental Dyslexia'. *Scientific Reports* 8 (1): 3153.

Zhu, P. J., and D. M. Lovinger. 2010. 'Developmental Alteration of Endocannabinoid Retrograde Signaling in the Hippocampus'. *Journal of Neurophysiology* 103 (2): 1123–9.

Ziegler, J. C., D. Bertrand, D. Tóth, et al. 2010. 'Orthographic Depth and Its Impact on Universal Predictors of Reading'. *Psychological Science* 21 (4): 551–9. https://doi.org/10.1177/0956797610363406.

Ziegler, J. C., C. Castel, C. Pech-Georgel, et al. 2008. 'Developmental Dyslexia and the Dual Route Model of Reading: Simulating Individual Differences and Subtypes'. *Cognition* 107 (1): 151–78.

Ziegler, J. C., and U. Goswami. 2005. 'Reading Acquisition, Developmental Dyslexia, and Skilled Reading Across Languages: A Psycholinguistic Grain Size Theory'. *Psychological Bulletin* 131 (1): 3–29. https://doi.org/10.1037/0033-2909.131.1.3.

Ziegler, J. C., C. Perry, and M. Zorzi. 2014. 'Modelling Reading Development through Phonological Decoding and Self-Teaching: Implications for Dyslexia'. *Philosophical Transactions of the Royal Society of London. Series B, Biological Sciences* 369 (1634): 20120397.

———. 2020. 'Learning to Read and Dyslexia: From Theory to Intervention Through Personalized Computational Models'. *Current Directions in Psychological Science* 29 (3): 293–300.

Zirk-Sadowski, J., C. Lamptey, A. Devine, M. Haggard, and D. Szűcs. 2014. 'Young-Age Gender Differences in Mathematics Mediated by Independent Control or Uncontrollability'. *Developmental Science* 17 (3): 366–75.

Zoccolotti, P., M. De Luca, C. V. Marinelli, and Do. Spinelli. 2020. 'Predicting Individual Differences in Reading, Spelling and Maths in a Sample of Typically Developing Children: A Study in the Perspective of Comorbidity'. *PloS One* 15 (4): e0231937.

Zoeller, R. T. 2005. 'Environmental Chemicals as Thyroid Hormone Analogues: New Studies Indicate That Thyroid Hormone Receptors Are Targets of Industrial Chemicals?' *Molecular and Cellular Endocrinology* 242 (1–2): 10–15.

Zorzi, M. 2010. 'The Connectionist Dual Process (CDP) Approach to Modelling Reading Aloud'. *The European Journal of Cognitive Psychology* 22 (5): 836–60.

Zorzi, M., C. Barbiero, A. Facoetti, et al. 2012. 'Extra-Large Letter Spacing Improves Reading in Dyslexia'. *Proceedings of the National Academy of Sciences of the United States of America* 109 (28): 11455–9.

Zorzi, M., G. Houghton, and B. Butterworth. 1998a. 'The Development of Spelling-Sound Relationships in a Model of Phonological Reading'. *Language and Cognitive Processes* 13 (2–3): 337–71.

1998b. 'Two Routes or One in Reading Aloud? A Connectionist Dual-Process Model'. *Journal of Experimental Psychology. Human Perception and Performance* 24 (4): 1131–61.

Zorzi, M., and A. Testolin. 2018. 'An Emergentist Perspective on the Origin of Number Sense'. *Philosophical Transactions of the Royal Society of London. Series B, Biological Sciences* 373 (1740). https://doi.org/10.1098/rstb.2017.0043.

Zorzi, M., A. Testolin, and I. P. Stoianov. 2013. 'Modeling Language and Cognition with Deep Unsupervised Learning: A Tutorial Overview'. *Frontiers in Psychology* 4 (August): 515.

Zorzi, M., Stoianov, I., & Umiltà, C. 2005. 'Computational Modeling of Numerical Cognition'. In J. I. D. Campbell (Ed.), *Handbook of Mathematical Cognition* (pp. 67–83). Psychology Press.

Zoubrinetzky, R., G. Collet, M.-A. Nguyen-Morel, S. Valdois, and W. Serniclaes. 2019. 'Remediation of Allophonic Perception and Visual Attention Span in Developmental Dyslexia: A Joint Assay'. *Frontiers in Psychology* 10 (July): 1502.

Zuijen, T. L. van, A. Plakas, B. A. M. Maassen, et al. 2013. 'Infant ERPs Separate Children at Risk of Dyslexia Who Become Good Readers from Those Who Become Poor Readers'. *Developmental Science* 16 (4): 554–63.

Zuk, J., P. Bishop-Liebler, O. Ozernov-Palchik, et al. 2017. 'Revisiting the "Enigma" of Musicians with Dyslexia: Auditory Sequencing and Speech Abilities'. *Journal of Experimental Psychology. General* 146 (4): 495–511.

Zuk, J., J. Dunstan, E. Norton, et al. 2021. 'Multifactorial Pathways Facilitate Resilience among Kindergarteners at Risk for Dyslexia: A Longitudinal Behavioral and Neuroimaging Study'. *Developmental Science* 24 (1): e12983.

Part XII

Aaron, P. G. 1997. 'The Impending Demise of the Discrepancy Formula'. *Review of Educational Research* 67 (4): 461–502. https://doi.org/10.3102/00346543067004461.

Abbott, S. P., and V. W. Berninger. 1999. 'It's Never Too Late to Remediate: Teaching Word Recognition to Students with Reading Disabilities in Grades 4–7'. *Annals of Dyslexia* 49: 223–50.

Abosi, O. 2007. 'Educating Children with Learning Disabilities in Africa'. *Learning Disabilities Research & Practice: A Publication of the Division for Learning Disabilities, Council for Exceptional Children* 22 (3): 196–201.

Abramowicz, H. K., and S. A. Richardson. 1975. 'Epidemiology of Severe Mental Retardation in Children: Community Studies'. *American Journal of Mental Deficiency* 80 (1): 18–39.

Abreu, P. M. J. Engel de, M. Baldassi, M. L. Puglisi, and D. M. Befi-Lopes. 2013. 'Cross-Linguistic and Cross-Cultural Effects on Verbal Working Memory and Vocabulary: Testing Language-Minority Children with an Immigrant Background'. *Journal of Speech, Language, and Hearing Research: JSLHR* 56 (2): 630–42.

Adams, M. J., B. R. Foorman, I. Lundberg, and T. Beeler. 1998. *Phonemic Awareness in Young Children: A Classroom Curriculum*. P.H. Brookes.

Agrawal, J., B. L. Barrio, B. Kressler, Y.-J. Hsiao, and R. K. Shankland. 2019. 'International Policies, Identification, and Services for Students with Learning Disabilities: An Exploration across 10 Countries'. *Learning Disabilities: A Contemporary Journal* 17 (1): 95–113.

Ainscow, M. 2016. 'Collaboration as a Strategy for Promoting Equity in Education: Possibilities and Barriers'. *Journal of Professional Capital and Community* 1 (2). https://doi.org/10.1108/JPCC-12-2015-0013.

Akers, K. G., A. Martinez-Canabal, L. Restivo, et al. 2014. 'Hippocampal Neurogenesis Regulates Forgetting during Adulthood and Infancy'. *Science* 344 (6184): 598–602.

Alberini, C. M., and A. Travaglia. 2017. 'Infantile Amnesia: A Critical Period of Learning to Learn and Remember'. *The Journal of Neuroscience: The Official Journal of the Society for Neuroscience* 37 (24): 5783–95.

Alloway, T. P., S. E. Gathercole, H. Kirkwood, and J. Elliott. 2009. 'The Cognitive and Behavioral Characteristics of Children with Low Working Memory'. *Child Development* 80 (2): 606–21.

Alnahdi, G. 2015. 'Teaching Reading for Students with Intellectual Disabilities: A Systematic Review'. *International Education Studies* 8 (9): 79.

Al Otaiba, S., K. Baker, P. Lan, et al. 2019. 'Elementary Teacher's Knowledge of Response to Intervention Implementation: A Preliminary Factor Analysis'. *Annals of Dyslexia* 69 (1): 34–53.

Altani, A., A. Protopapas, and G. K. Georgiou. 2018. 'Using Serial and Discrete Digit Naming to Unravel Word Reading Processes'. *Frontiers in Psychology* 9 (April): 524.

Altani, A., A. Protopapas, K. Katopodi, and G. K. Georgiou. 2020. 'From Individual Word Recognition to Word List and Text Reading Fluency'. *Journal of Educational Psychology* 112 (1): 22–35.

Amalric, M., and S. Dehaene. 2017. 'Cortical Circuits for Mathematical Knowledge: Evidence for a Major Subdivision within the Brain's Semantic Networks'. *Philosophical Transactions of the Royal Society of London. Series B, Biological Sciences* 373 (1740). https://doi.org/10.1098/rstb.2016.0515.

American Psychiatric Association. 2013. *Diagnostic and Statistical Manual of Mental Disorders (DSM-5®)*. American Psychiatric Association Publishing.

American Psychiatric Association, and American Psychiatric Association: Task Force on Nomenclature and Statistics. 1980. *Diagnostic and Statistical Manual of Mental Disorders*. American Psychiatric Association Publishing.

Anastasiou, D., R. Gardner, D. Michail, and et al. 2011. 'Ethnicity and Exceptionality'. In J. M. Kauffman, D. P. Hallahan, and P. Cullen Pullen, *Handbook of Special Education*, 742–55. Routledge.

Andellini, M., V. Cannatà, S. Gazzellini, B. Bernardi, and A. Napolitano. 2015. 'Test-Retest Reliability of Graph Metrics of Resting State MRI Functional Brain Networks: A Review'. *Journal of Neuroscience Methods* 253 (September): 183–92.

Anderson, K. G. 1997. 'Gender Bias and Special Education Referrals'. *Annals of Dyslexia* 47: 151–62. https://doi.org/10.1007/s11881-997-0024-8.

Anreiter, I., H. M. Sokolowski, and M. B. Sokolowski. 2018. 'Gene–environment Interplay and Individual Differences in Behavior'. *Mind, Brain and Education: The Official Journal of the International Mind, Brain, and Education Society* 12 (4): 200–11.

Anthony, J. L., and C. J. Lonigan. 2004. 'The Nature of Phonological Awareness: Converging Evidence From Four Studies of Preschool and Early Grade School Children'. *Journal of Educational Psychology* 96 (1): 43–55. https://doi.org/10.1037/0022-0663.96.1.43.

Anthony, J. L., C. J. Lonigan, S. R. Burgess, et al. 2002. 'Structure of Preschool Phonological Sensitivity: Overlapping Sensitivity to Rhyme, Words, Syllables, and Phonemes'. *Journal of Experimental Child Psychology* 82 (1): 65–92.

Anthopolos, R., J. S. Kaufman, L. C. Messer, and M. L. Miranda. 2014. 'Racial Residential Segregation and Preterm Birth: Built Environment as a Mediator'. *Epidemiology* 25 (3): 397–405.

Araújo, S., and L. Faísca. 2019. 'A Meta-Analytic Review of Naming-Speed Deficits in Developmental Dyslexia'. *Scientific Studies of Reading* 23 (5). https://doi.org/10.1080/10888438.2019.1572758.

Araújo, S., Al. Reis, K. M. Petersson, and L. Faísca. 2015. 'Rapid Automatized Naming and Reading Performance: A Meta-Analysis'. *Journal of Educational Psychology* 107 (3): 868–83. https://doi.org/10.1037/edu0000006.

Arens, A. K., H. W. Marsh, R. G. Craven, et al. 2016. 'Math Self-Concept in Preschool Children: Structure, Achievement Relations, and Generalizability across Gender'. *Early Childhood Research Quarterly* 36 (July): 391–403.

Arens, A. K., and F. Preckel. 2018. 'Testing the Internal/external Frame of Reference Model with Elementary School Children: Extension to Physical Ability and Intrinsic Value'. *Contemporary Educational Psychology* 54 (July): 199–211.

Arnold, A. P., J. Xu, W. Grisham, et al. 2004. 'Minireview: Sex Chromosomes and Brain Sexual Differentiation'. *Endocrinology* 145 (3): 1057–62.

Artelt, C., J. Naumann, and W. Schneider. 2010. 'Lesemotivation Und Lernstrategien'. https://core.ac.uk/display/144486827.

Artiles, A. J. 1998. 'The Dilemma of Difference: Enriching the Disproportionality Discourse with Theory and Context'. *The Journal of Special Education* 32 (1): 32–6.

———. 2019. 'Fourteenth Annual Brown Lecture in Education Research: Reenvisioning Equity Research: Disability Identification Disparities as a Case in Point'. *Educational Researcher* 48 (6): 325–35.

Arulmani, Gideon. 2004. *Career Counselling: A Handbook*. McGraw-Hill Education (India) Pvt Limited.

Asfaha, Y. M., D. Beckman, J. Kurvers, and S. Kroon. 2009. 'L2 Reading in Multilingual Eritrea: The Influences of L1 Reading and English Proficiency'. *Journal of Research in Reading* 32 (4): 351–65.

Aster, M.l G. von, and R. S. Shalev. 2007. 'Number Development and Developmental Dyscalculia'. *Developmental Medicine and Child Neurology* 49 (11): 868–73.

Atherton, O. E., L. R. Zheng, W. Bleidorn, and R. W. Robins. 2019. 'The Codevelopment of Effortful Control and School Behavioral Problems'. *Journal of Personality and Social Psychology* 117 (3): 659–73. https://doi.org/10.1037/pspp0000201.

Aunola, K., E. Leskinen, M.-K. Lerkkanen, and J.-E. Nurmi. 2004. 'Developmental Dynamics of Math Performance From Preschool to Grade 2'. *Journal of Educational Psychology* 96 (4): 699–713.

Baddeley, A. D., and G. Hitch. 1974. 'Working Memory'. In *Psychology of Learning and Motivation*, edited by Gordon H. Bower, 8:47–89. Academic Press.

Badian, N. A. 1986. 'Nonverbal Disorders of Learning: The Reverse of Dyslexia?' *Annals of Dyslexia* 36 (1): 253–69.

1994. 'Preschool Prediction: Orthographic and Phonological Skills, and Reading'. *Annals of Dyslexia* 44 (1): 1–25.

1999. 'Persistent Arithmetic, Reading, or Arithmetic and Reading Disability'. *Annals of Dyslexia* 49 (1): 43.

Bailey, D. 2019. 'Chapter 13 – Explanations and Implications of Diminishing Intervention Impacts Across Time'. In *Cognitive Foundations for Improving Mathematical Learning*, edited by D. C. Geary, D. B. Berch, and K. M. Koepke, 5:321–46. Academic Press.

Bailey, D., G. J. Duncan, C. L. Odgers, and W. Yu. 2017. 'Persistence and Fadeout in the Impacts of Child and Adolescent Interventions'. *Journal of Research on Educational Effectiveness* 10 (1): 7–39.

Bailey, D. H., G. J. Duncan, F. Cunha, B. R. Foorman, and D. S. Yeager. 2020. 'Persistence and Fade-Out of Educational-Intervention Effects: Mechanisms and Potential Solutions'. *Psychological Science in the Public Interest: A Journal of the American Psychological Society* 21 (2): 55–97.

Bailey, D. H., G. J. Duncan, T. Watts, D. H. Clements, and J. Sarama. 2018. 'Risky Business: Correlation and Causation in Longitudinal Studies of Skill Development'. *The American Psychologist* 73 (1): 81–94.

Bailey, D. H., L. S. Fuchs, J. K. Gilbert, D. C. Geary, and D. Fuchs. 2020. 'Prevention: Necessary but Insufficient? A 2-Year Follow-up of an Effective First-Grade Mathematics Intervention'. *Child Development* 91 (2): 382–400.

Bailey, D. H., T. Nguyen, J. M. Jenkins, et al. 2016. 'Fadeout in an Early Mathematics Intervention: Constraining Content or Preexisting Differences?' *Developmental Psychology* 52 (9): 1457–69.

Bailey, D. H., T. W. Watts, A. K. Littlefield, and D. C. Geary. 2014. 'State and Trait Effects on Individual Differences in Children's Mathematical Development'. *Psychological Science* 25 (11): 2017–26.

Bailey, S. K., K. S. Aboud, T. Q. Nguyen, and L. E. Cutting. 2018. 'Applying a Network Framework to the Neurobiology of Reading and Dyslexia'. *Journal of Neurodevelopmental Disorders* 10 (1): 37.

Baker, L., and A. Wigfield. 1999. 'Dimensions of Children's Motivation for Reading and Their Relations to Reading Activity and Reading Achievement'. *Reading Research Quarterly* 34 (4): 452–77.

Bal, A., J. Betters-Bubon, and R. E. Fish. 2019. 'A Multilevel Analysis of Statewide Disproportionality in Exclusionary Discipline and the Identification of Emotional Disturbance'. *Education and Urban Society* 51 (2): 247–68.

Balu, R., P. Zhu, F. Doolittle, et al. 2015. 'Evaluation of Response to Intervention Practices for Elementary School Reading. NCEE 2016-4000'. *National Center for Education Evaluation and Regional Assistance*, November. http://files.eric.ed.gov/fulltext/ED560820.pdf.

Barahmand, Usha. 2008. 'Arithmetic Disabilities: Training in Attention and Memory Enhances Arithmetic Ability'. *Research Journal of Biological Sciences* 3 (11): 1305–12.

Barbaresi, W. J., S. K. Katusic, R. C. Colligan, A. L. Weaver, and S. J. Jacobsen. 2005. 'Math Learning Disorder: Incidence in a Population-Based Birth Cohort, 1976–82, Rochester, Minn'. *Ambulatory Pediatrics: The Official Journal of the Ambulatory Pediatric Association* 5 (5): 281–9.

Barbiero, C., M. Montico, I. Lonciari, et al. 2019. 'The Lost Children: The Underdiagnosis of Dyslexia in Italy. A Cross-Sectional National Study'. *PloS One* 14 (1): e0210448.

Barnett, W. S. 2011. 'Effectiveness of Early Educational Intervention'. *Science* 333 (6045): 975–8.

Barnett, W. S., K. Jung, D. J. Yarosz, et al. 2008. 'Educational Effects of the Tools of the Mind Curriculum: A Randomized Trial'. *Early Childhood Research Quarterly* 23 (3): 299–313.

Barrett, S., and C. Fudge. 1981. *Policy and Action: Essays on the Implementation of Public Policy.* Methuen.

Barrouillet, P., and M. Fayol. 1998. 'From Algorithmic Computing to Direct Retrieval: Evidence from Number and Alphabetic Arithmetic in Children and Adults'. *Memory & Cognition* 26 (2): 355–68.

Barth, H. C., and A. M. Paladino. 2011. 'The Development of Numerical Estimation: Evidence against a Representational Shift'. *Developmental Science* 14 (1): 125–35.

Bastos, J. A., A. M. T. Cecato, M. R. I. Martins, K. R. R. Grecca, and R. Pierini. 2016. 'The Prevalence of Developmental Dyscalculia in Brazilian Public School System'. *Arquivos de Neuro-Psiquiatria* 74 (3): 201–6.

Battleday, R. M., T. Muller, M. S. Clayton, and R. Cohen Kadosh. 2014. 'Mapping the Mechanisms of Transcranial Alternating Current Stimulation: A Pathway from Network Effects to Cognition'. *Frontiers in Psychiatry / Frontiers Research Foundation* 5 (November): 162.

Bauermeister, J. J., P. E. Shrout, L. Chávez, et al. 2007. 'ADHD and Gender: Are Risks and Sequela of ADHD the Same for Boys and Girls?' *Journal of Child Psychology and Psychiatry, and Allied Disciplines* 48 (8): 831–9.

Bauer, P. J. 2006. 'Constructing a Past in Infancy: A Neuro-Developmental Account'. *Trends in Cognitive Sciences* 10 (4): 175–81.

Becker, J. R. 1981. 'Differential Treatment of Females and Males in Mathematics Classes'. *Journal for Research in Mathematics Education* 12 (1): 40–53. https://doi.org/10.5951/jresematheduc.12.1.0040.

Bell, L. C., and C. A. Perfetti. 1994. 'Reading Skill: Some Adult Comparisons'. *Journal of Educational Psychology* 86 (2): 244–55. https://doi.org/10.1037/0022-0663.86.2.244.

Belsky, D. W., T. E. Moffitt, D. L. Corcoran, et al. 2016. 'The Genetics of Success: How Single-Nucleotide Polymorphisms Associated With Educational Attainment Relate to Life-Course Development'. *Psychological Science* 27 (7): 957–72.

Benavides-Varela, S., Callegher, C. Z., Fagiolini, B., Leo, I., Altoè, G., and Lucangeli, D. (2020). Effectiveness of digital-based interventions for children with mathematical learning difficulties: A meta-analysis. Computers & Education 157, 103953. https://doi.org/10.1016/j.compedu.2020.103953.

Ben-Yehudah, G., E. A. Hirshorn, T. Simcox, C. A. Perfetti, and J. A. Fiez. 2019. 'Chinese-English Bilinguals Transfer L1 Lexical Reading Procedures and Holistic Orthographic Coding to L2 English'. *Journal of Neurolinguistics* 50: 136–48. https://doi.org/10.1016/j.jneuroling.2018.01.002.

Berch, D. B., and M. M. M. Mazzocco. 2007. *Why Is Math So Hard for Some Children?: The Nature and Origins of Mathematical Learning Difficulties and Disabilities.* Paul H. Brookes Publishing Company.

Bergen, E. van, P. F. de Jong, B. Maassen, and A. van der Leij. 2014. 'The Effect of Parents' Literacy Skills and Children's Preliteracy Skills on the Risk of Dyslexia'. *Journal of Abnormal Child Psychology* 42: 1187–200. https://doi.org/10.1007/s10802-014-9858-9.

Berkeley, S., W. N. Bender, L. G. Peaster, and L. Saunders. 2009. 'Implementation of Response to Intervention'. *Journal of Learning Disabilities* 42 (1): 85–95. https://doi.org/10.1177/0022219408326214.

Berkout, O. V., J. N. Young, and A. M. Gross. 2011. 'Mean Girls and Bad Boys: Recent Research on Gender Differences in Conduct Disorder'. *Aggression and Violent Behavior* 16 (6): 503–11.

Berman, P., and M. W. McLaughlin. 1974. 'Federal Programs Supporting Educational Change: Vol. I, A Model of Educational Change,' January. www.rand.org/pubs/reports/R1589z1.html.

Berninger, V. W., W. D. Winn, P. Stock, et al. 2008. 'Tier 3 Specialized Writing Instruction for Students with Dyslexia'. *Reading and Writing* 21 (1): 95–129.

Bhattacharya, A., and L. C. Ehri. 2004. 'Graphosyllabic Analysis Helps Adolescent Struggling Readers Read and Spell Words'. *Journal of Learning Disabilities* 37 (4): 331–48.

Bialystok, E., G. Luk, K. F. Peets, and S. Yang. 2010. 'Receptive Vocabulary Differences in Monolingual and Bilingual Children'. *Bilingualism* 13 (4): 525–31.

Bian, L., S.-J. Leslie, and A. Cimpian. 2017. 'Gender Stereotypes about Intellectual Ability Emerge Early and Influence Children's Interests'. *Science* 355 (6323): 389–91. https://doi.org/10.1126/science.aah6524.

Bindman, S. W., A. H. Hindman, R. P. Bowles, and F. J. Morrison. 2013. 'The Contributions of Parental Management Language to Executive Function in Preschool Children'. *Early Childhood Research Quarterly* 28 (3): 529–39.

Bindman, S. W., E. M. Pomerantz, and G. I. Roisman. 2015. 'Do Children's Executive Functions Account for Associations between Early Autonomy-Supportive Parenting and Achievement Through High School?' *Journal of Educational Psychology* 107 (3): 756–70.

Birgisdottir, F., S. Gestsdottir, and G. J. Geldhof. 2020. 'Early Predictors of First and Fourth Grade Reading and Math: The Role of Self-Regulation and Early Literacy Skills'. *Early Childhood Research Quarterly* 53 (October): 507–19.

Bishop, D. V. M. 2010. 'Which Neurodevelopmental Disorders Get Researched and Why?' *PloS One* 5 (11): e15112.

Bishop, K. M., and D. Wahlsten. 1997. 'Sex Differences in the Human Corpus Callosum: Myth or Reality?' *Neuroscience & Biobehavioral Reviews*. 21 (5): 581–601. https://doi.org/10.1016/s0149-7634(96)00049-8.

Bjorklund, D. F., and K. B. Causey. 2017. *Children's Thinking: Cognitive Development and Individual Differences*. SAGE Publications.

Bjorklund, D. F., and A. D. Pellegrini. 2000. 'Child Development and Evolutionary Psychology'. *Child Development* 71 (6): 1687–708.

Björn, P. M., M. T. Aro, T. K. Koponen, L. S. Fuchs, and D. H. Fuchs. 2016. 'The Many Faces of Special Education Within RTI Frameworks in the United States and Finland'. *Learning Disability Quarterly* 39 (1): 58–66. https://doi.org/10.1177/0731948715594787.

Blair, C., and C. C. Raver. 2014. 'Closing the Achievement Gap through Modification of Neurocognitive and Neuroendocrine Function: Results from a Cluster Randomized Controlled Trial of an Innovative Approach to the Education of Children in Kindergarten'. *PloS One* 9 (11): e112393.

Blair, C., and R. P. Razza. 2007. 'Relating Effortful Control, Executive Function, and False Belief Understanding to Emerging Math and Literacy Ability in Kindergarten'. *Child Development* 78 (2): 647–63.

Blanchett, W. J. 2010. 'Telling It like It Is: The Role of Race, Class, & Culture in the Perpetuation of Learning Disability as a Privileged Category for the White Middle Class.' *Disability Studies Quarterly: DSQ* 30 (2). https://doi.org/10.18061/dsq.v30i2.1233.

Bleeker, M. M., and J. E. Jacobs. 2004. 'Achievement in Math and Science: Do Mothers' Beliefs Matter 12 Years Later?' *Journal of Educational Psychology* 96 (1): 97–109. https://doi.org/10.1037/0022-0663.96.1.97.

Blevins-Knabe, B., and L. Musun-Miller. 1996. 'Number Use at Home by Children and Their Parents and Its Relationship to Early Mathematical Performance'. *Early Development and Parenting: An International Journal of Research and Practice* 5 (1): 35–45.

Blumenthal, Y., S. Voß, S. Sikora, and B. Hartke. 2019. 'Selected Findings of the First Large-Scale Implementation of Response to Intervention in Germany'. In Kollosche, D., Marcone, R., Knigge, M., Penteado, M., Skovsmose, O. (eds.) *Inclusive Mathematics Education*. Springer. https://doi.org/10.1007/978-3-030-11518-0_10.

Blum, W., and S. Schukajlow. 2018. 'Selbständiges Lernen Mit Modellierungsaufgaben – Untersuchung von Lernumgebungen Zum Modellieren Im Projekt DISUM'. In *Evaluierte Lernumgebungen Zum Modellieren*, edited by S. Schukajlow and W. Blum, 51–72. Springer Fachmedien Wiesbaden.

Boada, R., and B. F. Pennington. 2006. 'Deficient Implicit Phonological Representations in Children with Dyslexia'. *Journal of Experimental Child Psychology* 95 (3): 153–93.

Boehner, J. A. 2002. *No Child Left Behind Act of 2001*. https://www.congress.gov/bill/107th-congress/house-bill/1.

Boer, M. van den, and P. F. de Jong. 2015. 'Parallel and Serial Reading Processes in Children's Word and Nonword Reading'. *Journal of Educational Psychology* 107 (1): 141–51.

Bolger, D. J., C. A. Perfetti, and W. Schneider. 2005. 'Cross-Cultural Effect on the Brain Revisited: Universal Structures plus Writing System Variation'. *Human Brain Mapping* 25 (1): 92–104.

Booth, J. R., D. D. Burman, J. R. Meyer, et al. 2002. 'Functional Anatomy of Intra- and Cross-Modal Lexical Tasks'. *NeuroImage* 16 (1): 7–22.

Booth, J. R., D. D. Burman, J. R. Meyer, et al. 2004. 'Brain-Behavior Correlation in Children Depends on the Neurocognitive Network'. *Human Brain Mapping* 23: 99–108. https://doi.org/10.1002/hbm.20051.

Booth, J. R., D. Lu, D. D. Burman, et al. 2006. 'Specialization of Phonological and Semantic Processing in Chinese Word Reading'. *Brain Research* 1071 (1): 197–207. https://doi.org/10.1016/j.brainres.2005.11.097.

Borckardt, J. J., Z. H. Nahas, J. Teal, et al. 2013. 'The Painfulness of Active, but Not Sham, Transcranial Magnetic Stimulation Decreases Rapidly Over Time: Results From the Double-Blind Phase of the OPT-TMS Trial'. *Brain Stimulation* 6 (6): P925–8. https://doi.org/10.1016/j.brs.2013.04.009.

Borleffs, E., B. A. M. Maassen, H. Lyytinen, and F. Zwarts. 2017. 'Measuring Orthographic Transparency and Morphological-Syllabic Complexity in Alphabetic Orthographies: A Narrative Review'. *Reading and Writing* 30 (8): 1617–38.

Botswana, Republic of. 2015. '*Education & Training Sector Strategic Plan (ETSSP 2015–2020)*'. Government Printers Gaborone, Botswana.

Bower, C., L. Zimmermann, B. Verdine, et al. 2020. 'Piecing Together the Role of a Spatial Assembly Intervention in Preschoolers' Spatial and Mathematics Learning:

Influences of Gesture, Spatial Language, and Socioeconomic Status'. *Developmental Psychology* 56 (4): 686–98.

Bowers, J. S. 2020. 'Reconsidering the Evidence That Systematic Phonics Is More Effective Than Alternative Methods of Reading Instruction'. *Educational Psychology Review* 32 (3): 681–705.

Bowers, P. N., J. R. Kirby, and S. Hélène Deacon. 2010. 'The Effects of Morphological Instruction on Literacy Skills: A Systematic Review of the Literature'. *Review of Educational Research* 80 (2): 144–79.

Boyce, W. T., and M. S. Kobor. 2015. 'Development and the Epigenome: The "Synapse" of Gene-Environment Interplay'. *Developmental Science* 18 (1): 1–23.

Boyce, W. T., J. Obradovi, N. R. Bush, et al. 2012. 'Social Stratification, Classroom Climate, and the Behavioral Adaptation of Kindergarten Children'. *Proceedings of the National Academy of Sciences* 109 (6178): 17168–73. https://doi.org/10.1073/pnas.1201730109.

Boyes, M. E., S. Leitão, M. Claessen, et al. 2020. 'Piloting "Clever Kids": A Randomized-Controlled Trial Assessing Feasibility, Efficacy, and Acceptability of a Socioemotional Well-Being Programme for Children with Dyslexia'. *The British Journal of Educational Psychology*, December, e12401.

Bradley, L., and P. E. Bryant. 1983. 'Categorizing Sounds and Learning to Read – a Causal Connection'. *Nature* 301: 419–21. https://doi.org/10.1038/301419a0.

Brady, S. A., and D. P. Shankweiler. 2013. *Phonological Processes in Literacy: A Tribute to Isabelle Y. Liberman*. Routledge.

Breznitz, Z., O. Rubinsten, V. J. Molfese, and D. L. Molfese, eds. 2012. *Reading, Writing, Mathematics and the Developing Brain: Listening to Many Voices*. 2012 ed. Literacy Studies 6. Springer.

Brighina, F., V. Raieli, L. M. Messina, et al. 2019. 'Non-Invasive Brain Stimulation in Pediatric Migraine: A Perspective From Evidence in Adult Migraine'. *Frontiers in Neurology* 10. https://doi.org/10.3389/fneur.2019.00364.

Brinkman, W. B., S. N. Sherman, A. R. Zmitrovich, et al. 2009. 'Parental Angst Making and Revisiting Decisions about Treatment of Attention-Deficit/Hyperactivity Disorder'. *Pediatrics* 124 (2): 580–9.

Brown, M. C., D. E. Sibley, J. A. Washington, et al. 2015. 'Impact of Dialect Use on a Basic Component of Learning to Read'. *Frontiers in Psychology* 6 (March): 196.

Bruce, S. M., and K. Venkatesh. 2014. 'Special Education Disproportionality in the United States, Germany, Kenya, and India'. *Disability & Society* 29 (6): 908–21.

Brunoni, A. R., B. Sampaio-Junior, A. H. Moffa, et al. 2019. 'Noninvasive Brain Stimulation in Psychiatric Disorders: A Primer'. *Revista Brasileira de Psiquiatria (Sao Paulo, Brazil: 1999)* 41 (1): 70–81.

Brunoni, A. Ru., and M.-A. Vanderhasselt. 2014. 'Working Memory Improvement with Non-Invasive Brain Stimulation of the Dorsolateral Prefrontal Cortex: A Systematic Review and Meta-Analysis'. *Brain and Cognition* 86 (April): 1–9.

Bryant, B. R., D. Pe. Bryant, J. Porterfield, et al. 2016. 'The Effects of a Tier 3 Intervention on the Mathematics Performance of Second Grade Students With Severe Mathematics Difficulties'. *Journal of Learning Disabilities* 49 (2): 176–88.

Bryant, D. P., B. R. Bryant, G. Roberts, et al. 2011. 'Early Numeracy Intervention Program for First-Grade Students with Mathematics Difficulties'. *Exceptional Children* 78 (1): 7–23.

Bryant, P. 2002. 'It Doesn't Matter Whether Onset and Rime Predicts Reading Better Than Phoneme Awareness Does or Vice Versa'. *Journal of Experimental Child Psychology* 82 (1): 41–6. https://doi.org/10.1006/jecp.2002.2672.

Bub, D. N., M. Arguin, and A. R. Lecours. 1993. 'Jules Dejerine and His Interpretation of Pure Alexia'. *Brain and Language* 45 (4): 531–59.

Buchweitz, A., S. V. Shinkareva, R. A. Mason, T. M. Mitchell, and M. A. Just. 2012. 'Identifying Bilingual Semantic Neural Representations across Languages'. *Brain and Language* 120 (3): 282–9. https://doi.org/10.1016/j.bandl.2011.09.003.

Buckingham, J., R. Beaman, and K. Wheldall. 2014. 'Why Poor Children Are More Likely to Become Poor Readers: The Early Years'. *Educational Review* 66 (4): 428–46. https://doi.org/10.1080/00131911.2013.795129.

Bueren, N. E. R. van, T. L. Reed, V. Nguyen, et al. 2021. 'Personalized Closed-Loop Brain Stimulation for Effective Neurointervention Across Participants'. *PLOS Computational Biology* 17(9): e1008886. https://doi.org/10.1101/2021.03.18.436018.

Bulajić, A., M. Despotović, and T. Lachmann. 2019. 'Understanding Functional Illiteracy from a Policy, Adult Education, and Cognition Point of View: Towards a Joint Referent Framework'. *Zeitschrift Für Neuropsychologie* 30 (2): 109–22. https://doi .org/10.1024/1016-264x/a000255.

Bull, R., and G. Scerif. 2001. 'Executive Functioning as a Predictor of Children's Mathematics Ability: Inhibition, Switching, and Working Memory'. *Developmental Neuropsychology* 19 (3): 273–93.

Bulthé, J., J. Prinsen, J. Vanderauwera, et al. 2019a. 'Multi-Method Brain Imaging Reveals Impaired Representations of Number as Well as Altered Connectivity in Adults with Dyscalculia'. *NeuroImage* 190: 289–302. https://doi.org/10.1016/j.neuroimage .2018.06.012.

———. 2019b. 'Multi-Method Brain Imaging Reveals Impaired Representations of Number as Well as Altered Connectivity in Adults with Dyscalculia'. *NeuroImage* 190 (April): 289–302.

Bunea, I. M., A. Szentágotai-Tătar, and A. C. Miu. 2017. 'Early-Life Adversity and Cortisol Response to Social Stress: A Meta-Analysis'. *Translational Psychiatry* 7 (12): 1–8.

Burgess, A. P., C. Witton, L. Shapiro, and J. B. Talcott. 2018. 'From Subtypes to Taxons: Identifying Distinctive Profiles of Reading Development in Children'. In *Reading and Dyslexia: From Basic Functions to Higher Order Cognition*, edited by T. Lachmann and T. Weis, 213–33. Springer International Publishing.

Bus, A. G., and M. H. van IJzendoorn. 1999. 'Phonological Awareness and Early Reading: A Meta-Analysis of Experimental Training Studies'. *Journal of Educational Psychology* 91 (3): 403–14. https://doi.org/10.1037/0022-0663.91.3.403.

Busch, J., C. Schmidt, and D. Grube. 2015. 'Arithmetic Fact Retrieval'. *Zeitschrift Für Psychologie* 223 (2): 110–19.

Buschmann, A., B. Jooss, A. Rupp, et al. 2009. 'Parent Based Language Intervention for 2-Year-Old Children with Specific Expressive Language Delay: A Randomised Controlled Trial'. *Archives of Disease in Childhood* 94 (2): 110–16.

Butterworth, B., and Y. Kovas. 2013. 'Understanding Neurocognitive Developmental Disorders Can Improve Education for All'. *Science* 340 (6130): 300–5.

Calcus, A., I. Hoonhorst, C. Colin, P. Deltenre, and R. Kolinsky. 2018. 'The 'Rowdy Classroom Problem' in Children with Dyslexia: A Review'. In *Reading and Dyslexia: From Basic Functions to Higher Order Cognition*, edited by T. Lachmann and T. Weis, 183–211. Springer International Publishing.

Calhoon, M. B., D. Greenberg, and C. Vincent Hunter. 2010. 'A Comparison of Standardized Spelling Assessments: Do They Measure Similar Orthographic Qualities?' *Learning Disability Quarterly: Journal of the Division for Children with Learning Disabilities* 33 (3): 159–70.

Camilli, G., S. Vargas, S. Ryan, and W. S. Barnett. 2010. 'Meta-Analysis of the Effects of Early Education Interventions on Cognitive and Social Development'. *Teachers College Record* 112 (3): 579–620.

Campbell, F. A., and C. T. Ramey. 1994. 'Effects of Early Intervention on Intellectual and Academic Achievement: A Follow-up Study of Children from Low-Income Families'. *Child Development* 65 (2): 684–98.

Campbell, F. A., C. T. Ramey, E. Pungello, J. Sparling, and S. Miller-Johnson. 2002. 'Early Childhood Education: Young Adult Outcomes From the Abecedarian Project'. *Applied Developmental Science* 6 (1): 42–57.

Campbell, F., G. Conti, J. J. Heckman, et al 2014. 'Early Childhood Investments Substantially Boost Adult Health'. *Science* 343 (6178): 1478–85.

Cantlon, J. F. 2012. 'Math, Monkeys, and the Developing Brain'. *Proceedings of the National Academy of Sciences of the United States of America* 109 Suppl 1 (June): 10725–32.

Cao, F., M. Vu, D. H. L. Chan, et al. 2013. 'Writing Affects the Brain Network of Reading in Chinese: A Functional Magnetic Resonance Imaging Study'. *Human Brain Mapping* 34: 1670–84. https://doi.org/10.1002/hbm.22017.

Cao, F., X. Yan, Z. Wang, et al. 2017. 'Neural Signatures of Phonological Deficits in Chinese Developmental Dyslexia'. *NeuroImage* 146 (February): 301–11.

Caplan, G. 1964. 'Principles of Preventive Psychiatry' 304. https://psycnet.apa.org/fulltext/1965-02239-000.pdf.

——— 1974. *Support Systems and Community Mental Health: Lectures on Concept Development.* Behavioral Publications.

Cappelletti, M., and C. J. Price. 2014. 'Residual Number Processing in Dyscalculia'. *NeuroImage. Clinical* 4: 18–28.

Caravolas, M. 2004. 'Spelling Development in Alphabetic Writing Systems: A Cross-Linguistic Perspective'. *European Psychologist* 9 (1): 3–14.

Caravolas, M., C. Hulme, and M. J. Snowling. 2001. 'The Foundations of Spelling Ability: Evidence from a 3-Year Longitudinal Study'. *Journal of Memory and Language* 45 (4): 751–74. https://doi.org/10.1006/jmla.2000.2785.

Caravolas, M., A. Lervåg, S. Defior, G. S. Málková, and C. Hulme. 2013. 'Different Patterns, but Equivalent Predictors, of Growth in Reading in Consistent and Inconsistent Orthographies'. *Psychological Science* 24 (8): 1398–1407.

Caravolas, M., A. Lervåg, P. Mousikou, et al. 2012. 'Common Patterns of Prediction of Literacy Development in Different Alphabetic Orthographies'. *Psychological Science* 23 (6): 678–86.

Carey, S., and D. Barner. 2019. 'Ontogenetic Origins of Human Integer Representations'. *Trends in Cognitive Sciences* 23 (10): 823–35.

Carlisle, J. F. 2003. 'Morphology Matters in Learning to Read: A Commentary'. *Reading Psychology* 24 (3–4): 291–322.

Carreiras, M., J. A. Duñabeitia, and M. Perea. 2007. 'Reading Words, NUMB3R5 and YMßOL'. *Trends in Cognitive Sciences* 11 (11): 454–5.

Carrol, J. M., M. J. Snowling, J. Stevenson, and C. Hulme. 2003. 'The Development of Phonological Awareness in Preschool Children'. *Developmental Psychology* 39 (5): 913.

Carroll, J. M., B. Maughan, R. Goodman, and H. Meltzer. 2005. 'Literacy Difficulties and Psychiatric Disorders: Evidence for Comorbidity'. *Journal of Child Psychology and Psychiatry, and Allied Disciplines* 46 (5): 524–32.

Casey, B. M., C. M. Lombardi, D. Thomson, et al. 2018. 'Maternal Support of Children's Early Numerical Concept Learning Predicts Preschool and First-Grade Math Achievement'. *Child Development* 89 (1): 156–73.

Casey, B. M., R. L. Nuttall, and E. Pezaris. 1997. 'Mediators of Gender Differences in Mathematics College Entrance Test Scores: A Comparison of Spatial Skills with Internalized Beliefs and Anxieties'. *Developmental Psychology* 33 (4): 669–80. https://doi.org/10.1037/0012-1649.33.4.669.

Castle, M. N. 2004. *Individuals with Disabilities Education Improvement Act of 2004.* www.congress.gov/bill/108th-congress/house-bill/1350.

Castles, A., and M. Coltheart. 2004. 'Is There a Causal Link from Phonological Awareness to Success in Learning to Read?' *Cognition* 91 (1): 77–111.

Castles, A., K. Rastle, and K. Nation. 2018. 'Ending the Reading Wars: Reading Acquisition from Novice to Expert'. *Psychological Science in the Public Interest*, 19 (1), 5–51. https://doi.org/10.1177/1529100618772271.

Castro, M. V. de, M. A. S. Bissaco, B. M. Panccioni, S. C.M. Rodrigues, and A. M. Domingues. 2014. 'Effect of a Virtual Environment on the Development of Mathematical Skills in Children with Dyscalculia'. *PloS One* 9 (7): e103354.

Cattaneo, Z., A. Pisoni, and C. Papagno. 2011. 'Transcranial Direct Current Stimulation over Broca's Region Improves Phonemic and Semantic Fluency in Healthy Individuals'. *Neuroscience* 183: 64–70. https://doi.org/10.1016/j.neuroscience.2011.03.058.

Catts, H. W., A. McIlraith, M. Sittner Bridges, and D. Corcoran Nielsen. 2017. 'Viewing a Phonological Deficit within a Multifactorial Model of Dyslexia'. *Reading and Writing* 30 (3): 613–29.

Catts, H. W. 1993. 'The Relationship between Speech-Language Impairments and Reading Disabilities'. *Journal of Speech and Hearing Research* 36 (5): 948–58.

Ceci, S. J., D. K. Ginther, S. Kahn, and W. M. Williams. 2014. 'Women in Academic Science: A Changing Landscape'. *Psychological Science in the Public Interest: A Journal of the American Psychological Society* 15 (3): 75–141.

Chan, D. W., C. S.-H. Ho, S.-M. Tsang, S.-H. Lee, and K.K. H. Chung. 2007. 'Prevalence, Gender Ratio and Gender Differences in Reading-related Cognitive Abilities among Chinese Children with Dyslexia in Hong Kong'. *Educational Studies* 33 (2): 249–65.

Changizi, M. A., Q. Zhang, H. Ye, and S. Shimojo. 2006. 'The Structures of Letters and Symbols throughout Human History Are Selected to Match Those Found in Objects in Natural Scenes'. *The American Naturalist* 167 (5): E117–39.

Chan, W. W. Lan, T. K. Au, and J. Tang. 2013. 'Developmental Dyscalculia and Low Numeracy in Chinese Children'. *Research in Developmental Disabilities* 34 (5): 1613–22.

Chaplin, T. M., and A. Aldao. 2013. 'Gender Differences in Emotion Expression in Children: A Meta-Analytic Review'. *Psychological Bulletin* 139 (4): 735–65. https://doi.org/10.1037/a0030737.

Chapman, J. W., W. E. Tunmer, and R. Allen. 2003. 'Findings from the International Adult Literacy Survey on the Incidence and Correlates of Learning Disabilities in New Zealand: Is Something Rotten in the State of New Zealand?' *Dyslexia* 9 (2): 75–98.

Cheam, F., and C. W. L. Jocelyn. 2009. 'Early Intervention for Pupils At-Risk of Mathematics Difficulties'. In *Mathematics Education*, 2: 370–86.Series on Mathematics Education. WORLD SCIENTIFIC.

Chenault, B., J. Thomson, R. D. Abbott, and V. W. Berninger. 2006. 'Effects of Prior Attention Training on Child Dyslexics' Response to Composition Instruction'. *Developmental Neuropsychology* 29 (1): 243–60.

Cheng, D., Q. Xiao, J. Cui, et al. 2020. 'Short-Term Numerosity Training Promotes Symbolic Arithmetic in Children with Developmental Dyscalculia: The Mediating Role of Visual Form Perception'. *Developmental Science* 23 (4): e12910.

Cheng, D., Q. Xiao, J. Cui, C. Chen, and J. Zeng. 2020. 'Short-term Numerosity Training Promotes Symbolic Arithmetic in Children with Developmental Dyscalculia: The Mediating Role of Visual Form Perception'. *Developmental Science* 23 (4): e12910. https://onlinelibrary.wiley.com/doi/abs/10.1111/desc.12910?casa_token=gcwt UsLsolkAAAAA:VABRViSQSsNpY2Gnhl69jhw9OlN-efxC74Qatk2yVCOJFFqI FypUzECm5l5rDr8k8eIMWpcc6yLSEFA.

Chen, H.-Yu, E. C. Chang, S. H. Y. Chen, Y.-C. Lin, and D. H. Wu. 2016. 'Functional and Anatomical Dissociation between the Orthographic Lexicon and the Orthographic Buffer Revealed in Reading and Writing Chinese Characters by fMRI'. *NeuroImage* 129 (1): 105–16. https://doi.org/10.1016/j.neuroimage.2016.01.009.

Chen, H., X.-H. Gu, Y. Zhou, et al. 2017. 'A Genome-Wide Association Study Identifies Genetic Variants Associated with Mathematics Ability'. *Scientific Reports* 7 (1): 1–9.

Chen, Q., and J. Li. 2014. 'Association between Individual Differences in Non-Symbolic Number Acuity and Math Performance: A Meta-Analysis'. *Acta Psychologica* 148 (May): 163–72.

Cheung, C.-N., J. Y. Sung, and S. F. Lourenco. 2020. 'Does Training Mental Rotation Transfer to Gains in Mathematical Competence? Assessment of an at-Home Visuospatial Intervention'. *Psychological Research* 84 (7): 2000–17.

Cheung, H., H.-C. Chen, C. Y. Lai, O. C. Wong, and M. Hills. 2001. 'The Development of Phonological Awareness: Effects of Spoken Language Experience and Orthography'. *Cognition* 81 (3): 227–41. https://doi.org/10.1016/s0010-0277(01) 00136-6.

Chia, N. K. H. n.d. 'An Investigative Study on the Learning Difficulties in Mathematics Encountered by Primary 4 Children: In Search of a Cognitive Equation for Mathematics Learning'. Accessed April 15, 2021. http://aasep.org/fileadmin/user_upload/Protected_Directory/JAASEP/2011_Winter/Investigative_Study_on_Learning_Difficulties_in_Mathematics_Encountered_by_Primary_4_Children-In_Search_of_Cognitive_Equation_for_Mathematics_Learning.pdf.

Chia, N. K. H., A. G. T. Ng, S. S. K. Tan, and L. H. Wee. 2014. 'A Comparison of Cognitive Equations of Mathematics Learning Process between the American and Singaporean Students with Dyscalculia'. *Educational Research International* 1 (3): 1–14.

Chodura, S., J.-T. Kuhn, and H. Holling. 2015. 'Interventions for Children With Mathematical Difficulties'. *Zeitschrift Für Psychologie* 223 (2): 129–44.

Chou, T.-L., M. H. Davis, W. D. Marslen-Wilson, and J. R. Booth. 2006. 'Phonological Priming in Visual Word Recognition for English Words: An Event-Related Functional MRI Study'. *Chinese Journal of Psychology* 48 (4): 329–46.

Chu, F. W., K. vanMarle, and D. C. Geary. 2015. 'Early Numerical Foundations of Young Children's Mathematical Development'. *Journal of Experimental Child Psychology* 132 (April): 205–12.

Cipora, K., K. Patro, and H.-C. Nuerk. 2015. 'Are Spatial-Numerical Associations a Cornerstone for Arithmetic Learning? The Lack of Genuine Correlations Suggests No'. *Mind, Brain and Education: The Official Journal of the International Mind, Brain, and Education Society* 9 (4): 190–206.

Cirillo, G., G. Di Pino, F. Capone, et al. 2017. 'Neurobiological after-Effects of Non-Invasive Brain Stimulation'. *Brain Stimulation* 10 (1): 1–18.

Claessens, A., G. Duncan, and M. Engel. 2009. 'Kindergarten Skills and Fifth-Grade Achievement: Evidence from the ECLS-K'. *Economics of Education Review* 28 (4): 415–27. https://doi.org/10.1016/j.econedurev.2008.09.003.

Clark, C. A. C., T. D. Sheffield, S. A. Wiebe, and K. A. Espy. 2013. 'Longitudinal Associations between Executive Control and Developing Mathematical Competence in Preschool Boys and Girls'. *Child Development* 84 (2): 662–77.

Clayton, S., and C. Gilmore. 2015. 'Inhibition in Dot Comparison Tasks'. *ZDM: The International Journal on Mathematics Education* 47 (5): 759–70.

Clements, A. M., S. L. Rimrodt, J. R. Abel, et al. 2006. 'Sex Differences in Cerebral Laterality of Language and Visuospatial Processing'. *Brain and Language* 98 (2): 150–8.

Clements, D. H., and J. Sarama. 2007. 'Effects of a Preschool Mathematics Curriculum: Summative Research on the Building Blocks Project'. *Journal for Research in Mathematics Education* 38 (2): 136–63.

Clements, D. H., J. Sarama, C. B. Wolfe, and M. E. Spitler. 2013. 'Longitudinal Evaluation of a Scale-Up Model for Teaching Mathematics With Trajectories and Technologies: Persistence of Effects in the Third Year'. *American Educational Research Journal* 50 (4): 812–50.

Coard, B. 1971. 'How the West Indian Child Is Made Educationally Subnormal in the British School System: The Scandal of the Black Child in Schools in Britain'. *ERIC*. https://eric.ed.gov/?id=ED054281.

Coburn, C. E. 2003. 'Rethinking Scale: Moving Beyond Numbers to Deep and Lasting Change'. *Educational Researcher* 32 (6): 3–12. https://doi.org/10.3102/0013189x032006003.

Cohen Kadosh, R., K. Cohen Kadosh, T. Schuhmann, et al. 2007. 'Virtual Dyscalculia Induced by Parietal-Lobe TMS Impairs Automatic Magnitude Processing'. *Current Biology: CB* 17 (8): 689–93.

Cohen Kadosh, R., A. Dowker, A. Heine, L. Kaufmann, and K. Kucian. 2013. 'Interventions for Improving Numerical Abilities: Present and Future'. *Trends in Neuroscience and Education* 2 (2): 85–93.

Cohen Kadosh, R., N. Levy, J. O'Shea, N. Shea, and J. Savulescu. 2012. 'The Neuroethics of Non-Invasive Brain Stimulation'. *Current Biology: CB* 22 (4): R108–11.

Cohen Kadosh, R., S. Soskic, T. Iuculano, R. Kanai, and V. Walsh. 2010. 'Modulating Neuronal Activity Produces Specific and Long-Lasting Changes in Numerical Competence'. *Current Biology: CB* 20 (22): 2016–20.

Colé, P., L. G. Duncan, and A. Blaye. 2014. 'Cognitive Flexibility Predicts Early Reading Skills'. *Frontiers in Psychology* 5 (June): 565.

Coltheart, M. 1996. 'Phonological Dyslexia: Past and Future Issues'. *Cognitive Neuropsychology* 13 (6): 749–62.

2014. 'The Neuronal Recycling Hypothesis for Reading and the Question of Reading Universals'. *Mind & Language* 29 (3): 255–69.

Conn, K. M. 2017. 'Identifying Effective Education Interventions in Sub-Saharan Africa: A Meta-Analysis of Impact Evaluations'. *Review of Educational Research* 87 (5): 863–98.

Connor, D. J., and B. A. Ferri. 2010. 'Introduction to DSQ Special Issue: 'Why Is There Learning Disabilities?' – Revisiting Christine Sleeter's Socio-Political Construction of Disability Two Decades on'. *Disability Studies Quarterly: DSQ* 30 (2). https://doi.org/10.18061/dsq.v30i2.1229.

Cooperstock, M., and J. Campbell. 1996. 'Excess Males in Preterm Birth: Interactions with Gestational Age, Race, and Multiple Birth'. *Obstetrics & Gynecology* 88 (2): 189–93. https://doi.org/10.1016/0029-7844(96)00106-8.

Cormier, E. 2012. 'How Parents Make Decisions to Use Medication to Treat Their Child's ADHD: A Grounded Theory Study'. *Journal of the American Psychiatric Nurses Association* 18 (6): 345–56.

Cornu, V., C. Hornung, C. Schiltz, and R. Martin. 2017. 'How Do Different Aspects of Spatial Skills Relate to Early Arithmetic and Number Line Estimation?' *Journal of Numerical Cognition* 3 (2): 309–43.

Coslett, H. B., and N. Monsul. 1994. 'Reading with the Right-Hemisphere: Evidence from Transcranial Magnetic Stimulation'. *Brain and Language* 46 (2): 198–211. https://doi.org/10.1006/brln.1994.1012.

Costanzo, F., D. Menghini, C. Caltagirone, M. Oliveri, and S. Vicari. 2013. 'How to Improve Reading Skills in Dyslexics: The Effect of High Frequency rTMS'. *Neuropsychologia* 51 (14): 2953–59.

Costanzo, F., S. Rossi, C. Varuzza, et al. 2019. 'Long-Lasting Improvement Following tDCS Treatment Combined with a Training for Reading in Children and Adolescents with Dyslexia'. *Neuropsychologia* 130 (July): 38–43.

Costanzo, F., C. Varuzza, S. Rossi, et al. 2016a. 'Evidence for Reading Improvement Following tDCS Treatment in Children and Adolescents with Dyslexia'. *Restorative Neurology and Neuroscience* 34 (2): 215–26.

Costanzo, F., C. Varuzza, S. Rossi, et al. 2016b. 'Reading Changes in Children and Adolescents with Dyslexia after Transcranial Direct Current Stimulation'. *Neuroreport* 27 (5): 295–300.

Costenbader, V., and S. Markson. 1998. 'School Suspension: A Study with Secondary School Students'. *Journal of School Psychology* 36 (1): 59–82.

Cotton, S. M., D. P. Crewther, and S. G. Crewther. 2005. 'Measurement Error: Implications for Diagnosis and Discrepancy Models of Developmental Dyslexia'. *Dyslexia* 11 (3): 186–202.

Coupé, C., Y. Oh, D. Dediu, and F. Pellegrino. 2019. 'Different Languages, Similar Encoding Efficiency: Comparable Information Rates across the Human Communicative Niche'. *Science Advances* 5 (9). https://doi.org/10.1126/sciadv.aaw2594.

Cui, J., Y. Zhang, S. Wan, C. Chen, J. Zeng, and X. Zhou. 2019. 'Visual Form Perception Is Fundamental for Both Reading Comprehension and Arithmetic Computation'. *Cognition* 189 (August): 141–54.

Cunningham, A. J., A. P. Burgess, C. Witton, J. B. Talcott, and L. R. Shapiro. 2021. 'Dynamic Relationships between Phonological Memory and Reading: A Five Year Longitudinal Study from Age 4 to 9'. *Developmental Science* 24 (1): e12986. https://doi.org/10.1111/desc.12986.

Cvencek, D., A. N. Meltzoff, and A. G. Greenwald. 2011. 'Math-Gender Stereotypes in Elementary School Children'. *Child Development* 83 (3): 766–79. https://doi.org/10.1111/j.1467-8624.2010.01529.x.

Dackermann, T., U. Fischer, H.-C. Nuerk, U. Cress, and K. Moeller. 2017. 'Applying Embodied Cognition: From Useful Interventions and Their Theoretical Underpinnings to Practical Applications'. *ZDM: The International Journal on Mathematics Education* 49 (4): 545–57.

Dackermann, T., S. Huber, J. Bahnmueller, H.-C. Nuerk, and K. Moeller. 2015. 'An Integration of Competing Accounts on Children's Number Line Estimation'. *Frontiers in Psychology* 6. https://doi.org/10.3389/fpsyg.2015.00884.

Da, J. 2004. 'A Corpus-Based Study of Character and Bigram Frequencies in Chinese E-Texts and Its Implications for Chinese Language Instruction'. In *Proceedings of the Fourth International Conference on New Technologies in Teaching and Learning Chinese*, 501–11. Citeseer.

Daley, S. G., and G. Rappolt-Schlichtmann. 2018. 'Stigma Consciousness Among Adolescents With Learning Disabilities: Considering Individual Experiences of Being Stereotyped'. *Learning Disability Quarterly* 41 (4): 200–12. https://doi.org/10.1177/0731948718785565.

Dann, H.-D., T. Diegritz, and H. S. Rosenbusch. 1999. *Gruppenunterricht im Schulalltag: Realität und Chancen.* Universitätsbibliothek.

David Hill, W., S. P. Hagenaars, R. E. Marioni, et al. 2016. 'Molecular Genetic Contributions to Social Deprivation and Household Income in UK Biobank'. *Current Biology: CB* 26 (22): 3083–9.

Davidson, K., K. Eng, and D. Barner. 2012. 'Does Learning to Count Involve a Semantic Induction?' *Cognition* 123 (1): 162–73.

Deary, I. 2003. 'Population Sex Differences in IQ at Age 11: The Scottish Mental Survey 1932'. *Intelligence* 31 (6): 533–42. https://doi.org/10.1016/s0160-2896(03)00053-9.

Deater-Deckard, K. 2014. 'Family Matters: Intergenerational and Interpersonal Processes of Executive Function and Attentive Behavior'. *Current Directions in Psychological Science* 23 (3): 230–6.

DeFrancis, J. 1989. *Visible Speech: The Diverse Oneness of Writing Systems.* University of Hawaii Press.

Dehaene, S. 1992. 'Varieties of Numerical Abilities'. *Cognition* 44 (1-2): 1–42.

Dehaene, S., and L. Cohen. 2007. 'Cultural Recycling of Cortical Maps'. *Neuron* 56 (2): 384–98.

Dehaene, S., F. Pegado, L. W. Braga, et al. 2010. 'How Learning to Read Changes the Cortical Networks for Vision and Language'. *Science* 330 (6009): 1359–64.

Déjerine, J. 1891. 'Sur Un Cas de Cécité Verbale Avec Agraphie Suivi D'autopsie'. *Mémoires de La Société de Biologie* 3: 197–201.

De Jong, P. F., and A. Van der Leij. 1999. 'Specific Contributions of Phonological Abilities to Early Reading Acquisition: Results from a Dutch Latent Variable Longitudinal Study'. *Specific Contributions of Phonological Abilities to Early Reading Acquisition: Results from a Dutch Latent Variable Longitudinal Study* 91 (3): 450.

Deming, D. 2009. 'Early Childhood Intervention and Life-Cycle Skill Development: Evidence from Head Start'. *American Economic Journal. Applied Economics* 1 (3): 111–34.

Deno, S. L. 1985. 'Curriculum-Based Measurement: The Emerging Alternative'. *Exceptional Children* 52, 219–232 https://doi.org/10.1177/001440298505200303.

Desoete, A., H. Roeyers, and A. De Clercq. 2004. 'Children with Mathematics Learning Disabilities in Belgium'. *Journal of Learning Disabilities* 37 (1): 50–61.

D'Esposito, M., and B. R. Postle. 2015. 'The Cognitive Neuroscience of Working Memory'. *Annual Review of Psychology*. https://doi.org/10.1146/annurev-psych-010814-015031.

Devine, A., F. Soltész, A. Nobes, U. Goswami, and D. Szűcs. 2013. 'Gender Differences in Developmental Dyscalculia Depend on Diagnostic Criteria'. *Learning and Instruction* 27 (October): 31–9.

DeWitt, I., and J. P. Rauschecker. 2012. 'Phoneme and Word Recognition in the Auditory Ventral Stream'. *Proceedings of the National Academy of Sciences of the United States of America* 109 (8): E505–14.

Diamanti, V., N. Goulandris, R. Campbell, and A. Protopapas. 2018. 'Dyslexia Profiles Across Orthographies Differing in Transparency: An Evaluation of Theoretical Predictions Contrasting English and Greek'. *Scientific Studies of Reading: The Official Journal of the Society for the Scientific Study of Reading* 22 (1): 55–69.

Diamond, A., and D. S. Ling. 2016. 'Conclusions about Interventions, Programs, and Approaches for Improving Executive Functions That Appear Justified and Those That, despite Much Hype, Do Not'. *Developmental Cognitive Neuroscience* 18 (April): 34–48.

Di Ianni, M., C. R. Wilsher, M. S. Blank, et al. 1985. 'The Effects of Piracetam in Children with Dyslexia'. *Journal of Clinical Psychopharmacology* 5 (5): 272–8.

Dilling, H., and H. J. Freyberger. 2019. *Taschenführer Zur ICD-10-Klassifikation Psychischer Störungen*.

Dilnot, J., L. Hamilton, B. Maughan, and M.J. Snowling. 2017. 'Child and Environmental Risk Factors Predicting Readiness for Learning in Children at High Risk of Dyslexia'. *Development and Psychopathology* 29 (1): 235–44.

Dinkel, P. J., K. Willmes, H. Krinzinger, K. Konrad, and J. W. Koten Jr. 2013. 'Diagnosing Developmental Dyscalculia on the Basis of Reliable Single Case FMRI Methods: Promises and Limitations'. *PloS One* 8 (12): e83722.

Döhnert, M., and E. D. Englert. 2003. 'Das Irlen-Syndrom – Gibt Es Pathophysiologische Korrelate Und Wissenschaftliche Evidenz Für Das "Lesen Mit Farben"?' *Zeitschrift Fur Kinder- Und Jugendpsychiatrie Und Psychotherapie* 31 (4): 305–9.

Dolean, D., M. Melby-Lervåg, I. Tincas, C. Damsa, and A. O. Lervåg. 2019. 'Achievement Gap: Socioeconomic Status Affects Reading Development beyond Language and Cognition in Children Facing Poverty'. *Learning and Instruction* 63 (October): 101218.

Dowker, A. 2004. 'What Works for Children with Mathematical Difficulties?,' January. www.researchgate.net/publication/253032270.

——— 2019. *Individual Differences in Arithmetic: Implications for Psychology, Neuroscience and Education*. Routledge.

Dowker, A., and H.-C. Nuerk. 2016. 'Editorial: Linguistic Influences on Mathematics'. *Frontiers in Psychology* 7 (July): 1035.

Dudley-Marling, C. 2004. 'The Social Construction of Learning Disabilities'. *Journal of Learning Disabilities* 37 (6): 482–9.

Dumas, D., D. McNeish, J. Sarama, and D. Clements. 2019. 'Preschool Mathematics Intervention Can Significantly Improve Student Learning Trajectories Through Elementary School'. *AERA Open* 5 (4). https://doi.org/10.1177/2332858419879446.

Duncan, G. J., C. J. Dowsett, A. Claessens, et al. 2007. 'School Readiness and Later Achievement'. *Developmental Psychology* 43 (6): 1428–46. https://doi.org/10.1037/0012-1649.43.6.1428.

Duncan, R. J., S. A. Schmitt, and D. Lowe Vandell. 2019. 'Additive and Synergistic Relations of Early Mother-Child and Caregiver-Child Interactions for Predicting Later Achievement'. *Developmental Psychology* 55 (12): 2522–33.

Dunn, L. M. 1968. 'Special Education for the Mildly Retarded – Is Much of It Justifiable?' *Exceptional Children* 35 (1): 5–22.

Ebbinghaus, H. 1885. *Über das Gedächtnis: Untersuchungen zur experimentellen Psychologie.* Duncker & Humblot.

Education Equity Research Initiative. 2017. 'Mainstreaming Equity in Education'. Education Equity Research Initiative. October 27, 2017. www.fhi360.org/sites/default/files/media/documents/resource-mainstreaming-equity-education.pdf.

'Education Policy Outlook in Norway'. 2020. OECD Education Policy Perspectives. Organisation for Economic Co-Operation and Development (OECD). https://doi.org/10.1787/8a042924-en.

Ehlert, A., and A. Fritz. 2013. 'Evaluation of Maths Training Programme for Children with Learning Difficulties'. *South African Journal of Childhood Education* 3 (1): 117–40.

Ehlert, A., U. Schroeders, and A. Fritz-Stratmann. 2012. 'Kritik Am Diskrepanzkriterium in Der Diagnostik von Legasthenie Und Dyskalkulie'. *Lernen Und Lernstörungen* 1 (3): 169–84. https://doi.org/10.1024/2235-0977/a000018.

Ehri, L. C., S. R. Nunes, S. A. Stahl, and D. M. Willows. 2001. 'Systematic Phonics Instruction Helps Students Learn to Read: Evidence from the National Reading Panel's Meta-Analysis'. *Review of Educational Research* 71 (3): 393–447.

Ehri, L. C., S. R. Nunes, D. M. Willows, et al. 2001. 'Phonemic Awareness Instruction Helps Children Learn to Read: Evidence From the National Reading Panel's Meta-Analysis'. *Reading Research Quarterly* 36 (3): 250–87. https://doi.org/10.1598/rrq.36.3.2.

Eimeren, L. van, S. N. Niogi, B. D. McCandliss, I. D. Holloway, and D. Ansari. 2008. 'White Matter Microstructures Underlying Mathematical Abilities in Children'. *Neuroreport* 19 (11): 1117–21.

Einarsdóttir, J. T., A. Björnsdóttir, and I. Símonardóttir. 2016. 'The Predictive Value of Preschool Language Assessments on Academic Achievement: A 10-Year Longitudinal Study of Icelandic Children'. *American Journal of Speech-Language Pathology / American Speech-Language-Hearing Association* 25 (1): 67–79.

Elbro, C., and D. K. Petersen. 2004. 'Long-Term Effects of Phoneme Awareness and Letter Sound Training: An Intervention Study With Children at Risk for Dyslexia'. *Journal of Educational Psychology* 96 (4): 660–70. https://doi.org/10.1037/0022-0663.96.4.660.

Elder, T., D. Figlio, S. Imberman, and C. Persico. 2019. 'School Segregation and Racial Gaps in Special Education Identification'. National Bureau of Economic Research. https://doi.org/10.3386/w25829.

Eliot, Lise. 2011. 'The Trouble with Sex Differences'. *Neuron* 72 (6): P895–8. https://doi.org/10.1016/j.neuron.2011.12.001.

Elliott, J. G., and E. L. Grigorenko. 2014. *The Dyslexia Debate.* Cambridge University Press.

Elliott, L., L. Feigenson, J. Halberda, and M. E. Libertus. 2019. 'Bidirectional, Longitudinal Associations between Math Ability and Approximate Number System Precision in Childhood'. *Journal of Cognition and Development: Official Journal of the Cognitive Development Society* 20 (1): 56–74.

Else-Quest, N. M., J. S. Hyde, and M. C. Linn. 2010. 'Cross-National Patterns of Gender Differences in Mathematics: A Meta-Analysis'. *Psychological Bulletin* 136 (1): 103–27.

Engle, P. L., M. M. Black, J. R. Behrman, et al. 2007. 'Strategies to Avoid the Loss of Developmental Potential in More than 200 Million Children in the Developing World'. *The Lancet* 369 (9557): 229–42.

Ennemoser, M., P. Marx, J. Weber, and W. Schneider. 2012. 'Spezifische Vorläuferfertigkeiten Der Lesegeschwindigkeit, Des Leseverständnisses Und Des Rechtschreibens'. *Zeitschrift Fur Entwicklungspsychologie Und Padagogische Psychologie* 44 (2): 53–67.

Erbeli, F., S. A. Hart, R. K. Wagner, and J. Taylor. 2018. 'Examining the Etiology of Reading Disability as Conceptualized by the Hybrid Model'. *Scientific Studies of Reading: The Official Journal of the Society for the Scientific Study of Reading* 22 (2): 167–80.

'Ernst Klett Verlag – Zahlenbuch – Frühförderprogramm Ausgabe Ab 2009 – Lehrwerk Konzeption'. n.d. Accessed July 29, 2021. https://www.klett.de/lehrwerk/zahlen buch-fruehfoerderprogramm-ausgabe-ab-2009/konzeption.

Espinoza, O. 2007. 'Solving the Equity–equality Conceptual Dilemma: A New Model for Analysis of the Educational Process'. *Educational Research* 49 (4): 343–63. https://doi.org/10.1080/00131880701717198.

European Commission/EACEA/Eurydice (2020). *Compulsory Education in Europe – 2020/21*. Eurydice Facts and Figures. Luxembourg: Publications Office of the European Union. Retrieved from https://eacea.ec.europa.eu/national-policies/eurydice/con tent/compulsory-education-europe-202021_en.

Evans, B. J. W., R. Patel, A. J. Wilkins, et al. 2008. 'A Review of the Management of 323 Consecutive Patients Seen in a Specific Learning Difficulties Clinic'. *Ophthalmic & Physiological Optics: The Journal of the British College of Ophthalmic Opticians* 19 (6): 454–66.

Eyal, G. 2013. 'For a Sociology of Expertise: The Social Origins of the Autism Epidemic'. *The American Journal of Sociology* 118 (4): 863–907.

Fan, J., B. Mccandliss, J. Fossella, J. Flombaum, and M. Posner. 2005. 'The Activation of Attentional Networks'. *NeuroImage* 26 (2): 471–9. https://doi.org/10.1016/j.neuroimage.2005.02.004.

Faramarzi, S., A. Yarmohamadian, M. Malekpour, P. Shirzadi, and M. Qasemi. 2016. 'The Effect of Neuropsychological Interventions on Language Performance in Preschool Children with Specific Language Impairment (SLI): A Case Study'. *Middle Eastern Journal of Disability Studies* 6: 304–16.

Farmer, M. E., and R. M. Klein. 1995. 'The Evidence for a Temporal Processing Deficit Linked to Dyslexia: A Review'. *Psychonomic Bulletin & Review* 2 (4): 460–93.

Farrington-Flint, L., S. Vanuxem-Cotterill, and J. Stiller. 2009. 'Patterns of Problem-Solving in Children's Literacy and Arithmetic'. *British Journal of Developmental Psychology* 27 (4): 815–34. https://doi.org/10.1348/026151008x383148.

Fawcett, A. J. 2002. 'Dyslexia, the Cerebellum and Phonological Skill'. In *Basic Functions of Language, Reading and Reading Disability*, edited by E. Witruk, A. D. Friederici, and T. Lachmann, 265–79. Springer US.

Feingold, A. 1994. 'Gender Differences in Variability in Intellectual Abilities: A Cross-Cultural Perspective'. *Sex Roles* 30 (1): 81–92.

Feng, J., I. Spence, and J. Pratt. 2007. 'Playing an Action Video Game Reduces Gender Differences in Spatial Cognition'. *Psychological Science* 18 (10): 850–5.

Ferraz, E., T. Dos Santos Gonçalves, T. Freire, et al. 2018. 'Effects of a Phonological Reading and Writing Remediation Program in Students with Dyslexia: Intervention for Specific Learning Disabilities'. *Folia Phoniatrica et Logopaedica: Official Organ of the International Association of Logopedics and Phoniatrics* 70 (2): 59–73.

Fertonani, A., C. Ferrari, and C. Miniussi. 2015. 'What Do You Feel If I Apply Transcranial Electric Stimulation? Safety, Sensations and Secondary Induced Effects'. *Clinical Neurophysiology* 126 (11): 2181–8. https://doi.org/10.1016/j.clinph.2015.03.015.

Fiez, J. A., D. A. Balota, M. E. Raichle, and S. E. Petersen. 1999. 'Effects of Lexicality, Frequency, and Spelling-to-Sound Consistency on the Functional Anatomy of Reading'. *Neuron* 24 (1): P205–218. https://doi.org/10.1016/s0896-6273(00)80833-8.

Finisguerra, A., R. Borgatti, and C. Urgesi. 2019. 'Non-Invasive Brain Stimulation for the Rehabilitation of Children and Adolescents With Neurodevelopmental Disorders: A Systematic Review'. *Frontiers in Psychology* 10 (February): 135.

Fiori, V., M. Coccia, C. V. Marinelli, et al. 2011. 'Transcranial Direct Current Stimulation Improves Word Retrieval in Healthy and Nonfluent Aphasic Subjects'. *Journal of Cognitive Neuroscience* 23 (9): 2309–23.

Fischbach, A., K. Schuchardt, J. Brandenburg, et al. 2013. 'Prävalenz von Lernschwächen Und Lernstörungen: Zur Bedeutung Der Diagnosekriterien'. *Lernen Und Lernstörungen* 2 (2): 65–76.

Fischer, F. W., I. Y. Liberman, and D. Shankweiler. 1978. 'Reading Reversals and Developmental Dyslexia: A Further Study'. *Cortex: A Journal Devoted to the Study of the Nervous System and Behavior* 14 (4): 496–510.

Fischer, M. Y., and M. Pfost. 2015. 'Wie Effektiv Sind Maßnahmen Zur Förderung Der Phonologischen Bewusstheit?' *Zeitschrift Für Entwicklungspsychologie Und Pädagogische Psychologie* 47: 35–51. https://doi.org/10.1026/0049-8637/a000121.

Fishbein, B., M. O. Martin, I. V. S. Mullis, and P. Foy. 2018. 'The TIMSS 2019 Item Equivalence Study: Examining Mode Effects for Computer-Based Assessment and Implications for Measuring Trends'. *Large-Scale Assessments in Education* 6 (11). https://doi.org/10.1186/s40536-018-0064-z.

Fish, R. E. 2017. 'The Racialized Construction of Exceptionality: Experimental Evidence of Race/ethnicity Effects on Teachers' Interventions'. *Social Science Research* 62 (February): 317–34.

——— 2019. 'Standing Out and Sorting In: Exploring the Role of Racial Composition in Racial Disparities in Special Education'. *American Educational Research Journal* 56 (6): 2573–608.

——— 2022. "Stratified Medicalization of Children's Schooling Difficulties." Paper presented at the Interdisciplinary Training Program Fellows Conference, University of Wisconsin.

Fivush, R., and K. Nelson. 2004. 'Culture and Language in the Emergence of Autobiographical Memory'. *Psychological Science* 15 (9): 573–7.

Flannery, K. A., J. Liederman, L. Daly, and J. Schultz. 2000. 'Male Prevalence for Reading Disability Is Found in a Large Sample of Black and White Children Free from Ascertainment Bias'. *Journal of the International Neuropsychological Society* 6 (4): 433–420. https://doi.org/10.1017/s1355617700644016.

Fletcher, J. M., R. Savage, and S. Vaughn. 2020. 'A Commentary on Bowers (2020) and the Role of Phonics Instruction in Reading'. *Educational Psychology Review* 33: 1249–74. November. https://doi.org/10.1007/s10648-020-09580-8.

Flowers, L., M. Meyer, J. Lovato, F. Wood, and R. Felton. 2001. 'Does Third Grade Discrepancy Status Predict the Course of Reading Development?' *Annals of Dyslexia* 51 (1): 49–71.

'Förderboxen Für KiTa Und Anfangsunterricht – Mengen, Zählen, Zahlen (MZZ) – Die Welt Der Mathematik Verstehen – Koffer Mit Fördermaterialien Und Handreichungen (80 S.)'. n.d. Accessed 24 August 2021. /www.cornelsen.de/produkte/foerder boxen-fuer-kita-und-anfangsunterricht-mengen-zaehlen-zahlen-mzz-die-welt-der-mathematik-verstehen-koffer-mit-foerdermaterialien-und-handreichungen-80-s-9783060800155.

Foy, J. G., and V. A. Mann. 2013. 'Executive Function and Early Reading Skills'. *Reading and Writing* 26 (3): 453–72.

Francis, D. J., J. M. Fletcher, K. K. Stuebing, et al. 2005. 'Psychometric Approaches to the Identification of LD'. *Journal of Learning Disabilities* 38 (2): 98–108. https://doi.org/10.1177/00222194050380020101.

Franco, A., N. Malhotra, and G. Simonovits. 2014. 'Social Science. Publication Bias in the Social Sciences: Unlocking the File Drawer'. *Science* 345 (6203): 1502–5.

Frankland, P. W., S. Köhler, and S. A. Josselyn. 2013. 'Hippocampal Neurogenesis and Forgetting'. *Trends in Neurosciences* 36 (9): 497–503.

Frederick, A., and D. Shifrer. 2019. 'Race and Disability: From Analogy to Intersectionality'. *Sociology of Race and Ethnicity* 5 (2): 200–14.

Fredricks, J. A., and J. S. Eccles. 2002. 'Children's Competence and Value Beliefs from Childhood through Adolescence: Growth Trajectories in Two Male-Sex-Typed Domains'. *Developmental Psychology* 38 (4): 519–33.

Freud, S. 1924. A General Introduction to Psychoanalysis. Washington Square Press.

Frick, A. 2019. 'Spatial Transformation Abilities and Their Relation to Later Mathematics Performance'. *Psychological Research* 83 (7): 1465–84.

Friso-van den Bos, I., E. H. Kroesbergen, J. E. H. Van Luit, et al. 2015. 'Longitudinal Development of Number Line Estimation and Mathematics Performance in Primary School Children'. *Journal of Experimental Child Psychology* 134 (June): 12–29.

Frith, U. 2017. 'Beneath the Surface of Developmental Dyslexia'. In *Surface Dyslexia*. Routledge. https://doi.org/10.4324/9781315108346-18.

Frith, U. 1999. 'Paradoxes in the Definition of Dyslexia'. *Dyslexia* 5 (4): 192–214.

Froehlich, T. E., J. Fogler, W. J. Barbaresi, et al. 2018. 'Using ADHD Medications to Treat Coexisting ADHD and Reading Disorders: A Systematic Review'. *Clinical Pharmacology and Therapeutics* 104 (4): 619–37.

Fuchs, L. S., D. L. Compton, D. Fuchs, et al. 2005. 'The Prevention, Identification, and Cognitive Determinants of Math Difficulty'. *Journal of Educational Psychology* 97 (3): 493–513.

Fuchs, L. S., and D. Fuchs. 1986. 'Effects of Systematic Formative Evaluation: A Meta-Analysis'. *Exceptional Children* 53 (3): 199–208. https://doi.org/10.1177/001440298605300301.

Fuchs, L. S., D. Fuchs, D. L. Compton, et al. 2006. 'The Cognitive Correlates of Third-Grade Skill in Arithmetic, Algorithmic Computation, and Arithmetic Word Problems'. *Journal of Educational Psychology* 98 (1): 29–43.

Fuchs, L. S., D. Fuchs, C. L. Hamlett, S. K. Hope, et al. 2006. 'Extending Responsiveness-to-Intervention to Math Problem-Solving at Third Grade'. *TEACHING Exceptional Children* 38 (4): 59–63. https://doi.org/10.1177/004005990603800409.

Fuchs, L. S., S. R. Powell, P. M. Seethaler, et al. 'The Effects of Strategic Counting Instruction, with and without Deliberate Practice, on Number Combination Skill among Students with Mathematics Difficulties'. *Learning and Individual Differences* 20 (2): 89–100.

Fuhs, M. W., and N. M. McNeil. 2013. 'ANS Acuity and Mathematics Ability in Preschoolers from Low-Income Homes: Contributions of Inhibitory Control'. *Developmental Science* 16 (1): 136–48.

Fuhs, M. W., K. Turner Nesbitt, D. Clark Farran, and N. Dong. 2014. 'Longitudinal Associations between Executive Functioning and Academic Skills across Content Areas'. *Developmental Psychology* 50 (6): 1698–709.

Fuhs, M. W., N. Tavassolie, Y. Wang, et al. 2021. 'Children's Flexible Attention to Numerical and Spatial Magnitudes in Early Childhood'. *Journal of Cognition and Development: Official Journal of the Cognitive Development Society* 22 (1): 22–47.

Furman, T., and O. Rubinsten. 2012. 'Symbolic and Non Symbolic Numerical Representation in Adults with and without Developmental Dyscalculia'. *Behavioral and Brain Functions: BBF* 8 (November): 55.

Furnes, B., and S. Samuelsson. 2009. 'Preschool Cognitive and Language Skills Predicting Kindergarten and Grade 1 Reading and Spelling: A Cross-Linguistic Comparison'. *Journal of Research in Reading* 32 (3): 275–92.

——— 2011. 'Phonological Awareness and Rapid Automatized Naming Predicting Early Development in Reading and Spelling: Results from a Cross-Linguistic Longitudinal Study'. *Learning and Individual Differences* 21 (1): 85–95.

Gabel, S. L., S. Curcic, J. J. W. Powell, K. Khader, and L. Albee. 2009. 'Migration and Ethnic Group Disproportionality in Special Education: An Exploratory Study'. *Disability & Society* 24 (5): 625–39.

Gabrieli, J. D. E. 2009. 'Dyslexia: A New Synergy between Education and Cognitive Neuroscience'. *Science* 325 (5938): 280–3.

Galaburda, A. M. 1993. 'Neurology of Developmental Dyslexia'. *Current Opinion in Neurobiology* 3 (2): 237–42.

Galaburda, A. M. (2018). The Role of Rodent Models in Dyslexia Research: Understanding the Brain, Sex Differences, Lateralization, and Behavior. In T. Lachmann & T. Weis (Eds.), *Literacy Studies. Reading and Dyslexia* (Vol. 16, pp. 83–102). Cham: Springer International Publishing. https://doi.org/10.1007/978-3-319-90805-2_5

Galaburda, A. M., G. F. Sherman, G. D. Rosen, F. Aboitiz, and N. Geschwind. 1985. 'Developmental Dyslexia: Four Consecutive Patients with Cortical Anomalies'. *Annals of Neurology* 18 (2): 222–33.

Gallagher, A., U. Frith, and M. J. Snowling. 2000. 'Precursors of Literacy Delay among Children at Genetic Risk of Dyslexia'. *Journal of Child Psychology and Psychiatry, and Allied Disciplines* 41 (2): 203–13.

Galuschka, K., R. Görgen, J. Kalmar, et al. 2020. 'Effectiveness of Spelling Interventions for Learners with Dyslexia: A Meta-Analysis and Systematic Review'. *Educational Psychologist* 55 (1): 1–20.

Galuschka, K., E. Ise, K. Krick, and G. Schulte-Körne. 2014. 'Effectiveness of Treatment Approaches for Children and Adolescents with Reading Disabilities: A Meta-Analysis of Randomized Controlled Trials'. *PloS One* 9 (2): e89900.

Garland-Thomson, R. 2020. 'Integrating Disability, Transforming Feminist Theory'. In C. R. McCann, S.-K. Kim, E. Ergun (eds.) *Feminist Theory Reader*. https://doi.org/10.4324/9781003001201-22.

Gathercole, S. E., and A. D. Baddeley. 2014. *Working Memory and Language*. Psychology Press.

Geary, D. C. 1989. 'A Model for Representing Gender Differences in the Pattern of Cognitive Abilities'. *The American Psychologist* 44 (8): 1155–6.

———. 2010. 'Missouri Longitudinal Study of Mathematical Development and Disability'. In *BJEP Monograph Series II, Number 7-Understanding Number Development and Difficulties*, 31:31–49. British Psychological Society.

———. 2011. 'Cognitive Predictors of Achievement Growth in Mathematics: A 5-Year Longitudinal Study'. *Developmental Psychology* 47 (6): 1539–52.

———. n.d. 'Missouri Longitudinal Study of Mathematical Development and Disability'. Accessed July 23, 2021. http://citeseerx.ist.psu.edu/viewdoc/summary?doi=10.1.1.473.6330.

Geary, D. C., D. B. Berch, and K. M. Koepke. 2014. *Evolutionary Origins and Early Development of Number Processing*. Academic Press.

Geary, D. C., and K. vanMarle. 2018. 'Growth of Symbolic Number Knowledge Accelerates after Children Understand Cardinality'. *Cognition* 177 (August): 69–78.

Geary, D. C. 1993. 'Mathematical Disabilities: Cognitive, Neuropsychological, and Genetic Components'. *Psychological Bulletin* 114 (2): 345–62.

Geeler, S. K., U. Grob, A. Heinze, et al. 2021. 'Längsschnittliche Messung Numerischer Kompetenzen von Kindergartenkindern'. *Diagnostica* 67 (2): 62–74.

Geiger, E. F., and M. E. Brewster. 2018. 'Development and Evaluation of the Individuals With Learning Disabilities And/or Difficulties Perceived Discrimination Scale'. *The Counseling Psychologist* 46 (6): 708–37. https://doi.org/10.1177/0011000018794919.

Gelfand, J. R., and S. Y. Bookheimer. 2003. 'Dissociating Neural Mechanisms of Temporal Sequencing and Processing Phonemes'. *Neuron* 38 (5): P831–42. https://doi.org/10.1016/s0896-6273(03)00285-x.

Georgiou, G. K., and R. Parrila. 2020. 'What Mechanism Underlies the Rapid Automatized Naming–reading Relation?' *Journal of Experimental Child Psychology* 194 (June): 104840.

Gerber, M. M. 2005. 'Teachers Are Still the Test: Limitations of Response to Instruction Strategies for Identifying Children with Learning Disabilities'. *Journal of Learning Disabilities* 38 (6): 516–24.

Gerlach, M., A. Fritz, G. Ricken, and S. Schmidt. 2007. Kalkulie. Diagnose- und Trainingsprogramm für rechenschwache Kinder. [Kalkulie. Diagnostic and Training]. https://www.cornelsen.de/reihen/kalkulie-diagnose-und-trainingsprogramm-fuer-rechenschwache-kinder-360002290000.

Gerlach, M., A. Fritz, and D. Leutner. 2013. *Mathematik- und Rechenkonzepte im Vor- und Grundschulalter – Training: MARKO-T; Manual*. Hogrefe.

Gersten, R., D. J. Chard, M. Jayanthi, et al. 2009. 'Mathematics Instruction for Students With Learning Disabilities: A Meta-Analysis of Instructional Components'. *Review of Educational Research* 79 (3): 1202–42.

Gibbs, S. J., and J. G. Elliott. 2020. 'The Dyslexia Debate: Life without the Label'. *Oxford Review of Education* 46 (4): 487–500.

Gibson, D. J., E. A. Gunderson, and S. C. Levine. 2020. 'Causal Effects of Parent Number Talk on Preschoolers' Number Knowledge'. *Child Development* 91 (6): e1162–77.

Gilmore, C., N. Attridge, S. Clayton, et al. 2013. 'Individual Differences in Inhibitory Control, Not Non-Verbal Number Acuity, Correlate with Mathematics Achievement'. *PloS One* 8 (6): e67374.

Ginsburg, A., and M. S. Smith. 2016. 'Do Randomized Controlled Trials Meet the "Gold Standard"'. *American Enterprise Institute*. www.carnegiefoundation.org/wp-content /uploads/2016/03/Do-randomized-controlled-trials-meet-the-gold-standard.pdf.

Giofrè, D., G. Cumming, L. Fresc, I. Boedker, and P. Tressoldi. 2017. 'The Influence of Journal Submission Guidelines on Authors' Reporting of Statistics and Use of Open Research Practices'. *PloS One* 12 (4): e0175583.

Given, B. K., J. D. Wasserman, S. A. Chari, K. Beattie, and G. F. Eden. 2008. 'A Randomized, Controlled Study of Computer-Based Intervention in Middle School Struggling Readers'. *Brain and Language* 106 (2): 83–97.

Göbel, S. M., K. Moeller, S. Pixner, L. Kaufmann, and H.-C. Nuerk. 2014. 'Language Affects Symbolic Arithmetic in Children: The Case of Number Word Inversion'. *Journal of Experimental Child Psychology* 119 (March): 17–25.

Goldin-Meadow, S., S. C. Levine, L. V. Hedges, et al. 2014. 'New Evidence about Language and Cognitive Development Based on a Longitudinal Study: Hypotheses for Intervention'. *The American Psychologist* 69 (6): 588–99.

Golinkoff, R. M., D. D. Can, M. Soderstrom, and K. Hirsh-Pasek. 2015. '(Baby)Talk to Me: The Social Context of Infant-Directed Speech and Its Effects on Early Language Acquisition'. *Current Directions in Psychological Science* 24 (5): 339–44.

González, J. E. J., and A. I. Garcia Espínel. 1999. 'Is IQ-Achievement Discrepancy Relevant in the Definition of Arithmetic Learning Disabilities?' *Learning Disability Quarterly: Journal of the Division for Children with Learning Disabilities* 22 (4): 291–301.

Goodwin, A. P., and S. Ahn. 2010. 'A Meta-Analysis of Morphological Interventions: Effects on Literacy Achievement of Children with Literacy Difficulties'. *Annals of Dyslexia* 60 (2): 183–208.

———. 2013. 'A Meta-Analysis of Morphological Interventions in English: Effects on Literacy Outcomes for School-Age Children'. *Scientific Studies of Reading: The Official Journal of the Society for the Scientific Study of Reading* 17 (4): 257–85.

Gordanier, J., O. Ozturk, B. Williams, and C. Zhan. 2020. 'Free Lunch for All! The Effect of the Community Eligibility Provision on Academic Outcomes'. *Economics of Education Review* 77 (August): 101999.

Görgen, R., E. De Simone, G. Schulte-Körne, and K. Moll. 2021. 'Predictors of Reading and Spelling Skills in German: The Role of Morphological Awareness'. *Journal of Research in Reading* 44 (1): 210–27.

Görgen, R., S. Huemer, G. Schulte-Körne, and K. Moll. 2020. 'Evaluation of a Digital Game-Based Reading Training for German Children with Reading Disorder'. *Computers & Education* 150 (June): 103834.

Goswami, U., and P. Bryant. 2016. *Phonological Skills and Learning to Read*. Psychology Press.

Goswami, U., J. C. Ziegler, and U. Richardson. 2005. 'The Effects of Spelling Consistency on Phonological Awareness: A Comparison of English and German'. *Journal of Experimental Child Psychology* 92 (4): 345–65.

Gottlieb, J., M.Alter, B. W. Gottlieb, and J. Wishner. 1994. 'Special Education in Urban America: It's Not Justifiable for Many'. *The Journal of Special Education* 27 (4): 453–65.

Gough, P. B., and W. E. Tunmer. 1986. 'Decoding, Reading and Reading Disability: Remedial and Special Education'. *Remedial and Special Education* 7(1): 6–10. doi:10.1177 /074193258600700104.

Goulandris, N. K., M. J. Snowling, and I. Walker. 2000. 'Is Dyslexia a Form of Specific Language Impairment? A Comparison of Dyslexic and Language Impaired Children as Adolescents'. *Annals of Dyslexia* 50 (1): 103–20.

Graham, L., and J. E. Pegg. 2010. 'Hard Data to Support the Effectiveness of 'QuickSmart' Numeracy'. https://rune.une.edu.au/web/handle/1959.11/7389.

———. 2011. 'Evaluating the QuickSmart Numeracy Program: An Effective Australian Intervention That Improves Student Achievement, Responds to Special Educational Needs, and Fosters Teacher Collaboration'. *The Journal of Educational Administration* 29(2): 87–102.

Groen, O. van der, and N. Wenderoth. 2016. 'Transcranial Random Noise Stimulation of Visual Cortex: Stochastic Resonance Enhances Central Mechanisms of Perception'. *The Journal of Neuroscience: The Official Journal of the Society for Neuroscience* 36 (19): 5289–98.

Gross-Tsur, V., O. Manor, and R. S. Shalev. 1996. 'Developmental Dyscalculia: Prevalence and Demographic Features'. *Developmental Medicine & Child Neurology* 38 (1): 25–33.

Grube, D., and M. Hasselhorn. 2006. *Längsschnittliche Analysen Zur Lese-, Rechtschreib- Und Mathematikleistung Im Grundschulalter: Zur Rolle von Vorwissen, Intelligenz, Phonologischem Arbeitsgedächtnis Und Phonologischer Bewusstheit*. na.

Gualtieri, T., and R. E. Hicks. 1991. 'An Immunoreactive Theory of Selective Male Affliction'. In *1986 Annual Progress In Child Psychiatry*. Routledge. https://doi .org/10.4324/9780203450499-13.

Guidi, L. G., A. Velayos-Baeza, I. Martinez-Garay, et al. 2018. 'The Neuronal Migration Hypothesis of Dyslexia: A Critical Evaluation 30 Years on'. *The European Journal of Neuroscience* 48 (10): 3212–33.

Guiso, L., F. Monte, P. Sapienza, and L. Zingales. 2008. 'Culture, Gender, and Math'. *Science* 320 (5880): 1164.

Gunderson, E. A., and S. C. Levine. 2011. 'Some Types of Parent Number Talk Count More than Others: Relations between Parents' Input and Children's Cardinal-Number Knowledge'. *Developmental Science* 14 (5): 1021–32.

Gunderson, E. A., Daeun Park, E. A. Maloney, S. L. Beilock, and S. C. Levine. 2018. 'Reciprocal Relations among Motivational Frameworks, Math Anxiety, and Math Achievement in Early Elementary School'. *Journal of Cognition and Development: Official Journal of the Cognitive Development Society* 19 (1): 21–46.

Gunderson, E. A., G. Ramirez, S. L. Beilock, and S. C. Levine. 2012. 'The Relation between Spatial Skill and Early Number Knowledge: The Role of the Linear Number Line'. *Developmental Psychology* 48 (5): 1229–41.

Gunderson, Elizabeth A., Gerardo Ramirez, Susan C. Levine, and Sian L. Beilock. 2012. 'The Role of Parents and Teachers in the Development of Gender-Related Math Attitudes'. *Sex Roles* 66: 153–66. https://doi.org/10 .1007/s11199-011-9996-2.

Gustafson, S., L. Fälth, I. Svensson, T. Tjus, and M. Heimann. 2011. 'Effects of Three Interventions on the Reading Skills of Children With Reading Disabilities in Grade 2'. *Journal of Learning Disabilities* 44 (2): 123–35.

Gustafson, S., J. Ferreira, and J. Rönnberg. 2007. 'Phonological or Orthographic Training for Children with Phonological or Orthographic Decoding Deficits'. *Dyslexia* 13 (3): 211–29.

Gutkin, Terry B., and Cecil R. Reynolds. 2008. *The Handbook of School Psychology, 4th Edition*. Wiley Global Education.

Halberda, J., and L. Feigenson. 2008. 'Developmental Change in the Acuity of the 'Number Sense': The Approximate Number System in 3-, 4-, 5-, and 6-Year-Olds and Adults'. *Developmental Psychology* 44 (5): 1457–65.

Halpern, D. F., C. P. Benbow, D. C. Geary, et al. 2007. 'The Science of Sex Differences in Science and Mathematics'. *Psychological Science in the Public Interest: A Journal of the American Psychological Society* 8 (1): 1–51.

Haman, M., K. Lipowska, M. Soltanlou, et al. 2020. 'The Plural Still Counts: Cross-Linguistic Study of the Symbolic Numerical Magnitude Comparison Task in Polish- and German-Speaking Preschoolers'. PsyArXiv. August 11.https://doi.org/10.31234/osf.io/ge8zq.

Hanf, K., & Scharpf, F. W. (1978). 'Interorganizational Policy Making Limits to Coordination and Central Control. London, Beverly Hills Sage Publications. – References – Scientific Research Publishing'. Accessed July 29, 2021. https://www.scirp.org/reference/referencespapers.aspx?referenceid=2594690.

Hannon, B. 2014. 'Are There Gender Differences in the Cognitive Components of Adult Reading Comprehension?' *Learning and Individual Differences* 32: 69–79. https://doi.org/10.1016/j.lindif.2014.03.017.

Hannula, M. M., J. Lepola, and E. Lehtinen. 2010. 'Spontaneous Focusing on Numerosity as a Domain-Specific Predictor of Arithmetical Skills'. *Journal of Experimental Child Psychology* 107 (4): 394–406.

Hanushek, E. A., and D. D. Kimko. 2000. 'Schooling, Labor-Force Quality, and the Growth of Nations'. *The American Economic Review* 90 (5): 1184–208.

Harry, B., and J. Klingner. 2007. 'Discarding the Deficit Model'. *Educational Leadership: Journal of the Department of Supervision and Curriculum Development, N.E.A* 64 (5): 16.

——— 2014. *Why Are So Many Minority Students in Special Education?, 2nd Edition*. Teachers College Press.

Hasselhorn, M., O. Köller, K. Maaz, and K. Zimmer. 2014. 'Implementation Wirksamer Handlungskonzepte Im Bildungsbereich Als Forschungsaufgabe'. *Psychologische Rundschau; Ueberblick Uber Die Fortschritte Der Psychologie in Deutschland, Oesterreich, Und Der Schweiz* 65 (3): 140–4.

Hasselhorn, M., and C. Mähler. 2006. 'Diagnostik von Lernstörungen'. *Handbuch Der Psychologischen Diagnostik*, 618–25.

Hasselhorn, M., W. Schneider, and U. Trautwein, eds. 2014. *Lernverlaufsdiagnostik*. 1st ed. Jahrbuch der pädagogisch-psychologischen Diagnostik. Tests und Trends. Hogrefe Verlag.

Hatcher, P. J., C. Hulme, and A. W. Ellis. 1994. 'Ameliorating Early Reading Failure by Integrating the Teaching of Reading and Phonological Skills: The Phonological Linkage Hypothesis'. *Child Development* 65 (1): 41–57. https://doi.org/10.2307/1131364.

Hattie, J. 2008. *Visible Learning: A Synthesis of Over 800 Meta-Analyses Relating to Achievement*. Routledge.

Hawes, Z., and D. Ansari. 2020. 'What Explains the Relationship between Spatial and Mathematical Skills? A Review of Evidence from Brain and Behavior'. *Psychonomic Bulletin & Review* 27 (3): 465–82.

Hawes, Z., J. Moss, B. Caswell, S. Naqvi, and S. MacKinnon. 2017. 'Enhancing Children's Spatial and Numerical Skills through a Dynamic Spatial Approach to Early Geometry Instruction: Effects of a 32-Week Intervention'. *Cognition and Instruction* 35 (3): 236–64.

Hawes, Z., N. Nosworthy, L. Archibald, and D. Ansari. 2019. 'Kindergarten Children's Symbolic Number Comparison Skills Relates to 1st Grade Mathematics Achievement: Evidence from a Two-Minute Paper-and-Pencil Test'. *Learning and Instruction* 59 (February): 21–33.

Hawke, J. L., R. K. Olson, E. G. Willcut, S. J. Wadsworth, and J. C. DeFries. 2009. 'Gender Ratios for Reading Difficulties'. *Dyslexia* 15 (3): 239–42. https://doi.org/10.1002/dys.389.

Hayashi, Y., H. Okita, M. Kinoshita, K. Miyashita, and M. Nakada. 2014. 'Functional Recovery from Pure Dyslexia with Preservation of Subcortical Association Fiber Networks'. *Interdisciplinary Neurosurgery* 1 (3): 59–62. https://doi.org/10.1016/j.inat.2014.06.004.

Hayek, M., A. Karni, and Z. Eviatar. 2019. 'Transcoding Number Words by Bilingual Speakers of Arabic: Writing Multi-Digit Numbers in a Units-Decades Inverting Language'. *Writing Systems Research* 11 (2): 188–202.

Hecht, S. A., S. R. Burgess, J. K. Torgesen, R. K. Wagner, and C. A. Rashotte. 2000. 'Explaining Social Class Differences in Growth of Reading Skills from Beginning Kindergarten through Fourth-Grade: The Role of Phonological Awareness, Rate of Access, and Print Knowledge'. *Reading and Writing* 12 (1): 99–128.

Heckman, J. J. 2012. 'Invest in Early Childhood Development: Reduce Deficits, Strengthen the Economy'. *The Heckman Equation* 7: 1–2.

Hedges, L., and A. Nowell. 1995. 'Sex Differences in Mental Test Scores, Variability, and Numbers of High-Scoring Individuals'. *Science* 269 (5220): 41–5. https://doi.org/10.1126/science.7604277.

Heim, S., J. Tschierse, K. Amunts, et al. 2008. 'Cognitive Subtypes of Dyslexia'. *Acta Neurobiologiae Experimentalis* 68 (1): 73–82.

Heine, A., J. Wissmann, S. Tamm, et al. 2013. 'An Electrophysiological Investigation of Non-Symbolic Magnitude Processing: Numerical Distance Effects in Children with and without Mathematical Learning Disabilities'. *Cortex: A Journal Devoted to the Study of the Nervous System and Behavior* 49 (8): 2162–77.

Hein, J., M. W. Bzufka, and K. J. Neumärker. 2000. 'The Specific Disorder of Arithmetic Skills. Prevalence Studies in a Rural and an Urban Population Sample and Their Clinico-Neuropsychological Validation'. *European Child & Adolescent Psychiatry* 9 Suppl 2: II87–101.

Hellstrand, H., J. Korhonen, K. Linnanmäki, and P. Aunio. 2020. 'The Number Race: Computer-Assisted Intervention for Mathematically Low-Performing First Graders'. *European Journal of Special Needs Education* 35 (1): 85–99.

Helmreich, I., J. Zuber, S. Pixner, et al. 2011. 'Language Effects on Children's Nonverbal Number Line Estimations'. *Journal of Cross-Cultural Psychology* 42 (4): 598–613.

Hensch, T. K. 2004. 'Critical Period Regulation'. *Annual Review of Neuroscience* 27 (1): 549–79.

Herbers, J. E., J. J. Cutuli, L. M. Supkoff, et al. 2012. 'Early Reading Skills and Academic Achievement Trajectories of Students Facing Poverty, Homelessness, and High Residential Mobility'. *Educational Researcher* 41 (9): 366–74.

Hess, K. 2003. *Lehren – zwischen Belehrung und Lernbegleitung: Einstellungen, Umsetzungen und Wirkungen im mathematischen Anfangsunterricht.* h.e.p. Verlag.

Heth, I., and M. Lavidor. 2015. 'Improved Reading Measures in Adults with Dyslexia Following Transcranial Direct Current Stimulation Treatment'. *Neuropsychologia* 70 (April): 107–13.

Hibel, J., G. Farkas, and P. L. Morgan. 2010. 'Who is Placed into Special Education?' *Sociology of Education* 83 (4): 312–32.

Hibel, J., and A. D. Jasper. 2012. 'Delayed Special Education Placement for Learning Disabilities Among Children of Immigrants'. *Social Forces; a Scientific Medium of Social Study and Interpretation* 91 (2): 503–30.

Leiß, D. 2007. '"Hilf Mir, Es Selbst Zu Tun". Lehrerinterventionen Beim Mathematischen Modellieren'. Accessed July 29, 2021. www.fachportal-paedagogik.de/literatur/vollanzeige.html?FId=901385.

Hinshelwood, J. 1900. 'Congenital Word-Blindness'. *The Lancet* 155 (4004): 1506–8.

Hirvonen, R., A. Tolvanen, K. Aunola, and J.-E. Nurmi. 2012. 'The Developmental Dynamics of Task-Avoidant Behavior and Math Performance in Kindergarten and Elementary School'. *Learning and Individual Differences* 22 (6): 715–23.

Hjetland, H. N., E. I. Brinchmann, R. Scherer, C. Hulme, and M. Melby-Lervåg. 2020. 'Preschool Pathways to Reading Comprehension: A Systematic Meta-Analytic Review'. *Educational Research Review* 30 (June): 100323.

Ho, C. S.-H., D. W. Chan, K. K. H. Chung, S.-H. Lee, and S.-M. Tsang. 2007. 'In Search of Subtypes of Chinese Developmental Dyslexia'. *Journal of Experimental Child Psychology* 97 (1): 61–83. https://doi.org/10.1016/j.jecp.2007.01.002.

Ho, C. S.-H., and P. Bryant. 1997. 'Phonological Skills Are Important in Learning to Read Chinese'. *Developmental Psychology* 33 (6): 946–51. https://doi.org/10.1037/0012-1649.33.6.946.

Ho, C. S.-H., D. W.-O. Chan, S.-H. Lee, S.-M. Tsang, and V. H. Luan. 2004. 'Cognitive Profiling and Preliminary Subtyping in Chinese Developmental Dyslexia'. *Cognition* 91 (1): 43–75. https://doi.org/10.1016/s0010-0277(03)00163-x.

Ho, C. S.-H., and K.-M. Fong. 2005. 'Do Chinese Dyslexic Children Have Difficulties Learning English as a Second Language?' *Journal of Psycholinguistic Research* 34: 603–18. https://doi.org/10.1007/s10936-005-9166-1.

Hollingworth, L. S. 1926. *Gifted Children: Their Nature and Nurture.* Macmillan . https://doi.org/10.1037/10599-000.

Holloway, I. D., and D. Ansari. 2009. 'Mapping Numerical Magnitudes onto Symbols: The Numerical Distance Effect and Individual Differences in Children's Mathematics Achievement'. *Journal of Experimental Child Psychology* 103 (1): 17–29.

Holm, A., and B. Dodd. 1996. 'The Effect of First Written Language on the Acquisition of English Literacy'. *Cognition* 59 (2): 119–47.

Honig, M. I., ed. 2006. *New Directions in Education Policy Implementation: Confronting Complexity.* State University of New York Press.

Horwitz, B., J. M. Rumsey, and B. C. Donohue. 1998. 'Functional Connectivity of the Angular Gyrus in Normal Reading and Dyslexia'. *Proceedings of the National Academy of Sciences* 95 (15): 8939–44. https://doi.org/10.1073/pnas.95.15.8939.

Huang, Y.-Z., M.-K. Lu, A. Antal, et al. 2017. 'Plasticity Induced by Non-Invasive Transcranial Brain Stimulation: A Position Paper'. *Clinical Neurophysiology: Official Journal of the International Federation of Clinical Neurophysiology* 128 (11): 2318–29.

Huber, C., and M. Grosche. 2012. 'Das Response-to-Intervention-Modell Als Grundlage Für Einen Inklusiven Paradigmenwechsel in Der Sonderpädagogik'. *Zeitschrift Für Heilpädagogik* 63 (8): 312–22.

Huettig, F., R. Kolinsky, and T. Lachmann. 2018. 'The Culturally Co-Opted Brain: How Literacy Affects the Human Mind'. *Language, Cognition and Neuroscience* 33 (3): 275–7. https://doi.org/10.1080/23273798.2018.1425803.

Huettig, F., T. Lachmann, A. Reis, and K. M. Petersson. 2018. 'Distinguishing Cause from Effect – Many Deficits Associated with Developmental Dyslexia May Be a Consequence of Reduced and Suboptimal Reading Experience'. *Language, Cognition and Neuroscience* 33 (3): 333–50. https://doi.org/10.1080/23273798.2017.1348528.

Hughes, J. A., G. Phillips, and P. Reed. 2013. 'Brief Exposure to a Self-Paced Computer-Based Reading Programme and How It Impacts Reading Ability and Behaviour Problems'. *PloS One* 8 (11): e77867.

Hull, C., and B. Hjern. 1982. 'Helping Small Firms Grow: An Implementation Analysis of Small Firm Assistance Structures'. *European Journal of Political Research* 10 (2): 187–98.

Hulme, C., K. Goetz, D. Gooch, J. Adams, and M. J. Snowling. 2007. 'Paired-Associate Learning, Phoneme Awareness, and Learning to Read'. *Journal of Experimental Child Psychology* 96 (2): 150–66.

Hulme, Charles, Peter J. Hatcher, Kate Nation, et al. 2002. 'Phoneme Awareness Is a Better Predictor of Early Reading Skill than Onset-Rime Awareness'. *Journal of Experimental Child Psychology* 82 (1): 2–28.

Hulme, C., and M. J. Snowling. 2013. *Developmental Disorders of Language Learning and Cognition*. John Wiley & Sons.

———. 2015. 'Learning to Read: What We Know and What We Need to Understand Better'. *Child Development Perspectives* 7 (1): 1–5.

Hulme, C., V. V. Muter, and M. Snowling. 1998. 'Segmentation Does Predict Early Progress in Learning to Read Better than Rhyme: A Reply to Bryant'. *Journal of Experimental Child Psychology* 71 (1): 39–44.

Hung, Y.-H., S. J. Frost, and K. R. Pugh. 2018. 'Domain Generality and Specificity of Statistical Learning and Its Relation with Reading Ability'. In *Reading and Dyslexia: From Basic Functions to Higher Order Cognition*, edited by T. Lachmann and T. Weis, 33–55. Springer International Publishing.

Hurwitz, S., B. Perry, E. D. Cohen, and R. Skiba. 2020. 'Special Education and Individualized Academic Growth: A Longitudinal Assessment of Outcomes for Students With Disabilities'. *American Educational Research Journal* 57 (2): 576–611.

Hutchison, J. E., I. M. Lyons, and D. Ansari. 2019. 'More Similar Than Different: Gender Differences in Children's Basic Numerical Skills Are the Exception Not the Rule'. *Child Development* 90 (1): e66–79.

Hu, W., H. L. Lee, Q. Zhang, et al. 2010. 'Developmental Dyslexia in Chinese and English Populations: Dissociating the Effect of Dyslexia from Language Differences'. *Brain: A Journal of Neurology* 133 (Pt 6): 1694–706.

Hyde, D. C., and E. S. Spelke. 2012. 'Spatiotemporal Dynamics of Processing Nonsymbolic Number: An Event-Related Potential Source Localization Study'. *Human Brain Mapping* 33 (9): 2189–203.

Hyde, J. S. 2005. 'The Gender Similarities Hypothesis'. *The American Psychologist* 60 (6): 581–92.

Hyde, J. S., and N. M. McKinley. 1997. 'Gender Differences in Cognition'. In *Gender Differences in Human Cognition*, Oxford Scholarship Online. https://doi.org/10.1093/acprof:oso/9780195112917.003.0002.

Hyde, J. S., S. M. Lindberg, M. C. Linn, A. B. Ellis, and C. C. Williams. 2008. 'Diversity. Gender Similarities Characterize Math Performance'. *Science* 321 (5888): 494–5.

Hyde, J. S., and M. C. Linn. 1988. 'Gender Differences in Verbal Ability: A Meta-Analysis'. *Psychological Bulletin* 104 (1): 53.

'ICD-10 Version:2019'. n.d. Accessed June 10, 2021. https://icd.who.int/browse10/2019/en.

'ICD-11'. n.d. Accessed July 29, 2021. https://icd.who.int/.

Imbo, I., C. V. Bulcke, J. De Brauwer, and W. Fias. 2014. 'Sixty-Four or Four-and-Sixty? The Influence of Language and Working Memory on Children's Number Transcoding'. *Frontiers in Psychology* 5 (April): 313.

'Individuelle Lernunterstützung in Schülerarbeitsphasen. Eine Videobasierte Analyse Des Unterstützungsverhaltens von Lehrpersonen Im Mathematikunterricht'. n.d. Accessed July 29, 2021. https://www.fachportal-paedagogik.de/literatur/vollan zeige.html?FId=880554.

Ingram, H. A. P. 1978. 'Soil Layers in Mires: Function and Terminology'. *Journal of Soil Science* 29 (2): 224–7.

Ise, E., and G. Schulte-Körne. 2013. 'Symptomatik, Diagnostik Und Behandlung Der Rechenstörung'. *Zeitschrift Für Kinder- Und Jugendpsychiatrie Und Psychotherapie* 41 (4): 271–82. https://doi.org/10.1024/1422-4917/a000241.

Iuculano, T., and R. Cohen Kadosh. 2014. 'Preliminary Evidence for Performance Enhancement Following Parietal Lobe Stimulation in Developmental Dyscalculia'. *Frontiers in Human Neuroscience* 8 (February): 38.

Jacobson, L., M. Koslowsky, and M. Lavidor. 2012. 'tDCS Polarity Effects in Motor and Cognitive Domains: A Meta-Analytical Review'. *Experimental Brain Research. Experimentelle Hirnforschung. Experimentation Cerebrale* 216 (1): 1–10.

James, W. H. 2000. 'Why Are Boys More Likely to Be Preterm than Girls? Plus Other Related Conundrums in Human Reproduction'. *Human Reproduction* 15 (10): 2108–11.

Jamison, Eliot A., Dean T. Jamison, and Eric A. Hanushek. 2007. 'The Effects of Education Quality on Income Growth and Mortality Decline'. *Economics of Education Review* 26 (6): 771–88.

Jiménez, J. E., C. G. de la Cadena, L. S. Siegel, et al. 2011. 'Gender Ratio and Cognitive Profiles in Dyslexia: A Cross-National Study'. *Reading and Writing* 24 (7): 729–47.

Jimenez, J. E., M. del Rosario Ortiz, M. Rodrigo, et al. 2003. 'Do the Effects of Computer-Assisted Practice Differ for Children with Reading Disabilities With and Without IQ – Achievement Discrepancy?' *Journal of Learning Disabilities* 36 (1): 34–47.

Jirout, J. J., and N. S. Newcombe. 2015. 'Building Blocks for Developing Spatial Skills: Evidence from a Large, Representative US Sample'. *Psychological Science* 26 (3): 302–10.

Joel, D., and A. Fausto-Sterling. 2016. 'Beyond Sex Differences: New Approaches for Thinking about Variation in Brain Structure and Function'. *Philosophical*

Transactions of the Royal Society of London. Series B, Biological Sciences 371 (1688): 20150451.

Johnson, E., D. F. Mellard, D. Fuchs, and M. A. McKnight. 2006. 'Responsiveness to Intervention (RTI): How to Do It. [RTI Manual]'. *National Research Center on Learning Disabilities*, August. http://files.eric.ed.gov/fulltext/ED496979.pdf.

Jones, M. G., and J. Wheatley. 1990. 'Gender Differences in Teacher-Student Interactions in Science Classrooms'. *Journal of Research in Science Teaching* 27 (9): 861–74. https://doi.org/10.1002/tea.3660270906.

Jong, P. F. de, and E. van Bergen. 2017. *Issues in Diagnosing Dyslexia*. John Benjamins Publishing Company. https://benjamins.com/catalog/z.206.21dej.

Jordan, N. C., J. Huttenlocher, and S. C. Levine. 1992. 'Differential Calculation Abilities in Young Children from Middle- and Low-Income Families'. *Developmental Psychology* 28 (4): 644–53. https://doi.org/10.1037/0012-1649.28.4.644.

Jordan, N. C., D. Kaplan, M. N. Locuniak, and C. Ramineni. 2007. 'Predicting First-Grade Math Achievement from Developmental Number Sense Trajectories'. *Learning Disabilities Research & Practice* 22 (1): 36–46. https://doi.org/10.1111/j.1540-5826.2007.00229.x.

Jordan, N. C., D. Kaplan, C. Ramineni, and M. N. Locuniak. 2009a. 'Early Math Matters: Kindergarten Number Competence and Later Mathematics Outcomes'. *Developmental Psychology* 45 (3): 850–67. https://doi.org/10.1037/a0014939.

2009b. 'Early Math Matters: Kindergarten Number Competence and Later Mathematics Outcomes'. *Developmental Psychology* 45 (3): 850–67.

Joshi, R. M. 2018. 'Simple View of Reading (SVR) in Different Orthographies: Seeing the Forest with the Trees'. In *Reading and Dyslexia: From Basic Functions to Higher Order Cognition*, edited by T. Lachmann and T. Weis, 71–80. Springer International Publishing.

Joshi, R. M., and K. Wijekumar. 2020. 'Introduction to the Special Issue: "Teacher Knowledge of Literacy Skills."' *Dyslexia* 26 (2): 117–19.

Josselyn, S. A., and P. W. Frankland. 2012. 'Infantile Amnesia: A Neurogenic Hypothesis'. *Learning & Memory* 19 (9): 423–33.

Jovanović, G., Z. Jovanović, J. Banković-Gajić, et al. 2013. 'The Frequency of Dyscalculia among Primary School Children'. *Psychiatria Danubina* 25 (2): 170–74.

Joyce, T., and S. R. Borgwaldt. 2013. 'Typology of Writing Systems'. *Typology of Writing Systems* 51: 1–12. https://doi.org/10.1075/bct.51.01joy.

Józsa, K., and K. Caplovitz Barrett. 2018. 'Affective and Social Mastery Motivation in Preschool as Predictors of Early School Success: A Longitudinal Study'. *Early Childhood Research Quarterly* 45 (October): 81–92.

Jussim, L., and J. S. Eccles. 1992. 'Teacher Expectations: II. Construction and Reflection of Student Achievement'. *Journal of Personality and Social Psychology* 63 (6): 947–61. https://doi.org/10.1037/0022-3514.63.6.947.

Kang, C. Y., G. J. Duncan, D. H. Clements, J. Sarama, and D. H. Bailey. 2019. 'The Roles of Transfer of Learning and Forgetting in the Persistence and Fadeout of Early Childhood Mathematics Interventions'. *Journal of Educational Psychology* 111 (4): 590–603.

Karbach, J., T. Strobach, and T. Schubert. 2015. 'Adaptive Working-Memory Training Benefits Reading, but Not Mathematics in Middle Childhood'. *Child Neuropsychology: A Journal on Normal and Abnormal Development in Childhood and Adolescence* 21 (3): 285–301.

Karlsen, J., S.-A. Halaas Lyster, and A. Lervåg. 2017. 'Vocabulary Development in Norwegian L1 and L2 Learners in the Kindergarten-School Transition'. *Journal of Child Language* 44 (2): 402–26.

Kaufmann, L., P. Handl, and B. Thöny. 2003. 'Evaluation of a Numeracy Intervention Program Focusing on Basic Numerical Knowledge and Conceptual Knowledge: A Pilot Study'. *Journal of Learning Disabilities* 36 (6): 564–73.

Kaufmann, L., H. C. Nuerk, M. Graf, H. Krinzinger, M. Delazer, and K. Willmes. 2009. 'TEDI-MATH: Test Zur Erfassung Numerisch-Rechnerischer Fertigkeiten Für 4-8 Jährige'. https://uni-salzburg.elsevierpure.com/en/publications/tedi-math-test-zur-erfassung-numerisch-rechnerischer-fertigkeiten.

Kaufmann, L., and S. Pixner. 2012. 'New Approaches to Teaching Early Number Skills and to Remediate Number Fact Dyscalculia'. In *Reading, Writing, Mathematics and the Developing Brain: Listening to Many Voices*, edited by Z. Breznitz, O. Rubinsten, V. J. Molfese, and D. L. Molfese, 277–94. Springer Netherlands.

Kay, J., and D. Yeo. 2012. *Dyslexia and Maths*. David Fulton Publishers. https://doi.org/10.4324/9780203459478.

Kekic, M., E. Boysen, I. C. Campbell, and U. Schmidt. 2016. 'A Systematic Review of the Clinical Efficacy of Transcranial Direct Current Stimulation (tDCS) in Psychiatric Disorders'. *Journal of Psychiatric Research* 74 (March): 70–86.

Keller, K., and V. Menon. 2009. 'Gender Differences in the Functional and Structural Neuroanatomy of Mathematical Cognition'. *NeuroImage* 47 (1): 342–52.

Kelly, Steven N. 1998. 'Preschool Classroom Teachers' Perceptions of Useful Music Skills and Understandings'. *Journal of Research in Music Education* 46 (3): 374–83. https://doi.org/10.2307/3345549.

Kennedy, N. I., W. H. Lee, and S. Frangou. 2018. 'Efficacy of Non-Invasive Brain Stimulation on the Symptom Dimensions of Schizophrenia: A Meta-Analysis of Randomized Controlled Trials'. *European Psychiatry: The Journal of the Association of European Psychiatrists* 49 (March): 69–77.

Keong, W. K., V. Pang, C. K. Eng, and T. C. Keong. 2016. 'Prevalence Rate of Dyscalculia According to Gender and School Location in Sabah, Malaysia'. In *7th International Conference on University Learning and Teaching (InCULT 2014) Proceedings*, 91–100. Springer Singapore.

Kersey, A. J., E. J. Braham, K. D. Csumitta, M. E. Libertus, and J. F. Cantlon. 2018. 'No Intrinsic Gender Differences in Children's Earliest Numerical Abilities'. *NPJ Science of Learning* 3 (July): 12.

Kersey, A. J., K. D. Csumitta, and J. F. Cantlon. 2019. 'Gender Similarities in the Brain during Mathematics Development'. *NPJ Science of Learning* 4 (November): 19.

Kershner, J. R. 2019. 'Neurobiological Systems in Dyslexia'. *Trends in Neuroscience and Education* 14 (March): 11–24.

Khong, L. Y.-L., and P. T. Ng. 2005. 'School–Parent Partnerships in Singapore'. *Educational Research for Policy and Practice* 4: 1–11. https://doi.org/10.1007/s10671-005-5617-6.

Kiger, D., D. Herro, and D. Prunty. 2012. 'Examining the Influence of a Mobile Learning Intervention on Third Grade Math Achievement'. *International Journal of Information and Communication Technology Education: An Official Publication of the Information Resources Management Association* 45 (1): 61–82.

Kim, S. Y., L. Liu, and F. Cao. 2017. 'How Does First Language (L1) Influence Second Language (L2) Reading in the Brain? Evidence from Korean-English and Chinese-English Bilinguals'. *Brain and Language* 171 (August): 1–13.

Kim, S. Y., T. Qi, X. Feng, G. Ding, L. Liu, and Fan Cao. 2016. 'How Does Language Distance between L1 and L2 Affect the L2 Brain Network? An fMRI Study of Korean–Chinese–English Trilinguals'. *NeuroImage* 129: 25–39. https://doi.org/10.1016/j.neuroimage.2015.11.068.

Kirschner, P. A., J. Sweller, and R. E. Clark. 2006. 'Why Minimal Guidance During Instruction Does Not Work: An Analysis of the Failure of Constructivist, Discovery, Problem-Based, Experiential, and Inquiry-Based Teaching'. *Educational Psychologist* 41 (2): 75–86.

Kita, Y., H. Yamamoto, K. Oba, et al. 2013. 'Altered Brain Activity for Phonological Manipulation in Dyslexic Japanese Children'. *Brain: A Journal of Neurology* 136 (Pt 12): 3696–708.

Kivirauma, J., and K. Ruoho. 2007. 'Excellence through Special Education? Lessons from the Finnish School Reform'. *International Review of Education. Internationale Zeitschrift Fur Erziehungswissenschaft. Revue Internationale de Pedagogie* 53 (3): 283–302.

Kjeldsen, A.-C., P. Niemi, and Å. Olofsson. 2003. 'Training Phonological Awareness in Kindergarten Level Children: Consistency Is More Important than Quantity'. *Learning and Instruction* 13 (4): 349–65. https://doi.org/10.1016/s0959-4752(02)00009-9.

Kjeldsen, A.-C., L. Educ, S. K. Saarento-Zaprudin, and P. O. Niemi. 2019. 'Kindergarten Training in Phonological Awareness: Fluency and Comprehension Gains Are Greatest for Readers at Risk in Grades 1 Through 9'. *Journal of Learning Disabilities* 52 (5): 366–82. https://doi.org/10.1177/0022219419847154.

Kjeldsen, A.-C., A. Kärnä, P. Niemi, Å. Olofsson, and K. Witting. 2014. 'Gains From Training in Phonological Awareness in Kindergarten Predict Reading Comprehension in Grade 9'. *Scientific Studies of Reading* 18 (6): 452–67. https://doi.org/10.1080/10888438.2014.940080.

Klatte, M., K. Bergström, C. Steinbrink, M. Konerding, and T. Lachmann. 2018. 'Effects of the Computer-Based Training Program Lautarium on Phonological Awareness and Reading and Spelling Abilities in German Second-Graders'. In *Reading and Dyslexia: From Basic Functions to Higher Order Cognition*, edited by T. Lachmann and T. Weis, 323–39. Springer International Publishing.

Klatte, M., J. Spilski, J. Mayerl, et al. 2017. 'Effects of Aircraft Noise on Reading and Quality of Life in Primary School Children in Germany: Results From the NORAH Study'. *Environment and Behavior* 49 (4): 390–424.

Kleemans, T., M. Peeters, E. Segers, and L. Verhoeven. 2012. 'Child and Home Predictors of Early Numeracy Skills in Kindergarten'. *Early Childhood Research Quarterly* 27 (3): 471–7.

Klein, E., J. Suchan, K. Moeller, et al. 2016. 'Considering Structural Connectivity in the Triple Code Model of Numerical Cognition: Differential Connectivity for Magnitude Processing and Arithmetic Facts'. *Brain Structure & Function* 221 (2): 979–95.

Klibanoff, R. S., S. C. Levine, J. Huttenlocher, M. Vasilyeva, and L. V. Hedges. 2006. 'Preschool Children's Mathematical Knowledge: The Effect of Teacher "Math Talk."' *Developmental Psychology* 42 (1): 59–69.

Klingner, J. K. 2006. 'The Special Education Referral and Decision-Making Process for English Language Learners: Child Study Team Meetings and Staffing,' May. https://nepc.colorado.edu/publication/special-education-referral-and-decision-making-process-english-language-learners-child-s.

Klock, H. 2020. *Adaptive Interventionskompetenz in Mathematischen Modellierungsprozessen: Konzeptualisierung, Operationalisierung und Förderung*. 1st ed. Studien Zur Theoretischen Und Empirischen Forschung In der M. Springer Spektrum.

Koeda, T., A. Seki, H. Uchiyama, and N. Sadato. 2011. 'Dyslexia: Advances in Clinical and Imaging Studies'. *Brain & Development* 33 (3): 268–75.

Kohn, J., L. Rauscher, K. Kucian, et al. 2020. 'Efficacy of a Computer-Based Learning Program in Children With Developmental Dyscalculia. What Influences Individual Responsiveness?' *Frontiers in Psychology* 11 (July): 1115.

Kolinsky, R., R. Gabriel, C. Demoulin, et al. 2020. 'The Influence of Age, Schooling, Literacy, and Socioeconomic Status on Serial-Order Memory'. *Journal of Cultural Cognitive Science* 4 (3): 343–65.

Kollosche, D., R. Marcone, M. Knigge, et al., eds. 2019. *Inclusive Mathematics Education: State-of-the-Art Research from Brazil and Germany*. 1st ed. Springer Nature.

Konerding, M., K. Bergström, T. Lachmann, and M. Klatte. 2020. 'Effects of Computerized Grapho-Phonological Training on Literacy Acquisition and Vocabulary Knowledge in Children with an Immigrant Background Learning German as L2'. *Journal of Cultural Cognitive Science* 4: 367–83. https://doi.org/10.1007/s41809-020-00064-3.

Kong, A., G. Thorleifsson, M. L. Frigge, et al. 2018. 'The Nature of Nurture: Effects of Parental Genotypes'. *Science* 359 (6374): 424–8.

Koponen, T., M. Aro, A.-M. Poikkeus, et al. 2018. 'Comorbid Fluency Difficulties in Reading and Math: Longitudinal Stability Across Early Grades'. *Exceptional Children* 84 (3): 298–311.

Koponen, T., K. Aunola, T. Ahonen, and J.-E. Nurmi. 2007. 'Cognitive Predictors of Single-Digit and Procedural Calculation Skills and Their Covariation with Reading Skill'. *Journal of Experimental Child Psychology* 97 (3): 220–41.

Korucu, I., E. Rolan, A. R. Napoli, D. J. Purpura, and S. A. Schmitt. 2019. 'Development of the Home Executive Function Environment (HEFE) Scale: Assessing Its Relation to Preschoolers' Executive Function'. *Early Childhood Research Quarterly* 47 (April): 9–19.

Kosc, L. 1974. 'Developmental Dyscalculia'. *Journal of Learning Disabilities* 7 (3): 164–77.

Koshmider, J. W., and M. H. Ashcraft. 1991. 'The Development of Children's Mental Multiplication Skills'. *Journal of Experimental Child Psychology* 51 (1): 53–89.

Koumoula, A., V. Tsironi, V. Stamouli, et al. 2004. 'An Epidemiological Study of Number Processing and Mental Calculation in Greek Schoolchildren'. *Journal of Learning Disabilities* 37 (5): 377–88.

Kovas, Y., I. Voronin, A. Kaydalov, S. B. Malykh, P. S. Dale, and R. Plomin. 2013. 'Literacy and Numeracy Are More Heritable Than Intelligence in Primary School'. *Psychological Science* 24 (10): 2048–56.

Koyama, M. S., P. C. Hansen, and J. F. Stein. 2008. 'Logographic Kanji versus Phonographic Kana in Literacy Acquisition'. *Annals of the New York Academy of Sciences* 1145 (1): 41–55. https://doi.org/10.1196/annals.1416.005.

Krajewski, K., G. Nieding, and W. Schneider. 2008. 'Kurz- Und Langfristige Effekte Mathematischer Frühförderung Im Kindergarten Durch Das Programm "Mengen,

Zählen, Zahlen"'. *Zeitschrift Für Entwicklungspsychologie Und Pädagogische Psychologie* 40 (3): 135–46. https://doi.org/10.1026/0049-8637.40.3.135.

Krajewski, K., and W. Schneider. 2009a. 'Early Development of Quantity to Number-Word Linkage as a Precursor of Mathematical School Achievement and Mathematical Difficulties: Findings from a Four-Year Longitudinal Study'. *Learning and Instruction* 19 (6): 513–26. https://doi.org/10.1016/j.learninstruc.2008.10.002.

———. 2009b. 'Exploring the Impact of Phonological Awareness, Visual–spatial Working Memory, and Preschool Quantity–number Competencies on Mathematics Achievement in Elementary School: Findings from a 3-Year Longitudinal Study'. *Journal of Experimental Child Psychology* 103 (4): 516–31. https://doi.org/10.1016/j.jecp.2009.03.009.

Kramarski, B., Z. R. Mevarech, and M. Arami. 2002. 'The Effects of Metacognitive Instruction on Solving Mathematical Authentic Tasks'. *Educational Studies in Mathematics* 49 (2): 225–50.

Krapohl, E., and R. Plomin. 2015. 'Genetic Link between Family Socioeconomic Status and Children's Educational Achievement Estimated from Genome-Wide SNPs'. *Molecular Psychiatry* 21 (3): 437–43.

Krause, B., and R. Cohen Kadosh. 2014. 'Not All Brains Are Created Equal: The Relevance of Individual Differences in Responsiveness to Transcranial Electrical Stimulation'. *Frontiers in Systems Neuroscience* 8 (February): 25.

Kroeger, L., and R. D. Brown. 2018. 'Enhancing Mathematical Cognitive Development Through Educational Interventions'. In *Neuroscience of Mathematical Cognitive Development: From Infancy Through Emerging Adulthood*, edited by R. Douglas Brown, 119–36. Springer International Publishing.

Kroesbergen, E. H., and J. E. H. van Luit. 2002. 'Teaching Multiplication to Low Math Performers: Guided versus Structured Instruction'. *Instructional Science* 30 (5): 361–78.

Kroesbergen, E. H., and J. E. H. van Luit. 2003. 'Mathematics Interventions for Children with Special Educational Needs'. *Remedial and Special Education: RASE* 24 (2): 97–114.

Krull, J., J. Wilbert, and T. Hennemann. 2014. 'The Social and Emotional Situation of First Graders with Classroom Behavior Problems and Classroom Learning Difficulties in Inclusive Classes'. *Learning Disabilities–A Contemporary Journal* 12 (2). www.researchgate.net/profile/Juergen_Wilbert2/publication/269391716_The_Social_and_Emotional_Situation_of_First_Graders_with_Classroom_Behavior_Problems_and_Classroom_Learning_Difficulties_in_Inclusive_Classes/links/5488407d0cf268d28f08b9c5.pdf.

Kucian, K., and M. von Aster. 2015. 'Developmental Dyscalculia'. *European Journal of Pediatrics* 174 (1): 1–13.

Kuhn, J.-T., and H. Holling. 2014. 'Number Sense or Working Memory? The Effect of Two Computer-Based Trainings on Mathematical Skills in Elementary School'. *Advances in Cognitive Psychology / University of Finance and Management in Warsaw* 10 (2): 59–67.

Lachmann, T. 2002. 'Reading Disability as a Deficit in Functional Coordination'. In *Basic Functions of Language, Reading and Reading Disability*, edited by E. Witruk, A. D. Friederici, and T. Lachmann, 165–98. Springer US.

Lachmann, T. 2008. 'Experimental Approaches to Specific Disabilities in Learning to Read: The Case of Symmetry Generalization in Developmental Dyslexia'. In

N. Srinivasan, A. K. Gupta, and J. Pandey (eds.), *Advances in Cognitive Science*, 321–42. Sage Publications.

2018. 'Reading and Dyslexia: The Functional Coordination Framework'. In *Reading and Dyslexia: From Basic Functions to Higher Order Cognition*, edited by T. Lachmann and T. Weis, 271–96. Springer International Publishing.

Lachmann, T., S. Berti, T. Kujala, and E. Schröger. 2005. 'Diagnostic Subgroups of Developmental Dyslexia Have Different Deficits in Neural Processing of Tones and Phonemes'. *International Journal of Psychophysiology: Official Journal of the International Organization of Psychophysiology* 56 (2): 105–20.

Lachmann, T., and C. van Leeuwen. 2014. 'Reading as Functional Coordination: Not Recycling but a Novel Synthesis'. *Frontiers in Psychology* 5 (September): 1046.

Lachmann, T., and C. Van Leeuwen. 2008. 'Different Letter-Processing Strategies in Diagnostic Subgroups of Developmental Dyslexia'. *Cognitive Neuropsychology* 25 (5): 730–44. https://doi.org/10.1080/02643290802309514.

Lachmann, T., and T. Weis. 2018. *Reading and Dyslexia: From Basic Functions to Higher Order Cognition*. Springer International Publishing.

Lambert, K., and B. Spinath. 2014. 'Do We Need a Special Intervention Program for Children with Mathematical Learning Disabilities or Is Private Tutoring Sufficient?' *Waxmann*. https://doi.org/10.25656/01:8841/ https://nbn-resolving.org/urn:nbn:de:0111-opus-88416.

2018. 'Are WISC IQ Scores in Children with Mathematical Learning Disabilities Underestimated? The Influence of a Specialized Intervention on Test Performance'. *Research in Developmental Disabilities* 72: 56–66. https://doi.org/10.1016/j.ridd.2017.10.016.

Landerl, K., H. H. Freudenthaler, M. Heene, et al. 2019. 'Phonological Awareness and Rapid Automatized Naming as Longitudinal Predictors of Reading in Five Alphabetic Orthographies with Varying Degrees of Consistency'. *Scientific Studies of Reading* 23 (3): 230–4. https://doi.org/10.1080/10888438.2018.1510936.

Landerl, K., and H. Wimmer. 2008. 'Development of Word Reading Fluency and Spelling in a Consistent Orthography: An 8-Year Follow-Up'. *Journal of Educational Psychology* 100 (1): 150–61. https://doi.org/10.1037/0022-0663.100.1.150.

Landerl, K., H. Wimmer, and U. Frith. 1997. 'The Impact of Orthographic Consistency on Dyslexia: A German-English Comparison'. *Cognition* 63 (3): 315–34.

Laycock, R., D. P. Crewther, P. B. Fitzgerald, and S. G. Crewther. 2009. 'TMS Disruption of V5/MT+ Indicates a Role for the Dorsal Stream in Word Recognition'. *Experimental Brain Research. Experimentelle Hirnforschung. Experimentation Cerebrale* 197 (1): 69–79.

Layes, S., R. Lalonde, Y. Bouakkaz, and M. Rebai. 2018. 'Effectiveness of Working Memory Training among Children with Dyscalculia: Evidence for Transfer Effects on Mathematical Achievement-a Pilot Study'. *Cognitive Processing* 19 (3): 375–85.

Lazonder, A. W., and R. Harmsen. 2016. 'Meta-Analysis of Inquiry-Based Learning'. *Review of Educational Research* 86 (3): 681–718.

Lazzaro, G., F. Costanzo, C. Varuzza, et al. 2020. 'Individual Differences Modulate the Effects of tDCS on Reading in Children and Adolescents with Dyslexia'. *Scientific Studies of Reading* 25 (6): 470–85. https://doi.org/10.1080/10888438.2020.1842413.

Leahy, A. M. 1961. 'Nature-Nurture and Intelligence'. In J. Jenkins and D. G. Paterson (Eds.), *Studies in Individual Differences: The Search for Intelligence*, pp. 376–95. https://doi.org/10.1037/11491-031.

Le Corre, M., and S. Carey. 2007. 'One, Two, Three, Four, Nothing More: An Investigation of the Conceptual Sources of the Verbal Counting Principles'. *Cognition* 105 (2): 395–438.

Lee, K.-M. 2004. 'Functional MRI Comparison between Reading Ideographic and Phonographic Scripts of One Language'. *Brain and Language* 91 (2): 245–51.

Lee Swanson, H., and C. Sachse-Lee. 2000. 'A Meta-Analysis of Single-Subject-Design Intervention Research for Students with LD'. *Journal of Learning Disabilities* 33 (2): 114–36.

Lefevre, J.-A., C. J. Lira, C. Sowinski, et al. 2013. 'Charting the Role of the Number Line in Mathematical Development'. *Frontiers in Psychology* 4 (September): 641.

LeFevre, J.-A., S.-L. Skwarchuk, B. L. Smith-Chant, et al. 2009. 'Home Numeracy Experiences and Children's Math Performance in the Early School Years'. *Canadian Journal of Behavioural Science. Revue Canadienne Des Sciences Du Comportement* 41 (2): 55–66.

Lekgoko, O., and H. Winskel. 2008. 'Learning to Read Setswana and English: Cross-Language Transference of Letter Knowledge, Phonological Awareness and Word Reading Skills'. *Perspectives in Education* 26 (4): 57–73.

Lê, M.-L. T., and M.-P. Noël. 2020. 'Transparent Number-Naming System Gives Only Limited Advantage for Preschooler's Numerical Development: Comparisons of Vietnamese and French-Speaking Children'. *PloS One* 15 (12): e0243472.

Lenhard, A., W. Lenhard, M. Schug, and A. Kowalski. 2011. 'Computerbasierte Mathematikförderung Mit Den "Rechenspielen Mit Elfe Und Mathis I"'. *Zeitschrift Für Entwicklungspsychologie Und Pädagogische Psychologie* 43 (2): 79–88. https://doi.org/10.1026/0049-8637/a000037.

Leonard, B. D., and P. Conrad. 1978. 'Identifying Hyperactive Children: The Medicalization of Deviant Behavior'. *Contemporary Sociology* 7 (6): 746–7. https://doi.org/10.2307/2065693.

Lervåg, A. 2005. *Prediction of Development in Beginning Reading and Spelling: A Norwegian Latent Variable Study*. Unipub, Univ. of Oslo, Fac. of Education.

——— 2020. 'Editorial: Some Roads Less Travelled-Different Routes to Understanding the Causes of Child Psychopathology'. *Journal of Child Psychology and Psychiatry, and Allied Disciplines* 61 (6): 625–7.

Lervåg, A., and V. G. Aukrust. 2010. 'Vocabulary Knowledge Is a Critical Determinant of the Difference in Reading Comprehension Growth between First and Second Language Learners'. *Journal of Child Psychology and Psychiatry, and Allied Disciplines* 51 (5): 612–20.

Lervåg, A., I. Bråten, and C. Hulme. 2009. 'The Cognitive and Linguistic Foundations of Early Reading Development: A Norwegian Latent Variable Longitudinal Study'. *Developmental Psychology* 45 (3): 764–81.

Lervåg, A., and C. Hulme. 2009. 'Rapid Automatized Naming (RAN) Taps a Mechanism That Places Constraints on the Development of Early Reading Fluency'. *Psychological Science* 20 (8): 1040–8.

Leung, F. K. S. 2014. 'What Can and Should We Learn from International Studies of Mathematics Achievement?' *Mathematics Education Research Journal* 26 (3): 579–605.

Levine, S. C., J. Huttenlocher, A. Taylor, and A. Langrock. 1999. 'Early Sex Differences in Spatial Skill'. *Developmental Psychology* 35 (4): 940–9. https://doi.org/10.1037 /0012-1649.35.4.940.

Levine, S. C., K. R. Ratliff, J. Huttenlocher, and J. Cannon. 2012. 'Early Puzzle Play: A Predictor of Preschoolers' Spatial Transformation Skill'. *Developmental Psychology* 48 (2): 530–42.

Levine, S. C., L. W. Suriyakham, M. L. Rowe, J. Huttenlocher, and E. A. Gunderson. 2010. 'What Counts in the Development of Young Children's Number Knowledge?' *Developmental Psychology* 46 (5): 1309–19.

Lewis, C., G. J. Hitch, and P. Walker. 1994. 'The Prevalence of Specific Arithmetic Difficulties and Specific Reading Difficulties in 9- to 10-Year-Old Boys and Girls'. *Journal of Child Psychology and Psychiatry, and Allied Disciplines* 35 (2): 283–92.

Libertus, M. E., L. Feigenson, and J. Halberda. 2013. 'Is Approximate Number Precision a Stable Predictor of Math Ability?' *Learning and Individual Differences* 25 (June): 126–33.

Libertus, M. E., D. Odic, L. Feigenson, and J. Halberda. 2016. 'The Precision of Mapping between Number Words and the Approximate Number System Predicts Children's Formal Math Abilities'. *Journal of Experimental Child Psychology* 150 (October): 207–26.

Liederman, J., L. Kantrowitz, and K. Flannery. 2005. 'Male Vulnerability to Reading Disability Is Not Likely to Be a Myth: A Call for New Data'. *Journal of Learning Disabilities* 38 (2): 109–29.

Lindberg, S. M., J. Shibley Hyde, J. L. Petersen, and M. C. Linn. 2010. 'New Trends in Gender and Mathematics Performance: A Meta-Analysis'. *Psychological Bulletin* 136 (6): 1123–35.

Lin, Y., X. Zhang, Q. Huang, et al. 2020. 'The Prevalence of Dyslexia in Primary School Children and Their Chinese Literacy Assessment in Shantou, China'. *International Journal of Environmental Research and Public Health* 17 (19). https://doi.org/10 .3390/ijerph17197140.

Lipsky, M. 1971. 'Street-Level Bureaucracy and the Analysis of Urban Reform'. *Urban Affairs Quarterly* 6 (4): 391–409.

Little, T. D. 2013. *Longitudinal Structural Equation Modeling*. Guilford Press.

Liu, K.-Y., M. King, and P. S. Bearman. 2010. 'Social Influence and the Autism Epidemic'. *AJS; American Journal of Sociology* 115 (5): 1387–434.

Liu, L., R. Tao, W. Wang, et al. 2013. 'Chinese Dyslexics Show Neural Differences in Morphological Processing'. *Developmental Cognitive Neuroscience* 6: 40–50. https://doi.org/10.1016/j.dcn.2013.06.004.

Liu, P. D., C. Mcbride-Chang, T. T.-Y. Wong, H. Shu, and A. M.-Y. Wong. 2013. 'Morphological Awareness in Chinese: Unique Associations of Homophone Awareness and Lexical Compounding to Word Reading and Vocabulary Knowledge in Chinese Children'. *Applied Psycholinguistics* 34 (4): 755–75. https://doi.org/10.1017/s014271641200001x.

Lloyd, J. W., J. M. Kauffman, T.J. Landrum, and D. L. Roe. 1991. 'Why Do Teachers Refer Pupils for Special Education? An Analysis of Referral Records'. *Exceptionality* 2 (3): 115–26.

Logan, S., and R. Johnston. 2009. 'Gender Differences in Reading Ability and Attitudes: Examining Where These Differences Lie'. *Journal of Research in Reading* 32 (2): 199–214.

——— 2010. 'Investigating Gender Differences in Reading'. *Educational Review* 62 (2): 175–87.

Logan, S., and E. Medford. 2011. 'Gender Differences in the Strength of Association between Motivation, Competency Beliefs and Reading Skill'. *Educational Research* 53 (1): 85–94. https://doi.org/10.1080/00131881.2011.552242.

Looi, C. Y., J. Lim, F. Sella, et al. 2017. 'Transcranial Random Noise Stimulation and Cognitive Training to Improve Learning and Cognition of the Atypically Developing Brain: A Pilot Study'. *Scientific Reports* 7 (1): 1–10.

Lopez, M., M. O. Ruiz, C. R. Rovnaghi, et al. 2021. 'The Social Ecology of Childhood and Early Life Adversity'. *Pediatric Research* 89 (2): 353–67.

Losen, D. J., and K. G. Welner. 2001. 'Disabling Discrimination in Our Public Schools: Comprehensive Legal Challenges to Inappropriate and Inadequate Special Education Services for Minority Children'. *The Harvard Civil Rights – Civil Liberties Law Review*. 36: 407.

Loveless, T. 2015. '2015 Brown Center Report on American Education: How Well Are American Students Learning?' Brookings. March 24, 2015. www.brookings.edu/research/2015-brown-center-report-on-american-education-how-well-are-american-students-learning/.

Lovett, M. W., L. Lacerenza, and S. L. Borden. 2000. 'Putting Struggling Readers on the PHAST Track: A Program to Integrate Phonological and Strategy-Based Remedial Reading Instruction and Maximize Outcomes'. *Journal of Learning Disabilities* 33 (5): 458–76.

Lovett, M. W., L. Lacerenza, M. De Palma, and J. C. Frijters. 2012. 'Evaluating the Efficacy of Remediation for Struggling Readers in High School'. *Journal of Learning Disabilities* 45 (2): 151–69.

Lovett, M. W., L. Lacerenza, K. A. Steinbach, and M. De Palma. 2014. 'Development and Evaluation of a Research-Based Intervention Program for Children and Adolescents with Reading Disabilities'. *Perspectives on Language and Literacy* 40 (3): 21–31.

Luby, J. L., T. Z. Baram, C. E. Rogers, and D. M. Barch. 2020. 'Neurodevelopmental Optimization after Early-Life Adversity: Cross-Species Studies to Elucidate Sensitive Periods and Brain Mechanisms to Inform Early Intervention'. *Trends in Neurosciences* 43 (10): 744–51.

Luciano, M., D. M. Evans, N. K. Hansell, et al. 2013. 'A Genome-Wide Association Study for Reading and Language Abilities in Two Population Cohorts'. *Genes, Brain, and Behavior* 12 (6): 645–52.

Ludwig, K. U., J. Schumacher, G. Schulte-Körne, et al. 2008. 'Investigation of the DCDC2 Intron 2 Deletion/compound Short Tandem Repeat Polymorphism in a Large German Dyslexia Sample'. *Psychiatric Genetics* 18 (6): 310–12.

Luke, K.-K., H.-L. Liu, Y.-Y. Wai, Y.-L. Wan, and L. H. Tan. 2002. 'Functional Anatomy of Syntactic and Semantic Processing in Language Comprehension'. *Human Brain Mapping* 16 (3): 133–45.

Lundberg, I., J. Frost, and O.-P. Petersen. 1988. 'Effects of an Extensive Program for Stimulating Phonological Awareness in Preschool Children'. *Reading Research Quarterly* 23 (3): 263–84. https://doi.org/10.1598/rrq.23.3.1.

Lu, Y., M. Ma, G. Chen, and X. Zhou. 2021. 'Can Abacus Course Eradicate Developmental Dyscalculia'. *Psychology in the Schools* 58 (2): 235–51.

Lyons, I. M., and S. L. Beilock. 2011. 'Numerical Ordering Ability Mediates the Relation between Number-Sense and Arithmetic Competence'. *Cognition* 121 (2): 256–61.

Macizo, P., A. Herrera, P. Román, and M. Cruz Martín. 2011. 'The Processing of Two-Digit Numbers in Bilinguals'. *British Journal of Psychology* 102 (3): 464–77.

Mahé, G., C. Pont, P. Zesiger, and M. Laganaro. 2018. 'The Electrophysiological Correlates of Developmental Dyslexia: New Insights from Lexical Decision and Reading Aloud in Adults'. *Neuropsychologia* 121 (December): 19–27.

Maïonchi-Pino, N., A. Magnan, and J. Ecalle. 2010. 'The Nature of the Phonological Processing in French Dyslexic Children: Evidence for the Phonological Syllable and Linguistic Features' Role in Silent Reading and Speech Discrimination'. *Annals of Dyslexia* 60 (2): 123–50.

Makita, K. 1968. 'The Rarity of Reading Disability in Japanese Children'. *The American Journal of Orthopsychiatry* 38 (4): 599–614.

Mann, B. 2014. 'Equity and Equality Are Not Equal'. *The Education Trust*. https://edtrust.org/the-equity-line/equity-and-equality-are-not-equal/.

Manolitsis, G., G. K. Georgiou, and N. Tziraki. 2013. 'Examining the Effects of Home Literacy and Numeracy Environment on Early Reading and Math Acquisition'. *Early Childhood Research Quarterly* 28 (4): 692–703.

Marchesotti, S., J. Nicolle, I. Merlet, L. H. Arnal, J. P. Donoghue, and A.-L. Giraud. 2020. 'Selective Enhancement of Low-Gamma Activity by tACS Improves Phonemic Processing and Reading Accuracy in Dyslexia'. *PLoS Biology* 18 (9): e3000833.

Marioni, R. E., G. Davies, C. Hayward, et al. 2014. 'Molecular Genetic Contributions to Socioeconomic Status and Intelligence'. *Intelligence* 44 (May): 26–32.

Marjou, Xavier. 2019. 'OTEANN: Estimating the Transparency of Orthographies with an Artificial Neural Network'. *arXiv [cs.CL]*. arXiv. http://arxiv.org/abs/1912.13321.

Mark, W., and A. Dowker. 2015. 'Linguistic Influence on Mathematical Development Is Specific rather than Pervasive: Revisiting the Chinese Number Advantage in Chinese and English Children'. *Frontiers in Psychology* 6 (February): 203.

Maroto, M., D. Pettinicchio, and A. C. Patterson. 2019. 'Hierarchies of Categorical Disadvantage: Economic Insecurity at the Intersection of Disability, Gender, and Race'. *Gender & Society: Official Publication of Sociologists for Women in Society* 33 (1): 64–93.

Marshall, A. T., S. Betts, E. C. Kan, R. McConnell, B. P. Lanphear, and E. R. Sowell. 2020. 'Association of Lead-Exposure Risk and Family Income with Childhood Brain Outcomes'. *Nature Medicine* 26 (1): 91–7.

Marsh, H. W., A. S. Abduljabbar, P. D. Parker, et al. 2015. 'The Internal/External Frame of Reference Model of Self-Concept and Achievement Relations: Age-Cohort and Cross-Cultural Differences'. *American Educational Research Journal* 52 (1): 168–202.

Martin, A., M. Kronbichler, and F. Richlan. 2016. 'Dyslexic Brain Activation Abnormalities in Deep and Shallow Orthographies: A Meta-analysis of 28 Functional Neuroimaging Studies'. *Human Brain Mapping* 37 (7): 2676–99. https://doi.org/10.1002/hbm.23202.

Massand, E. and A. Karmiloff-Smith. 2015. 'Cascading Genetic and Environmental Effects on Development: Implications for Intervention'. In K. J. Mitchell (ed.), *The Genetics of Neurodevelopmental Disorders*, 275–88. John Wiley & Sons, Inc.

Master, A., S. Cheryan, A. Moscatelli, and A. N. Meltzoff. 2017. 'Programming Experience Promotes Higher STEM Motivation among First-Grade Girls'. *Journal of Experimental Child Psychology* 160: 92–106. https://doi.org/10.1016/j.jecp.2017.03.013.

Maughan, B., and J. Carroll. 2006. 'Literacy and Mental Disorders'. *Current Opinion in Psychiatry* 19 (4): 350.

Mayes, S. D., and S. L. Calhoun. 2006. 'Frequency of Reading, Math, and Writing Disabilities in Children with Clinical Disorders'. *Learning and Individual Differences* 16 (2): 145–57.

Mazzocco, M. M. M., L. Feigenson, and J. Halberda. 2011. 'Preschoolers' Precision of the Approximate Number System Predicts Later School Mathematics Performance'. *PloS One* 6 (9): e23749.

McArthur, G., A. Castles, S. Kohnen, et al. 2015. 'Sight Word and Phonics Training in Children With Dyslexia'. *Journal of Learning Disabilities* 48 (4): 391–407.

McArthur, G., P. M. Eve, K. Jones, et al. 2012. 'Phonics Training for English-Speaking Poor Readers'. *Cochrane Database of Systematic Reviews* 12 (December): CD009115.

McArthur, G., Y. Sheehan, N. A. Badcock, et al. 2018. 'Phonics Training for English-speaking Poor Readers'. *Cochrane Database of Systematic Reviews*, no. 11. https://doi.org/10.1002/14651858.CD009115.pub3.

McArthur, G., S. Kohnen, K. Jones, et al. 2015. 'Replicability of Sight Word Training and Phonics Training in Poor Readers: A Randomised Controlled Trial'. *PeerJ* 3 (May): e922.

McBride, C., Y. Wang, and L. M.-L. Cheang. 2018. 'Dyslexia in Chinese'. *Current Developmental Disorders Reports* 5 (4): 217–25.

McBride-Chang, C. 1999. 'The ABCs of the ABCs: The Development of Letter-Name and Letter-Sound Knowledge'. *Merrill-Palmer Quarterly* 45 (2): 285–308.

McBride-Chang, C., J.-R. Cho, H. Liu, et al. 2005. 'Changing Models across Cultures: Associations of Phonological Awareness and Morphological Structure Awareness with Vocabulary and Word Recognition in Second Graders from Beijing, Hong Kong, Korea, and the United States'. *Journal of Experimental Child Psychology* 92 (2): 140–60.

McBride-Chang, C., K. K. H. Chung, and X. Tong. 2011. 'Copying Skills in Relation to Word Reading and Writing in Chinese Children with and without Dyslexia'. *Journal of Experimental Child Psychology* 110 (3): 422–33. https://doi.org/10.1016/j.jecp.2011.04.014.

McBride-Chang, C., F. Lam, C. Lam, et al. 2011. 'Early Predictors of Dyslexia in Chinese Children: Familial History of Dyslexia, Language Delay, and Cognitive Profiles'. *Journal of Child Psychology and Psychiatry* 52 (2): 204–11. https://doi.org/10.1111/j.1469-7610.2010.02299.x.

McCaskey, U., M. von Aster, R. O'Gorman Tuura, and K. Kucian. 2017. 'Adolescents with Developmental Dyscalculia Do Not Have a Generalized Magnitude Deficit – Processing of Discrete and Continuous Magnitudes'. *Frontiers in Human Neuroscience* 11. https://doi.org/10.3389/fnhum.2017.00102.

McCrink, K., and K. Wynn. 2004. 'Large-Number Addition and Subtraction by 9-Month-Old Infants'. *Psychological Science* 15 (11): 776–81.

McElvany, N., M. Kortenbruck, and M. Becker. 2008. 'Lesekompetenz Und Lesemotivation'. *Zeitschrift Für Pädagogische Psychologie* 22 (34): 207–19. https://doi.org/10.1024/1010-0652.22.34.207.

McEwen, B. S., N. P. Bowles, J. D. Gray, et al. 2015. 'Mechanisms of Stress in the Brain'. *Nature Neuroscience* 18 (10): 1353–63.

McGee, R., M. Prior, S. Williams, D. Smart, and A. Sanson. 2002. 'The Long-Term Significance of Teacher-Rated Hyperactivity and Reading Ability in Childhood: Findings from Two Longitudinal Studies'. *Journal of Child Psychology and Psychiatry* 43 (8): 1004–17. https://doi.org/10.1111/1469-7610.00228.

McLeskey, J., N. L. Waldron, and S. A. Wornhoff. 1990. 'Factors Influencing the Identification of Black and White Students with Learning Disabilities'. *Journal of Learning Disabilities* 23 (6): 362–66.

Meaburn, E. L., N. Harlaar, I. W. Craig, L. C. Schalkwyk, and R. Plomin. 2008. 'Quantitative Trait Locus Association Scan of Early Reading Disability and Ability Using Pooled DNA and 100K SNP Microarrays in a Sample of 5760 Children'. *Molecular Psychiatry* 13 (7): 729–40.

Meaney, M. J. 2010. 'Epigenetics and the Biological Definition of Gene × Environment Interactions'. *Child Development*. https://doi.org/10.1111/j.1467-8624.2009.01381.x.

Mehan, H., A. Hertweck, and J. L. Meihls. 1986. *Handicapping the Handicapped: Decision Making in Students' Educational Careers*. Stanford University Press.

Meier, M. H., W. S. Slutske, A. C. Heath, and N. G. Martin. 2011. 'Sex Differences in the Genetic and Environmental Influences on Childhood Conduct Disorder and Adult Antisocial Behavior'. *Journal of Abnormal Psychology* 120 (2): 377–88.

Mejía-Rodríguez, A. M., H. Luyten, and M. R. M. Meelissen. 2020. 'Gender Differences in Mathematics Self-Concept Across the World: An Exploration of Student and Parent Data of TIMSS 2015'. *International Journal of Science and Mathematics Education* 19: 1229–50. https://doi.org/10.1007/s10763-020-10100-x.

Mejias, S., J. Grégoire, and M.-P. Noël. 2012. 'Numerical Estimation in Adults with and without Developmental Dyscalculia'. *Learning and Individual Differences* 22 (1): 164–70.

Melby-Lervåg, M., and A. Lervåg. 2012. 'Oral Language Skills Moderate Nonword Repetition Skills in Children With Dyslexia: A Meta-Analysis of the Role of Nonword Repetition Skills in Dyslexia'. *Scientific Studies of Reading: The Official Journal of the Society for the Scientific Study of Reading* 16 (1): 1–34.

Melby-Lervåg, M., T. S. Redick, and C. Hulme. 2016. 'Working Memory Training Does Not Improve Performance on Measures of Intelligence or Other Measures of 'Far Transfer': Evidence From a Meta-Analytic Review'. *Perspectives on Psychological Science: A Journal of the Association for Psychological Science* 11 (4): 512–34.

Melhuish, E., L. Quinn, K. Sylva, et al. 2013. 'Preschool Affects Longer Term Literacy and Numeracy: Results from a General Population Longitudinal Study in Northern Ireland'. *School Effectiveness and School Improvement* 24 (2): 234–50.

Meng, Z.-L., T. N. Wydell, and H.-Y. Bi. 2019. 'Visual-Motor Integration and Reading Chinese in Children With/without Dyslexia'. *Reading and Writing* 32: 493–510. https://doi.org/10.1007/s11145-018-9876-z.

Menon, V. 2016. 'Working Memory in Children's Math Learning and Its Disruption in Dyscalculia'. *Current Opinion in Behavioral Sciences* 10 (August): 125–32.

Mercer, J. R. 1973. *Labeling the Mentally Retarded: Clinical and Social System Perspectives on Mental Retardation*. University of California Press.

Michels, L., R. O'Gorman, and K. Kucian. 2018. 'Functional Hyperconnectivity Vanishes in Children with Developmental Dyscalculia after Numerical Intervention'. *Developmental Cognitive Neuroscience* 30 (April): 291–303.

Michie, S., D. Fixsen, J. M. Grimshaw, and M. P. Eccles. 2009. 'Specifying and Reporting Complex Behaviour Change Interventions: The Need for a Scientific Method'. *Implementation Science* 4 (40). https://doi.org/10.1186/1748-5908-4-40.

Miciak, J., and J. M. Fletcher. 2019. 'The Identification of Reading Disabilities'. In Kilpatrick, D., Joshi, R., and Wagner, R. (eds) *Reading Development and Difficulties*. Springer. https://doi.org/10.1007/978-3-030-26550-2_7.

Miles, C. 1895. 'A Study of Individual Psychology'. *The American Journal of Psychology* 6 (4): 534–58.

Miles, T. R., M. N. Haslum, and T. J. Wheeler. 1998. 'Gender Ratio in Dyslexia'. *Annals of Dyslexia* 48 (1): 27–55.

Miller, B., K. Taylor, and R. Ryder. 2019. 'Introduction to Special Topic: Serving Children with Disabilities Within Multitiered Systems of Support'. *AERA Open* 5 (2). https://doi.org/10.1177/2332858419853796.

Miller, D. I., and D. F. Halpern. 2014. 'The New Science of Cognitive Sex Differences'. *Trends in Cognitive Sciences*. https://doi.org/10.1016/j.tics.2013.10.011.

Miller, E. B., G. Farkas, D. Lowe Vandell, and G. J. Duncan. 2014. 'Do the Effects of Head Start Vary by Parental Preacademic Stimulation?' *Child Development* 85 (4): 1385–1400.

Miller, K. F., M. Kelly, and X. Zhou. 2005. 'Learning Mathematics in China and the United States: Cross-Cultural Insights into the Nature and Course of Preschool Mathematical Development'. In *Handbook of Mathematical Cognition*, edited by J. I. D. Campbell, 508: 163–77. Psychology Press.

Mix, K. S. 2019. 'Why Are Spatial Skill and Mathematics Related?' *Child Development Perspectives* 13 (2): 121–6.

Mix, K. S., S. C. Levine, Y.-L. Cheng, et al. 2016. 'Separate but Correlated: The Latent Structure of Space and Mathematics across Development'. *Journal of Experimental Psychology. General* 145 (9): 1206–27.

Mo, C., M. Yu, C. Seger, and L. Mo. 2015. 'Holistic Neural Coding of Chinese Character Forms in Bilateral Ventral Visual System'. *Brain and Language* 141: 28–39. https://doi.org/10.1016/j.bandl.2014.11.008.

Moeller, K., U. Fischer, U. Cress, and H.-C. Nuerk. 2012. 'Diagnostics and Intervention in Developmental Dyscalculia: Current Issues and Novel Perspectives'. In *Reading, Writing, Mathematics and the Developing Brain: Listening to Many Voices*, edited by Z. Breznitz, O. Rubinsten, V. J. Molfese, and D. L. Molfese, 233–75. Springer Netherlands.

Moeller, K., S. Shaki, S. M. Göbel, and H.-C. Nuerk. 2015. 'Language Influences Number Processing–a Quadrilingual Study'. *Cognition* 136 (March): 150–5.

Moeller, K., J. Zuber, N. Olsen, H.-C. Nuerk, and K. Willmes. 2015. 'Intransparent German Number Words Complicate Transcoding: A Translingual Comparison with Japanese'. *Frontiers in Psychology* 6 (June): 740.

Mohd, S., N. Elleeiana, N. A. Hamzaid, B. Pingguan Murphy, and E. Lim. 2016. 'Development of Computer Play Pedagogy Intervention for Children with Low Conceptual Understanding in Basic Mathematics Operation Using the Dyscalculia Feature Approach'. *Interactive Learning Environments* 24 (7): 1477–96.

Mohr, J. P. 2006. 'Broca's Area and Broca's Aphasia (1976)'. *Broca's Region*. Oxford Scholarship online: https://doi.org/10.1093/acprof:oso/9780195177640 .003.0027.

Moll, K., F. Ramus, J. Bartling, et al. 2014. 'Cognitive Mechanisms Underlying Reading and Spelling Development in Five European Orthographies'. *Learning and Instruction* 29 (February): 65–77.

Monei, T., and A. Pedro. 2017. 'A Systematic Review of Interventions for Children Presenting with Dyscalculia in Primary Schools'. *Educational Psychology in Practice* 33 (3): 277–93.

Mononen, R., P. Aunio, T. Koponen, and M. Aro. 2015. 'A Review of Early Numeracy Interventions for Children at Risk in Mathematics'. *International Journal of Early Childhood Special Education*, 6, 25–54.

Mononen, R., P. Aunio, T. Koponen, et al. 2014. 'Investigating RightStart Mathematics Kindergarten Instruction in Finland'. *Journal of Early Childhood Education Research* 3 (1): 2–26. https://helda.helsinki.fi/bitstream/handle/10138/232677/Mononen_Aunio_Koponen_issue3_1b.pdf?sequence=1.

Moody, H. A., J. T. Darden, and B. W. Pigozzi. 2016. 'The Relationship of Neighborhood Socioeconomic Differences and Racial Residential Segregation to Childhood Blood Lead Levels in Metropolitan Detroit'. *Journal of Urban Health: Bulletin of the New York Academy of Medicine* 93 (5): 820–39.

Moore, D. S. 2017. 'Behavioral Epigenetics'. *Wiley Interdisciplinary Reviews: Systems Biology and Medicine* 9 (1): e1333.

Moore, D. S., and D. Shenk. 2017. 'The Heritability Fallacy'. *Wiley Interdisciplinary Reviews: Cognitive Science* 8 (1–2): e1400.

Moran, A. S., H. L. Swanson, M. M. Gerber, and W. Fung. 2014. 'The Effects of Paraphrasing Interventions on Problem-Solving Accuracy for Children at Risk for Math Disabilities'. *Learning Disabilities Research & Practice: A Publication of the Division for Learning Disabilities, Council for Exceptional Children* 29 (3): 97–105.

Moreau, D., A. J. Wilson, N. S. McKay, K. Nihill, and K. E. Waldie. 2018. 'No Evidence for Systematic White Matter Correlates of Dyslexia and Dyscalculia'. *NeuroImage. Clinical* 18 (February): 356–66.

Morgan, P. L., G. Farkas, M. M. Hillemeier, et al. 2015. 'Minorities Are Disproportionately Underrepresented in Special Education: Longitudinal Evidence Across Five Disability Conditions'. *Educational Researcher* 44 (5): 278–92.

Morishita, H., and T. K. Hensch. 2008. 'Critical Period Revisited: Impact on Vision'. *Current Opinion in Neurobiology* 18 (1): 101–7.

Morris, A. P., B. F. Voight, T. M. Teslovich, et al. 2012. 'Large-Scale Association Analysis Provides Insights into the Genetic Architecture and Pathophysiology of Type 2 Diabetes'. *Nature Genetics* 44 (9): 981–90.

Morris, R. D., M. W. Lovett, M. Wolf, et al. 2012. 'Multiple-Component Remediation for Developmental Reading Disabilities: IQ, Socioeconomic Status, and Race as Factors in Remedial Outcome'. *Journal of Learning Disabilities* 45 (2): 99–127.

Morsanyi, K., B. M. C. W. van Bers, T. McCormack, and J. McGourty. 2018. 'The Prevalence of Specific Learning Disorder in Mathematics and Comorbidity with Other Developmental Disorders in Primary School-Age Children'. *British Journal of Psychology* 109 (4): 917–40.

Mughal, M. K., C. S. Ginn, R. L. Perry, and K. M. Benzies. 2016. 'Longitudinal Effects of a Two-Generation Preschool Programme on Receptive Language Skill in Low-Income Canadian Children to Age 10 Years'. *Early Child Development and Care* 186 (8): 1316–26.

Müller, B., G. Schaadt, J. Boltze, et al. 2017. 'ATP2C2andDYX1C1are Putative Modulators of Dyslexia-Related MMR'. *Brain and Behavior* 7 (1): e00851. https://doi.org/10.1002/brb3.851.

Murphy, K. A., J. Jogia, and J. B. Talcott. 2019. 'On the Neural Basis of Word Reading: A Meta-Analysis of fMRI Evidence Using Activation Likelihood Estimation'. *Journal of Neurolinguistics* 49 (February): 71–83.

Murphy, M. M., M. M. M. Mazzocco, L. B. Hanich, and M. C. Early. 2007. 'Cognitive Characteristics of Children With Mathematics Learning Disability (MLD) Vary as a Function of the Cutoff Criterion Used to Define MLD'. *Journal of Learning Disabilities* 40 (5): 458–78. https://doi.org/10.1177/00222194070400050901.

Muter, V., C. Hulme, M. J. Snowling, and J. Stevenson. 2004. 'Phonemes, Rimes, Vocabulary, and Grammatical Skills as Foundations of Early Reading Development: Evidence from a Longitudinal Study'. *Developmental Psychology* 40 (5): 665–81.

Muter, V., and M. Snowling. 1998. 'Concurrent and Longitudinal Predictors of Reading: The Role of Metalinguistic and Short-Term Memory Skills'. *Reading Research Quarterly* 33 (3): 320–37.

Muter, V., C. Hulme, M. Snowling, and S. Taylor. 1998. 'Segmentation, Not Rhyming, Predicts Early Progress in Learning to Read'. *Journal of Experimental Child Psychology* 71 (1): 3–27.

Nagel, Stuart. 1994. *Encyclopedia of Policy Studies*, 2nd ed. CRC Press.

Nag, S. 2013. 'Low Literacy Attainments in School and Approaches to Diagnosis: An Exploratory Study'. *Contemporary Education Dialogue* 10 (2): 197–221.

Nag, S., S. Chiat, C. Torgerson, and M. J. Snowling. 2014. 'Literacy, Foundation Learning and Assessment in Developing Countries'. DFID Publication. www.globalreadingnetwork.net/sites/default/files/media/file/Literacy-foundation-learning-assessment.pdf.

Nag, S., and M. J. Snowling. 2011. 'Cognitive Profiles of Poor Readers of Kannada'. *Reading and Writing* 24 (6): 657–76.

Nag, S., S.r B. Vagh, K. M. Dulay, and M. J. Snowling. 2018. 'Home Language, School Language and Children's Literacy Attainments: A Systematic Review of Evidence from Low- and Middle-income Countries'. *Review of Education* 7 (1): 91–150. https://doi.org/10.1002/rev3.3130.

Nag, S., and M. J. Snowling. 2012. 'School Underachievement and Specific Learning Difficulties'. https://www.neuroscience.ox.ac.uk/publications/672400.

Nag, S. (2011). Re-thinking support: the hidden school-to-work challenges for individuals with Special Needs. International Journal of Educational and Vocational Guidance. 11(2), 125 – 137. doi: 10.1007/s10775-011-9203-6

Nagy, W., V. Berninger, R. Abbott, K. Vaughan, and K. Vermeulen. 2003. 'Relationship of Morphology and Other Language Skills to Literacy Skills in At-Risk Second-Grade Readers and At-Risk Fourth-Grade Writers'. *Journal of Educational Psychology* 95 (4): 730–42.

Nakamura, K., W.-J. Kuo, F. Pegado, et al. 2012. 'Universal Brain Systems for Recognizing Word Shapes and Handwriting Gestures during Reading'. *Proceedings of the National Academy of Sciences of the United States of America* 109 (50): 20762–67.

Näslund, J. C., and W. Schneider. 1991. 'Longitudinal Effects of Verbal Ability, Memory Capacity, and Phonological Awareness on Reading Performance'. *European Journal of Psychology of Education*. https://doi.org/10.1007/bf03172772.

National Center on Response to Intervention. 2010. Essential Components of RTI – A Closer Look at Response to Intervention. US Department of Education, Office of Special Education Programs, National Center on Response to Intervention. http://files .eric.ed.gov/fulltext/ED526858.pdf.

National Early Literacy Panel (US). 2008. *Developing Early Literacy: Report of the National Early Literacy Panel*. https://lincs.ed.gov/publications/pdf/NELPReport09.pdf.

'National Education Policy, 2020'. n.d. Accessed July 29, 2021. www.education.gov.in/sites/ upload_files/mhrd/files/NEP_Final_English_0.pdf.

National Reading Panel (US). 2000. Report of the National Reading Panel: Teaching Children to Read: An Evidence-Based Assessment of the Scientific Research Literature on Reading and Its Implications for Reading Instruction: Reports of the Subgroups. www.nichd.nih.gov/publications/pubs/nrp/smallbook.

National Research Council. 2002. *Minority Students in Special and Gifted Education*. Edited by M. S. Donovan and C. T. Cross. The National Academies Press.

Nation, K. 2005. 'Children's Reading Comprehension Difficulties'. In M. J Snowling and C. Hulme (eds.), *The Science of Reading: A Handbook*, chapter 14. Blackwell Publishing Ltd . https://doi.org/10.1002/9780470757642.ch14.

Nelson, J. R., Y. Liu, J. Fiez, and C. A. Perfetti. 2009. 'Assimilation and Accommodation Patterns in Ventral Occipitotemporal Cortex in Learning a Second Writing System'. *Human Brain Mapping* 30: 810–20. https://doi.org/10.1002/hbm.20551.

Nelson, K., and R. Fivush. 2004. 'The Emergence of Autobiographical Memory: A Social Cultural Developmental Theory'. *Psychological Review* 111 (2): 486–511.

Newcombe, N. S., M. E. Lloyd, and K. R. Ratliff. 2007. 'Development of Episodic and Autobiographical Memory: A Cognitive Neuroscience Perspective'. *Advances in Child Development and Behavior* 35: 37–85.

Newstead, K. 1998. 'Aspects of Children's Mathematics Anxiety'. *Educational Studies in Mathematics* 36 (1): 53–71.

Nguyen, T., T. W. Watts, G.J. Duncan, et al. 2016. 'Which Preschool Mathematics Competencies Are Most Predictive of Fifth Grade Achievement?' *Early Childhood Research Quarterly* 36 (July): 550–60.

Nicolson, R. I., and A. J. Fawcett. 2007. 'Procedural Learning Difficulties: Reuniting the Developmental Disorders?' *Trends in Neurosciences* 30 (4): 135–41.

Nieder, A., and E. K. Miller. 2003. 'Coding of Cognitive Magnitude: Compressed Scaling of Numerical Information in the Primate Prefrontal Cortex'. *Neuron* 7 (1): 149–57.

Niklas, F., and W. Schneider. 2014. 'Casting the Die before the Die Is Cast: The Importance of the Home Numeracy Environment for Preschool Children'. *European Journal of Psychology of Education* 29 (3): 327–45.

Nitsche, M. A., K. Fricke, U. Henschke, et al. 2003. 'Pharmacological Modulation of Cortical Excitability Shifts Induced by Transcranial Direct Current Stimulation in Humans'. *The Journal of Physiology* 553 (Pt 1): 293–301.

Noort, M. den, M. den Noort, E. Struys, and P. Bosch. 2015. 'Transcranial Magnetic Stimulation Research on Reading and Dyslexia: A New Clinical Intervention Technique for Treating Dyslexia?' *Neuroimmunology and Neuroinflammation* 2: 145–52. https://doi.org/10.4103/2347-8659.157967.

Norbury, C. F., D. Gooch, C. Wray, et al. 2016. 'The Impact of Nonverbal Ability on Prevalence and Clinical Presentation of Language Disorder: Evidence from a Population Study'. *Journal of Child Psychology and Psychiatry, and Allied Disciplines* 57 (11): 1247–57.

Nores, M., and W. S. Barnett. 2010. 'Benefits of Early Childhood Interventions across the World: (Under) Investing in the Very Young'. *Economics of Education Review* 29 (2): 271–82.

Nosworthy, N., S. Bugden, L. Archibald, B. Evans, and D. Ansari. 2013. 'A Two-Minute Paper-and-Pencil Test of Symbolic and Nonsymbolic Numerical Magnitude Processing Explains Variability in Primary School Children's Arithmetic Competence'. *PLoS ONE* 87 (7): e67918. https://doi.org/10.1371/journal.pone.0067918.

Novick, M. R. 1966. 'The Axioms and Principal Results of Classical Test Theory'. *Journal of Mathematical Psychology* 3 (1): 1–18.

Nuerk, H.-C., K. Patro, U. Cress, U. Schild, C. K. Friedrich, and S. M. Göbel. 2015. 'How Space-Number Associations May Be Created in Preliterate Children: Six Distinct Mechanisms'. *Frontiers in Psychology* 6 (March): 215.

Nys, J., P. Ventura, T. Fernandes, et al. 2013. 'Does Math Education Modify the Approximate Number System? A Comparison of Schooled and Unschooled Adults'. *Trends in Neuroscience and Education* 2 (1): 13–22.

Ober, T. M., P. J. Brooks, B. D. Homer, and D. Rindskopf. 2020. 'Executive Functions and Decoding in Children and Adolescents: A Meta-Analytic Investigation'. *Educational Psychology Review* 32: 1–29.

O'Connor, P. D., F. Sofo, L. Kendall, and G. Olsen. 1990. 'Reading Disabilities and the Effects of Colored Filters'. *Journal of Learning Disabilities* 23 (10): 597–603, 620.

Odden, A. R., ed. 1991. *Education Policy Implementation*. SUNY Series, Educational Leadership. State University of New York Press.

Odic, D., and A. Starr. 2018. 'An Introduction to the Approximate Number System'. *Child Development Perspectives* 12 (4): 223–29.

OECD. 2011. *Starting Strong III: A Quality Toolbox for Early Childhood Education and Care: A Quality Toolbox for Early Childhood Education and Care*. OECD Publishing.

———. 2019. *PISA 2018 Results (Volume I): What Students Know and Can Do: What Students Know and Can Do*. OECD Publishing.

Okbay, A., J. P. Beauchamp, M. A. Fontana, et al. 2016. 'Genome-Wide Association Study Identifies 74 Loci Associated with Educational Attainment'. *Nature* 533 (7604): 539–42.

Oliver, M. L., T. M. Shapiro, and T. Shapiro. 2006. *Black Wealth, White Wealth: A New Perspective on Racial Inequality*. Taylor & Francis.

Olsson, L., R. Östergren, and U. Träff. 2016. 'Developmental Dyscalculia: A Deficit in the Approximate Number System or an Access Deficit?' *Cognitive Development* 39 (July): 154–67.

O'Malley, K. J., D. J. Francis, B. R. Foorman, J. M. Fletcher, and P. R. Swank. 2002. 'Growth in Precursor and Reading-Related Skills: Do Low-Achieving and IQ-Discrepant Readers Develop Differently?' *Learning Disabilities Research & Practice: A Publication of the Division for Learning Disabilities, Council for Exceptional Children* 17 (1): 19–34.

O'Malley, Patricia, Sandi Jenkins, Brooke Wesley, et al. 2013. 'Effectiveness of Using iPads to Build Math Fluency'. Paper presented at 2013 Council for Exceptional Children Annual Meeting in San Antonio, Texas. http://files.eric.ed.gov/fulltext/ED541158.pdf.

Ong-Dean, C. 2006. 'High Roads and Low Roads: Learning Disabilities in California, 1976–1998'. *Sociological Perspectives: SP: Official Publication of the Pacific Sociological Association* 49 (1): 91–113.

2009. *Distinguishing Disability: Parents, Privilege, and Special Education*. University of Chicago Press.

Osher, D., D. L. Kelly, N. Tolani-Brown, L. Shors, and C.-S. Chen. 2009. 'UNICEF Child Friendly Schools Programming: Global Evaluation Final Report'. *Washington, DC: American Institutes for Research*. http://humanitarianlibrary.org/sites/default/files/2014/02/cfs_executive_summary_v2r.pdf.

Oswald, D. P., M. J. Coutinho, A. M. Best, and N. Nguyen. 2001. 'Impact of Sociodemographic Characteristics on the Identification Rates of Minority Students as Having Mental Retardation'. *Mental Retardation* 39 (5): 351–67.

Palm, U., F. M. Segmiller, A. N. Epple, et al. 2016. 'Transcranial Direct Current Stimulation in Children and Adolescents: A Comprehensive Review'. *Journal of Neural Transmission* 123 (10): 1219–34.

Park, J., V. Bermudez, R. C. Roberts, and E. M. Brannon. 2016. 'Non-Symbolic Approximate Arithmetic Training Improves Math Performance in Preschoolers'. *Journal of Experimental Child Psychology* 152 (December): 278–93.

Parsons, S., J. Bynner, and National Research and Development Centre for Adult Literacy and Numeracy. 2005. Does Numeracy Matter More? https://core.ac.uk/download/pdf/111651.pdf.

Partanen, M., and L. S. Siegel. 2014. 'Long-Term Outcome of the Early Identification and Intervention of Reading Disabilities'. *Reading and Writing* 27: 665–84. https://doi.org/10.1007/s11145-013-9472-1.

Partanen, M., L. S. Siegel, and D. E. Giaschi. 2019. 'Longitudinal Outcomes of an Individualized and Intensive Reading Intervention for Third Grade Students'. *Dyslexia*, no. dys.1616 (April). https://doi.org/10.1002/dys.1616.

Passolunghi, M. C., B. Vercelloni, and H. Schadee. 2007. 'The Precursors of Mathematics Learning: Working Memory, Phonological Ability and Numerical Competence'. *Cognitive Development* 22 (2): 165–84. https://doi.org/10.1016/j.cogdev.2006.09.001.

Pastore, N. 1949. *The Nature-Nurture Controversy*. King's Crown Press.

Paulesu, E., E. McCrory, F. Fazio, et al. 2000. 'A Cultural Effect on Brain Function'. *Nature Neuroscience* 3: 91–6. https://doi.org/10.1038/71163.

Paulesu, E., L. Danelli, and M. Berlingeri. 2014. 'Reading the Dyslexic Brain: Multiple Dysfunctional Routes Revealed by a New Meta-Analysis of PET and fMRI Activation Studies'. *Frontiers in Human Neuroscience* 8 (November): 830.

Paulesu, E., J. F. Démonet, F. Fazio, et al. 2001. 'Cultural Diversity and Biological Unity in Dyslexia'. *NeuroImage* 13 (6): 584. https://doi.org/10.1016/s1053-8119(01)91927-5.

Paxson, C., and N. Schady. 2007. 'Cognitive Development among Young Children in Ecuador'. *The Journal of Human Resources XLII* (1): 49–84.

Peacock, J. L., L. Marston, N. Marlow, S. A. Calvert, and A. Greenough. 2012. 'Neonatal and Infant Outcome in Boys and Girls Born Very Prematurely'. *Pediatric Research* 71 (3): 305–10.

Pearman, F. A., M. P. Springer, M. Lipsey, et al. 2020. 'Teachers, Schools, and Pre-K Effect Persistence: An Examination of the Sustaining Environment Hypothesis'. *Journal of Research on Educational Effectiveness* 13 (4): 547–73.

Pedhazur, E. J. 1997. *Multiple Regression in Behavioral Research: Explanation and Prediction*. Wadsworth Publishing Company.

Peng, P., K. Lee, J. Luo, et al. 2021. 'Simple View of Reading in Chinese: A One-Stage Meta-Analytic Structural Equation Modeling'. *Review of Educational Research* 91 (1): 3–33.

Peng, P., J. Namkung, M. Barnes, and C. Sun. 2016. 'A Meta-Analysis of Mathematics and Working Memory: Moderating Effects of Working Memory Domain, Type of Mathematics Skill, and Sample Characteristics'. *Journal of Educational Psychology* 108 (4): 455–73.

Peng, P., M. Barnes, C. Wang, et al. 2018. 'A Meta-Analysis on the Relation between Reading and Working Memory'. *Psychological Bulletin* 144 (1): 48–76. https://doi.org/10.1037/bul0000124.

Peng, P., C. Wang, S. Tao, and C. Sun. 2017. 'The Deficit Profiles of Chinese Children with Reading Difficulties: A Meta-Analysis'. *Educational Psychology Review* 29: 513–64. https://doi.org/10.1007/s10648-016-9366-2.

Pennington, B. F. 2006. 'From Single to Multiple Deficit Models of Developmental Disorders'. *Cognition* 101 (2): 385–413.

Pennington, B. F., L. Santerre-Lemmon, J. Rosenberg, et al. 2012. 'Individual Prediction of Dyslexia by Single versus Multiple Deficit Models'. *Journal of Abnormal Psychology* 121 (1): 212–24.

Perfetti, C. 2007. 'Reading Ability: Lexical Quality to Comprehension'. *Scientific Studies of Reading: The Official Journal of the Society for the Scientific Study of Reading* 11 (4): 357–83.

Perfetti, C. A., Y. Liu, and L. H. Tan. 2005. 'The Lexical Constituency Model: Some Implications of Research on Chinese for General Theories of Reading'. *Psychological Review* 112 (1): 43–59. https://doi.org/10.1037/0033-295x.112.1.43.

Pesco, D., A. A. A. N. MacLeod, E. Kay-Raining Bird, et al. 2016. 'A Multi-Site Review of Policies Affecting Opportunities for Children with Developmental Disabilities to Become Bilingual'. *Journal of Communication Disorders* 63 (September): 15–31.

Peterchev, A. V., R. Jalinous, and S. H. Lisanby. 2008. 'A Transcranial Magnetic Stimulator Inducing near-Rectangular Pulses with Controllable Pulse Width (cTMS)'. *IEEE Transactions on Bio-Medical Engineering* 55 (1): 257–66.

Petermann, F. 2014. 'Implementationsforschung: Grundbegriffe Und Konzepte'. *Psychologische Rundschau* 65 (3): 122–8. https://doi.org/10.1026/0033-3042/a000214.

Peters, L., and B. De Smedt. 2018. 'Arithmetic in the Developing Brain: A Review of Brain Imaging Studies'. *Developmental Cognitive Neuroscience* 30): 265–79. https://doi.org/10.1016/j.dcn.2017.05.002.

Peterson, R. L., A. B. Arnett, B. F. Pennington, et al. 2018. 'Literacy Acquisition Influences Children's Rapid Automatized Naming'. *Developmental Science* 21 (3): e12589.

Peterson, R. L., and B. F. Pennington. 2012. 'Developmental Dyslexia'. *The Lancet* 379 (9830): 1997–2007.

Peyre, H., C-L Gérard, I. Dupong Vanderhorst, et al. 2018. 'Rééducation Oculomotrice Informatisée Dans La Dyslexie: Essai Clinique Randomisé En Crossover En Population Pédiatrique'. *L'Encéphale* 44 (3): 247–55.

Pfahl, L., and J. J. W. Powell. 2011. 'Legitimating School Segregation. The Special Education Profession and the Discourse of Learning Disability in Germany'. *Disability & Society* 26 (4): 449–62.

Pfost, M., K. Blatter, C. Artelt, P. Stanat, and W. Schneider. 2019. 'Effects of Training Phonological Awareness on Children's Reading Skills'. *Journal of Applied Developmental Psychology* 65: 101067. https://doi.org/10.1016/j.appdev.2019.101067.

Piazza, M., P. Pica, V. Izard, E. S. Spelke, and S. Dehaene. 2013. 'Education Enhances the Acuity of the Nonverbal Approximate Number System'. *Psychological Science* 24 (6): 1037–43.

'PIRLS 2001 International Report'. n.d. Accessed July 22, 2021. https://www.iea.nl/publications/study-reports/international-reports-iea-studies/pirls-2001-international-report.

'PIRLS 2006 International Report'. n.d. Accessed July 22, 2021. https://timss.bc.edu/pirls2006/intl_rpt.html.

'PIRLS 2016 – Report'. n.d. Accessed July 22, 2021. http://timssandpirls.bc.edu/pirls2016/international-results/.

Pixner, S., J. Zuber, V. Heřmanová, et al. 2011. 'One Language, Two Number-Word Systems and Many Problems: Numerical Cognition in the Czech Language'. *Research in Developmental Disabilities* 32 (6): 2683–9.

Plante, I., R. de la Sablonnière, J. M. Aronson, and M. Théorêt. 2013. 'Gender Stereotype Endorsement and Achievement-Related Outcomes: The Role of Competence Beliefs and Task Values'. *Contemporary Educational Psychology* 38 (3): 225–35. https://doi.org/10.1016/j.cedpsych.2013.03.004.

Poldrack, R. A., J. E. Desmond, G. H. Glover, and J. D. Gabrieli. 1998. 'The Neural Basis of Visual Skill Learning: An fMRI Study of Mirror Reading'. *Cerebral Cortex* 8 (1): 1–10.

Posner, M. I., and M. K. Rothbart. 2017. 'Integrating Brain, Cognition and Culture'. *Journal of Cultural Cognitive Science* 1 (1): 3–15.

Powell, D., and L. Atkinson. 2020. 'Unraveling the Links between Rapid Automatized Naming (RAN), Phonological Awareness, and Reading'. *Journal of Educational Psychology* 113 (4): 706–18. https://doi.org/10.1037/edu0000625.

Preßler, A. L., T. Könen, M. Hasselhorn, and K. Krajewski. 2014. 'Cognitive Preconditions of Early Reading and Spelling: A Latent-Variable Approach with Longitudinal Data'. *Reading and Writing* 27 (2): 383–406.

Pressman, J. L. and A. Wildavsky. 1984. *Implementation*. University of California Press. Accessed July 29, 2021. https://www.ucpress.edu/book/9780520053311/implementation.

Price, G. R., I. Holloway, P. Räsänen, M. Vesterinen, and D. Ansari. 2007. 'Impaired Parietal Magnitude Processing in Developmental Dyscalculia'. *Current Biology* 17 (24): PR1042–R1043. https://doi.org/10.1016/j.cub.2007.10.013.

Priest, N., Y. Paradies, B. Trenerry, et al. 2013. 'A Systematic Review of Studies Examining the Relationship between Reported Racism and Health and Wellbeing for Children and Young People'. *Social Science & Medicine* 95 (October): 115–27.

Prior, M., D. Smart, A. Sanson, and F. Oberklaid. 2001. 'Longitudinal Predictors of Behavioural Adjustment in Pre-Adolescent Children'. *The Australian and New Zealand Journal of Psychiatry* 35 (3): 297–307.

Pritulsky, C., C. Morano, R. Odean, et al. 2020. 'Spatial Thinking: Why It Belongs in the Preschool Classroom'. *Translational Issues in Psychological Science* 6 (3): 271–82.

Pröscholdt, M. V., A. Michalik, W. Schneider, et al. 2013. 'Effekte Kombinierter Förderprogramme Zur Phonologischen Bewusstheit Und Zum Sprachverstehen Auf Die Entwicklung Der Phonologischen Bewusstheit von Kindergartenkindern

Mit Und Ohne Migrationshintergrund'. *Frühe Bildung* 2 (3): 122–32. https://doi.org /10.1026/2191-9186/a000099.

Protopapas, A., A. Altani, and G. K. Georgiou. 2013. 'RAN Backward: A Test of the Visual Scanning Hypothesis'. *Scientific Studies of Reading: The Official Journal of the Society for the Scientific Study of Reading* 17 (6): 453–61.

Protopapas, A., K. Katopodi, A. Altani, and G. K. Georgiou. 2018. 'Word Reading Fluency as a Serial Naming Task'. *Scientific Studies of Reading: The Official Journal of the Society for the Scientific Study of Reading* 22 (3): 248–63.

Protzko, J. 2016. 'Does the Raising IQ-Raising G Distinction Explain the Fadeout Effect?' *Intelligence* 56 (May): 65–71.

Pruden, S. M., S. C. Levine, and J. Huttenlocher. 2011. 'Children's Spatial Thinking: Does Talk about the Spatial World Matter?' *Developmental Science* 14 (6): 1417–30.

Pugh, K. R., W. E. Mencl, A. R. Jenner, et al. 2000. 'Functional Neuroimaging Studies of Reading and Reading Disability (Developmental Dyslexia)'. *Mental Retardation and Developmental Disabilities Research Reviews* 6 (3): 207–13. https://doi.org/10 .1002/1098-2779(2000)6:3<207::aid-mrdd8>3.0.co;2-p.

Pugh, K. R., W. E. Mencl, B. A. Shaywitz, et al. 2000. 'The Angular Gyrus in Developmental Dyslexia: Task-Specific Differences in Functional Connectivity Within Posterior Cortex'. *Psychological Science*. https://doi.org/10.1111/1467-9280.00214.

Pugh, K., and L. Verhoeven. 2018. 'Introduction to This Special Issue: Dyslexia Across Languages and Writing Systems'. *Scientific Studies of Reading: The Official Journal of the Society for the Scientific Study of Reading* 22 (1): 1–6.

Purpura, D. J., L. E. Hume, D. M. Sims, and C. J. Lonigan. 2011. 'Early Literacy and Early Numeracy: The Value of Including Early Literacy Skills in the Prediction of Numeracy Development'. *Journal of Experimental Child Psychology* 110 (4): 647–58.

Purpura, D. J., A. R. Napoli, E. A. Wehrspann, and Z. S. Gold. 2017. 'Causal Connections between Mathematical Language and Mathematical Knowledge: A Dialogic Reading Intervention'. *Journal of Research on Educational Effectiveness* 10 (1): 116–37.

Purpura, D. J., and E. E. Reid. 2016. 'Mathematics and Language: Individual and Group Differences in Mathematical Language Skills in Young Children'. *Early Childhood Research Quarterly* 36 (July): 259–68.

Quinn, J. M. 2018. 'Differential Identification of Females and Males with Reading Difficulties: A Meta-Analysis'. *Reading and Writing* 31: 1039–61. https://doi.org /10.1007/s11145-018-9827-8.

Rabiner, D., and J. D. Coie. 2000. 'Early Attention Problems and Children's Reading Achievement: A Longitudinal Investigation'. *Journal of the American Academy of Child & Adolescent Psychiatry* 39 (7): P859–867. https://doi.org/10.1097 /00004583-200007000-00014.

Rack, J. P. 2017. 'Dyslexia: The Phonological Deficit Hypothesis'. In A. Fawcett and R. Nicolson (eds.), *Dyslexia in Children*, 5–37. Routledge.

Ramaa, S., and I. P. Gowramma. 2002. 'A Systematic Procedure for Identifying and Classifying Children with Dyscalculia among Primary School Children in India'. *Dyslexia* 8 (2): 67–85.

Ramani, G. B., E. N. Daubert, G. C. Lin, et al. 2020. 'Racing Dragons and Remembering Aliens: Benefits of Playing Number and Working Memory Games on Kindergartners' Numerical Knowledge'. *Developmental Science* 23 (4): e12908.

Ramani, G. B., M. L. Rowe, S. H. Eason, and K. A. Leech. 2015. 'Math Talk during Informal Learning Activities in Head Start Families'. *Cognitive Development* 35 (July): 15–33.

Ramani, G. B., and R. S. Siegler. 2008. 'Promoting Broad and Stable Improvements in Low-Income Children's Numerical Knowledge through Playing Number Board Games'. *Child Development* 79 (2): 375–94.

Ramirez, G., E. A. Gunderson, S. C. Levine, and S. L. Beilock. 2013. 'Math Anxiety, Working Memory, and Math Achievement in Early Elementary School'. *Journal of Cognition and Development: Official Journal of the Cognitive Development Society* 14 (2): 187–202.

Ramus, F., Rosen, S., Dakin, S. C., Day, B. L., Castellote, J. M., White, S., & Frith, U. (2003). Theories of developmental dyslexia: Insights from a multiple case study of dyslexic adults. *Brain: A Journal of Neurology*, 126(Pt 4), 841–865. https://doi.org/10.1093/brain/awg076.

Ranpura, A., E. Isaacs, C. Edmonds, et al. 2013. 'Developmental Trajectories of Grey and White Matter in Dyscalculia'. *Trends in Neuroscience and Education* 2 (2): 56–64.

Räsänen, P., Jonna Salminen, A. J. Wilson, P. Aunio, and S. Dehaene. 2009. 'Computer-Assisted Intervention for Children with Low Numeracy Skills'. *Cognitive Development* 24 (4): 450–72.

Rastle, K., and J. S. H. Taylor. 2018. 'Print-Sound Regularities Are More Important than Print-Meaning Regularities in the Initial Stages of Learning to Read: Response to Bowers & Bowers (2018)'. *Quarterly Journal of Experimental Psychology* 71 (7): 1501–5.

Re, A. M., M. Pedron, P. E. Tressoldi, and D. Lucangeli. 2014. 'Response to Specific Training for Students With Different Levels of Mathematical Difficulties'. *Exceptional Children* 80 (3): 337–52.

Reigosa-Crespo, V., M. Valdés-Sosa, B. Butterworth, et al. 2012. 'Basic Numerical Capacities and Prevalence of Developmental Dyscalculia: The Havana Survey'. *Developmental Psychology* 48 (1): 123–35.

Reilly, D., D. L. Neumann, and G. Andrews. 2019. 'Gender Differences in Reading and Writing Achievement: Evidence from the National Assessment of Educational Progress (NAEP)'. *The American Psychologist* 74 (4): 445–58.

Reis, A., S. Araújo, I. S. Morais, and L. Faísca. 2020. 'Reading and Reading-Related Skills in Adults with Dyslexia from Different Orthographic Systems: A Review and Meta-Analysis'. *Annals of Dyslexia* 70 (3): 339–68.

Ren, K., and E. A. Gunderson. 2021. 'The Dynamic Nature of Children's Strategy Use after Receiving Accuracy Feedback in Decimal Comparisons'. *Journal of Experimental Child Psychology* 202 (February): 105015.

Ren, K., Y. Lin, and E. A. Gunderson. 2019. 'The Role of Inhibitory Control in Strategy Change: The Case of Linear Measurement'. *Developmental Psychology* 55 (7): 1389–99.

Resnick, L. B. 1989. 'Developing Mathematical Knowledge'. *American Psychologist* 44 (2): 162–69. https://doi.org/10.1037/0003-066x.44.2.162.

Restori, A. F., G. S. Katz, and H. B. Lee. 2009. 'A Critique of the IQ / Achievement Discrepancy Model for Identifying Specific Learning Disabilities'. *Europe's Journal of Psychology* 5 (4): 128–45.

Ribeiro, F. S., and F. H. Santos. 2020. 'Persistent Effects of Musical Training on Mathematical Skills of Children With Developmental Dyscalculia'. *Frontiers in Psychology* 10: 2888.

Richards, B. A., and P. W. Frankland. 2017. 'The Persistence and Transience of Memory'. *Neuron* 94 (6): 1071–84.

Richlan, F. 2014. 'Functional Neuroanatomy of Developmental Dyslexia: The Role of Orthographic Depth'. *Frontiers in Human Neuroscience*. https://doi.org/10.3389/fnhum.2014.00347.

Richlan, F., M. Kronbichler, and H. Wimmer. 2009. 'Functional Abnormalities in the Dyslexic Brain: A Quantitative Meta-Analysis of Neuroimaging Studies'. *Human Brain Mapping* 30: 3299–308. https://doi.org/10.1002/hbm.20752.

Rietveld, C. A., S. E. Medland, J. Derringer, et al. 2013. 'GWAS of 126,559 Individuals Identifies Genetic Variants Associated with Educational Attainment'. *Science* 340 (6139): 1467–71.

Rios, D. Me., M. C. Rios, I. D. Bandeira, et al. 2018. 'Impact of Transcranial Direct Current Stimulation on Reading Skills of Children and Adolescents With Dyslexia'. *Child Neurology Open* 5 (October): 2329048X18798255.

Ritchie, S. J., and T. C. Bates. 2013. 'Enduring Links from Childhood Mathematics and Reading Achievement to Adult Socioeconomic Status'. *Psychological Science* 24 (7): 1301–8.

Ritchie, S. J., S. Della Sala, and R. D. McIntosh. 2011. 'Irlen Colored Overlays Do Not Alleviate Reading Difficulties'. *Pediatrics* 128 (4): e932–38.

Roberts, G., J. Quach, M. Spencer-Smith, et al. 2016. 'Academic Outcomes 2 Years After Working Memory Training for Children With Low Working Memory: A Randomized Clinical Trial'. *JAMA Pediatrics* 170 (5): e154568–e154568.

Robinson, G. L., and R. N. Conway. 1990. 'The Effects of Irlen Colored Lenses on Students' Specific Reading Skills and Their Perception of Ability: A 12-Month Validity Study'. *Journal of Learning Disabilities* 23 (10): 589–96.

Robinson, G. L., and P. J. Foreman. 1999. 'Scotopic sensitivity/Irlen Syndrome and the Use of Coloured Filters: A Long-Term Placebo Controlled and Masked Study of Reading Achievement and Perception of Ability'. *Perceptual and Motor Skills* 89 (1): 83–113.

Rodic, M., X. Zhou, T. Tikhomirova, et al. 2015. 'Cross-Cultural Investigation into Cognitive Underpinnings of Individual Differences in Early Arithmetic'. *Developmental Science* 18 (1): 165–74.

Rogde, K., M. Melby-Lervåg, and A. Lervåg. 2016. 'Improving the General Language Skills of Second-Language Learners in Kindergarten: A Randomized Controlled Trial'. *Journal of Research on Educational Effectiveness* 9 (sup1): 150–70.

Rose, J 2006. *Independent Review of the Teaching of Early Reading: Final Report*. Department for Education and Skills.

Rosenberg-Lee, M., S. Ashkenazi, T. Chen, et al. 2015. 'Brain Hyper-Connectivity and Operation-Specific Deficits during Arithmetic Problem Solving in Children with Developmental Dyscalculia'. *Developmental Science* 18 (3): 351–72. https://doi.org/10.1111/desc.12216.

Roßbach, H.-G., and M. Hasselhorn. 2014. 'Lernumwelten in vorschulischen Kindertageseinrichtungen'. In *Pädagogische Psychologie*, 387. Beltz.

Rossi, S., M.Hallett, P. M. Rossini, A. Pascual-Leone, and Safety of TMS Consensus Group. 2009. 'Safety, Ethical Considerations, and Application Guidelines for the Use of Transcranial Magnetic Stimulation in Clinical Practice and Research'. *Clinical Neurophysiology: Official Journal of the International Federation of Clinical Neurophysiology* 120 (12): 2008–39.

Rothe, J., G. Schulte-Körne, and E. Ise. 2014. 'Does Sensitivity to Orthographic Regularities Influence Reading and Spelling Acquisition? A 1-Year Prospective Study'. *Reading and Writing* 27 (7): 1141–61.

Ruan, Y., G. K. Georgiou, S. Song, Y. Li, and H. Shu. 2018. 'Does Writing System Influence the Associations between Phonological Awareness, Morphological Awareness, and Reading? A Meta-Analysis'. *Journal of Educational Psychology* 110 (2): 180–202. https://doi.org/10.1037/edu0000216.

Rubinsten, O., and R. Tannock. 2010. 'Mathematics Anxiety in Children with Developmental Dyscalculia'. *Behavioral and Brain Functions* 6 (46). https://doi.org/10.1186/1744-9081-6-46.

Rueckl, J. G., P. M. Paz-Alonso, P. J. Molfese, et al. 2015. 'Universal Brain Signature of Proficient Reading: Evidence from Four Contrasting Languages'. *Proceedings of the National Academy of Sciences of the United States of America* 112 (50): 15510–15.

Rufener, K. S., K. Krauel, M. Meyer, H.-J. Heinze, and T. Zaehle. 2019. 'Transcranial Electrical Stimulation Improves Phoneme Processing in Developmental Dyslexia'. *Brain Stimulation* 12 (4): 930–37.

Rutter, M. 2010. 'Gene–environment Interplay'. *Depression and Anxiety* 27 (1): 1–4.

Rutter, M., A. Caspi, D. Fergusson, et al. 2004. 'Sex Differences in Developmental Reading Disability: New Findings from 4 Epidemiological Studies'. *JAMA: The Journal of the American Medical Association* 291 (16): 2007–12.

Rutter, M., T. E. Moffitt, and A. Caspi. 2006. 'Gene-Environment Interplay and Psychopathology: Multiple Varieties but Real Effects'. *Journal of Child Psychology and Psychiatry, and Allied Disciplines* 47 (3-4): 226–61.

Rutter, M., and W. Yule. 1975. 'The Concept of Specific Reading Retardation'. *Journal of Child Psychology and Psychiatry, and Allied Disciplines* 16 (3): 181–97.

Saatcioglu, A., and T. M. Skrtic. 2019. 'Categorization by Organizations: Manipulation of Disability Categories in a Racially Desegregated School District'. *The American Journal of Sociology* 125 (1): 184–260.

Sabatier, P. A. 1986. 'Top-Down and Bottom-Up Approaches to Implementation Research: A Critical Analysis and Suggested Synthesis'. *Journal of Public Policy* 6 (1): 21–48.

Sabel, C. 2012. 'Individualised Service Provision and the New Welfare State'. *Promoting Inclusive Growth*. https://doi.org/10.1787/9789264168305-5-en.

Sampson, R. J., J. D. Morenoff, and T. Gannon-Rowley. 2002. 'Assessing 'Neighborhood Effects': Social Processes and New Directions in Research'. *Annual Review of Sociology* 28 (1): 443–78.

Sánchez-León, C. A., I. Cordones, C. Ammann, et al. 2021. 'Immediate and after Effects of Transcranial Direct-Current Stimulation in the Mouse Primary Somatosensory Cortex'. *Scientific Reports* 11 (1): 3123.

Sandefur, Justin. 2016. 'Internationally Comparable Mathematics Scores for Fourteen African Countries'. *SSRN Electronic Journal*. Center for Global Development Working Paper No. 444. https://doi.org/10.2139/ssrn.2893768.

Sanetti, L. M. Hagermoser, S. Charbonneau, A. Knight, et al. 2020. 'Treatment Fidelity Reporting in Intervention Outcome Studies in the School Psychology Literature from 2009 to 2016'. *Psychology in the Schools* 57 (6): 901–22.

Sanfilippo, J., M. Ness, Y. Petscher, et al. 2020. 'Reintroducing Dyslexia: Early Identification and Implications for Pediatric Practice'. *Pediatrics* 146 (1). https://doi.org/10.1542/peds.2019-3046.

Sarnecka, B. W. 2014. 'On the Relation between Grammatical Number and Cardinal Numbers in Development'. *Frontiers in Psychology* 5 (October): 1132.

Savage, R., K. Cornish, T. Manly, and C. Hollis. 2006. 'Cognitive Processes in Children's Reading and Attention: The Role of Working Memory, Divided Attention, and Response Inhibition'. *British Journal of Psychology* 97 (Pt 3): 365–85.

Sax, L., and K. J. Kautz. 2003. 'Who First Suggests the Diagnosis of Attention-Deficit/hyperactivity Disorder?' *Annals of Family Medicine* 1 (3): 171–4.

Scalise, N. R., E. N. Daubert, and G. B. Ramani. 2020. 'Benefits of Playing Numerical Card Games on Head Start Children's Mathematical Skills'. *Journal of Experimental Education* 88 (2): 200–20.

Scarr, S., and K. McCartney. 1983. 'How People Make Their Own Environments: A Theory of Genotype → Environment Effects'. *Child Development* 54 (2): 424–35.

Scheirer, M. A., M. C. Shediac, and C. E. Cassady. 1995. 'Measuring the Implementation of Health Promotion Programs: The Case of the Breast and Cervical Cancer Program in Maryland'. *Health Education Research* 10 (1): 11–25. https://doi.org/10.1093/her/10.1.11.

Schiefele, U., E. Schaffner, J. Möller, and A. Wigfield. 2012. 'Dimensions of Reading Motivation and Their Relation to Reading Behavior and Competence'. *Reading Research Quarterly* 47 (4): 427–63.

Schmitt, S. A., G. John Geldhof, D. J. Purpura, R. Duncan, and M. M. McClelland. 2017. 'Examining the Relations between Executive Function, Math, and Literacy during the Transition to Kindergarten: A Multi-Analytic Approach'. *Journal of Educational Psychology* 109 (8): 1120–40.

Schneider, W. 2019. 'Programme Zur Förderung Kognitiver Fähigkeiten in Vorschule Und Schule: Wie Effektiv Sind Sie, Und Wie Gut Sind Die Verfahren Praktisch Implementiert?' *Zeitschrift Für Pädagogische Psychologie* 33 (1): 5–16. https://doi.org/10.1024/1010-0652/a000231.

Schneider, W., and M. Bullock. 2009. 'The Development of Reading and Spelling: Relevant Precursors, Developmental Changes, and Individual Differences'. In Schneider and Bullock. (eds.) *Human Development from Early Childhood to Early Adulthood*, 209–30. Psychology Press.

Schneider, W., P. Küspert, E. Roth, M. Visé, and H. Marx. 1997. 'Short- and Long-Term Effects of Training Phonological Awareness in Kindergarten: Evidence from Two German Studies'. *Journal of Experimental Child Psychology* 66 (3): 311–40. https://doi.org/10.1006/jecp.1997.2384.

Schneider, W., E. Roth, and M. Ennemoser. 2000. 'Training Phonological Skills and Letter Knowledge in Children at Risk for Dyslexia: A Comparison of Three Kindergarten Intervention Programs'. *Journal of Educational Psychology* 92 (2): 284–95. https://doi.org/10.1037/0022-0663.92.2.284.

Schneider, W., and C. Stengard. 2000. *Inventory of European Longitudinal Studies of Reading and Spelling: A COST Action A8 Project*. Office for Official Publications of the European Communities.

Schrader, J., M. Hasselhorn, P. Hetfleisch, and A. Goeze. 2020. 'Stichwortbeitrag Implementationsforschung: Wie Wissenschaft Zu Verbesserungen Im Bildungssystem

Beitragen Kann'. *Zeitschrift Für Erziehungswissenschaft* 23: 9–59. https://doi.org/10 .1007/s11618-020-00927-z.

Schroeder, P. A., T. Dresler, J. Bahnmueller, et al. 2017. 'Cognitive Enhancement of Numerical and Arithmetic Capabilities: A Mini-Review of Available Transcranial Electric Stimulation Studies'. *Journal of Cognitive Enhancement* 1 (1), 39–47. https://doi.org/10.1007/s41465-016-0006-z.

Schulte, A., and G. D. Borich. 1984. 'Considerations in the Use of Difference Scores to Identify Learning-Disabled Children'. *Journal of School Psychology* 22 (4): 381–90.

Schulte-Körne, G. 2010. 'Diagnostik Und Therapie Der Lese-Rechtschreib-Störung'. *Deutsches Ärzteblatt* 107 (41): 718–26.

Schwaighofer, M., F. Fischer, and M. Bühner. 2015. 'Does Working Memory Training Transfer? A Meta-Analysis Including Training Conditions as Moderators'. *Educational Psychologist* 50 (2): 138–66.

Schwartz, A. E., B. G. Hopkins, and L. Stiefel. 2021. 'The Effects of Special Education on the Academic Performance of Students with Learning Disabilities'. *Journal of Policy Analysis and Management: [the Journal of the Association for Public Policy Analysis and Management]* 40 (2): 480–520.

Schwering, S. C., and M. C. MacDonald. 2020. 'Verbal Working Memory as Emergent from Language Comprehension and Production'. *Frontiers in Human Neuroscience* 14 (March): 68.

Scruggs, T. E., M. A. Mastropieri, S. Berkeley, and J. E. Graetz. 2010. 'Do Special Education Interventions Improve Learning of Secondary Content? A Meta-Analysis'. *Remedial and Special Education: RASE* 31 (6): 437–49.

Segers, E., C. M. P. Damhuis, E. van de Sande, and L. Verhoeven. 2016. 'Role of Executive Functioning and Home Environment in Early Reading Development'. *Learning and Individual Differences* 49: 251–9. https://doi.org/10.1016/j .lindif.2016.07.004.

Seidenberg, M. 2018. *Language at the Speed of Sight: How We Read, Why So Many Can't, and What Can Be Done About It*. Basic Books.

Seitzman, B. A., C. Gratton, T. O. Laumann, et al. 2019. 'Trait-like Variants in Human Functional Brain Networks'. *Proceedings of the National Academy of Sciences of the United States of America* 116 (45): 22851–61.

Sella, F., P. Tressoldi, D. Lucangeli, and M. Zorzi. 2016. 'Training Numerical Skills with the Adaptive Videogame 'The Number Race': A Randomized Controlled Trial on Preschoolers'. *Trends in Neuroscience and Education* 5 (1): 20–9.

Sen, A, et al. 1979. 'Equality of What'. *The Tanner Lecture on Human Values* 22. http:// tannerlectures.utah.edu/_documents/a-to-z/s/sen80.pdf.

Sénéchal, M., and J.-A. LeFevre. 2002. 'Parental Involvement in the Development of Children's Reading Skill: A Five-Year Longitudinal Study'. *Child Development* 73 (2): 445–60.

Seymour, P. H. K., M. Aro, J. M. Erskine, in collaboration with COST Action A8 Network. 2003. 'Foundation Literacy Acquisition in European Orthographies'. *British Journal of Psychology* 94 (2): 143–74. https://doi.org/10.1348/000712603321661859.

Shakeshaft, N. G., M. Trzaskowski, A. McMillan, et al. 2013. 'Strong Genetic Influence on a UK Nationwide Test of Educational Achievement at the End of Compulsory Education at Age 16'. *PloS One* 8 (12): e80341.

Shakespeare, T. 2013. *Disability Rights and Wrongs Revisited*. Routledge.

Shankweiler, D., W. E. Mencl, D. Braze, et al. 2008. 'Reading Differences and Brain: Cortical Integration of Speech and Print in Sentence Processing Varies with Reader Skill'. *Developmental Neuropsychology* 33 (6): 745–75.

Share, D. L. 1996. 'Word Recognition and Spelling Processes in Specific Reading Disabled and Garden-Variety Poor Readers'. *Dyslexia* 2 (3): 167–74. https://doi.org/10.1002/(sici) 1099-0909(199611)2:3<167::aid-dys167>3.0.co;2-o.

———. 2008. 'On the Anglocentricities of Current Reading Research and Practice: The Perils of Overreliance on an 'Outlier' Orthography'. *Psychological Bulletin* 134 (4): 584–615. https://doi.org/10.1037/0033-2909.134.4.584.

Share, D. L., M. Shany, and O. Lipka. 2019. 'Developmental Dyslexia in Hebrew'. In Verhoeven, L., Perfetti, C., & Pugh, K. (Eds.). *Developmental Dyslexia across Languages and Writing Systems*. Cambridge University Press, 152–75.

Share, D. L. 1995. 'Phonological Recoding and Self-Teaching: Sine qua Non of Reading Acquisition'. *Cognition* 55 (2): 151–218; discussion 219–26.

Sharkey, P., and F. Elwert. 2011. 'The Legacy of Disadvantage: Multigenerational Neighborhood Effects on Cognitive Ability'. *AJS: American Journal of Sociology* 116 (6): 1934–81.

Shaywitz, S. E., J. M. Fletcher, J. M. Holahan, et al. 1999. 'Persistence of Dyslexia: The Connecticut Longitudinal Study at Adolescence'. *Pediatrics* 104 (6): 1351–59.

Shaywitz, S. E., B. A. Shaywitz, R. K. Fulbright, et al. 2003. 'Neural Systems for Compensation and Persistence: Young Adult Outcome of Childhood Reading Disability'. *Biological Psychiatry* 54 (1): P25–33. https://doi.org/10.1016/s0006-3223(02)01836-x.

Shaywitz, S., B. Shaywitz, L. Wietecha, et al. 2017. 'Effect of Atomoxetine Treatment on Reading and Phonological Skills in Children with Dyslexia or Attention-Deficit/Hyperactivity Disorder and Comorbid Dyslexia in a Randomized, Placebo-Controlled Trial'. *Journal of Child and Adolescent Psychopharmacology* 27 (1): 19–28.

Shaywitz, S. E. 1998. 'Dyslexia'. *The New England Journal of Medicine* 338 (5): 307–12.

Shaywitz, S. E., M. D. Escobar, B. A. Shaywitz, J. M. Fletcher, and R. Makuch. 1992. 'Evidence That Dyslexia May Represent the Lower Tail of a Normal Distribution of Reading Ability'. *The New England Journal of Medicine* 326 (3): 145–50.

Shaywitz, S. E., B. A. Shaywitz, J. M. Fletcher, and M. D. Escobar. 1990. 'Prevalence of Reading Disability in Boys and Girls. Results of the Connecticut Longitudinal Study'. *JAMA: The Journal of the American Medical Association* 264 (8): 998–1002.

Shifrer, D. 2018. 'Clarifying the Social Roots of the Disproportionate Classification of Racial Minorities and Males with Learning Disabilities'. *The Sociological Quarterly* 59 (3): 384–406.

Shifrer, D., and R. Fish. 2020. 'A Multilevel Investigation into Contextual Reliability in the Designation of Cognitive Health Conditions among U.S. Children'. *Society and Mental Health* 10 (2): 180–97.

Shmueli, G. 2010. 'To Explain or to Predict?' *Statistical Science* 25 (3): 289–310.

Shu, H., X. Chen, R. C. Anderson, N. Wu, and Y. Xuan. 2003. 'Properties of School Chinese: Implications for Learning to Read'. *Child Development* 74 (1): 27–47.

Siegel, L. S., and N. Himel. 1998. 'Socioeconomic Status, Age and the Classification of Dyslexics and Poor Readers: The Dangers of Using IQ Scores in the Definition of Reading Disability'. *Dyslexia* 4 (2): 90–104.

Siegel, L. S., and E. B. Ryan. 1989. 'Subtypes of Developmental Dyslexia: The Influence of Definitional Variables'. *Reading and Writing* 1 (3): 257–87.

Siegel, L. S., and I. S. Smythe. 2005. 'Reflections on Research on Reading Disability with Special Attention to Gender Issues'. *Journal of Learning Disabilities* 38 (5): 473–77. https://doi.org/10.1177/00222194050380050901.

Siegel, L. S. 1992. 'An Evaluation of the Discrepancy Definition of Dyslexia'. *Journal of Learning Disabilities* 25 (10): 618–29.

Siegler, R. S., and J. L. Booth. 2004. 'Development of Numerical Estimation in Young Children'. *Child Development* 75 (2): 428–44.

Siegler, R. S., and D. W. Braithwaite. 2017. 'Numerical Development'. *Annual Review of Psychology* 68 (January): 187–213.

Siegler, R. S., and H. Lortie-Forgues. 2014. 'An Integrative Theory of Numerical Development'. *Child Development Perspectives* 8 (3): 144–50. https://doi.org/10.1111/cdep.12077.

Siegler, R. S., and J. E. Opfer. 2003. 'The Development of Numerical Estimation: Evidence for Multiple Representations of Numerical Quantity'. *Psychological Science* 14 (3): 237–43.

Siegler, R. S., and G. B. Ramani. 2009. 'Playing Linear Number Board Games – but Not Circular Ones – Improves Low-Income Preschoolers' Numerical Understanding'. *Journal of Educational Psychology* 101 (3): 545–60.

Simanowski, S., and K. Krajewski. 2019. 'Specific Preschool Executive Functions Predict Unique Aspects of Mathematics Development: A 3-Year Longitudinal Study'. *Child Development* 90 (2): 544–61.

Simms, V., S. Clayton, L. Cragg, C. Gilmore, and S. Johnson. 2016. 'Explaining the Relationship between Number Line Estimation and Mathematical Achievement: The Role of Visuomotor Integration and Visuospatial Skills'. *Journal of Experimental Child Psychology* 145 (May): 22–33.

Simons, D. J., W. R. Boot, N. Charness, et al. 2016. 'Do "Brain-Training" Programs Work?' *Psychological Science in the Public Interest: A Journal of the American Psychological Society* 17 (3): 103–86.

Simonsmeier, B. A., R. H. Grabner, J. Hein, U. Krenz, and M. Schneider. 2018. 'Electrical Brain Stimulation (tES) Improves Learning More than Performance: A Meta-Analysis'. *Neuroscience and Biobehavioral Reviews* 84 (January): 171–81.

Simos, P. G., K. Kanatsouli, J. M. Fletcher, et al. 2008. 'Aberrant Spatiotemporal Activation Profiles Associated with Math Difficulties in Children: A Magnetic Source Imaging Study'. *Neuropsychology* 22 (5): 571–84.

Simos, P. G., J. I. Breier, J. M. Fletcher, et al. 2001. 'Age-Related Changes in Regional Brain Activation during Phonological Decoding and Printed Word Recognition'. *Developmental Neuropsychology* 19 (2): 191–210.

Simos, P. G., J. M. Fletcher, E. Bergman, et al. 2002. 'Dyslexia-Specific Brain Activation Profile Becomes Normal Following Successful Remedial Training'. *Neurology* 58 (8): 1203–13.

Siok, W. T., F. Jia, C. Y. Liu, C. A. Perfetti, and L. H. Tan. 2020. 'A Lifespan fMRI Study of Neurodevelopment Associated with Reading Chinese'. *Cerebral Cortex* 30 (7): 4140–57.

Siok, W. T., Z. Jin, P. Fletcher, and L. H. Tan. 2003. 'Distinct Brain Regions Associated with Syllable and Phoneme'. *Human Brain Mapping* 18: 201–7. https://doi.org/10.1002/hbm.10094.

Siok, W. T., J. A. Spinks, Z. Jin, and L. H. Tan. 2009. 'Developmental Dyslexia Is Characterized by the Co-Existence of Visuospatial and Phonological Disorders in Chinese Children'. *Current Biology* 19 (1): PR890–R892. https://doi.org/10.1016/j.cub.2009.08.014.

Siok, W. T., and P. Fletcher. 2001. 'The Role of Phonological Awareness and Visual-Orthographic Skills in Chinese Reading Acquisition'. *Developmental Psychology* 37 (6): 886–99.

Siok, W. T., Z. Niu, Z. Jin, C. A. Perfetti, and L. H. Tan. 2008. 'A Structural-Functional Basis for Dyslexia in the Cortex of Chinese Readers'. *Proceedings of the National Academy of Sciences* 105 (14): 18391194. https://doi.org/10.1073/pnas.0801750105.

Sirin, Selcuk R. 2005. 'Socioeconomic Status and Academic Achievement: A Meta-Analytic Review of Research'. *Review of Educational Research* 75 (3): 417–53. https://doi.org/10.3102/00346543075003417.

Skeide, M. A. (ed.) 2022. *The Cambridge Handbook of Dyslexia and Dyscalculia*. Cambridge University Press.

Skeide, M. A., H. Kirsten, I. Kraft, et al. 2015. 'Genetic Dyslexia Risk Variant Is Related to Neural Connectivity Patterns Underlying Phonological Awareness in Children'. *NeuroImage* 118 (September): 414–21.

Skeide, M. A., I. Kraft, B. Müller, et al. 2016. 'NRSN1associated Grey Matter Volume of the Visual Word Form Area Reveals Dyslexia before School'. *Brain* 139 (10): 2792–803. https://doi.org/10.1093/brain/aww153.

Skiba, R. J., L. Poloni-Staudinger, A. B. Simmons, L. R. Feggins-Azziz, and C.-G. Chung. 2005. 'Unproven Links: Can Poverty Explain Ethnic Disproportionality in Special Education?' *The Journal of Special Education* 39 (3): 130–44.

Skwarchuk, S.-L., C. Sowinski, and J.-A. LeFevre. 2014. 'Formal and Informal Home Learning Activities in Relation to Children's Early Numeracy and Literacy Skills: The Development of a Home Numeracy Model'. *Journal of Experimental Child Psychology* 121 (May): 63–84.

Sleeter, C. 2010. 'Why Is There Learning Disabilities? A Critical Analysis of the Birth of the Field in Its Social Context'. *Disability Studies Quarterly: DSQ* 30 (2). https://doi.org/10.18061/dsq.v30i2.1261.

Sniekers, S., S. Stringer, K. Watanabe, et al. 2017. 'Genome-Wide Association Meta-Analysis of 78,308 Individuals Identifies New Loci and Genes Influencing Human Intelligence'. *Nature Genetics* 49 (7): 1107–12.

Snowling, M., and C. Hulme. 1989. 'A Longitudinal Case Study of Developmental Phonological Dyslexia'. *Cognitive Neuropsychology* 6 (4): 379–401. https://doi.org/10.1080/02643298908253289.

Snowling, M. J. 2019. *Dyslexia*. Oxford University Press.

Snowling, M. J., A. Gallagher, and U. Frith. 2003. 'Family Risk of Dyslexia Is Continuous: Individual Differences in the Precursors of Reading Skill'. *Child Development* 74 (2): 358–73.

Snowling, M. J., M. E. Hayiou-Thomas, H. M. Nash, and C. Hulme. 2020. 'Dyslexia and Developmental Language Disorder: Comorbid Disorders with Distinct Effects on Reading Comprehension'. *Journal of Child Psychology and Psychiatry, and Allied Disciplines* 61 (6): 672–80.

Snowling, M. J., and C. Hulme. 2011. 'Evidence-Based Interventions for Reading and Language Difficulties: Creating a Virtuous Circle'. *British Journal of Educational Psychology* 81 (1): 1–23. https://doi.org/10.1111/j.2044-8279.2010.02014.x.

Snowling, M. J., A. Lervåg, H. M. Nash, and C. Hulme. 2019. 'Longitudinal Relationships between Speech Perception, Phonological Skills and Reading in Children at High-Risk of Dyslexia'. *Developmental Science* 22 (1): e12723.

Sokolowski, Andrzej. 2018. *Scientific Inquiry in Mathematics – Theory and Practice: A STEM Perspective*. Springer.

Sokolowski, H. M., and D. Ansari (2018). Understanding the Effects of Education through the Lens of Biology'. *NPJ Science of Learning* 3 (1) (October): 17. https://doi.org/10.1038/s41539-018-0032-y.

Sokolowski, H. M., H. M. Sokolowski, W. Fias, C. B. Ononye, and D. Ansari. 2017. 'Are Numbers Grounded in a General Magnitude Processing System? A Functional Neuroimaging Meta-Analysis'. *Neuropsychologia* 105: 50–69. https://doi.org/10.1016/j.neuropsychologia.2017.01.019.

Sokolowski, M. B., and D. Wahlsten. 2001. 'Gene-Environment Interaction and Complex Behavior'. In H. R. Chin and S. O. Moldin (eds.), *Methods in Genomic Neuroscience*, 3–28. CRC Press.

Solan, H. A., J. Shelley-Tremblay, A. Ficarra, M. Silverman, and S. Larson. 2003. 'Effect of Attention Therapy on Reading Comprehension'. *Journal of Learning Disabilities* 36 (6): 556–63.

Solar Energy Research Inst., Golden, CO (USA). 1980. 'Studying the Implementation of Public Programs'. https://doi.org/10.2172/5487716.

Solis, M., S. Ciullo, S. Vaughn, et al. 2012. 'Reading Comprehension Interventions for Middle School Students With Learning Disabilities: A Synthesis of 30 Years of Research'. *Journal of Learning Disabilities* 45 (4): 327–40.

Soltanlou, M., C. Artemenko, T. Dresler, et al. 2019. 'Math Anxiety in Combination With Low Visuospatial Memory Impairs Math Learning in Children'. *Frontiers in Psychology* 10 (January): 89.

Sommer, I. E. C. 2004. 'Do Women Really Have More Bilateral Language Representation than Men? A Meta-Analysis of Functional Imaging Studies'. *Brain* 127 (8): 1845–52. https://doi.org/10.1093/brain/awh207.

Sommer, I. E., A. Aleman, M. Somers, M. P. Boks, and R. S. Kahn. 2008. 'Sex Differences in Handedness, Asymmetry of the Planum Temporale and Functional Language Lateralization'. *Brain Research* 1206 (April): 76–88.

Song, S., A. Zilverstand, W. Gui, H.-J. Li, and X. Zhou. 2019a. 'Effects of Single-Session versus Multi-Session Non-Invasive Brain Stimulation on Craving and Consumption in Individuals with Drug Addiction, Eating Disorders or Obesity: A Meta-Analysis'. *Brain Stimulation* 12 (3): P606–18. https://doi.org/10.1016/j.brs.2018.12.975.

Song S, Zhang Y, Shu H, Su M and McBride C (2020) 'Universal and Specific Predictors of Chinese Children With Dyslexia – Exploring the Cognitive Deficits and Subtypes'. *Front. Psychol.* 10:2904. doi: 10.3389/fpsyg.2019.02904.

Spaepen, E., E. A. Gunderson, D. Gibson, S. Goldin-Meadow, and S. C. Levine. 2018. 'Meaning before Order: Cardinal Principle Knowledge Predicts Improvement in Understanding the Successor Principle and Exact Ordering'. *Cognition* 180 (November): 59–81.

Spencer, M., R. K. Wagner, C. Schatschneider, et al. 2014. 'Incorporating RTI in a Hybrid Model of Reading Disability'. *Learning Disability Quarterly: Journal of the Division for Children with Learning Disabilities* 37 (3): 161–71.

Sprick, J. T., E. C. Bouck, T. R. Berg, and C. Coughlin. 2020. 'Attendance and Specific Learning Disability Identification: A Survey of Practicing School Psychologists'.

Learning Disabilities Research & Practice: A Publication of the Division for Learning Disabilities, Council for Exceptional Children 35 (3): 139–49.

Squires, K. E., and J. A. Wolter. 2016. 'The Effects of Orthographic Pattern Intervention on Spelling Performance of Students With Reading Disabilities: A Best Evidence Synthesis'. *Remedial and Special Education: RASE* 37 (6): 357–69.

Stanovich, K. E. 1994. 'Annotation: Does Dyslexia Exist?' *Journal of Child Psychology and Psychiatry, and Allied Disciplines* 35 (4): 579–95.

Stanovich, K. E. 1991. 'Discrepancy Definitions of Reading Disability: Has Intelligence Led Us Astray?' *Reading Research Quarterly* 26 (1): 7–29.

———. 2005. 'The Future of a Mistake: Will Discrepancy Measurement Continue to Make the Learning Disabilities Field a Pseudoscience?' *Learning Disability Quarterly: Journal of the Division for Children with Learning Disabilities* 28 (2): 103–6.

Steinbrink, C., H. Ackermann, T. Lachmann, and A. Riecker. 2009. 'Contribution of the Anterior Insula to Temporal Auditory Processing Deficits in Developmental Dyslexia'. *Human Brain Mapping* 30 (8): 2401–11.

Steinbrink, C., and T. Lachmann. 2014. *Lese-Rechtschreibstörung*. Springer. https://doi.org /10.1007/978-3-642-41842-6.

Steinbrink, C., S. Schwanda, M. Klatte, and T. Lachmann. 2010. 'Sagen Wahrnehmungsleistungen Zu Beginn Der Schulzeit Den Lese-Rechtschreiberfolg in Klasse 1 Und 2 Voraus?' *Zeitschrift Fur Entwicklungspsychologie Und Padagogische Psychologie* 42 (4): 188–200.

Stein, J. F., A. J. Richardson, and M. S. Fowler. 2000. 'Monocular Occlusion Can Improve Binocular Control and Reading in Dyslexics'. *Brain: A Journal of Neurology* 123 (Pt 1) (January): 164–70.

Stein, J. 2018. 'The Magnocellular Theory of Developmental Dyslexia'. *Literacy Studies* 16. https://doi.org/10.1007/978-3-319-90805-2_6.

Stein, J. F. 2018. 'Does Dyslexia Exist?' *Language, Cognition and Neuroscience* 33 (3): 313–20.

Stevens, E. A., M. A. Rodgers, and S. R. Powell. 2018. 'Mathematics Interventions for Upper Elementary and Secondary Students: A Meta-Analysis of Research'. *Remedial and Special Education: RASE* 39 (6): 327–40.

Steyer, R., A.-M. Majcen, P. Schwenkmezger, and A. Buchner. 1989. 'A Latent State-Trait Anxiety Model and Its Application to Determine Consistency and Specificity Coefficients'. *Anxiety Research* 1 (4): 281–99.

Storch, S. A., and G. J. Whitehurst. 2002. 'Oral Language and Code-Related Precursors to Reading: Evidence from a Longitudinal Structural Model'. *Developmental Psychology* 38 (6): 934–47. https://doi.org/10.1037/0012-1649.38.6.934.

Storebø, O. J., J. M. Stoffers-Winterling, B. A. Völlm, et al. 2018. 'Psychological Therapies for People with Borderline Personality Disorder'. *The Cochrane Library* 2: CD012955, February. https://doi.org/10.1002/14651858.cd012955.

Strand, S., and G. Lindsay. 2009. 'Evidence of Ethnic Disproportionality in Special Education in an English Population'. *The Journal of Special Education* 43 (3): 174–90.

Stuebing, K. K., J. M. Fletcher, J. M. LeDoux, et al. 2002. 'Validity of IQ-Discrepancy Classifications of Reading Disabilities: A Meta-Analysis'. *American Educational Research Journal* 39 (2): 469–518. https://doi.org/10.3102/00028312039002469.

Stutz, F., E. Schaffner, and U. Schiefele. 2016. 'Relations among Reading Motivation, Reading Amount, and Reading Comprehension in the Early Elementary Grades'.

Learning and Individual Differences 45: 101–13. https://doi.org/10.1016/j
.lindif.2015.11.022.

Suggate, S. P. 2016. 'A Meta-Analysis of the Long-Term Effects of Phonemic Awareness, Phonics, Fluency, and Reading Comprehension Interventions'. *Journal of Learning Disabilities* 49 (1): 77–96. https://doi.org/10.1177/0022219414528540.

Sun, Z., L. Zou, J. Zhang, et al. 2013. 'Prevalence and Associated Risk Factors of Dyslexic Children in a Middle-Sized City of China: A Cross-Sectional Study'. *PloS One* 8 (2): e56688.

Swanson, H. 2015. 'Cognitive Strategy Interventions Improve Word Problem Solving and Working Memory in Children with Math Disabilities'. *Frontiers in Psychology* 6: 1099.

Swanson, H. L. 1999. 'Reading Research for Students with LD: A Meta-Analysis of Intervention Outcomes'. *Journal of Learning Disabilities* 32 (6): 504–32.

Swanson, H. L. 2011. 'Working Memory, Attention, and Mathematical Problem Solving: A Longitudinal Study of Elementary School Children'. *Journal of Educational Psychology* 103 (4): 821–37.

Swanson, H. L., A. Moran, C. Lussier, and W. Fung. 2014. 'The Effect of Explicit and Direct Generative Strategy Training and Working Memory on Word Problem-Solving Accuracy in Children at Risk for Math Difficulties'. *Learning Disability Quarterly: Journal of the Division for Children with Learning Disabilities* 37 (2): 111–23.

Takala, M., E. Silfver, Y. Karlsson, and M. Saarinen. 2020. 'Supporting Pupils in Finnish and Swedish Schools – Teachers' Views'. *Scandinavian Journal of Educational Research* 64 (3): 313–32. https://doi.org/10.1080/00313831.2018.1541820.

'TALIS 2018 Results (volume I): Teachers and School Leaders as Lifelong Learners'. n.d. Accessed July 29, 2021. https://www.oecd-ilibrary.org/education/talis-2018-results -volume-i_1d0bc92a-en.

Tallal, Paula. 1980. 'Auditory Temporal Perception, Phonics, and Reading Disabilities in Children'. *Brain and Language* 9 (2): 182–98. https://doi.org/10.1016/0093-934x (80)90139-x.

Tan, L. H., J. A. Spinks, G. F. Eden, C. A. Perfetti, and W. T. Siok. 2005. 'Reading Depends on Writing, in Chinese'. *Proceedings of the National Academy of Sciences* 102 (24). https://doi.org/10.1073/pnas.0503523102.

Tan, L. H., A. R. Laird, K. Li, and P. T. Fox. 2005. 'Neuroanatomical Correlates of Phonological Processing of Chinese Characters and Alphabetic Words: A Meta-Analysis'. *Human Brain Mapping* 25 (1): 83–91.

Tan, L. H., J. A. Spinks, C.-M. Feng, et al. 2003. 'Neural Systems of Second Language Reading Are Shaped by Native Language'. *Human Brain Mapping* 18: 158–66. https://doi.org/10.1002/hbm.10089.

Tarone, E., and M. Bigelow. 2005. 'Impact of Literacy on Oral Language Processing: Implications for Second Language Acquisition Research'. *Annual Review of Applied Linguistics* 25: 77–97. https://doi.org/10.1017/s0267190505000048.

Temple, E., R. A. Poldrack, J. Salidis, et al. 2001. 'Disrupted Neural Responses to Phonological and Orthographic Processing in Dyslexic Children: An fMRI Study'. *Neuroreport* 12 (2): 299–307. https://doi.org/10.1097/00001756-200102120-00024.

Tenenbaum, H. R., and M. D. Ruck. 2007. 'Are Teachers' Expectations Different for Racial Minority than for European American Students? A Meta-Analysis'. *Journal of Educational Psychology* 99 (2): 253–73.

Terney, D., L. Chaieb, V. Moliadze, A. Antal, and W. Paulus. 2008. 'Increasing Human Brain Excitability by Transcranial High-Frequency Random Noise Stimulation'. *The Journal of Neuroscience: The Official Journal of the Society for Neuroscience* 28 (52): 14147–55.

Thomas Boyce, W., M. B. Sokolowski, and G. E. Robinson. 2020. 'Genes and Environments, Development and Time'. *Proceedings of the National Academy of Sciences of the United States of America* 117 (38): 23235–41.

TIMSS, and PIRLS International Study Center at Boston College. n.d. 'TIMSS 2019 International Results in Mathematics and Science'. Accessed July 29, 2021. https://timssandpirls.bc.edu/timss2019/.

Tobia, V., and G. M. Marzocchi. 2014. 'Predictors of Reading Fluency in Italian Orthography: Evidence from a Cross-Sectional Study of Primary School Students'. *Child Neuropsychology: A Journal on Normal and Abnormal Development in Childhood and Adolescence* 20 (4): 449–69.

Toh, T. L., and B. Kaur. 2019. 'Low Attainers and Learning of Mathematics'. In Toh, T., Kaur, B., and Tay, E. (eds) *Mathematics Education in Singapore. Mathematics Education – An Asian Perspective*. Springer. https://doi.org/10.1007/978-981-13-3573-0_13.

Topping, K. J., D. Miller, P. Murray, S. Henderson, C. Fortuna, and N. Conlin. 2011. 'Outcomes in a Randomised Controlled Trial of Mathematics Tutoring'. *Educational Research* 53 (1): 51–63.

Torgesen, J. K. 2000. 'Individual Differences in Response to Early Interventions in Reading: The Lingering Problem of Treatment Resisters'. *Learning Disabilities Research & Practice: A Publication of the Division for Learning Disabilities, Council for Exceptional Children* 15 (2000): 55–64.

Törmänen, M. R. K., and M. Takala. 2009. 'Auditory Processing in Developmental Dyslexia: An Exploratory Study of an Auditory and Visual Matching Training Program with Swedish Children with Developmental Dyslexia'. *Scandinavian Journal of Psychology* 50 (3): 277–85.

Torppa, M., K. Georgiou, M.-K. Lerkkanen, et al. 2016. 'Examining the Simple View of Reading in a Transparent Orthography: A Longitudinal Study From Kindergarten to Grade 3'. *Merrill-Palmer Quarterly* 62 (2): 179–206. https://doi.org/10.13110/merrpalmquar1982.62.2.0179.

Toste, J. R., D. L. Compton, D. Fuchs, et al. 2014. 'Understanding Unresponsiveness to Tier 2 Reading Intervention: Exploring the Classification and Profiles of Adequate and Inadequate Responders in First Grade'. *Learning Disability Quarterly: Journal of the Division for Children with Learning Disabilities* 37 (4): 192–203.

Toth, G., and L. S. Siegel. 2020. 'A Critical Evaluation of the IQ-Achievement Discrepancy Based Definition of Dyslexia'. *Current Directions in Dyslexia Research*. Garland Science. https://doi.org/10.1201/9781003077411-4.

Tucker-Drob, E. M., and T. C. Bates. 2016. 'Large Cross-National Differences in Gene × Socioeconomic Status Interaction on Intelligence'. *Psychological Science* 27 (2): 138–49.

Turkeltaub, P. E., J. Benson, R. H. Hamilton, et al. 2012. 'Left Lateralizing Transcranial Direct Current Stimulation Improves Reading Efficiency'. *Brain Stimulation* 5 (3): 201–7.

Turkeltaub, P. E., L. Gareau, D. L. Flowers, T. A. Zeffiro, and G. F. Eden. 2003a. 'Development of Neural Mechanisms for Reading'. *Nature Neuroscience* 6: 767–73. https://doi.org/10.1038/nn1065.

2003b. 'Development of Neural Mechanisms for Reading'. *Nature Neuroscience* 6 (7): 767–73.

Tzeng, Y.-L., C.-H. Hsu, W.-H. Lin, and C.-Y. Lee. 2018. 'Impaired Orthographic Processing in Chinese Dyslexic Children: Evidence From the Lexicality Effect on N400'. *Scientific Studies of Reading: The Official Journal of the Society for the Scientific Study of Reading* 22 (1): 85–100.

Ulferts, H., K. M. Wolf, and Y. Anders. 2019. 'Impact of Process Quality in Early Childhood Education and Care on Academic Outcomes: Longitudinal Meta-Analysis'. *Child Development* 90: 1474–89. https://doi.org/10.1111/cdev.13296.

Uno, A., T. N. Wydell, N. Haruhara, M. Kaneko, and N. Shinya. 2009. 'Relationship between Reading/writing Skills and Cognitive Abilities among Japanese Primary-School Children: Normal Readers versus Poor Readers (Dyslexics)'. *Reading and Writing* 22 (7): 755–89.

United Nations, and United Nations (UN). 2009. 'Convention on the Rights of Persons with Disabilities'. *Jahrbuch Für Wissenschaft Und Ethik* 14 (1). https://doi.org/10.1515 /9783110208856.203.

'UQ eSpace'. n.d. Accessed July 29, 2021. https://espace.library.uq.edu.au/view/UQ: 733076.

Usami, S., K. Murayama, and E. L. Hamaker. 2019. 'A Unified Framework of Longitudinal Models to Examine Reciprocal Relations'. *Psychological Methods* 24 (5): 637–57. https://dx.doi.org/10.1037/met0000210.

US Department of Education, Office of Special Education, and Office of Special Education Programs Rehabilitative Services. 2020. '41st Annual Report to Congress on the Implementation of the Individuals with Disabilities Education Act, 2019'. Education Publications Center Washington, DC.

Uttal, D. H., and C. A. Cohen. 2012. 'Chapter Four – Spatial Thinking and STEM Education: When, Why, and How?' In *Psychology of Learning and Motivation*, edited by Brian H. Ross, 57:147–81. Academic Press.

Uttal, D. H., N. G. Meadow, E. Tipton, et al. 2013. 'The Malleability of Spatial Skills: A Meta-Analysis of Training Studies'. *Psychological Bulletin* 139 (2): 352–402.

Vaessen, A., D. Bertrand, D. Tóth, et al. 2010. 'Cognitive Development of Fluent Word Reading Does Not Qualitatively Differ between Transparent and Opaque Orthographies'. *Journal of Educational Psychology* 102 (4): 827–42. https://doi .org/10.1037/a0019465.

Vágvölgyi, R., K. Bergström, A. Bulajić, et al. 2021. 'Functional Illiteracy and Developmental Dyslexia: Looking for Common Roots. A Systematic Review'. *Journal of Cultural Cognitive Science* 5: 159–79. https://doi.org/10.1007/s41809-021-00074-9.

Vágvölgyi, R., A. Coldea, T. Dresler, J. Schrader, and H.-C. Nuerk. 2016. 'A Review about Functional Illiteracy: Definition, Cognitive, Linguistic, and Numerical Aspects'. *Frontiers in Psychology* 7 (November): 1617.

Valdois, Sylviane, Carole Peyrin, Delphine Lassus-Sangosse, et al. 2014. 'Dyslexia in a French–Spanish Bilingual Girl: Behavioural and Neural Modulations Following a Visual Attention Span Intervention'. *Cortex* 53 (April): 120–45. https://doi.org/10 .1016/j.cortex.2013.11.006.

Van den Broeck, W. 2002. 'The Misconception of the Regression-Based Discrepancy Operationalization in the Definition and Research of Learning Disabilities'. *Journal of Learning Disabilities* 35 (3): 194–204.

Van Luit, J. E. H., and E. A. M. Schopman. 2000. 'Improving Early Numeracy of Young Children with Special Educational Needs'. *Remedial and Special Education: RASE* 21 (1): 27–40.

'Vanuatu Inclusive Education (IE) Policy / Republic of Vanuatu, Ministry of Education'. 2011. Accessed July 29, 2021. https://education.gov.vu/docs/policies/Vanuatu%20Inclusive%20Education%20Policy_2011.pdf.

VanVoorhis, C. R. W., B. L. Morgan, and Others. 2007. 'Understanding Power and Rules of Thumb for Determining Sample Sizes'. *Tutorials in Quantitative Methods for Psychology* 3 (2): 43–50.

Vaughn, S., and L. S. Fuchs. 2003. 'Redefining Learning Disabilities as Inadequate Response to Instruction: The Promise and Potential Problems'. *Learning Disabilities Research and Practice* 18 (3): 137–46. https://doi.org/10.1111/1540-5826.00070.

Veenstra, R., S. Lindenberg, F. Tinga, and J. Ormel. 2010. 'Truancy in Late Elementary and Early Secondary Education: The Influence of Social Bonds and Self-Control – the TRAILS Study'. *International Journal of Behavioral Development* 34 (4): 302–10. https://doi.org/10.1177/0165025409347987.

Ventura, P., C. Pattamadilok, T. Fernandes, et al. 2008. 'Schooling in Western Culture Promotes Context-Free Processing'. *Journal of Experimental Child Psychology* 100 (2): 79–88.

Verdine, B. N., R. M. Golinkoff, K. Hirsh-Pasek, and N. S. Newcombe. 2017. 'Spatial Skills, Their Development, and Their Links to Mathematics'. *Monographs of the Society for Research in Child Development* 82 (1): 7–30.

Verhoeven, L., and C. Perfetti. 2017. *Learning to Read across Languages and Writing Systems*. Cambridge University Press.

Verhoeven, L., C. Perfetti, K. Pugh, et al. 2019. *Developmental Dyslexia across Languages and Writing Systems*. Cambridge University Press.

Verpalen, A., F. Van de Vijver, and A. Backus. 2018. 'Bias in Dyslexia Screening in a Dutch Multicultural Population'. *Annals of Dyslexia* 68 (1): 43–68.

Visscher, P. M., M. A. Brown, M. I. McCarthy, and J. Yang. 2012. 'Five Years of GWAS Discovery'. *American Journal of Human Genetics* 90 (1): 7–24.

Visser, L., J. Kalmar, J. Linkersdörfer, et al. 2020. 'Comorbidities between Specific Learning Disorders and Psychopathology in Elementary School Children in Germany'. *Frontiers in Psychiatry*. https://doi.org/10.3389/fpsyt.2020.00292.

Viterbori, P., L. Traverso, and M. C. Usai. 2017. 'The Role of Executive Function in Arithmetic Problem-Solving Processes: A Study of Third Graders'. *Journal of Cognition and Development: Official Journal of the Cognitive Development Society* 18 (5): 595–616.

Viterbori, P., M. C. Usai, L. Traverso, and V. De Franchis. 2015. 'How Preschool Executive Functioning Predicts Several Aspects of Math Achievement in Grades 1 and 3: A Longitudinal Study'. *Journal of Experimental Child Psychology* 140 (December): 38–55.

Vogel, S. A. 1990. 'Gender Differences in Intelligence, Language, Visual-Motor Abilities, and Academic Achievement in Students with Learning Disabilities'. *Journal of Learning Disabilities* 23 (1): 44–52. https://doi.org/10.1177/002221949002300111.

Volkmer, S., K. Galuschka, and G. Schulte-Körne. 2019. 'Early Identification and Intervention for Children with Initial Signs of Reading Deficits – A Blinded Randomized Controlled Trial'. *Learning and Instruction* 59 (February): 1–12.

Voss, S., Y. Blumenthal, K. Mahlau, et al. 2016. *Der Response-to-Intervention-Ansatz in der Praxis: Evaluationsergebnisse zum Rügener Inklusionsmodell.* Waxmann Verlag GmbH.

Wagner, J. B., and S. C. Johnson. 2011. 'An Association between Understanding Cardinality and Analog Magnitude Representations in Preschoolers'. *Cognition* 119 (1): 10–22.

Wagner, R. K., and J. K. Torgesen. 1987. 'The Nature of Phonological Processing and Its Causal Role in the Acquisition of Reading Skills'. *Psychological Bulletin* 101 (2): 192–212. https://doi.org/10.1037/0033-2909.101.2.192.

Wagner, R. K., J. K. Torgesen, and C. A. Rashotte. 1994. 'Development of Reading-Related Phonological Processing Abilities: New Evidence of Bidirectional Causality from a Latent Variable Longitudinal Study'. *Developmental Psychology* 30 (1): 73–87. https://doi.org/10.1037/0012-1649.30.1.73.

Wai, J., D. Lubinski, and C. P. Benbow. 2009. 'Spatial Ability for STEM Domains: Aligning over 50 Years of Cumulative Psychological Knowledge Solidifies Its Importance'. *Journal of Educational Psychology* 101 (4): 817–35.

Wallentin, M. 2009. 'Putative Sex Differences in Verbal Abilities and Language Cortex: A Critical Review'. *Brain and Language* 108 (3): 175–83. https://doi.org/10.1016/j.bandl.2008.07.001.

Walley, A. C., J. L. Metsala, and V. M. Garlock. 2003. 'Spoken Vocabulary Growth: Its Role in the Development of Phoneme Awareness and Early Reading Ability'. *Reading and Writing* 16 (1): 5–20.

Wang, E., S. Qin, M. Chang, and X. Zhu. 2015. 'Digital Memory Encoding in Chinese Dyscalculia: An Event-Related Potential Study'. *Research in Developmental Disabilities* 36C (January): 142–49.

Washington, J. A., D. L. Compton, and P. McCardle. 2020. *Dyslexia: Revisiting Etiology, Diagnosis, Treatment, and Policy.* Paul H. Brookes Publishing Company.

Watts, T. W., G. J. Duncan, R. S. Siegler, and P. E. Davis-Kean. 2014. 'What's Past Is Prologue: Relations between Early Mathematics Knowledge and High School Achievement'. *Educational Researcher* 43 (7): 352–60.

Webb, N. M., K. M. Nemer, and M. Ing. 2006. 'Small-Group Reflections: Parallels between Teacher Discourse and Student Behavior in Peer-Directed Groups'. *Journal of the Learning Sciences* 15 (1): 63–119.

Weber, J., P. Marx, and W. Schneider. 2007. 'Die Prävention von Lese-Rechtschreibschwierigkeiten'. *Zeitschrift Für Pädagogische Psychologie* 21 (1): 1664–2910. https://doi.org/10.1024/1010-0652.21.1.65.

Wellesley College: Center for Research on Women. 1992. *How Schools Shortchange Girls: The AAUW Report: A Study of Major Findings on Girls and Education.* AAUW Educational Foundation. https://wcwonline.org/images/pdf/how-schools-shortchange-girls-executive_summary.pdf.

Wendt, H., W. Bos, C. Selter, et al. 2016. *TIMSS 2015: mathematische und naturwissenschaftliche Kompetenzen von Grundschulkindern in Deutschland im internationalen Vergleich.* Waxmann.

Wernicke, C. 1874. *Der aphasische Symptomencomplex: eine psychologische Studie auf anatomischer Basis.* Cohn & Weigert.

Werning, R., J. M. Löser, and M. Urban. 2008. 'Cultural and Social Diversity: An Analysis of Minority Groups in German Schools'. *The Journal of Special Education* 42 (1): 47–54.

Wheldall, K., and L. Limbrick. 2010. 'Do More Boys Than Girls Have Reading Problems?' *Journal of Learning Disabilities* 43 (5): 418–29. https://doi.org/10.1177/0022219409355477.

White, B. 2007. 'Are Girls Better Readers than Boys? Which Boys? Which Girls?' *Canadian Journal of Education / Revue Canadienne de L'éducation* 30 (2): 554–81. https://doi.org/10.2307/20466650.

Whitehurst, G. J., and C. J. Lonigan. 1998. 'Child Development and Emergent Literacy'. *Child Development* 69 (3): 848–72.

White, I. R., J. Carpenter, and N. J. Horton. 2012. 'Including All Individuals Is Not Enough: Lessons for Intention-to-Treat Analysis'. *Clinical Trials* 9 (4): 396–407.

Whitley, J., and T. Hollweck. 2020. 'Inclusion and Equity in Education: Current Policy Reform in Nova Scotia, Canada'. *Prospects*, September, 1–16.

Willmes, K., E. Klein, and H.-C. Nuerk. 2013. 'Akalkulie'. In *Funktionelle MRT in Psychiatrie Und Neurologie*, edited by F. Schneider and G. R. Fink, 577–86. Springer Berlin Heidelberg.

Willms, J. L., K. A. Shapiro, M. V. Peelen, et al. 2011. 'Language-Invariant Verb Processing Regions in Spanish–English Bilinguals'. *NeuroImage* 57 (1): 251–61. https://doi.org/10.1016/j.neuroimage.2011.04.021.

Wilsher, C. R., and E. A. Taylor. 1994. 'Piracetam in Developmental Reading Disorders: A Review'. *European Child & Adolescent Psychiatry* 3 (2): 59–71.

Wilsher, C. R., D. Bennett, C. H. Chase, et al. 1987. 'Piracetam and Dyslexia: Effects on Reading Tests'. *Journal of Clinical Psychopharmacology* 7 (4): 230–7.

Wilson, A. J., S. K. Revkin, D. Cohen, L. Cohen, and S. Dehaene. 2006. 'An Open Trial Assessment of 'The Number Race', an Adaptive Computer Game for Remediation of Dyscalculia'. *Behavioral and Brain Functions: BBF* 2 (1): 20.

Wimmer, H., and H. Mayringer. 2002. 'Dysfluent Reading in the Absence of Spelling Difficulties: A Specific Disability in Regular Orthographies'. *Journal of Educational Psychology* 94 (2): 272–7. https://doi.org/10.1037/0022-0663.94.2.272.

Wimmer, H., H. Mayringer, and K. Landerl. 2000. 'The Double-Deficit Hypothesis and Difficulties in Learning to Read a Regular Orthography'. *Journal of Educational Psychology* 94 (4): 668–80. https://doi.org/10.1037/0022-0663.92.4.668.

Wimmer, H., K. Landerl, R. Linortner, and P. Hummer. 1991. 'The Relationship of Phonemic Awareness to Reading Acquisition: More Consequence than Precondition but Still Important'. *Cognition* 40 (3): 219–49.

Witkowski, M., E. Garcia-Cossio, B. S. Chander, et al. 2016. 'Mapping Entrained Brain Oscillations during Transcranial Alternating Current Stimulation (tACS)'. *NeuroImage* 140 (October): 89–98.

Wolf, K. M., U. Schroeders, and K. Kriegbaum. 2016. 'Metaanalyse Zur Wirksamkeit Einer Förderung Der Phonologischen Bewusstheit in Der Deutschen Sprache'. *Zeitschrift Für Pädagogische Psychologie* 30 (1): 1664–2910. https://doi.org/10.1024/1010-0652/a000165.

Wong, A. C.-N., C. M. Bukach, J. Hsiao, et al. 2012. 'Holistic Processing as a Hallmark of Perceptual Expertise for Nonface Categories Including Chinese Characters'. *Journal of Vision* 12 (7). https://doi.org/10.1167/12.13.7.

Wong, T. T.-Y., C. S.-H. Ho, and J. Tang. 2017. 'Defective Number Sense or Impaired Access? Differential Impairments in Different Subgroups of Children With Mathematics Difficulties'. *Journal of Learning Disabilities* 50 (1): 49–61.

Wu, C.-Y., M.-H. R. Ho, and S.-H. A. Chen. 2012. 'A Meta-Analysis of fMRI Studies on Chinese Orthographic, Phonological, and Semantic Processing'. *NeuroImage*. https://doi.org/10.1016/j.neuroimage.2012.06.047.

Wu, S. S., E. G. Willcutt, E. Escovar, and V. Menon. 2014. 'Mathematics Achievement and Anxiety and Their Relation to Internalizing and Externalizing Behaviors'. *Journal of Learning Disabilities* 47 (6): 503–14.

Wydell, T. N. 2019. 'Developmental Dyslexia in Japanese'. In Verhoeven, L., Perfetti, C., & Pugh, K. (Eds.), *Developmental Dyslexia across Languages and Writing Systems*, 176–99. Cambridge University Press.

Wydell, T. N., and T. Kondo. 2003. 'Phonological Deficit and the Reliance on Orthographic Approximation for Reading: A Follow-up Study on an English-Japanese Bilingual with Monolingual Dyslexia'. *Journal of Research in Reading* 26 (1): 33–48. https://doi.org/10.1111/1467-9817.261004.

Wydell, T. N., and B. Butterworth. 1999. 'A Case Study of an English-Japanese Bilingual with Monolingual Dyslexia'. *Cognition* 70 (3): 273–305.

Wynd, D. 2015. *'It Shouldn't Be This Hard': Children, Poverty and Disability*. Child Poverty Action Group.

Wynn, K. 1990. 'Children's Understanding of Counting'. *Cognition* 36 (2): 155–93.

Wynn, K. 1992b. 'Children's Acquisition of the Number Words and the Counting System'. *Cognitive Psychology* 24 (2): 220–51.

Wyschkon, A., J. Kohn, K. Ballaschk, and G. Esser. 2009. 'Sind Rechenstörungen Genau so Häufig Wie Lese-Rechtschreibstörungen?' *Zeitschrift Fur Kinder- Und Jugendpsychiatrie Und Psychotherapie* 37 (6): 499–512.

Wyse, D., and U. Goswami. 2008. 'Synthetic Phonics and the Teaching of Reading'. *British Educational Research Journal* 34 (6): 691–710.

Xu, M., D. Baldauf, C. Q. Chang, R. Desimone, and L. H. Tan. 2017. 'Distinct Distributed Patterns of Neural Activity Are Associated with Two Languages in the Bilingual Brain'. *Science Advances* 3 (7): e1603309.

Xu, M., L. H. Tan, and C. Perfetti. 2019. 'Developmental Dyslexia in Chinese'. In L. Verhoeven, C. Perfetti, and K. Pugh (eds.), *Developmental Dyslexia across Languages and Writing Systems* (pp. 200–226). Cambridge University Press. https://doi.org/10.1017/9781108553377.010.

Xu, M., J. Yang, W. T. Siok, and L. H. Tan. 2015. 'Atypical Lateralization of Phonological Working Memory in Developmental Dyslexia'. *Journal of Neurolinguistics* 33: 67–77. https://doi.org/10.1016/j.jneuroling.2014.07.004.

Yang, Y., Y. H. Yang, J. Li, M. Xu, and H.-Y. Bi. 2020. 'An Audiovisual Integration Deficit Underlies Reading Failure in Nontransparent Writing Systems: An fMRI Study of Chinese Children with Dyslexia'. *Journal of Neurolinguistics* 54: 100884. https://doi.org/10.1016/j.jneuroling.2019.100884.

Yoon, H. W., K.-D. Cho, and H. W. Park. 2005. 'Brain Activation of Reading Korean Words and Recognizing Pictures by Korean Native Speakers: A Functional Magnetic Resonance Imaging Study'. *The International Journal of Neuroscience* 115 (6): 757–68.

Young, T., and W. D. Lewis. 2015. 'Educational Policy Implementation Revisited'. Educational Policy. https://doi.org/10.1177/0895904815568936.

Zaphiris, P., and A. Ioannou. 2016. *Learning and Collaboration Technologies: Third International Conference, LCT 2016, Held as Part of HCI International 2016, Toronto, ON, Canada, July 17–22, 2016, Proceedings*. Springer International Publishing.

Zell, E., Z. Krizan, and S. R. Teeter. 2015. 'Evaluating Gender Similarities and Differences Using Metasynthesis'. *The American Psychologist* 70 (1): 10–20.

Zhang, J., and D. A. Norman. 1995. 'A Representational Analysis of Numeration Systems'. *Cognition* 57 (3): 271–95.

Zhang, X., and D. Lin. 2015. 'Pathways to Arithmetic: The Role of Visual-Spatial and Language Skills in Written Arithmetic, Arithmetic Word Problems, and Nonsymbolic Arithmetic'. *Contemporary Educational Psychology* 41 (April): 188–97.

Zhang, Y., and X. Zhou. 2016. 'Building Knowledge Structures by Testing Helps Children With Mathematical Learning Difficulty'. *Journal of Learning Disabilities* 49 (2): 166–75.

Zhou, X., C. Chen, Y. Zang, et al. 2007. 'Dissociated Brain Organization for Single-Digit Addition and Multiplication'. *NeuroImage* 35 (2): 871–80.

Zhou, X., W. Wei, Y. Zhang, J. Cui, and C. Chen. 2015. 'Visual Perception Can Account for the Close Relation between Numerosity Processing and Computational Fluency'. *Frontiers in Psychology* 6 (September): 1364.

Zhukova, M., and E. Grigorenko. 2019. 'Developmental Dyslexia in Russian'. In L. Verhoeven, C. Perfetti, and K. Pugh (eds.), *Developmental Dyslexia across Languages and Writing Systems* (pp. 133–51). Cambridge University Press. https://doi.org/10.1017/9781108553377.007.

Ziegler, J. C., D. Bertrand, D. Tóth, et al. 2010. 'Orthographic Depth and Its Impact on Universal Predictors of Reading'. *Psychological Science* 21 (4): 551–9. https://doi.org/10.1177/0956797610363406.

Ziegler, J. C., and U. Goswami. 2005. 'Reading Acquisition, Developmental Dyslexia, and Skilled Reading Across Languages: A Psycholinguistic Grain Size Theory'. *Psychological Bulletin* 131 (1): 3–29. https://doi.org/10.1037/0033-2909.131.1.3.

Ziegler, J. C., C. Perry, A. Ma-Wyatt, D. Ladner, and G. Schulte-Körne. 2003. 'Developmental Dyslexia in Different Languages: Language-Specific or Universal?' *Journal of Experimental Child Psychology* 86 (3): 169–93. https://doi.org/10.1016/s0022-0965(03)00139-5.

Ziemann, U., and H. R. Siebner. 2015. 'Inter-Subject and Inter-Session Variability of Plasticity Induction by Non-Invasive Brain Stimulation: Boon or Bane?' *Brain Stimulation* 8 (3): P662–3. https://doi.org/10.1016/j.brs.2015.01.409.

Zippert, E. L., and B. Rittle-Johnson. 2020. 'The Home Math Environment: More than Numeracy'. *Early Childhood Research Quarterly* 50 (January): 4–15.

Zuber, J., S. Pixner, K. Moeller, and H.-C. Nuerk. 2009. 'On the Language Specificity of Basic Number Processing: Transcoding in a Language with Inversion and Its Relation to Working Memory Capacity'. *Journal of Experimental Child Psychology* 102 (1): 60–77.

Index

CPSIA information can be obtained
at www.ICGtesting.com
Printed in the USA
LVHW060738150822
725948LV00005B/168